THE LORE OF
NEW MEXICO

University of New Mexico Press | Albuquerque

THE LORE OF
NEW MEXICO

 ABRIDGED EDITION

MARTA WEIGLE *and* **PETER WHITE**

Library of Congress Cataloging-in-Publication Data

Weigle, Marta.
The lore of New Mexico / Marta Weigle and Peter White.—
Abridged ed.
    p. cm.
Includes bibliographical references and index.
ISBN 0-8263-3157-2 (pbk. : alk. paper)
    1. Folklore—New Mexico.
    2. Hispanic Americans—Folklore.
    3. Indians of North America—New Mexico—Folklore.
    4. New Mexico—Social life and customs.
    I. White, Peter, 1947–
    II. Title.
GR110.N6 W45 2003
398.2'09789—dc21
2003006265

Printed and bound by Edwards Brothers, Inc.
Design and composition: Robyn Mundy
Typeset in Bembo 11/13.5

CONTENTS

PREFACE

In 1988 when the first edition of *The Lore of New Mexico* was published by the University of New Mexico Press as a volume in the Publications of the American Folklore Society, New Series, with Larry Danielson as general editor, we presented it as "the first book-length state folklore of New Mexico," which, "like other books of state folklore, is part history, ethnography, and folklore and part anthology, exhibition catalogue, and guidebook." With examples drawn from Native American, Hispanic, and Anglo cultures, it was "intended first of all for the people of this state" but also "addressed to a wider public interested in Southwestern and American culture and to students and scholars of art, history, literature, anthropology, and, especially, folklore and American studies." Fourteen years later, it remains the only comprehensive book of New Mexico state folklore but has been out of print for almost six years, since the original 535-page volume proved too daunting for reprint and the negatives were destroyed.

The first edition was published in three parts: (1) "Between Sipapu and Trinity—Symbol and Theme in New Mexico Folklore," with four chapters and four focal places; (2) "Visual, Verbal, and Musical Folk Arts of New Mexico," with three chapters: "Homescape—Material Culture in the Domestic Setting," "Namescape—The Verbal Arts," and "Soundscape—The Musical Arts"; and (3) "Place, Person, and Celebration—New Mexico Folklife," also with three chapters. An appendix of "Selected Resources for New Mexico Folklore" preceded the notes and indexes.

The present abridged edition eliminates the original part 2 on genres of New Mexico folklore and the appendix, which has become dated due to newly published resources and changes in the various repositories. All text, illustrations, and notes to the original parts 1 and 3 appear here as parts I and II. The earlier acknowledgments are reprinted in this new preface, which is followed by a slightly revised introduction to accommodate the omission of the original part 2 and the appendix.

The December 1986 Acknowledgments

This book grew out of the national and regional concerns of the fields of folklore and American studies with their interdisciplinary perspectives on sociocultural and symbolic systems. It results from an unusual and very satisfying collaboration between colleagues of quite different academic backgrounds: Marta Weigle, who was trained as a folklorist with an anthropological and sociolinguistic orientation, and Peter White, who holds a master's degree in popular culture and a doctorate in colonial American literary and cultural studies and who has for ten years conducted fieldwork on Hispanic and Anglo New Mexican fiddlers. Weigle has been associated with the departments of anthropology and English at the University of New Mexico since 1972, White with the latter department since 1978; both have been members of the Department of American Studies since 1982.

Although planning began several years before, we did not begin work until July 1983, and the first year was one of familiarizing ourselves with the resources available and with each other's intellectual perspectives. A University of New Mexico Research Allocations Committee faculty research grant to Peter White enabled us to work at the libraries, archives, and museums in Santa Fe, where Marta Weigle lives, and particularly to explore the still only partially tapped resources in the New Mexico Federal Writers' Project/Writers' Program files. These valuable documents had previously been inventoried by Weigle as part of a 1979–81 grant to her and William Wroth from the National Endowment for the Humanities.

Work in Albuquerque centered on the similarly valuable collections of E. W. Baughman and J. D. Robb at the University of New Mexico. In the spring of 1984, we co-taught a graduate seminar on American folklore and folklife for the Department of American Studies, thus bringing together many semesters of separately taught classes in folklore and folklife, mythology, literature, Southwest studies, and American studies.

Peter White's second University of New Mexico faculty research grant and, in the fall of 1984, a sabbatical and a university presidential fellowship allowed him to make regular trips to Santa Fe to begin writing with Weigle. After realizing the symbolic and thematic coherence of the crucial, formative period for New Mexico's expressive culture, we completed the first version of part 1 in July, August, and September 1984. Our discovery of the symbolic continuity from mythic emergence to the birth of the nuclear age marked the turning point in the book's conception and the beginning of its realization.

As the symbols, themes, texts, and focal points of part 1 coalesced, we knew we had veered from our original intention to write a more generically oriented, tricultural overview of New Mexican folklore and folklife. Still, we did not entirely abandon the earlier ambition and continued to work together and individually during 1984 and 1985. Weigle wrote the chapter on verbal arts and White the chapter on musical arts [neither in this abridged edition]. All other chapters and sections in the book are truly collaborative efforts.

Throughout this challenging and often exhilarating experience, we have been extended every courtesy by the always gracious and helpful staff members in the Departments of American Studies, English, and Anthropology at the University of

New Mexico, especially Maria K. Warren and Margaret Gilmore of American Studies; the New Mexico State Records Center and Archives, Santa Fe, particularly Kay Dorman, Arlene Padilla, Don Padilla, and J. Richard Salazar; and the History Library and Photo Archives at the Museum of New Mexico, Santa Fe, notably Arthur Olivas, Orlando Romero, and Richard Rudisill. Jan Barnhart, Mary Blumenthal, Mary Ellen Hanson, Bill Tydeman, and James Wright from the library system at the University of New Mexico should also be noted gratefully, as should Judith Sellars, librarian at the Museum of International Folk Art, Santa Fe. Marc Simmons generously opened his files and offered his invaluable and unique historian's and material culture specialist's viewpoints on this state and its colonial and territorial heritage.

Beth Hadas of the University of New Mexico Press has remained supportive and patient throughout. Copyeditors Fae Korsmo and Floyce Alexander did a superb job on the manuscript and photographs. The Composition Department of the University of New Mexico Printing Plant skillfully accomplished the difficult typesetting. We owe a special debt to Emmy Ezzell for her splendid design of this complicated volume.

Our debt to our predecessors in this vast area will be apparent in the text, notes, and appendix to this [1988] volume. To this should be added our gratitude for guidance and inspiration from fellow New Mexico Folklore Society members and University of New Mexico English Department colleagues Ernie and Frances Baughman and Katherine Simons. We mark with regret the recent passing of T. M. ("Matt") Pearce, Professor Emeritus of English, who was a pioneer in Southwest studies at the university and a founding member of the New Mexico Folklore Society in 1931.

Friends and family also contributed substantially throughout these several years. Especially, we owe a great deal to Marta's colleagues in folklore, Chuck Perdue and Nan Martin-Perdue of the University of Virginia and Beverly Stoeltje of Indiana University, and to Peter's folk music and violin-making associates, Albuquerqueans Ken Keppeler, Jeanie McLerie, and John T. Honeycutt.

The June 2002 Acknowledgments

Since the 1988 publication of *The Lore of New Mexico,* which in 1989 won the Historical Society of New Mexico's Ralph Emerson Twitchell Award for "significant contribution to the field of history," both authors have devoted more time to university administration—Weigle as chair of the Department of Anthropology from 1995 to 2002 and White as associate dean in the College of Arts and Sciences and now dean of University College. Luther Wilson of the University of New Mexico Press made it possible for us to undertake this abridged edition despite our administrative obligations. Editor David Holtby, supervising editors Amy Elder and Evelyn Schlatter, scanners and proofreaders Adam Kane and Sondra Birkenes, and designer Robyn Mundy ably saw it through production.

We remain indebted to the special friends cited at the end of the December 1986 acknowledgments. To these Marta adds Mary Powell of Ancient City Press while Peter adds Wendy Swedick, and all the old-time musicians in the Southwest.

INTRODUCTION

Any state folklore study must present the unique expressive culture—the peculiarly characteristic stories, songs, sayings, artifacts, landmarks, events, peoples, and lifestyles—from an essentially arbitrary, artificially bounded area. New Mexico is no exception. It did not achieve statehood until 1912, and the officially proclaimed boundaries did not correspond to long-standing tribal, colonial, or territorial political and cultural realities. The texts in this book have been chosen to illustrate these traditional realities, which continue to exist informally alongside the formal symbols of the state—a "Mexican" seal codified in 1913, an "Anglo" state song adopted in 1915, and an "Indian-Spanish" flag legislated in 1925.

The title of this book, *The Lore of New Mexico,* is a deliberate play on lore and lure. It suggests four centuries of imposed identities for the state—from the sixteenth-century conquistadors seeking cities of gold to the twentieth-century promoters of tourism and recreation. The latter, who drew on scholarly and popular work by anthropologists, folklorists, historians, architects, artists, writers, and people of commerce, fabricated an image for the state that persists today, when New Mexico is popularly considered a place rich in folklore, arts, and multiethnic identities. Some of these relatively recent, popular culture notions are thus included in almost every chapter of this book as important elements in New Mexican lore.

The Lore of New Mexico presents the state's folklore from two different, but overlapping and complementary, perspectives, which correspond to the book's two parts: "Between Sipapu and Trinity—Symbol and Theme in New Mexico Folklore" and "Place, Person, and Celebration—New Mexico Folklife." Part I is a historical, thematic, and symbolic analysis of various forms of story, song, saying, ritual, and artifact. Part II's folklife descriptions are organized to illustrate worldviews—the sense of place, significant persons, and notions of ritual and ordinary time that characterize traditional Native American, Hispanic, and Anglo cultures. Introductions explain the contents and organization of each part.

Each part of this book could be read separately as a complete folklore/folklife study. Every chapter includes Native American (Pueblo, Navajo, and/or Apache), Hispanic, and Anglo texts drawn from different time periods. Although some more recent materials are included, the unofficial terminus of the book is 1940, the year of the Coronado Cuarto Centennial, a contrived statewide and regional celebration commemorating Coronado's 1540 *entrada* into New Mexico. World War II and the detonation of the world's first atomic bomb at Trinity site in White Sands on July 16, 1945, mark an important turning point, so most of the texts come from or are characteristic of New Mexicans and New Mexico before the nuclear age and the postwar boom.

These texts are drawn from a wide range of material: field-collected stories, songs, sayings, artifacts, and other genres of folklore and material culture; ethnographic accounts and photographs of ritual and everyday life; verbal and visual images from popular culture; and creative, popular, and scholarly discussion and analysis. It has not always been possible to find reliable texts that fairly represent all the cultures and subcultures in New Mexico and that address important considerations of gender, social class, and urban-rural differences. Nevertheless, every effort has been made to present examples from the best sources available, to document them carefully, and to contextualize them as fully as possible.

The various New Deal federal projects to document and foster the arts through state work relief projects in the 1930s through the beginning of World War II provide important resources for the study of New Mexico folklore and folklife. These projects—notably the Federal Art Project, the Federal Music Project, and the Federal Writers' Project—and other contemporary, government-sponsored documentary work—especially in the Historic American Buildings Survey, the Tewa Basin Study, and the Historical Section of the Farm Security Administration—comprise a pivotal and heretofore underutilized body of data on New Mexico ethnohistory, ethnography, and folklore. Examples from all these projects, especially firsthand and personal accounts collected by workers on the New Mexico Federal Writers' Project (NMFWP) and photographs by Farm Security Administration (FSA) photographers, appear throughout *The Lore of New Mexico*. They add significantly to the strong record of anthropological and folklore research since the 1880s. Most of the other photographs come from the Photo Archives at the Museum of New Mexico (MNM), Santa Fe.

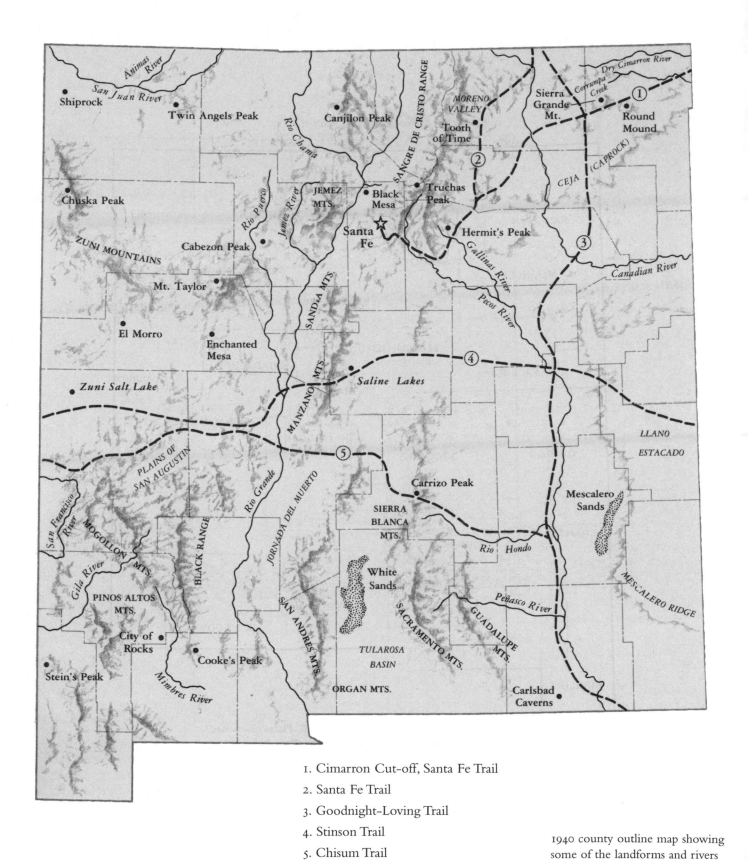

1. Cimarron Cut-off, Santa Fe Trail
2. Santa Fe Trail
3. Goodnight-Loving Trail
4. Stinson Trail
5. Chisum Trail

1940 county outline map showing
some of the landforms and rivers
mentioned in the text.

3

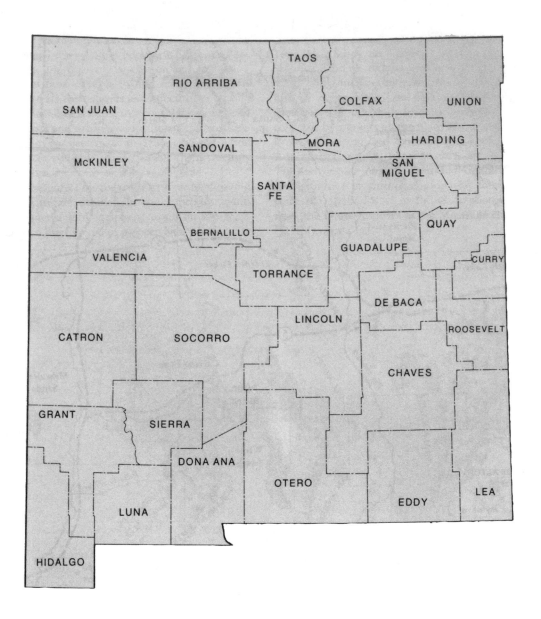

County outline map of New Mexico, 1940. Places mentioned in the text are located by county in the index. See also two valuable resources: T. M. Pearce, ed., *New Mexico Place Names: A Geographical Dictionary* (Albuquerque: University of New Mexico Press, 1965); and Jerry L. Williams, ed., *New Mexico in Maps,* 2d ed. (Albuquerque: University of New Mexico Press, 1986).

PART ONE

BETWEEN SIPAPU AND TRINITY

Symbol and Theme in New Mexico Folklore

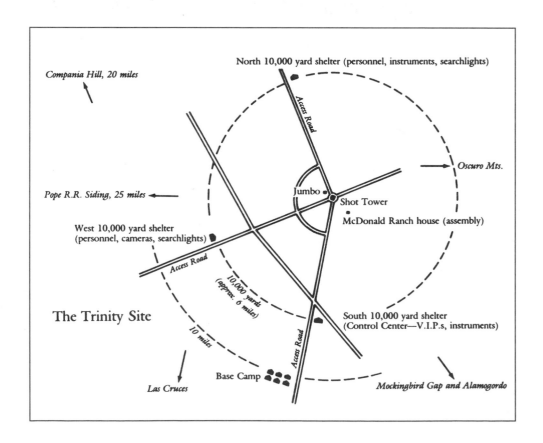

Navajo drypainting from Blessingway rite, showing circular yellow Emergence Place in center, encircled by domesticated plants, triangular clouds toward four sacred (circular) mountains with pollen footprints above and surrounded by yellow-and-blue Sunray supernatural. Collected in 1946–1947 by Maud Oakes from Jake Anderson, age sixty-eight, of Mariano Lake, New Mexico. (From Leland C. Wyman, *Blessingway* [Tucson: University of Arizona Press, 1970], Fig. 16, p. 87. Used with permission.)

The Trinity Site

Compania Hill, 20 miles

North 10,000 yard shelter (personnel, instruments, searchlights)

Access Road

Oscuro Mts.

Pope R.R. Siding, 25 miles

Jumbo

Shot Tower

McDonald Ranch house (assembly)

West 10,000 yard shelter (personnel, cameras, searchlights)

Access Road

10,000 yards (approx. 6 miles)

South 10,000 yard shelter (Control Center—V.I.P.s, instruments)

10 miles

Access Road

Las Cruces

Base Camp

Mockingbird Gap and Alamogordo

Trinity Site, after a schematic diagram by Guy Fleming, in Lansing Lamont, *Day of Trinity* (New York: Atheneum, 1965).

INTRODUCTION TO PART ONE

"Between Sipapu and Trinity" outlines the evolution of New Mexico's expressive culture from mythic times to the nuclear age. Sipapu, the place of emergence from the underworlds into this world according to Tewa Pueblo Indian belief, represents myths common to all pueblos and to the Navajo and Apache peoples. Trinity stands for the Christian culture of the Spanish and later the Anglo Americans as well as for Trinity site in White Sands, where the world's first atomic bomb was detonated on July 16, 1945.

The major themes and symbols in New Mexico folklore are explored in four chapters involving: (1) myths of dangerous journeying between worlds ("Sky Looms: Texts of Transformation and Sacred Worlds"), (2) epics of traditional travel in this world ("Royal Roads: Texts of Migration, Adventure, and Commerce"), (3) legends of climatology, railroading, and tourist accommodations ("Steel Rails: Texts of Health-Seeking and Tourism"), and (4) promotions for automobile tourism ("Land of Enchantment: Texts of Color and Spectacle"). The symbols and themes developed in each chapter are echoed in the alternating portfolios of texts about "focal places" (Shiprock and Four Corners, El Santuario de Chimayó, Pecos Pueblo and Mission, and Carlsbad Caverns). The wide-ranging "texts" in both chapters and portfolios—myths, legends, songs, sayings, and descriptive accounts that are historical, ethnographic, political, commercial, even geological—present a continuum of belief, practice, and art that epitomizes the changing expressive cultures of the so-called three peoples of the state: Native Americans, Hispanos, and Anglos.

Part I traces the *lore* of New Mexico from that created and shared by people afoot, on horseback, or in animal-drawn vehicles who visit, confront, trade, entertain, or communicate personally with one another, to the manufactured *lure* of a colorful spectacle of stereotyped "folk" who are viewed through the windows of a train or car by strangers in transit or watched impersonally in unfamiliar settings.

The following chapters and portfolios describe an important symbolic metamorphosis—from the terrifying, uncertain passage of humankind's mythic emergence from beneath the earth to the myth's modern inversion, the car-borne tourists' tamed descent and streamlined ascent from Carlsbad Caverns.

1 *SKY LOOMS*

TEXTS OF TRANSFORMATION AND SACRED WORLDS

Oh our Mother the Earth, oh our Father the Sky,
Your children are we, and with tired backs
We bring you the gifts that you love.
Then weave for us a garment of brightness;
May the warp be the white light of morning,
May the weft be the red light of evening,
May the fringes be the falling rain,
May the border be the standing rainbow.
Thus weave for us a garment of brightness
That we may walk fittingly where birds sing,
That we may walk fittingly where grass is green,
Oh our Mother the Earth, oh our Father the Sky!

—Herbert Joseph Spinden, trans., *Songs of the Tewa,* 1933.[1] Sky looms are the small desert rains that resemble a loom hung between the sky and the earth. They appear as symbolic decorations on Pueblo Indian pottery and on the white cotton mantle of ceremonial dress.

Cochiti Pueblo pot showing bird, deer, and sky loom designs. Photo by Wyatt Davis. (MNM Neg. No. 44018.)

New Mexicans have always lived in what they believe to be a sacred world, a center set apart from all Other. Whether they call their world the Middle Place or the land between the sacred mountains, whether they name it the Land of the Seven Cities of Cibola or simply *"mi placita,"* or whether they designate it the Well Country, the Land of Enchantment, or "our claim," New Mexico becomes through singing, telling, and celebrating a place of tremendous spiritual power and peril. New Mexicans have danced and sung, chanted and processed, narrated and prayed in their search for *salvus* and salvation. Through their lore, drama, and ritual they have created the expressive means of renewal and regeneration.

Native New Mexican Erna Fergusson, defining *Our Southwest* in 1940, wrote: "The arid Southwest has always been too strong, too indomitable for most people. Those who can stand it have had to learn that man does not modify this country; it transforms him, deeply. . . . It is magnificence forever rewarding to a man courageous enough to seek to renew his soul."[2]

In Native American songs and mythology of emergence and healing, this courage is expressed by the first people, who move upward into this world, and by the culture heroes and heroines who journey through unfamiliar domains, learning to protect and enrich their peoples. Hispanic colonists raised crosses throughout the harsh new land and annually disciplined themselves in symbolic reenactments of the sorrowful Passion and heroic journey of their savior-protector. Those who navigated the Great Plains by wagon and rail sought revitalization in new fields under boundless skies and found strength in the fellowship of work and worship. Such journeys are mythic in their affective and imaginative scope and voice an archetypal experience that runs thematically through all New Mexicans' lore.

Emergence and the Heroics of Culture

Pueblo, Apache, and Navajo peoples share a belief in this world as one of several. The present world is a mediator between one or more underworlds within the earth mother, from whom the first people emerged, and the upper worlds of the sun, moon, and stars. These celestial realms are inhabited by deities of thunder, lightning, and other transformative, creative powers. Journeying between these worlds is perilous and usually undertaken with the help of guides.

In an Acoma Pueblo version of the emergence myth, both the tutelary deity Tsichtinako and the first human beings in the underworld of Shipapu are female. Their long pilgrimage up into this world of light is one of uncertainty and anxiety, as shown in the following telling recorded by Matthew W. Stirling from a group of Acomas visiting the Smithsonian Institution in 1928:

> In the beginning two female human beings were born. These two children were born underground at a place called Shipapu. As they grew up, they began to be aware of each other. There was no light and they could only feel each other. Being in the dark they grew slowly.
>
> After they had grown considerably, a Spirit whom they afterward called Tsichtinako spoke to them, and they found that it would give them nourishment. After they had grown large enough to think for themselves, they spoke to the Spirit when it had come to them one day and asked it to make itself known to them and to say whether it was male or female, but it replied only that it was not allowed to meet with them. They then asked why they were living in the dark without knowing each other by name, but the Spirit answered that they were nuk'timi (under the earth); but they were to be patient in waiting until everything was ready for them to go up into the light. So they waited a long time, and as they grew they learned their language from Tsichtinako.

"Acoma Roadway," 1904 (Plate
570). Photo by Edward S. Curtis.
(MNM Neg. No. 117080.)

When all was ready, they found a present from Tsichtinako, two baskets of seeds and little images of all the different animals (there were to be) in the world. The Spirit said they were sent by their father . . . and that he wished them to take their baskets out into the light, when the time came. . . .

[The women planted unseen seeds from their baskets, and the trees grew slowly toward the light. Before their emergence, when, thanks to their helpers Badger and Locust, they could see the light above, Tsichtinako "taught them the prayers and the creation song, which they were to sing," and the animals helped them to the surface.] . . .

The earth was soft and spongy under their feet as they walked, and they said, "This is not ripe." They stood waiting for the sun, not knowing where it would appear. Gradually it grew lighter and finally the sun came up. Before they began to pray, Tsichtinako told them they were facing east and that their right side, the side their best aim was on, would be known as kū'ā'mē (south) and the left ti dyami (north) while behind at their backs was the direction pūna'me (west) where the sun would go down. They had already learned while underground the direction nŭk'ŭm' (down) and later, when they asked where their father was, they were told tyunami (four skies above). . . .

They now prayed to the Sun as they had been taught by Tsichtinako, and sang the creation song. Their eyes hurt for they were not accustomed to the strong light. For the first time they asked Tsichtinako why they were on earth and why they were created. Tsichtinako replied, "I did not make you. Your father, Uchtsiti, made you, and it is he who has made the world, the sun which you have seen, the sky, and many other things which you will see. But Uchtsiti says the world is not yet completed, not yet satisfactory, as he wants it. This is the reason he has made you. You will rule and bring to life the rest of the things he has given you in the baskets." The sisters then asked how they themselves had come into being. Tsichtinako answered saying, "Uchtsiti first made the world. He threw a clot of his own blood into space and by his power it grew and grew until it became the earth. Then Uchtsiti planted you in this and by it you were nourished as you developed. Now that you have emerged from within the earth, you will have to provide nourishment for yourselves. I will instruct you in this." Then they asked where their father lived and . . . why Tsichtinako did not become visible to them. . . . And they asked again how they were to live, whether they could go down once more under the ground, for they were afraid of the winds and rains and their eyes were hurt by the light. Tsichtinako replied that Uchtsiti would take care of that and would furnish them means to keep warm and change the atmosphere so that they would get used to it.

At the end of the first day, when it became dark they were much frightened, for they had not understood that the sun would set and thought that Tsichtinako had betrayed them. "Tsichtinako! Tsichtinako! You told us we were to come into the light," they cried, "Why, then, is it dark?" So Tsichtinako explained, "This is the way it will always be. The sun will go down and the next day come up anew in the east. When it is dark you are to rest and sleep as you slept when all was dark." So they were satisfied and slept. They rose to meet the sun, praying to it as they had been told, and were happy when it came up again, for they were warm and their faith in Tsichtinako was restored.[3]

Navajo accounts of their emergence dramatically portray the long and arduous upward journey of primordial beings through subterranean domains numbering anywhere from two to fourteen. As the emerging beings move from a lower platter or hemisphere to one above, they repeatedly fall into a pattern of transgression and failure, followed by destruction and flight into the next world. Each vertical movement represents another of their desperate attempts to flee the omnipotence of powers who live in the four directions and who become thoroughly disgusted and exasperated with the first beings' inability to live peacefully and harmoniously. They ascend to escape great walls of water or sometimes to avoid the fire converging upon them. In short, the people are initially well intentioned, then they become disorderly and violent, only to see their subterranean worlds, one after another, wracked by flood or conflagration.[4]

With the birth of Changing Woman a more lasting order and blessing begins to be possible. Her children, twin gods fathered by the Sun, travel to the Sky to obtain instruction and protection from their father and Grandmother Spider. Upon return to this world, they embark on their mission to tame the malevolent forces which imperil yet-to-be-created Navajos. Changing Woman's twin sons thus stand as models for the culture heroes and heroines whose courageous journeys to other worlds provide knowledge of new ways of healing and protection for the Navajos of this world.

Among these other worlds is the Land-beyond-the-sky, where dwell "extra-powerful storm elements—Winter, Pink and Spotted Thunders, Big Winds, and Whirlwinds, [who] run a school for novices learning the ritual of the Male Shooting, Hail, Water, and Feather chants; the pupils are conducted thither and back by other gods."[5] The hero of the Navajo Windway myth, in a version recorded by Father Berard Haile from Black Mustache in 1929, disregards ritual injunctions and comes face to face with these devastating other-world forces:

Then [the hero] left for that place of which it had been told him, "You must not go there," toward the Black Range (Jemez Mountains). He reached that mountain and walked along a slope. There was a heavy stand of pine mixed with spruce, they say. Then it happened that above him a cloud appeared which began to spread out, and it was almost midday at the time. . . .

And so it seems, that when the rain began to splash this way he was thinking, "Under which one shall I run, shall I go under a pine perhaps, perhaps under a spruce?" he thought to himself. And then he ran toward a tall spruce which stood there, which alone (happened to have) thick boughs, to this he ran. But it seems that it might not have happened if he had placed the arrows, which he was carrying, with their tips upward, but in matter of fact he leaned them with their pointed ends downward. At that instant a flash of lightning struck him, even the messenger who had been given to him had not warned him in time, they say. Thunder had shattered him, his former flesh had been scattered about in small pieces. He did not return home at sunset, and that night he was missed. "Where can he have gone to!" they were saying as they discussed this all night long, they say.[6]

The Way of the Cross: Passion and Penance

The heroic journey of the Christian culture hero is commemorated in the Stations of the Cross, a processional devotion nurtured in New Mexico by the Franciscan missionaries who acted as spiritual guides for the early Spanish colonists. In later years, when fewer clergy shepherded a growing diocesan population, lay Penitente brotherhoods carried on the Franciscan tradition in communal Holy Week observances of the Way of the Cross, the Encuentro, or Encounter, between Jesus and His Mother on the path to Calvary, the simulated Crucifixion, and the evening Tenebrae or "earthquake" services marking the cosmological disruptions that followed the death of Jesus.

During Holy Week, the most significant transformational time of the Roman Catholic Church calendar, worshippers in New Mexico pray and sing long and mournful *alabados,* or hymns, of the Passion. The following stanzas are from an alabado collected by Reyes N. Martínez in Arroyo Hondo during the late 1930s. It was "sung at any procession of the Via Crucis, during Lent, and at the wakes held during that season of the year, [or at] a wake of a deceased person who was a member of the fraternity of the Penitentes."

On that dolorous way,	*En la calle amarga,*
With Dimas and Jestas,	*Con Dimas y Jestas*
He fell three times,	*Tres veces cayo*
With the cross uphill.	*Con la cruz acuestas.*
With gall and vinegar	*Con hiel y vinagre*
They strengthened Him,	*Le fortalecieron,*
It was when on the cross	*Fue cuando en la cruz*
Hanging there they saw Him.	*Pendiente lo vieron.*
Adore the cross	*Adora la cruz*
That He drags along	*Que lleva arrastrando,*
Splashed with His blood	*Pinta con su sangre*
That He goes shedding.	*Que va derrarmando.*
Adore the garments	*Adora el rofrage*
With which He is dressed,	*Que lleva vestido,*
With His own blood	*Con su misma sangre*
I saw him dyed.	*Yo lo vi tenido.*
O precious blood!	*O preciosa sangre!*
Alleviate my suffering	*Alivia mis males*
And let me drink	*Y dadme a beber*
From your precious chalice.	*De tu precioso caliz.*[7]

(Opposite). "An altar in the church. The prevailing colors are grey and blue. A Coca-Cola bottle is used as a candle holder." FSA photo by John Collier, Las Trampas, January 1943. (LC-USW 3-17872-C.)

Devotion to the Blood of Christ was especially important to Hermanos, or Brothers, of the Penitente Brotherhood, a lay religious society whose members pledged themselves to year-round acts of Christian charity and to performing the rituals and disciplines of Holy Week. Some of their public practices included penitential processions of flagellants and cross-bearers. In many Hispanic communities a Penitente Brother was chosen to participate in a symbolic reenactment of the Crucifixion, the quintessential moment of Christ's heroism and the supreme confirmation of Christian belief.

During the 1920s Santa Fe poet Alice Corbin Henderson and her husband, artist William Penhallow Henderson, were invited to join the villagers at Abiquiú and witness this penitential sacrifice. They stood before the Brothers' *morada* (meetinghouse) and watched as two Hermanos dug a hole to receive the cross.

For some time nothing happened. Then, finally, a group of men came out carrying a small wooden platform on which stood the almost life-sized *Cristo* in a red dress. Again the door opened, and the heavy cross, with a living man bound upon it, was carried out, with its crossbeam upward, through the door and laid upon the ground with its foot on the edge of the hole made ready to receive it. Slowly and carefully the cross was raised into place, turned facing the *Morada*, and made firm; and on the cross hung the supreme penitent, in imitation of his Saviour. Facing the penitent on the cross stood the red-robed *Cristo*, who, with eyes no longer blindfolded, thus acknowledged His living disciple. At the foot of the cross, the *Hermano Mayor* and other leaders of the Brotherhood knelt praying. The black-cowled figure on the cross wore only the white cotton drawers rolled up as a loincloth. His wrists and arms were bound to the main timber by a horse-hair rope. Around his chest, a band of linen supplemented the rope, and eased the strain somewhat.

For ten, fifteen, seventeen minutes—and they seemed ages long as we waited—the figure hung on the cross; then the black-cowled head suddenly fell forward, the body slumped, and the men slowly lowered the cross and carried it into the *Morada* with the limp figure hanging upon it. The men with the *Cristo* followed singing and the door closed upon them.

Meanwhile, the sun sinking at our backs had turned the cliffs across the valley into splendid cathedral shapes of rose and saffron beauty—a beauty that is touched here in this country with a sometimes terrible sense of eternity, loneliness, and futility. For all the gay laughter of youth on the hillside, the stark parable of the Crucifixion is close to the country's soul. It eats into the heart, this terror; and it is not difficult to imagine how the early Franciscans felt, as they gazed upon this terrible afternoon light on bare mesa and peak, and felt the thorns of this eternal loneliness pressing into their souls. Actual mortification of the flesh is perhaps less poignant. What, one wondered, in such a stark primeval landscape, could call for an artificial terror—for a theatrically induced tragic sense of life and death? Yet we were to have this too, presently, in the symbolic Tinieblas.[8]

Las Tinieblas, the so-called earthquake or Tenebrae service of Good Friday night, is the Brothers' last public ritual during Holy Week. Together with most villagers and often a fair number of outsiders, the Brothers gather in the church or morada for a devotion similar to the official church ritual that commemorates the chaos following Jesus's death. This tumult is evoked in a verse from the alabado, "Salve de Dolores," or "Hail, Lady of Sorrows," sung at Arroyo Hondo for wakes and during Lent, from a version collected by Reyes N. Martínez in 1940:

The rocks break in two	*Las piedras se parten*
And the winds howl	*Y braman los aires*
Children become frightened	*Tortubean los hijos*
Sepulchres break open.	*Los sepulcros se abren.*[9]

At the beginning of the Tinieblas, the only light comes from thirteen to seventeen candles, which are placed in a triangular, white, standing candelabrum; in a special, black, *tenebrario* holder; or on the altar. Each candle or pair of candles, which symbolizes the desertion of the apostles, is extinguished following the singing of an alabado verse. Lorin W. Brown describes what happens in Córdova when the last light, representing the dead Lord, is removed or covered:

Suddenly, a voice calls out *"Ave María,"* whereupon a deafening tumult breaks out. It is the clapping of hands added to the clattering racket of the *matracas* [ratchets] in the hands of the Brethren. When the noise dies down, someone is heard saying:
—*Un sudario en el nombre de Dios por l'alma del difunto José———.* (A prayer for the repose of the soul of the deceased José———, in the name of God.)
A subdued murmur is heard as most of the assembly join in the semi-whispered response to the request. Another name is called out, and the request is complied with. Perhaps three or more requests for prayers are called out and complied with when the same voice again calls out *"Ave María,"* and the clapping of hands is resumed with the accompanying sounds as before . . . [including] the rattling of heavy chains. [10]

The alternating cacophony and prayer lasts nearly an hour before the single remaining light is returned and the others relighted from it. If the service is held in a church, the Brothers leave first, facing the altar and walking backward until out of the door; if at a morada, nonmembers depart immediately.

The Tinieblas is a dramatic highpoint in the village year. Families and neighbors literally huddle together in the din-filled, disorienting darkness—in the midst of chaos. At the same time, they symbolically take a stand in the face of this disintegration and are, in a sense, "heartened." In calling out the names of their beloved departed, they vividly recall the foundations and human history of their community. [11]

Wind and Fire: Sacrifice on the Plains

Both Hispano and Anglo settlers on the vast eastern grasslands, known as the Llano Estacado or Staked Plains, recalled the beginnings of their lonely communities in poignant songs and tales of the culture hero buffalo hunters and cowboys who had discovered the water sources that made later ranch and homestead life possible. These accounts commemorate the sacrifice of legendary figures who confront their destiny in dramatic encounters on the open plains. Such stories give transcendent meaning to an otherwise harsh existence wrested from inhospitable, desolate territory. Singers, storytellers, and their audiences participate in the discipline of *ciboleros,* or buffalo hunters, like the tragic Manuel Maes from Galisteo, who died on the Llano in 1873 and whose last words are imaginatively recreated in a *corrido,* or ballad, collected by Lorin W. Brown in 1937:

Oh my sorrel colored horse,	*Caballo alazan tostado*
That you should have been my death!	*Que tu la muerte me dites*
I found that I was tired	*me vide tan fatigiado*
And lost my hold on my lance	*Saltar la lanza me hicisteis*
And so the prairie sod is drenched	*El suelo quedo regado*
With my blood. You dyed it. . . .	*Con mi sangre lo tiniesteis. . . .*
Near the shores of a lake	*A orillas de una laguna*
Where they are going to bury me.	*De ande me iban enterrar*
Like a prickly pear plant without its fruit.	*Como al nopal sin la tuna*
Youth! here you'll remain.	*Joven te vas a quedar.*
"Cañon de l'Agua" to all well known	*Cañon del agua mentado*
You'll be my resting place	*Tu fuistes mi habitación*
And of my beloved parents	*Y de mis padres amados*
I wish their blessing	*Espero su bendición*
I hope they will commend	*Que me haigan encomendado*
That my soul should have absolution.	*Que mi alma tenga perdón.*
My heart had warned me	*Mi corazón me avisaba*
That death was imminent	*La muerte se te apodera*
On this Staked Plain	*En este llano estacado*
I will leave my skeleton.	*Vienes a hacer calavera.*[12]

Both Spanish and Anglo buffalo hunters were followed by trail blazers of another sort—the cowboys who herded cattle over dangerous terrain along the Goodnight-Loving Trail. The perils of cowboy life are expressed in "Little Joe, the Wrangler," one of America's most famous cowboy songs, which Jack Thorp composed on the trail from Chimney Lake, New Mexico, to Higgins, Texas, and first performed in Uncle Johnny Root's saloon in Weed, New Mexico. Folklorists Austin and Alta Fife call Little Joe "one of a constellation of heroes who, as a group, make up the mythical image of the cowboy—in this particular case the image of an abused youth whose loyalty in the crisis of a cattle stampede leads to a hero's death."[13]

Thorp opens his 1908 collection, *Songs of the Cowboys,* with "Little Joe, the Wrangler," whom he portrays as "a little 'Texas Stray'" who wanders into camp "all alone." The trail boss, who "sorter liked the little stray somehow," guides him in the lore of the cow camp, but disaster intervenes:

B. F. Pankey Ranch, "El Chico,"
Lamy, ca. 1915. Photo by T.
Harmon Parkhurst. (MNM Neg.
No. 12733.)

We'd driven to red river and the weather had been fine;
  We were camped down on the south side in a bend
When a norther commenced blowing and we doubled up
    our guards
  For it took all hands to hold the cattle then.

Little Joe the wrangler was called out with the rest
  And scarcely had the kid got to the herd
When the cattle they stampeded; like a hail storm, long
    they flew
  And all of us were riding for the lead.

'Tween the streaks of lightning we could see a horse far
    out ahead
  'Twas little Joe the wrangler in the lead;
He was riding "old Blue Rocket" with his slicker 'bove
    his head
  Trying to check the leaders in their speed.

At last we got them milling and kinder quieted down
  And the extra guard back to the camp did go
But one of them was missin' and we all knew at a glance
  'Twas our little Texas stray poor wrangler Joe.

 Next morning just at sunup we found where Rocket fell
  Down in a washout twenty feet below
Beneath his horse mashed to a pulp his horse had rung
    the knell
  For our little Texas stray—poor wrangler Joe.[14]

The ranchers and farmers who followed their culture heroes onto the "great American desert," as the Llano Estacado was known in the nineteenth century, settled first near old water sources and later sought others, drilling into the "desert" and harnessing the power of the omnipresent wind. May Price Mosley, who was raised in Lea County, speaks of her hunter and rancher neighbors as shrewd and even visionary individuals who first established themselves beside life-giving springs and then dug wells and built in ever-expanding radii. She recounts their emergence as a mythic penetration of the apparently barren earth:

> Thus did a few ex-buffalo hunters with their pick-axes and "dinimite" explode the long accepted theory of the Llano Estacado being a part of the "great American desert," and bit by bit uncover the fact that it was and is underlaid with one of the most remarkable and inexhaustible water supplies known to the continent. Sheet water, which at the few depressions of the plains reached to the surface in slight seeps, or very near the surface in shallow water spots. Water all through the centuries, for man's taking in exchange for a few moments' or a few hours' labor. Water beneath all its prairies, which but awaited the perfection of the well drill, the windmill, and the pumping plant to make this desert bloom.[15]

Roland Dickey remembers the sound of the windmills, "those Martian flowers that once sucked subsurface water from the plains," in eastern New Mexico:

> In those days, long before the deep primordial water table was being drained by electric pumps and circular irrigation systems, our lives centered around the windmill, a veritable polestar. We kept one ear on the wind, and although the big wheel and tail of the mill machinery would yaw automatically—that is, turn sideways in rising wind and reduce speed—it could be ripped apart like a loose sail.
>
> At the first sound of pump rods plunging up and down at a suicidal rate, we would rush to draw down the cable that furled the long fletched tail against the wheel, narrow-edge to the wind. During a gale this called for the weight and strength of two people on the 2-by-4 cut-off brake. The steel wheel would squawk and groan as it fought the wind, turning this way and that like an animal cornered.[16]

The same winds that helped turn desert into garden could transform Eden into an apocalyptic inferno, as in Curry County:

> But here ill winds do blow, and about November 15, 1906, a prairie fire started west of Melrose. The people in the Grady and Belleview country saw it coming for two nights and one day before it struck them about sunrise after the second night. Four hours more put this fire in Hereford [Texas]. Then the wind changed. The fire [was] going south to north side of the Santa Fe R.R. A slight wind change sent the fire west traveling along the railroad to a plowed field west to Melrose where the settlers gathered with water to wet sacks with which to fight it. They won.

In 1938, Mrs. Lena S. Maxwell collected old-timers' stories like the one above and told Mrs. Belle Kilgore her own reminiscences of that catastrophe and "hard times" around her hometown of Grady:

I remember about the prairie fire that swept everything from the face of the earth reaching from the southwest of Grady and Belleview to the northwest and as far as Clayton, New Mexico. One boy was caught out with his mules. The child's face was burned so badly and only his teeth on one side was left. The mules were so badly burned that they had to be killed.

Storms! An electric storm where we lived, four miles south of Grady and six miles directly south of the edge of the caprock. It was sometime in August. A big cloud stretched from east to west which was the blackest and angriest that I have ever seen. . . . When we went into the house and closed the doors there were little sparks of electricity all through the room just like sassafras wood sparks from an open fireplace popping from the fire. The lightning got continually worse. We took the metal hairpins out of our hair and I took off my corset which had steel staves in it. We put on our night dress and crawled into a fifty-pound feather bed. My daughter put her arms around me. I said, "Do not do that dear, if I am struck and killed it will kill you too." She cried, "Mama if you are killed I do not want to live." So we lay clasped in each other's arms until the electrical display had passed over, which seemed at least an hour. That is the most terrible experience that I have ever gone through with. That was perhaps in 1914 or '15.[17]

Trinity Site: Initiation into the Nuclear Age

A pinprick of a brilliant light punctured the darkness, spurted upward in a flaming jet, then spilled into a dazzling cloche of fire that bleached the desert to a ghastly white. It was precisely 5:29:45 a.m.

. . . Across the test site everything suddenly became infinitely tiny. Men burrowed into the sand like ants. Oppenheimer in that blinding instant thought of fragments from the sacred Hindu epic, Bhagavad-Gita:

> If the radiance of a thousand suns
> Were to burst at once into the sky,
> That would be like the splendor
>   of the Mighty One . . .
> I am become Death,
> The shatterer of worlds.

For a fraction of a second the light in that bell-shaped fire mass was greater than any ever produced before on earth. Its intensity was such that it could have been seen from another planet.[18]

Thus journalist Lansing Lamont describes July 16, 1945, the "Day of Trinity," when all people of this world emerged into the terrible light of the nuclear age. Acutely aware that this thunderous explosion of the world's first atomic bomb portends both deliverance and destruction, Lamont portrays the instant of transformation as one of awesome descent and ascent, of sublime terror, majesty, and fear:

First atomic bomb, White Sands, 1945. (MNM Neg. No. 71128. Los Alamos National Laboratory Collections in the Museum of New Mexico.)

For a split second after the moment of detonation the fireball, looking like a monstrous convoluting brain, bristled with spikes where the shot tower and balloon cables had been vaporized. Then the dust skirt whipped up by the explosion mantled it in a motley brown. Thousands of tons of boiling sand and dirt swept into its maw only to be regurgitated seconds later in a swirling geyser of debris as the fireball detached itself from the ground and shot upward. As it lifted from the desert, the sphere darkened in places, then opened as fresh bursts of luminous gasses broke through its surface.

At 2000 feet, still hurtling through the atmosphere, the seething ball turned reddish yellow, then a dull blood-red. It churned and belched forth smoking flame in an elemental fury. Below, the countryside was bathed in golden and lavender hues that lit every mountain peak and crevasse, every arroyo and bush with a clarity no artist could capture. At 15,000 feet the fireball cleaved the overcast in a bubble of orange that shifted to a darkening pink. Now, with its flattened top, it resembled a giant mushroom trailed by a stalk of radioactive dust. Within another few seconds the fireball had reached 40,000 feet and pancaked out in a mile-wide ring of graying ash. The air had ionized around it and crowned it with a lustrous purple halo. As the cloud finally settled, its chimney-shaped column of dust drifted northward and a violet afterglow tinged the heavens above Trinity.[19]

Conclusion

These four sets of mythic texts, taken in the broadest sense, reveal the sacred nature of New Mexico. They distill generations of human thought and experience within this land and show the common understandings among peoples of very different historical periods and cultures. Through these texts all New Mexicans participate in emergence, journey, pilgrimage, and mystery, guided by the lore of courageous culture heroes. Inspired by such lore, they no longer inhabit ordinary space and time but live imaginatively in a holy place and a renewed time.

New Mexico is a place of emergence. For Native Americans this means their birth as a people from the earth mother. In the Christian tradition, emergence is rebirth through sacrificial blood. New Mexico is also the place of another awesome or awful emergence. Here the world entered the nuclear age.

Emergence is not an end but a process. Mythologically, this process is usually symbolized by journey. In these New Mexico texts the journey between worlds is imagined as vertical movement. The most tangible symbols of this movement are the trees by which the people ascended from the underworlds, the cross upon which Jesus was crucified, the windmill that brought the life-giving waters from beneath the surface, and the bomb tower that held the device that blasted the desert into the sky. A more evanescent symbol of ascent and descent is the lightning that strikes the hero of the Navajo Windway myth, that stampedes the cattle on the open range, and that threatens the life of mother and daughter in their plains homestead.

Journey is conceived as a process of varying duration. The Acoma sisters grew slowly in the darkness of Shipapu and gradually learned the ways of emergence. The Holy Week Passion marked the culmination of a Lenten season of forty days' discipline. When time becomes calendrical, journeys take place in days, months, and years. But the flash of lightning in the Navajo Windway myth and the precise chronometry of detonation at Trinity symbolize journey as a sudden instant or microsecond of transformation.

The heroes of these mythic texts are pilgrims who endure difficult transformations in their journeying. The Navajo shattered by thunder, the Penitente Brother elevated on the village cross, the homesteader rooted at the base of the windmill, and the scientist mesmerized by his atomic pyrotechnics must sacrifice during their search for knowledge and renewal. Their trials bring them face to face with the ambivalence of a fascinating but terrible power, visions of promise and threat, salvation and damnation, creation and destruction.

The pilgrim is also a pupil, an initiate undergoing rites of passage, whose goal is new knowledge, whether of a healing rite, a new home, or a new perspective with enriched forms of lore—more moving song, speech, symbol, and celebration. The hero of the Navajo Windway chant violated the interdiction against going to Black Mountain (the Jemez Mountains where the nuclear scientists later designed their bomb). Although struck by lightning, he yet brought back rites of healing.

The passage of the pilgrim-pupil becomes a confrontation with what theologian Rudolf Otto describes as *"Das Heilige"* or "The Sacred." This encounter inspires "the *feeling of terror* before the sacred, before the awe-inspiring mystery *(mysterium tremendum),* the majesty *(majestas)* that emanates an overwhelming superiority of power . . . [and] *religious fear* before the fascinating mystery *(mysterium fascinans)* in which perfect fullness of being flowers."[20] Terror in the presence of the sacred is evoked when the two sisters in the Acoma emergence myth cower with uncertainty about the cycle of day and night, when Hispano villagers huddle in the darkness of the Tinieblas, when plains farmers gaze at the approaching holocaust for two nights and one day, and when scientists burrow to escape the irradiating fire mass.

The Tewa Indians imagine the connection between worlds as woven with rain on a sky loom. The people bring gifts and Mother Earth and Father Sky communicate with bright garments of light and rain in a reciprocal and repetitious process that enables them to "walk fittingly" in their sacred home. But the explosion at Trinity that sent fire and dust mushrooming forty thousand feet into the air wove a fearful garment on the modern loom of science and technology. The instantaneous inversion of the traditional sky loom means that all New Mexicans must undertake new journeys to seek new knowledge and bring back new gifts, that they may continue the process of emergence and "walk fittingly" in the nuclear age.

Cochiti Pueblo pottery designs, by Kenneth Chapman. (MNM Neg. No. 22300.)

FOCAL PLACE ONE

Shiprock and Four Corners

The mythic texts in chapter 1, "Sky Looms," recount sacred connections and journeys between this earth and the under and upper worlds. Shiprock and nearby Four Corners in northeastern New Mexico focus these themes. While the geological texts presented below echo the theme of emergence, the mythological texts describe the origin of landforms that reach into the sky and the exploits of culture heroes who climb toward that domain.

Shiprock is a natural landmark with multiple, powerful mythic connotations for the Navajo people. By contrast, Four Corners is a completely artificial surveyors' construct of arbitrary, political boundaries.

Tourists visiting the Shiprock area today are forbidden to climb the rock formations, but they may participate in the area's commerce by attending the Navajo Fair or buying the Yeibichai and Two Grey Hills rugs characteristic of this part of the Navajo Reservation. They may also drive to Four Corners and purchase goods from Navajo and Ute vendors and go from that contrived intersection to the Four Corners Power Plant, whose smoke was visible to the naked eye of culture hero astronauts who had journeyed beyond earth and sky to the moon itself.

Geological Texts

The Cretaceous Period (70 to 135 m.y. ago) was one of great contrast in New Mexico. . . .

As the Cretaceous seas withdrew from New Mexico, the Cenozoic Era dawned, and never again have marine waters shaped the landscapes. The rocks, Precambrian, Paleozoic, Mesozoic, and Cenozoic, and their ancient movements determine New Mexico's spectacular landscapes. They tell tales of the endless war between erosion and hard rock, show the deposition of sediments, their uplift, and

Shiprock, Navajo riders. Photo by Will Pennington. (MNM Neg. No. 89512.)

their eventual destruction. The result is striking scenery—volcanic mountains, as Mount Taylor, Sierra Blanca, Valle Grande—fresh lava flows near Carrizozo and Grants—volcanic necks like Shiprock and Cabezon—White Sands, the work of the wind—El Morro, Enchanted Mesa, Acoma, and badlands near Santa Fe, the result of weathering and erosion—great fault-line escarpments of the Sandia, Manzano, San Andres, and Sacramento mountains—the work of underground waters at Carlsbad Caverns. And man adds his erosive powers—the huge open-pit copper mine at Santa Rita and countless excavations for rock to build homes, to straighten highways.[1]

The last phase of the Paleogene Period, about 25 to 40 m.y. ago, was an earth-shaking time in New Mexico—and the first explosion of an atomic bomb in 1945 on the Jornada del Muerto between Socorro and Carrizozo was a relatively low-energy-yield event compared with the late Paleogene earth movements. . . . This widespread volcanic activity continued into the Neogene Period which began about 25 m.y. ago. . . . Mount Taylor, towering up to 11,389 feet near Grants and visible on the western skyline from Albuquerque, is a Neogene volcanic pile, as are parts of the Sangre de Cristo range northeast of Taos. Shiprock and Cabezon Peak, landmarks in northwestern New Mexico, are volcanic necks—the eroded cores of ancient volcanoes.[2]

Shiprock! A buttressed needle, towering 1450 vertical feet above Navajoland, with walls of black igneous rock radiating from its feet like spikes on a wheel. This dark-colored spire once filled the throat of a volcano. Where are the piles of rocks, hundreds of feet thick, that once surrounded it? Down the river they went, down the San Juan to the Colorado River, and thence to the ocean.[3]

Mythological Texts

At Mesa Verde National Park in 1928, Navajo chief Sandoval, or Hastin Tlo'tsi hee (Old Man Buffalo Grass), recounted to Aileen O'Bryan (Nusbaum) the Navajo emergence myth told him by his grandmother, Esdzan Hosh kige. Her story includes the following account about the origin of Shiprock and other mountains:

First Man and First Woman formed six sacred mountains from the soil that First Man had gathered from the mountains in the Third World and kept in his medicine bag. . . .

After First Man and First Woman had made and dressed the six mountains they found that there was still a little earth left in the medicine bag, so Tseya kan', the Hog Back Mountains, and the mesas south of them were formed. . . .

The last of the earth was used to form Nltsa dzil, Strong Rain Mountain, the Carrizos. They made this great mountain with its legs to the South and its head to the North. It has for its dress Strong Goods, meaning many rocks for its clothing. This mountain has three other names: it is called Yolgai dzil, Bead Mountain; Nil tliz dzil, Mixed Chips Mountain; and Ta di din dzil, Strong Pollen Mountain. It holds the pollen of all the plants. And it was planned by First Man that the people should use this mountain, so he made it a strong mountain. First Man and First Woman set arrows around it to guard it. These are the rock formations such as Shiprock.[4]

According to both Washington Matthews's *Navaho Legends* (1897) and the Franciscan Fathers' Navajo dictionary of 1910, Shiprock is called Tse bida'i, or Winged Rock, in Navajo.[5] Gladys A. Reichard summarizes several anthropological texts collected during the nineteenth and twentieth centuries in the following account of Cliff Monster or Throwing Monster (tsé nenáxa'li'), who became Shiprock. He was an "unpersuadable deity" who was

conceived by the self-abuse of a chief's daughter with a feather quill [and] was thrown after birth into an alkali bed. He became the monster He-throws-against-the rocks, named from his habit of catching people in his long sharp claws and throwing them to his children lower down among the rocks. He had a long beak and large eyes; something like feathers grew on his shoulders. The male caught his prey, carried it to the highest ledge of a rock like Shiprock, and threw it down to his wife, who wore beautiful earstrings. The children waited for their food below the mother.

Monster Slayer [the elder twin culture hero] carried the paunch filled with Burrowing Monster's blood as bait for Cliff Monster. The male, seeing Monster Slayer traveling with it slung over his shoulder, swooped down and carried him high, then let him fall to the nest at the very top of the cliff. Monster Slayer was saved by a life feather given him by Spider Woman, and the blood flowing from the broken paunch made the monster think the boy had been killed. Monster Slayer found himself among the young, from whom he learned the parents' names. Monster Slayer killed the mother and father monsters, tossing them down to the children to eat, just as many Earth People had been treated. . . .

The father monster was transformed into Shiprock, which is thought to look like a poised eagle. The young were transformed into the eagles and owls that today furnish many forms of ceremonial property. Monster Slayer took feathers for his trophies. After all these things had happened, he found himself high on a ledge with no way to get down. Bat Woman appeared, carried him down, and was rewarded with a basket of down feathers that subsequently became birds.[6]

Shiprock was called Needles before 1848. The Place Names Project sponsored by the New Mexico Folklore Society, 1948–1951, yielded three contemporary "folk myths" associated with the "majestic rock called by the Navajos *tse bida' hi,* 'rock with wings' . . . : one that the Navajos crossed a narrow sea beyond the setting sun and landed among an unfriendly people which caused the Great Spirit to send a stone ship to carry them to this spot; another is that they were brought by a great bird which was turned into stone when the mission was finished; the third is that the Navajos were cast up from the earth at this spot and the ship is a symbol of their voyage."[7]

Tourist Texts

SHIPROCK . . . was established in 1903 as a northern Navajo Indian agency and remains a center for Navajo tribal business, trading, health care, and industry such as the large helium plant and a uranium processing facility.

Nearly every fall since 1903, the Navajo nation has held its Northern Navajo Fair in Shiprock. Exceptional arts and crafts are exhibited, and rodeos and rides provide the thrills. Some older men and many women wear traditional dress to the events of the fair.[8]

Typical of the Shiprock area are the Yei and Yeibichai rugs, portraying religious figures—tall, slender, sticklike, with stylized arms and legs, usually lacking true religious significance. The rugs generally are woven with commercially dyed yarn, and may be coarse or fine in texture.

Two other locally produced types of [Navajo] rugs are also available in Shiprock, easily identifiable as to origin. Teec Nos Pos, an area close to the Four Corners Monument, produces a bright and busy rug with a broad, figured border and intricate geometric designs, largely using commercially dyed wool. It is said that a missionary to the area early in the twentieth century circulated pictures of Persian rugs among weavers, influencing them to adopt a similar style. One of the most popular and most costly regional rug types is the Two Grey Hills rug, named for a trading post twenty-five miles south of Shiprock. This style emerged in the twentieth century after area weavers threw off an attempt by a trader from Crystal to introduce bright commercial colors. The Two Grey Hills rug uses black, a commercial color, and the natural colors of brown, gray, and white, woven with a dark (usually black) border and strong, geometric designs within the border. Some of the finest Two Grey Hills rugs can be classified as tapestries rather than floor coverings; the works of Daisy Tauglechee, for example, may have 120 threads of her hand-spun wool to the inch and a buttery texture.[9]

As the traveler heads south from the town of Shiprock, the monolithic formation called Shiprock (because of its resemblance to a sailing craft with wind-filled sheets) looms to the west. . . . As with all such rock monuments in Navajo country, it is forbidden to climb the Shiprock because of its religious significance.[10]

Four Corners

New Mexico's artificial identity as a state is focused near Shiprock, at Four Corners, the only point in the United States where four states come together. Accessible only by road, miles from any dwelling, and now ringed by vendors and picnic tables, this surveyor's and cartographer's intersection made manifest with a flat monument is also visible from outer space, according to a current New Mexico guide:

The Four Corners Power Plant is an enormous electricity-generating unit on the south side of Morgan Lake. The adjacent Navajo Mine is the largest open-pit coal mine in the western United States. Tours are given on a regular schedule. In keeping with the grand scale of these operations, it is said that the smoke from the Four Corners Plant was the only manmade phenomenon visible with the naked eye to the astronauts on the moon.[11]

Retablo showing Santiago.
Photo by Truman Matthews.
(MNM Neg. No. 21292.)

2 ROYAL ROADS

TEXTS OF MIGRATION, ADVENTURE, AND COMMERCE

Of arms I sing and of the man heroic;	*Las armas y el varon heroico canto,*
The being, valor, prudence, and high effort	*El ser, valor, prudencia, y alto esfuerço,*
Of him whose endless, never-tiring patience,	*De aquel cuya paciencia no rendida,*
Over an ocean of annoyance stretching,	*Por un mar de disgustos arrojada,*
Despite the fangs of foul, envenomed envy	*A pesar de la inuidia ponçoñosa*
Brave deeds of prowess ever is achieving;	*Los hecos y prohesas va encumbrando.*
Of those brave men of Spain, conquistadores,	*De aquellos Españoles valerosos,*
Who, in the Western India nobly striving,	*Que en la Occidental India remontados,*
And searching out all of the world yet hidden,	*Descubriendo del mundo lo que esconde,*
Still onward press their glorious achievements,	*Plus vltra con braueza van diziendo,*
By their strong arm and deeds of daring valor,	*A fuerça de valor y braços fuertes,*
In strife of arms and hardships as enduring	*En armas y quebrantos tan sufridos,*
As, with rude pen, worthy of being honored.	*Quanto de tosca pluma celebrados;*
And thee I supplicate, most Christian Philip,	*Suplicoos Christianissimo Filipo,*
Since of New Mexico thou art the Phoenix	*Que pues de nueva Mexico soys fenix,*
Of late sprung forth and in thy grandeur risen	*Nueuamente salido y producido,*
From out the mass of living flame and ashes	*De aquellas viuas llamas y cenizas,*
Of faith most ardent, in whose glowing embers	*De ardentísima fee, en cuyas brasas,*
Thy own most holy father and our master	*A vuestro sacro Padre, y señor nuestro,*
We saw unwrapped, devoured by sacred fervor—	*Todo deshecho y abrasado vimos*
To move some little time from off thy shoulders	*Suspendais algun tanto de los hombres (hombros),*
The great and heavy weight, that thee oppresses,	*El grande y graue peso que os impide,*
Of that terrestrial globe which in all justice	*De aquese inmenso globo que en justicia,*
Is by thine own strong arm alone supported;	*Por solo vuestro braço se sustenta,*
And giving, gracious king, attentive hearing,	*Y prestando gran Rey atento oido,*
Thou here wilt see the weight of weary labors,	*Vereis aqui la fuerça de trabajos,*
And grievous calumnies with which is planted	*Calumnias y aflicciones con que planta,*

The holy gospel and the faith of Jesus	El Euangelio santo y Fé de Christo
By that Achilles who by royal order	Aquel Christiano Achiles que quisistes,
Devotes himself to such heroic service.	Que en obra tan heroica se ocupase,
And if I may by rare access of fortune	Y si por qual que buena suerte alcanço,
Have thee, most noble Philip, for a hearer,	A teneros Monarca por oiente,
Who doubts that with a universal impulse	Quien duda que con admirable espanto,
The whole world will hold its breath to listen	La redondez del mundo todo escuche,
To that which holds so great a king's attention?	Lo que a tan alto Rey atento tiene.

—Gaspar Pérez de Villagrá, *Historia de la Nueva México,* 1610, Canto One, trans. Hubert Howe Bancroft, 1889.[1] Soldier-poet Villagrá chronicled the first authorized colonizing expedition to New Mexico, led by Don Juan de Oñate in 1598.

Heroes and heroines of all sorts—explorers, traders, trail drivers, migrants, prospectors, trappers, hunters, stagecoach drivers, Indian runners—have woven a tapestry of trails across New Mexico. Whether fascinated by visions of the fabulous, lured by prospects of legendary wealth, or compelled toward a homeland, these adventurous travelers relentlessly traversed and retraversed this land. For such journeyers the process of discovery and migration was tantamount to sacred pilgrimage, but here with a concentration on temporal, terrestrial movement testing individual mettle and fulfilling collective destinies. From the earliest times this mobility also generated an ongoing commerce among peoples eager to communicate, to participate, to compete, to exchange, to learn about themselves and others, and to celebrate their travels in story, song, and ceremony.

Footpaths

In Apache, Navajo, and Pueblo mythology, migrations over this earth follow the emergence from the underworlds. Santa Clara Pueblo Turtle Dancers sing of their journey from the north:

> Long ago in the north
> Lies the road of emergence!
> Yonder our ancestors live,
> Yonder we take our being.
>
> Yet now we come southwards.
> For cloud flowers blossom here
> Here the lightning flashes,
> Rain water here is failing![2]

The Cochiti Indians tell an origin myth of their wandering before they came to Cochiti Mesa:

The people lived together in Frijoles Canyon. They used to dance every night. Two of the koshare were playing; they were on the house roofs, and they were playing at throwing a little baby from one to the other. The baby slipped from the hands of the koshare who was "throwing" him, and fell to the ground and was killed. Then both of the koshare jumped down after the baby, and they were all killed. The people decided to leave that place.

They came to the mesa of the Stone Lions. They remained there four days and danced the Red Tse'atcuwa. From there they came on and stopped at Nokahe'a. They remained there four days and danced the Black Tseatcuwa. From there they came on and stopped at Red Paint Mountain. They remained there four days and danced the Red Tseatcuwa. From there they came on and stopped at Rabbit's Place (Lakia). They remained there four days and danced the Black Tseatcuwa. They came on and stopped at Water Dripping Place (Stĭrshtĭkana). There the koshare danced by themselves. The footprints of the people and their turkeys are there yet. They came on and came to Cochiti mesa, and they danced all their dances. They lived there. [3]

Matilda Coxe Stevenson collected a version of the Zunis' emergence and migration in the late nineteenth century. It is chanted by a masked figure known as Kyaklo:

Following their road of exit, they stooped over
  and came out.
They walked this way.
They came to the gaming-stick spring.
They came to the gaming-ring spring.
They came to the Ne'wekwe baton spring.
They came to the spring with prayer plume standing.
They came to the cat-tail place.
They came to the moss spring.
They came to the muddy spring.
They came to the sun-ray spring.
They came to the spring by many aspens.
They came to shell place.
They came to dragon-fly place.
They came to flower place.
They came to the place of trees with drooping limbs.
They came to fish spring.
They came to young-squash spring.
They came to listening spring.

Yäm o'neya'ʰhlan kwai'ina i'tinakna, kwai'ikĭa.
[Their great road exit stoop, come out.]
Kĭa'ʰla a'wakĭa.
[This way come.]
Yä'munĕ ʰkĭai' akwi a'wikĭa
[Gaming-stick spring come to.]
ʰSĭ'kon ʰkĭai' akwi a'wikĭa.
[Gaming-ring spring come to.]
Tä'nin ʰkĭai' akwi a'wikĭa.
[Ne'wekĭwe baton spring come to.]

Ta′melän ′kĭai′akwi a′wikĭa.
[Prayer plume standing spring come to.]
Ke′yatiwa kwi a′wikĭa.
[Cat-tail place come to.]
A′wisho ′kĭai′ akwi a′wikĭa.
[Moss spring come to.]
Pä′nanulin ′kĭai′ akwi a′wikĭa.
[Muddy spring come to.]
La′tŏw ′kĭai′akwi a′wikĭa.
[Sunbeam spring come to.]
′Hlän′ihlkoha ′kĭai′akwi a′wikĭa.
[Aspen spring come to.]
U′pul′lema kwi a′wikĭa.
[Shell place come to.]
Pä′sie shi′na kwi a′wikĭa.
[Dragon fly name place come to.]
U′teyan ĭn′kwi a′wikĭa.
[Flower place come to.]
Ta′piliyänkyu kwi a′wikĭa.
[Tree with drooping limbs place come to.]
Käsh′ita ′kĭai′akwi a′wikĭa.
[Fish spring place come to.]
Mo′län ′kia′akwi a′wikĭa.
[Young squash spring come to.]
Hä′tina ′kĭai′akwi a′wikĭa.
[Listen spring come to.][4]

This account, known to the Zunis as "Kyaklo an penanne," the Word of Kyaklo, is an especially important narration of their peregrination from the place of emergence to their Middle Place, or homeland. According to Dennis Tedlock:

> Kyaklo is a person, a Zuni, who witnessed some of the events of the beginning. He comes once each four or eight years to give his word. He is a stubborn, cranky cripple who must be carried everywhere he goes by the ten clowns who accompany him, and he always demands that the smallest one do it. He always comes into town by the same path, the same path he has followed since the beginning. There is a new subdivision whose streets do not follow his path, so he must be carried through people's yards. There is a house that sits in his path, so he must be carried up over the roof and down the other side. When they come to the river, just before entering the old part of town, he insists that the clowns wade through the ice and mud of the river rather than taking the bridge. He wears the finest clothes, but they always manage to drop him in the river. . . . The people who want to hear his word assemble in six different ceremonial chambers, or kivas. . . . He goes from one building to the next, still chanting even while being carried through the streets; no one person hears the whole word on one occasion, except for the clowns who carry him. . . . To wear Kyaklo's mask, a person must devote his whole life, for one year, to studying for the part.[5]

Footraces are another means of recreating important movement. In *Indian Running*, Peter Nabokov explains that: "Gods and animals ran long before Indian men and women ever did. Thereafter the gods told people to do it, and the animals showed them how. 'There is nothing that Indians like so well as to run races,' a Zuni Indian told Anna Risser. 'Maybe that is because the gods in the far past settled so many difficult questions by races.'"[6]

Every Jicarilla Apache youth, after he has reached puberty but before he has married, must participate at least once in autumn ceremonial relay races. Half of the runners are selected to represent the "Llanero" (the moon and the plants), while the others are chosen to portray the "Ollero" (the sun and the animals). In 1934–1935 Morris Edward Opler learned the myth of the origin of the races:

> The reason for the first ceremonial race was that there was too much food of both kinds, meat and plants, at the same time. The food was all mixed up and people didn't know how to use it. The food did not come in season then as it does now. Sun and Moon decided that it must be divided up and that there should be seasons for the different kinds of food.
>
> Moon said, "I'll bet all my fruits against you."
>
> Sun said, "I'll bet all my animals." . . .
>
> The sun's side kept ahead and won the race.
>
> So the sun won, and his side was able to hunt all kinds of animals and had a great deal of meat to eat that year. . . . The sun and the moon agreed that they were going to run like this every year for four years. The second year the moon's side won. The third year the sun's side won. And the fourth year the moon won again. The sun and the moon took turns winning because people can't eat meat all the time, and they can't eat vegetables all the time. It was to insure both kinds of food for mankind.
>
> After the fourth race the ceremony was handed to these Apaches. They were watching it during these four years, so Sun, Moon, White God, Ancestral Man, Monster Slayer, and Water's Child decided to give it to them. "This is your ceremony now," they told the Apache. "If you stop holding this ceremony you will starve." That is why the Jicarilla are afraid to stop holding this ceremony.[7]

Opler noted that while there was good-natured rivalry during the ceremonial relay races, the objectives were collective and cooperative, not competitive.

Nevertheless, southwestern Indian lore includes many example of how human movement could be intensely contested. The Acoma Indians told Bernhart A. Reuter in the 1920s about a legendary episode that took place on the most difficult trail ascending Acoma Mesa:

> There is a story about a wager between a woman and a man who used to climb this trail often because they liked the thrill it gave them to bring their loads up its difficult sections. The woman wagered her jewelry against his buckskins that she could, with a large pot full of water on her head and without spilling a drop, follow him anywhere that he could climb with a deer on his back. The contest, of course, had to wait until he killed a deer. On his next hunt he was lucky in shooting a fine buck, and when the deer was brought to the mesa, he laid it at the foot of this

trail and notified the woman and the people of the village that he was ready for the wager. The woman was not long appearing at the foot of the trail, where the deer lay, with her tinaja of water.

After resting a short time, the man put the deer on his back in true Indian fashion. (The Indians skin back hide from the lower leg bones leaving the dew-claws on the hide for knots. The bones are then removed at the knees and hocks. Then the hide of the left front leg and the right hind leg are tied together and the other two legs the same fashion. A man can then insert his arms in between the fastened legs much as he puts on a pair of suspenders, so that the leg skins knotted together will lie between his shoulders and the deer's body across his hips.) In this fashion, the man mounted the deer on his back and began the laborious ascent; and the woman followed close behind with the olla of water perched on her head.

By this time the people of the village had gathered around the edge of the cliff to watch the outcome. The man moved along at a fair pace at first, for the lower part of the trail is neither difficult nor dangerous. On reaching the point where the trail ascends at a greater angle and hangs on the side of the mesa wall, the two moved cautiously; for any faltering in their footwork might send them to their doom. With great effort and caution the man with his deer reached the part of the trail near the summit which is most difficult to make with any sort of load. The man was now beginning to feel the strain of the ascent with his load of 150 pounds or more.

The woman seemed fresh, for hers was a feat of skill more than toil. After resting a little, the man tackled this last and most difficult part of his trip with the woman close behind. Just as the man with his deer was straining every muscle of his body to force his way over this last desperate stretch, his feet slipped, and with his heavy load fell backward over the woman with the jar of water and both were hurled to the floor of the gulch below. Thus ended the lives of the two hardiest souls of the village.[8]

Conquistadors

In the first half of the sixteenth century, Spanish exploration and conquest of Central and South America gave rise to a complex of legend and report about the fabulous. The Mexican expeditions of Hernán Cortés (1519–1521), were

> exploits . . . duplicated in a measure in Central America, where the noted Pedrarias conquered the natives with a cruel and ruthless hand; in Guatemala, where Pedro de Alvarado subjugated a kingdom; in Peru, where Francisco de Pizarro, descendant of a family so poor and lowly that he has been called the Swineherd of Estremadura, broke the power of the Inca Empire and reduced it to allegiance to Spain; in Chile, where Pedro de Valdivia began the conquest of the indomitable Araucanian Indians; or in New Granada (the modern Colombia), where Gonzalo Jiménez de Quesada established the power of the Spanish king in the fabled land of the Chibchas. Here originated the tale of El Dorado, popularized by Adolph Bandelier as *The Gilded Man* [1893], where, in a religious ceremonial, a native chieftain, bedaubed with mud and sprayed with gold dust, dived into a lake to wash off the golden dust and so propitiate the gods.[9]

"Spring foot-races, Pueblo of Isleta, N.M.," 1891. Photo by Charles F. Lummis. (Lummis Collection, Coronado Room, General Library, University of New Mexico. Used with permission.)

During the late 1520s, while Cortés was in Spain answering charges of treason and abuse, two expeditions were launched simultaneously: Pánfilo de Narváez in the Floridas and Nuño de Guzmán northward from Mexico City. Guzmán and his men were seeking the Isle of the Amazons and the legendary Seven Golden Cities, which fourteenth-century Portuguese navigators had sought in the Atlantic. In March 1536 some of Guzmán's band were startled to encounter in northern Mexico the bedraggled remnants of Narváez's ill-fated eastern expedition. Four survivors among Narváez's original force of three hundred—Alvar Núñez Cabeza de Vaca, the Black Estevánico, Andrés Dorantes, and Alonso del Castillo Maldonado—had trekked more than six thousand miles in eight years. Guzmán escorted the fortunate Europeans to Culiacán and then to Mexico City, where they related tales of their fabulous exploits to the new viceroy, Antonio de Mendoza, and renewed Spanish interest in the lands north of the Aztec Empire.

Cabeza de Vaca appeared before King Charles I of Spain to deliver a report of his adventures and subsequently released a printed version in October 1542. In that version he describes his encounters with Indians in present-day southern New Mexico:

> We showed them the copper rattle we had recently been given, and they told us that many layers of this material were buried in the place whence it came, that this [metal] was highly valued, and that the people who made it lived in fixed dwellings. We conceived the country they spoke of to be on the South Sea, which we had always understood was richer in mineral resources than that of the North. . . .

MIGRATION, ADVENTURE, AND COMMERCE 37

They [of the Tularosa village] guided us [down the Tularosa, then south] through more than fifty leagues, mostly over rugged mountain desert so dry there was a dearth of game, and we suffered great hunger. . . .

Many of the people began to sicken from the privation and exertion of negotiating those sterile, difficult ridges. Our escort, however, conducted us across a thirty-league plain. . . , and we found many persons come a long distance on the trail to greet us . . . and welcomed us like those before. . . .

We told our new hosts that we wished to go where the sun sets; but they said people in that direction were remote. We commanded them to send and make known our coming anyway. They stalled and made various excuses, because the people to the west were their enemies, whom they wanted to avoid. . . .

We told them, then, to conduct us northward. They answered as before: there were no people in that direction for a very long distance, nothing to eat, and no water. When we remained adamant, they still excused themselves as best they could, and our gorge rose.[10]

Cabeza de Vaca follows a pattern common to the travel narratives of the Spanish New World, as John Francis Bannon elucidates:

The Indians were quick to sense the greed-inspired gullibility of their unwelcome guests and they fed this credulity with consummate skill. What the Spaniard sought was regularly "just a little farther on"—*poco más allá*. And the very interesting aspect of this whole matter is that the native Americans—north, south, east, and west—on both continents and on either seaboard, seem to have the almost identical answer. Whether it was El Dorado or the Amazons or the White King, the Land of Chicora or Cíbola or Quivira, the Mountain of Silver or dozens more, the Indians fitted their misinformation to tantalize Spanish hopes and to keep alive Spanish get-rich-quick dreams. First contacts with the Borderlands of the future sprang from the incurable optimism of the conquistadores.[11]

In March 1539, Fray Marcos de Niza, guided by Estevánico, set out from Culiacán to explore the interior, to verify Cabeza de Vaca's stories, and to search for the Seven Cities. Estevánico pushed ahead of the main party, informing Fray Marcos of his progress by sending back Christian crosses of increasing size:

That is, if Estevánico found good news, he was to send back an Indian bearing a small cross; if more important news, a larger cross; and if he should discover a country richer than Mexico itself, a great cross. Lo and behold, four days later an Indian messenger brought Fray Marcos a cross "as high as a man" and urged the friar to push forward at once. Fray Marcos did so, and is supposed finally to have approached Zuñi in New Mexico, but to have seen the pueblo only from a distance, for the Zuñians were hostile, had killed Estevánico, and his fleeing companions did not need to urge Fray Marcos to flee for his life. It may be that he had seen Zuñi in a mirage, a common characteristic of the dry, mountain country, as all of us who have lived in it can testify. In any case, Fray Marcos, on his return to Mexico, gilded his narrative profusely with stories of rich cities. The Seven Cities, indeed, were given the name Cíbola, a new word which he had heard

Map of New Mexico. Painting by Bernardo Miera y Pacheco, 1760. (MNM Neg. No. 92062; MNM Artifact No. 9599/45.)

from the Indians. Ever since then it has been applied to Zuñi and the group of pueblos that surrounded it in ancient times.[12]

On September 2, 1539, Fray Marcos reported his findings to Mendoza in Mexico City. The viceroy meanwhile had determined that Francisco Vásquez de Coronado would lead a formal "entrada de conquista" to the north.

Instead of finding a city "larger than the city of Mexico," as Fray Marcos had portrayed it, Coronado found the Zuni Pueblo of Hawikuh and discovered that the "Seven Cities were seven little villages, all within a radius of four leagues." Disappointed but undaunted, Coronado dispatched a group of soldiers under Pedro de Tovar to journey farther north into Tusayan, where they became the first white men to see the Hopi towns of northeastern Arizona.

Another party under Hernando de Alvarado was dispatched to the east: "En route they passed the famous 'sky city' of Ácoma; thence they advanced into the province of Tiguex, the future Albuquerque area. At that point they were in the heart of Pueblo country. They pushed on to Cicuye [Pecos] and next ventured beyond the mountains toward the Texas Panhandle, where they got their first look at that amazing creature, the American buffalo—the 'shaggy cows' of the Cabeza de Vaca story. At Cicuye they met the Indian whom they dubbed 'The Turk,' who was to influence their lives and those of their companions for the next ten or so months—and profoundly. His was the story of Quivira, a land lying to the north and east whose riches made former dreams of the Seven Cities conservative by comparison."[13] In his history of the Coronado expedition, Pedro de Castañeda reports that

> the Turk claimed that in his land there was a river, flowing through plains, which was two leagues wide, with fish as large as horses and a great number of very large canoes with sails, carrying more than twenty oarsmen on each side. The nobles, he said, traveled in the stern, seated under canopies, and at the prow there was a large golden eagle. He stated further that the lord of that land took his siesta under a large tree from which hung numerous golden jingle bells, and he was pleased as they played in the wind. He added that the common table service of all was generally of wrought silver, and that the pitchers, dishes, and bowls were made of gold. He called gold *acochis*. At first he was believed on account of the directness with which he told his story and also because, when they showed him jewels made of tin, he smelled them and said that it was not gold, that he knew gold and silver very well, and that he cared little for other metals.[14]

The Coronado expedition wintered in Tiguex, and in the spring of 1541 they moved eastward onto the Llano Estacado. Both Coronado and Pedro de Castañeda kept detailed records of the Spaniards' route across the Llano and their methods of navigating across that unusual terrain. The party took its direction from the compass, and one member was detailed to count his footsteps each day. Coronado described the Llano as being "as bare of landmarks as if we were surrounded by the sea. Here the guides lost their bearings because there is nowhere a stone, hill, tree, bush, or anything of the sort."[15] According to Castañeda, even hunters learned the treachery of the plains:

> many of the men who went hunting got lost and were unable to return to the camp for two or three days. They wandered from place to place without knowing how to find their way back. . . . It must be remarked that since the land is so level, when they had wandered aimlessly until noon, following the game, they had to remain by their kill, without straying, until the sun began to go down in order to learn which direction they then had to take to get back to their starting point.[16]

It was also "necessary to stack up piles of bones and dung of the cattle at various distances in order that the rear guard could follow the army and not get lost."[17] Having traveled as far as present-day Wichita, Kansas, in search of Quivira, the temporarily discouraged expedition returned to the Rio Grande for the winter of 1541–42. Coronado's injury in a riding accident finally forced the now disillusioned explorers to return south to New Spain in the spring of 1542.

Although Quivira "became an established point on the maps of European mapmakers . . . [who] might locate it anywhere from Kansas to California,"[18] it did not again figure significantly in New Mexican lore until the first colonizing expedition of Don Juan de Oñate in 1598. Oñate and his men explored the pueblos from the Jumano in the Estancia Valley, northward up the Rio Grande to Taos, and west to the Jemez, Acoma, Zuni, and Moqui (Hopi) regions. Even though they discovered neither gold nor great cities, Oñate still wrote his resolve to King Felipe III on April 7, 1599: "I trust in God that I shall give your majesty a new world, greater than New Spain, to judge from the reports I have received and from what I have seen and explored, and I shall persevere in this effort to the end of my life."[19] Among these reports were renewed testimonies about Quivira, and in the summer of 1601 Oñate followed essentially the same eastward route onto the plains taken by Coronado sixty years before. An optimistic Oñate returned to the Rio Grande: "Not only had they found a land of surpassing fertility and promise, but they had heard of other lands and kingdoms farther on—'más allá'—as the Spanish reads—which could be explored from Quivira."[20]

The Horse

Coronado, Oñate, and other Spanish adventurers who came on horseback in search of Quivira ironically bestowed great wealth—the horse itself—upon those whom they intended to plunder. The Zuni Indians initially believed that the Spaniards'

Navajo riders. Photo by J. R. Willis. (MNM Neg. No. 98187.)

horses were anthropophagous, or man-eating. Castañeda reported that the Acoma Indians descended from their mesa to greet Coronado and "made their peace ceremonies by approaching the horses, taking their sweat and anointing themselves with it." Castañeda interpreted this as a sign of submission since the Indians made "crosses with the fingers of their hands,"[21] but it is more likely that "the Pueblo tribes, equally amazed with the unknown animal . . . smeared their own bodies with the fluid, doubtless with the idea of transferring to themselves something of the magic of the Great Dog of the white men."[22]

By the time of Oñate's colonizing expedition in 1598, the Pueblo Indians had become accustomed to the new animals. Oñate arrived at San Juan Pueblo with 256 mares and 995 stallions, and the Spanish colonists, known to be excellent horse breeders, could have nurtured their original stock into a herd of more than 5,000 horses, with as many as 1,600 mares, in ten years of encampment at San Juan.[23] Indian servants helped tend the horses, and "some of the older Indians (Tewa) at San Juan believed that the horse had always been present at their pueblos. . . . [They told] many stories of deeds on horseback, almost mythological in character, so that we must assume a marked cultural impact caused by the intensity of horse culture at San Gabriel (Yunque) now included in the San Juan Pueblo structure."[24]

The Spaniards moved their capital in 1610 from San Gabriel to Santa Fe, which became a major center for the distribution of horses to non-Pueblo tribes. New Mexican Apaches acquired horses sometime between 1600 and 1638, while those Southern Athapascans who became known as Navajos were definitely established as horsemen sometime after 1680. According to LaVerne Harrell Clark, "the acquiring of horses by the Southern Athapascans was of major importance to their lifeways. It brought greater mobility and freedom of movement to those semi-nomadic people who had previously known only the tedious foot journeys of a few miles a day with all their possessions carried on their backs or loaded on slow pack dogs."[25] The introduction of the horse increased opportunities for commerce, hunting, and the acquisition of wealth and social status.

Both Navajo and Apache mythologists quickly incorporated the horse and all it symbolized into story, song, art, ritual, belief, and practice. Morris Opler, for example, has recorded origin myths from the Lipan and Mescalero Apaches, recounting how the culture hero created the first horse in the upper world of the sky.[26] "The War God's Horse Song," sung by the Navajo Tall Kia ah'ni and interpreted below by Louis Watchman, glorifies the horse in mythological terms:

> *I am the Turquoise Woman's son.*
> *On top of Belted Mountain*
> *Beautiful horses—slim like a weasel!*
> *My horse has a hoof like striped agate;*
> *His fetlock is like a fine eagle-plume;*
> *His legs are like quick lightning.*
> *My horse's body is like an eagle-plumed arrow;*
> *My horse has a tail like a trailing black cloud.*
> *I put flexible goods on my horse's back;*
> *The Little Holy Wind blows through his hair.*

His mane is made of short rainbows.
My horse's ears are made of round corn.
My horse's eyes are made of big stars.
My horse's head is made of mixed waters
(From the holy springs—he never knows thirst).
My horse's teeth are made of white shell.
The long rainbow is in his mouth for a bridle,
* And with it I guide him.*
When my horse neighs, different-colored horses follow.
When my horse neighs, different-colored sheep follow.
* I am wealthy, because of him.*

Before me peaceful,
Behind me peaceful,
Under me peaceful,
Over me peaceful,
All around me peaceful—
Peaceful voice when he neighs.
I am Everlasting and Peaceful.
I stand for my horse.[27]

Horses were no less important to the *vaqueros* and cowboys of the Southwest. The following sentiments expressed by Jack Thorp echo an old range adage that "a man on foot is no man at all"[28]:

Singin' was amusement for the cowboy's times of ease, but what really mattered in the cow country was ridin'. The horse was the main thing in a cowboy's life. . . . A good cow horse . . . was supper and breakfast, wife and sweetheart, pal, means of conveyance, the main tool and brains of the cow business, and sometimes life itself. "I've bought 'em by the thousand, I've owned 'em everywhere." The ones that had brains and stamina are remembered, as individuals, even after the names and faces of some of the old bunkhouse mates begin to fade—my little horse, Catchem for instance. When he made the run that saved my life he did sixty miles between sundown and sun-up, over wild country, alone, without saddle, bridle, or rider, nothing on him but his hobble rope and my note.[29]

A horse similar to Catchem figures in a song sung by Frances Dwire of Taos for Margaret Larkin around 1930. A black mustang named Plantonio safely carries a military rider across the plains and through an Indian attack to save New Mexico:

I'll tell you a story,
There is one I know,
Of a horse I once owned
In New Mexico.

Swift as an antelope,
Black as a crow,

Star on his forehead
Was whiter than snow.

His arched neck was hidden
By a long flow of mane,
They called him Plantonio
The Pride of the Plain.

The country was new
And the settlers were scarce,
And the Indians on the warpath
Were savage and fierce.

The captain stepped up,
Said someone must go
For the aid and protection
Of New Mexico.

A dozen young fellows
Straightforward said "Here!"
But the captain saw me,
I was standing quite near.

"You're good for the ride,
You're the lightest one here,
On the back of that mustang
You've nothing to fear."

They all shook my hand
As I nodded my head,
Rode down the dark pathway,
And north turned his head.

The black struck a trot
And he kept it up all night,
And just as the east
Was beginning to light

Not a great ways behind
There arose a fierce yell,
And I knew that the redskins
Were hot on my trail.

I jingled the bells
At the end of his rein,
Spoke his name softly
And struck his dark mane.

He answered my call
With a toss of his head.
His dark body lengthened
And faster he sped.

The arrows fell 'round us
Like torrents of rain.
Plantonio, Plantonio,
The Pride of the Plain.

I delivered my message,
And tried to dismount,
But the pain in my foot
Was so sharp I could not.

The arrow you see
Hanging there on the wall,
Had passed through my foot,
Stirrup, saddle and all.

With New Mexico saved
We'd not ridden in vain,
Plantonio, Plantonio,
The Pride of the Plain.[30]

Traffic and Trade

From the first, commerce was an integral part of the adventure of the trail. Saltwater shells and pottery were traded throughout the prehistoric Southwest, "and by A.D. 1000 turquoise, copper, and macaws were added to the continuing exchange of stone, marine shell, and ceramics."[31] Pre-Columbian New Mexico was the site of two major centers of trade—Chaco Canyon and the salines of the Estancia Basin.

J. J. Brody points out that "Chaco Canyon is seen now as the center of an economic, ritual, and social system that extended over an area of 30,000 square miles. The 100 or more outlying communities known to have been a part of that system were linked by hundreds of miles of roads and a complex network of signaling stations."[32] Navajo Indians living in Chaco Canyon knew of the roads, which archeologists only began to study systematically in the 1970s. The system was built to accommodate foot traffic, and, according to Linda Cordell: "The roads are not contoured to topographic relief. Changes in direction are accomplished with a sharp angular turn rather than a curve." Cliffs and ledges are surmounted with ramps or stairways, which "vary in form from shallowly pecked finger- and toe-holds, to masonry steps consisting of two or three stones . . . , to well-constructed flights of wide steps with treads and risers cut out of the bedrock."[33]

Robert H. Lister and Florence C. Lister contend that "no other aboriginal land communication system of such magnitude and purpose has been recognized north of Mexico. Certainly it was a product of group organization, controls, and a lot of human energy."[34] Linda Cordell suggests that one model for this trade center and network is likely the various Mesoamerican "long-distance trade networks," claiming: "Among the Aztec, a special class of people referred to as *pochteca* acted as long-distance traders, middlemen, and sometimes spies. Enjoying political immunity, they traversed Mesoamerica. The Aztec, of course, ruled Mexico long after Casas Grandes and Chaco Canyon had been abandoned, but the idea of *pochteca* serves as an analogy." She notes that "the suggested items of trade include live macaws and copper bells from Mesoamerica in exchange for turquoise from the Southwest."[35]

Pueblo descendants of the Chaco people have preserved in their folklore more contemporary evidence of the importance and power of commerce. According to Richard I. Ford, "macaws and parrot feathers reached the northern Rio Grande Pueblos from Opata, Zuni, and Santo Domingo traders . . . [and] San Juan provided the Jicarilla with songbird feathers."[36] A folktale from Taos Pueblo, collected by Elsie

"A Scene at Zuni Pueblo," ca. 1879–1880. Photo by John K. Hillers. (MNM Neg. No. 5037.)

Clews Parsons and published in 1940, tells of the quest of Little Bleary-eye and his younger brother for such exotic goods. The kiva Gophers send the two on an impossible mission to obtain the skin of a whole parrot. Following Spider Grandmother's directions, Little Bleary-eye proceeds alone to the Big House at the north lake where he encounters people who give him the parrot, a bowl of dried meat, bow and arrows, green corn, and out-of-season fruits. The people tell him:

"Now you go back home! All this fruit is for your wife and you to eat. When you get home, peel this fruit and throw all the waste outside of your house, so the people (natetain) will see it." This was in the midst of winter. Then he took him outside. And he got to where his little brother was lying sadly. From there they went back home. When they got home, his wife spoke with surprise about the green corn and the fruit he brought since it was in the midst of winter. He said this was given to him by the people in the big lake and also the parrot was given to him to present to the Gophers. His wife husked the corn and peeled the fruit and threw the waste outside of the house for the people to see. Then in the morning he was seen by the people who said, "Little Bleary-eye has got back home. We sent him whence he would never return. He is a powerful medicine man. Come and look outside! Look! He has husks of corn and peels of fruit thrown outside his house, in the midst of winter!" They were surprised, they could never do anything with him. Then at nightfall he went to the kiva with his parrot for the kiva Gophers. He gave it to them, and they thanked him. Then he went out. Then the Gophers said, "He is very powerful. We can never do what we want to him. We sent him whence he could not return, but he got the parrot and returned. Men are poor, but some men have very powerful ways of doing. Although they are poor they are lucky, having power (itoayemu). We expect to live long through him. The people are living at the cottonwood, and thus we remain." [37]

Salt was the object of other important pilgrimages. Both Laguna and Zuni Indians obtained salt from their own salt lakes. In the 1920s, Acoma Indians told Leslie White about early salt gathering:

When they were living at Kacikatcut[ya] (White House) in the north there was a woman named Mina Koya. She was the Salt Woman. She quarreled with the people. They quarreled with her because she was so dirty. So she left and went to the south. She stopped at various places on the way, but kept on going southwest. Finally she stopped where the Zuñi salt lake is now. She stopped there to rest and turned into the salt lake.

   The people at Acoma used to send out expeditions to the Zuñi salt lake to get salt. Only men from the Pumpkin and Parrot clans went. One or more of the war chiefs went with them, however. When they got to the salt lake they bathed. They made prayer sticks and prayed. The headmen of the clans had a ho'nani. Wearing only a breechcloth, the men went into the lake to gather the salt. No one laughed during the time they were at work; it was a very solemn occasion. When they came back to Acoma with the salt every house had the sign of its clan painted on the wall by the door. The Parrot and Pumpkin men distributed salt to each house. [38]

Many more Indians relied on pre-Columbian trade around the seventy saline lakes of the Estancia Basin. During the thirteenth century, Pueblo Indians from the west, Plains Indians from the east, and Jumano Indians from the south journeyed to this region to obtain valuable salt. According to Paul M. Kraemer, a recognizable pattern of salt trade begins to emerge at this time:

> The Indians, and especially the Pueblo groups, then as now, had a society and culture that did not encourage private individualistic enterprise. In particular, individuals did not travel for long distances except when on missions concerned with tribal affairs. Nevertheless, a tiny minority of Indian men did not belong to any cohesive tribal group. They traveled alone from group to group, carrying trade goods on their backs. No one trader covered a very large area. However, the itinerant traders as a whole served a relay function so that items such as parrot feathers from Yucatan and sea shells from the California or Gulf coasts were, in effect, exchanged for items such as turquoise from the mines south of Santa Fe. In the same way, baskets of salt from the salines of Estancia were dispersed over a wide area.[39]

By the fourteenth century, Piro-speaking Pueblo Indians from the lower Rio Grande established a non-exclusive claim to the salt lakes because they settled on the western and southern rims of the Basin and learned to harvest, transport, and trade high quality salt. They prospered, and when the Spanish arrived in the sixteenth century, ten Saline Pueblos occupied the area between present-day Chilili and Gran Quivira National Monument. Throughout the Spanish and Mexican periods salt from this region continued to be a prized commodity in the developing commerce between New Mexico and Mexico City.

Two kinds of roads carried this growing traffic: *caminos de la herradura* (horseshoe roads suitable for pedestrians and pack animals) and *caminos de rueda* (wheel roads that could accommodate ox- and mule-cart caravans). Four main highways, or *caminos reales,* emanated from Mexico City. The longest, which ran north about twelve hundred miles to Santa Fe, was known as *el camino de tierra adentro,* or the road from the interior.[40] During the 1600s periodic mission supply trains traveled this route and, after the 1696 reconquest, government caravans organized by private contractors brought supplies to the colonists.

A system of trade fairs, whose participants were protected in their journeyings by a declared "Truce of God," was established in the eighteenth century and linked with similar, more elaborate annual gatherings to the south. The first of these were officially established at Taos and Pecos Pueblos by royal decree in 1723. By the 1790s the major trade fairs were designated for specific tribes—Taos for Comanches, Santa Clara and Santa Fe for Utes, Pecos for Jicarilla Apaches, Jemez and Acoma for Navajos, and El Paso for Mescalero Apaches. Rio Grande traders then headed south for fairs such as San Juan de los Lagos in Nueva Galicia, San Juan del Río in Durango, Saltillo in Coahuila, and Valle de San Bartolomé south of Chihuahua City.[41]

New Mexicans organized annual *conductas,* or convoys, to travel the Camino Real. They assembled at Sevillita de la Joya, now La Joya, south of Albuquerque. Regular soldiers and militiamen escorted these convoys, which included wagon and pack animals as well as sheep for sale in the mining communities of northern

Carreta at Tesuque Pueblo. (MNM Neg. No. 11826.)

Mexico. "Five hundred persons was considered the minimum number needed to insure safe passage through the country of hostile Apaches," and, according to Marc Simmons, "the merchants often took their entire families on the trail, since that was far safer than leaving them at home, unprotected and at the mercy of the Indians. The caravans thus became traveling societies in miniature and were witness to births, marriages, and deaths." Arthur L. Campa notes that "historians give varying figures regarding the size of the annual New Mexico–Chihuahua trade, but they all agree that it was one of the largest and most important events in the otherwise prosaic lives of the isolated settlers."[42]

Caravans were supervised by a *mayordomo*, an overseer who had the major responsibility for the entire venture. A *cargador*, or head packer, assisted the mayordomo and directed the *arrieros*, or muleteers, in their work. The success of the conducta depended upon these men, who loaded, unloaded, and cared for the mules, who protected the caravan from marauders, and who virtually insured safe conveyance of cargo in their charge:

> The arriero was a tough individualist. . . . Other citizens, who led less strenuous and less mobile lives, looked upon him with awe. He had his own songs and folk-sayings, many of which traced their origin back to earlier arrieros in the mountains of Spain.
>
> Above all, the arriero of colonial days was noted for his honesty. It was part of the rigorous code by which he lived. An Anglo traveler in New Mexico during

the 1840s spoke of him as "a man whose word may invariably be depended upon and who looks to the interest of those who employ him with scrupulous care, taking every precaution to guard the goods entrusted to his charge from being stolen or damaged, and despising lying and deceit."

. . . The mule trains that were once so prominent a feature of life in the Rio Grande valley have been gone a hundred years or more. Most of the rich lore surrounding the packing profession has been lost. But one of the old sayings that does survive expresses the true spirit of the plucky muleteer: "Better to be an arriero than to be rich. [43]

Singing was an integral part of traditional caravan life. According to Arthur L. Campa:

the long trips by pack trains of mules and horses were made less monotonous and dreary by the songs that the troubadour sang around the campfires. Every caravan, so tradition tells us, boasted a good bard who not only sang for the traders but who composed all sorts of humorous verse based on anecdotes of happenings along the road. The *pueta* made sport of any weakness shown by members of the expedition by singing *coplas* of satiric intent accompanying himself on his *vihuela*.

The more romantically inclined insisted on love songs that brought solace to their lonesome hearts, for many of these traders were young men out to prove their mettle. It was customary in those days for a young man who asked for a girl's hand in marriage to make the trip to Chihuahua in order to prove to the family that he was a man worthy of a wife. The troubadour had a rich store for such young men.

When the Santa Fe Trail was opened to New Mexicans and ox carts met, "the *mayordomos* arranged a camp holiday so that the men coming from home might tell news to those returning from the east. The whole affair wound up in the evening with a contest in which the troubadours from each outfit were pitted against each other."[44]

In the Anglo tradition, the romance of the Santa Fe Trail is expressed in a cowboy song that Doughbelly Price of Taos first learned on the Cross L outfit near Folsom at the turn of the century. John D. Robb recorded this version of the "Santa Fee Trail" from Price on December 10, 1950:

1.
Say Pard, have you sighted a schooner
Way back on the Santa Fee Trail
They made it there Monday or sooner
With a water keg tied on the tail.
There was pa and ma and de musy [sic]
And somewhere alongside the way
Was a tow headed gal on a pinto.
They was janglin' for old Santa Fee Trail
Hey, hey, hey!
They was janglin' for old Santa Fee.

2.
Well, I seen her ride down the arroyo
Way back on the Arkansas sand
She had a smile like an acre of sunflowers
She had a little brown quirt in her hand.
She mounted her pinto so airy
And she rode like she carried the mail
And her eyes they set fire to the prairie
Alongside of the Santa Fee Trail.
Hey, Hey, Hey!
Alongside of the Santa Fee Trail.

Santa Fe Trail ruts near Fort Union, ca. 1900. (MNM Neg. No. 12845.)

3.
Well, I know a gal down by the border
That I ride to El Paso to see.
She's a member of a high flyin' order
And I've sometimes kissed some girls good-bye
But, God, they're all cockerels and deedin's.
(They serve afternoon tea by the pail.)
Compared to the chord of stampedin'
That I got on that Santa Fee Trail
Hey, Hey, Heyee,
Alongside of that Santa Fee Trail.

4.
Well, I don't [know] her name on the prairie
And a-lookin' for one girl it's some wide
As it reaches from hell to West Baden
As you can see on that Santa Fee ride
Maybe we'll find water by sundown
And a camp may be made in the swale
And come on a gal on a pinto
Camped alongside the Santa Fee Trail,
Hey, Hey, Heyee,
Camped alongside the Santa Fee Trail.[45]

The Santa Fe Trail was opened to Anglo-Americans on September 1, 1821, when Captain William Becknell embarked from Franklin, Missouri, and arrived in Santa Fe two and a half months later on November 16. Mexico had declared its independence from Spain on August 24, 1821, and officials of the new government, unlike their predecessors, welcomed the outsider. Becknell's party returned to Missouri laden with Mexican silver, and its leader thus became known as the "Father of the Santa Fe Trail."

It was merchant Josiah Gregg, however, who crossed and recrossed the great southern plains four times between 1831 and 1840, whose 1844 *Commerce of the Prairies* became "the epic of the Santa Fe Trail."[46] He described the arrival of the American wagon train in Santa Fe:

The caravan at last hove in sight, and, wagon after wagon was seen pouring down the last declivity at about a mile's distance from the city. To judge from the clamorous rejoicings of the men, and the state of agreeable excitement which the muleteers seemed to be laboring under, the spectacle must have been as new to them as it had been to me. It was truly a scene for the artist's pen to revel in. Even the animals seemed to participate in the humor of their riders, who grew more and more merry and obstreperous as they descended towards the city. I doubt, in short, whether the first sight of the walls of Jerusalem were beheld by the crusaders with much more tumultuous and soul-enrapturing joy.

The arrival produced a great deal of bustle and excitement among the natives. *"Los Americanos!"—"Los carros!"—"La entrada de la caravana!"* were to be heard in every direction; and crowds of women and boys flock around to see the new-comers; while crowds of *léperos* hung about as usual to see what they could pilfer. The wagoners were by no means free from excitement on this occasion. Informed of the 'ordeal' they had to pass, they had spent the previous morning in 'rubbing up;' and now they were prepared, with clean faces, sleek combed hair, and their choicest Sunday suit, to meet the 'fair eyes' of glistening black that were sure to stare at them as they passed. There was yet another preparation to be made in order to 'show off' to advantage. Each wagoner must tie a bran new 'cracker' to the lash of his whip; for, on driving through the streets and the *plaza pública*, every one strives to outvie his comrades in the dexterity with which he flourishes this favorite badge of authority.[47]

Josiah Gregg's epic vision of his mercantile pilgrimage to Santa Fe is epitomized by his sweeping view from atop Round Mound in northeastern New Mexico:

At last, some of the most persevering of our adventurers succeeded in ascending the summit of the Round Mound, which commands a full and advantageous view of the surrounding country, in some directions to the distance of a hundred miles or more. Looking southward a varied country is seen, of hills, plains, mounds, and sandy undulations; but on the whole northern side, extensive plains spread out, studded occasionally with variegated peaks and ridges. Far beyond these, to the north-westward, and low in the horizon a silvery stripe appears upon an azure base, resembling a list of chalk-white clouds. This is the perennially snowcapped summit of the eastern spur of the Rocky Mountains. . . .

As the caravan was passing under the northern base of the Round Mound, it presented a very fine and imposing spectacle to those who were upon its summit. The wagons marched slowly in four parallel columns, but in broken lines, often at intervals of many rods between. The unceasing 'crack, crack,' of the wagoners' whips, resembling the frequent reports of distant guns, almost made one believe that a skirmish was actually taking place between two hostile parties: and a hostile engagement it virtually was to the poor brutes, at least; for the merciless application of the whip would sometimes make the blood spirt from their sides—and that often without any apparent motive of the wanton *carrettieri*, other than to amuse them-selves with the flourishing and loud popping of their lashes![48]

Gregg's heroic journeys across the plains contrast with the more dreamlike and lyrical recollections of Marian Russell. In the 1930s, she told her daughter-in-law about a trip over the Santa Fe Trail in 1852, when she was only a child of seven:

Minute impressions flash before me; the sun-bonnetted women, the woolen-trousered men, little mother in her flounced gingham, brother Will walking in long strides by our driver, voices of the lonely and homeless singing around blazing campfires. Because I was one of the youngest, I may today be the only one left of that band to tell of the old, old trail that, like a rainbow, led us westward. . . .

Scenes of the old trail come flooding back to me: Places where the earth was like a Persian rug, the lavender, red and yellow wild flowers mingling with the silvery green prairie grass. There were places where we saw wild turkeys among the cottonwood trees, and where the wild grapevine ran riot. Always there were buffalo. Sometimes we saw them walking slowly in single file along their narrow paths on the way to some distant water hole. The buffalo are gone now; gone, too, the sea of grass. When the railroads came the old trail was neglected. Weeds sprang up along its rutted way. The old trail, the long trail over which once flowed the commerce of a nation, lives now only in the memory of a few old hearts. It lives there like a lovely, oft repeated dream.[49]

Marian Russell also recalled storytelling as a moving part of her trail experience:

Each night there were two great circles of wagons. . . . Inside those great circles the mules were turned after grazing, for ropes were stretched between the wagons and thus a circular corral made. Inside the corral were the cooking fires, one for each wagon. After the evening meal we would gather around the little fires. The men would tell stories of the strange new land before us, tales of gold and of Indians. The women would sit with their long skirts drawn up over a sleeping child on their laps. Overhead brooded the night sky, the little camp fires flickered, and behind us loomed the dark hulks of the covered wagons.

Their famous wagonmaster Captain Francis Xavier Aubry one night came to their fireside and announced their arrival in New Mexico Territory. "'This is the land,' said Captain Aubry, 'where only the brave or the criminal come. This is called, "the Land without Law." But it is a land that has brought healing to the hearts of many. Many an invalid I have had in my caravans, but before they reached Santa Fe they were eating buffalo meat raw and sleeping soundly under their blankets. There is something in the air of New Mexico that makes the blood red, the heart to beat high and the eyes to look upward. Folks don't come here to die—they come to live and they get what they come for.'"[50]

Conclusion

Not far from Hawikuh, or Zuni, where the conquistadors first sought the legendary Cíbola, stands an ancient geological landmark. This massive formation of soft sandstone rises some two hundred feet above the valley floor, and on its top lie the ruins of Atsinna, an abandoned prehistoric Zuni Pueblo whose Zuni name means "writing on rock." Seventeenth-century Spanish conquistadors camped at the foot of Atsinna and called it El Morro, meaning "headland" or "bluff." By the mid-nineteenth century, Anglo traders, soldiers, immigrants, and other travelers had named the formation Inscription Rock after the numerous petroglyphs and Spanish writings inscribed on its soft surface.

On September 17 and 18, 1849, army engineer Lieutenant J. H. Simpson and Philadelphia artist R. H. Kern approached the face of the rock "and sure enough, here were inscriptions, and some of them very beautiful . . . one of them dating as far back as 1606, all of them very ancient, and several of them very deeply as well as beautifully engraven . . . the greater portion . . . in Spanish . . . and the remainder in hyeroglyphics [sic], doubtless of Indian origin."[51] The Americans saw Spanish

inscriptions made by conquistadors like General Don Diego de Vargas in 1692, missionaries, soldiers, traders, and other adventurers. The earliest Spanish text was incised by Oñate on his return from a 1604 excursion to the Gulf of California:

> "Pasó por aquí el adelantado Don Juan de Oñate del descubrimiento de la mar del sur a 16 de Abril de 1605."—"Passed by here the Governor Don Juan de Oñate from the discovery of the Sea of the South on the 16th of April, 1605."

The only poem on the rock was written in 1629:

> Aqui (llego el Señor) y Gobernador
> Don Francisco Manuel de Silva Nieto
> Que lo imposible tiene ya subjeto
> Su brazo indubitable y su valor
> Con los carros del Rey Nuestro Señor
> Cosa que solo el puso en este efecto
> De Agostos 5 (Mil) Seiscientos Veinte Nueve
> Que se Bien a Zuñi pasa y la Fe lleve.

El Morro, showing Indian petroglyphs and a Spanish inscription that reads in translation: "We passed by here, the Sergeant Major and Captain Juan de Archuleta and Adjutant Diego Martin Barba and ensign Agustin de Ynojos, the year of 1636." (MNM Neg. No. 6198.)

Here arrived the Señor and Governor
Don Francisco Manuel de Silva Nieto
Whose indubitable arm and valor
Have overcome the impossible
With the wagons of the King our Lord
A thing which he alone put into this effect
August 5, 1629 that one may well to Zuñi
pass and carry the faith.

The last dated Spanish inscription was by Andrés Romero, who marked his passage in 1774.[52]

Among the earliest English carvings is the precisely crafted "P. Gilmer Breckenridge/1859." Breckenridge had ridden west to California after graduation from Virginia Military Institute. He first saw El Morro in 1857, when he was in charge of the twenty-five camels being tested for use in the American deserts by Lieutenant Edward Beale's expedition.

In the summer of 1858, Williamson, Holland, John Udell, and J. L. Rose, members of the first emigrant wagon train to pass Inscription Rock on the way to California, carved their names in the sandstone. The forty families in that train were attacked by Mojave Indians on the Colorado River, and the survivors, among them the elderly Baptist preacher John Udell and his sixty-four-year-old wife, walked back to Albuquerque in November 1858. They then joined Lieutenant Beale's 1859 caravan, which reached California safely by way of El Morro.[53]

El Morro is but one of many landmarks throughout New Mexico—from the Rio Grande itself to Shiprock, Round Mound, Wagon Mound, the Caprock, and the southwestern mountains of the Gila River region. Folklore texts suggest that such landmarks are perceived differently by Native American and Euro-American travelers. According to A. Irving Hallowell, the Saulteaux Indians from the Great Lakes, for example, "always move from one point to another, rather than in a given direction toward a goal, [and] directional orientation usually functions as the wider frame of reference to facilitate the step by step procedure."[54] The migrations recorded in Southwestern Native American mythology likewise indicate a pattern of movement from point to point or landmark to landmark—from Frijoles Canyon to the mesa of the Stone Lions to Cochiti, from "moss spring" to "the shell place," and from Taos Pueblo to the "north lake."

Spanish and Anglo travelers also note landmarks, but their journeys are directed toward more distant and nebulous objectives like the fabulous Cíbola, Quivira, and even Santa Fe itself. They expressed their experiences as heroic quests. Villagrá's epic glorifies Oñate's "being, valor, prudence, and high effort" and his "most Christian" monarch Philip, whom he praises as the Phoenix of New Mexico. Later, those who engaged in commerce over the prairies to Santa Fe and south to Mexico City saw themselves as romantic adventurers in the service of civil government or in search of personal gain. Cowboys, muleteers, wagonmasters, and traders figured in story, song, and saying.

The historic traversing of New Mexico by foot, horseback, and wagon has always generated a fundamental commerce of tangibles and intangibles, a continual process through which people exchanged natural and manufactured products and art

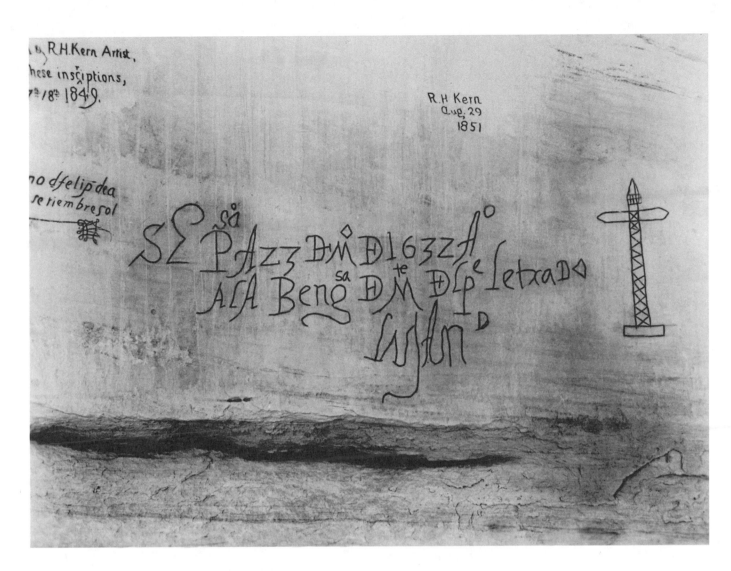

and shared ideas, customs, and folklore. At various times in New Mexico history, commerce centered in places like Chaco, the Salines, and the trade fair sites. These places became similar to the ancient Greek "agora on the boundary," a neutral marketplace that was set aside on boundaries between communities for religious festivity and economic exchange.[55]

By the mid-nineteenth century, Santa Fe, with its Plaza and Adobe Palace, resembled the "agora within the city," a place of commerce and civil government best exemplified by the Athenian Agora with its *stoas,* or open-sided markets, military headquarters, courts, council chambers, and official residences. Marian Russell describes it as a supply center where "freight wagons pulled in daily from the Staked Plains of Texas, from Fort Union and California. Great caravans were leaving for the east, west and south. Friendly Indians came in for the trading. Often the narrow streets became choked with a wiggling mass of humanity." She vividly recalls:

The market place in Santa Fe was a wonder. In open air booths lay piles of food stuffs. Heaps of red and green peppers vied with heaps of red and blue corn and heaps of golden melons. There were colorful rugs woven by the hands of the

El Morro, showing 1849 and 1851 inscriptions by Philadelphia artist R. H. Kern and Spanish inscription, which reads in translation: "They passed on the 23rd of March, 1632, to the avenging of the death of the Father Letrado.— Lujan." (MNM Neg. No. 57367.)

Mexicans and deep-fringed shawls, gay with embroidery. There were massive Indian jars filled to the brim with Mexican beans. There were strings of prayer beads from old Mexico, beads worn smooth and shiny to a patina by many praying hands. Mexican turquoise in heavy settings of silver. Silver was then cheaper than tin. Here was to be found exquisite Mexican drawn work and intricate Indian bead work.

In deep, old hand-carved frames were pictures, mottoes, wreaths of flowers all cunningly fashioned of human hair, red, black, brown and yellow. There were beaded moccasins and chamois coats, leather trousers, silver trimmed saddles, spurs and knapsacks; great hand-carved chests and cupboards, Indian baskets and jars without number. So many things that were fine and splendid; so many things that were rude and clumsy, the Santa Fe market afforded.

If one were in quest of a pair of Indian moccasins he might hunt among booths until he was dizzy, only at last to come to a heap of footwear of every size, shape and quality and in such abundance as to make him forget what he came for.

Long lines of burros all but hidden under enormous bundles of fagots made headway in and out among the children, taking good care not to step on them.

This was old Santa Fe, asleep among the red hills. Sheep grazed on distant mesas, a hot wind blew across the mesquite. There were saw-tooth mountains silhouetted against the sky. Through a great wooden gateway flowed the Santa Fe trail from across a wide, hot valley.[56]

FOCAL PLACE TWO

El Santuario de Chimayó

The epic and legend texts in chapter 2, "Royal Roads," describe traditional forms of movement over the land—by foot, on horseback, in animal-drawn vehicle—for migration, adventure, and commerce. Pilgrimage is the most sacred way to travel through this world. The pilgrim consciously and with discipline undertakes a religious journey. Commerce is also involved, and pilgrims share stories, songs, ideas, and adventure; they exchange and purchase relics, holy objects, and other goods.

A religious procession approaching the Santuario, Chimayó, ca. 1917. Photo by Jesse Nusbaum. (MNM Neg. No. 14379.)

In New Mexico, El Santuario de Chimayó—the famous healing shrine at El Potrero, a *placita* of Chimayó some twenty-six miles northeast of Santa Fe—has been the destination of pilgrims since prehistoric times. First Native Americans, then Hispanos, and later Anglos too traveled there to seek health and renewal. It continues to attract pilgrims today, especially on Good Friday.

Ethnographic and Historical Texts

"Chimayó" comes from the Tewa Indian designation, according to John Peabody Harrington's ethnography of the early 1900s:

> *Tsimajo, Tsimajobu'u* 'flaking stone of superior quality' 'town of the flaking stone of superior quality' (*tsi'i* 'flaking stone' of any variant; *majo* 'superior' 'chief' . . . ; *bu'u*, 'town'). . . . Just why the name was originally applied has been forgotten. No obsidian or other flaking stone is known to exist at the place. . . .
> The Indians say that Chimayó used to be a Tewa Indian pueblo, then called *Tsimajo'ǫŋwi* (*'ǫŋwi* 'pueblo'). This pueblo was situated where the church now is, the informants stated. The church is on the south side of the creek. Where the church now is there used to be a pool, they say, called *Tsimajop̣okwi̱* (*p̣okwi̱* 'pool' . . .). The earth or mud of this pool has healing properties.[1]

A nearby, flat-topped hill, *Tsi Mayoh,* is sacred to the San Juan Pueblo Indians. It was created by the *T'owa e* of the directions, deities who guard the Pueblo world from atop each of four mountains and four such *Tsin,* or flat-topped hills. Alfonso Ortiz writes that "each of these hills is sacred because it is particularly dark and foreboding; each has a cave and/or labyrinths running through it."[2]

In the 1950s, Stephen F. de Borhegyi interviewed María Martínez, the famous potter of San Ildefonso Pueblo, who told him that *"Tzimmayo* in the Tewa dialect means 'place where the big stones stand.'" She also recounted legends in which

> the site of the present Santuario in Chimayó was originally an Indian shrine but the origin of the curative powers of this earth [was] lost in the past. Chimayó is believed to have been a place where fire, smoke, and hot water belched forth in ancient times. The pit of the sacred earth was a pool. . . . However, according to Tewa legend, when the twin war gods killed the giant, fire burst out at many places, and the healing, hot mud springs atop Black Mesa, at Tsimmayo (Chimayó), and Obuhegi dried up and only mud was left. The Indians continued to visit the site of the hot spring and used the mud for healing, calling it *nam po'uare* (*nam,* "earth," *po'uare,* "blessed").[3]

Borhegyi also notes that in the early 1920s, Ina Sizer Cassidy spoke with the cacique of San Ildefonso and learned that "the fire burst out from the earth at San Ildefonso, Nambé and Cabezón."

Chimayó's first Hispanic settlement is now known as Plaza del Cerro, first mentioned in 1714 documents and definitely established as Tzimayó by the 1740s. E. Boyd prepared a descriptive history for the New Mexico preservation plan of 1971:

Santuario de Chimayó, ca. 1911.
Photo by Jesse Nusbaum. (MNM
Neg. No. 13751.)

Originally, the Plaza del Cerro was a square enclosed by contiguous adobe buildings. The only entrance ways were two or possibly three alleys . . . wide enough to
admit only animals and people on foot and therefore easily defensible. The fortified
colonial plaza plan is shown better here than in any other plaza extant in New
Mexico. . . . Also running through the plaza is the *acequia madre*, or main irrigation
ditch. . . . Although it is now [1971] surrounded by a barn, the original *torreón*, or
defensive watch tower, still stands south of the plaza in good condition. The central ground, which was once held communally, is divided by fences and planted in
fruit trees and small garden plots. In some of these plots the Chimayó chili is grown,
for which the area is famous. A few of the fruit trees in and around the plaza are
wild plum, indigenous to the region and predating Spanish settlement.

The Chimayó area was known for its "fine crops of fruit and chili in addition to the
staple corn and frijoles, and the weaving of blankets and other wool textiles."

Between 1813 and 1816 the Santuario de Nuestro Señor de Esquipulas was built
just down the road from the plaza, bringing in many pilgrims and greatly
augmenting the economic standing of the plaza. Another chapel near the
Santuario, built in the 1860's, further stimulated business and other activity. Also,
by this time the San Luis Valley in Colorado had been settled, and Chimayó had a
good trade with towns there, exchanging fruit and chili for wheat and potatoes.
Before the new Santa Fe–Taos highway was built in 1917, following the Rio
Grande Canyon, travel from Santa Fe to Taos used the Chimayó–Las
Truchas–Peñasco route whenever weather permitted, making Chimayó a stop on
a major road.[4]

Fieldworkers for the 1935 Tewa Basin Study also found evidence of Chimayó's cultural and commercial importance:

> The people of Chimayó are . . . go-getters. Very proud are they of the fact that the Chimayosos never loaf, and of the fact that the products of this pleasant valley have been justly famous among the natives of New Mexico since the reconquest (1692), and among the natives of Colorado and Arizona since before the coming of the railroad. The date of the building of the Denver & Rio Grande spur from Alamosa, Colorado, to Santa Fe is a memorable time mark all over the region. Prior to the World War it was the annual custom of the people to load their surplus chili, fruit, and blankets into covered wagons, and trains of 5, 6, 7, and as many as 12 would be taken to Colorado—San Luis Valley, especially—and thus the good exchanged for the products of that region. . . . Trade was on a barter basis, and customary prices evolved. Thus one almud (16 pounds) of beans is worth 2 strings of chili to this day. One fanega (140 pounds) of wheat was worth 2 strings of chili.[5]

Chimayó's commerce was stimulated by its status as a pilgrimage center. In 1916, Paul A. F. Walter described it as "a New Mexico Lourdes" and gave the following version of the Santuario legend:

> It was some years after the Chimayó rebellion in 1837, that a priest came to the settlements on the upper Santa Cruz, which are known under the collective name of Chimayó. He ministered to the people who were without a church, and after a while asked them to build a chapel on a spot he had selected. But the people were too indifferent and refused to heed the admonition. One day the priest disappeared and the next morning, from a cottonwood tree that stood on the spot designated by the priest for a chapel, there protruded a foot. The people were so impressed with the miracle that they built the chapel and made it the most beautiful church in all of New Mexico.[6]

El Santuario was in danger of being dismantled in 1929, when three members of the Cháves family, among them María de los Angeles Cháves, Bernardo Abeyta's granddaughter, could no longer afford their property. Members of the Society for the Preservation and Restoration of New Mexico Mission Churches and what was then known as the Society for the Revival of Spanish Arts, notably Santa Feans E. Dana Johnson, John Gaw Meem, Alice Corbin Henderson, Frank Applegate, and Mary Austin, arranged for an anonymous donation, which was given to Don José Cháves by Archbishop Albert T. Daeger on October 15, 1929, the same day that official incorporation papers for the Spanish Colonial Arts Society were signed. Writer Mary Austin "was able to find a Catholic benefactor who made possible the purchase of the building and its contents, to be held in trust by the Church for worship and as a religious museum, intact, and no alterations to be made in it without our consent."[7]

Legend Texts: Esquípulas

Trader Don Bernardo Abeyta (1771–1856), a wealthy and influential resident of El Potrero who probably traveled at least to Mexico on more than one occasion, appears to have introduced the Esquípulas healing cult of the Santuario into the Chimayó area very early in the nineteenth century. The cult is related to a Guatemalan prototype that originated after 1524 as a syncretistic Mayan-Spanish devotion involving geophagy, or earth-eating, and an image known as *El Cristo Negro de Esquípulas,* or the Black Christ of Esquípulas. According to William Wroth: "Tradition records that the cross of *Our Lord of Esquípulas* miraculously sprouted fresh green leaves and branches, symbolizing Christ's power of spiritual regeneration. Images of *Our Lord of Esquípulas* are often dark in complexion, following the original which is especially revered by the Guatemalan Indians."[8]

Abeyta built a small *hermita,* or hermitage, at El Potrero to house the Esquípulas crucifix he miraculously discovered there. He applied to build a chapel, now El Santuario de Chimayó, in 1813, and it was finished in 1816. The cult of Esquípulas spread quickly, and "there are evidences of it at Nambé, Santa Cruz, La Puebla, Cundiyó, Truchas, Trampas, Pojoaque, Santa Fe, Agua Fría, Abeytas, and Tomé, [as well as] the Indian pueblos of Santa Clara, San Juan, San Lorenzo de Picurís, San Ildefonso, and Isleta."[9]

In 1931, Elizabeth Willis DeHuff recounted a legend about how Abeyta discovered the shrine's patron saint:

> The story is told that in the early part of the nineteenth century, Don Bernardo Abeyta, who owned many acres along the little stream of the Holy Cross and many sheep, became *muy enfermo,* so ill that no one dared to hope for his recovery. One day, when the sunshine reflected, warm and comfortable, from the recessed *portale* of his ranch home, Don Bernardo was bundled in his Chimayó blankets and set upon his porch, whence he could look down from the *potrero,* upon which his ranch house was situated, to the little winding stream gurgling over his weir dam, as it silently sent half of its water gliding into his *acequia madre* to nourish his beans, corn and chili pepper plants. It was a goodly sight and Don Bernardo began to meditate upon his many blessings. Then suddenly, down near the meandering *acequia,* there appeared to him the image of his Patron Saint, San Esquípula, beckoning to him. With great effort, the sick man threw off his blankets, arose and hobbled with difficulty in obedience to the summoning of the Saint; but before he could cross the ditch, the image of the Saint vanished and Don Bernardo fell upon his knees on the spot where San Esquípula had stood. Immediately he was made well.
>
> There was great rejoicing among his family and friends and news of his miraculous cure spread through the countryside, bringing others who were sick to the blessed spot. They, too, were healed, and so to commemorate this greatest of all blessings to him, Don Bernardo built an adobe chapel, enshrining the sacred spot in a room beside the altar.[10]

Juan Abeita of Isleta Pueblo had told Elsie Clews Parsons a different version in 1925:

Santuario, altar, and main reredos, painted by Molleno. Top panels (l. to r.) depict Holy Cross with five wounds of Jesus and lance; Franciscan emblem with crossed arms of Christ and St. Francis; Holy Cross of Jerusalem. Curtain, geometric, wheat and grape designs below flank crucifix of Our Lord of Esquípulas. Color postcard by Mike Roberts. (MNM Neg. No. 40325.)

Interior of El Santuario, ca. 1911.
Photo by Jesse Nusbaum. (MNM
Neg. No. 13754.)

One time when a man was out herding sheep he found Escapu'la, a little head sticking out from the ground. He dug this santu out from the ground and carried him all the time on his back while he was herding. He went home. "My wife," he said, "I found this pastor. I am going to keep him. Wherever I go he shall go with me." "All right." They kept him in that little hole. When the man went herding, he carried him on his back again. The santu was right there with him. Then the man went and told the priest that he had found him. The priest told him to carry him to Santa Fe. He carried him there. When he came home, he found him back in his little hole. "Well, come out herding with me," he said to him. The old woman said, "Some day I am going to burn him up." "No!" The man went herding. On his return he found his wife all crooked, her mouth pulled to one side. He prayed and she prayed, to the santu, to make her look as she did before. So she got well again. So people say that when they make a promise to San Escapu'la they must keep it.

Abeita also told Parsons:

At Chimayó, the traditional home of the Tewa immigrants to the Hopi, there is preserved in a room of the church a hole in the ground of which the clay has in Indian opinion potent medicinal value, "good for pains in the body, and for being sad," said my Isletan informant. Twice he had visited the "san(c)tuario" or Shamno, as it is called from the man of Picurís (Shamnoag) who first found the saint.

He was out herding sheep. With his crook he was tapping some rocks and there by a big rock he found the saint, Sant Istipula. He was made of clay. The old herder took the image and placed it overnight by his pillow. In the morning the saint had disappeared; he had gone back to his rock where the herder sought and found him. This time he carried the saint to Picurís for all to see. But from there, too, the morning after, the saint disappeared. The herder returned to the rock and there was the saint. So the herder thought there was no use carrying the saint away and on that spot he built a shade for him. Later in some way the Mexicans got possession of this place.[11]

In the early 1950s, Father José Cubbels helped Stephen F. de Borhegyi collect the following versions:

A granddaughter of Bernardo Abeyta still lives in La Puebla near Chimayó. According to her story, with which most of my informants in Chimayó agree, it was during a Holy Week when Bernardo Abeyta, a good member of the fraternity of Jesús Nazareno or Penitentes, was performing the customary penances of the society around the hills of Potrero that he suddenly saw a bright light shining from a hole in the ground near the Santa Cruz river. He rushed to the spot and with his bare hands dug out the miraculous crucifix of Our Lord of Esquípulas. He called all the people of El Potrero to see and venerate the precious finding. They soon notified Father Sebastián Alvarez, and a procession was organized to take the crucifix to Santa Cruz. It was placed in the niche of the main altar. Next morning the crucifix disappeared from its niche and was found again in the same hole where it was first discovered. Another procession was formed to carry it back to Santa Cruz, but the same thing happened this time and once more after it had been taken to Santa Cruz for the third time. By this everyone understood that the crucifix wished to remain in El Potrero, and, to venerate it properly, a chapel was built above the hole. Another version of the legend has it that a young girl named María Ignacia Martínez, a relative of Don Bernardo, found the crucifix in a hollow tree while fetching water from the river. Her father, Francisco Martínez, went on muleback to Santa Cruz to tell about the discovery. This, as might be expected, is the version of the Martínez family.

According to another story, there was a very kind and devout priest, rather small in stature, who traveled about the countryside carrying with him a large cross. He was killed by the Indians and was buried with his cross by the Spaniards near El Potrero. When the Santa Cruz river overflowed its banks sometime in the early part of the Nineteenth Century, people discovered the burial and the cross which had been washed out and notified the priest. From there the story is much the same as the other versions with the three miraculous trips of the cross back to its original location. . . . [12]

Legend Texts: El Niño

Stephen F. de Borhegyi continues his history of El Santuario with an account of how *El Santo Niño de Atocha,* the Holy Child of Atocha, came to replace Our Lord of Esquípulas as the area's patron healer.

> Apparently, after the death of Bernardo Abeyta [in 1856], a jealous neighbor wished to capitalize on the fame and revenue of the Santuario and so established a private chapel dedicated to the Santo Niño de Atocha. The story goes that a member of this family, Severiano Medina, went down to Fresnillo, Zacatecas, Mexico, where is located a shrine to the Santo Niño de Atocha and upon his return with a statue of the Santo Niño he built a chapel next door to the Santuario of Esquípulas. I was not able to find out the exact date of the construction of this chapel, but, according to the present [1954] owner, Ramon Medina, it was built sometime between 1850 and 1860. A close study of this celebrated Santo Niño reveals that it is actually a German papier maché doll that was forced into a sitting position on a wooden chair to resemble the Santo Niño de Atocha. In spite of this, the spreading fame of the Santo Niño and his nocturnal activities threatened to usurp the fame of the Santuario with its Lord of Esquípulas. In a desperate attempt to rescue the dwindling revenue the owners of the Santuario, the Cháves family, obtained another Santo Niño figure and announced that in the Santuario, not only the Santo Niño but San José, San Rafael, and Santiago also traveled through the country at night and needed new shoes. . . . Unfortunately . . . instead of the small wooden bulto being that of the Santo Niño de Atocha, it is the Holy Child of Prague who carries in his right hand a small globe. They placed this statue . . . in the chamber where the pit of sacred earth is located, thus completing the confusion that already existed. The Santo Niño now reigns supreme in both churches and is credited with the healing power that originally belonged to the earth and the miraculous crucifix of Our Lord of Esquípulas. There are now only a few elderly people in the village of Chimayó who still remember "San Esquípulas" and some even know that it is actually the crucifix behind the altar. However, even they attribute the healing power of the earth to the Santo Niño.[13]

According to E. Boyd, the Holy Child of Atocha was originally a Spanish manifestation of the Christ Child, who is depicted wearing "a brimmed hat with a pilgrim's cockleshell, a robe, and mantle, [bearing] the pilgrim's staff with a gourd, and [carrying] a small basket. In most versions He is seated in a chair."[14] In the 1920s or 1930s, a "devout member" of the Chimayó community told Nina Otero:

> Each year the tiny statue needs and is provided with new shoes. Last year's shoes are worn and shabby, for He runs and plays with the children of the poor and their laugh rings out as the brook that runs through this village. . . .
>
> The Holy Child tears his clothes, wears them out. People make pilgrimages to His shrine and frequently do not find Him. He is out among the people.

Sometime in the late 1940s or early 1950s, a student folklore collector from Highlands University submitted the following account:

Prayer Room of El Santuario, showing several figures of El Niño de Atocha, June 21, 1974. Photo by Robert Brewer. (MNM Neg. No. 65141.)

My aunt from Taos Pueblo asked me to drive her to Chimayó on a mission. She had been married ten years and had not conceived. She took the Santo Niño de Praga at El Santuario a pair of beaded white moccasins she had made herself. She said el Niño wore out his shoes pacing the church at night and doing all those favors for people. She stayed in the church all afternoon praying beside this little statue and left her moccasins there. She now has a seven-year-old boy and a three-year-old little girl.[15]

In 1979, newspaper reporter David Roybal interviewed Father Casimir Roca, priest at El Santuario, and members of the Medina family, who confirmed the Niño's history in Chimayó:

A daughter of Elena Medina, Enisdel Medina de Chavez of La Puebla, is a very religious woman who claims the Santo Niño statue in Chimayó must be recognized. It was the center of worship during a period lasting more than a century, she said. She added, "Besides it is not the statue that performs the miracles. It is the faith of the people."

The local faith in the statue dates back to 1856. It is said that in that year, Blas Seberiano Medina of El Potrero learned through a revelation that a statue of El Santo Niño de Atocha existed in the central Mexican town of Fresnillo.

Medina is said to have suffered from severe rheumatism. He reportedly prayed to El Santo Niño de Atocha, promising to seek the statue in Fresnillo if he was cured of his rheumatism. Legend reports Medina was cured and that early one day he set out on a burro to the mining-era Mexican town. . . .

According to the story, Medina took six months to return to El Potrero, where he arrived with the statue on Feb. 15, 1857. Reportedly overjoyed with the statue's presence, María Dolores Trujillo, Francisco Antonio Trujillo and Juan Martínez donated land for construction of a church. In 1858 the parish priest Juan de Jesús Trujillo is said to have obtained ornaments and permission to celebrate the Catholic Mass.

Miracles since attributed to the local statue include one which was reportedly experienced by a young Sombrillo boy said to have been lost in area hills while picking pinon. It is claimed the boy, upon being found and seeking the statue, told his parents it had given him water while he was lost.[16]

Pilgrimage Texts

In 1916, Paul A. F. Walter reports:

> Stories are told of the cures effected by the holy clay from the little chapel of San Rafael [sic], where a good-sized well or kiva has been dug in the floor by believers removing the sanctified earth. A few weeks ago, a woman from Galisteo, who had been a paralytic for ten years, who had been at a sanitarium in Santa Fe, and who had been pronounced incurable by physicians, made a pilgrimage to Chimayó. She had been unable to walk for years, but upon her return from Sanctuario, while near Pojoaque, she leaped from the wagon to the great joy of relatives with her, and since then has been able to walk and work as she did before she had been stricken with paralysis.

This sacred earth motif is amplified in a legend recounted by the Chimayó aunt of a Highlands University student folklore collector in 1952. The aunt claimed that "people take tons of dirt every year but no matter how much dirt is taken, the hole remains the same size." Amy Passmore Hurt notes that in 1934, "'the well' [was] merely a deep hole in the dirt floor which tradition says was filled by the *Santo Niño*, the Christ Child. . . . I learned that [in Hispanic belief] married women were not permitted to dip into the well."[17]

María Martínez of San Ildefonso Pueblo remembered her girlhood pilgrimage to Chimayó in 1890. Her mother had promised her ten-year-old daughter's participation in return for the child's recovery from smallpox. María told Alice Marriott that an old Spanish man let her and her mother in.

> There were votive lights blooming like yellow yucca flowers on an iron stand before the altar, as the old man led María and her mother down the aisle. Then the man turned to his left and unlocked a grilled iron door beside the altar. There was darkness behind the door—darkness and a sense of depth. Mother drew María towards it. The child smelled an earthen dampness, like the darkness of the

El Santuario, room with "*El posito*," hole or sacred well from which healing earth obtained, ca. 1920. (MNM Neg. No. 14618.)

storeroom at home, and it surprised her. Most churches smelled of dry dust, not wet.

"There are steps going down," said Mother. "You must go down them. When you get to the bottom, take off all your clothes. Don't be afraid, because nobody can see you. Then take this holy medal and scrape off the earth on the sides of the hole. Rub the earth all over your body. That's what makes you well."

"Will you go with me?" María asked.

"Just you can go. This is your pilgrimage. After you have rubbed yourself with the sacred earth and dressed again, take the medal and dig out enough earth to fill your water bottle. That much you can take home with you, to drink there to make you well. While you are doing this, you should say your 'Our Father.' Don't think about any thing but your prayers and the Santo Niño." . . .

[Afterward, María] left the offerings and crossed herself in front of the carved and painted figure of the Santo Niño that stood on the great altar. Then she turned and walked back to her mother, who was kneeling now in the aisle of the church. From the side aisle on the left of the church, Father and Tío Tilano also rose. Together they all four went out into the sunset.

"Give me the bottle of earth, please," Mother said, and María handed it to her.

"What will you do with it?" she asked.

"You will have to mix it in water and drink it before breakfast every morning for the next four days," her mother answered. "This is good earth. The Indians knew about it and how it use it a long time ago. Then the padres came and learned about its power, and the Santo Niño came and told them what to do, so they built the church here. Everybody knows that the earth is good. It makes everyone well who drinks it, for the rest of his life."[18]

3 *STEEL RAILS*

TEXTS OF HEALTH-SEEKING AND TOURISM

*Of the beaten paths in our Far Southwest, few are of the kind we all know.
More are of a very different sort.*

*The few are the steel ribbons of the railroads, following lines of least resistance across immensity. The many are the paths of the Indians, worn inches deep
in solid rock by moccasined feet; the ways of the sandalled padres and steel-clad
soldiers of Spain; the trails of the fur-capped mountain men; and the broad
tracks blazed by those in buckskin and deepened under the dust clouds of plodding pack trains and Covered Wagons.*

*It is with the latter that this folder has to deal. They lead away into the
hinterlands of New Mexico and Arizona, far from the familiar beaten path of
the railroad. They criss-cross a last frontier that has taken 350 years to subdue.
They find out buried cities that flourished when Britons crouched in caves, reach
medieval Spain dreaming away the centuries in the mountains of America, and
string together age-old Indian pueblos where one may "catch archaeology alive."
They seek out the mines, the lumber camps, the open ranges and the painted
canyons of the least-known and most fascinating corner of the United States.*

*Those who are passing on into the setting sun made the Southwest safe.
The railroad made its gateways accessible. It needed only the automobile, dragging better roads behind it, to let down the last barriers of time and distance,
discomfort and inconvenience, that for so long barred the Southwest to any but
the pioneer. . . .*

*Harveycar Motor Cruises reach every part of the Southwest. They hold the
only key to exploration in comfort of an amazing territory.*

—Harveycar Motor Cruises: off the beaten path in the Great Southwest,
1 January 1929.

October 1929

Cover of the October 1929 reprint of the first (62-page) Indian Detours brochure of April 1926. (Private collection.)

Beginning in the late nineteenth century, railroad publicists carefully crafted images of the Southwest for a new type of American traveler who wanted all of the adventure and none of the adversity of pilgrimage or pioneering "off the beaten path." These image-makers were part of a complex commercial enterprise that in this century succeeded in creating and marketing a new mythology for the Southwest. The best-known mythmakers were writers, artists, architects, and designers employed by the Fred Harvey Company and the Atchison, Topeka & Santa Fe Railway. Fred Harvey became known as the "Civilizer of the West," while the Santa Fe was called "the Railroad that Built an Empire." Both companies were in large part responsible for the wholesale manufacture of a compelling new myth expressed architecturally, artistically, and ritualistically, but above all artificially.

"The Land of Sunshine": Chasing the Cure

Both the Santa Fe Railway and the Harvey system owed some of their early success to New Mexico's outstanding reputation among health-seekers in the nineteenth and early twentieth centuries. Claims about the territory's salubrity were routinely included in publicity from the Bureau of Immigration.[1] In 1881 Grant County boosters proclaimed: "For all pulmonary complaints there is not a more congenial spot on the top of the green earth. Here you inhale the pure, fresh, lifegiving and invigorating air." Bureau of Immigration writers reported that the Las Vegas Hot Springs contained "the great national laboratory, that sends gushing from its side those hot and healing waters, limpid and pure, a nectar fit for the Gods themselves. There the halt and the infirm can come and quaff this innocent beverage." As a result, R. W. Wiley proclaimed, "A few heard the story of the miracle of sun and air and mountains in the time before Koch had discovered the tubercle basillus [sic], and when the engineers of the Santa Fe drove the stakes of the first survey in New Mexico, they found there a few men, camped in the hills and on the mesas 'chasing the cure' the best they knew, but with only a limited knowledge of its proper pursuit."[2]

For centuries, Native Americans and Hispanos had used the hot springs at Gallinas, not far from Hermit's Peak near Las Vegas, for various curative purposes. In 1846 the invading United States Army established a hospital there. The Atchison, Topeka & Santa Fe Railway bought the hot springs and built a spur line from Las Vegas in 1882. On April 17, 1882, the railroad opened an elegant three-hundred-room hotel operated by Fred Harvey—the Montezuma, so named because the Aztec ruler was supposed to have bathed there.

Hot springs and bath houses with the Phoenix (Montezuma) atop the hill in back, Las Vegas Hot Springs, ca. 1884–85. Photo by J. R. Riddle. (MNM Neg. No. 2458.)

Contemporary railroad brochures proclaimed the benefits of drinking the waters and bathing in the springs and mud:

> The following diseases are almost invariably cured: Chronic Rheumatism, Gout, Scrofula, Stiff Joints, Skin diseases as a class, Ulcerations and enlargements of the Glands, General Physical Debility, Mental Exhaustion, Spinal Diseases, Sciatica, Lumbago, Paralysis, St. Vitus Dance, and all neuralgic or Nervous Affections, Catarrh or Ozena in all forms, Dyspepsia, Liver Disorders, Early Stages of Bright's Disease, Diabetes, Goitre, Specific Locomotor Ataxia, Spurious vaccination, all Blood poisons and Female Diseases. Pulmonary Diseases not too far advanced are very successfully treated, but the purity of the atmosphere and the mild, equable temperature no doubt contributing to the general good result in such cases.[3]

After the Montezuma burned and was rebuilt as the Phoenix in 1886, its inaugural brochure claimed that "The Phoenix has every appliance of luxury, amusement, health, social life and solid comfort. Outdoor life amid natural beauty that can not be improved, is attainable by ladies, children and invalids, without fatigue or hardship, while malaria, all epidemics, and the extremes of heat and cold are forever barred. It is in immediate proximity to the renowned medicinal baths, and is the ideal health residence, summer or winter."[4]

The Phoenix prospered during the Era of Climatology, "the belief that climate produces and cures levels of illness, a theory that flourished in the medical community from the 1880s until germ theory eclipsed it around the turn of the century."[5] The railroads were largely responsible for popularizing this notion of health and identifying beneficial locales along the lines from Colorado to New Mexico. In 1881, F. C. Nims, ticket agent of the Denver and Rio Grande Western Railroad, published *Health, Wealth and Pleasure in Colorado and New Mexico, A Reliable Treatise on the Famous Pleasure and Health Resorts, and the Rich Mining and Agricultural Regions of the Rocky Mountains,* a 130-page booklet which served as the model for a flood of promotional tracts during the late nineteenth and early twentieth centuries. The introduction promised climatological remedies to railroad passengers:

> For people from the East who seek health through a change of climate and associations, the country traversed by the Denver and Rio Grande Railway offers inducements that are nowhere surpassed. The pure, dry air of the plains and mountains, rarefied by an elevation of from one to two miles above the sea, and often in a high degree electrical, is bracing and exhilarating to the lungs. For asthma it is an almost unfailing specific, as hundreds of persons, confirmed asthmatics before coming to Colorado, but here able to breathe with comfort, and in the enjoyment of health, will make haste to testify. Those who have weak lungs, or who are in the incipient stages of consumption, seldom fail of relief in this climate, especially if they live out of doors as much as possible, and are not afraid of the sunshine, which is one of the crowning glories of Colorado. Nowhere in America are so many fine days. During some seasons a cloudy day is almost as rare as an eclipse, and there can be no doubt that cheerfulness and bodily and mental activity are promoted by absence of dark days, fogs, mists and dampness. If, as Longfellow sings, "Some days must be dark and dreary," in this climate they are

reduced to the minimum, and during some years happily missed from the calendar altogether.[6]

Colorado doctors Samuel Fish, Samuel Solly, and Charles Dennison, themselves recovered tuberculars, wrote promotional medical journal pieces in the 1880s describing the "southwest climate as the best-known therapy for tuberculosis, asthma, and hay fever, and hot springs as therapy for rheumatism, eczema, psoriasis, and acne." The American Climatological Association of eastern and western physicians was founded in 1884. Lungers and hackers, as consumptives were called, followed the railroads to spas, hospitals, sanitoriums, and resorts, and "seekers of physical health accounted for one-fifth to one-half of all immigration to [New Mexico] between 1870 and 1910," although up to 60 percent of tubercular patients died during their first years in what was called "The Well Country."[7]

Albuquerque advertised itself as "in the heart of the well country." In a booklet prepared for the Health Department of the Albuquerque Commercial Club, forerunner of the Chamber of Commerce, R. W. Wiley sent a "distinctly humanitarian message to those who are sufferers from health impairment, bidding them come to this land and find in its unequaled climate new life and hope and to learn its gospel of health":

And then there began to accumulate a great mass of undisputable evidence. Medical men spent years in investigating and marshalling facts to prove the superiority of the climate of the Southwest over that of all other sections in the cure of tuberculosis. From the results that were obtained here a majority of physicians in all sections of the country came to the inevitable conclusion that, while some portions of the West were blessed with the necessary altitude and pure air, many of the localities theretofore regarded with favor were too great in humidity and subject to too violent extremes in temperature. Also, the great benefit of altitude in the cure of tuberculosis had been so thoroughly demonstrated that the plains, deserts, and seashores came to be exempted when the advice "Go West" was given to a patient. It can be seen, therefore, that it has been a natural course of disclosures that has finally placed outside the geographical boundaries of the Well Country such points as Denver and Colorado Springs, because of high humidity, and southern California, and parts of Arizona and Texas, because of low altitude. Generally speaking, we can say that this land of which we are writing extends from Albuquerque, its heart, in every direction a distance of about four hundred miles.[8]

Cover: *Las Vegas Hot Springs, New Mexico.* "Prepared for the Information of Tourists, Tired People, Invalids of all Classes, and those who seek a Summer or Winter Resort, with the Benefit to be derived from Medicinal Baths and Mineral Waters." Passenger Department, Santa Fe Route, 1887. (MNM Neg. No. 122059.)

"The Railroad That Built an Empire" and "The Civilizer of the West"

The Atchison, Topeka & Santa Fe Railway was founded by Colonel Cyrus K. Holliday (1826–1900). On October 30, 1868, Colonel Holliday, together with Kansas Senator Edmund G. Ross (later governor of New Mexico, 1885–1889), turned the first spadeful of earth and prophesied a mighty railroad between Kansas and the Pacific Ocean and Gulf of Mexico. The tracks reached the New Mexico state line on December 7, 1878, and operations were opened at Las Vegas on July 4, 1879; at Galisteo Junction (Lamy) on February 9, 1880; at Santa Fe the following week, on February 16; at Albuquerque on April 15, 1880; at Fort Wingate on February 13, 1881; and at Holbrook, Arizona, on September 24 of that year. The Santa Fe connected with the Southern Pacific at Needles, California, thus establishing a West Coast connection, on August 8, 1883. With the Santa Fe came the Fred Harvey Company's famous system of dining, lodging, and marketing. As Will Rogers proclaimed: "Buffalo fed the west for years and they put it on a nickel. Fred Harvey took up where the buffalo left off."[9]

Born in London on June 27, 1835, Frederick Henry Harvey emigrated to the United States in 1850 and worked in New York City, New Orleans, and St. Louis restaurants before opening his own in 1856. He became a U.S. citizen in 1858 and two years later married Barbara Sarah Mattas, the daughter of Bohemian immigrants. The couple moved to Leavenworth, Kansas, and Harvey began work for the Chicago, Burlington and Quincy Railroad, traveling extensively but suffering unappetizing food and uncomfortable sleeping conditions along the railroads. He decided all travelers shared his tribulations and longed for fine, home-cooked meals and clean rooms. Harvey first brought his idea to the Burlington and then approached the Santa Fe, which responded favorably with a verbal contract. The first track of the Atchison, Topeka & Santa Fe Railway connected Topeka and Burlingame, Kansas, in September 1869, and Fred Harvey opened his first railroad-connected lunchroom at Topeka in 1876. He signed his first formal contract with the Santa Fe on January 1, 1878.[10]

The second formal contract between the Atchison, Topeka & Santa Fe Railroad Company and Fred Harvey was signed on May 1, 1889, and ran for a period of five years. "It granted to Fred Harvey the exclusive right, with some minor reservations, to manage and operate the eating houses, lunch stands, and hotel facilities which the company then owned, leased, or was to lease at any time in the future upon any of its railroads west of the Missouri River, including all lines then leased or operated in the name of the Atchison, Topeka and Santa Fe. Coal, ice, and water were to be provided by the railroad; employees and supplies were to be hauled free. Profits arising from the operations were to go to Fred Harvey in full for all services rendered by him in such business."[11] By 1895 the Harvey system of railroad accommodations was consolidated, and the Fred Harvey Company continued as a family operation following its founder's death in 1901.

Among Harvey's more famous establishments was the Montezuma Hotel near Las Vegas, New Mexico. During the grand opening banquet on April 17, 1882, Miguel A. Otero, Jr., delivered an oration describing "how the emperor, Montezuma, had 'disappeared from view amid clouds' but with a promise that he would return

"The Atchison, Topeka and Santa Fe railroad streamliner 'Super Chief' stopping for five minutes' servicing at the depot." FSA photo by Jack Delano, Albuquerque, March 1943.
(LC-USW 3-20414-D.)

Fred Harvey (1835–1901), known as "The Civilizer of the West." (Harvey Collection, Special Collections, General Library, University of New Mexico. Used with permission.)

in 'glory from the East' . . . [and concluding] that 'Tonight we hail his coming in the new and splendid halls of Montezuma.'" Harvey imported fresh fruit and vegetables from Mexico for the hotel, and "when the Santa Fe's Sonora System was completed to Guaymas on the Gulf of California, [he] contracted with the chief of a local tribe of Yaqui Indians to supply the Montezuma with green turtles to be kept in tanks until ready for use."[12]

Other hotels in the Harvey system were named after Spanish explorers: El Tovar (opened 1905) at the Grand Canyon; the Fray Marcos at Williams, Arizona; the Castañeda at Las Vegas, New Mexico (opened 1898); and the Cardenas at Trinidad, Colorado. Frank Waters calls these and others "the only true inns of the West and in the Western tradition." He claims that "the Harvey House was not only a haven in the wilderness, but an institution that had no parallel in America. Perhaps more than any single organization, the Fred Harvey system introduced America to Americans."[13]

Albuquerque boasted the Alvarado, owned by the railroad and operated by Fred Harvey.

> The shining jewel in the Santa Fe's crown was the Alvarado Hotel, begun in 1901 and named for Coronado's lieutenant, Hernando de Alvarado. Built at a cost of $200,000 alongside the tracks facing First Street, it was touted as the finest railroad hotel on earth. The design adhered to the California Mission style, which made use of towers, balconies, and arcades supported by arches. Inside, carved beams, massive fireplaces, and black oak paneling in the dining room lent an elegant tone to the southwestern theme. On May 11, 1902, the press announced that the newly completed Alvarado opened in "a burst of rhetoric, a flow of red carpet, and the glow of myriad brilliant electric lights." Instantly, it became the social center of Albuquerque and, among other things, the host of the glamorous Montezuma Ball held yearly.

A steadily growing number of train travelers necessitated the enlargement of the Alvarado in 1922, when "new rooms were added, as were shaded patios, water lily pools, and trickling fountains all carefully calculated to create the romantic atmosphere of old Spain."[14]

The influence of the Alvarado was such that in 1963 Lawrence Clark Powell proclaimed Albuquerque "the midway point, roughly equidistant between Fort Worth and Los Angeles, between Taos and El Paso, in the heart of the Indian country between Pueblo and Plains peoples, Spanish in origin and still bi-cultural, now molded by space-age developments; proliferating city on the river at the edge of the great plains, guarded by the Sandia range, a melting pot of the Southwestern elements." In his *Southwestern Book Trails: A Reader's Guide to the Heartland of New Mexico & Arizona,* Powell acknowledges Harvey's legacy as follows:

> Where do I take my stand when I survey the Southwest? Not in coastal Malibu where I live, nor in Los Angeles where I work; both are marginal vantage points, as were Dobie's in Austin, Campbell's in Norman. It is at the heart that I take my stand; at the heart of hearts, the *cor cordium* in Albuquerque, New Mexico, that ancient crossing on the Rio Grande. I will be even more precise and say just where

Alvarado Hotel (1902–1970), Harvey House on the station platform at Albuquerque. (Harvey Collection, Special Collections, General Library, University of New Mexico. Used with permission.)

Train visitors purchasing wares from Indians outside the Fred Harvey Indian Building (1902–1970), Albuquerque, showing towers of Alvarado Hotel to the right, ca. 1912. (Harvey Collection, Special Collections, General Library, University of New Mexico. Used with permission.)

it would be in Albuquerque: on the station platform of the Alvarado, one of the last of the Harvey Houses and the most beautiful of them all, old gray stucco with the turquoise trim, its cool courts and shady patios inviting siesta, its Indian museum packed with old Pueblo artifacts, its slow heartbeat the coming and going of the Santa Fe trains.[15]

From the beginning in 1876, service in Fred Harvey establishments was ritualized and carefully paced so patrons from the trains always had time to finish the elegant meals, with menus rotated every four days throughout the system to insure variety. Initially, food was local, but later, trains carried delicacies and specialties from around the country to grace the lavish menus. Coffee was especially important to Fred Harvey, so he formed a ninety-nine-year association with Chase and Sanborn to provide special coffee blends of uniformly high quality, adjusted to the local water systems.

At first Harvey himself made legendary surprise inspections of his establishments, wiping his pocket handkerchief over windows and door tops or snatching the tablecloth from under defective place settings. In 1881, inspectors' visits to Las Vegas and Raton, New Mexico, caused fights among the male waiters. When Tom Gable was hired to manage the Raton operation, he suggested that Harvey hire waitresses, who came to be legendary as well.

Harvey girls, "young women, 18 to 30 years of age, of good character, attractive and intelligent," were rigorously trained and strictly chaperoned. They wore severe uniforms—long, plain black dresses with white "Elsie" collars, long white aprons, black bows, stockings, low-heeled black shoes, and plain hairdos with white ribbons. "Many Harvey Girls were former schoolmarms. All were upright and moral, or so it went. This trait of virtue was epitomized in the 1946 Judy Garland movie musical 'The Harvey Girls'. . . . [They] weren't paid extravagantly, but the benefits were good. Will Rogers once said Fred Harvey and his girls 'kept the West in food and wives.' Legend has it that 20,000 of the handmaidens wound up as brides to western ranchers, cowboys and railroaders."[16]

Male patrons of Harvey houses and eating establishments were also expected to observe decorum. "One of Fred Harvey's most sacred regulations was his well-known 'coat rule.' From his earliest days it was accepted that all dining room men patrons should wear dinner jackets. To insure that no one was turned away because of improper dress, a supply of dark alpaca coats was always kept on hand. For nearly half a century, Americans ranging from gunmen to presidents obeyed the rule."[17] Harvey himself was known as a stern but even-handed enforcer of his own codes of conduct. Legend places the following incident at the Montezuma, the Castañeda, or the depot lunchroom at Las Vegas:

Cowpokes occasionally made trouble, desiring to show off by riding ponies into dining rooms and firing off pistols to astonish pilgrims aboard trains. Sometimes they demanded to be fed coatless. . . . Some cowhands and their foreman rode into the dining room, shot off a few bottlenecks and demanded food in loud and profane language.

Mr. Harvey, who was present, maintained his dapper serenity, stepped forward and raised a white hand. "Gentlemen," he said, "ladies dine here. No swearing or foul language is permitted. You must leave quietly at once." The cowhands, shamed, walked their horses out of the room, being careful that the screen door did not slam, and their foreman later apologized for them. Mr. Harvey, never a man to hold a grudge, set the men up to a fine lunch and would accept no payment, though insisting that his guests wear coats.[18]

When trains became faster in the late 1880s, Fred Harvey also took over the franchise for dining cars and news "butchering" or vending. The railroad in 1900 advertised its "dining service under the management of Fred Harvey [as] the best in the world." Indeed, "Harvey was in top form on his diners, serving West Coast specialties like citrus fruit and shellfish to California-bound travelers and midwestern favorites like Kansas City steaks to patrons heading east."[19]

German immigrant Herman Schweizer started as a sixteen-year-old news butcher or vendor on the trains and was at seventeen promoted to manage the Harvey lunchroom at Coolidge, New Mexico. From the first, Schweizer bought Navajo silver and blankets, and as early as 1899 commissioned new pieces using old pawn silver as models for items to sell to Harvey customers. The pawned Navajo silver

Patio of El Ortiz, with a Harvey girl in costume barely visible under portal to the right. From a May 1937 Indian Detours brochure. (Private collection.)

had proved to be too heavy for sale to the tourists, who wanted lighter jewelry which they could wear in the East. In 1899 Mr. Herman Schweizer . . . asked a turquoise-mine owner in Nevada to cut stones into flat, square, and oblong shapes for Indian use. Schweizer took these stones and some silver to a trading post at

Thoreau, New Mexico. He asked the trader there to have Navajo smiths make jewelry lighter in weight than that which they made for their own use. This method of "farming out" to the trading posts silver and turquoise, which had been polished and cut to the right size and shape, proved to be a very satisfactory method of obtaining jewelry for the tourist trade. Therefore, the Harvey Company sent the raw materials to other posts to be made into rings, bracelets, beads, and other jewelry. The traders at Sheep Springs, Smith Lake, and Mariano Lake gave this silver to the Navajo silversmiths and paid them by the ounce for the finished products. The Harvey Company sold these bracelets, rings, and beads on the trains which traveled over the Santa Fe line and in stands in the stations along the route.[20]

Herman Schweizer continued for years in charge of the Harvey Company curio department and served as the major collector for what became the Fred Harvey Fine Arts Collection of Native American, Mexican, Spanish Colonial, and some European pieces of art found in the New World.[21] Schweizer was headquartered in Albuquerque, where he was joined by Minnie Harvey Huckel and her anthropologist-businessman husband John Frederick Huckel, who was assigned to head the Fred Harvey Indian Department in 1902. Together they worked out many details of collection and commerce that served the whole Harvey system in good stead.

The Santa Fe Railway had not featured Indians in its advertising until the turn of the century, in part because trains were still equipped with Winchester rifles against raids as late as the 1880s, and in part because the metaphor and means of marketing had not been developed. However, by the turn of the century, Schweizer and another key Harvey employee, architect and designer Mary Elizabeth Jane Colter (1869–1958), had begun to create a commercially feasible image of southwestern Native American cultures. Colter designed the interiors for the Indian Building built between the Albuquerque train depot and the Alvarado Hotel in 1902.

The Indian Building itself contained an exhibition room for fine items not offered for sale, a workroom for Indian artisans to demonstrate their skills, and salesrooms. Schweizer and Colter arranged the Albuquerque complex so that visitors alighted from their train, walked through the Indian Building museum room, then entered the demonstration area and saw the natives at work. Thus when they finally entered the salesrooms, armed with their new-found appreciation of Indian artistry, they were ready to purchase articles resembling the exhibited originals, before going to lunch. Although for many years Schweizer had to stand outside the Indian Building and induce arriving passengers to enter, the venture finally paid off in Albuquerque and elsewhere in the Harvey System.[22]

Having mastered an effective method of merchandising the Indians, the Harvey Company now faced the challenge of incorporating Spanish colonial culture into their marketable version of the Southwest. New Mexico's capital city of Santa Fe, already publicized as the "City different," the "City of a Thousand Wonders," and the "Granada of America," was the center for the Hispanic Southwest. Ironically,

the tale that the Atchison, Topeka & Santa Fe Rail Road somehow never reached its namesake city of Santa Fe has become one of New Mexico's most durable legends. In spite of the persistence of the story, the facts in the matter are quite to the contrary. In fact, the railroad extended its tracks to the Ancient City at the earliest possible opportunity, the first train arriving there on February 9, 1880, and regular service of one class or another continuing from that date to the present.[23]

After October 1880, Pullman trains bypassed Santa Fe in favor of Albuquerque, but a local passenger train continued daily runs between the capital city and Lamy (earlier, Galisteo) junction. There, in 1910, Kansas City architect Louis Curtiss designed a small Harvey hotel, El Ortiz, in the emerging regional Spanish-Pueblo style. Mary Colter planned the interior using a predominantly Mexican-Spanish motif. Visitor Owen Wister, author of *The Virginian*, wrote his compliments to Jacob Stein, the manager. He described El Ortiz as

> like a private house of someone who had lavished thought and care upon every nook. . . . In the patio of this hacienda, pigeons were picking in the grass by the little center fountain. This little oasis among the desert hills is a wonder of taste to be looked back upon by the traveler who has stopped there, and forward to by the traveler who is going to stop there. The temptation was to give up all plans and stay a week for the pleasure of living and resting in such a place.[24]

In Santa Fe itself, however, the company constructed its fullest representation of New Mexico's colonial culture. La Fonda Hotel on the old Santa Fe Plaza, acquired by the Railroad in 1925 and leased to the Fred Harvey Company in 1926, became the showcase for what became a tricultural blend of architecture, interior decoration, and the merchandising of food, ambience, arts, crafts, and even local residents. One of the first La Fonda brochures proclaimed:

El Ortiz (1910–1943), Harvey House on the station platform at Lamy. From a May 1937 Indian Detours brochure. (Private collection.)

This old-time city is in the very heart of a region acclaimed by experienced travelers as of continuing and surpassing interest, regardless of the length or season of one's visit. The hospitable doors of La Fonda swing wide the year 'round, for in Old Santa Fe and the surrounding country there is no month of the twelve without its peculiar charm.

From La Fonda radiate tree-bordered avenues and 'dobe-lined byways. Within it comfort and luxury go hand in hand with the true atmosphere of a land where the Past lives on happily with the Present. About it are the things that Kit Carson and Lew Wallace knew—the mountains, the ageless Indian pueblos, the picturesque settlements born in America of a medieval Spain.

Santa Fe's crude fondas of other days were famous as the End of the Trail. La Fonda of today was created to be both the End and Beginning of Trails—for those who would step aside for a time from accustomed things, to follow a hundred new and old ways into the hidden corners of a singularly beautiful and interesting section of our country as yet undisturbed and unspoiled by the rush of modern life.[25]

Mary Colter urged architect John Gaw Meem to modify the hotel's lines in his refinement of and addition to the existing structure, designed in 1920 by the Rapp and Rapp architectural firm. Meem had established his design by July 1927, noting: "The exterior of the hotel will be in the Spanish-Pueblo style . . . [with] the emphasis . . . more on mass than ornament. Its numerous set backs and ornaments will recall the terracing in the more ancient Pueblos of Taos and Acoma."[26]

Colter oversaw the interior decoration of the 156 rooms, each unique in color and design but all predominantly Mexican, especially the public rooms. According to Virginia L. Grattan, Colter was recovering from a Kansas City auto accident and supervised this work from a wheelchair:

A friend asked her if she was at all apprehensive about decorating a major hotel in Santa Fe, a town full of artists. Colter confided, "I'm scared to death of these Santa Fe artists." She needn't have worried. Fred Harvey opened the remodeled La Fonda in 1929, and it soon became a landmark. Not only did it become a mecca for tourists to the Southwest, but it was a haunt for Santa Feans as well.[27]

La Fonda's dining room became the only one in the Fred Harvey system that did not require men to wear a coat and tie, since the Bohemian art colonists would not allow the company to enforce its longstanding rule.

La Fonda was the site of yet another Fred Harvey innovation for transcontinental train travelers: Indian Detours, "an unusual outing-by-motor through the Spanish and Indian Southwest, available [at a cost of forty to sixty dollars per person] as a pleasant break in the long all-rail journey." Major R. Hunter Clarkson, a native of Edinburgh, Scotland, conceived the idea of setting up three-day motor trips between the Castañeda Harvey House in Las Vegas and the Alvarado in Albuquerque, with an intermediate stop at La Fonda. The first Detour brochure, written and designed by Roger W. Birdseye, advised:

It is the purpose of the Indian Detour to take you through the very heart of all this, to make you feel the lure of the Southwest that lies beyond the pinched horizons of your train window. In no other way can you hope to see so much of a vast, fascinating region in so short a time—and with the same economy, the same comfort, the same leisurely intimacy and the same freedom from all trivial distraction. ...It is 3 days and 300 miles of sunshine and relaxation and mountain air, in a land of unique human contrasts and natural grandeur.[28]

The first tourist-carrying Indian Detours Harveycar embarked from Las Vegas on Saturday, May 15, 1926. Couriers, "young women with intimate personal knowledge of the region supplemented by special training," accompanied each Harveycar. Erna Fergusson, who earlier had organized her own guided Koshare Tours to Indian dances, was hired to train the Couriers. They were "expected to be young women of education and some social grace, able to meet easily and well all kinds of people [and] expected to be intelligent enough to learn many facts about this country and to impart them in a way to interest intelligent travelers." An Advisory Board "of nationally known authorities on the archaeology, ethnology and history of the Southwest," including Dr. Edgar Lee Hewett, director of the Museum of New Mexico and the School of American Research, and Charles F. Lummis, selected, instructed, and examined Couriers. This preparation was in keeping with the Harvey spirit heralded in an *Albuquerque Morning Journal* editorial of August 21, 1925:

> Fred Harvey had in fact the true spirit of the collector and antiquarian. He insisted on authenticity. He discouraged the fairy stories that too often passed current to astonish the gullible tourist. If Fred Harvey showed an old Spanish bell there was no doubt of its age. If one of his agents related an historical incident or an Indian legend, its veracity could be relied on. Because of the insistence on authenticity which Mr. Harvey drilled in his organization, we may be sure the planned tours will not be vulgarized. The tourists will not be regaled with fanciful stories and amused with "fake" objects of interest. They will have presented to them the life of New Mexico both as it has been and as it still is.[29]

The Harvey Company was not only concerned with the Couriers' ability to inform tourists but with their capacity to project a distinctive Southwestern image. A 1929 brochure told tourists what to expect:

> Couriers' attractive outing uniforms, rich in Navajo hammered silver and turquoise jewelry, are characteristic of the Southwestern Indian country. Greeting guests on arrival by train, it is thereafter the Couriers' privilege to fill the pleasant dual role of hostesses as well as guides. Their information is not intruded; it is simply a store of remarkably interesting facts from which casually to develop the full interest of a strange country. Friendships with representative Indians in many pueblos assure their guests intimate glimpses of Indian life not otherwise obtainable.
>
> Couriers assume responsibility for all hotel and similar details en route and in many other ways add to the comfort and pleasure of Cruise guests.[30]

Couriers, drivers, cars, and promotional brochures were all adorned with the thunderbird emblem of the Indian Detours. It was described in the July 1926 issue of *National Motor Bus and Taxicab Journal* as "an enigmatic black fowl upon a vivid

(Left). Back cover: July 1929 La Fonda brochure, showing plumed serpent and sky loom motifs. Designed by Gerald Cassidy. (Private collection.)

(Center). Front cover: July 1929 La Fonda brochure, designed by Gerald Cassidy. (Private collection.)

(Opposite). Cover: La Fonda brochure, ca. 1949, showing incorporation of Hispanic and Indian motifs. (Private collection.)

orange background. This Thunderbird is a creature of early American mythology whose obsidian feathers clash against each other as he flies, making the thunder of the summer showers, so life giving to the crops. He is considered a harbinger of abundant harvests and is the symbol of good luck."[31]

The Harvey Company selected a genteel cowboy motif for its Harveycar drivers. "A uniform was designed for the drivers which made them look like polo players inspired by Zane Grey. They went outfitted in English riding boots and breeches, a colorful cowboy shirt and silk neckerchief, and a Tom Mix-size ten-gallon hat. They managed to look dashing enough, and their strong silent act inspired confidence in the tourists." A 1930 Harveycar brochure reassured travelers that their drivers were efficient and disciplined: "Steering wheels know no more reliable, clean-cut men. They are courteous and thoughtful of the little things—for they, too, have been through the mill of Harveycar training and experience. They are expert mechanics, every one, and after years of mountain and desert driving the emergency beyond their resource and skill has yet to arise."[32]

All in all, the Harveycar Indian Detours used the automobile to package more and more of the Southwest for outsiders' consumption. They claimed that the Courier Corps was one of the most popular aspects of their combined rail-motor service. "The Courier idea, long taken for granted as part of European tour service," claimed publicists in another brochure, "has here been developed along unique lines, adding immensely to the interest and pleasure of exploring what is still practically a virgin frontier territory of vast area."[33]

By the time of his death in 1901, Fred Harvey was known as the Civilizer of the West. His mystique is summed up in a 1949 *Collier's Magazine* article by Dickson Hartwell, "Let's Eat with the Harvey Boys":

If the .45 revolver was the peacemaker of the Southwest, Fred Harvey, founder of the empire was its civilizer. Working with the vast, longest-in-U.S. Santa Fe railroad—some say the Santa Fe made Harvey, others stoutly declare Harvey made the Santa Fe—he carried Delmonico food standards west of the Mississippi. He gave America the Harvey girl, immortalized by M-G-M, and he sold enough Indian curios to put a touch of Navajo or Hopi in every U.S. home.[34]

An undying, legendary figure, "Mr. Harvey: still in charge" excited speculation by an anonymous writer for *The Hotel Monthly* in December 1951:

> "What Mr. Harvey would think" about any new project is clear in the minds of many of the executives of the system—even though Fred Harvey died in 1901. Thus the ideas of a businessman who has been dead for half a century are today not a retarding influence, but a dynamic factor. Fred Harvey was a dealer in new ideas, new methods, new business projects—and his organization and his descendants are carrying on in that tradition. It is probably safe to say that if Fred Harvey could have had a long extension of life, and were still at the head of the Harvey system today, the Harvey operation would be very much the same as it is.

This rhetoric echoes Elbert Hubbard's eulogy. Hubbard pronounced Fred Harvey a "miracle":

> Fred Harvey is dead, but his spirit still lives. The standard of excellence he set can never go back. He has been a civilizer and benefactor. He has added to the physical, mental and spiritual welfare of millions. No sermon can equal a Fred Harvey

example—no poet can better a Fred Harvey precept. Fred Harvey simply kept faith with the public. He gave pretty nearly a perfect service. I did not know Fred Harvey, but I know this: he must have been an honest man, a good man—for the kind of a business a man builds up is a reflection of himself—spun out of his heart. Man, like Deity, creates in his own image. I take off my hat to Fred Harvey, who served the patrons of the Santa Fe so faithfully and well, that dying, he yet lives, his name a symbol of all that is honest, hygienic, beautiful and useful.[35]

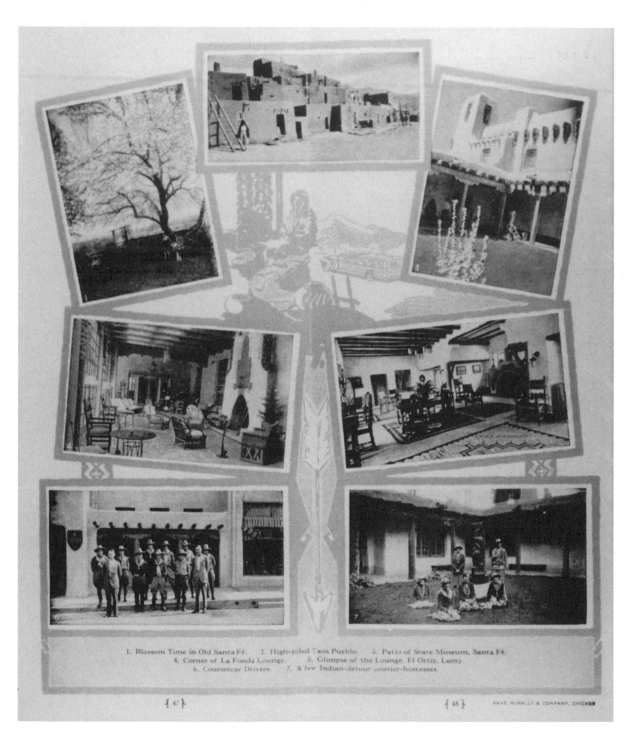

1. Blossom Time in Old Santa Fé.   2. High-piled Taos Pueblo.   3. Patio of State Museum, Santa Fé.
4. Corner of La Fonda Lounge.   5. Glimpse of the Lounge. El Ortiz, Lamy
6. Couriercar Drivers   7. A few Indian-detour courier-hostesses.

{ 47 }   { 48 }   RAND McNALLY & COMPANY, CHICAGO

Conclusion

Between 1879 and 1941, the Santa Fe Railway, the Fred Harvey Company, and numerous civic and commercial organizations manufactured and marketed a coherent and compelling regional identity for New Mexico and the Southwest. They portrayed a regenerative land and climate where exotic native peoples and historic sites of conquest and exploration were on view to pampered observers. Tourists were shuttled on modern conveyances between elegant hotels and carefully orchestrated spectacles of Native American and Hispano life.

This commercial packaging was made possible initially by catering to late-nineteenth-century American notions of travel. Early Anglo tourism in what came to be known as The Great Southwest was undertaken by health seekers and the wealthy, attuned to European and largely aristocratic models of national health spas like Bath, England, or Baden-Baden, Germany, of Mediterranean and Adriatic rivieras, and of casinos like Monte Carlo. Stage and rail travel was dangerous and above all expensive, so women and families did little tourist travel until the 1880s, when the orientation was toward elite travel in exquisite Pullmans to the grand hotels of the West like San Francisco's Palace, Denver's Windsor, and the Manitou and Broadmoor complex of Colorado Springs.

Would-be Saratogas like the Montezuma and the Castañeda in Las Vegas were also familiar and fit the expectation of finding the East Coast and Europe in the Western United States—Italy in California (Pasadena's Hotel Green promising "the conveniences of New York hotel life" with "the semi-tropical beauties of Italy, and the fruits and flowers of southern California") and Switzerland in the Colorado Rockies, for example. As often as not, one would also find wealthy Easterners and Europeans of known social class and habits.[36]

Anglo tourists inherited the eighteenth-century British institution of the Grand Tour. Nelson Graburn traces the cultural, educational, and political impetus for such travel to "the post-medieval decline of the universities and the great public and grammar schools as institutions of liberal learning," which brought about "the rise of alternative means of instruction: the tutor and the tour were the two principal ones." The aristocrat "went abroad not only to see the classical sights, but to learn languages, manners and accomplishments, riding, dancing, and other social graces. The tour was deemed a very necessary part of the training of future political and administrative leaders, as well as patrons of the arts."[37]

Those who launched the advertising campaign on behalf of New Mexico and the Southwest had to create a visit to rival the Grand Tour. However, in the so-called American desert, at the Grand Canyon, at cliff dwellings, Indian pueblos, and isolated Hispanic villages, *nothing* was familiar. The railroads and the Fred Harvey Company had to endow this alien landscape and its inhabitants with images of Western antiquity, sacredness, and culture. The Native American world had to assume a cultural significance equal to the ancient worlds of Babylon, Egypt, Greece, and Rome.[38] Tourists had to be educated to understand Indian and Spanish colonial arts and crafts as equivalent to the products of the European Renaissance. Hispanic villagers had to assume royal stature as noble descendants of Coronado and the conquistadors.

The advertisers' goal was endorsed by Indian Detours founder R. Hunter Clarkson, speaking at an August 29, 1925, La Fonda Hotel dinner meeting of New

Mexicans interested in the newest Harvey venture. According to the *Albuquerque Morning Journal* of August 30:

> Highlights in Clarkson's talk were:
>
> There is more of historic, prehistoric, human and scenic interest in New Mexico than in any other similar area in the world, not excepting India, Egypt, Europe or Asia.
>
> From 10,000 to 12,000 ticket agents will become media advertising Santa Fe and New Mexico.
>
> The influx of tourists will mean more prosperity for everyone.
>
> The big idea is not only to let people know what is in Northern New Mexico but to tell them what it is when they see it.[39]

While the original vision of New Mexico promoters was aristocratic, European, and highly structured, they soon began to cater to an increasing number of middle-class tourists who were out to "See America First"—adventurous "pioneers" mimicking the heroism of the Santa Fe Trail. These would-be frontiersmen first ventured into the Southwest along "the steel ribbons of the railroads" and then were led "off the beaten path" and into the "hinterlands" by "cowboys" and "Navajo" Courier guides. Their trek was made efficient, comfortable, safe, and convenient by entrepreneurs of transportation and accommodation.

Fred Harvey's predecessor and counterpart in the British Isles was a Baptist minister and social reformer named Thomas Cook who, "taking advantage of the new railway system, in 1842 organized an all-inclusive tour to a temperance meeting. Other successful and morally uplifting tours followed; Cook combined his visions of democratic travel and the pomotion of sobriety, with the chance to profit financially from the opportunities for taking townspeople to the countryside or abroad. . . . Promoting railway expansion everywhere, and the standardization of hotels and restaurants, Cook's coupons and later traveler's checks made travel easy for the masses, opening approved parts of the world to the inspection and edification of the educated middle classes." Like Cook, Harvey designed what Graburn calls "travel-made-easy [which] followed closely on the heels of imperial and commercial expansion."[40]

Daniel J. Boorstin observes a peculiarity of middle-class American tourists in the twentieth century, who came to "expect our two-week vacation to be romantic, exotic, cheap and effortless. We expect a faraway atmosphere if we go to a nearby place; and we expect everything to be relaxing, sanitary, and Americanized if we go to a faraway place."[41]

Fred Harvey and the railroads first succeeded in Americanizing the "far" Southwestern experience. Then, as it was brought "near," these enterprising mythmakers presented the Great Southwest as the exotic habitat of colorful but tamed natives. Couriers were even asked "Why did the Indians build their pueblos so far from the railroad?" Brochures alerted train travelers to the fascinating possibility of witnessing in March or April Penitente flagellation alongside the railroad tracks.[42] In a little over fifty years, then, the Santa Fe and the Fred Harvey organization packaged and publicized what had previously been local, traditional, and often circumspect native and folk cultures.

These and other traffickers in Southwestern imagery took a complex of expressive symbols and cultures and skillfully manufactured a commodity for national consumption. Their enduring legacy is America's contemporary notion of New Mexico as the healthy Land of Enchantment, the home of the naturally artistic Indian, the quaint Spaniard, the laconic white-hatted cowboy, the lonely prospector ever dreaming of gold, and the bohemian artists and literati. A picture-perfect spectacle of land and sky, New Mexico has now been made the setting for orchestrated ordeals, a place where hunter, hiker, skier, health seeker, and tourist can go through the motions of recreation and regeneration.

Taos Indian-Detour map by Behn. From the 1933 reprint of an Indian Detours brochure first published in 1930. (Private collection.)

FOCAL PLACE THREE

Pecos Pueblo and Mission

The historical and commercial texts in chapter 3, "Steel Rails," present a successfully marketed, national image for the Southwest and New Mexico. Building on the commerce of the Chihuahua and Santa Fe Trails, Santa Fe Railroad and Fred Harvey Company entrepreneurs provided services to travelers-become-tourists.

The state's first tourist "trap" was Pecos Pueblo and Mission, a safe and spectacular spot along the Santa Fe Trail eighteen miles southeast of Santa Fe on a natural gateway to the plains. Visited by conquistadors, colonists, travelers, politicians, and later tourists, it was the focus of both indigenous and invented legends about the Aztec leader Montezuma.

Historical Texts

Coronado visited Pecos Pueblo in 1541, and later conquistadors followed suit. Missionaries were assigned there from the time of Oñate's colonization in 1598, and archeologists have discovered that four seventeenth- and eighteenth-century mission churches occupied the site of what was once one of the largest and most impressive pueblos in New Mexico.[1] The last Indians abandoned Pecos in 1838, joining inhabitants of Jemez Pueblo, the only other Indians speaking their Towa language.

John L. Kessell summarizes what happened after 1838, when "the era of Pecos as monument" began:

> While the last of the Pecos "kept the faith" at Jemez, a motley procession of traders, soldiers, and tourists was tracking through the ruins of their former homes, scratching graffiti, pocketing souvenirs, and recounting the fantastic tales of "a lost civilization."

The Old Pecos Church, September 1880. Photo by George C. Bennett, published by W. Henry Brown. (MNM Neg. No. 6503.)

If Thomas James heard the tales in 1821, he did not repeat them. Ten years later, Albert Pike heard them all right—Montezuma, the eternal fire in a cave, and worship of a giant snake—but he did not fix them precisely on Pecos. That came soon enough. An article by "El Doctor Masure" in the *Santa Fe Republican* of September 24, 1847, told of a visit in 1835 to the "furnace of Montezuma" at Pecos. . . .

Ever since the sixteenth century, Spanish chroniclers had associated ruins north of Mexico with the origin of the Aztecs and with Montezuma. The legendary pre-conquest feathered serpent [Quetzalcoatl] had slithered northward even earlier.[2] When, in the romantic atmosphere of the nineteenth century, Pecos became a bona fide and easily accessible ruin, it is no wonder that such specters took up residence here. "Ere the May-flower drifted to Plymouth's snowy rock, this vestal flame was burning. . . . and yet till Montezuma shall return—so ran the charge—that fire must burn."

Contemporary anthropologists and historians were somewhat more skeptical, however:

> Pondering Montezuma's alleged birth at Pecos and his vow to return, the astute Adolph F. Bandelier in 1880 ascribed the tale to "an evident mixture of a name with the Christian faith in a personal redeemer, and dim recollections of Coronado's presence and promise to return." Of course it may also have been a convenient ruse employed by the Pueblos to mislead inquisitive whites. Lt. John G. Bourke, contemporary of Bandelier and ethnologist in his own right, found the Montezuma story "among the Pueblos who have had most to do with Americans and Mexicans and among no others." No matter, thought historian Ralph Emerson Twitchell in 1910. "This story is the veriest rot."[3]

Marc Simmons claims that many mid-nineteenth-century visitors were influenced by William H. Prescott's monumental 1843 history, *The Conquest of Mexico*. "Widely read in the U.S., it first brought the attention of the reading public to the stirring events surrounding Montezuma's encounter with Cortez and the overthrow of the Aztec empire."[4] The impressive, accessible Pecos ruins thus came to symbolize another encounter between newcomers and native Mexicans—this time between Anglo Americans and native New Mexicans. Soldiers particularly and many territorial politicians were aware of this new confrontation. When Secretary of the Territory William G. Ritch designed a seal for New Mexico's first legislative manual or "Blue Book" in 1882, he chose to depict two eagles—a larger, American one sheltering a smaller bird adapted from that on the seal of the Republic of Mexico.

Nineteenth-century travelers over the Santa Fe Trail—whether merchants, soldiers, immigrants or stagecoach passengers—almost invariably stopped at Pecos because there was a good supply of water, grass, and wood, and it was then only one hard day's drive to Santa Fe. They recorded many impressions in their journals, letters, articles, and books. Nearby, Captain Andrew (sometimes, Napolean; actually Martin) Kozlowski, a Polish immigrant who came to New Mexico after 1846 as an officer with the Missouri Volunteers, ranched, farmed, and operated a stage station built from "materials scavenged from the ruined Pecos mission and Indian Pueblo one mile away. Meals provided to stage passengers by his wife, including fresh trout from the Pecos River, were said to be the best on the western end of the trail."[5]

Adolph F. Bandelier visited Pecos and documented its ruins and nearby inhabitants in the late summer of 1880. According to John L. Kessell:

> The great Swiss-American pioneer ethnologist had only just arrived in the Southwest a few days before. From the train, he had caught his first glimpse of Pecos. . . .
>
> To alert the less observant tourist, the Santa Fe Railway Company later erected on the north side of the tracks opposite the ruins an immense signboard proclaiming Pecos a wonder of the Southwest. In a sense, Bandelier did the same thing. His notably meticulous report—even to mention of the broken Anheuser-Busch beer bottles—based on ten exhilerating [*sic*] days of field investigation alerted the archaeologist to the potentials of the Southwest.

The railroad was also important in stimulating twentieth-century tourism, especially after the 1915 Panama-California Expositions in San Diego and San Francisco. Those who attended the Panama-California Exposition in San Diego were alerted to the wonders of the Pecos by "a sixteen-foot-long model of the mesa top showing reconstructed church, South Pueblo, and main Quadrangle" in the New Mexico Building exhibits overseen by Museum of New Mexico director Edgar Lee Hewett.[6]

Pecos received further national attention when Willa Cather included a literary account of the pueblo's last days and its sacred fire and serpent in her popular Southwestern novel, *Death Comes for the Archbishop* (1927). She drew her material primarily from library research, but some Pecos visitors before and after her book appeared reported essentially field-collected, folklore texts about Montezuma, the fire, and the serpent. Their fieldwork did not resume after World War II, when Pecos was definitely secured as a monument.

Serious archeological work had not begun until excavations by Alfred V. Kidder and Jesse L. Nusbaum in 1915. The pueblo and surrounding land had been acquired by Gross, Kelly, and Company, a Santa Fe mercantile firm, in 1902. "In 1920, 67 acres encompassing the Pueblo ruins and mission were deeded to the Archdiosese of Santa Fe, which, in turn donated the parcel to the School of American Research. Designated a state monument in 1935, Congress established it as a national monument by an act of 1965, after the state donated the land to the federal government."[7]

Political Texts

John L. Kessell claims that no nineteenth-century visitor to Pecos recorded an account to top that by "young Pvt. Josiah M. Rice, who passed by in 1851 with Col. Edwin V. Sumner's command. 'There are,' claimed Rice, 'many traditions connected with this old church, one of which is that it was built by a race of giants, fifty feet in height. But these, dying off, they were succeeded by dwarfs, with red heads who, being in their turn exterminated, were followed by the Aztecs.'"

Lieutenant William H. Emory's *Notes of a Military Reconnaissance* of August 17, 1846, present a less fantastic soldier's description:

> Pecos, once a fortified town, is built on a promontory or rock, somewhat in the shape of a foot. Here burned, until within seven years, the eternal fires of Montezuma, and the remains of the architecture exhibit, in a prominent manner, the engraftment of the Catholic church upon the ancient religion of the country. . . . The fires from the *"estuffa"* burned and sent their incense through the same altars from which was preached the doctrine of Christ. Two religions so utterly different in theory, were here, as in all of Mexico, blended in harmonious practice until about a century since, when the town was sacked by a band of Indians.
>
> Amidst the havoc of plunder of the city, the faithful Indian managed to keep his fire burning in the *"estuffa"*; and it was continued till a few years since—the tribe became almost extinct. Their devotions rapidly diminished their numbers, until they became so few as to be unable to keep their immense estuffa (forty feet in diameter) replenished, when they abandoned the place and joined a tribe of the original race over the mountains, about sixty miles south. There, it is said, to this

day they keep up their fire, which has never yet been extinguished. The labor, watchfulness, and exposure to heat consequent on this practice of their faith, is fast reducing this remnant of the Montezuma race; and a few years will, in all probability, see the last of this interesting people.[8]

Hon. W. G. Ritch, Secretary of the Territory, appended an essay entitled "Introductory. New Mexico. A Sketch of Its History and Review of Its Resources." to his 1882 compilation for the Twenty-fifth Session of the Territorial Legislature, *Legislative Blue-Book, of the Territory of New Mexico, with the Rules of Order, Fundamental Law, Official Register and Record, Historical Data, Compendium of Facts, Etc., Etc.* This "Resources" text includes an account of the Montezuma tradition and the coat of arms Ritch designed for the book's cover:

TRADITION

A written record of which is to be found in some of the pueblos, is that Pecos pueblo was the birth-place of Montezuma; that after he had grown to man's estate he showed himself possessed of supernatural powers; that he at a certain time assembled a large number of his people and started from New Mexico on a journey south, Montezuma riding on the back of an eagle; and thus riding in advance, was to his people, as was the star to the wise men of the East. Wherever the eagle stopped at night there was planted an Indian pueblo. The sign of arriving at the site of the great city and capital of the Aztec nation was to be the "alighting of the eagle upon a cactus bush and devouring a serpent." This event took place when the eagle arrived at the site of the present city of Mexico, then first made a city and capital.

Seal of the State. (MNM Neg. No. 89928.)

COAT OF ARMS

The legend has been made memorable by the action of the Republic of Mexico in adopting the alighting eagle as the design of the national seal. The same design is like-wise stamped on Mexican coins. The founding of the city of Mexico is dated 1325. The memory of the legend is perpetuated in New Mexico by including the design as part of the coat of arms of this Territory. The seal of New Mexico it will thus be noticed is the eagle, as represented on the seal of Mexico, resting under the wing or shadowing care of the American eagle. The reader we think will say it is not only highly interesting, but likewise most appropriate.[9]

The Daily New Mexican (Santa Fe) of January 1, 1882, announced Ritch's design for the "New Territorial Seal," which "was engraved expressly for the Legislative Manual or Blue Book . . . now in press," as follows:

The design of the Great Seal of the Territory is the eagle, as represented in the coat of arms of the republic of Mexico, perched on a cactus bush, under the protective or shadowing wing of the eagle, as represented in the coat of arms of the United States, with the Latin motto *"Crescit Eundo,"* and the date "MDCCCL," the latter dating the organic act. . . . In the vignette, Mr. Ritch has added a sunrise scene for a background, with an Aztec standing upon the top of his house, his hand shadowing his eyes, watching with interest for the coming of Montezuma, and which tradition has assured him he will some time, with the rising of the sun. The wreath surrounding the above scene is suggestive of the possibilities of New Mexico in viniculture and horticulture. The scenes to the right and left are mineral and pastoral, mountain and plain, and speak for themselves.

The vignette is the first engraving of its character ever made of the coat of arms of New Mexico; it is wonderfully suggestive to the antiquarian, as well as suggestive of the material resources of the Territory, and when compared with the vignettes of other States and Territories must be regarded as equal to the best and is most satisfactory to our people at home.

The Great Seal of the State of New Mexico was selected by a commission named in joint Legislative Resolution No. 11, passed on March 13, 1913. It represents a modification of Ritch's design and is officially described in these terms: "The coat of arms of the State shall be the Mexican eagle grasping a serpent in its beak, the cactus in its talons, shielded by the American eagle with outspread wings, and grasping arrows in its talons; the date 1912 under the eagles and on the scroll, the motto: 'Crescit Eundo.' The great seal of the State shall be a disc bearing the coat of arms and having around the edge the words, 'Great Seal of the State of New Mexico.'" The official translation of the motto reads: "We grow as we go."[10]

Travel Texts

In September 1839, "the irrepressible Matthew C. Field, actor, journalist, and rover, spent the night with Dr. David C. Waldo in the Pecos church" and wrote an article about the "dilapidated town called *Pecus*" for the New Orleans *Picayune*. An old man fed them "a supper of hot porridge made of pounded corn and goat's milk, which we drank with a shell spoon from a bowl of wood, sitting upon the ground at the foot of the ruined altar by the light of a few dimly burning sticks of pine." The old man told of a summertime "pestilential disorder" that left only three people to tend the Sacred Fire—a chief, his daughter, and her betrothed. The chief died. Just before the couple died the young man took a brand from the fire and led his betrothed outside the cave. "A light then rose in the sky which was not the light of morning, but the heavens were red with the flames that roared and crackled up the mountain side. And the lovers lay in each other's arms, kissing death from each other's lips, and smiling to see the fire of Montezuma mounting up to heaven."

> He told it in glowing words and with a rapt intensity which the writer has endeavored to imitate, but he feels that the attempt is a failure. The scene itself—the ruined church—the feeble old man bending over the ashes, and the strange tones of his thin voice in the dreary midnight—all are necessary to awaken such interest as was felt by the listeners. Such is the story, however, and there is no doubt but that the legend has a strong foundation, in truth; for there stands the ruined town, well known to the Santa Fe traders, and there lives the old man, tending his goats on the hill side during the day, and driving them into the church at night. . . . It was imperative upon us to leave the place before day light that we might reach our destination (San Miguel) early the next morning, so that we could not gratify our curiosity by

descending the cavern ourselves, but we gave the old man a few bits of silver, and telling him that the story with which he had entertained us should be told again in the great United States, we each pocketed a cinder of the sacred fire and departed.[11]

Josiah Gregg had visited Pecos before Field and recorded the following passage in his *Commerce of the Prairies* (1844):

Many curious tales are told of the singular habits of this ill-fated tribe, which must no doubt have tended to hasten its utter annihilation. A tradition was prevalent among them that Montezuma had kindled a holy fire, and enjoined their ancestors not to suffer it to be extinguished until he should return to deliver his people from the yoke of the Spaniards. In pursuance of these commands, a constant watch had been maintained for ages to prevent the fire from going out; and, as tradition further informed them, that Montezuma would appear with the sun, the deluded Indians were to be seen every clear morning upon the terraced roofs of their houses, attentively watching for the appearance of the "king of light," in hopes of seeing him "cheek by jowl" with their immortal sovereign. I have myself descended into the famous *estufas,* or subterranean vaults, of which there were several in the village, and have beheld this consecrated fire, silently smouldering under a covering of ashes, in the basin of a small altar. Some say that they never lost hope in the final coming of Montezuma until, by some accident or other, or a lack of a sufficiency of warriors to watch it, the fire became extinguished; and that it was this catastrophe that induced them to abandon their villages, as I have before observed.

The task of tending the sacred fire was, it is said, allotted to the warriors. It is further related, that they took the watch by turns for two successive days and nights, without partaking of either food, water, or sleep; while some assert, that instead of being restricted to two days, each guard continued with the same unbending severity of purpose until exhaustion, and very frequently death, left their places to be filled by others. A large portion of those who came out alive were generally so completely prostrated by want of repose and the inhalation of carbonic gas that they very soon died; when, as the vulgar story asseverates, their remains were carried to the den of a monstrous serpent, which kept itself in excellent condition by feeding upon these delicacies. This huge snake (invented no doubt by the lovers of the marvellous to account for the constant disappearance of the Indians) was represented as the idol which they worshipped, and as subsisting entirely upon the flesh of his devotees: live infants, however, seemed to suit his palate best. The story of this wonderful serpent was so firmly believed in by many ignorant people, that on one occasion I heard an honest ranchero assert, that upon entering the village very early on a winter's morning, he saw the huge trail of the reptile in the snow, as large as that of a dragging ox.[12]

Eighteen-year-old Susan Shelby Magoffin accompanied her new husband, veteran trader Samuel Magoffin, over the Santa Fe Trail from Missouri to New Mexico in 1846–1847. She kept a detailed diary of the adventure and on August 29, 1846, made the following entry:

Ruins of Church at Pecos in 1846

I have visited this morning the ruins of an ancient pueblo, or village, now desolate and a home for the wild beast and bird of the forest.

It created sad thoughts when I found myself riding almost heedlessly over the work of these once mighty people. There perhaps was pride, power and wealth, carried to its utter most limit, for here tis said the great Montezuma once lived, though tis probably a false tradition, as the most learned and ancient American historians report that great monarch to have resided much farther south than any portion of New Mexico.

At any rate these pueblos believed in and longlooked for the coming of their king to redeem them from the *Spanish yoke*. And I am told by persons who saw it, that tis only within some two or three years since it was inhabited by one family only, the last of a once numerous population. These continued to keep alive "Montezuma's fire," till it was accidently extinguished, and they abandoned the place, believing that *Fate* had turned her hand against them.[13]

After a lithograph, "Ruins of Pecos Aztek Church," in W. H. Emory, *Notes of a Military Reconnoissance* (1848). (Ancient City Press Collection.)

Literary Texts

Willa Cather includes a version of the Pecos serpent legend in Book IV, "Snake Root," of *Death Comes for the Archbishop* (1927), her famous, fictionalized "saint's legend" about Archbishop Jean Baptiste Lamy (whom she calls Jean Marie Latour). To escape a blizzard, Latour spends a disturbing night with his Pecos Indian guide Jacinto near the pueblo in a "terrible" cave below "two giant stone lips." They find

Cochiti Pueblo pottery called
"Rare Specimens Ancient
Montezuma Pottery," for sale by
L. Fisher, ca. 1881. Photo by Ben
Wittick. (MNM Neg. No. 16296.)

ashes of a dead fire, and the cavern resounds with "the oldest voices on earth"—"not a rushing noise, but the sound of a great flood moving with majesty and power." Later, Latour vows that "no tales of wonder . . . would ever tempt him into a cavern hereafter," but he does ask trader Zeb Orchard about such stories:

> Orchard said that the legend about the undying fire was unquestionably true; but it was kept burning, not in the mountain, but in their own pueblo. It was a smothered fire in a clay oven, and had been burning in one of the kivas ever since the pueblo was founded, centuries ago. About the snake stories, he was not certain. . . .
>
> "They do keep some sort of varmint out in the mountain, that they bring in for their religious ceremonies," the trader said. "But I don't know if it's a snake or not. No white man knows anything about Indian religion, Padre."[14]

Artist Frank G. Applegate lived in Santa Fe from 1921 until his death in 1931. He ends his literary *Indian Stories from the Pueblos* (1929) with a romanticized story "told me by a son of the last living Pecos Indian":

> Montezuma, before leaving Pecos, lighted a sacred fire on the Sun Altar and commanded that this fire must be fed and kept burning continuously, day and night, by twelve virgin daughters of the head men of the pueblo, and he told the head men that as long as this fire was kept burning Pecos would prosper, and that some time he himself would return and again rule over the pueblo.
>
> This sacred fire was kept alive and ceremonies were held yearly in honor of Montezuma for many centuries. But one night the twelve virgins, made drowsy by the heat of the fire, fell asleep, and the sacred flame died and the altar became cold.
>
> For their negligence the virgins were punished, disgraced and made outcasts, but from that time the prosperity of the pueblo quickly diminished, and the population declined so much that the men of Pecos came to the conclusion that the Pueblo was accursed because the sacred fire had gone out, and decided to abandon Pecos and go and live with their kinsmen at Jemez, a pueblo which Montezuma had founded with the overflow of population from Pecos, and where yearly their descendants still perform some of the ceremonies brought from the home of their fathers.[15]

Folklore Texts

In 1880, Adolph F. Bandelier interviewed Mariano Ruiz, who had been adopted by the Pecos Indians, and Mrs. Andrew Kozlowski about Pecos legends. He wrote in his journal on September 3, 1880:

> Very fine, went out with Bennett to photograph and then to Kozlowski's and to Ruiz. Called at Señor Mariano Ruiz. Found him after considerable trouble and search. Sat down under a tree and talked. He came in 1837 from Jemez, when there were but eighteen Indians left. Was adopted *como hijo del pueblo* [as a son of the pueblo]. In 1838, the *capitán de la guerra* [war captain] of Jemez came over, having heard that the Indians of Pecos were fast dying, as well as their flocks. The sickness was fiebre [influenza], commencing with tembladas [chills], and closing with calen-

turas [fever]. The Pecos then were not willing to leave, but in 1839 they sold the flocks and everything, and made a deed to Ruiz for the land. This deed is now in the hands of Major Sena at Santa Fe. In 1840, the gobernador, the capitán and the cacique of Jemez, with two or three other Indians, came over again, and the Pecos, five in number, with their families, left for Jemez. Their houses were still standing, three stories high. They kept their holy embers (not fire) alive in the great room at the north wing, and met in the estufa, but Ruiz was never permitted to assist. Every year an Indian was elected *para cuidar del fuego* [to care for the fire], and the tale was, that if anyone who had ever taken care of the fire left the tribe, he would die. On that account, Ruiz always refused to take charge of the fire. They were idolators, and Ruiz says that the report was that they worshipped a [large] serpent (una vivora grande) which they kept concealed. He presumed that they took both the embers and the snake to Jemez. . . .

I then went back to Mrs. Kozlowski, who confirmed the veracity of the old man. She has been here for twenty-two years and saw the houses still perfect. The church with its roof and complete. Kozlowski tore parts of it down to build stables and houses.[16]

In 1924, Mariano Ruiz's grandson told photographer Edward S. Curtis a story his grandfather had told him.

The snake, he said, was kept in an underground room in the village, and at stated intervals a newborn infant was fed to it. The elder Ruiz was asked to assume the duty of custodian of the sacred fire, an annual office, which he declined because he had observed that the firekeeper always died soon after being released from confinement in the subterranean chamber where the fire burned. (Whether the fire and the serpent were housed in the same cell the grandson did not know, but possibly such was the case and the refusal of Ruiz to accept the proffered position was really due to his horror at the idea of spending the year in proximity to the reptile. But there appears to be no good reason why he should not have imparted this information to Bandelier, if such was the case.) Strolling about the environs of the village, Ruiz one day came upon his most intimate friend bowed in grief. To the Mexican's inquiry the Indian responded that his newborn child had been condemned to be fed to the snake, that already he had been forced to yield several children to the sacrifice, and had vainly hoped that this one would be spared. This was the first time Ruiz had heard that children were fed to the snake. He proposed that they hoodwink the priests, and acting on his advice the Indian poisoned a newborn kid with certain herbs, wrapped it up as if it were a baby, and threw it to the reptile. That night terrifying sounds issued from the den as the great snake writhed in its death agony, and in the morning it lay with the white of its belly exposed. The populace was utterly downcast, for this presaged the extinction of the tribe.[17]

Helen H. Roberts spent the summers "of 1929 and 1930 collecting songs in three Rio Grande pueblos and by the second season had made considerable progress in cementing real friendship with a number of Indian families, particularly at San Ildefonso." Ignacio Aguilar, "a San Ildefonso Indian about seventy years old," became "a warm friend" who told her the following story:

Ignacio's grandfather had told him the incident, of which he had been a witness. The old man had relatives in Cicuye or Pecos and had visited there often in the days when the pueblo was inhabited. The Cicuye Indians had a snake god which they kept in a kiva and which enabled them to obtain all of the things they asked for. In return for these favors the hunters went every day to procure fresh meat for it. The snake was very hungry and required much meat. It was just after a war, and the kiva men were very busy, or perhaps for some other reason they did not feed the snake god. The snake called for food, but they paid no attention to him. Finally he became angry, so he told the kiva men, "Since you will give me no food, I cannot stay and help the people any longer. I must go away from here." The kiva men still paid no attention to the snake, so when they were all asleep, he left the kiva and started down the arroyo. He was so huge that he left a track like a small arroyo.

Ignacio's grandfather and a party of San Ildefonso Indians were hunting down by Galisteo. They were surprised to see two Cicuye Indians coming down the river. They wore almost no clothes but were clad only with loin cloths as when hunting and seemed very excited. So some of the San Ildefonso Indians went to ask them what was the matter. The Cicuye Indians asked them if they had seen this snake god, but the San Ildefonso Indians had not. The Cicuye Indians told them, "It is well that you did not, for he might have bitten you. We have tracked him this far, but we cannot find him."

The two from Cicuye went on down the valley, following the snake's track as far as Domingo. There the snake had gone into the water and disappeared. They could find no more track on either side of the river. When they returned to their pueblo without having found the snake god, all the people said, "There is no use of our staying here because no more good can come to the Pueblo with our snake god gone." So they moved and went to live with the people of Jemez. The people of Galisteo were relatives of those of Cicuye and had been accustomed to come there to ask favors of the snake god. They too felt that disaster had befallen their pueblo with its departure from Cicuye, and being friends of the people of Domingo, went to live with them there and deserted their own home.[18]

On May 26, 1939, Bernhardt A. Reuter of Pecos submitted to the New Mexico Federal Writers' Project an account of the "two caves in this district which it is claimed the Pecos Indians held as sacred, and in which they at times held special ceremonies." Reuter explored both caves. The first "is located some fifteen miles north of the old Pecos village on the west side of the river and just above the mouth of the Holy Ghost canyon."

I made the trip to this cave and explored it for the purpose of ascertaining if there were any pictographs symbolic of the purpose for which the Indians held it sacred, and if possible to locate any shrines where prayer-plumes or artifacts might be deposited. I took with me my daughter Ruth Reuter and my son-in-law Mr. Naumer, so as to facilitate a thorough investigation of all parts of the cave. We were served with a powerful gas lantern and two flash lights and examined all sections carefully, but found nothing worthy of note excepting here and there a square hole in the dirt floor of the cavern. I anticipated finding such holes, if the floor of the cave permitted, for I knew that some Pueblos bury their prayer-plumes for such ceremonies. I do not have personal knowledge of all the Pueblos but I do know that many of the tribes have symbolic cipap's [sipapu] and at certain times perform ceremonies in them. As a rule these symbolic places are in caves, but if no cave can be found within approximately twenty-five miles of the Pueblo, the officials select a place for the ceremony.

From all I could find out, it is true that the Pecos division of the Jemez Pueblo keeps up the practice of visiting the cave in certain years and on such occasions performs rites in it. Mr. Ralph Litrell who with his father operated a dairy close to the cave told an acquaintance of mine that once when the Indians came to go into the cave, he requested permission to go in with them. The Indians responded by saying: "Yes, you can go in with us but you may not come out again." I tried to find out if any one had gone into the cave shortly after the Indians departed and a Mr. Gapp who operates the dairy that once belonged to the Litrells told me of a man that went in right after the Indians had come out and gone away. He said that all this man found was a hole which the Indians had dug and covered and the remainder of a small fire which they had built. He dug out the hole and found some little sticks with feathers tied to them, which of course were none other than prayer-plumes. I am personally acquainted with this man of whom Mr. Gapp told me, and I have done considerable driving in an attempt to make contact with him but with no result. This man is a miner, an Italian by nationality. I have never seen his name written and I may make a bad job of spelling it but it sounds as if it were written Tsu-cetty.

The second cave "is situated high up on a bluff on the east side of the Pecos canyon about two miles north-east of the Pecos Pueblo . . . in full view, to the south-east of the Harrison's country store at Pecos, and is just over the line of my place on the land recently owned by Tex Austin and now by Mr. Currier."

According to stories told by local people the Pecos Indians in past times made frequent visits to this cave but as far as is known they have not visited it in more than a decade. I have lived in my present home for sixteen years and though my house is within one-half mile of the cave I have neither seen nor heard of Indians visiting the cave in my time of living here.

This cave has of late years largely lost its character as a sacred place of Indian worship. It is now called José Vaca's cave because of the almost insane activities of this treasure hunting native in his attempt to explore its depths. The story about José Vaca's activities are fairly well covered by J. Frank Dobie in his volume, "Coronado's Children," and is a most striking example of how the enthusiasm of an ignorant man can lead him into interpreting almost any chance markings of nature as the very symbols given on a map or recited in a writing, . . . [indicating] the burial of some treasure.

Reuter laments that "an important landmark sacred to the Indians has thus been destroyed by the hands of an ignorant man."[19]

4 LAND OF ENCHANTMENT

TEXTS OF COLOR AND SPECTACLE

Just a show! The Southwest is the great playground of the white American. The desert isn't good for anything else. But it does make a fine national playground. And the Indian, with his long hair and his bits of pottery and blankets and clumsy home-made trinkets, he's a wonderful live toy to play with. More fun than keeping rabbits, and just as harmless. Wonderful, really, hopping round with a snake in his mouth. Lots of fun! Oh, the wild west is lots of fun: the Land of Enchantment. Like being right inside the circus-ring: lots of sand, and painted savages jabbering, and snakes and all that. Come on, boys! Lots of fun! The great Southwest, the national circusground. Come on, boys; we've every bit as much right to it as anybody else. Lots of fun!

—D. H. Lawrence, "Just Back from the Snake Dance," 1924.[1]

Both camera and motorcar mark the beginning of contemporary tourism, which requires neither professional guide-interpreter nor chauffeur. The camera makes each visitor an artist-journalist. The automobile frees the tourist from timetable and tracks.

The economic and expressive potential in both these new technologies initially was harnessed by the Atchison, Topeka & Santa Fe Railway and the Fred Harvey Company and later exploited by the New Mexico State Highway Department and the State Tourist Bureau. By 1937 the latter had dubbed New Mexico "The Land of Enchantment" on highway maps. In the late 1930s, New Mexico workers on the New Deal Federal Writers' Project documented those highways for tourists in cars and proclaimed the state "colorful" in their contribution to the American Guide Series, *New Mexico: A Guide to the Colorful State.*

Back of Santa Fe Chamber of
Commerce stationery, 1940s.
Designed by Wilfred Stedman.
(Private collection.)

Land of Enchantment

In the 1920s the State Highway Department began to consider the possibilities in tourist promotion. The first issue of *New Mexico Highway Journal* appeared in July 1923 and included the following notice on page 10:

> While automobile tourists seek the attractions of local scenery, there is another big element in drawing them. That is the condition of the roads. A state that keeps its roads in good order is going to get a great deal more vacation travel from now on than it ever had before. This will go far toward paying for keeping the highways in good condition.

In 1931, this official publication changed its name to *New Mexico: The Sunshine State's Recreational and Highway Magazine* and was regularly printing literary features and folklore.

The Highway Department started a Service Bureau to answer tourists' inquiries in 1930 and, in June 1933, initiated the highway patrol to assure safety on the roads and to aid tourists by offering information, goodwill, and welcome. Relief workers on the New Deal's Public Works Project began roadside beautification in March 1934, and they also erected signs and markers for tourists. An advertising program was launched in 1934 with help from an association of state businessmen known as

Albuquerque Stage bus by Navajo hogan, 1925. Photo by T. Harmon Parkhurst. (MNM Neg. No. 11715.)

the Tourist Development League. Finally, in 1935, newly inaugurated Governor Clyde Tingley reorganized the Highway Department and created the New Mexico Tourist Bureau to coordinate all state and civic activities aimed at developing tourism. Tingley's "move marked the first definite and official effort to bring tourists to the state. It encouraged them to visit—perhaps even to remain in the state."[2]

The Highway Department and the Tourist Bureau emphasized two names for New Mexico in their 1930s promotions. *Roads to Cibola* was the title of a thirty-two-page Highway Commission brochure in 1931, and a sixteen-page Tourist Bureau pamphlet was entitled *Welcome to the Land of Enchantment* in 1937, which was also the year when "Land of Enchantment" first appeared on a road map. The *Cibola* epithet is clearly related to treasure tales and conquistador imagery, but the term *enchantment* was not originally derived from the sort of enchantment popularly associated with witchcraft and magic tales. Apparently, Tourist Bureau personnel were influenced by two publications, Lilian Whiting's 1906 travel book, *The Land of Enchantment: From Pike's Peak to the Pacific* and Eugene Manlove Rhodes's 1911 short story, "A Number of Things." In these, "enchantment" is a spectacle to be *seen*.

Lilian Whiting, who dedicates *The Land of Enchantment* to Major John Wesley Powell, "the great explorer," takes as her book's epigraph "The Fairest enchants me; / The Mighty commands me." She describes for the sightseer what she calls "four centres of sublime and unparalleled scenic sublimity which stand alone and unrivalled in the world"—in southern California, Arizona, Colorado, and New Mexico (primarily the environs of Santa Fe). Rhodes also relates enchantment to vision in "A Number of Things," a story describing the Socorro area of 1900:

> A land of mighty mountains, far seen, gloriously tinted, misty opal, purple, blue and amethyst; a land of enchantment and mystery. Those same opalescent hills, seen closer, are decked with barbaric colors—reds, yellows or pinks, brown or green or gray; but, from afar, shapes and colors ebb and flow, altered daily, hourly, by subtle sorcery of atmosphere, distance and angle; deepening, fading, combining into new and fantastic forms and hues—to melt again as swiftly into others yet more bewildering.[3]

The experience of variable, visual "enchantment" is part of travel by foot, horseback, wagon, and automobile, *not* of rail travel. Like pre-rail methods of transportation, cars, which theoretically can be slowed, accelerated, turned, and stopped virtually at will, allow driver and passengers to leave their vehicle to attend to physical needs. They thus see more people than from a train window and often must interact with them. This kind of touring was the primary concern of the organizers and writers of the Federal Writers' Project American Guide Series between 1935 and 1942.

The Colorful State

Like other state guides, *New Mexico: A Guide to the Colorful State* was designed "to turn the attention of Americans to their own land, and to promote their knowledge of America as a whole, and to arouse the interest of the public in the history, the natural resources, recreational facilities, economic and cultural developments of the

"Gas station price analysis." FSA photo by Dorothea Lange, Santa Fe, August 1938. (LC-USF 34-19787-E.)

State, its folk-lore, art and literature, and to disseminate this information for the use of the [automobile-traveling] public."[4] Above all, guides were intended to boost tourism by car, and the individual tours (twenty-five for New Mexico's guide) were designed for automobile travelers. This was fitting for a work relief project, since, "between 1933 and 1942, federal relief agencies spent four billion dollars on road and street construction . . ., [and] the mileage of surfaced highways, which doubled between 1921 and 1930, doubled again between 1930 and 1940"—an increase partly the result of organized efforts by a growing number of motorists and car owners, according to John A. Jakle:

> The number of private automobiles in the United States increased from 8,000 in 1900 to 458,000 in 1910, to 8 million in 1920, and to 23 million in 1930. . . . Automobile production reflected high living standards and the leisure time to make automobile ownership practical. As the historian Foster Dulles observes about the United States, "A car for the family to be used primarily for pleasure was accepted as a valid ambition for every member of the American democracy."[5]

Katharine Kellock, the national tour editor for the Federal Writers' Project, "insisted that the guides satisfy all travelers, whether drivers on interstate highways or hardy trail explorers, and that they cover every mile of the country." She demanded a departure from the Baedeker European guidebooks with their loop tours from capital cities and chose instead the north-to-south and east-to-west standard used by airlines and compass-oriented maps. Both meticulous, accurate coverage and an entertaining style were stressed. Manuscript copy for tours was returned to New Mexico from Washington on April 22, 1936, with the criticism that: "We also feel that in the manuscripts submitted there is a tendency to write about the Points of Interest from a remote viewpoint whereas the tourist will read the Guide material on the spot. Consequently, care should be taken to convey the impression made on the tourist and to lead him around from point to point."[6]

On January 17, 1936, the national director of the Federal Writers' Project, Henry G. Alsberg, wrote to New Mexico director Ina Sizer Cassidy about the kind of visual description expected of the New Mexico project workers: "We are particularly interested in scenic or human interest subjects—traditions, folklore, oldest settlers, ghost stories—anything that can be visualized as a halo to illuminate some objects which travelers can gaze on with horror or delight or some other form of emotion. We are always trying to keep before us the thought and effort to make people 'see America first.'" On June 13, 1939, Alsberg was even more explicit in a letter to Cassidy's replacement, acting New Mexico director Aileen Nusbaum:

> Try to make the readers see the white mid-summer haze, the dust that rises in unpaved New Mexican streets, the slithery red earth roads of winter, the purple shadows of later afternoon, the brilliant yellow of autumn foliage against brilliant blue skies, the pseudo-cowboys in the tourist centers, the blank-faced Indians who are secretly amused by white antics, the patched and irregular walls of the older adobes; make him understand the social cleavages and jealousies, the strangely rotarianized "Indian dances," the life of the transplanted Oklahomans, Texans, Mexicans, Greenwich Villagers, and so on.

Harveycar at unidentified pueblo, 1929. Photo by Edward Kemp. (MNM Neg. No. 47185.)

"Navajo Lodge formerly an old ranch house in the mountains. About thirty years ago the rancher [Ray Morley] who owned it had it dismantled and moved it piece by piece and rebuilt it at its present location [on U.S. 60 and N.M. 12]. He is now dead and the house is used as a hotel principally for summer visitors." FSA photos by Russell Lee, Datil, April 1940. (LC-USF 34-35886-D; interior: LC-USF 34-35893-D.)

A letter of July 20, 1939, reiterates the earlier request, emphasizing that "we want the type of visual description that Steinbeck would give—that is, descriptions of the types of buildings common to smaller New Mexican towns, mention of color, smells, sounds, signs, and above all, of the types of people seen along the streets."[7]

New Mexico: A Guide to the Colorful State also incorporates folklore collected from "people seen along the streets." The book's subtitle was chosen in part to reflect these concerns. According to then state director Charles Ethrige Minton, who oversaw the final details: "There is no official State Name, and we found at least eight names that have been applied, such as 'Sunshine State,' 'Cactus State,' and so on, each worse than the other; so, because it is the most colorful of all the states in various ways, we decided on that subtitle, although we don't think it especially good."[8] The choice proved significant because it distinguishes New Mexico's guide from all others, many of which characterize their states with epithets derived from physical features, flora, fauna, history, or inhabitants.[9] Only the New Mexico guide suggests a "folk" cast to the state's "colorful" lore and life.

The first essay in the guidebook, "The State Today," opens with a remarkable paean to this colorfulness:

New Mexico today represents a blend of three cultures—Indian, Spanish, and American—each of which has had its time upon the stage and dominated the scene. The composite of culture which now, in the union of statehood, presents a harmonious picture upon casual inspection, is deceptive, for the veneer of Americanization in places runs thin indeed. It is difficult to think of a modern

Santa Clara Pueblo Eagle dancers ringed by spectators and Harveycars, ca. 1928. (MNM Neg. No. 46939.)

America in a village of the Pueblo Indians, while the inhabitants dance for rain. To be sure, a transcontinental train may thunder by, or an airplane soar overhead; but the prayers never stop, the dance goes on, and the fantastic juxtaposition seems to widen the gap between. Who could dream of the American Way in a mountain hamlet where the sound of the Penitente flute is heard above the thud of the scourges, and Spanish-American villagers perform medieval rites of redemption in Holy Week?

These are extremes of incongruity, but they are true. They diminish in the vicinity of the larger towns and cities and vanish altogether in some places; but their existence, strong or weak, colors the contemporary scene. New Mexico is a favorite camping-ground of the anthropologists because here they can study the living Indians in connection with their ancient, unbroken past and possible future. They can learn much about how people lived in medieval Spain by studying the ways of life in the remote Spanish-American villages of modern New Mexico; it has been said that if a Spaniard of those times should come to earth today, he could understand the Spanish spoken in New Mexico more readily than the modern language of his native land.

The interaction of the diverse elements of the population is slowly working toward homogeneity, dominated more and more by the irresistible middle current of Anglo-American civilization and the modern American tempo.[10]

Yet "homogeneous, New Mexico is not," the anonymous writers proclaim four paragraphs later. In this opening essay and the remainder of the book, variety, fiestas, spirituality, art, antiquity, ethnicity, Bohemianism, exoticism, and quaintness are shown to make up the "colorful" quality of New Mexico.

Other New Mexican color is suggested in the four-page "Coronado Cuarto Centennial Folk Festival Calendar (Giving Principal Events from May 15 to November 1940)." It precedes the essays in the New Mexico guide, which was sponsored by the University of New Mexico and the Coronado Cuarto Centennial Commission. Folklore and folklife played an important role in these Cuarto Centennial events, which were planned as "educational" attractions for residents and tourists, primarily those in cars and buses. The Cuarto Centennial was to include Coronado historical pageants and some "two hundred folk festivals scattered throughout the State all during the summer"—a time when "colorful New Mexico will be more colorful than ever," and "even tourists crossing the State in a few hours can hardly miss contact some way or other with the 400th anniversary celebration."[11]

Conclusion

In *The Image: A Guide to Pseudo-Events in America,* Daniel J. Boorstin explains a critical change—"From Traveler to Tourist: The Lost Art of Travel"—a development that began in the mid-nineteenth century and culminated in the mid-twentieth century. Boorstin points out that "formerly travel required long planning, large expense, and great investments of time. It involved risks to health or even to life. The traveler was active. Now he became passive. Instead of an athletic exercise, travel became a spectator sport."[12]

For centuries, journeying in New Mexico was conceived as spiritual pilgrimage and social communion. Reciprocity in kind was generally expected from travelers and visitors. May Price Mosley explains why pioneer ranchers on the Staked Plains of southeastern New Mexico entertained both neighbors and strangers:

> The hospitality of welcoming all passers to one's habitat was not entirely or merely a social function. It was an obligatory custom born of necessity, for save where the traveller had full camp equipment he journeyed at the mercy of such hospitality. There was not a place where lodging and food could be bought in the whole broad land which, with the mode of travel of that time, required a week to cross. . . .
>
> Occasional travellers through this section, when it was wholly a ranch country, often wondered why, with money in their pockets, they could not buy food from the ranchers. If you were out of bread, the rancher, though he might have a thousand pounds of flour, would not consider selling you so much as a pound. He would, however, loan you all you needed if you were a neighboring rancher, or give you enough to appease your hunger if you were a travelling stranger. The difficulty of hauling commodities the hundred or more miles from the railroad, and the long intervals between times that "the wagon went to town" account for this custom, and also explain why *"paying back what you borrowed"* was the crucial test of Plains morality and religion.[13]

This is travel in the old sense of the word, as Boorstin explains:

> The old English noun "travel" (in the sense of a journey) was originally the same word as "travail" (meaning "trouble," "work," or "torment"). And the word "travail," in turn, seems to have been derived, through the French, from a popular Latin or Common Romanic word trepalium, which meant a three-staked instrument of torture. To journey—to "travail," or (later) to travel—then was to do something laborious or troublesome. The traveler was an active man at work.

The tourist, on the other hand, is a passive observer of staged spectacles, undergoing no rite of passage, sacrificing nothing and exercising no discipline. According to Boorstin:

> The tourist is passive; he expects interesting things to happen to him. He goes "sight-seeing" (a word, by the way, which came in about the same time, with its first use recorded in 1847). He expects everything to be done to him and for him.[14]

Staged celebrations are important tourist expectations.

Traditionally, visitors to communities and ceremonies were participants, not spectators. Native American dances and other ceremonials involved everyone either as prayerful audience or dancer, sandpainter, singer, or drummer. They participated imaginatively in the specific communal aim of the occasion, whether to pray for rain, harvest, hunting or healing. Implicit in all such ceremonies was the first journey, the traveling up or emergence from the underworlds into this world, a dangerous and sacred quest of tremendous significance for blessing and centering all aspects of life.

Visitors to Hispanic communities participated in a crucial symbolic journey as

well. Observances during Holy Week, culminating on Good Friday with the recreation of Jesus' sorrowful way to Calvary, served as the most important expression of the sacred foundation of Hispanic community life. Everyone attended prayerfully.

Publicists for the Santa Fe Railway, the Fred Harvey Company, the New Mexico Tourist Bureau, and the New Mexico Federal Writers' Project theatricalized such indigenous celebrations to accommodate new, arbitrary, outsiders' times. A different, non-seasonal, non-rite-of-passage, non-liturgical schedule was invented for the amusement and convenience of spectators who demanded to know precisely when and where "Indian dances" and "fiestas" were to take place. The traditional sense of time and event was altered, and soon these invented traditions came to be accepted as authentic.[15]

Cameras facilitated this change. T. C. McLuhan notes that

American families, at the turn of the century, began to take up photography for themselves through mass-produced and inexpensive Kodaks. ("You press the button; we do the rest!") This development produced an interesting and unexpected dividend. Many of the first tourists to the Southwest brought with them their new Kodaks and showed no inhibition about using them. . . . In 1906, an editorial writer commented:

Harveycar and tourists at Santa Clara Pueblo. (MNM Neg. No. 46940.)

About half the tourists jump from the trains almost as soon as they stop and run from one place to another in search of souvenir postal cards, flop themselves down in the waiting-room or on the brick curb and write feverishly, hunt around for some place to buy stamps and then mail their cards, and by that time have only a few minutes left to patronize the lunch counter. Meanwhile, the greater portion of the other half are taking snapshots of the hotel or station, or are posing against one of the buildings for someone else's picture. It's as good as a circus to watch them.[16]

Nelson H. H. Graburn, who analyzes tourism as a profane spirit quest, observes that tourists bring back photographs and souvenirs as evidence of their communication with what they consider the sacred. "The Holy Grail is the myth sought on the journey, and the success of the holiday is proportionate to the degree that the myth is realized."[17]

D. H. Lawrence articulates similar themes of alienated, secular journey and transformative, sacred mystery in his 1931 *Survey Graphic* essay, "New Mexico":

Superficially, the world has become small and known. Poor little globe of earth, the tourists trot round you as easily as they trot round the Bois or round Central Park. There is no mystery left, we've been there, we've seen it, we know all about it. We've done the globe, and the globe is done. . . .

Yet the more we know, superficially, the less we penetrate, vertically. . . .

The same is true of land travel. We skim along, we get there, we see it all, we've done it all. And as a rule, we never once go through the curious film which railroads, ships, motorcars, and hotels stretch over the surface of the whole earth. Peking is just the same as New York, with a few different things to look at; rather more Chinese about, etc. Poor creatures that we are, we crave for experience, yet we are like flies that crawl on the pure and transparent mucous-paper in which the world like a bon-bon is wrapped so carefully that we can never get at it, though we see it there all the time as we move about it, apparently in contact, yet actually as far removed as if it were the moon.

As a matter of fact, our great-grandfathers, who never went anywhere, in actuality had more experience of the world than we have, who have seen everything. When they listened to a lecture with lantern-slides, they really held their breath before the unknown, as they sat in the village school-room. We, bowling along in a rickshaw in Ceylon, say to ourselves: "It's very much what you'd expect." We really know it all.

We are mistaken. The know-it-all state of mind is just the result of being outside the mucous-paper wrapping of civilization. Underneath is everything we don't know and are afraid of knowing.

I realized this with shattering force when I went to New Mexico.

New Mexico, one of the United States, part of the U.S.A. New Mexico, the picturesque reservation and playground of the eastern states, very romantic, old Spanish, Red Indian, desert mesas, pueblos, cowboys, penitentes, all that film-stuff. Very nice, the great South West, put on a sombrero and knot a red kerchief round your neck, to go out in the great free spaces!

That is New Mexico wrapped in the absolutely hygienic and shiny mucous-paper of our trite civilization. That is the New Mexico known to most of the Americans who know it all. But break through the shiny sterilized wrapping, and actually touch the country, and you will never be the same again.[18]

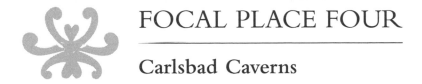

FOCAL PLACE FOUR

Carlsbad Caverns

The automobile made Carlsbad Caverns a tourist mecca to rival the Grand Canyon. At the turn of the century, cowboy-explorer James Larkin White left the brilliant sunshine of the upper world and was lowered into the "black stillness" of the now famous caves. His heroic descent was soon duplicated by others, who publicized and made accessible the subterranean wonders.

Shortly after the Caverns were proclaimed a national monument in 1923, Charles L. White, a farsighted Loving entrepreneur of oil and gasoline, filed for land at the entrance to the federal preserve. There he established White's City, a complex of roadside tourist accommodations and attractions.

At the caves themselves, visitors were led beneath the ground by National Park Service Rangers. Their descent was orchestrated as secular pilgrimage—a contemporary inversion of the first people's emergence from Sipapu and a safe encounter with the mysterious now made commercial and "interesting."

Commercial Texts

The town of Carlsbad on the Pecos River was "organized in 1888 and first named for John A. and Charles B. Eddy, brothers who held large ranch interests and promoted railroad building and townsites in this section. . . . When it was learned that the mineral content of a spring [northwest] of town rivaled that of the Carlsbad springs in Bohemia [Czechoslovakia], agitation arose to change the name. . . . At an election on May 23, 1899, the change was voted. The city was officially proclaimed Carlsbad by Gov. W. E. Lindsey on Mar. 25, 1918."[1]

In 1892, Walter Stevens visited Eddy and wrote:

The streets of Eddy are full of people who have come to the Pecos to prolong life. This is a climate so dry that to die means to dry up, not to decay. . . . In and about Eddy are a former railroad builder from Chicago, a retired army officer, two doctors from Ft. Wayne, Ind., a retired merchant from La Cross, Wisc., another doctor from Van Wert, O[hio], an Oakland (Ill.) merchant, a nephew of the late William H. Seward, Lincoln's Secretary of State, an Englishman and a Scotchman of means, a New Yorker, a civil engineer from St. Louis, and a real estate man from the same place. . . . It isn't true that everybody in the Pecos Valley has come for health. Occasionally there is a man who has found this a place to make money.[2]

Three decades later, Kentucky-born Charles L. White proved to be such a man.

White's City, named for entrepreneur Charles L. White (no relation to James White), is eighteen miles southwest of Carlsbad near the entrance to the Carlsbad Cavern National Park. According to an undated (1984) *White's City Gazette and Souvenir Menu:*

Charlie L. White, founder of one of the best known tourist centers in the southwest, was born in Cyclone, Kentucky in 1889. After completing grade school and training at the normal school at Bowling Green, Ky. he became a teacher in a country school at age of 18. Two years later, ill health forced him to leave Kentucky for a drier climate. He came to New Mexico in 1909 as an instructor in the first school in the now-booming oil section of southeastern New Mexico. He taught until 1914, when he opened a mercantile company in Loving, New Mexico and soon installed the first handoperated gasoline pump in the town.

"I saw gasoline was the coming product of the century as more and more cars were purchased so I began distributing gasoline," Charlie recalled. He and four associates owned the first bank in Loving with Charlie as cashier. When the bank failed with so many others he stayed on until all the depositors were paid in full.

In 1926 he and his family were on an outing to see the much talked about bat cave when he was struck with the idea of acquiring the land at the mouth of the canyon leading to the caverns. Not even waiting to visit the caves, he rushed to Carlsbad, the county seat, to file homestead papers. So with lots of foresight and very little money, and plenty of "Savy" he built the "White's Cavern Camp" which consisted of a home, 13 units for visitors and a filling station. In the years to come he added a garage, cafe, grocery store, drug store and museum.

In 1937 he built the first modern tourist court to handle the ever growing crowds of visitors to the Carlsbad Caverns. The city now consists of three modern motels, the Velvet Garter Saloon and Restaurant, Fast Jack's, Curio and Gift Shop, Grocery Store, Million Dollar Museum, Park Entrance RV Parks and major oil service stations. For years each evening Charlie White entertained guests of White's City with a lecture on the early history of the Carlsbad Caverns and the surrounding country. He gave the lecture every night in the museum until his death in 1962.

(Opposite). Thomas Boles and group, Dome Room, Carlsbad Caverns, ca. 1951. Photo by Ferenz Fedor. (MNM Neg. No. 57362.)

Geological Text

How were the Caverns formed? The story began about 240 million years ago, during the Permian Period. At that time, the two limestone formations in which the caverns occur—the Tansill Formation and Capitan Limestone—were deposited as part of an organic reef complex at the edge of a warm shallow sea.

During subsequent periods, other seas brought in sedimentary material that covered the reef. About 60 million years ago, earth movements, which were responsible for the uplift of the area, fractured the reef and permitted surrounding ground water to enter along fracture lines and begin work in fashioning the caverns. The water at first dissolved small crevices in the limestone. As more water came in, the crevices enlarged to cavities, called solution pockets. Then the walls, floors, and ceilings of the pockets dissolved and collapsed, joining the pockets, while the solution process continued, eventually forming the huge rooms seen today.

Beginning about 3 million years ago and into recent times, the uplift of the local Guadalupe Mountains and changing climates lowered the water table. Water that had been inside the caverns drained away and was replaced by air. Most solution stopped, but large sections of partly dissolved walls and ceilings collapsed under their own weight. Stability was finally achieved, however, and probably no rock has fallen within the caverns during the last several thousand years.

Even before the collapsing ended, another phase of cavern development had begun. Rain water and snow melt slowly seeped into the caverns. Droplets of water, each holding a minute quantity of dissolved limestone, appeared upon the ceilings. Exposed to the air, the droplets evaporated and left their mineral content as calcite and aragonite—crystalline forms of limestone. Over centuries, this process of evaporation and deposition has built a myriad of crystalline stalactites of all shapes and sizes. Water that dripped to the floor evaporated and deposited the calcite and aragonite to build stalagmites. When joined together, stalactites and stalagmites become columns, or pillars. In the scenic rooms, conditions existed that brought about the creation of helicites—twisted formations that seem to defy gravity in their growth. Color in the cave formations, shades of brown, red, and yellow, result from the presence of small amounts of iron oxide and other minerals.[3]

Exploration Texts

The plaque in the Visitor Center at Carlsbad Caverns National Park is dedicated to James Larkin White (1882–1946). It reads: "Beginning in 1901, Jim White made the first known extensive explorations of the Carlsbad Caverns. He was chiefly responsible for bringing the attention of the public, scientific groups and the federal government to the importance and significance of the Caverns."

By one account, bats emerging from what became the Caverns entrance led White to the discovery. According to Blanche C. Grant's 1928 version:

> A tall lank youth of eighteen, a cowboy, was building a drift fence to hold cattle back on the slopes of the Guadalupe mountains in southeastern New Mexico and came upon the eighth wonder of the world—the Carlsbad Caverns. . . .

"I built lots of drift fences of wire and, after a while, a law wuz passed for rollin' it up." It was such a fence that Jim White and two Mexican helpers were building back in the days of 1900 [*sic*]. They laid off for a day and went wandering over the mesquite grown hills when suddenly they came upon the great hole under long slabs of yellow and gray stone. Jim looked eagerly into the darkness of the cave and then turned away. That fence must be finished, so the next day he went on working for the Lucas brothers—Dan and John. But he could not forget the cave.

A few days later he found his way again, in and out of the dark green mesquite, to the mouth of the cave. With him were two Mexicans. They wandered over to a ledge. There lay a skeleton. Near by were bits of tarpaulin. They pondered for awhile. Here was evidently the remains of a man who had "disappeared" many years before, a man who had probably been murdered and hidden in the fearful awesome cave.

Undaunted by his gruesome find, White started on his trip. "I got them to let me down on a rope," he said, as he began to live it all over again. "We had two ropes. We tied them to rocks, and made loops in one so I could rest when I climbed up." Finally securely tied about the waist, he was lowered into the cave. He had no gun, nothing but a jack knife and a coal oil lantern, for Jim White has never known fear.

No dread of ghosts held Jim from going on into the darkness ahead to the east where the silence was broken only by the stir of thousands of sleeping bats which he could not see. Then he turned the other way and, climbing over great boulders, was soon lost in utter darkness except where his feeble oil light cut here and there.

Great walls towered into the black stillness. Thin, whitish columns caught the light but White knew they were not ghosts. He had no time for fear. He was bent on discovery. Finally he reached the edge of a huge hole where lay huge rocks in great disorder. Here he thought he had gone far enough. He was then about a mile in the cave. The one boy with his flickering torch little dreamed that some day he would be able to telephone from near that spot to those waiting in the bright sunshine of the upper world.

Following the trail he had blazed with black marks on the gray stone, Jim reached the long rope, pulled himself up and joined his Mexican comrades. He went on then about his work but again he could not forget the cave and the dark that lay beyond the great dip in the floor which he soon named "The Devil's Den."[4]

James White's stories attracted attention from the United States General Land Office. In April 1922, a mineral examiner, Robert A. Holley, was sent to investigate the caverns' potential as a national monument. The day before White lowered him into the cave for the first time, Holley told the cowboy: "We didn't feel as though this cave was of much importance, but the Department thought I'd better run down and measure it, so they could know if it is big enough for them to consider." After a month's survey work, Holley began his report as follows:

I enter upon this task with a feeling of temerity as I am wholly conscious of the feebleness of my efforts to convey in words the deep conflicting emotions, the feeling of fear and awe, and the desire for an inspired understanding of the Divine Creator's work that presents to the human eye such a complex aggregate of natural wonders in such a limited space.[5]

Like Holley, geologist Willis T. Lee recommended that the cave be recognized, and on October 25, 1923, President Calvin Coolidge signed the proclamation establishing Carlsbad Cave National Monument. Dr. Lee published an influential article on his explorations in the January 1924 *National Geographic* with pictures by himself and Ray V. Davis. President Herbert Hoover signed the bill establishing Carlsbad Caverns National Park on May 14, 1930. Trails and lights were installed in the late 1920s, with the first two elevators in service in 1931.[6]

James White claims to have taken the original tour group of thirteen into the caverns, one by one, in a bucket used by one of the companies that mined guano. Each member of that first party agreed to pay one dollar for Mrs. White's trouble in feeding and housing them. According to Blanche C. Grant:

> Now [1928] Jim White acts as chief guide through the great caverns and plans to explore other dark recesses hoping to find more wonders and eventually another way out for the even temperature of from 55 degrees to 50 degrees the year round and the clear pure air argues another entrance to the caves.
>
> No one knows as much about the caves as does Jim White. When he is asked about them and especially to tell of his discovery of the place he modestly assures his audience that there must have been other cowboys who had seen the big entrance before his time. Old settlers agree with him and say that the entrance was first found during the sixties. White is of the opinion that an Indian was the earliest explorer for on his first venture far in the cave he found a skeleton lying on a small ledge. No metal lay near. An examination of the skull led White to believe it once belonged to an Indian. He carried his gruesome find above and gave it finally to a doctor in town. The other bones have been carried away.
>
> Still young, tall, wiry and sharp of feature, Jim White keeps his kindly gray eyes keen for any new find in his beloved caves as well as watching carefully all those who go down into the darkness under his guidance.
>
> "I take care of the sick ones, the old ones and the kids," he said the other day, as he walked away from the cave entrance to the land of his pride—the Land of the Great Fantastic, the Eighth Wonder of the World.[7]

Tourist Texts

In *Piñon Country,* his 1941 contribution to the American Folkways Series edited by Erskine Caldwell, Haniel Long compares visiting Fred Harvey's Grand Canyon complex with a descent into "The Cavern":

> The Carlsbad Caverns are an event of inward and outward living in a different way from the Grand Canyon. Other visitors to the Canyon at the time you are there can hardly matter much to you. You do not brush elbows with them; most of them you do not even see, and those you do see you are not likely to see twice. . . . The Canyon is a somewhat formal affair, too. The scenic views are along forest boulevards or stone walks that seem to have been there a long time, and all the buildings melt into the timelessness of the fir groves that envelop

them. There is a great hush, and a great air of decorum, as though an important personage had just died. As a young man said, you see the Canyon in a top hat.

This loneliness and formality and sense of being cut off from the comforts of your kind help make the Canyon a deep experience. The Cavern can be as deep an experience, but you do not continue on your way thinking only of the fantasia of substance under the surface of the earth. You have in mind also the people you went underground with, for they give you as much cause for thought as the stalactites and stalagmites. Going through the Cavern is a folk festival. You must be at the Cavern at a set time, and become part of a group of hundreds of people; and with this party, under the eye of the rangers, take a walk of six subterranean miles.

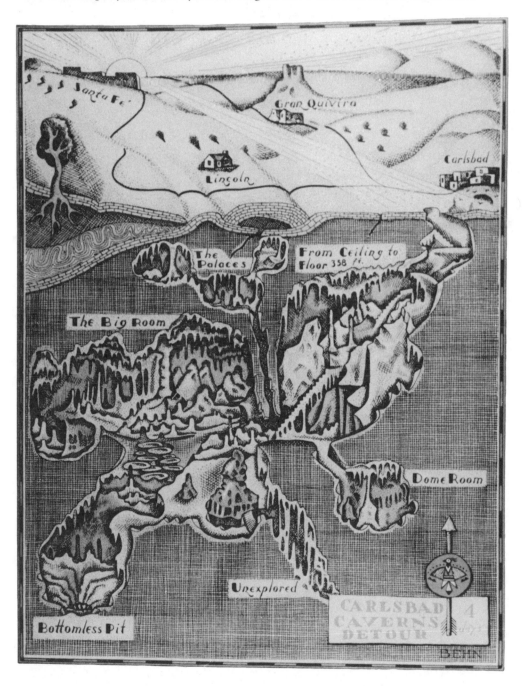

Carlsbad Caverns Detour map by Behn. From the 1933 reprint of an Indian Detours brochure first published in 1930. (Private collection.)

Tourists at Carlsbad Caverns entrance, May 7, 1932. (MNM Neg. No. 57345.)

In the course of descending, ascending, hurrying, pausing, sauntering, sidling, you stop for a forty-five-minute luncheon at a cafeteria in an enormous and well-lighted chamber. If you aren't acquainted with a dozen or so people by now, it will happen here, or else what a pity.[8]

Long's experience was made possible by an elaborate and ritualized tour of the caves, orchestrated by the National Park Service. It is described in the 1940 edition of *New Mexico: A Guide to the Colorful State* as follows:

CARLSBAD CAVERNS NATIONAL PARK . . . *Three daily conducted tours with guide service, $1.50 per person for those over 16; elevator fee 25¢; elevator trip 12:30 to Big Room for those unable to walk; chief daily tour is 10:30 A.M.; lunch on tour, 50¢; comfortable walking shoes and light sweater recommended; temperature in Caverns, 56° summer and winter.*

. . . A TOUR OF THE CAVERNS
A siren is sounded at starting time and visitors assemble at the entrance where a large opening gives a view into the dim interior, from which rises the cool, slightly dank odor of undersurface regions. The dome-shaped entrance, rocky and discolored, gives a hint of what is to come, but is no preparation for it. After an

introductory talk by one of the rangers, the line forms two abreast and moves slowly down toward the first objective, the Auditorium. Far below can be seen the place near which it is located, and the descending, expectant line can be seen below and above—those who have entered and those who are about to—moving like pilgrims toward a shrine. At a turn in the path a ranger clicks the attendance, while above at the Pay Station data is being compiled giving the States and foreign countries from which those registering have come, with the number from each section. . . .

Past MIRROR LAKE, another of the small, crystal-clear pools, looms the *Bottomless Pit,* 700 feet deep. Here the ceiling is 200 feet above the trail which now rises slightly, so that there is a view of the long serpentine line. Where the trail is moist from the dripping, a crunching sound of many feet is heard, but at other times—and for much the greater part—the trail is dry and the tread silent.

Ahead, on the right, is the *Shrine,* labeled and illumined, and beyond, another pool amid stalwart pillars. The largest growing stalagmite, *Crystal Spring Dome,* marks a point where the trail is damp again. From here the trail rises to a point at the *Rock of Ages,* an impressive stalagmite mass several millions of years old and second oldest in the Caverns, which stands to the left of the place where the group is now asked to be seated. . . .

The mind plays with the dimensions of the Big Room: 4,000 feet by 625 feet and 300 feet high, the largest in the known world, requiring one and one-half hours to encircle. Of the 25 separate light circuits in the caverns only one is now turned on. When all are seated, the guide explains that the lights will be switched off for 30 seconds, making the room completely dark. This is done. After 30

"Parking terraces at entrance to Carlsbad Caverns. Space for 500 cars," June 1, 1936. Note pattern resembling Navajo drypaintings of the emergence place. (MNM Neg. No. 52058.)

seconds a dim light illumines a formation far off across the room and a quartet is heard in the hymn, "Rock of Ages." During the singing of two verses other sections in front are lighted in succession. At the end the voices fade to silence before the lights go up. The ranger gives the attendance figures and names the States and foreign countries represented, with the number from each.

At word from the guide, the group rises and follows along the farther trail past the *Polar Regions,* so named because of the resemblance to photographs of the Byrd Polar Expedition, then back to the lunch room, where the party divides, those returning by elevator passing to the left and those walking out going to the right.

At the surface again, until eyes are adjusted to the strong afternoon light, a rest of a few minutes is advised before regaining the parked car or bus.[9]

PART TWO

PLACE, PERSON, AND CELEBRATION
New Mexico Folklife

INTRODUCTION TO PART TWO

New Mexico folklife—indeed, the folklife of any community or group—is characterized by a world view—some definable sense of place, of person, and of time. New Mexicans' world views are the subject of "Place, Person, and Celebration—New Mexico Folklife."

Legend, lore, and songs about light, water, weather, and traditional patterns of settlement are presented in chapter 5, "A Sense of Place: Texts of Settlement, Communication, and Confrontation." New Mexico spatial domains are symbolized by mountains and corn-meal trails in Native American cultures, by plazas and crosses in Hispanic culture, and by fences and post offices in Anglo culture. Significant place lore is also associated with those who approach, test, and cross boundaries, as do herders, hunters, traders, miners, and those who raid and wage war during periods of conquest, colonization, and immigration.

Others who test limits are heroes and heroines like those in chapter 6, "People of Power: Texts of Fear and Fascination." Poseyemu, the Franciscans, the later clergy, healers, lawmen, and those on the peripheries of society like witches, hermits, beggars, wanderers, outlaws, and murderers embody extraordinary powers—either to heal or to hurt. Both culture heroes and villains help define and illuminate ordinary human capabilities and social interactions.

A wide variety of descriptive accounts in chapter 7, "A Sense of Time: Texts of Community and Celebration," illustrate how New Mexicans have marked and passed time. The "sense of time" in any society is generated by different "times": occasional encounters and gatherings when people talk, visit, prepare and share food, contest with one another, or mark individual rites of passage like marriages and funerals; cyclical, seasonal, and liturgical celebrations; and periodic or sporadic, invented festivals. Although invented traditions like Old Timers Days, Santa Fe Fiesta, the Gallup Inter-Tribal Indian Ceremonial, and the 1940 Coronado Cuarto Centennial are of relatively recent, largely commercial origin, they have come to epitomize twentieth-century celebrations in New Mexico.

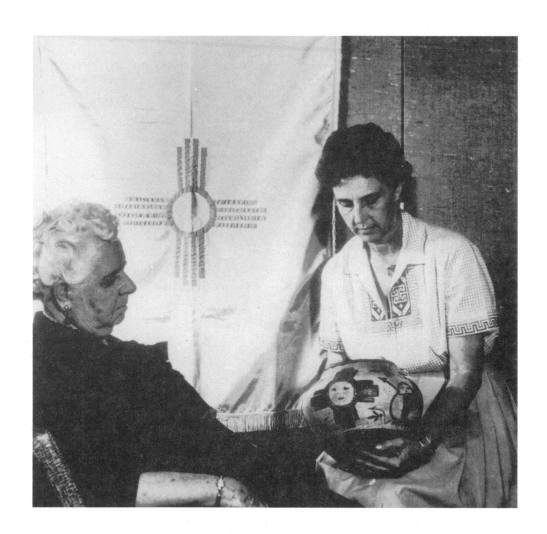

New Mexico flag with Mrs. H. P. Mera, who sewed the prototype, looking at inspirational Zia Pueblo pot held by Betty Toulouse. (MNM Neg. No. 50131.)

5 A SENSE OF PLACE

TEXTS OF SETTLEMENT, COMMUNICATION, AND CONFRONTATION

I wonder if somewhere in an eastern village a new chief
*   has arisen for the year,*

. . . .

Now chief, for this life-giving rain, you must love the
*   earth and the sky.*
We all receive the benefit from the rain,
It is the duty of the chief to look after his people,
This is what I ask you to do.

From the south it is raining,
From the east the water is coming in streams,
In front of the streams of water toward the west,
From there westward the lightning strikes the earth,
All of us receive crops.
Now here, chief, are crops. With this you may love your
*   people.*
This I ask of you.

—From an Acoma Pueblo song recorded from Philip Sanchez (Ho-ni-ya) for Dr. Matthew W. Stirling, at the Bureau of American Ethnology, Smithsonian Institution, Washington, D.C., 1928, and interpreted by Wilbert Hunt (Tse-gi-se-wa).[1]

Saint Isidore, Husbandman	*San Ysidro Labrador,*
Saintly patron of the farmer,	*Patrón de los labradores,*
May your favor grant us protection	*Que nos libre tu favor*
From locusts and temblors dread	*De langostas y temblores.*
. . . .	. . . .
When our Lord as punishment	*Cuando el Señor por castigo*
Sends adverse winds and hail,	*Nos manda mal temporal,*
We on your kind protecting grace	*Con tu bondadoso abrigo*
Rely to save our crops from harm.	*Nos vemos libre de mal.*

—From an *alabado* collected and translated by Lorin W. Brown in the Córdova area during the late 1930s.[2]

Under a sky of azure,
Where balmy breezes blow;
Kissed by the golden sunshine,
Is Nuevo Mejico.

Home of the Montezuma,
With fiery heart aglow,
State of the deeds historic,
Is Nuevo Mejico.

—From "O, Fair New Mexico," the official state song, adopted in 1915, with words and music composed in 1914 by Elizabeth Garrett, blind daughter of Pat Garrett and Apolinaria Gutiérrez Garrett.[3]

New Mexico officially became the forty-seventh state of the United States of America at 1:35 P.M. on January 6, 1912, when President William Howard Taft signed the proclamation of statehood in the White House. Taft then turned to the New Mexico delegates who had witnessed his signature and told them: "Well, it is all over. I am glad to give you life. I hope you will be healthy."[4]

New Mexico's first state flag, designed by historian Ralph Emerson Twitchell and authorized in 1915, reflected the state's territorial history. According to Richard L. Polese, "it consisted of a light blue field 'emblematic of the blue skies of New Mexico,' embodying a miniature flag of the United States in the upper left corner, a great seal of the state with the motto, 'The Sunshine State,' in the lower right corner, and upon the field running from lower left to upper right the words 'New Mexico' in white."[5] The number "47" appears in the upper right corner of this flag, which is displayed in the capitol rotunda in Santa Fe.

The New Mexico Daughters of the American Revolution sponsored an unsuccessful competition for a new flag in 1923, finally appealing for help to Santa Fe district public health officer Dr. Harry P[ercival] Mera (1875–1951). Mera, whose amateur interest in archeology led him to become curator at Santa Fe's Laboratory of Anthropology after it opened in 1931, chose a sun design painted on a Zia Pueblo pot. The original pot design showed a face inside the sun's circle, but this was rejected in favor of a plain center. Mera's wife Reba sewed a flag for presentation to the state legislature in 1925. Their legislative act, House Bill 164 of March 1925, precisely fixed the new symbol's field: "Said flag shall be the ancient Zia Sun Symbol of red in the center of a field of yellow. The colors shall be the red and yellow of old Spain." The official flag salute further focuses symbolic elements of Pueblo, Spanish (not Mexican), and Anglo traditions: "I salute the flag of the State of New Mexico, the Zia symbol of perfect friendship among united cultures."[6]

Officially imposed boundaries and invented symbols do not usually coincide—at least initially—with local and traditional realities of place. New Mexicans in long-standing and recent pueblos, plazas, ranches, homesteads, and railroad towns were accustomed to express their allegiance to entirely different communities, both socio-economic and spiritual. These customary, unofficial allegiances are the subject of this chapter.

A traditional sense of place includes recognition of climate, the use of water and land—both on and beneath the earth's surface, and notions of center, direction, and periphery. The sections that follow compare Native American, Hispanic, and Anglo approaches to New Mexico's atmosphere and aridity—its peculiarities of light, water, and weather. Contrasts in settlement and the use of land and water suggest different cultural ways of centering and bounding. Many of the profound, affective expressions of location and dislocation that so color New Mexican lore are also included.

When people move toward the peripheries of their space, they come close to, contact, or cross into the "wild," the "alien," the "foreign," or even the "supernatural." Traditionally, those who went out or beyond were herders of sheep and cattle, hunters and trappers, raiders and warriors, traders, freighters, and miners. They communicated with or confronted others outside the centers and in so doing connected and enriched or, conversely, intruded upon and plundered other territories.

Light

Corn-grinding songs were sung at dawn in nearly every pueblo. "In the early morning the women at Isleta grind the corn for household use. They sing at their work, and if some of the men are near they may join in the singing. As the women look at the rising sun they think of what may come to their people in the new day." Frances Densmore's interpreter told her that "the sun brings human lives to the earth and also takes them away." Densmore recorded the following corn-grinding song from Isletan Anthony Lucero sometime in the 1930s:

> Early this morning the coming of the sun,
> For what purpose is it coming?
> Perhaps for the cornmeal it is coming.
>> Yonder in the west at Shiawibat [Isleta]
>> All Isleta maidens, what do you think?
>> What do you say? Shall we sit and sing?
> Early this morning the coming of the sun,
> For what purpose is it coming?
> Perhaps for the yellow dust from the corntassels [pollen]
>> it is coming,
>> Yonder in the west at Shiawibat,

People of Shiawibat, what do you think?
What do you say? Shall we sit and sing?
Early this morning the coming of the sun,
For what purpose is it coming?
Perhaps for sons and daughters of the people it is
    coming.
Yonder in the west,
People, what do you think?
What do you say? Shall we sit and sing?[7]

At Zuni Pueblo, "in the olden times and sometimes today, a person who observes tewusu [Zuni religion] rises before dawn and finds his way to the east of the village where he stands by an anthill or a juniper or sage brush facing the east with a handful of prayer meal. He greets the sunrise, asking for protection for himself, his family, and the people and asking that even though 'some of his children' might wish to do harm to his people that this should not occur, so that 'we may all reach the ends of our roads together in happiness.'"[8]

Indians from Taos Pueblo observe similar customs. In January 1925, Carl G. Jung talked with Ochwiay Biano ("Mountain Lake," legally named Antonio Mirabal), a religious dignitary between forty and fifty years old. The man told Jung about the Sun father ("The sun is God. Everyone can see that."):

With a significant gesture he pointed to the sun.

    I felt that we were approaching extremely delicate ground here, verging on the mysteries of the tribe. "After all," he said, "we are a people who live on the roof of the world; we are the sons of Father Sun, and with our religion we daily help

Taos Pueblo, April 1936. FSA photo by Arthur Rothstein. (LC-USF 34-2724-E.)

our father to go across the sky. We do this not only for ourselves, but for the whole world. If we were to cease practicing our religion, in ten years the sun would no longer rise. Then it would be night forever."

I then realized on what the "dignity," the tranquil composure of the individual Indian, was founded. It springs from his being a son of the sun; his life is cosmologically meaningful, for he helps the father and preserver of all life in his daily rise and descent. If we set against this our own self-justifications, the meaning of our own lives as it is formulated by our reason, we cannot help but see our poverty.

The insight proved important to Jung, who concludes: "That man feels capable of formulating valid replies to the overpowering influence of God, and that he can render back something which is essential even to God, induces pride, for it raises the human individual to the dignity of a metaphysical factor. 'God and us'—even if it is only an unconscious *sous-entendu*—this equation no doubt underlies that enviable serenity of the Pueblo Indian. Such a man is in the fullest sense of the word in his proper place."[9]

All Native American tribes symbolically link color and direction. Among the Navajo, who consider color a dimension of light, these associations also include diurnal time and gender—white:male:east:dawn; blue:female:south:daylight; yellow:female:west:twilight; and black:male:north:night. According to Gary Witherspoon, in Navajo, color forms another language:

> The underworlds had no sun and were lighted only by single or individual colors. The first world was the darkest, and its color was black. The color of the second world was blue, the color of the third world was yellow, and the color of the fourth world was red. In the present fifth world, the sun combines all the colors of the underworlds into the light of daytime. Nighttime, being without sunlight, is symbolic of a return to the darkness and chaotic but formative conditions of the underworld. Thus ritual drama—which begins with a return to the underworlds and a reenactment of the undesirable events and resulting conditions found in episodes of culture heroes and concludes with a triumphant restoration of *hózhó* [usually translated "beauty" or "harmony"] and a glorious reemergence to the beautiful, colorfully light, cosmos of the fifth world—appropriately begins during the night and culminates with the healed patient going to greet the rising sun.
>
> Light, like sound, is closely associated with air, and color, like pitch with regard to sound, seems to be an inherent quality or attribute of light. The air masses which joined to create the mist beings or wind souls of the first world were each of a specific color, and all wind souls found in beings of the fifth world [our world] are colored. Light, like sound, is also transmitted through the air. It is sunlight which combines all colors in its brilliance and also makes the colors of all things visible. Darkness destroys or eliminates all sense or perception of color, and is thus a kind of noncommunicative silence.[10]

Hispanic New Mexicans viewed the sun as exerting "mysterious influences on individuals," according to Aurelio M. Espinosa. "The head of the bed must never be placed towards the rising sun, since it will cause the sleeper to rise with a bad headache, and even insanity may result. The sun is also the tooth-giver. When a tooth falls out or is extracted, the child takes the tooth, throws it at the sun with all possible force, and recites in sing-song fashion,—'Sol, sol, / Toma este diente / Y dame otro mejor.'" They also believe "that blondes cannot see the sun; and of one who is very fair, people say, *'Es tan huero que no puede ver al sol.'"*[11]

Like the Pueblo peoples, Hispanos traditionally greeted the dawn. Recalling her childhood in Arroyo Hondo during the late nineteenth century, Cleofas M. Jaramillo remembers her "Aunt Dolores' veneration for the old religious customs." The household would be awakened by her aunt's singing the *Canto del alba,* or "Hymn at dawn":

Let's sing the dawn,	*Coro: Cantémos él álba*
The light is coming;	*Yá viene él día.*
Let's give thanks,	*Darémos gracías,*
Ave Maria!	*Áve María!*
. . .	. . .
Born is the dawn, Maria,	*Náce él álba, María*
And the Ave comes after her;	*Y él Áve tras élla;*
Vanishing the night	*Desterrando lá nóche*
And our troubles.	*Y nuestras penas.*[12]

Marian imagery also informs other *alabados* or *alabanzas* sung at dawn. In the 1940s, Juan B. Rael collected four such hymns sung in praise of the Virgin at daybreak after vigils or wakes and in private homes: *Dios te salve, luna hermosa; Dios te salve, bella aurora; Buenos días, paloma blanca;* and *Alaben, cristianos.*[13] J. D. Robb collected a version of the first, "God Save Thee, Beautiful Moon!" in 1967 from Vicente T. Gallegos, age sixty-nine, of Albuquerque. The following are among its twelve verses:

1.
God save thee, beautiful moon!
God save thee, light of the day!
God save thee, sun and stars!
And God save thee, Mary!

4.
More beautiful than the moon
And lovelier than the sun art thou
Since the beginning of the world,
My lady, thou art blessed.

7.
In the east the sun arose
Giving beautiful light to the earth;
From thy mouth was born the dawn,
And from thy womb, Jesus.

1.
¡Dios te salve, luna hermosa!
¡Dios te salve, luz del día!

¡Dios te salve, sol y estrellas!
¡Y Dios te salve, María!

4.
Más hermosa que la luna
y más linda que el sol eres
desde el principio del mundo,
Señora, bendita tú eres.

7.
Del oriente nació el sol
dando al mundo hermosa luz;
de tu boca nació el alba,
y de tu vientre, Jesús.[14]

Writers and artists who came to the twentieth-century art colonies at Taos and Santa Fe often marveled at the light in New Mexico. Poet Winfield Townley Scott, a transplanted New Englander, writes in nautical terms: "In cozier country it seems that the sun rises and sets, the moon rises and sets, above a still and level world. But

"Service at the mission church. The painting on the retablo represents Nuestra Señora del Carmel." FSA photo by John Collier, Las Trampas, January 1943. (LC-USW 3-14618-E.)

here, as on a great ship, you are more aware of the voyaging planet—the mountains wheeling upward to the sun, and the winds like encountered currents breaking across the turning earth." He maintains that "in this staggering spaciousness of earth and sky, light is the vital force, the nervous or majestic rhythm, the master painter."[15]

The Spanish called Albuquerque's Sandia Mountains, *sandía,* or watermelon, because of their shape and color at sunset.[16] However, they did not, as both Winfield T. Scott and Willa Cather claim, name the Sangre de Cristo Mountains near Santa Fe for their sunset hues. Cather reworks a relatively recent tradition when she portrays a dying Bishop Latour (Lamy) contemplating: "Yes, Sangre de Cristo; but no matter how scarlet the sunset, those red hills never became vermilion, but a more and more intense rose-carnelian; not the colour of living blood, the Bishop had often reflected, but the colour of the dried blood of saints and martyrs preserved in old churches in Rome, which liquefies upon occasion."[17] In her 1917 poem, "A Legend of Sangre de Cristo," Clara D. True recounts how Padre Juan is slain at Kah-po, which she identifies as "an ancient Tewa Indian village near the site of the modern pueblo of Santa Clara," and while expiring calls out for a sign "that Death be lost in Victory":

A silence falls within the walls,
The gathering shadows grow to gloom,
Quiet the Red Men's mocking cries
The while a glory fills the skies.
A rosy glow has settled low
About Las Truchas' somber peaks;
Painting the world a crimson hue
Beneath a sky of dark'ning blue.
The splendor grows, the color glows,
Encarnardines the wide-flung range,
Towering in roseate glory now
As death-dews bathe the boy-priest's brow.

The martyred friar prophesies to the assembled Indians:

My body only has thou killed.
Blood of the Christ o'er mountains spread
Shall preach to you when I am dead.

In fact, however, the Spanish knew the Sangre de Cristo mountain range as the "Sierra Madre," or "Mother Range," and it was not called Sangre de Cristo until the late nineteenth century, when railroad publicists waged an intensive campaign to attract tourists and speculators by extolling the sights to be seen along their lines.[18]

Jill Warren compares artists' views of "New Mexico's famous light" with the perspectives of Los Alamos scientists, explaining that, at higher elevations, "there are fewer air molecules than at sea level because the heavy ones sink; dust particles drop out more easily because there is less density to support them," and aridity means less water vapor in air that is "easier to look through." Since "moisture and dust diffract, or scatter, light rays," thus dividing the spectrum into its component parts, colors become visible. "Because New Mexico air is low in moisture and dust (except when the wind blows), the light that reaches us is more like the way it was when it left the sun."

Warren reports a conversation with Ray Jones, a Los Alamos laser specialist:

> Because the air is less dense, there is less distortion of light rays here. That allows a
> clarity that makes colors seem more intense and makes distances less obvious. On
> a clear day in Los Alamos, you almost feel as though you could reach out and touch
> the Sangres in Santa Fe, even though they're about thirty miles away. Sunrises and
> sunsets may appear more intense because of the contrast of the other colors to the
> deep blue of the sky.

Painters are also looking through comparatively dry air, according to Los Alamos staff meteorologist Brent Bowen: "Santa Fe and Taos get about twelve inches of rain a year. . . . That compares to about forty-four inches per year for New York or Paris. The average humidity in New Mexico is 45 percent. That might seem high, but the figure includes mountain areas with their heavy snows. The average humidity in New York is 70 percent. We get sunlight about 65 percent of the time. The low moisture means there's almost unlimited visibility, and the stars at night look big and bright."[19]

Water and Weather

Santa Fe poet Haniel Long begins *Piñon Country,* his 1941 volume on the Southwest for the American Folkways Series edited by Erskine Caldwell, with minutes from a Navajo Tribal Council meeting in November 1939. At issue was a water rights dispute between the highway department and the tribe. The exchange about water epitomizes New Mexican folkways, as Long elaborates:

> The limited supply circumscribes the present and the future of Pueblo, Navajo, Hopi,
> Apache, Spanish American, Mormon, everybody. Far more space in the daily paper
> goes to water than to any other subject. The news items about it are of all kinds. At
> Tesuque a one-armed native (in the Southwest the "natives" are the Spanish
> Americans) kills his neighbor (with a rifle, too) for stealing water. At Carlsbad the
> body of a prominent rancher is at the undertaker's and over the Texas line another
> prominent rancher is being held without bail—a "water-right argument." Governor
> Miles of New Mexico orders the state police to break the locks on the water gates
> in the Virden valley; farmers came to him crying their water was shut off so that
> Arizona Indians could irrigate. President Roosevelt signs a compact that ends a thirty
> years' dispute among the states of Texas, New Mexico, and Colorado for use of the
> waters of the Rio Grande. The Senate approves an additional appropriation of
> $500,000 for the dam and canal on the Rio Grande which divides waters apportioned
> the United States from those due Mexico. At Silver City the water superintendent
> warns everybody to use water sparingly. The weather man at Albuquerque says rain
> is needed over most lower elevation ranges, and soil is beginning to blow in the east-
> ern dry-farming sections. A native named Sanchez sues the city of Albuquerque for
> four thousand dollars because a ditch overflowed into his home, and the jury disagrees
> over the justice of the claim. A three-year-old child at Pecos, Maria Barella, reaches
> too far out over a ditch for a floating stick, falls in, and is drowned.[20]

"Farm boy drinking at well." FSA photo by Russell Lee, Pie Town, June 1940. (LC-USF 34-36646-D.)

New Mexico's pervasive water lore originates in scarcity. Em Hall states: "Not much precipitation falls here. . . . What does come down falls unevenly over the state (8 inches in the barren plains, 30 inches on the mountain peaks), and at irregular times (mostly in July and August, seldom in June and October)." This "yields roughly 85 million acre-feet of water a year, or enough water to cover 85 million acres one foot deep . . . [putting] New Mexico very near the bottom of state rankings in terms of water produced for surface area." Only some three million acre-feet of the "comparatively puny" eighty-five million "appears annually as surface water running in streams."[21] Hall's statistics are but one contemporary expression of the long-standing recognition that survival in an arid environment requires ingenuity, luck, work, and ritual.

On the Staked Plains, Indians, traders, explorers, and buffalo hunters became intimately familiar with natural sources of water in an apparently barren landscape. When settlement began, the buffalo hunters turned to hunting water and selling land, according to May Price Mosley of the New Mexico Federal Writers' Project (NMFWP):

> With a market for every watering place developed, the buffalo hunters now turned to water hunting. Few of them found it profitable, for many dry holes were dug. Enough to make the business a gamble, and to make a good well valuable. Their methods and equipment were of necessity primitive. In digging one of the first wells the hunters drew dirt from the well in a lard bucket tied to a rope which was thrown over the tongue of their wagon for a pulley. . . . They had no well drills. . . . These water hunters learned by trial and error that on the Llano Estacado shallow water was more likely to be found at the west or north edge of a lake than elsewhere; and that if they dug far out on the level prairie they encountered impenetrable flint-like rock, which they called "granite," but no water.

Increased cattle raising in Texas, together with a two-year drouth there, brought more and more ranchers this way searching for water on the Llano Estacado that they might move their herds out on its well-grassed prairies. Ex-buffalo hunters did all in their power to supply this demand. Their general procedure seems to have been to dig a well and camp beside it till a buyer came along, then move along and look out another site. In some instances they dug for hire at points designated by the prospectors, but this doesn't seem to have happened often in the earliest settlement.[22]

In turn, the homesteaders who followed initially depended on the ranchers for their domestic water. Freighter Clyde Stanfield told J. Vernon Smithson (NMFWP) about a violent episode at "the only windmill for miles around . . . the 3T mill, situated in what is now [1936] known as the Pettigrew Lake, . . . owned by a [ranching] syndicate whose headquarters was at Prairie View." Stanfield recalled:

> One day there were about thirty wagons waiting for water at the 3T mill. All the men except one had twelve quart pails and this one had a bucket that would hold half a bushel. The other men became angry because he was getting more than his share of water, which had to be caught from the pipe. The mill was pumping very slowly and each man was jealous lest another should get more than he.
>
> The anger of these men finally resulted in a fight. The man possessing the large bucket was hurt quite badly and was forced to give up his big pail and used a twelve quart pail thereafter.[23]

When Uncle Charlie Smith arrived in the Melrose area in 1906 with "an immigrant car and enough groceries to last [him] twelve months," he recalled in an interview with Lena K. Maxwell: "I hauled every drop of water I used for four and one-half years. For my stock, cows, hogs, horses, chickens, and household purposes. Hauled all the water we had and paid ten cents a barrel, or three barrels for twenty-five cents, and hauled some of it five miles." By 1910, Smith was able to build his own well, which he proudly described to Maxwell:

> Mr. Pickens, the husband of the late Mrs. Pickens, used to run a tin-shop here, and made galvanized water-tanks, and galvanized casing for wells. I cased my well with deep well Artesian casing, and it is still there and will be there when Gabriel blows his horn. That well is one of the best in the country and was known by everybody far and near. Travelers would make it a point to stop there and get water. Its supply was inexhaustible. Can't be pumped dry. One day Oscar McGruder decided he'd pump that well dry, but he couldn't. He pumped for fourteen hours with a gasoline engine and it was still throwing as good a stream when he stopped as when he had been pumping for thirty minutes.[24]

Uncle Charlie Smith does not say how he decided where to dig his well, but water witching, or dowsing, is a frequent motif in Anglo water lore.

William M. Emery (NMFWP) describes how the Brookhart family used divination to determine where to dig a well on their Clayton area ranch north of the Dry Cimarron River:

"Forked stick twisting and pointing downward in the water witch's hands over the proper location for a well." FSA photo by Russell Lee, Pie Town, June 1940. (LC-USF 33-12751-M3.)

There was no spring or stream on the place, only a dry arroyo which lay about a half a mile from the house. As this arroyo lay at the foot of the slope on which the house was built, and was considerably lower than any of the rest of the land, it was chosen as the most suitable place to find water—even though it would have to be hauled about a half mile to the house. . . . They first "witched" for water along the banks of the arroyo. "Witching" for water is done by holding a forked stick—or crooked wire—tightly between the two hands. When water is located, the stick—or wire—turns over and over in the witch's hands. A branch of a peach tree is usually preferred, although in this country where peach tree branches are not always available a pinion branch is often used. Not everyone is possessed of this art—or talent—of witching for water, and those who are are known as "water witches." It is a common thing to witch for water in the Southwest, so that the success of the labor might be assured.[25]

When they first arrived in the early 1930s, homesteaders in west-central New Mexico hauled their water and rarely tried to drill wells because of the prohibitive cost. In his classic study of water witching in the community he calls Homestead [Fence Lake], whose settlers "defined themselves as pioneers, leaving the 'civilized' centers of Texas and Oklahoma to seek new homes on the 'frontier' west of the Continental Divide," Evon Z. Vogt tells how

one farmer suddenly "discovered" in 1933 that he had the "power" to witch for water. As a young boy in Texas he observed witching. One day he simply cut a forked stick from his wife's peach tree, tried out the technique as he remembered it, and it worked. He found two water veins on his farm, traced them to a point where they crossed each other, and had a successful well drilled at a depth of 230 feet. He rapidly achieved community-wide reputation as a water witch and successfully witched 18 wells in the next few years. Six wells were dowsed by a second water witch who lived in the community for a few years, making a total of 24 wells that were located in this manner. During the same period, however, the original water witch dowsed five locations where dry holes resulted after drilling; and he missed calculating the depth by as much as 200–400 feet. For, in addition to using the common technique for locating the water vein by walking over the ground with a forked twig and putting a stake in the ground where the rod dipped, he developed a special technique for determining depth. He would hold a thin, straight stick (5 feet in length) over the water vein, and it would "involuntarily" nod up and down. The number of nods indicated the depth in feet to the water. . . .

As time went on, the water witch killed his wife's lone peach tree by cutting witching sticks from it. He then made an adjustment to the New Mexican environment by shifting to the use of forked sticks from piñon trees. He explains his dowsing in terms of "electricity" and usually attributes errors to the presence of iron (like a knife in his pocket, or an old piece of farm machinery in the vicinity) or to the fact that he could not find a straight stick.[26]

By no means everyone in Homestead relied on dowsing, and during the same period, twenty-five successful and seven dry wells were dug without water witching.

Contemporary "water witches" are hydrologists, who speak what Em Hall calls "'waterese,' a new esoteric language . . . full of 'transmissivity and storage coefficents,' 'drawdowns,' 'recoveries,' 'simulations,' 'sustained yields,' and, indeed, 'sensitivities.'" Hydrological debates "take place not among the *mayordomos* of ancient community *acequias,* but among groundwater hydrologists carrying briefcases full of computer printouts in one hand, in the other, endless resumes."[27]

The Spanish word *acequia,* or irrigation ditch, from the Arabic *as-saquiya,* is but one of many Spanish water terms dating from the European country's Moorish occupation. Nevertheless, Spanish irrigation practices antedated the Moorish invasion, and their codified water law was a composite of Roman, Germanic, and Moorish influences.[28] Spanish colonial water law was based on traditional Iberian codes and practices. According to Marc Simmons, "the community acequias were organizations composed of all landowners holding property on a ditch [and] . . . the association of water users that had charge of an irrigation system was often one of the most highly integrated and efficient organizations in the community." Elected *mayordomos,* or ditch bosses, were figures of "authority and prestige" who "inspected and superintended repair of acequias, regulated the number of days labor required of each proprietor, distributed and aportioned water, adjudicated disputes, and searched for infractions of regulations."[29]

Annual ditch cleaning continues to the present. Called *la fatiga,* according to Arthur Campa, the demanding work is still supervised by a mayordomo. Nambe resident Orlando Romero describes a *fatiga* in 1979:

> As customary, the *mayordomo* begins the task of reading the names of the various members of this particular *acequia.* His authority, as described by the association's bylaws, includes the responsibility for making payment to laborers who substitute for absent members. The next most important man is the *rayador,* whose responsibility is to mark the section assigned to each individual cleaner. . . .
>
> As soon as the last section is finished, the *rayador* begins the process of assigning sections numerically all over again until the ditch is cleaned and repaired. It also is a way of telling who needs to go back to his previously assigned section and complete his work if the *mayordomo* is not satisfied with the individual or his work. In some sections the ditch needs more work than usual or extensive repair has to be completed. The *mayordomo* then assigns a group of men to continue necessary repairs while the main crew proceeds with the usual cleaning.
>
> Although the work is usually difficult, there is always occasion for conversation and socializing because time usually overlaps before the last section of the *acequia* is finished and the *rayador* marks off the new section. For many of the men it is time to renew old village conversations, to talk a little about life or just plain village gossip. For many of us, it offers the opportunity to converse with village patriarchs like Don Bernardo Baca, who in his eighties not only still participates in the spring ritual of the *acequias* but also has a good story to tell about life in the village, usually about days when there was so much water that people had trouble crossing the small Nambe stream, or about days when there was so little water that it was a miracle plants produced anything at all.[30]

The main, or mother, ditch is known as the *acequia madre,* while the secondary channels are called *contra acequias.* In the Spanish colonial period these smaller ditches were endowed with the religiously significant term *sangrias.* William Wroth notes that "just as the circulation of the blood animates the human body, sustaining its life, so the circulation of water from the *acequia madre* . . . through the system of secondary channels sustains vegetal life in the fields, providing the basis of human sustenance." These and other waterways like streams and creeks are symbolically related to *Sangre de Cristo,* the Blood of Christ, "which simultaneously sustains all mundane life and provides the means to salvation."[31]

Use of irrigation water was carefully monitored by the mayordomo and all members of the ditch association and community. Alfonso Ortiz claims that Hispanic farmers near San Juan Pueblo "until recent years . . . have all but forced the Tewa to cooperate, by early March, in cleaning and restoring the complex system of irrigation canals they share. Work must begin at this time because it takes more than two weeks to clean out the canals. When farming was done on a larger scale, and the population was smaller than today [1960s], work had to begin in late February if the wheat fields were to have water when it was needed most." The principal of the three ditches connecting the neighboring villages

is called "mother canal," and when it is opened in mid-March the moiety chiefs lead the water in from the last Spanish village. The Summer chief, who leads, scatters cornmeal along the way, while the Winter chief scatters fish scales, so there will be an abundance of fish. The fishing season, as such, begins at this time in Tewa belief, although fishing is also done in the river during the rest of the year. Henceforth also, the people obtain their water from the canals, and the springs are ritually closed until autumn.[32]

Confrontations and cooperation over water played an integral part in the life of every New Mexican community, as illustrated in the History of Grazing study conducted by the New Mexico Writers' Program in the early 1940s. S. F. Hassell writes:

Irrigating fields and orchards, El Cerrito, April 1941. Bureau of Agricultural Economics photo by Irving Rusinow. (Neg. No. 83-G-37849, National Archives.)

Nowhere in the United States is water so much appreciated and more eagerly looked for than in the Southwest. It is lifeblood, and the people here know it. A story an old Mormon in the little settlement of Ramah in western New Mexico likes to tell about a neighbor illustrates the value that people in the Southwest place on water.

Jim Link was the old Mormon's neighbor and was talking to him about another neighbor. Link said, "I would trust that man with all the money I have. I would trust him with my wife and I would trust him with my life." Here there was an impressive pause. "But," he continued, "I would not trust him up at that headgate."[33]

Drought was greatly feared, and much New Mexican weather lore teaches the signs of rain. John F. Kitchens of Albuquerque, who was born in southern New Mexico, notes: (1) "If the smoke from a newly made fire settles quickly from the chimney to the ground, it is going to rain"; (2) "Chickens sitting on the wood-pile are a sure sign of rain"; (3) "Terrapins crawling over the prairie are a sign of rain"; and (4) "Cowboys say a good sign of rain is to find their ropes stiff and inflexible in the morning." Pragmatism also found a place in Kitchens's lore:

Shooting at a cloud will help to make it rain—the bigger the caliber the better. Substantiated by the story of a local woman who tried the trick with a 12 gauge shot gun and caused a flash flood which washed away the stock tank. Her small son afterwards observed, "Ma, next time you better use the 22."[34]

In Placitas, Lou Sage Batchen (NMFWP) collected a folktale about "long, long ago [when] two wise men learned in the science of the sun, moon, and stars, and the weather climbed to the highest point of the Sandia Mountains to study the stars and solve some of their astrological problems." They encountered an old woman living there with her donkey. Disregarding her warning of rain because their instruments indicated otherwise, they set up their equipment, barely making it back before the skies opened up.

"Tell us," demanded one of the wise men, "how did you know it would rain tonight? We are wise men and read all signs. We saw no sign of rain."

"Because this afternoon my donkey told me," she said simply. "He went running and jumping all around the place. That always foretells rain very soon."

Early the next morning the two wise men left the house. The old woman went outside to see them off. To her surprise they turned to go back down the mountain.

"You are not going to stay to study the stars?" she asked.

"We are going back where we came from," answered one. "What's the use of all our scientific studies and our instruments to guide us when a burro knows more about the weather than science?"

"Who knows what God tells the animals?" the old woman inquired.[35]

Batchen's tale is similar to a contemporary incident reported by Barre Toelken:

A Navajo belief relating rain to burrowing animals was inadvertently "collected" by government agents in the 1950s when they proposed to get rid of prairie dogs on some parts of the reservation in order to protect the roots of the sparse desert grass and thereby maintain at least marginal grazing for sheep. Navajos objected strongly, insisting, "If you kill off the prairie dogs, there will be no one to cry for rain." Of course they were assured by the amused government that there was no conceivable connection between rain and prairie dogs, a fact that could be proven easily by a simple scientific experiment: a specific area would be set aside and all burrowing animals there would be exterminated. The experiment was carried out, over the continued objections of the Navajos, and its outcome was surprising only to the white scientists. Today the area (not far from Chilchinbito, Arizona) has become a virtual wasteland with very little grass. Apparently, without the ground-turning processes of the burrowing animals, the sand in the area has become solidly packed, causing a fierce run-off whenever it rains. What sparse vegetation was once there has been carried off by the flooding waters.[36]

Cleofas M. Jaramillo reports that in Arroyo Hondo, "if the ashes in the fireplace whirled around on a very quiet day the weather would turn bad." She says that

people watched strictly the changes of the moon as a weather bureau. If the old moon ended dry and the new moon set in dry there was no hope of rain during the whole month, but if the new moon appeared with *"los cuernos colgados"* (its horns turned down) the whole month would be rainy. Woe to the farmers if the moon turned up its horns. They would say *"ya bramo la luna"* (the moon has roared). A long drought would follow until lady moon would deign to turn her horns down again and let the water out.

Jaramillo's brother, Reyes N. Martínez (NMFWP), collected similar beliefs from shepherds in Taos County in 1940:

When a new moon first appears in the evening above the western horizon, if it is "colgada" (hanging), that is, if its points appear in a line perpendicular, or nearly so, to the earth's surface, it is going to let all the water run out, and the succeeding four weeks will be a rainy period. But if its ends appear in a line horizontal or parallel, or nearly so, to earth's surface, like an upturned saucer, it is going to hold all the water, and the ensuing period, throughout all its phases, is going to be dry. An "ojo de buey" (ox's eye), a patch in the sky resembling a small segment of a rainbow, indicates an unusually rainy period. In winter, when the coyotes howl vehemently at night, a storm is brewing.[37]

Lorin W. Brown (NMFWP) describes what such a storm was called:

On a dark and stormy night or a day when the blizzard sweeps across the country on a cold norther one will hear some of the older residents of New Mexico say: "Este es día de herejes" ("This is a day for the heretics"). This saying alludes to the time when the Indians chose just such inclement weather to launch a surprise attack or raid on the Spanish settlements, hoping to catch the men of the villages napping inside by the fireplace.[38]

Judd Lyons told Kenneth Fordyce (NMFWP) that people in northeastern New Mexico referred to 1880 as "the year of the *big wind*," when it "blew unusually hard for one hundred consecutive days," and "neither before nor since have the people of New Mexico known the wind to blow for such a long period with such unceasing velocity and fierceness as it did in that year." In "Chronicles of Neglected Time: Windscapes," Roland Dickey remembers his boyhood on the eastern plains in the twentieth century:

> Like the puffing Boreas that livens old maps, the Wind personified seems always to be lurking somewhere in my memories of eastern New Mexico. Channeled in the mountainless corridor that divides the continent from Canada to Mexico, the wind certainly was "the Force" in our lives, and we learned to stay tuned to its presence or absence. I never got used to the wind, and whenever it rose above a "cool summer breeze" it seemed the most hated and feared element that Nature concocts. "There's nothing between us and the North Pole but a barbed-wire fence," the saying goes, and wind on the high plains carries salvation and disaster, "chill factor" and moisture, desiccation and dust.[39]

According to Marc Simmons, "historians have tended to overlook the harmful impact which the Little Ice Age [1450–1850] had upon colonial New Mexico's economy." During the colonial period New Mexicans suffered "severe temperatures in winter, excessive snowfall, late thaws and early frosts, and regular freezing of the Rio Grande [with] the net result . . . a lowering of agricultural potential owing to a shortening of the growing season."[40] Rain was always a concern, even during shortened growing seasons, as Louise Lamphere emphasizes in her study of Southwestern Indian ceremonialism:

> The prevalence of water symbolism is striking in Pueblo religion, if only in contrast to the Yuman, Apache, and Navajo, where water symbolism is much less important.
>
> Examples are numerous. The Pueblo cosmos is often bordered by oceans or lakes. In the Tewa water-pouring ceremony, the kachinas emerge from these lakes before coming to the village. Zuni prayersticks are made from red willow because willow roots are connected to a common root stock, just as Zuni springs are connected to an underground water system. . . . The willows thus symbolize the bringing of long life and rain to humans. Sacred water is placed on Tewa altars contained in a bowl with jagged edges, indicating a cloud-shaped design. During the Cochiti Green Corn or Tablita Dance . . . dancers use gestures that invoke the rain-bringing kachinas, lightning, clouds, fog, and growing crops.[41]

From 1906 until 1970, ritually significant Blue Lake, high in the mountains above Taos Pueblo and the source of its water supply, was the subject of what Jemez Pueblo historian Joe S. Sando calls "one of America's epic stories . . . a symbol of the plight of the American Indian." In 1906, President Theodore Roosevelt declared Blue Lake part of Taos Forest Reserve, placing it "in so-called 'protective custody' . . . from encroachment by mining prospectors and other speculators." An executive order dated June 26, 1908, made it part of the Carson National Forest. On several occasions Taos Pueblo tried unsuccessfully to recover Blue Lake.[42]

On April 18, 1961, nine years before Congress returned 48,000 acres to the Taos Indians, Severino Martínez, then governor of the Pueblo, spoke to the Association on American Indian Affairs in New York City, proclaiming:

Zuni Pueblo women, ca. 1908. Photo by H. F. Robinson. (MNM Neg. No. 37366.)

> Blue Lake is the most important of all our shrines because it is a part of our life. It is our Indian church; . . . at the Blue Lake, we go there and talk to our Great Spirit in our own language, and talk to Nature and what is going to grow, and ask God Almighty, like anyone else would do. . . .
>
> We have to pray for what we receive from the sun that gives the light and the water we drink. They are provided by God. We are taking that water to give us strength so we can gain in knowledge and wisdom about the work that we are engaged in. Without energy provided by God, we are helpless. Religion is the most important thing to our life. That is the reason why this Blue Lake is so important to us.[43]

The Zuni people also consider local waterways to be sacred. The Zuni River is their "spiritual lifeline," and "nearly every aspect of the religious system is in some way tied to the river." In 1983, Zuni Edmund J. Ladd writes of his people's continuing belief

> that the spirit returns upon death to the place where this muddy little stream converges with the Little Colorado River, northwest of the town of Saint Johns, Arizona. The place is called *ko/lhu /wa/a la:wa*—"there to become one of the ancestors." The ancestors are said to return to *itiwann/a*—Zuni—by making their way up to the Zuni River in the form of ducks whenever the masked dances are performed. They also return in the form of rain in the summer and snow in the winter to replenish the stream, to provide protection, spiritual guidance, and abundant harvests and to give long life. The stream ties the living world—*ja/lona:/itiwann/a)*—with the other world—*ko/lhu/wa/a la:wa*.[44]

Mountains and Corn-Meal Trails: Native American Settlement

Centering: Southwestern Indian Concepts of Space

On February 22, 1882, six Zuni Indians left their pueblo to accompany anthropologist Frank Hamilton Cushing on a train trip to the East Coast. A Zuni tribal history states: "The six Zunis who went on the trip were Nai-iu-tchi (Senior Priest of the Bow), Lai-iu-ah-tsai-lu, Ba:lawahdiwa (the present governor and Cushing's brother by adoption), Lai-iu-ah-tsai-lun-k'ia (Cushing's father by adoption in the tribe and Priest of the Temple), Ki-a-si (Junior Priest of the Bow), and Nanahe (a Hopi adopted into the Zuni tribe). . . . They met President [Chester A.] Arthur and visited Washington Monument, where Ba:lawahdiwa said, from the top, that perspective changed, 'No longer the powerful Americans, but little men like ants creeping around on the ground below. . . .' They journeyed through New England seeing Boston, Harvard University and the Peabody Museum and stopped at Salem where Nai-iu-tchi made a speech."[45] On March 28, 1882, Boston mayor Dr. Samuel Abbot Green chartered a steamer to take the Zunis and 250 invited guests to Deer Island. There, they inducted Cushing into the Zuni kachina society and performed ceremonies scattering sacred corn meal on the water and planting prayer sticks. They filled demijohns with water from the "Ocean of Sunrise" and took these back to Zuni, where it was "used at the summer solstice to dampen the paint used on the plumes of prayer sticks."[46]

Zunis believe that the eastern ocean is one of four oceans bounding the earth's circular coastline. Cushing states that each ocean has at its center "a very ancient sacred place (Té-thlä-shi-na-kwïn), a great mountain peak, in the North . . . the Mountain Yellow, in the West the Mountain Blue, in the South the Mountain Red, in the East the Mountain White." According to Dennis Tedlock:

> The Sun Father has two houses, one in the eastern ocean and the other in the western. . . .
>   In the oceans live the yellow, blue, red, and white *kolo'wisi,* four giant feathered serpents who are capable of causing a world flood. . . . Along the shores of the oceans

L. to r.: Lai-iu-ah-tsai-lun-k'ia, Frank Cushing's foster father; Nai-tu-tchi, Senior Bow Priest; Frank Hamilton Cushing; Pa-lo-wa-ti-wa, also known as Patricio Pino, son of Pedro Pino, governor of Zuni from mid-1870s to mid or late 1880s; Ki-a-si, Junior Bow Priest; Na-na-he, a Hopi married to a Zuni woman. Photo probably by James Wallace Black, taken in his Boston studio, ca. March 23, 1882. (MNM Neg. No. 9146.)

and in springs live the *ʔuwanammi* (or *ʔuwanam ʔaˑšiwani* 'rain priests') of the six directions, who take the form of clouds, rainstorms, fog, and dew when they leave their homes. . . . Their *ʔaˑpiʔta ʔaˑšiwani* 'bow priests' (warriors), also of the six directions, make lightning and thunder . . . ; and their *pekʷiˑwe* 'spokesmen' . . . are the six *kʔašima wowe* 'water—bringing birds': oriole (north), Steller's jay (west), macaw (south), magpie (east), purple martin (zenith), and rough-winged swallow (nadir). . . .

The six orientation points of the Zunis also have their colors: north—yellow, west—blue, south—red, east—white, zenith—multicolored, and nadir—black. Zuni Pueblo itself is known as *ʔitiwanʔa,* or "the middle place," for it is equidistant from the four oceans. Some of the pueblo houses' innermost rooms hold *ʔettoˑwe,* or sacred bundles, and "at the center of the bundles, at the center of Zuni, there rests a stone on a permanent altar . . . , and inside this stone beats the heart of the world."[47]

The Tewa pueblos northeast of Zuni also identify the sacred center of their world. According to Alfonso Ortiz, at San Juan Pueblo, *Nang echu kwi nang sipu pingeh,* or "Earth mother earth navel middle place," is "the sacred center of the village, and the ring of stones representing it is on the south plaza." As with Zuni, the cardinal directions are associated with colors: north—blue/green, west—yellow, south—red, and east—white.[48]

Ortiz identifies three "micro-environments" surrounding San Juan Pueblo. The innermost is the woman's domain, and "consists of the village, the farmlands, and other lowlands near the village . . . [and] is given its spiritual dimension by four shrines at the outer periphery of the village, one in each cardinal direction . . . dedicated to the no-longer-*sæˑʈaˑ* spirits of departed ancestors, who are spiritual counterparts to the living *sæˑʈaˑ* people of the village. The shrines and this innermost circle are most accessible to the ordinary *sæˑʈaˑ* people, as, indeed, they must be."

The second circle, that of hills, mesas, and washes, is a mediating environment in every important sense. First, it is an area in which both men and women may be, but one into which women and children did not usually go unless accompanied by men. This environment is in the charge of men but does not exclude women. Both hunting and gathering are done there, by both sexes. In a spiritual sense, it is an area defined by four sacred mesas, or flat-topped buttes, one in each direction. Each of these mesas is believed to have a cave or labyrinth that permits entry into the *o'pá' nunæ*, or underworld; so the ritually unprepared, women and children both, may not venture too close, to avoid being drawn into the cave or labyrinth. . . .

The third concentric circle is the clearcut domain of men, as contrasted with the innermost circle, the domain of women. This is an area of purely male hunting and gathering, and the destination of purely male religious pilgrimages. Made People who are women may go on pilgrimages as well, but they go only as far as a shrine in the foothills of the middle space, which they have for their own ritual use.[49]

The entire Tewa world "is about 140 miles north to south, and thirty-five miles east to west," being bounded sixty miles to the north by Canjilon Peak, called *Tse Shu Pín,* or Shimmering Mountain; fifteen miles to the west by *Tsikomo,* or Obsidian-Covered Mountain; eighty miles to the south by Sandia Crest, called *Oku Pín,* or Turtle Mountain; and twenty miles to the east by Truchas Peak, called *Ku Sehn Pín,* or Stone Man Mountain.[50]

Like the Pueblos, both the Navajo and the Jicarilla Apache believe in an emergence from underworlds into this one. Unlike the Pueblos and Navajo, however, as Louise Lamphere notes, among most Apache groups "there is no clear model of the universe that lays out the relationship of geographical entities like mountains and rivers, in terms of color and directional symbolism with associated birds, animals, and supernatural creatures." Nevertheless, "among the Jicarilla, there is some indication of the bounding of territory by mountains and by four rivers (two male and two female . . .), and the human body is used as a model for structuring the natural environment, as indicated in the texts collected by [Pliny E.] Goddard." Lamphere contrasts this with the Navajo cosmos:

Navajo cosmology contains many of the same elements as are found among the Apache, but these are utilized in a more systematic and structured manner. The Navajo think of their cosmos as a circle where the "sky horizon edge" *(yák'ashbąąh)* meets the "earth horizon edge" *(ník'ashbąąh].* The circular horizon is divided into "light phenomena." Each has an "inner form" *(bii'gistíín)* that is male or female, and each is associated with one of the four directions and one of four colors. As one Navajo informant depicted the circle . . . , Dawn Man (associated with whiteness) lies on the horizon from east to south; Horizontal Blue Man lies from south to west; Evening Twilight Woman (associated with yellow) lies from west to north; and Darkness Woman (associated with black) lies from north to east. The Navajo world is also bounded by four sacred mountains, each associated with a direction and a color. Four precious stones, four types of corn, and four birds are also associated with the mountains. . . . The Navajo color-direction scheme has equations different from the Apache one [east—black, south—blue, west—yellow, north—white]. East is associated with white, south with blue, west with yellow and north with black.[51]

In a Navajo origin legend recorded by Washington Matthews in the late 1800s,[52] the sacred mountains are identified as Blanca Peak (Colorado) in the east, Mount Taylor (New Mexico) in the south, San Francisco Peak (Arizona) in the west, and Hesperus Peak (Colorado) in the north.

The Navajos were forcibly dislocated from their sacred land by the United States Army during the 1860s. In the fall of 1862, Brigadier General James H. Carleton was made military commander of New Mexico and began plans to subjugate the Indians. He established a new military post at Fort Sumner (also known as Bosque Redondo), where he intended to resettle captured Mescalero Apaches and Navajos. In April 1863 he warned Navajo leaders that they would have to move to Fort Sumner and in June of that year threatened an attack by the army under Colonel Christopher ("Kit") Carson if they did not comply by July 20. In February 1864, a convoy of 1,445 Navajos left Los Pinos for Fort Sumner, followed by some 2,500 more in March. By December 31, 1864, 8,354 Navajos had survived the Long Walk and were incarcerated at Fort Sumner, with 9,022 there in March 1865.

Conditions at Fort Sumner were deplorable, and those who managed to survive the forced march often died of illness, homesickness, exposure, and starvation. On May 28, 1868, General William T. Sherman and Colonel Samuel F. Tappan were sent to Fort Sumner as peace commissioners. They concluded a treaty with the Navajos on June 1, 1868, and Congress ratified it on July 25 of the same year, not long before the first Navajos returned to their sacred lands.[53]

Stories of Kit Carson and the soldiers' attacks, of the Long Walk, and of the miseries at Fort Sumner continue to be told by Navajos, as Robert A. Roessel emphasizes:

> Nothing in heaven or earth could have been more terrifying and traumatic to the Navajo than the experience of the Long Walk. They were a free people who lived in their own country with its sacred mountains and familiar landmarks. They were people who were independent and self-sufficient: a people who had a way of life that was satisfying and meaningful. They were people who related to Navajoland in a spiritual manner since it was given and made safe for them by the Holy People. To be forced to leave their beloved land with its sacred mountains and shrines, and to cross three rivers, all of which their traditions warned them never to do, was to subject the Navajo to unparalleled anguish and heartache. When this anguish and heartache is combined with the unequaled physical suffering experienced at Fort Sumner, a faint glimpse of the impact this tragedy had, and continues to have, for the Navajo may be realized. The experience at Fort Sumner could well have totally destroyed the heart and mind of a less determined people.[54]

Their courage and dignity is expressed in Chief Barboncito's negotiations with General Sherman. On May 28, 1868, Barboncito declared, through interpreters:

> The bringing of us here has caused a great decrease of our numbers, many of us have died, also a great number of our animals. Our Grand-fathers had no idea of living in any other country except our own and I do not think it right for us to do so as we were never taught to. When the Navajos were first created four mountains and four rivers were pointed out to us, inside of which we should live, that

was to be our country and was given to us by the first woman of the Navajo tribe. It was told to us by our forefathers, that we were never to move east of the Rio Grande or west of the San Juan rivers and I think that our coming here has been the cause of so much death among us and our animals. That our God when he was created (the woman I spoke of) gave us this piece of land and created it specially for us and gave us the whitest of corn and the best of horses and sheep.

The next day he proclaimed:

After we get back to our country it will brighten up again and the Navajos will be as happy as the land, black clouds will rise and there will be plenty of rain. Corn will grow in abundance and everything look happy. Today is a day that anything black or red does not look right everything should be white or yellow representing the flower and the corn.[55]

Corn-Meal Trails: Benevolent Passage

Barboncito's equation of corn and well-being is seen in Gladys A. Reichard's summary of corn meal's ritual significance for the Navajo:

Corn meal (na·dá·ká·n) is one of the commonest forms of corn in ceremony. It is coarsely ground, white for a man, yellow for a woman, mixed if there is a patient of each sex. Sometimes it must be ground by a virgin or at some particular place or time in the ritual cycle. It is invariably used for the hogan blessing, for sandpainting sprinkling, and as a drier after the bath in all the rites I have seen, Evil as well as Holy. Often it serves as a substitute for pollen, since corn meal is plentiful and pollen is scarce. It usually denotes the same thing, life and success along the road, exemplified by footprints laid in corn meal.[56]

Virtually all New Mexican Indian cultures express the literal and symbolic importance of corn through the ritual use of corn meal. Mescalero Apache girls participating in the girls' puberty ceremony are blessed with pollen obtained not from corn but from yellow cattails. Claire R. Farrer describes a dawn ceremony on the first day of five for the puberty ceremony from her 1974–1975 fieldwork.

The girls kneel, facing east, on their skin mats while a line forms to the southeast of them. The girls' mothers stand behind them holding burden baskets filled with food; their fathers and uncles stand to either side, inside the runway and directly in front of the holy lodge. Each Singer applies the yellow cattail pollen to the girl for whom he is singing: a tiny sprinkle to the east, south, west, north, thence from the west to the east (from the crown of her head to her forehead), to the south (on her right shoulder), to the north (on her left shoulder), and from south to north (across her nose). The movements form a cross, linking the four directions with the girl as the center.

Apache singer Bernard Second told Farrer:

Pollen is applied to them. They are blessed with pollen. Pollen is the color of yellow. The yellow color represents God's generosity. It also represents the south, from which the warm winds bring rain that a thirsty land might drink and bring forth its bounty of fruit and meat. And they are . . . blessed that they will be fruitful and bring forth strong sons that they will be mighty warriors . . . that they will bring forth strong daughters that will become the mothers of a warrior race; that they will perpetuate themselves in a good way, a holy way, with the Powers of the four directions.[57]

The Apaches also use corn meal in these and other ceremonies.

Among the Pueblo Indians, corn meal ritually ground by women "is used to bless every aspect of daily living and religious practice," according to Leonora S. M. Curtin, who began a search for "up-to-date" information on the "Preparation of Sacred Corn Meal in the Rio Grande Pueblos" in 1964. She had covered fourteen pueblos by the summer of 1966, concluding that "the data I received at Taos Pueblo [were] the most complete and significant." There, in July 1964, Cruz Martínez told her:

In March the young virgins (14- or 15-year olds) of the pueblo are conducted to the kiva (ceremonial lodge) and given small metates and manos with which they grind white corn into meal. During the process the *cacique* sings five songs.

Later in the season the girls go up into the sacred mountains of Taos (the Blue Lake area, or *Pa-we-chan-mo* to pick small bluebells (*Campanula rotundifolia,* or *pe-ce-pam,* its Indian name). These blossoms are then dried, crushed, and added to the corn meal.

Early in August the girls go to a cornfield. They hold a prayer stick adorned with a turkey feather in their right hands, with which they shake the stamen and pollen into pottery bowls held in their left hands while singing a secret song.

These three ingredients are mixed together to make sacred corn meal.[58]

Society room (?) with seed corn, Zuni Pueblo, ca. 1891–1896. Photo by Matilda Coxe Stevenson. (MNM Neg. No. 82362.)

Curtin's materials from the 1960s agree with earlier accounts, notably Elsie Clews Parsons's ethnography of Isleta Pueblo in 1925. Parsons reports:

> Corn meal or pollen (our informant uses the term indiscriminately) is in very general ritual use. It is sprinkled by everybody to the sun at sunrise. In ceremonials it is sprinkled to sun, moon, stars. It is sprinkled in all the directions, or in the direction of any spirit that is being addressed. It is sprinkled on prayer feathers, on the altar, and on the sun spot. It is placed in the basket or on the hand where sacrosanct objects are to be placed or given. It is thrown into the river or buried in the field. The meal and pollen are contained separately in buckskin in the pouch of the bandoleer. Corn pollen only is used; not as in some other places pollen from flowers. Corn pollen may be gathered by anybody, "with a song," asking one of the cornstalks in the row for it. "We always ask for what we gather."
>
> Ritual road (p'æide) making by sprinkling corn meal occurs as elsewhere. Persons are led in or out of the ceremonial room by sprinkling meal before them. The chakabede [kachina chief] makes a pollen road for łiwale [war chief] when he leads him into town. Similarly, the chiefs lead a returning war party, or an irrigating party, into town by sprinkling meal. . . . The town chief sprinkles meal for the sun in a line from east to south when the runners name the sun in their song, which sprinkling is "like calling him"; i.e., making a road for him. Similarly by meal road making, the deceased is summoned, as well as dismissed.[59]

Plazas and Crosses: Hispano Settlement

Proclaimed Spaces: Villas and Placitas

During his 1692 reconquest of northern New Mexico, Captain-General Diego de Vargas Zapata Luján Ponce de León y Contreras camped with his men not far from the Santa Fe plaza. On the morning of September 14, the feast of the Exaltation of the Holy Cross, he donned fine attire, eschewing his armor, and "rode out toward the city to the music of the band, accompanied by the alferez carrying the royal banner, by [Captain Roque] Madrid and the other military leaders, by the missionaries and the six residents from El Paso [where the colonists had retreated after the 1680 Pueblo Revolt]." According to J. Manuel Espinosa:

> A large five-foot cross had been planted in the patio. Vargas dismounted, approached it, fell to one knee, and kissed it. Thus assured, the people began to climb down from the roof tops, some of which were quite high, by means of wooden ladders. When all had come down the men and women divided into separate groups. General Vargas strode through their midst with the royal standard raised in one hand. He then addressed them, through an interpreter, as he had done on many previous occasions, asking them to be peaceful and happy to be pardoned; he wished them again to become vassals of the Spanish king and good Christians. Both demands were granted. Then the soldiers stood in line with swords unsheathed as Vargas took formal possession of the villa of Santa Fe. The royal standard was raised three times, and each time Vargas cried out:

Long live our king, Carlos the Second! May God spare him! King of Spain and of all this New World, and of the realm and provinces of New Mexico, and of these subjects newly won and conquered!

Each time his men answered, "May he live many years and rule happily!" In joy they tossed their hats into the air, while the missionaries fell to their knees and thanked God for their good fortune. Father Corvera intoned the *Te Deum Laudamus.*[60]

A version of this ritual was enacted every time Spaniards were granted land by the governor. The *alcalde mayor* of the appropriate jurisdiction handled the complicated process of entitlement. When the petition was cleared by the governor, according to Myra Ellen Jenkins, "the alcalde, two Spanish witnesses, and neighboring Indians then went to the location for the final ceremony. The alcalde pointed out the boundaries to the new grantee who tore up grass, and threw rocks. All present shouted 'Long Live the King,' thus signifying that the new owner was in undisputed possession."[61]

William A. Keleher notes that while Roman law allowed land to be delivered "by an instrument in writing at a distance from the land, without manual delivery," in medieval Europe, "there could be no valid vesting of title unless there was personal, manual delivery and investiture." Thomas J. Steele, S.J., explains that this emphasis on personal delivery, possession, and occupancy also stressed "centers rather than margins, which tended to be remarkably vague. The fertile valley in the case of a land grant, the house in the case of a piece of privately owned property, is central and determinative, and the boundaries are often derived from it." Pueblo grants were measured not by concentric domains between sacred mountains or mesas, but by four hundred leagues measured in each of four directions from the church. Since there was no church in most Spanish grants, "the boundaries around the valley are often described as running from such and such a tree to such and such a hill to such and such an arroyo, and eventually back to the starting point, a description . . . perfectly adequate for the time and place, though as later became clear it would leave too much to the imagination of persons who did not live there, or who had a vested interest in making the grant larger or smaller than was intended."[62]

The Hispanic *paisanos,* or countrymen, civilian settlers of the frontier, were encouraged to pioneer by such *mercedes reales,* or royal land grants, a *merced* being "any land given, sold, or otherwise alienated by the crown." According to Victor Westphall:

> Municipal and community grants were made to groups of persons who desired jointly to form a new settlement. . . .
>
> Each settler on community grants received an allotment of land for a house (*solar*) and one or more outlots for cultivation (*suertes*), as well as the right to use the unallotted land in common with the other settlers for pastures, watering places, wood, hunting, and gathering. . . .
>
> The common lands of community grants were classified according to use. The *dehesa* was pasture land, and the monte (grove) was used principally for gathering wood and natural foods. The ejido was located just outside the town and was used variously for recreation, as a threshing floor, as a garbage dump, or as a pound for stray cattle.[63]

Marc Simmons claims that "by tradition the Spaniard was a town dweller, accustomed to residing in communities welded into a unity by the practical necessity of defense and the common need to produce an adequate food supply." This did not work out ideally in essentially rural New Mexico, however, where no municipality attained the status of *ciudad,* or city, and only Santa Fè, Santa Cruz de la Canada, Albuquerque, and El Paso del Norte became *villas,* or administrative centers. Villas were structured by royal regulations, which specified fortifications, plazas, and a grid system of carefully marked streets. This pattern governed other communities too, according to Victor Westphall:

> *Poblaciones* were loosely grouped ranchos [households adjacent to farms and orchards, also called "houses of the field"], and were sometimes designated as plazas when consolidated for purposes of defense. This designation for a plaza was not universal. A dispersed settlement was frequently termed a plaza, or even a *placita* or *lugar* for smaller areas. At other times such settlements were referred to as *parajes* (encampments) or *puestos* (outposts).[64]

Talpa, Taos Valley, January 1943. FSA photo by John Collier. (LC-USW 3-13788-C.)

Indian communities also had plazas, and J. B. Jackson contrasts the two:

Unlike the Latin-American plaza the Pueblo Indian plaza is not the place where public announcements are made; these are shouted from some roof top. It is not a loitering place: When Pueblo Indian women take the air in the evening they go to one of the upper terraces of the house cluster. [Victor] Mindeleff in fact tells us that the third terrace is always reserved for just such a purpose. The Pueblo Indian plaza never contains a well or spring; it is not the site of markets and fairs. It is not the juncture of several streets or roads as it is with us; it is not a place of traffic. In Latin countries people spend hours watching the plaza activities, but in the Indian pueblo there are no doors or windows on the ground floor to look out of, and even if there were, what would there be to watch? Very little.

Jackson cites Victor Mindeleff's 1891 study of Hopi and Zuni architecture, in which Mindeleff writes that "in earlier times, so the priests relate, people were more devout and the houses were planned with their terraces fronting upon the court so that the women and children and all the people could be close to the masked dancers as they issued from the kiva." According to Jackson:

There is evidently nothing here about everyday uses for the plaza or court; and evidently the practice of enclosing the plaza with houses was thought of not as a precaution against enemies but as an expression of devotion and piety. Thus while the plaza may be ill-defined, topographically speaking, it seems to have a very well defined religious purpose.

We can call it a place where people watch the dances and where the dances take place; a place where there is a permanent shrine or kiva or religious marker of some sort. It is a kind of open air room; identified with the religious activities of the house clusters surrounding it.[65]

The village church or chapel is the equivalent in Hispanic folk culture.

Ecclesiastical Domains

Hispanic churches traditionally were built with the sanctuary at the east end, but this is rare in New Mexico, where they are more likely to face west or south, depending upon the favored scheduling of services. South-facing facades assured "an even lighting at the sanctuary during most of the day." The type of church architecture was formulated in the 1600s and basically persisted with some modification. According to George Kubler:

Coherent, organized architectural form characterizes these churches. The material is the soil itself piled high and thick, pierced by few windows, with a roof line that recalls the deck levels of ships at sea upon the desert. . . . The scale of these buildings dominates the urban profile; where the town buildings hug the landscape in low files, the churches stand forth in a scale that is neither human nor canonical, but military and hieratic. Inside, the treatment of light is theatrical: the nave is cool and dark, but at the sanctuary there prevails an intense daylight, focused and concentrated by vertical skylights installed at the difference of roof level between the nave and the sanctuary.[66]

In the 1700s, private chapels or oratories for the use of families and their servants and public chapels auxiliary to parish churches and open to all worshippers were modeled after domestic architecture, as were most Penitente Brotherhood *moradas*, or meetinghouses, after 1800.[67]

All such structures were important to villagers who were basically small farmers oriented to their fields while living in scattered ranchos and settlements.[68] According to Thomas J. Steele, S.J.:

> The village chapel was the ultimate focus of the people's lives, and the name of the chapel served as a designation of identity; the space of the village received its most profound and universal validation in the name of the saint. Since in contrast to the Indians, the Spanish attribute primacy to time rather than to space, the main function of the saint is to tie the chapel and the village and the people into the liturgical cycle of the Roman Catholic church.

By naming a community for a saint and constructing a chapel, villagers "therefore possessed a sacred name, and in this name the people sensed that they could survive and that they should survive." Steele claims that village membership was primary in a person's identity and that the chapel's saint focused that identity.[69]

Despite orders from Mexico in 1799, 1819, 1822, 1826, and 1833, most people were buried inside churches and chapels before 1833. Outside burial and cemeteries removed from church yards to sites away from town were innovations resisted by New Mexicans, who cited the "better protection inside churches from despoilment of graves by Indian raiders, as well as tradition and the difficulties of digging graves out of doors when the ground was frozen in winter. It is likely that prestige was also a factor, since the rich had until then the privilege of reposing in or close to the sanctuary."[70]

Until the nineteenth century, graves inside or outside the church were not marked, and "it is probable that the idea of grave markers was introduced to Spanish New Mexicans by those put up in memory of early traders who died in the territory, and later on by the simply inscribed slabs erected for American military graves." The first markers were decorative wooden ones, most in cruciform shape.

> In the 1880s, ready-mixed commercial paints, another novelty in New Mexico, were carried in general stores. These began to appear on cemetery markers, with or without carving, while others were merely whitewashed. A crown of thorns, small crosses, and a rose were popular ornaments with the name, dates, and "Pray For Him"(or "Her") lettered below. Towns along the railroad saw family plots of the *ricos* suddenly glorified by cast-iron railings with ornate gates surrounding a marble angel or obelisk, shipped from St. Louis founders or stonecutters. Thus, another style of village grave ornament was launched; the *cuna* (cradle) of wooden pickets (in some northern villages *cerquita,* little wooden fence), spindles, and scroll-sawn finials, usually whitewashed.[71]

Rural New Mexicans also began to copy the stone work of French and Italian stonecutters who came to build the new cathedral at Santa Fe in the 1860s.

In many locales, crosses and piles of stones, called *descansos,* were placed on the route between the church and the cemetery. Lorin W. Brown describes how *descansos* are erected to mark the site of a halt in the funeral procession:

> Some member or friend of the bereaved family has placed a small cross by the roadside to mark the site of the halt, at the base of which each mourner places a small stone.
>
> This cross will have inscribed on it a supplication to the passerby to say a prayer for the rest and peace of the soul of the deceased. If the passerby is heedful he will comply with the request and add his stone to the others supporting the cross. In time several crosses will decorate the same site, for it is the natural resting place, being midway from church to graveyard. The word *descanso* means a short halt or stop for rest, hence the name by which these places are known.[72]

"The graveyard outside the church." FSA photo by John Collier, Las Trampas, January 1943. (LC-USW 3-13692-C.)

Descansos were also placed in remote places, along riverbanks, or beside roads, marking the site of accidental deaths.

One ninety-mile stretch of desert road became legendary for its victims. The Jornada del Muerto, or Route of the Dead Man, which stretched south of Socorro on the Camino Real toward El Paso, was marked by *parajes,* or woodless, waterless, grassless campsites, about a half-day's journey apart. The dead man was German trader Bernardo Gruber, who arrived in New Mexico in 1668 and was soon jailed on heresy and witchcraft charges. According to Marc Simmons:

> Later with the aid of Indian servants, he escaped and fled south toward El Paso. But disaster soon befell him.
>
> A Spanish party on the Camino Real came upon Gruber's remains weeks afterward in the midst of the desert. Apparently he had been killed either by his servants or by Apache raiders. All that could be found was a few bones, gnawed on by animals, and some scraps of velvet clothing.
>
> The unusual episode impressed itself upon the minds of seventeenth century New Mexicans. To commemorate it, they called a nearby *paraje,* El Aleman, which means the German. As a place name, El Aleman survives today. But merely as a siding on the Santa Fe Railroad, which follows the path of the historic Camino Real through the Jornada.[73]

Although no crosses survived in the Jornada del Muerto, their presence along other waysides, atop chapels and churches, on home and church altars, in the popular Holy Week observances of open-air Stations of the Cross, and as symbols of conquest and community in Hispanic plazas across New Mexico establish and sustain a sense of place that is at once liturgical and actual.

(Below). "Marker of an accident on the highway." Note the more traditional cross (fallen) and stones to the left. FSA photo by Russell Lee, Bernalillo County, July 1940. (LC-USF 34-37171-D.)

(Right). Death in her cart. (Private collection.)

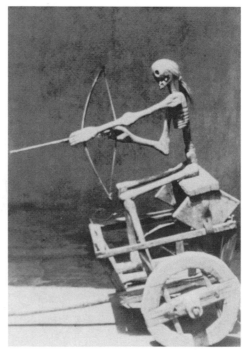

Fences and Post Offices: Anglo Settlement

Sectioned Space

On July 4, 1831, a caravan of traders who had left Independence, Missouri, in mid-May was camped at McNees Crossing (now known as Corrumpa Creek) on the Cimarron Cut-off of the Santa Fe Trail in northeastern New Mexico. Josiah Gregg describes their observance of the first Independence Day ever celebrated in New Mexico:

> Scarce had gray twilight brushed his dusky brow, when our patriotic camp gave lively demonstrations of that joy which plays around the heart of every American on the anniversary of this triumphant day. The roar of our artillery and rifle platoons resounded from every hill, while the rumbling of the drum and the shrill whistle of the fife, imparted a degree of martial interest to the scene which was well calculated to stir the souls of men. There was no limit to the huzzas and enthusiastic ejaculations of our people; and at every new shout the dales around sent forth a gladsome response. This anniversary is always hailed with heart-felt joy by the wayfarer in the remote desert; for here the strifes and intrigues of party-spirit are unknown: nothing intrudes, in these wild solitudes, to mar the harmony of feeling, and almost pious exultation, which every true-hearted American experiences on this great day.[74]

When Gregg and his party saw the land (now in Union County), it was, as many termed it, "a sea of grass." Indian, Spanish, and Anglo buffalo hunters on this "sea" were followed by open range cowmen and then sheepmen, who fenced some of the range and feuded with the cowmen. J. B. Jackson characterizes these post-1900 homesteaders who cut

> the entire sea of grass . . . into sections as if it had frozen and were to be stored away in ice houses. . . . Some of them are still there, monuments to a kind of geometrical folly which long obsessed our land offices. The Homesteaders come—many of them lured from prosperous farms back east, let it be remembered. . . . Their hideous little houses stand out conspicuously, like chessmen among the section-size squares.[75]

Union County's development paralleled that of many eastern and southwestern New Mexico livestock-raising domains outside the areas of longtime Pueblo and Spanish settlement. Open-range ranching held sway until the early 1900s. As elsewhere on the Great Plains, barbed wire of the kind invented by the legendary Illinois farmer Joseph Farwell Glidden in 1873 made enclosure fencing possible in areas devoid of trees and suitable hedging materials. Lula Collins Daudet and Ruth Collins Roberts recall their preacher father's work on the family homestead near Des Moines in the early twentieth century:

> The first improvement Daddy made on the homestead was to build a fence around our 320 acres. He hauled cedar posts from Sierra Grande Mountain and trimmed

them, and stretched four strands of barbed wire around the acreage, stapling the wire to the strong cedar posts. After sixty-two years, these posts are still standing, holding the very same barbed wire, now a collector's item. That fence is a silent monument to Daddy's hard work. The posts have aged with the passing years and are now hard as iron.

That barbed wire fence is still used by the ranchers, who eventually took over all of the homesteads of Lakeview Community—one of the first big land grabs![76]

The Collins's perceptions do not match Walter Prescott Webb's observation that "there is something primitive about the name 'barbed wire'—something suggestive of savagery and lack of refinement." Webb cites a verse from Edwin Ford Piper's *Barbed Wire and Wayfarers:*

> *They say that heaven is a free range land,*
> *Goodbye, goodbye, O fare you well;*
> *But it's barbed wire for the devil's hat band;*
> *And barbed wire blankets down in hell.*

This attitude is echoed in a story from the late 1870s about cattleman Charles Goodnight, who encountered some Taos Indians attempting to return to their pueblo via a different route through the Texas Panhandle after trading with Kiowas in Oklahoma Indian Territory. Their chief asked directions from Goodnight.

"Great Plains homesteads and a sheep barn." FSA photo by Dorothea Lange, vicinity of Claude, June 1938. (LC-USF 34-18270-C.)

For an Indian to put such a question to a white man was unheard of, and Goodnight could not understand the reason for it. "You surely know the way back to Taos," he countered. "Haven't you lived in this country all your life?" To this the chief answered sadly, "Alambre! alambre! alambre! todas partes!—wire! wire! wire! everywhere!" And in this moment Goodnight realized what barbed wire was doing to the Southwest, with new fences which cut up the terrain so that even native tribes of Indians could be confounded.[77]

For Hispanic New Mexicans, too, fences came to symbolize an alien approach to land tenure. The English proverb, "good fences make good neighbors," was transformed in a New Mexican *dicho,* or saying, *"Buen abogado, mal vecino* (A good lawyer makes a bad neighbor)," following the disproportionate influx of lawyers during the territorial period. Thomas J. Steele, S.J., sees these lawyers' legal manipulations of written documents as part of the print-oriented, visually biased Anglo culture.

> Visual emphasis, applied to land ownership, led to the practice of treating a written document as sufficient and necessary. . . . Land can be transferred by mere manipulation of paper. The new owner does not need to go and see if there is anything there, does not need to pull up grass and throw stones and cry "Long live [the president]!" so long as the map and the deed assures him there is a rectangle somewhere on the face of the earth that he has bought.

Steele contends this is manifest in visual art forms as well:

> The New Mexican Spanish art provides its own context of "picture-space" [the Renaissance notion of easel or panel pictures], but the panels are only approximately rectangular; and their land boundaries, though they form a complete enclosure in a way that the Pueblos' own did not, have an analogous way of being approximate, unmathematical, and at times very vague. The Anglo preference in art is for precise rectangularity in framing and for the creation of a self-sufficient "little world" with consistent lineal perspective in control throughout; and their land ownership displays the sort of lineal and mathematical exactness and the kind of literate "page-space" domination through maps and title deeds that comports precisely with their art.[78]

Like the homestead rectangles of Anglo settlement, railroads epitomize precision and linearity. Approximately 3,590,281 acres of New Mexican land were granted to railroads through 1891, nearly three times the 1,270,712 acres of public domain sold to individuals during that period, as Victor Westphall notes. Besides grazing land, railroads acquired right-of-way that was eventually formalized in a law of March 3, 1875, providing "for a 200-foot right-of-way and twenty acres for station grounds every ten miles." Such provisions in time produced what A. W. Conway calls "a peculiarly Western phenomenon"—the railroad town, "which comes into existence to serve a railroad . . . [unlike] the older part of the nation, east of the Mississippi, [where] the railroad is usually built to serve a community."[79]

The so-called "Magic City" of Clovis, originally called Riley Switch, is typical. It was brought into being by the 250-mile Belen cut-off of the Atchison, Topeka &

"Statue [of Lucien B. Maxwell, owner of northeastern Maxwell Land Grant] by a local artist." FSA photo by Russell Lee, Cimarron, August 1939. (LC-USF 34-34041-D.)

Santa Fe Railroad, constructed between 1903 and 1907. Clayton Reed, who homesteaded the quarter section north of Riley Switch, was persuaded to sign the deed over to the Santa Fe Land and Improvement Company by R. C. Reid, who also became

the man entirely responsible for the survey and sale of lots. The entire original townsite was laid out in checkerboard style from First Street north to Seventh Street, and from Thornton Street to Prince. Mr. Reid was also authorized to name the streets. Those running north and south were designated as "streets," while those running north and south [sic: should read "east and west"] were "avenues." With the history of New Mexico in mind, Mr. Reid named the streets after the territorial governors.[80]

On the final Clovis plat, "one full block was set aside for a school, bounded by Axtell, Wallace, Sixth and Seventh Streets, where the Eugene Field School is today. This conforms to "the almost perfect," hypothetical American town, as described by J. B. Jackson. Unlike Hispanic towns, where

the plaza, nine times out of ten, is surrounded by public buildings, . . . almost every American town laid out after (say) 1820 deliberately planted a public building in the center of its square. Sometimes it was a school, sometimes a city hall, more often a courthouse, and it was always approachable from all four sides and always as conspicuous as possible. . . .

Thus the Square ceased to be thought of in XIX Century America as a vacant space; it became a container or (if you prefer) a frame. A frame, so it happened, not merely for the Courthouse, but for all activity of a communal sort. Few esthetic experiments have ever produced such brilliantly practical results. A society which had long since ceased to rally around the individual leader and his residence and which was rapidly tiring of rallying around the meeting house or church all at once found a new symbol: local representative government, or the Courthouse.[81]

Postal Links

Towns not located on the railroad considered the highway the main street, and the development of county and state roads became crucial. May Price Mosley (NMFWP) describes the situation among homesteaders in Lea County, where "not a few of the more ingenious managed to become postmasters, each envisioning the town-to-be

Catron County, April 1940. FSA photo by Russell Lee. (LC-USF 34-35863-D.)

on his particular plot. While the ranchers had received their mail every month or so—by way of the 'first passing'—the homesteaders wanted a post office. Preferably in walking distance!" Mosley touches on a key reason for this orientation:

> Because Texas was home—where one might visit as well as transact business—and because of the heavy almost impassable sands to the west, the early settlers, ranchers and homesteaders alike, made very few trips to their county seat towns, Roswell and Carlsbad. A trip there and back took most of a week. And Santa Fe was practically out of their world![82]

As Margaret W. Reid says in her edited collection of Ruth Kessler Rice's *Letters from New Mexico, 1899–1904:* "When she was sixteen, Ruth Kessler was uprooted from the traditional life she had always known in a conservative, small town in Ohio [Troy] to go to the territory of New Mexico, to Roswell which had only acquired a railroad in 1894. . . . As an outlet for her grief at leaving Troy, Ruth turned almost immediately to letter writing."[83]

The United States Post office at Santa Fe was authorized on October 1, 1849, and 145 post offices were established through 1878. In the five years after the coming of the railroad in 1879, 304 were authorized. Another burst came in the first decade of the twentieth century, when 474 were established between 1900 and 1909.[84]

During territorial and statehood periods, 1,572 New Mexico post offices received federal authorization, thereby putting "the 'town' on the map, since an office was typically the lowest form of governmental organization and required the

Federal government to 'recognize' an official placename."[85] Tucumcari, for example, was briefly called Six-Shooter Siding, but its post office was first named Douglas in 1901, then changed to Tucumcari in 1902. The official placename supposedly came from "a folk tale credited to Geronimo . . . an Apache Indian maid named Kari had a sweetheart, Tocom, who was slain by Tonapon, a rival. After the death of Tocom, Kari is said to have killed Tonapon and then taken her own life. Whereupon, Wautonamoah, her father, stabbed himself, crying 'Tocom! Kari'" More likely, however, is a derivation from the Comanche word *tukamukaru,* "to lie in wait for someone or something to approach," according to Oklahoma linguist Elliott Canonge, whose Comanche informant Felix Kowena said that Tucumcari Mountain "was frequently used as a lookout by Comanche war parties." [86] In any case, according to A. W. Conway, Tucumcari represents the changing roads and rectangles of Anglo New Mexico:

> Tucumcari, New Mexico, is in many respects a typical railroad town. . . . In this kind of town, the "wrong side of the tracks" has a very definite meaning, for it is north of the tracks that the foreign workers on the roadbeds have settled, near the round-house and the yards.
>
> When all freight came and went by rail, the best location for a business was near the station and the freight yards; and there you will still find the stockyards, the warehouses, the wholesale fuel and feed and lumber companies; and "downtown" Tucumcari, like the downtown of any railroad community is clustered about the streets leading to the station.
>
> But like many other Western towns, Tucumcari has recently discovered the importance of the tourist and the highway. A highway improvement project has brought into existence in a matter of two or three years a whole new set of enterprises—tourist courts, drive-in restaurants, filling stations, used car lots—on what was formerly an unpaved back street. And near this new business center there is developing a new residential section, separate and distinct from the old one. The rise of a New Town to rival and perhaps eclipse the Old Town, even though both are part of the same municipality, has long been characteristic of the Southwest.[87]

Native American, Hispanic, and Anglo New Mexicans centered and bounded their territory differently. Raiders often violated these boundaries, which were crossed routinely by herders, hunters, traders, and miners. Horses, wheeled vehicles, roads, and railways facilitated this movement between center and periphery.

Herding

In January 1598, Don Juan de Oñate and his colonizing expedition started north to New Mexico. In his 1610 epic, *History of New Mexico,* Gaspar Pérez de Villagrá describes the embarkation as follows, in Gilberto Espinosa's translation:

> The stores and ammunition were loaded into eighty wagons which were formed in a long line. When all was in readiness, the march began amid a deafening screeching of the cart wheels and the applause of all. It was a noble sight indeed

to see this caravan go forth. The wagons led the way, and in the wheel tracks they left across the plain followed the oxen, of which there were a great number; then the goats, sheep, lambs, mares, mules, and last a great herd of horses.

The expedition marched "until we reached the banks of a mighty river whose swift waters teemed with fish" and which they called "Río de las Conchas," (now Rio Conchos, which flows northward and northeastward in eastern Chihuahua, entering the Rio Grande opposite Presidio, Texas), "because of the many and beautiful shells we found along its banks."[88]

At the river, Oñate performed one of his first acts of heroism as he shepherded his people and their livestock:

> Our first care was to find a place where the army could safely ford the stream with our wagons and baggage. The waters were so swift and the soundings showed such a depth that there were none who would dare attempt its passage. Many were for not attempting it, fearful lest they be engulfed in its turbulent waters and perish.
>
> Our general then, like Julius Caesar who it is said rode and tamed the wildest steeds with neither bit nor rein, leaped upon a prancing charger, and, knowing that no words can be as eloquent or effective as a personal example, rode before the men and cried: "Come, noble soldiers, knights of Christ, here is presented the first opportunity for you to show your mettle and courage and to prove that you are deserving of the glories in store for you."
>
> So saying, he turned his horse toward the rushing waters and plunged into the roaring waves. Guiding his steed to the opposite bank, he turned rein and once more braved the angry waters, returning to his men.

His men followed Oñate's example and managed to get the cattle and wagons across. However,

> when the sheep were being taken across, it soon became evident that, because of the weight of their wool which bore them down as soon as it was soaked with water, they were unable to swim across. The general gave orders that a bridge be built. This order caused great wonder, for we all doubted that this mighty river could be spanned with a substantial bridge with our limited resources.
>
> Oñate did not hesitate. first, he ordered that two dozen of the largest cart wheels be brought. These he securely anchored to rafts, two across, the entire width of the river. He then ordered that tall trees which grew along the river banks be cut and trimmed, and taking the longest and strongest branches, we laid these lengthwise and crosswise over the cart wheels, covering them with branches, bark, and earth.
>
> When the bridge was completed it was secure and strong. It easily supported the weight of the remaining animals and also of the remaining baggage which we carted across the bridge.[89]

Sheep

Like Coronado and other conquistadors before him, Oñate had brought sheep for wool and for food. Missionaries developed sheep husbandry in New Mexico. They trained Indians "to care for the sheep, to shear their wool and to make it into cloth. The Indians learned well. The closest examples of the *churros* [Spanish lowlands sheep] that originally came into New Mexico can be seen even today in some Navajo flocks."[90]

Contemporary ethnographers have commented on the importance of sheep to the Navajo way of life. In the 1960s, James F. Downs studied Navajos from what he called the Nez Ch'ii community:

> Sheep dominate the livestock economics of Nez Ch'ii and the Navajo reservation as a whole. The social and cultural life of a family owning even four or five sheep is largely determined by this ownership. In part this is owing to cultural patterns built around sheep keeping as a way of life and supporting the patterns of sheep keeping as the "right" way to live. Also, the possession of even a few sheep requires certain activities that are only intensified if the number of sheep is increased. Sheep keeping also requires herding and tending every day, so that the activities of man are dominated by the needs of the herd. When the herd can provide man with his needs, the system remains in balance. In recent years, income from livestock cannot meet the needs of the Navajo, a situation that produces social and psychological tensions and sets the stage for major cultural changes.

"Native art on adobe wall." FSA photo by Russell Lee, Amalia, July 1940. (LC-USF 34-37058-D.)

Mesa near El Cerrito, April 1941. Bureau of Agricultural Economics photo by Irving Rusinow. (Neg. No. 83-G-37861, National Archives.)

Water requirements for mid-day penning mean that the sheep must be corralled within a five-mile radius of the water source. Downs attributes the pattern of Navajo open range and close control herding of sheep to "a history of livestock keeping marked by raiding and counter-raiding, or perhaps because of the not inconsiderable fear most Navajo have of the dark, sheep are penned each night."[91]

Fray Angelico Chavez calls Spanish New Mexico "My Penitente Land," one where "the prevailing way of life was . . . *pastoral,* not agricultural, and there is a marked difference between the two which sets the shepherd or stockman distinctly apart from the farmer or merchant." In its pastoral and spiritual themes, New Mexico is like the Holy Land and Spain. "For Palestine, Castile, and Hispanic New Mexico—grazing lands all and most alike in their physical aspects—likewise share a distinctive underlying human mystique born of that very type of arid landscape. They all differ basically from the largely agrarian and industrial Western world that we know, in both their economic and their religious outlook." The Penitente Brotherhood exemplifies this religious outlook in Chavez's "reflections."[92]

Reyes N. Martínez describes the life of the often mystical, frequently Penitente, *pastor,* who tended his flocks away from settled communities and who governed his life by the seasons, the sheep, and the liturgical cycle, especially the *Pastores* plays at Christmas and the Holy Week retreat of the Penitente Brothers. Martínez opens his 1940 description of "A Sheepherd at Work in Taos County, New Mexico" with a sense of place:

It was the first week in May of the year 1896, when the writer, while yet a small boy, was taken by his father to "Las Cuchillas," the country immediately west of Tres Piedras, in Taos County, to help him lamb his sheep. . . .

In those days, the public domain was used as free range for grazing sheep. No restrictions, as those now imposed by Forest Service regulations, were then in force, although by common agreement among themselves, each owner of a flock of sheep reserved a certain section of the range for lambing. These lambing places came to be known, as time passed, by the name of the owner of the sheep that were first lambed there, and those names serve to designate the places to the present day. . . .

In this section of the country the sheepherder of Taos County plies his vocation, and a vocation it is, because a great part of the adult male population of Taos County chose or adopted, since many years past, sheep-herding as their calling or main occupation, in which kind of work they become very proficient, so much so, that even to this day, preference is shown by the big sheep-raisers of the states of Colorado and Wyoming for men from Taos County, to tend their sheep. (In this connection, a story is told of a man who came to love the work so much, that he spent several years in succession, tending sheep, without ever visiting a human settlement in all that length of time. His whole interest and attention so centered in his job, that it became part of his very existence; and it is said, that when he returned to his native village, his gait was indicative of the mode of walking of a sheep, straight forward, head lowered, and looking only at the ground and some people used to say that when walking alone, he would even bleat, in an undertone, like a sheep.)[93]

Drawing in part on her father's memories, Fabiola Cabeza de Baca describes sheep ranching and herding on the Ceja and Llano Estacado after 1840.

Shearing the sheep was done in the summer and there were professional shearers who went from camp to camp each year. This was a bright spot in the life of the herders, for then they had a touch of the outside world. Among the shearers and herders there were always musicians and poets, and I heard Papa tell of pleasant evenings spent singing and storytelling, and of *corridos* composed to relate events which had taken place. These poets and singers were like the troubadours of old. The *corridos* dealt with the life of the people in the communities and ranches; they told of unrequited love, of death, of tragedies and events such as one reads about in the newspapers today.

The sheepherder watched his flock by day, traveling many miles while the sheep grazed on the range. As his flock pastured, he sat on a rock or on his coat; he whittled some object or composed songs or poetry until it was time to move the flock to water or better pasture. Many of the *corridos* are an inheritance from the unlettered sheepherder. At night he moved his flock to camp, a solitary tent where he prepared his food and where he slept. If there were several camps close to each other, the herders gathered at one tent for companionship.[94]

J. D. Robb claims that, "In fact some of the finest folk melodies of New Mexico are shepherds' songs":

As New Mexico has been my home base for almost 30 years, most of my examples come from this region. A surprisingly large percentage of the men who have sung for me over the years have been sheep herders for at least a portion of their lives. Among these were (or are) the late Prospero Baca, of Bernalillo, New Mexico, who herded sheep in Utah, Colorado and Wyoming; David Frescas, of Taos, New Mexico, in Colorado; Garcelon Pacheco, of Cordova, New Mexico, in Wyoming; Salomon Ruiz, of Albuquerque, near Bluewater in New Mexico; Samuel Lavadie who told me he had herded sheep in Colfax County, New Mexico, in 1898; and Napoleon Trujillo of Bernalillo and Albuquerque, New Mexico, who had herded near Cabezon and Cuba, New Mexico, and Flagstaff and Wickenburg, Arizona.[95]

Clyde Smith, "born in 1899 on a homestead at Battleship Rock in Jemez Canyon (also known as Cañon de San Diego)," worked for Baca Location owners Fredrico and Mariano Otero in 1917 and 1918. In 1979 and 1980 interviews, Smith recalled that "for evening recreation, guitars, harmonicas and a deck of cards were necessities. Story and joke telling also frequently provided amusement around the campfires." *Pastores* also "devoted leisure hours to various crafts: braiding horsehair or leather reatas [ropes] and headstalls, making rawhide moccasins called *teguas* (although store-bought work shoes or boots eventually replaced this traditional footwear), and carving on the bark of aspen trees."[96]

In the 1960s, James B. DeKorne photographed the vanishing shepherds' *Aspen Art in the New Mexico Highlands,* preserving images of hand prints, people, horses, cattle, deer, owls, pumas, crosses, and other figures carved on aspen trees in northern New Mexico since at least 1898. Some carvings were *refranes,* or sayings, in Spanish and sometimes even English. Images of dogs were also common, and DeKorne cites Edward Norris Wentworth's *America's Sheep Trails* for some legend texts:

> One (sheep owner) tells of trailing three to four hundred young rams over a four-day route and losing five head the first day. One of his dogs was also missing and on delivering the band he returned to look for the strays. A day's drive behind the flock he found the dog, bringing the five rams, and farther back he found where the dog had bedded them down on the three different nights of the journey. Other stories are told of the sagacity of dogs in saving sheep in storms, of their ability to sort dry ewes from ewes with lambs, or their rescue of flocks trapped by forest or prairie fires, and of their forcing sheep to water holes when thirst madness made the flock utterly uncontrollable by man alone.[97]

Pastores herding their flock of some two thousand head, afoot, with the help of dogs, were part of a complex organization in Spanish sheep ranching. According to Edward N. Wentworth:

> A ranch staff included a *majordomo,* with suitable numbers of *caporals, vaqueros* and *pastores.* The *majordomo* had charge of all routine activities, going the rounds of the sheep camps, checking the condition of the flocks, discharging incompetent herders, hiring new ones, and overseeing the monthly accounts and reports of those under him. Each *caporal* supervised a group of three *vaqueros* and nine *pastores.*

A *caporal* spent most of his time in the saddle, except when preparing accounts or reports. He apportioned range for the different bands, directed or helped the search for lost, strayed or stolen sheep, inspected for disease and helped to treat it, and carried out all other routine ranch matters. Each *vaquero* oversaw three *pastores* or herders. He was required to keep constant watch and supervision over the flocks and was somewhat higher paid than the *pastore*.[98]

Wentworth identifies the names of Spanish families with large sheep holdings in the nineteenth century and the leadership in the New Mexico Wool Growers Association in the twentieth century as Armijo, Baca, Delgado, Jaramillo, Leyba, Luna, Otero, Pino, Perea, Romero, Sandoval, Santistevan, Vigil, Yrisarri, Chaves, Gallegos, Gonzales, Martínez, and Ortiz.

In 1980, Mariano Chavez, whose family had made a living from sheep in northeastern New Mexico since 1898, was interviewed at the Museum of New Mexico. Diana Ortega DeSantis notes that: "Only vestiges now remain of the bins and corrals where Harding County's shepherds once tended their sheep. Other place names have replaced the designations such as *Tequesquite, Aguaje* (the name for the Chavez family ranch), and other spots prominent during the sheepherding era." She summarizes the territorial period:

"Maclovia Lopez, wife of the majordomo (mayor), spinning wool by the light of the fire. The family has ten sheep and they spin the wool for blankets, which are woven for them in Cordova." FSA photo by John Collier, Las Trampas, January 1943. (LC-USW 3-17813-E.)

Although many sheep were lost to Indian raids in the mid-nineteenth century, the sheep population had increased rapidly by the 1880s. The railroad, instead of long-distance sheep drives, provided a new, more efficient outlet for wool and sheep. Mariano Chavez recalls placing sheep on the train at Springer for shipping to Kansas.

American ingenuity resulted in crossbreeding of the short-haired churros with the longer haired *merinos,* a development that also increased wool production. . . .

New Mexico's sheep industry experienced a steady decline after the beginning of the twentieth century. With the coming of the railroads, the cattle industry grew and began to compete with the sheep industry. The depletion of pasture lands led to legislation unfavorable to profitable sheepherding: use of water holes and springs was limited, and fencing heralded the final phase of a long tradition.[99]

Cattle

Railroads and fences also marked the end of the long cattle drives and the great cattle trails. According to Jack Thorp's 1936 NMFWP manuscript on "The New Mexico Cattle Industry":

> The Pecos country, when it was open range, probably was the greatest cow-producer and started out more trail herds than any other range district in the west. It was not unusual for from thirty to forty chuck-wagons to be working at one time. From the mountains on the west, the plains country on the east, and on the Pecos River proper, a trail herd of cattle was made up and started out almost daily from some point along the river during the spring and summer work. These works, drives, or roundups starting some hundred miles north of Pecos City, Texas, usually broke up or ended either at Ft. Sumner or Anton Chico, New Mexico, where the last trail herd was formed and different bunches of cattle, which had been held on the drive, were started for their home range.
>
> During these days Roswell and Eddy—or as it is now known, Carlsbad—were the principal points for the cow men, and wild and wooly they were. A large volume could be written covering the lurid side of the life one saw on the Pecos River forty years ago. The river was known by many as the river of sin, for when a man was killed in its vicinity he sometimes was weighted down and his body sunk in the stream. Hence the saying: "to Pecos him," or "he was Pecosed."[100]

In 1937, George Anderson told Vernon Smithson (NMFWP) about the "last great roundup of the Llano Estacado." Held in the spring of 1898 "in the country surrounding the present Tatum, New Mexico,"

> this roundup . . . covered some four or five hundred sections . . . on the old LFD range and lasted for forty days. All of the surrounding ranches were represented—the DZ's, the 9R's, and other, lesser ranchers. Everyone knew when the roundup was to be held, and they were arranged so that the men could go from one roundup to another and gather all the cattle that belonged to the ranch that they were representing. Roundups usually began in the southern part of the region and went north, as all the cattle drifted south during the winter months.

In the roundup of 1898 there were 125 men, and their horses totaled 2,700. A cowboy couldn't get by with less than 12 or 14 horses and the more one had the better. Horses were ridden hard in the early days and after a day's hard work a horse needed three or four days' rest. Riders frequently changed horses four or five times daily.

Anderson told Smithson that "there were cattle in every direction as far as you could see" and that "some size of the herd might be judged from the fact that they branded 1,000 head of strays that spring."[101]

Lead steers were an integral part of the trail and its lore. Colonel Jack Potter (1864–1950) of Clayton wrote extensively of his trail days. He begins a 1948 piece as follows:

> I have talked and written about lead steers so much that some of my old cow range amigos call me Lead Steer Potter. They claim that when I get to heaven I'll like as not squat down on my hunkers and explain to old St. Peter that I might never have made it up that trail either if there hadn't been a good lead steer in the herd to guide me to water on some of the dry drives. My wife don't even deny my story that it was a lead steer that first called my attention to what a purty little lady on horseback she was!
>
> Well, that's all right with me. I moved a good many longhorns over a heap of cattle trails, marked and unmarked, in my younger days, and there were mighty few times when the sense and sagacity of some old high-hipped steer out in the lead didn't help me to get the job done. I've had some purty fair cowhands poke fun at me for claiming that a man can savvy what a smart lead steer wants to tell him just as plain as if it was said in words. But a good many of them, like this hombre I'll call Ol' Trouble Maker, have finally had to acknowledge the truth. Old Charlie Goodnight, whose favorite lead steer, Old Blue, became famous all over the West, always agreed with me that a longhorn steer could be smarter than a man in natural knowledge.[102]

Ed Popejoy of Raton told Kenneth Fordyce (NMFWP) in 1937 about "a remarkable white steer":

> 'Lige Johnson lived at Johnson Park almost up to the Colorado–New Mexico state line back in the days when cattlemen had to drive the herds which they wanted to sell in to Dodge City, Kansas. New Mexico was an excellent place to fatten steers and many seasons 'Lige drove his saleable cattle through.
>
> 'Lige Johnson had a white steer that developed quite a reputation as a leader. When the drive to Dodge was ready to start, this white steer was placed in the lead and the steer would remain there leading the cattle all the way. It made the driving exceptionally easy for the "punchers," for the white steer could and did lead without error.
>
> The most remarkable part of the white steer's performance was that when the cattle were delivered in Dodge, the white steer was turned loose and would return to the ranch, arriving there almost as promptly as the drivers. The white steer led the herd through three different years.[103]

In the early 1950s, Lou Blachly asked octogenarian Henry Brock how an experienced cowhand recognized signs of a good lead steer. Brock replied:

> You can see that every one of 'em's awful alert. He's real alert and he's a big, husky, strong traveler, you know, and they just . . . they form themselves just like men would form in an organization and pick out leaders. These really though get theirs by force, you know; they hook aside any other common steer that come along. But they're right there. I've rode along a herd that was just gettin' strung out in the mornings, you know, and just after daylight sometimes I'd go along with 'em for bits . . . I remember one herd that I had one time I had a big . . . buckskin longhorn in there, you know, but his feet got a little sore and one morning I was away up toward the lead and I happened to notice him comin' in through this herd. He was just a-hikin' it as fast as he could to catch up with the lead. He was one of the pointers but his feet was sore. Now . . . these other steers, longhorns and likeathat, got in his road he just hooked him to one side. He didn't go around any of 'em, he just pushed 'em, hooked 'em out of his way, and he was a-makin' it up there to get in his place in the pointers. Now he'd been bedded down early, I judged he'd bedded down way back, his feet was sore, and the main herd moved on and he just laid there. . . . Well sir, I just, I rode along with him just to see how he acted, you know. He was doin' his best. He had to walk a little faster than ever and sorefooted to overtake the rest of 'em, right up through the middle of 'em. . . . Oh, he overtook 'em and stayed with 'em.

Leaders were also important during the day's rest stops:

> You just halt the leaders and that would check everything, you know, and just let 'em stand a bit. Some would sit down, because the walking had been pretty strong, you know, and if there'd be too hot a time for 'em to want to graze because cattle don't want to graze in the heat, you know, they'd rather graze in the forenoon and morning. . . . The leaders . . . will show that they want to graze, you know. Well, you just turn 'em off the road and be sure if there's any breeze a-blowing you want to turn 'em to the breeze, you know, no animal, wild animals and likeathat, will graze from the wind, you know, with the wind, none of 'em. You can't run any wild animal from the wind.

Brock further notes that when "you're driving a herd or holding a bunch of cattle they'll begin drifting just as soon as the rain begins hittin 'em and you can't keep 'em from moving, you know, they'll just push ya along if you don't get out of the road, you know, till they get wet and then after that they'll stand still."[104]

Brock began working for the Diamond A Ranch in southwestern New Mexico and northern Old Mexico in 1890, became foreman in 1904, and moved to Grant County in 1907. Brock describes the Diamond A as one of the largest ranches in the West, a spread of over four million acres, 120 miles by 60 miles. At its peak the Diamond A ran more than fifty thousand cattle, with as many as forty hands working the rangeland, the line camps, and the main headquarters.

In sixteen interviews extending over three years, Brock gave Lou Blachly detailed descriptions of herding, rounding up, and driving cattle. Crossing the international border with herds of cows was virtually routine. One year Brock rode to a Mexican valley where "they built a pasture as big as, oh, some countries . . . well, bigger than Rhode Island. . . . And they got four thousand that time when we went down and I want to tell ya that when I saw them four thousand spread out to graze my knees got weak."

I was responsible for . . . you know, the idea of passin' them through, checkin' 'em against both governments, you know, and keepin' down the ad valorem duty on 'em, you know, and they went by. . . . All we could do was have the herd way over here and men ride in and cut off what they could—fifty, seventy-five, or a hundred and start 'em up. And I'd be standing, say, over on this side and away out over there a ways would be the government man, you know, and these cattle passed through and there was all other government officials, soldiers, Mexican soldiers, and one thing and another. But I had to pass them through and check out so many two-year-olds when I didn't have any; so many staggy [old] steers when I didn't take them; and one thing and another to keep down the evaluation, you see.[105]

Brock marveled at the longhorns he frequently brought up from Mexico:

Some of 'em their horns was so long that you get 'em up to the car door and go up the chute they'd have to get their heads up so that their horns were above the top of the chute and slide along and get 'em to the door and if they could turn their head sideways so one horn could go in then they could get in. And some of 'em we couldn't do that and we'd just take an ax . . . put a rope on him and draw his head right tight to the fence and chop one horn off with an ax. . . .

Well, I don't think I ever saw any horns wider than six feet but I've heard of 'em as bein' nine feet and I've had pictures sent to me with longhorns on 'em saying they're nine and ten feet but I never saw any of that. Six feet makes you sit up and take notice when you see one six foot long. I've seen horns on those steers that I brought from Mexico—I brought thousands of 'em and always tried to bring two thousand at a time, you see—and they was a sight to see when they was on the trail, you know, and watching along. You'd ride along and watch 'em go by with the horns, some of 'em were dangerous to look at, they were hooked and bowed, kill a horse the first rip.[106]

Milling and stampeding cattle are powerful images in Brock's conversation. To stop the herd's movement, point riders would circle the leaders into the herd.

He'd let 'em run in a circle or he'd force 'em to run in a circle. . . . They keep a-turnin' from you, you know, all the time while they're running. They come around and these leaders overtake the drags, the rear end, you know. . . .

Then they begin coming in, running in a circle there, just around and around until they get packed in that you could toss your hat in there and it would never touch the ground till . . . that mill breaks. . . . And they'll groan and moan and their horns are all up above, stuck up above. If one gets his horns like that down in under the others he's tramped to death, you know. He can't get his head up, you know, and stumbles in a ditch or somethin' they run over, he's gone. . . .

Oh! You could take two thousand head and you'd swear that you'd lost half of 'em, that they wasn't there when they're in a mill, you know, they can just get so packed together. They're just right packed right like sardines and moan and groan and those on the outside are just a-running at full tilt while those in the center, you know, just turn around and around like a hub on a wheel. Now they can make some noise where they're running.

According to Brock, cowboys also made noise to turn the herd and start the milling. The cowboy

hollers, he really hollers. If it's in the nighttime . . . he calls and he hollers at these cattle so that the other fellers know where he's at and that he has the lead, you see. He does that just as soon as these [mills] start if he's going to take the lead. . . . They understand one another, these cowpunchers, and the steers understand them too.[107]

If the herd leaders were frightened, a stampede could occur instantly, Brock said:

You betcha! It's marvelous to see! Just be goin' along, you know, and give those leaders a fright, something you know does, and that there acts just like an electric current. It's right down that line instantly. . . .

Sometimes a fella's horse that he's riding on night guard, and he's goin' along and he'll shake himself and shake the saddle. Well, . . . now that'll start 'em, start nearly any herd, you know, that's really touchy. Something like that and men don't want to be around. That's why I never wanted the men to be close to 'em when they was riding around. . . .

Cattle drive through Roswell. (MNM Neg. No. 14797. Historical Society of New Mexico Collections in Museum of New Mexico.)

[It takes] just about the tick of a watch. They're on their feet right now. They move more like electricity than anything I ever saw. I've always been puzzled. Here's another peculiarity about 'em, and I've talked to lots of old trail men, cattlemen, and nobody knows why. In the summertime you'll be coming along and have a herd and it's bedded down, everything is quiet. You can hear the owls, little owls, prairie owls, and hear coyotes howl, and even katydids and insects like that, and everything seemed like peace in the world and all at once there'll be just like the world stops. That will all stop and right then when cowboys know anything, they know their business, they begin movin' back just right now because that bunch of cattle is gonna run, that herd's gonna run. It may not be bad and it may be, but they're going to run and you've got to mill 'em, move 'em back again if you can.

But what starts 'em . . . and why [do] they run invariably? And even gentle herds? . . . I've asked lots of men and some of 'em I thought might know somethin' . . . about the peculiarity, that phenomenon. Everything stops. There won't be a breath of air, there won't be a sound, while a bit before that you could hear all kinds of sounds, and the cattle instantly are just as quiet themselves, just at that same time, and you can bet they're gonna run and they will, they'll jump and run every time and nobody knows why. And nobody knows why all these sounds stop, coyotes, owls, katydids, anything that could squawk and make a noise at night, you know, all goin' along just nicely and all at once it just stops and right then cowboys begin movin' back away from that herd because it's a-goin' to run.[108]

Hunting

In 1879, a large wooden cross stood in the south plaza of Zia Pueblo. According to Leslie A. White:

This cross marks the spot and commemorates the occasion of the first baptism of pueblo Indians into the Christian faith, according to one informant. There are two stones in the south plaza. The western one . . . is called mokaitc, mountain lion; it represents all the animals of the six directions; they protect the pueblo against disease. The other stone . . . is called aiwa'na. It stands for the twin war gods, Masewi and Oyoyewi, and their eight helpers. They protect the village against witches and disease.[109]

Mountain Lion was the focus of various hunting rituals, as E. Adamson Hoebel notes:

The Hunters' Society (shayek) traditionally performed hunting rituals and supervised communal hunts to obtain deer and rabbit meat for the cacique's storehouse. Early in the twentieth century, its leader named young men to serve as herders for the Pueblo horses. He also supervised the communal horse corral. These activities have dropped into disuse and the society was nearly defunct, if not actually extinct, in 1978.[110]

Hunters from Cochiti visited a shrine north of their pueblo in what is now Bandelier National Monument. Governor L. Bradford Prince describes his nineteenth-century visit to this sanctuary of "the Two Great Stone Lions" as reminiscent of "the weird druidical remains of ancient Britain, at Stonehenge, Callernish and Stennis."

> The circle is eighteen feet in diameter on the inside, and the [stone] wall was about three feet in thickness. The entrance, which is on the southeast, is through a passage way twenty feet in length between walls similar to those of the circle. . . . The easterly half of the circle is vacant, but in the other, facing directly toward the rising sun, and with their heads just reaching the center line, are the Two Great Stone Lions. . . .
>
> The body of each lion is thirty-eight inches in length, and the broad flat tails, which stretch straight back, reach thirty-two inches more, making almost six feet in all. Each is about two and a half feet wide, with tails eight inches wide; and the distance between them is about one foot. . . . Until a few years since, these images were in perfect preservation. My guide said that he remembered them as they were fourteen or fifteen years before, and they were then entirely uninjured. But since that time, ignorant herdsmen, tending flocks in the vicinity, have often made this enclosure a resting place at night.

In 1880, Bandelier noted that hunters streaked these "pumas" with red *almagre* to assure themselves good eyesight, strength and agility, since "the puma is the best hunter of the animal kingdom in the Sierra." Charles H. Lange reports that between 1946 and 1953, "some older hunters [still took] the extra precaution of passing by the shrine of the Stone Lions, Potrero de las Vacas . . . where they sprinkle red ochre (*almagre,* or ya'katshe) on the eyes of the lions, thereby increasing their own visual powers and general good luck. (At present a special red ochre is obtained from the Hopi at a dollar per teaspoonful."[111]

Sam D. Gill emphasizes that "when considering Native American hunting practices, it is most important to understand that hunting is not an economic and occupational activity with religious overtones or with religious elements; hunting is first and foremost a religious activity based on a spiritual view of reality and of the relationship between humans and animals. . . . The hunt, the kill, the dressing of the carcass, the distribution of the meat, and the disposal of the bones usually follow a carefully prescribed and often ritual procedure."[112] Gary Witherspoon notes:

> According to Navajo cultural concepts each being in the world has the right to live, to eat, and to act for itself. These rights to life and freedom extend to plants and animals, as well as to human beings. Only real and immediate human need justifies the killing of an animal or the cutting down of a tree. On such occasions a prayer should be said to the plant or animal explaining one's need and asking for the pardon and indulgence of the soul of the animal or plant.

Among the Jicarilla Apache:

> The hunting of large game animals was the duty of the men. Training for this role began in childhood, when the use of a bow and arrow was first demonstrated by the grandfather. A young boy was taught the use of proper whistles to attract birds

and animals, the various trapping methods, and to recognize the animals and learn their habits. When the boy was proficient as a marksman, he was taken on his first big hunt in the company of experienced hunters. This was usually around the age of 12. During the first hunt, if the boy made a kill, this was the occasion to initiate him into the fraternity of hunters. He began learning all the elaborate and complex rules and rituals necessary to become a respected and lucky hunter. It was believed that each animal had its own habits and mystique, and it was imperative that they be respected. Even the wives and families had to observe strict rules of behavior while their men were out hunting.[113]

Most Southwest tribes hunted buffalo. Hunters from Santa Clara Pueblo went on buffalo hunts once a year.

Lengthy buffalo hunts occurred in the fall, when the animal was said to be in its prime. The Hunters' Society head or a war captain would lead a hunting party of 6 to 10 men, frequently augmented by Spanish-Americans and men from neighboring Pueblos, to the plains, where bands of Kiowa and Comanche might join the party. Hunters on horseback would ride close to the animal and shoot with bow and arrow, or, more rarely, with a lance. Meat was jerked, packed in skin sacks, and carried back to the villages in carts or on horseback.[114]

Hispanic buffalo hunters, known as *ciboleros,* scoured the plains of eastern New Mexico and western Texas in search of the game that would provide food to sustain their people through the long winters and to obtain valuable byproducts for exchange in the markets of Chihuahua. *Ciboleros* dressed distinctively, "in homemade leather shirts and short leather pants that just covered the knees. They were shod with *teguas,* the hard-soled hide moccasins characteristic of the New Mexican settlements. And on their heads they wore a curious pointed hat of leather adorned with a gracefully curving feather."[115]

Hunting parties, led by elected leaders who were assisted by *agregados,* or skinners, were highly organized, and *ciboleros,* like Native American hunters, ritualized their activities. As a child, Fabiola Cabeza de Baca listened to buffalo hunting stories told by former *agregado* El Cuate, cook on her father's Las Vegas area ranch. He remembered: "The hunters formed a group before dashing into the herd, bowed their heads in prayer and invoked Santiago, the patron saint of Spain, to help them and guide them in the hunt. After making the sign of the cross, into the herd they rode, jabbing their lances inside the left ribs of choice fat animals, directly into the heart. A run, or *corrida,* usually would be three miles, during which each hunter killed from fifteen to twenty-five animals."[116]

In 1936, Mary A. Fulgenzi interviewed former *cibolero* Don Julio Hurtado, "a 90-year-old native of San Miguel del Bado," who remembered when "there were so many of those shaggy black animals that the mountains and the plains looked black."

When a buffalo hunt was organized, about 50 or 60 men, *ciboleros,* came together from the different districts and elected a leader, or *commandante,* whom they obeyed without question. As soon as the men spotted a herd, the *commandante* called the *ciboleros* together and had them all recite *un credo,* the Apostle's Creed.

"Pueblo Indian, with throwing stick, ready for a rabbit hunt." From George Wharton James, *New Mexico: The Land of Delight Makers* (Boston: Page Company, 1920), facing p. 98.

Following that, he gave the signal to charge, exclaiming, "Ave, María Purísima" (Hail, Mary, Most Pure). The men then charged the buffalo on horseback. The horse had to have mettle and spirit, for if it did not it feared the buffaloes and would not charge. Don Julio told of one horse which stood on its hind legs and whistled through its nose, refusing to obey the spear, the bit, or the whip.

The only weapon used in the hunt was the *lanza,* a short lance, which had to be used with speed and dexterity. Despite all precautions some hunters were hurt. Don Julio was wounded once in the leg by a buffalo that charged him with its horns. Blood poisoning set in but an Indian gave him a simple remedy which brought immediate cure. The Indian told him to bake a cactus plant, *nopal,* which was then placed on the wound. It drew out the poison and the man's life was saved.

Although buffalo hunting was a dangerous sport, few *ciboleros* were killed while hunting. Don Julio, in the many hunts in which he took part, remembers only one man being killed, and he was not killed by a buffalo. His horse stumbled and he fell, stabbing himself with his own *lanza.*[117]

Ciboleros figured in song and story. Genevieve Chapin of Union County (NMFWP) submitted an unidentified folktale about Tomacito, a native "Tom Thumb . . . diminutive in size, but great in achievement and endearing in kindness," who

hated to be told he could not do all the things other men did. After insisting on being allowed to go with the rest of the men of the village on a buffalo hunt, he was allowed to accompany them, much against their will and better judgment. With his spear he attacked a huge buffalo as high up on one front ankle as he could reach. The creature swallowed him whole, thinking a bee had stung him. Terribly alarmed at first, he at last became reconciled to his plight after finding that he could have fresh buffalo liver for dinner every day. He also wove for himself a new serape, using a single thread for warp and woof.

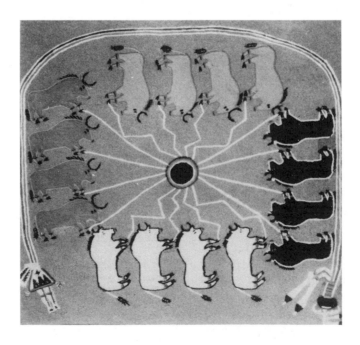

"Buffalo sandpainting, . . . one of the exhibits in the Hall of Ethnology in the State Museum of Santa Fe," 1942. From Navajo Shooting Chant. (MNM Neg. No. 36415.)

When the next season came the buffalo hunters again went out on the hunt, saddened by the absence of the merry little fellow who had accompanied them the previous year and whom they could never find though they searched every coyote and badger hole in the vicinity. What was their surprise, on cutting up for meat one of the huge creatures they had killed, to hear an angry little voice expostulating with them for ruining his house and spoiling his living! Great was the rejoicing in the village on his return and, at the feast they gave to celebrate the event, the tiny hunter drank nearly half a thimbleful of wine! Then, indeed, did the little man become boastful of his prowess! But it was noticed that he never again insisted on going with the hunters, but contented himself with spearing cockroaches in his mother's kitchen.[118]

As the United States expanded its territory, Anglo buffalo hunters were enlisted to supply buffalo meat for the military and the railroad workers. These hunters viewed their occupation pragmatically, as did General Sheridan, who pointed out that the hunters "are destroying the Indian's commissary" and urged: "Let them kill, skin, and sell until the herds are exterminated. Then your prairies can be covered with speckled cattle and the cowboy who follows the hunter." By 1880, hunters like Buffalo Bill Cody had virtually destroyed the plains buffalo population. According to Jean M. Burroughs:

Although today they are often regarded as little more than wanton slaughterers, in their own time and for decades afterward they were ranked among the folk heroes of the West, along with the Mountain Men, the great scouts, the gunslingers and the trail herders. Buffalo Bill Cody, of course, got his nickname from the large numbers of bison he was reputed to have killed, but camp gossip of the time had it that at least one other professional hunter had killed more buffalo than Cody. He was George (T. L.) Causey, and he is notable here because after 1880, when most of the southern buffalo herd had been slaughtered, he drifted westward into New Mexico and settled there.

In 1877, for example, George Causey and his brother John killed over ten thousand buffalo and that spring sold "11,000 hides, 6,000 tongues at $1 each, and 45,000 pounds of dried salted beef." The hunters used powerful rifles, and "Causey continued using his dependable Sharps .44 on the range though an unfortunate kick back to the shoulder caused such a serious infection that he almost lost his right arm."[119]

In July 1937, Belle Kilgore of Clovis (NMFWP) interviewed Buster (James Ervin) de Graftenreid, who accompanied George and John Causey on their last trip as commercial buffalo hunters in 1882.

At that time, however, there weren't many buffalo left of the countless thousands that once roamed the Great Plains. . . . By 1882 the great herds . . . were reduced to scattered bunches of five or six and seldom more than 10 or 12.

The hunters had to scour the countryside on horseback to find them. When they sighted a bunch they would maneuver to get on the downwind side, then they would sneak up on them, taking advantage of every bit of cover the country afforded. They would pick out a bull and shoot him, and while the others were milling around uncertainly or attacking the wounded animal they would shoot as rapidly as possible. Sometimes, however, the buffaloes would run. In that case the hunter would shoot as long as they were in sight, then chase them on horseback, jumping off to shoot every time they got within range.

"And the range was surprisingly long," said DeGraffenreid [sic]. "I've seen old man George Causey turn a buffalo end over end nearly a mile away. Those old .50 caliber buffalo guns shot an awfully big cartridge. The guns were so heavy-barreled that a man couldn't hold one up and shoot it like he would an ordinary gun. He had to stand a couple of sticks tied together to make a forked stand, and when he got off his horse to shoot it [he] would put those sticks in the ground for a rest. They shot them so fast that the barrel would get blistering hot and wouldn't shoot straight any more. They would pour water in them from a canteen and I've seen them hot enough to boil the water."

De Graftenreid also boasted of his own exploits on that excursion:

I've heard men tell of roping lots of buffalo, but I can say from experience that if a man roped one buffalo he wouldn't want to rope another. I took out one day after a "spike" bull about a three-year-old. I didn't have any gun but an old cap and ball pistol so I decided to rope him. I had to chase him about two miles and a half before I could throw my loop, but I made a lucky catch around his neck and one horn.

I threw him just like you would a steer, but he got right up and charged my horse. With those sharp horns he could have killed a horse in a minute. A lot of people imagine a longhorn steer would be dangerous, but . . . a buffalo was a lot more dangerous.

Well, I kept throwing that buffalo every time he got up, but he would jump up and come right back at me before I could wind him up in the rope. Finally my horse got so tired he could hardly get out of the way, and I was about to let that buffalo have my rope when I happened to throw him in such a way that one of his front feet was caught. I started dragging him with my horse keeping the rope as tight as I could. He gradually choked down, but even when he quit moving I kept dragging him.

Finally I was sure he was dead, but I still didn't want to get off and take that rope from around his neck. I just leaned over and cut my rope. When I went back to camp the boys didn't believe I had roped a buffalo, but I took them over there with me the next morning and there he was dead.[120]

Catron County in southwestern New Mexico was home to at least two celebrated hunters—Englishman Montague Stevens (1859–1953), who owned the SU Ranch and professionally hunted grizzlies, and Ben V. Lilly (1856–1936), who lived in the Alma area and, between 1913 and 1915, killed 110 mountain lions. Stevens had lost his left arm in a California goose hunting accident, but his prowess was not much affected. Marc Simmons provides the following account:

One day Stevens got word that the Jewett Gap grizzly had just run through a flock of sheep, killing about forty and carrying one two miles before eating it. Saddling up and turning his hounds loose, he took up the trail.

A few hours later, he ran on a freshly killed cow with its neck broken. Here the bear had eaten dinner. A few miles beyond the dogs jumped the grizzly, who had bedded down for the night.

Stevens chased it into some timber and got it cornered. With one arm he raised the rifle and fired at the bear's throat. At that instant the animal raised a fore-leg to swat at the dogs and took the shot in the paw. Then he sprinted straight for the hunter.

Struggling to cock his rifle Montague looked up to find the gaping jaws of the grizzly almost upon him. At the last possible moment he fired, breaking the bear's backbone and sending him rolling over and over downhill.

"Incidents such as that," he declared later, "have a tendency to undermine one's self-confidence, and self-confidence is an indispensible requisite in hunting grizzlies!"[121]

Perhaps the most famous hunter in the Gila Wilderness was Ben Lilly, who became the chief guide for President Theodore Roosevelt in 1907. Born in Alabama in 1856, Lilly learned the ways of the hunter in the bayous of Texas and Louisiana before moving west into south Texas and the Sierra Madre of Chihuahua and Sonora, and finally settling in the wilderness of southwestern New Mexico in 1911. According to Mogollon residents William Rakocy and Rosamond Shannon Jones:

Ben Lilly never did care much for crowds. He would go for months without getting a case of the "visits." He once said that it "made him as nervous as a long-tailed cat in a room full of rockers" to be in a crowd of people. Being out next to nature was ever so much more soothing, and besides, in Ben's opinion, man needed the occasional company of something wild in order to keep himself in the proper perspective.

In and around Cooney and Mogollon, Ben Lilly was well-known as a philosopher as well as hunter. . . .

Ben told us once that his only talent was hunting. Hunting had taken Ben from the canebreaks of Louisiana, where he killed black bears, to the mountains of Mexico to hunt the big grizzlies. All he ever took with him on the hunts were a pan, some salt and meal, an ax, a rifle and his dogs. He lived off the land for he knew flora as well as fauna. Edible plants were part of his daily menu and his seventy-plus years were a testimony of his good health.[122]

In 1985, *Albuquerque Journal* reporter M. H. Salmon interviewed Jack Hoover, a rancher from the Mimbres and Gila River regions, who knew Lilly and admired his skill: "Hell, in 1929, he got five lions in one month off our ranch alone." He told how Lilly had left a note on the grave of Crook, one of his favorite dogs, attesting that the animal had "helped kill 210 bear and 426 mountain lion since 1914." According to Hooker, "Ben Lilly was the best because he was at home in the wilds, as much as any hound or varmint":

In the woods Ben Lilly was a tougher man than you'll ever see. . . . I hunted with him; I knew Ben Lilly pretty good. I'd ride and he'd walk alongside, as fast as any horse, and he'd talk faster than that. Talk all day. He'd have half a dozen hounds at least, and he didn't tie his dogs; they obeyed him. When the race would start and go to rough country, you couldn't keep up with him, afoot or horseback.[123]

Kit Carson, legendary frontiersman—hunter, trapper, teamster, Indian scout, and prototypical Mountain Man—provides the symbolic model for lives like Lilly's. Born in Kentucky in 1809 and raised in the Boone's Lick district of Missouri, Christopher Carson was apprenticed at age fifteen to saddler David Workman after the accidental death of the boy's father. The next year, Carson joined a wagon train for Santa Fe, where he lived for a time before moving to Taos. After a series of false starts and deep disappointments, Kit finally met Ewing Young of Taos. Young hired him to cook but later discovered that he showed promise as a trapper and Indian fighter. In August 1829, Carson accompanied Young and his party on a trapping expedition that took them through the Gila River region and eventually to California and back. They trapped, traded, and fought with various Indians. According to Jack K. Boyer, this first venture

> made him a man. During this period, he had demonstrated his ability as a leader and hard worker, his quick, sound thinking, his coolheadedness and fearlessness in times of danger, and his dependability. Kit had left Taos in 1829 on this trip as an inexperienced and unknown youth of 20 and returned as a seasoned trapper not quite 22 years old. He was now accepted by the Mountain Men, and many of them in the coming years would join him to become known as Carson Men, which is a story in itself. Kit was now a full-fledged member of that exclusive club of Mountain Men![124]

Carson roamed the West, trapping with men like Tom Fitzpatrick, Captain Richard Lee, Joe Meek, Jim Bridger, and others of wide reputation. At a rendezvous on the Green River in 1835, Boyer claims, "probably the event that was to make the best story about Kit's trapping days occurred":

> This was the historic duel between Kit and the French Canadian trapper called Shunar or Shuman. Our best authority on this duel is the Reverend Samuel Parker who was at the rendezvous en route to Oregon. Shunar was a giant of a man and a great bully who had whipped every man in his group under Captain Dripps and all other men who had displeased Shunar in his camp section at the rendezvous. Now he threatened to do likewise to the Americans. Kit quickly told Shunar that he was the smallest of the Americans but that he was not afraid of him and challenged Shunar to a battle. Shunar, grabbing his rifle, leaped onto his horse. Kit, grabbing the first weapon handy—a pistol, mounted his horse and rode up close to Shunar. Both men fired their weapons at the same time; Shunar's ball passed close to Kit's head, cutting his hair; Kit's ball pierced Shunar's hand and passed through his arm above the elbow. They had no further trouble in camp with the bully. According to family tradition and to friends quoting Kit later, the real trouble which caused the duel was over an Arapaho maiden upon whom Shunar was trying to force his attention. This maiden was to be Kit's first wife and was named "Waa-Nibe or Grass Singing," but was called Alice by Kit. This story is probably true because it was about 1835 that Kit married Waa-Nibe, and about a year later their daughter, Adaline, was born.[125]

Carson later served as a guide and then as a United States Indian agent between 1854 and 1861, when he resigned to join the Union army. He died of a hemorrhage on May 23, 1868, at Fort Lyons, Colorado.

When contemporaries met the Carson about whom they had heard so much, they were often disappointed. General William Tecumseh Sherman met him in 1849: "I cannot express my surprise at beholding a small, stoop-shouldered man, with reddish hair, freckled face, soft blue eyes, and nothing to indicate extraordinary courage or daring." Jessie Benton Fremont, who hired Carson to guide his Rocky Mountain and California expeditions in 1842 and 1843–1844, and whose reports of those trips contributed substantially to the growing legend, described Kit in 1897 as "perfectly Saxon, clear and fair . . . very short, and unmistakably bandy-legged; long-bodied and short-limbed, a man of great strength and vitality." The generation of frontiersmen who followed Carson were influenced by the famous hero, according to Kent Ladd Steckmesser: "William F. 'Buffalo Bill' Cody named his son Kit Carson Cody and featured Kit in his (ghostwritten) *Story of the Wild West . . . A Full and Complete History of the Renowned Pioneer Quartette, Boone, Crockett, Carson and Buffalo Bill* (1888). Carson was also the boyhood idol of James Butler 'Wild Bill' Hickok. There is a story that the two became friends and Kit introduced young Hickok to Santa Fe night life."[126]

Carson also figured in local legends throughout the Southwest. The *Gallup, New Mexico, Gazette* of November 16, 1939, reports two Kit Carson inscriptions at El Morro and one at Kit Carson's Cave east of Gallup. Steckmesser notes that "Kit Carson Peak near Raton, New Mexico, is said to have gotten its name when Kit was

Kit Carson (1809–1868), St. Louis, Missouri, December 1864. (MNM Neg. No. 58388.)

attacked there by Comanches while on his way back to Taos from a visit with Dick Wootton," and he quotes a 1938 manuscript by Manville Chapman (NMFWP):

> He made for this peak, tied the reins of his horse to the saddle pommel, and whipped it off in the direction of Taos by way of Red River Canyon. Then he scrambled on foot up the sides of the peak to the top where there is a natural fortification of rock. Here he held off the Indian band for two or three days. The horse went on to Taos, pawed at the corral gate and roused Carson's family. A party was made up and went to Carson's relief.[127]

Kent Ladd Steckmesser sees Carson as "a practical but unimaginative man," noting James F. Meline's testimony in his 1867 *Two Thousand Miles on Horseback* that Carson's answers to questions "were all marked by great distinctness of memory, simplicity, candor, and a desire to make some one else, rather than himself, the hero of his story." Steckmesser concludes "The Carson Legend in Perspective" as follows:

> For Kit Carson, then, less of a gap exists between history and the legend than is the case with other Western characters, particularly the outlaws and gunfighters. He did perform some notable exploits, although he had no great historical significance. He was virtuous, although somewhat less so than the legend claims. He spoke of his exploits with becoming modesty, and he was respected by most of his contemporaries. Thus he could become a model for his group, and he did. The prominence of the mountain man as a type in the literature and legend of the West is linked with the popular representations of Kit Carson.[128]

In the eyes of many native New Mexicans, however, it was Carson's deeds as an Indian fighter while a colonel in the first New Mexico Volunteer Infantry Regiment that earned him a place of honor or infamy in their lore.

Raiding, Captivity, and Warfare

Kit Carson figured in an 1849 Jicarilla Apache attack in northeastern New Mexico. With his family and five companions, Missouri trader James White had decided to hurry on toward Santa Fe from Clayton in advance of the main wagon train. East of modern Springer, the Jicarillas attacked, killing the men and abducting Mrs. White, her ten-year-old daughter, and the family's black female servant. Major William Grier and the 1st U.S. Dragoons set out from Taos, guided by Carson and mountain man Antoine Leroux. They tracked the Apaches for twelve days but failed to surprise the band when they did not attack immediately as Carson urged. Mrs. White was killed by her abductors as the soldiers rushed the camp. Later, Carson told of finding among Mrs. White's possessions a dime novel about his exploits as an Indian slayer. "I have often thought that Mrs. White must have read it, and knowing that I lived nearby, must have prayed for my appearance in order that she might be saved. I did come, but I lacked the power to persuade those that were in command to follow my plan for her rescue. They would not listen to me and they failed." On their return, the soldiers captured an Apache woman who told them that the black servant had been killed and the Whites' daughter traded to the Utes. Despite repeated congressional efforts, the girl was never found.[129]

The Jicarillas who attacked the White party may have been acting as either warriors or raiders. Apaches used different terminology to distinguish between warfare to avenge Apache casualties and raiding. According to Morris E. Opler:

> A raid was undertaken to acquire enemy horses and booty. The object was to avoid encounters with the enemy. The ritual associated with the raid was directed toward enhancing successful concealment and thwarting pursuit. Those who led a raid were persons who felt that the possessions of the encampment, particularly horses, were in short supply. Of course, raiders, if discovered, had to be prepared to fight, but even then the emphasis was on successful escape with as much booty and as few casualties as possible rather than upon confrontation.

Both Navajos and Apaches justified their raiding with stories, as LaVerne Harrell Clark notes:

> The myths and tales of the Navajo and Apache record the mythical and economic reasons for the cycle of steady horse raids which began as soon as the people had acquired their first mounts. They remind us that while it was true that the Indian's culture hero had finally been given some horses for his people, the white man's benefactor had nevertheless received the marvelous gift first. Having this advantage, the white people now possessed horses in great numbers, while the Indians did not have enough to meet their barest needs. A Chiricahua Apache tale says that this was why "Child-of-the-Water had to steal from his own uncle." . . .
>
> In legend and in life, they stole the horses of the Mexicans and the Anglos. They stole from their Indian enemies too. But the records show that the raid for horses was more than just a grand horse theft. Because the raids grew from the economic necessities of the people, the Navajo and Apache came to look on them as sacred missions to bring home "the things by which men lived"—missions they believed they could accomplish successfully only by using the proper magic and ritual.[130]

Mid-nineteenth-century residents of the Rio Grande Valley suffered many successful Navajo raids. Marc Simmons reports that, "according to one estimate, in the four years from 1846 to 1850, the Navajos had plundered the Rio Grande Valley of more than 450,000 sheep, 31,000 cattle, 12,000 mules, and 7,000 horses." In the 1920s, a San Juan Pueblo man about sixty years old told Elsie Clews Parsons about horse-raiding Navajos' *pinang,* or magical powers.

> One year Navaho stole some horses in the mountains. The snow was so high [indicating half-foot]. They stole lots of horses, and the Tewa started after them. They went into the big mountains where there were lots of big trees. There they lost the tracks. They searched for them, they said, "Wonder where they took the horses, underground or up into the sky flying?" The Navaho had driven the horses on top of the fallen trees, jumping them from one fallen tree to another, so on the ground there were no tracks. . . . After they stole horses Navaho would make wind and

snow, through their *pinang*. They had arrow-points, large ones, and they made wind by waving these arrow-points around this way [sunwise circuit]. That is the way they did, long ago, the old men said.

Among the ceremonial figures important to Navajo horse raiding were Bear and Big Snake, given to the people by Changing Woman to protect them on their journeys among many peoples.[131]

Apache horse-raiding rituals were shamanic, given to men who encountered a guardian horse spirit. Such spirits "could approach an Apache at any time and offer him its power, sometimes . . . when a man and a horse had gone through some emotional crisis together." They would address the human using kinship terms, and thereafter would be treated as relatives, subject to kinship taboos, including injunctions against slaying them.

> The Apache considered a knowledge of horse power an essential part of any raid leader's background for many reasons. First of all, it was believed that if a leader possessed such powers, he would not only be successful in conducting his men on a safe journey, he would also be successful in helping them acquire horses. Remembering how he had employed his power advantageously on raids, an elderly Chiricahua Apache boasted to [Morris E.] Opler that he could always depend on it, even after his raiding days were over: "[My] power told me that I was going to get something if I went out on the raid. If I go out and look for something, my power gives me the ability to get horses and mules. The power sends me out and tells me, 'You are going to get this.'" He elaborated in detail too about how this same power of his had protected him from the enemy: "My power told me that the enemy was coming. It told me, 'If you want the enemy to see you, they are going to see you. If you want to see the enemy, you will see them. If you don't want to meet the enemy, they will swing around the other way.'"
>
> [The leader] likewise conducted a brief ceremony, previous to departure, for the benefit of the men going on the expedition. As one Chiricahua Apache explained it, the raiders needed his songs and prayers, so that "good horses [would] fall into their hands, so that their horses [would] be strong and carry them through, and so that all in the party [would] have good luck."[132]

Apache raiding continued well into the nineteenth century, and local legends about "the last Indian raid," usually for horses, played an important part in Hispanic and Anglo lore.

Humans as well as livestock were taken captive in raids and warfare, and the history of slave trade between tribes and races is a bitter one in New Mexico. Marc Simmons sketches the Spanish practices in his biography of Indian fighter Manuel Antonio Chaves, who spent his youth in Cebolleta.

> One aspect of Cebolleta's history . . . concerns the proclivity of that town's citizenry to engage in slave raids against the Navajos. How early the practice began and to what degree it inflamed the Indians against the townspeople is difficult to ascertain. Slaving expeditions were common in New Mexico during colonial times and fully accepted as just retaliation for Indian raids. Since this activity was

strictly forbidden by Spanish law, the colonists carefully avoided designating their captives as slaves and referred to them euphemistically as *criados* or servants. In fairness it should be noted that hostile Navajo, Ute, Comanche, and Apache in a like manner seized Spanish captives for their own use, and numerous instances existed of these becoming completely acculturated and reconciled to Indian life.

The sketchy records available strongly suggest that slaving was practiced by the Cebolletans from their days of first settlement in the Navajo country. In any case, by the mid-nineteenth century it was firmly fixed as a way of life, so that most New Mexican communities recognized a band or company of men known as "Cebolleteños" whose principal occupation was stealing Navajo children to sell in other towns. By established custom, whenever a wealthy father arranged for the marriage of a daughter, he commissioned the "Cebolleteños" to bring in a Navajo boy or girl to be given as a bridal gift. Moreover, youths of Cebolleta and other border villages often went on forays alone or with a few loyal companions to secure a captive child to serve their own bride-to-be. Since such enterprises were attended with considerable risk, many young swains failed to return. Manuel's son Amado [Chaves], writing about this business in later years, mentioned laconically,

Manuel Chaves y Garcia de Noriega (1818–1889), *El Leoncito,* The Little Lion, 1848. (MNM Neg. No. 9833.)

> On arriving home [after a slaving expedition] the first thing to do was to take the children to the priest to baptize them and give them a name. They would naturally take your name and as they grew up they would consider you and your wife as their parents. If you did not have the pluck to go after Indian children yourself you could buy one for five hundred dollars. It must be remembered that many parties that went after servants never returned. The Indians killed them all.[133]

When contemporary Navajos recount stories of their ancestors, they merge tales of slave trade with oral histories of the Long Walk and the chantway myths of culture heroes and heroines. In the late 1960s, the Navajo Community College in Chinle, Arizona, conducted an oral history project during which "some 40 Navajos, most of them elderly, . . . did their parts magnificently by taping (in the Navajo language) their versions of the Long Walk and other events which occurred more than a hundred years ago and which had come down to them by word of mouth." Ruth Roessel, then director of the Community College's Navajo Studies Program, describes this collection, which was published in 1973 as *Navajo Stories of the Long Walk Period.*

> As one reads these stories, a most revealing factor is the close identification, on the part of the Navajo storytellers, of the events with their religion. Time and again the Holy People come to the aid of the Navajos and are responsible for assisting them in returning home and being restored to their land. . . .
>
> Other penetrating perceptions into Navajos' interpretation of their own history include the extreme awareness felt by the Navajos in connection with being alone in the world—beset, besieged and surrounded by enemies.
>
> The stories in this book are full of the attacks and raids by other Indian tribes and Mexicans, as well as by the Army, against the Navajos. There is almost a feeling of persecution on the part of the Navajos in terms of the raids directed against them by others.[134]

Unidentified Navajo, Bosque
Redondo era, ca. 1864–1868.
(MNM Neg. No. 38200.)

Few Hispanic or Anglo captivity narratives are couched in such powerful religious terms. Nevertheless, on February 29, 1852, for example, New Mexico Governor James S. Calhoun addressed a letter to U.S. Secretary of State Daniel Webster, proclaiming that "it is a lamentable fact that [Indian raids] are increasing rapidly, to such an extent, that if such outrages continue much longer, our Territory, instead of becoming settled with an industrious and thriving population, will be left a howling wilderness, with no other inhabitants than the wolf, and the birds of prey hovering over the mangled remains of our murdered countrymen."[135] However, most captivity lore was individualized and matter-of-fact in reporting a fairly common experience.

In July 1936, Clay W. Vaden (NMFWP) interviewed Don Roque Ramos of Placita, near Monticello. Ramos was born in 1852 in Sonora, Mexico, and when quite young went to work on his oldest brother's ranch. There he was captured by Apaches, who took him north.

> For three years young Ramos was kept a captive with the Indians ruled over by their Apache chief, Chiz [Cochise], near Ojo Caliente. During this time he tried his very best to get along peaceably with them but when they spoke to him in their own language and he could not understand they often beat him cruelly. One day while cutting timber his Indian guard gave him an order which he could not understand and the guard became so angry that he struck the young lad over the head with a spear. An inch scar is still to be seen on the right side of his head. Another Mexican boy captive that Roque recognized told him every time he tried to escape the Indians punished him severely, so the young boys did not make many attempts to escape. Whenever the Indians saw the two Mexican boys talking together they would separate them. Then, too, the little girl Chonita begged him not to escape unless he could take her with him. . . .
>
> At the time he did finally make his escape he and the other two captives were separated so he never learned what became of the other Spanish boy or the little girl Chonita. The Indians had a camp near what is now Perfecto Silva's ranch a few miles north of Monticello. At times the Indians were friendly with the Spanish settlers at Monticello and Placitas, and on these occasions the young captive had become acquainted with several of the Spaniards living in these villages. Seeing that the Indians were all getting drunk and preparing to go on one of their raids against the whites, the young boy decided to take advantage of their drunken condition and run away at night. He did so and ran to the ranch where an old Spaniard joined him and together they ran along the creek in Monticello canyon until they reached the home of Jesus Garcia at Placita. Garcia took him on horseback to Paraje, a village below San Marcial. . . . Gregorio Sedillos, a wealthy Spaniard living there, adopted Roque Ramos and Garcia returned to his home at Placitas that same night so the Indians would not suspect him of helping the boy to escape.

Ramos later wrote to his oldest brother, who "all his lifetime blamed himself for what had happened," and the latter made the trip to New Mexico to try unsuccessfully to persuade his sibling to return.[136]

A saga of two brothers from a ranch on the Mimbres River in southeastern New Mexico became a well-known part of regional folklore. In September 1885, ten-year-old Jimmy McKinn and his older brother Martin were rounding up the family stock when they were surprised by Apaches from Geronimo's band. Martin was killed and Jimmy taken captive. He was held for several months in Mexico, and when General George Crook, Lieutenant John G. Bourke, photographer C. S. Fly, and other members of the United States army and peace delegation arrived to negotiate with Geronimo, they were astonished to find the young white captive "among the group of little Apache boys romping freely and carelessly together." Later, at Fort Bowie in southeastern Arizona, *Los Angeles Times* war correspondent Charles F. Lummis reported:

Apache captive Jimmy (Santiago) McKinn. Photo by C. S. Fly. (MNM Neg. No. 11649.)

Santiago [Jimmy] McKinn, this poor child, scaly with dirt, wild as a coyote, made my eyes a bit damp. His is a pathetic case. The sorrow of it is that he has become so absolutely Indianized. He understands English and Spanish, but it was like pulling eye-teeth to get him to speak either. He has learned the Apache language and talks it exclusively. When told that he was to be taken back to his father and mother, Santiago began boo-hooing with great vigor. He said in Apache that he didn't want to go back; he wanted always to stay with the Indians. All sorts of rosy pictures of his home were drawn, but he would have none of them, and acted like a young wild animal in a trap. When they lifted him into the wagon, he renewed his wails, and was still at them as he disappeared from our view.

As a grown man, McKinn became a blacksmith, working for the W. A. Tenney Freight Company in Silver City in 1908, and eventually moving to Phoenix, where he died in the mid-1950s. According to Marc Simmons: "In his last years McKinn was not eager to talk about his boyhood episode among the Indians. One of his sons married a Chiricahua Apache, and although Jimmy could speak to her in her own language there was always a tone of hostility in his voice."[137]

General Crook had not expected to find Jimmy McKinn because he was actually looking for young Charlie McComas, the son of prominent territorial judge H. C. McComas. The judge, his wife, and their six-year-old son were attacked by the San Carlos Apache leader Chato on March 28, 1883, on the road between Lordsburg and Silver City. The Apaches killed both parents and took Charlie with them to join Geronimo in the Sierra Madre Mountains of Mexico. Crook never located young McComas; captives he interrogated claimed the boy either starved or was shot during the general's raid. Nevertheless, rumors about the boy's fate persisted well into the twentieth century, including tales that little Charlie escaped Crook's attack and eventually became a leader of the remaining "broncos," or free Apaches.

In April 1930 a news dispatch carried by the United States press reported that a party of these aging "broncos" had raided a settlement in northern Sonora just below the Arizona border and had killed and scalped three persons. Eight years later an archeological expedition suddenly came upon this Indian remnant far up in the Sierra Madre. From a brief glimpse before the strange people disappeared the scholars observed that the leader had blue eyes and red hair! Their discovery rekindled speculation about Charlie McComas: as improbable as it appeared, could he have lived to become the last chief of the last free Apaches?[138]

Apache hostilities in southwestern New Mexico were intensified by mining interests. "In 1852 Americans wanted to reopen the Santa Rita copper mines in Eastern Chiricahua country, and Fort Webster was established nearby to protect them. Then gold was discovered at Pinos Altos, not far from Santa Rita, and there was an influx of prospectors to that site [whose] immediate contribution to Indian-American relations was to flog and thoroughly alienate Mangas Coloradas, the most prominent leader of his time of the Eastern Chiricahua band." During the Civil War, according to Morris E. Opler, "one of the more dubious achievements of [General James H.] Carleton's forces was to lure the Eastern Chiricahua chief, Mangas Coloradas, into custody under a flag of truce and a promise of treaty talks on January 17, 1863, and to torture and shoot him the next day."[139] An ailing Cochise died in 1874, but Victorio and Geronimo fueled the legends and tales of southern New Mexico for generations.

The United States Army's war with Victorio, who learned his skills from Mangas Coloradas, officially began on September 4, 1879, when Victorio and sixty men attacked soldiers near Ojo Caliente, killing eight men and capturing their horses and mules. The so-called buffalo soldiers, or blacks in blues, of the Ninth and Tenth Cavalry pursued Victorio's warriors through the mountains of southern New Mexico and into Texas. According to Robert Utley, these "black soldiers . . . endured some of the most punishing ordeals in the history of the Indian wars. . . . Yet despite a condition of almost constant exhaustion, the blacks kept at the task, four times prompting Victorio to drop into Mexico to rest and refit, ultimately setting the stage for his demise [at Tres Castillos, on October 15, 1880] at the hands of Mexican troops." Warm Springs Apache James Kaywaykl (died 1963), one of seventeen survivors of the Tres Castillos massacre, told Eve Ball about the eulogy for Victorio given by the warrior Nana:

Nana talked to us. The chief had died as he would have wished—in the defense of his people. He was the greatest of all Apache chiefs, yes, of all Indian chiefs. He had died as he had lived, free and unconquerable. We knew well the fate of Mangas Coloradas and of Cochise. They, too, would have preferred death in battle; they would have envied Victorio. So—we were not to mourn for him. He had been spared the ignominy of imprisonment and slavery, and for that he would have been thankful to Ussen [deity]. His courage was to be the inspiration of those left to

Geronimo before surrender, ca. 1885. Photo by C. S. Fly. (MNM Neg. No. 14272.)

carry on our race, and fortunately there were enough women and warriors that our people might increase.[140]

Geronimo was not captured until he surrendered to General Nelson A. Miles on September 3, 1886. Until then, he too terrorized Hispanic and Anglo New Mexicans. A Deming resident who had emigrated from Little Rock, Arkansas, in 1883, recalled the "early days" when "the Indians under Geronimo had been causing the settlers a lot of trouble stealing horses and killing people that were not around town [and] the people of Deming united and began to drill to wipe out the Indians as they were tired of the depredations and raids." In 1938 she still had "some pictures taken of the Indians on the war path with their bodies painted and the trousers that the government had given them, cut off above the knees. In the day time we would watch them on the mountains with the field glasses and at night could see their fires."[141]

Throughout New Mexico, newspaper editors in the 1880s articulated anxieties felt by all citizens of the territory. Given the conditions of hostility,

their minimum demand was "war, relentless, merciless war, till the savage devils are content to promise good behavior [and] abide by their promises." As conditions became worse, editors became more extreme in their demands: "exterminate them from branch to root as you would rattlesnakes." When United States Army efforts were not immediately successful, the editors encouraged the use of other methods. "The citizens of Silver City have subscribed $2,000 which they will cheerfully pay out at the rate of $100 per head for every Indian killed and brought in. There is a royalty for wolf scalps and why not for Indian scalps," asked the Las Vegas *Daily Optic*. Under warlike conditions these editors often recommended extermination as an economy measure, for as they pointed out, "a live indian cost the government twenty dollars a head per annum; a dead one nothing. Sabe?" When Geronimo was perpetrating his harshest acts, most territorial editors believed "it would be justice to slaughter all of the bucks in Geronimo's little band of Apaches, when they are captured. The Indian tribes must be abolished and this is an opportunity to get rid of them." Even after hostilities had abated, some territorial editors demanded death for the Apaches: "let them be hunted to death. . . . We kill mad dogs and mountain lions on sight. Of the beast and the Indian which is the worst?"[142]

In the summer of 1885 Geronimo attacked settlements within several miles of Fort Bayard and Silver City. Cowboy, hunter, and guide James H. Cook claimed that the Apaches killed "sixteen in all . . . several of them being women and children. One or two of the children were tortured to death by being hung up on spikes outside their houses." Cook had ridden over one hundred miles in twelve hours in a futile attempt to warn residents of the Silver City area.[143]

Utes posed a problem to settlers in northeastern New Mexico. William M. Emery (NMFWP) interviewed Sarah Jane-Gleason of Folsom in 1936, when she was the oldest resident of Union County. As a young homesteader with an infant daughter, she and neighboring women gathered with their children at the home of W. P. Duncan.

The men were all away from home on the roundup. . . . Shortly before sundown a cowboy rode up the canyon of the Dry Cimarron river with the warning that Indians were coming up that way. The women hastily finished the outside chores and barricaded themselves inside of the rock house. Doors and windows were locked and a pillow stuffed into a broken window; trunks and other heavy furniture were piled against them for added protection. Guns were loaded and placed in convenient places; fire and lights were extinguished and everything settled down to a night of watchful waiting.

The children were put to bed, but their sleep was often broken by a cry. . . . The night wore on; stories of other Indian scares and attacks were told by the older women, thus increasing the fear of the younger women and older children who were allowed to stay up. The dogs began barking in the middle of the night, and nearby a coyote howled, but no moving object could be detected in the inky blackness of the night. . . .

[The next morning,] under the windows were found the footprints of moccasined feet, but the main band . . . had left the Cimarron Canyon by way of Cow Canyon about five miles below. . . . That day the men returned home with the news that the Indians were only fighting among themselves.[144]

Mrs. Gleason's brother, Mr. William F. Sumpter of Folsom, told Emery about the last Ute raid, which he claimed was on July 4, 1874. Three shepherds were killed near Los Alamos followed by two cowboys at a Corrumpa Creek cowcamp belonging to the Cross-Ell Ranch.

One of the men killed was Jim Roberts, an Englishman. . . . In the spring of 1874, the Hall Brothers had trailed a herd of cattle to Denver. It lay between Jim Roberts and W. F. Sumpter as to who should go with the cattle and who should go to the cow-camp on the Corrumpa. It was finally decided that Sumpter should go with the cattle, providing he would leave his pet saddle horse—a very fine animal— with Roberts. When the Indians killed Roberts they also stole this horse. Sumpter searched for the horse for a long time but could never get any trace of it.

Roberts and his partner both lie buried on the banks of the Corrumpa creek near the spot where they were killed. This is now [1936] the site of one of the noted ranches and fishing resorts of this section, the Weatherby Ranch and Dam— formerly known as the James Ranch and Dam. Few who visit this resort know the story of the tragedy which took place here a little more than fifty years ago or of the two isolated graves within sight of their fishing grounds.[145]

Coincidentally, it was Englishmen who became the first victims of another common form of violence generated by threats to land and livelihood in territorial New Mexico. According to Robert J. Rosenbaum:

On the morning of April 27, 1889, the owners of a ranch near San Geronimo, twelve miles west of Las Vegas, awoke to find their four miles of new barbed wire fence cut. Cut is a mild word. It was destroyed, the fence posts chopped to kindling and the wire strewn in glittering fragments. The partners—two English adventurers trying their luck at Wild West ranching—were the first victims of a civil war that raged across San Miguel County for the next eighteen months. Wearing white masks or caps—*gorras blancas*—bands of native New Mexicans—*mexicanos*—struck at night, leveling fences, destroying crops, burning buildings, and, not infrequently, shooting people. By the summer of 1890, according to one English language newspaper, *Las Gorras Blancas* had brought business in Las Vegas to a standstill.

Few fences stood, and lumbermen could not cut timber on the common land. In August 1890, a new political party, El Partido del Pueblo, was formed using the issues and organization of Las Gorras Blancas and soon usurping the latter's influence. Nevertheless, "local bands of *Las Gorras Blancas* rode sporadically, at least until 1926, as *los extranjeros* continued to usurp chunks of common land."[146]

What Las Gorras Blancas symbolized in territorial New Mexico, Pancho Villa exemplified in the early twentieth century, when marauding escalated to an international scale, transcending localized boundary issues. New Mexicans figured in the Spanish-American War of 1898, when four hundred men were recruited for a regiment of cavalry made up of what the War Department called "the wild riders and riflemen of the Rockies and the Great Plains." This first Regiment of United States Volunteer Cavalry was commanded by Colonel Leonard Wood and Lieutenant Colonel Theodore Roosevelt. They were trained near San Antonio, Texas, where newspaper reporters impressed by their skills dubbed them "Roosevelt's Rough Riders." Ironically, their horses could not be shipped from Florida to Cuba, so they entered battle on foot. The victorious troopers agreed to a New Mexico reunion the following June. Las Vegas raised more money and boasted better hotels, notably the Fred Harvey Castañeda, so it was selected for the first reunion.[147]

The Mexican Revolution of 1910–1920 brought further difficulties along the borderlands. Mindful of American investments south of the border, the United States recognized Venustiano Carranza as president of Mexico in October 1915. This political decision provoked the wrath of one of the most famous guerrilla foes of Carranza, the notorious *jefe* Pancho Villa, whose real name was Dorotello Arango. Born during a thunderstorm in Durango on June 5, 1878, of *peón* parents, Arango learned the arts of horsemanship and cattle raising as a youth. According to legend, he was not the natural son of Agustín Arango but the illegitimate offspring of a rich Spanish *hacendado* or a famous Mexican general.[148]

When he became enmeshed in Mexican revolutionary politics at the age of seventeen, Arango took the name Francisco ("Pancho") Villa, by some accounts because of his grandfather, Jesús Villa. However, according to Haldeen Braddy:

> The most persistent folk explanation is that earlier in the era, fifty years before the birth of Dorotello, there flourished a rare old bandit chief called Pancho Villa. Possibly the boy was distantly, dimly related to him through his granddad Villa. The lustre of this brawny old character still commanded fearful respect in Dorotello's youth. In those days many a tough *hombre* was doubtless styled "Pancho Villa," just as today on the Mexican border the redoubtable monicker is used as a nickname for a *bravo*.[149]

By 1915, incidents of marauding along the international border had intensified and Villa's name had become synonymous with such raiding. "In the opinion of General [John J.] Pershing, Villistas bore the guilt for the main boundary violations.

Pancho Villa by a train in Mexico. (MNM Neg. No. 117657.)

Pershing noted also that Villa pillaged American ranches and settlements at Red House Ferry, Progress Post Office, and Las Paladas—all within a few months; he observed that the invader then escaped punishment in both Mexico and the United States. Again, the American general charged that ruthless bestiality and savage acts of mutilation characterized the assaults." When Mexican government troops were transported on American railroad trains to quell Villa's attack on Agua Prieta near Douglas, Arizona, in October 1915, Villa interpreted this as an act of treachery and "publicly vowed to 'lay waste to the Colossus of the North.'"[150]

The most celebrated upshot of this boast was the pre-dawn invasion of Columbus, New Mexico, on March 9, 1916. Much of the town was burned to the ground. Eighteen Americans were killed, including ten civilians, one of them a woman, and eight soldiers. Pancho Villa lost ninety men and some forty horses. The following day, American cavalrymen cremated the bodies. The clock at the Columbus station was stopped by a bullet at the moment of the raid, 4:11 A.M. Betty Reich (NMFWP) reports that the Columbus postmaster in 1916, Mr. L. L. Burkhead, "had an interesting souvenir made of this event . . . a metal watch fob in the shape of the state of New Mexico. On one side is a map of New Mexico with a star marking the location of Columbus and with the words: Souvenir of Villa Raid on

Columbus N.M. March 9th 1916. On the other side are the words, '9 citizens & 7 soldiers of 13th cavalry killed Town looted & burned Raiders driven into Mexico after 2 hr. fight leaving more than 80 dead.' There were several thousand of the watch fobs made but there are very few left in this part of the country."[151]

Reich also interviewed Jesse Fuller, who in 1937 was mayor of Columbus. During the raid he "was living in the business district of Columbus in a small house back of the Ford garage. He was awakened in the early hours . . . by the sounds of gunfire. He barricaded the door with a 50-gallon barrel of water and waited, gun in hand, for the enemy, but his home was unmolested—probably because Villa's men thought it was the home of a Mexican. From his window he could plainly see the bugler of Villa's band as he blew the signal for retreat from Columbus [by 7:15 A.M.]." However, Jack W. Breen, Jr., of Tucson, Arizona, told Haldeen Braddy that a bullet struck the rain barrel when Fuller was crouched behind it. "Fuller believed he had been shot to death, for he could feel something moist trickling down his shirt. The 'blood' of course turned out to be water; and in this manner Fuller escaped with no more than a bad scare."[152]

Another story of the raid claims: "A true heroine of the Columbus raid was Mrs. G[arnett] E. Parks, the telephone operator, who stayed at her switchboard, with her baby clasped to her breast, and summoned aid and gave continuing information to Deming as bullets ripped into her home and pieces of shattered glass pierced her body. Mrs. Parks survived and was later honored for her deeds." Betty Reich collected tales of residents' attempts to escape the surprise assault:

During the raid the Ravel Hotel was burned. This hotel was operated by a Mr. W. P. Ritchie. Mr. Ritchie was killed and his body was badly burned. There was also an unidentified man killed in the hotel. He was registered in the hotel but the register burned and no one knew who he was. Mr. Ritchie's daughter, Edna, was the only person beside himself that knew the combination of the safe. She was so frightened that she could not open it. The Mexicans took Mrs. Ritchie's rings. A Mexican boy that she judged to be about twelve years old held a gun in her ribs and shouted, "Pronto! Pronto!" while other Villistas beat her on the hands with the butts of their guns because she could not get her rings off quick enough. After the raid she got her rings back by mail but she never knew who sent them or their history after they were stolen. . . .

The Paige family hid in an outhouse during the raid. Three times the Mexicans set fire to their house and each time Mr. Paige put the fire out as soon as the Mexicans had left. Eighty bullet holes were found in their piano. There were some portraits hanging on the walls that Mrs. Paige had painted. The Mexicans shot around the faces of these until the faces fell out.

The longest account was given by Mr. and Mrs. A. J. Evans of Columbus, who at the time owned the local Ford garage and lived with their four children in a small house at the foot of the strategic hill on the east side, occupied by Villa's machine gunners, and later known as Villa Hill.

Mr. Evans was awakened by the sound of men going past his house. He looked out the window and saw Mexicans passing in a stooping position. They were so close that he could have reached out and touched them. In just a few minutes he heard some of them run into a wire fence. Mr. Evans awakened his wife and whispered to her not to scream but that there were Mexicans all around them. About that time the first shot was fired and then no one would have heard her if she had screamed because every Mexican in Villa's band began shooting and shouting, "Viva Villa! Viva Mexico!" The machine gunners on the hill began shooting over their house into the army camp. They were aiming at the place where they knew the army guns were locked up for the night.

A good many bullets went through the roof of their house but only one went through the house below the ceiling. This was a soft-nosed bullet, used by the Mexicans, which entered the south wall and did a great deal of damage to the house but hurt no one. The Evans had a Ford car in their garage in the yard but they knew they would be shot before they could reach it.

They were more afraid of American bullets than they were of the Mexican bullets, because they knew the Americans had better ammunition. The whole family—the oldest child was nine and the baby was six months old—got down on the floor on the west side of the house (next to the Mexicans) and stood a mattress up between them and the American bullets. . . .

No one entered their house. None of the doors were locked, just the screens were fastened. Once they heard someone rattle one of the screens but no other effort was made to enter the house. . . .

Every time there was a lull in the shooting they could hear a Mexican somewhere nearby playing a violin.

When the Mexicans set fire to some of the buildings in the business district it became as light as day in their house and one of the children whispered to their mother to put out the light.[153]

Not only the Evans family but other beleaguered citizens tried, not always successfully, to reach their automobiles. Ironically, when General "Blackjack" Pershing pursued Villa's horsemen into Mexico, he "organized the world's first motorized cavalry. It consisted of a fleet of four-wheel-drive Nash and Jeffry automobiles, assisted by eight observation biplanes, the first U.S. Army air force. . . . All of the vehicles and the airplanes soon perished in the desert and were never recovered. Decades later, adventurers trying to retrace the U.S. Army's invasion route found concrete bridges over ravines, rusted heaps of Jerry cans that transported gasoline, but little else." Villa's guerrilla band evaded Pershing's troops through expert horsemanship. According to Haldeen Braddy:

Horses had always been the key to Villa's lightning mobility. . . . The fact is that Villa prized good horses. A number of those he owned live on in legend to illuminate his prowess as "The Centaur of the North." They include the famous roan *Taurino*, probably his mount at Columbus; and the most celebrated of all, the white horse *Siete Leguas* (Seven Leagues). Most Americans wrongly claim that he rode a white horse on the raid.[154]

Historians advance various theories to explain Villa's apparently quixotic raid. According to Charles H. Harris and Louis R. Sadler, "these theses include: Villa's desire not only to retaliate against the Americans but also to provoke their intervention in Mexico, thus creating a situation on which he could capitalize; his intention to loot Columbus and the nearby 13th Cavalary encampment for munitions, remounts, and provisions; his desire for vengeance against certain Columbus businessmen who had allegedly defrauded him of money and arms; and, finally, the provocative theory that German agents manipulated Villa into attacking Columbus in order to embroil the United States in a war with Mexico." Others propose "that Pathe News, a hyper-aggressive movie newsreel outfit of the days before radio and TV, had paid Pancho to stage the raid for the cameras . . . , [and] yet another version . . . says that the raid was financed by $80,000 in gold supplied by U.S. agents to provide the U.S. Army with some combat training in preparation for World War I." Whatever Villa's actual motivations, his 1916 raid lives in oral tradition and is commemorated in Pancho Villa State Park, established in 1959, "the only public park in the U.S. ever named for a foreign invader."[155]

Trading

Between 1786 and the 1870s, New Mexicans maintained an amicable alliance with Comanches along their eastern frontier, freely visiting one another's villages, settling in one another's communities, and joining in campaigns against the Apaches. According to Charles Kenner:

> While the Comanches engaged in considerable trade during their visits, a much greater commerce was carried on in the Comanche camps by itinerant traders known as *Comancheros.* Their activities were so widescale that as early as 1820 Stephen Long, an American officer trekking across the Southwest, reported that a well-beaten trail containing more than twenty bridle paths followed the Canadian River eastward from New Mexico toward the plains. By the 1840s the *Comanchero* traffic had broadened the pack trails observed by Long into full-fledged cart roads. . . . A gold seeker with [Captain Randolph B.] Marcy's [1849] caravan . . . wrote [of the upper Canadian], "you find large, broad wagon trails made by the . . . Comanche traders, which lead you to the settlements."[156]

An eighty-seven-year-old ex-Comanchero, Señor Vicente Romero of Córdova, was interviewed by Lorin W. Brown (NMFWP) in 1937. Romero recalled his youthful exploits on the eastern plains:

> Four times I have been on trading trips to the Comanches and three times to the plains on buffalo hunts. We used bows and arrows and the lance as weapons when hunting at first. Later we were able to trade for guns at Santa Fe. . . .
> The first two trips to the Comanches I went with my uncle Guadalupe Marquez, who was the *comandante* or leader. I learned enough of the language and customs so that the last two trips I went as *comandante.* Our first trip took us about three months. We took salt, blankets, and strips of iron for arrowheads. We also took big packs of a very hard bread, which our wives baked especially for trading to the Indians. Another article of trade was dried apples and plums. . . .

Comanche Dance (?) set-up, San Juan Pueblo. Rex Studio Collection. (MNM Neg. No. 88325.)

After a sort of feast with the Indians we started in to trade. This would take a long time because there would be much talk over each trade. Sometimes an Indian and one of us would fix up a horse race. They liked to bet and that way we won many articles from them.

We did not stay in the same camp but traveled from spot to spot with our customers, following the buffalo trading as we went. I enjoyed this life very much. It was very new to me; we were always watchful and on our guard for some acts of treachery on the part of the Indians. But they had need of the goods we had to trade so they treated a trading party with a certain regard and usually avoided any act which might cause trouble. We were more careful than they were perhaps, always thinking of our families and the goods we were to take home with us.[157]

Despite assertions like a Chiricahua Apache's to Morris E. Opler that "you are ashamed to borrow . . . for that shows you are not a real man and have not been on the raid and obtained things for yourself," most southwestern Indians preferred trade to raiding and the expensive and unpredictable results of warfare. Exchange within a village or encampment included intracommunity lending, borrowing, and sharing; informal, occasional, and voluntary gambling and gaming; the redistribution of food and goods through ceremony; and trading parties from elsewhere. Trading parties from neighboring villages were often treated as guests, not strangers, by their hosts. According to Richard I. Ford: "The next degree removed from this guest-host relation was best observed in the Eastern Pueblos where the close proximity of neighboring villages permitted itinerant traders, usually with very specific items such as specialty foods, plant medicines, or jewelry, to visit several Pueblos on the same day and to trade their products at a seemingly fixed rate."[158]

Strangers came from greater distances, and "within the community each member was protected by charms against potential harm brought by the stranger . . . [an] anxiety, a fear of involvement . . . was always present despite a proven need for maintaining trade relations." Those who traveled out from the community carried charms and observed various supernatural precautions, and "since the farther from home one traveled, the more perilous the journey, women rarely went on these trips, ceremonialists were forbidden to go, and many men preferred to send their goods with others, [because] attacks and accidents could waylay even the most experienced trader, despite superb knowledge of the trails, water supplies and pasturage." Trading was also dangerous afterward, and "virtually every tribe had a ceremony to protect travelers before departing and a purification rite upon returning to protect the community from any bad spirits that might have accompanied the trader."[159]

No commodity served as money among southwestern Indians. However, particularly among Navajos and Pueblos, "long and short strings of shell beads *(hishi)* were convertible into good at any time . . . [and] T. R. Frisbie . . . has argued that a standard 30-inch length was a form of money." By the end of the nineteenth century, Navajo blankets served a similar function. In any case, recorded lists of exchange rates or equivalencies of hides, blankets, livestock, guns, and the like, "which demonstrate a remarkable homogeneity and near universal knowledge of the rates, suggest that bargaining was quite restricted, although not absent."[160]

Spanish colonial settlers developed a system of barter known as *cambalache.* Traders on the Chihuahua Trail carried pelts, hides, wool, textiles, dried fruit, nuts, and other items for exchange. Arthur L. Campa states that

> *cambalache* was replaced by coined currency when the latter became available, although the term is still known by old-timers today. The *jola,* which originally meant one eighth of a *real,* remained current among the folk around La Joya, New Mexico, where the Chihuahua traders prepared their *conductas* in colonial days, but today *jola* means one cent. *No tengo jolas* also means, "I have no money."

Even after a money economy was introduced, Hispano traders prospered, despite Córdova salt trader Don Higinio Torrez's contention to Lorin W. Brown:

> The tale is true that when God was passing out gifts to the different races he granted *Los Americanos* the gift of riches which they asked for. And us Mexicans we asked for enjoyment of life in the form of wine, women, and song. That is why we find ourselves so poor but enjoying life.[161]

Among those who found riches along the "extended" Chihuahua Trail was Don Felipe Chávez of Belen, who joined his older brothers in the Santa Fe Trail trade. According to Marc Simmons:

At the time of his death in 1905, Don Felipe was regarded as one of the richest men in New Mexico. Indeed, he was commonly known by the nickname, *"El Millonario."* Legend has it that twice a year he hauled his horde of gold and silver coins onto the patio of his house. There he gave them a good airing, as he said, to prevent rust.

One time Edward Glasgow, of a St. Louis commercial house where Chávez did business, mistook the latter's want list, thinking he wanted *una casa grande,* a big house, not *un caso grande,* a large kettle. Later, after being billed fifteen thousand dollars for the St. Louis mansion Glasgow purchased for him, Chávez visited the merchant and discovered the error on the original list.

> Felipe Chávez paid for the house and years afterward Glasgow sold it for him—at a price of $80,000. In telling of the incident later Don Felipe always said, with a twinkle in his eye, "What was a bad mistake worked out in the end." With luck like that, it is no wonder that he became *"El Millonario."*[162]

Most early merchants were like Edward Glasgow. As May Price Mosley (NMFWP) notes, early ranchers' "want lists, or 'bills' as they were termed, grew long" between the "annual or semi-annual shopping schedule" of those who were "not town-minded." She adds that "bills . . . were not expected to be paid oftener than once a year, no matter how often the rancher visited his merchant." Mosley describes a drummer, or itinerant salesman, in southeastern New Mexico—Ira J. Jeter, "one of the first business institutions of the South Plains, . . . never successfully imitated." Driving a mule-drawn wagon of dry goods and hardware, Jeter "would pull up at some ranch and spend the night; much of which would be spent in outfitting the family of the small rancher. . . . Next morning, after much weighing and debating, changing and figuring, father would write a check . . . and the argosy of trade would move on."[163]

Many Jewish merchants came to New Mexico during the nineteenth century. Among the best known were the Gusdorfs in Taos; the Seligmans, Spiegelbergs, and Staabs in Santa Fe; the Bibos in Bernalillo; and the Ilfelds in Las Vegas and Albuquerque. Louis Ilfeld (1857–1938) of Albuquerque opened a branch store in Thoreau near Fort Wingate. There, according to his daughter Beatrice Ilfeld Meyer, Billy the Kid and his gang appeared one night and demanded "grub, clothes, ammunition and whiskey." The Kid promised to pay later, and Ilfeld made an itemized accounting. A few weeks passed before Billy appeared at midnight, "asked for his account and paid it in full—in gold," with no questions "asked as to the original owners of the gold." Meyer credits her father with another legendary transaction, this one during the difficult days of depression in the twentieth century:

> At the time of the run on the First National Bank (in the 1930's), there were long queues of people waiting to withdraw their money. The situation was serious, when the [bank] president, Jack Reynolds, called on Don Luis for help. He walked through the crowds with several thousand dollars in his hand and deposited it to his account. When people saw Louis Ilfeld depositing rather than withdrawing his money, many left the bank, satisfied that their money was also safe, which it was. A run on the bank had been diverted.[164]

Most of the Jewish merchants opened branch stores in various communities and employed "drummers" to travel to more remote areas and sell their merchandise. William J. Parish describes both the Jewish drummers and the merchants they traveled for:

> The goods he possessed or commanded, and the understanding and sympathy that came with his cosmopolitanism, brought easy entrance to every door. His solid education and his acuteness in its use made it second nature for him to exert leadership in family and community problems. Solomon Floersheim, while traveling the countryside in the collection of sheep accounts, became widely known as "Doctor" because of his commonsense application of a minimum of medical knowledge. All these merchants were scribes for a population that was more than half illiterate. Any serious family problem from sickness to divorce or murder to burial was as likely as not to produce a call to the man who had helped them so many times in so many ways before. The dominant position that these merchants held for so many years, and their direct and rather intimate relationships with all segments of the economy, suggests the probability of their more than casual influence on the peaceful mingling of Spanish, Indian, and American cultures.[165]

By the late nineteenth century, Hispanic *varilleros* still operating what Arthur L. Campa calls "traveling dime stores" required some cash purchases. First from the back of burros and then from wagons called *ambulanzas,* the *varillero* plied his trade,

> a traveling salesman of the nineteenth century who supplied the housewives with sewing thread, the men with straw hats, and the children with toys and candy. He sold for cash, occasionally bartered, but did not have to shout his wares in order to trade. The people on his route knew him by name, and he in turn was well acquainted with the principal ranchos, where he customarily stopped at regular intervals during the spring, summer, and fall.

Their visits were very welcome in isolated rural communities, for

> these *varilleros,* aside from providing essential and much-needed merchandise to the customers, also provided them with the latest news from the outside world. The buying and selling was interspersed with a running news commentary about people who lived farther upriver or up the trail—marriages, deaths and other informative tidbits of interest to his customers. Those who came in contact with traders from Mexico City also brought news and information of wider interest.

Most *varilleros* were Spaniards, referred to as *gachúpines* or *españoles,* and some, like Don José, "would play and sing not only the regional folk songs he learned in his travels but also those that he labeled *de la madre patria,* 'from the mother country,' meaning his own country and, by extension, the country of all who spoke Spanish." Although "the *varilleros* were said to accrue large earnings from their trade,...people did not begrudge them their profits when they were men like Don José *el gachupin.*"[166]

Others who traded in New Mexico from the south were gypsies, known locally as *los turcos,* Turks, or *los árabes,* Arabs. Reyes N. Martínez remembered

Gypsies, possibly in New Mexico. (MNM Neg. No. 640.)

the summer of 1890, [when] a trio of "Arabs" (as they were called by the natives), wearing their baggy trousers and tasseled fezzes, the typical garb of the races of southern Asia, passed through the villages of Taos County. Two of them carried musical instruments folded and tucked under their arms. They stood these musical instruments on the ground and inflated them to the level of their chins by blowing air into them, causing them to assume the shape of oversized bagpipes. The third man led a muzzled black bear at the end of a light chain.

Arriving in front of the post office or the local store, they inflated their balloon-like instruments and started to play their strange music to draw the attention of the residents of the village. . . . After performing for two or three minutes, the bear ceased dancing and passed a cap held between its front paws among the gathering. . . . Another piece of music was then played . . . alternating . . . till no more coins were dropped into the cap. This closed the show and the trio of "Arabs," with their bear trailing behind them, resumed their journey northward. A group of children followed after them, at a safe distance from the bear, through the village streets until they reached the open highway.

Arabs, or whatever they may have been, were a strange sight in this part of the country. For it seemed that they neither spoke nor understood Spanish.

William J. Parish notes that "during the 'nineties in New Mexico, some concern was being expressed for the influx of *Los Árabes,* a Middle-Eastern gypsy-like people who had come to the United States along with the new waves of immigration from central, southern, and eastern Europe. With pack on back they trudged from place to place trading, principally in sheep. They were centered first in the Puerto de Luna area."[167]

Gypsy caravans were well known in the Southwest, but, Reyes N. Martínez claims, "it was not till the year 1910 that they began to travel in greatly augmented numbers."

In the years before 1917, they used to travel in wagons, on horseback, and afoot. Several wagons on which were loaded their tents, bedding, and cooking utensils and on which also traveled the women and the children and some of the men, composed the advance of the caravan. The rest of the men, on horseback and afoot, leading some of the other horses, brought up the rear. They usually sought (as they still do now [1937]) the neighborhood of the river to put up camp, where they could obtain firewood for cooking their meals. . . . The women and the older girls then got busy at their trade of fortune-telling, curing(?) the sick, etc. They spread throughout the village and visited every home into which they could gain admittance, accosting the residents for money and telling, in return, the fortune of those who paid the fee [ten to twenty-five cents minimum] that they asked. . . .

The men of the caravan engaged themselves mostly in trading horses. They always had some beautiful specimens. Their method was to give one of their horses in trade for another horse, receiving an extra consideration in cash to boot.

These caravans were always under the direction or management of an elderly man or woman. Two or three days was the usual stay. . . . Their leaving was like the passing of a circus. Reminiscences both pleasant and otherwise were left in their wake in the minds of the residents.

According to a 1982 article by Marc Simmons:

Samuel Lucero, who resides at San Jose on the Pecos River and is now in his 80s, recalls his first sight of the gypsies when he was a small boy. They came in a large caravan of bright red wagons pulled by horses. They set up camp between the village and the river and remained a week. That was about the length of time the local people could tolerate them. . . .

An elderly neighbor of mine in Cerrillos tells me that when she was a girl, trains of gypsy wagons came to town at least once a year. The women, she claims, would strike up conversations with the townsfolk, while the men would slip behind the houses and steal chickens.

The many tricks and schemes of the gypsies seem to have left the strongest impressions. Fortunetelling was a principal activity of the older girls and women, and they used it in a variety of ways to fleece the gullible.

Upon arrival, they fanned out through town gossiping and talking with everyone they met. This was part of their strategy—to pick up as much local information as possible, and use it later as bogus evidence of their fortunetelling powers.

World War I brought an end to the gypsy caravans. When they resumed in 1920, it was by automobile.

At first they came through in old, almost dilapidated touring cars, but about since 1930 they seem to have prospered to the extent that they now travel in late-model coaches and sedans, although their mode of camping, fortune-telling and style of dress is the same as it was in their first years of journeying through this section of New Mexico. Their foreign accent in their speech still seems to linger with them.[168]

Long John Dunn (1857–1953)
of Taos, 1932. Photo by Will
Connell. (MNM Neg. No.
59760.)

With growing automobile travel, the development of roads, highways, and bridges became increasingly important, particularly as would-be gypsies, the bohemian artists and literati and the tourists, "discovered" New Mexico after the turn of the century. Taos was one of the original places of their "discovery," and its tourist industry is in part associated with "John H. (Huntley [*sic: actually, Harris*]) Dunn [1857–1953)], known to the old timers and traveling public as 'Long John' and to the natives as 'Juan Largo.'" Dunn had been involved in the mining boom at Elizabethtown, but, "hearing of Taos, and visiting the old town at intervals, [he] saw the possibilities in the freighting and stage business and decided to move" there in the spring of 1893. He bought the toll bridge and road franchise across the Rio Grande and hauled freight and passengers from the Denver and Rio Grande Railroad at Tres Piedras, Servilleta, and occasionally Embudo. "The bridge was burned down in 1908, probably by hoboes camping underneath, and John rebuilt it, as the old Spaniards used to say, 'at his own expense,' and continued to operate the toll bridge until 1912 when he sold out to the Territory [*sic*] of New Mexico, who made it a free bridge."[169]

James A. Burns (NMFWP), himself a well-known Taos character, details the saga that followed:

> By the time he had sold out the toll bridge at Rio Hondo, the influx of artists and tourists from the East coming by way of Santa Fe, and the automobile becoming a practicable machine, Dunn turned his attention to this source of business, bought himself an automobile, learned to drive it, and went after that business. At first he made the trip in two days, stopping over-night at Velarde, later increasing the speed to three round trips a week, down to Santa Fe one day and back the next. . . .
>
> At that time the road down Taos Canyon was nothing but a pack trail, where now two cars can pass anywhere. It was the old Ladrones (robbers) trail where outlaws used to camp at the foot of the hill and climb up the canyon to Taos Valley and harass the farmers of Ranchos de Taos, driving off their stock and at times killing the settlers. . . .
>
> By continual agitation and making a general nuisance of himself around the State Capitol, John Dunn finally succeeded in getting the burro trails up Taos Canyon widened into a passable road, and later on as the value of tourist traffic began to be appreciated, succeeded in getting the highway graded from the foot of the hill to Embudo. . . . One of the commonest questions asked by tourists in driving down through the Cañon with John was foolish question No. 41144, "Do cars roll off the grade into the bottom of the canyon very often?" To which John would reply with his nasal drawl, "No, *only once*."[170]

Dunn continued to haul freight until new regulations forced him to quit in 1928, but he handled several mail routes from 1920 through the 1930s. According to Max Evans, he drove all the people coming to Taos until 1930 and continued to believe until his death on May 22, 1953, that artists and three others had made Taos what it is:

> The artists, first and foremost, because they advertised Taos across the Atlantic and across the Pacific and in between the two oceans. They never made a complaint about all the hardships, and they had many. I'm satisfied they're the easiest bunch of people to get along with it has ever been my privilege to meet.

Writer Mabel Dodge Lujan contributed a great deal to the poor people of Taos. She gave us the hospital, bandstand, and many other things. . . .

Next on the list is John Harris Dunn. I hauled 'em in, and I took care of 'em on the way. Finally there's that fine man and merchant, Gerson Gusdorf. He took care of 'em after they arrived.

With a lifelong devotion to Taos doyenne Mabel Dodge Luhan, who first arrived in 1916, Dunn "attended anything Mabel Dodge asked him to, and there is little doubt that she felt great pride in his tall, almost arrogant figure, with his direct, salty, nasal-whanging tales to entertain her friends from all parts of the world."[171]

Mining

Taos visitors and residents alike were fascinated by lore about another local character, land and mining speculator Arthur Rochford Manby, an Englishman. According to Den Galbraith: "All towns have a favorite story and in Taos one of the first stories an out-of-towner hears is the mystery of Arthur R. Manby, an eccentric bunco artist whose decapitated body was discovered July 3, 1929, behind locked doors. Ask a dozen people about that mystery and you'll get twelve widely different theories."[172]

James A. Burns (NMFWP) describes Manby as "a man of medium height, of stocky build, with a deep chest and a large head and short thick neck. . . . While around Taos, he usually dressed roughly: an old slouch hat, a shooting jacket or mackinaw coat, breeches, puttees and heavy shoes. . . . He was curt and business-like in ordinary conversations, transacting his business without any waste of words or time." Burns begins his 1936 sketch with a judicious assessment of the Englishman's Taos career, which began soon after he arrived in New Mexico in 1883:

> The wave of speculation in Spanish Grants, which struck New Mexico in the last decade of the nineteenth century, brought to Taos one of the most colorful characters in the ninety years since the American occupation. In a community noted or notorious in the state and nation for the rugged individualism of its citizens, he stood out like Saul "head and shoulders above his countrymen" as one of the most individualistic of them all. A man who made a few strong friends and a host of enemies. A man who gave to the people of Taos a thousand acres of land for a playground, who lined the main avenue of the residence district of the town with big cottonwood trees; autumnal beauty of which is the wonder and delight of artists and tourists from all over the world. He it was who defended the rights of the Spanish settlers against the encroachments of Washington bureaucrats for the water of their mountain streams that they had been using since "the memory of man runneth not to the contrary." When the pioneer physicians of Taos County were performing operations on kitchen tables by the light of kerosene lamps, with their hearts in their throats for fear the ether they were using might explode and blow them and their patients to kingdom come, this man planned a forty-room hospital for Taos, a plan which is only now coming to fruition through the generosity and public spirit of another of Taos' misunderstood individualists, Mabel Dodge Luhan.

In this and other matters Manby was forty years ahead of his time, but his habit of always looking out for Manby, from his intelligent self-interest, if such it was, [and] his way of following the advice of Robert Burns "to gather gear by every wile that's justified by honor," and perhaps some that were *not* so justified, he made many enemies in the community, some of whom almost rejoiced at his tragic and untimely death.

One of the primary reasons for this enmity, Burns relates, was Manby's dispossession of prominent Taoseño Don Juan de los Reyes Santistevan:

> At the time Manby came to Taos, Don Juan Santistevan, an old timer merchant and banker, of the old regime and highly respected, had a general store at the southwest corner of the Taos Plaza. Old Don Juan, though a shrewd trader of the old school, had failed to keep up with the march of events and the modern business methods and had gotten into financial difficulties. He owned what is now known as the Manby Tract (Survey No. 125 P. 4) and his old home just north of the Hotel Martin [now Taos Inn]. In some way Manby got himself appointed assignee of Don Juan's business to liquidate it. Just what financial and legal jugglery was employed would be hard to trace but the effect was easily seen. Like the monkey who adjudicated the suit between the two cats and kept nibbling at the two hunks of cheese to make them balance, Manby nibbled at Don Juan's hunk of cheese to such good effect that the final outcome was that Manby came into possession of the entire property, which he turned over to his Colonial Bond & Security Company.[173]

Manby also gained control of the Antonio Martínez and the Antoine Leroux, or Los Luceros, land grants in Taos County. According to Burns, he tried to develop a hot springs and sanitarium in the northwest corner of the latter, in the Rio Grande canyon. "The water of these springs has temperature of about 110 degrees and the analysis shows the mineral contents to resemble in variety and quantity those of Ojo Caliente in the southwestern part of Taos County. Other parties had done some pioneer work on the springs, . . . [and] after getting control of the Martinez Grant, Manby . . . had them cleaned out and built sheds over them, widening the trail leading down to the springs from the rim of the cañon." According to Reyes N. Martínez's 1936 account, in his construction "Manby ran true to his reputation, which was a mysterious and macabre one. A visitor to the springs in 1922 described the interior as eerie. . . . Lighted only by a small window in the rock wall, the black waters, spotted with weird glints of light, give the immediate impression of some dim prehistoric pool, fitly chosen for sacrificial rites."[174]

Manby named the site La Bajada Hot Springs and produced a two-page typescript giving their particulars, a chemical analysis of the waters, a pencil sketch of "two old Aztec inscriptions on each side of Spring, signifying perpetual life," and various items of lore to support his contention that "should it develop these springs are the long lost springs of the Aztecs, and the fact coupled with history seems to indicate that such a belief is well founded, then these springs, located as they are, amid magnificent scenery, and the bright sunshine of New Mexico, should ultimately develop into one of the world's great resorts." He identified his springs with Montezuma's birthplace.[175]

During the 1920s, Manby formed a secret society known as the "United States Secret and Civil Service Society, Self-Supporting Branch—Grand House Service Number 10." His longtime friend Teracita Ferguson was president, and meetings were held near her tourist camp. The society was supposed to be a branch of the United States Intelligence Department in Washington. According to Frank Waters:

> Manby gave the new members strange missions to perform. One of them was required to stealthily follow a businessman in town all day and make a detailed report of everything he did and everyone he met. Another was instructed to saddle his horse at daybreak and ride up a mountain canyon, waving a red flag as a signal to invisible secret agents hiding on the slopes. No one questioned these missions. Manby himself flashed signals by raising and lowering the American flag he flew from the roof of his house. Often at night he placed a lantern on the roof too. This, he explained, was for the benefit of a strange new-style air-ship, the *Garibaldi,* which periodically landed on his back pasture with messages of international importance and disappeared before morning. It was understood that the *Garibaldi* was flown from Italy.
>
> Failure of the members in the performance of their duties was punishable by death. Manby was not backward in showing them how it might be performed. Leading them out into the orchard, he would go through the motions of shooting a victim, stamping on his body, and cutting off his head.[176]

On many nights, Manby was seen and heard digging in his garden. After his grisly death was discovered, Teracita and her lover Carmen Duran moved into the house and began digging in the garden for Manby's allegedly hidden money. They were not questioned because "for the first few days after Manby's body had been found and buried, it was assumed that he had died from natural causes and that his dog had chewed off his head." However, conjecture soon escalated that the body so hastily buried was not Manby's.

> Victor Higgins, the watercolor painter, also held the opinion that Manby had killed and mutilated another man to leave in his place. . . .
>
> Joseph Sharp, the noted painter of Indians, returned to town after a long voyage with his wife. The couple was greatly disturbed upon hearing the wild conjectures abut Manby's alleged murder. In Italy both of them had seen Manby on a street in Florence and had quickly walked over to greet him. Manby, however, had ducked into a store and escaped through the back door.
>
> More evidence that Manby had fled was given by runty Doughbelly Price, the colorful real estate agent whose "Goddamn it, my word's as good as my dollar!" had established his reputation for veracity. He positively had seen Manby furtively slouching past his office two days after his alleged death. Elmer, the son of Alvin Burch, reported that a friend of his in Mexico who knew Manby well, Jesus Mares y Maesta, had seen him in Ojinaga, Chihuahua two years after his reported death. All these statements seemed to be confirmed by the telegram and letter received by Governor Dillon from Miles Plemmons stating that Manby had checked out of the country a week after he had been reported murdered, and offering to produce a passport photograph of him.[177]

Arthur R. Manby and dog, Taos. Courtesy Kit Carson Memorial Foundation, Inc.

Still others began to report seeing "an apparition, said to be Manby's, sometimes headless, [who] wanders around the grounds of his old house and its vicinity. Witnesses say it is a vile presence, filled with evil intent and malevolence."[178]

During the course of his investigations into the Manby case, Santa Fe detective Herman Charles (Bill) Martin discovered the decapitated remains of Bill Wilkerson, one of Manby's old partners in the Mystic and Ajax mines, who was murdered on September 28, 1921. The skull lay at the portal of the Mystic mine.

> A week or more later [in July 1929] Martin drove back alone to Mt. Baldy, taking [old prospector Thomas] Brankfort's advice to poke around some more. Here, as he recorded in his personal notes, he found a heap of bones and skulls, with their owners' remnants of clothes and belongings, that turned out to be skeletons of seven other men. Taking them back to Elizabethtown, he found a man who identified them. He was an elderly man named McIntyre who in the mining camp's prosperous days had run a hotel and livery stable, a saloon and a store, staking prospectors and selling them their outfits. According to him, all seven men had been associated with Manby in some way.[179]

Columbus Ferguson, Teracita's father, and William Stone had formed a partnership to mine the Mystic and Ajax claims in the 1870s. Wilkerson, whose real first name might have been Frank or George, arrived on the scene and became a partner around 1890. He had a bad reputation, having been implicated in a Kansas killing. "Old timers considered him a high-grader: a man who made it his profession to steal out from any mine in which he was working pieces of high-grade ore to dispose of at good profit through dishonest assayers or outside buyers." Owners of the failing Aztec mine nearby claimed the partners high-graded their ore. According to Frank Waters: "Old Stone, a simple man, became disgruntled and kept aloof in his own secluded cabin. One morning his mutilated body was found near the portal of the Mystic. No inquiry was made, and the cause of his death remained unknown."[180] Manby became the new partner.

Violence erupted frequently in mining camps. According to James A. Burns: "Among the gold miners, especially the placer miners, the most detested crime, and warranting instant death if caught in the act, was the stealing of Amalgam (quicksilver and gold) from the riffles in the sluice boxes. These were of necessity left exposed in the open until the regular weekly or monthly clean-up, when the Amalgam was gathered from the riffles, retorted, the quick returned to the riffles and the gold, the miners' harvest, shipped to the mint."[181] Harry E. Anderson of Raton told Burns of an 1889 incident in the Moreno Valley, where a young night watchman, E. H. Johnson, arrested his own mine superintendent, E. L. Hall, when the latter came too near the sluice boxes.

Moreno Valley mining began in 1866, when Ute Indians trading at Fort Union offered copper they had picked up on Baldy Mountain. Captain William Moore and William Kroenig went to investigate and then sent Lawrence F. Bronson, Peter Kinsinger, and a man named Kelley to do assessment work on the Mystic mine that fall. Kelley chanced to find gold, and the three carved DISCOVERY TREE in a nearby ponderosa and returned to Fort Union to await spring. Hundreds of prospectors followed them in 1867, including some three hundred soldiers who quit Fort Union. "Goldseekers found color at places like Spanish Bar, Michigan Gulch, Pine Tree

Ravine, St. Louis Gulch, Nigger Gulch and Humbug Gulch. Four hundred claims had been filed within an eight-mile radius of old Baldy by July and a steam sawmill was belching smoke and whirring out 4000 feet of lumber a day." According to Paige W. Christianson:

> With all the hectic activity and confusion, it was time for a town to be built. The new settlement was named Elizabethtown, after the oldest daughter of John Moore, one of its founders. E'town, as it was soon nicknamed, became a town of tents and log cabins and rough lumber shacks almost overnight. In 1869 and 1870, the boom was at its peak: Elizabethtown had a population of about 2,000, and another 2,000 lived in the immediate surroundings. By late 1870, the population reached 7,000. . . .
>
> The truth of the wealth of Elizabethtown lies somewhere between these extremes. A rich district for a brief period in the late 1860s and early 1870s, an estimated $2,000,000 worth of gold was produced in its placers, and perhaps as much more in the lodes. For New Mexico, that was a fabulous amount—more than had ever been seen in so short a span of time.

Ralph Looney notes that "E'town's growth was so phenomenal that by 1870 it became the first incorporated town in New Mexico Territory, with a mayor, a council and practically all the other frills of civilization . . . [and] next . . . the seat of a new county, carved out of Mora County and named in honor of Vice President-elect Schuyler Colfax."[182]

Virtually a ghost town by 1875 (although briefly revived around 1900), in its heyday Elizabethtown was the scene of much commerce and violence. In the fall of 1870, Charles Kennedy, who lived twenty miles away with his Ute wife at the foot of Palo Flechado Pass on the road to Taos, was found to have murdered some fourteen travelers, who had been lured to his cabin for dinner, and even one or two of his own children. Brought to trial in Elizabethtown on October 3, Kennedy was lynched by outraged miners three days later. Philip Varney recounts two versions of the aftermath of this mob action:

> one says that his skeleton was wired together and sent to the Smithsonian for study, as Kennedy's skull was "peculiar." Another version states that Kennedy's corpse was decapitated and the head was presented to Henry (Henri) Lambert, once a cook to Grant and Lincoln, formerly an Elizabethtown hosteler, and at that time proprietor of the well-known St. James in Cimarron. Lambert was ordered to hang it outside as a grisly reminder to those who would consider such evil acts. The head stayed so long on the corral fence that it mummified.[183]

Later, the skull disappeared from the noted Santa Fe Trail hotel.

Isolated from major transportation routes and population centers and with insufficient water for mining, Elizabethtown did not survive. Pinos Altos in southwestern New Mexico, where gold was discovered by '49ers returning from California in 1859, fared much better. Almost destroyed in September 1861 by an Apache attack led by Cochise and Mangas Coloradas, Pinos Altos was chartered as a mining company by Thomas Marston in 1866.[184]

After the Civil War, prospectors became an integral part of New Mexican life and lore. In *Black Range Tales* (1936), James A. ("Uncle Jimmie") McKenna recalls their contributions in religious terms:

> The Indian feared the prospector, yet he persecuted him. It was the prospector's cabin that was burned; it was his stock that was stolen; and his life was always in danger. The men of this group who are left are now between the ages of seventy and eighty-five. Who will deny that they deserve the care of their Government? Soon they will be forgotten, though every dale, every ridge, and every gulch of the Southwest bears their mark. Cowboys and hunters often come upon abandoned cabins, shafts, and drifts in lonely spots that were deserted by hunted owners more than fifty years ago. Will their places ever be filled?
>
> Something bigger than gold was behind the search of the old-time prospector and led him up and down the world looking for the hidden treasures of the earth. Leading the solitary life of a hermit for months at a time, frugal, hard-working, observant, kind, thoughtful, and brave—did he not take to himself virtue from the mighty works of God among which he wandered? Was he the vagabond he is sometimes made out, or was he, perhaps, a soul reaching out for the Creator, like all humans, as St. Augustine says, "Restless till we rest in Him"?[185]

McKenna claims that most prospectors "were men who helped to build the Continental railroads in the early eighties. Not a few Texans drove their herds of cattle into the mountains, took up ranches around water holes and later on became prospectors. And why not? There is the story of the cowboy who picked up a nugget of pure gold to throw at a mean cow, and he was only one of many who struck it rich by a turn of good luck."[186]

McKenna himself learned prospecting in Elizabethtown in 1877: "It was there that I panned my first gold, came to know what was meant by a diggings, and stored away bits of mining lore that I picked up here and there among veteran prospectors. It was there that I sat for the first time before a golden camp-fire and listened to blood-curdling tales of raiding Indians, of heartless cutthroats, of daring outlaws, of dashing cowboys, of painted women, of dead shots, and of regular old sourdoughs and desert rats, some good and some bad." He pushed southwest from E-town, then "got into placer mining near Hillsboro, but I did not stay there long, going on to Silver City, Pinos Altos, and Tombstone, back to Lake Valley, down to Hachita, and up again into the Black Range, becoming, like all other prospectors, a rover. . . . Many a time I was carried along in a round of excitement that went with a strike."[187]

A "Statement of the Bullion product of Grant County N. Mx. for the Year ending June 30th 1876" details seven shippers, among them L. T. Ancheta, moving gold worth $50,361.33, silver worth $422,829.00, and "208,000 Lbs of copper valued at 41,600$." In the accompanying letter to Secretary of the Territory William G. Ritch, C. P. Crawford of the office of H. M. Porter, Banker and Merchant, Silver City, wrote: "I must ask you to not allow the publication of anything but the totals. For obvious reasons parties shipping bullion do not wish a statement of their business made public." Originally called San Vicente de la Ciénaga when it was founded about 1870, Silver City was renamed by mining boom Anglos, and "before the railroad was built in 1881, twelve- and fourteen-horse teams hauled ore and bullion into

"Gold prospector blowing away dirt in order to find the gold in his pan, while a visiting prospector looks on." FSA photo by Russell Lee, Pinos Altos, May 1940. (LC-USF 33-12701-M2.)

the city, and bricks of gold and silver were stacked on sidewalks outside shipping offices."[188]

Kingston, known as the "Gem of the Black Range," was named for the area's first silver strike, the Iron King mine. "It was said that Kingston was the only place in the country where a man could sit down to breakfast a pauper and have dinner a millionaire." Englishwoman Sarah Jane Creech ("Sadie") Orchard arrived in 1885 or 1886 and set up a brothel on Kingston's Virtue Avenue, then moved to Hillsboro to establish one on a hillside overlooking the town. While in Hillsboro, she married James W. Orchard, owner of the Mountain Pride Line of stagecoaches and wagons.[189]

Betty Reich (NMFWP) reports that in 1937 Mrs. Orchard told her how:

In 1888 Mr. and Mrs. S. J. Orchard bought the Kingston stagecoach line. At that time they owned a stage line that served Silver City, Pinos Altos and Mogollon. Not wishing to give up their contract with the government for carrying the mail, Mr. Orchard continued to operate the Silver City line for two years, while Mrs. Orchard went to Kingston to operate the new line.

Mrs. Orchard often drove the great Concord coach herself and many of the passengers said that they would rather ride with her than any of the drivers she employed. She also broke many of the stagecoach horses. Ranchers sent in horses to them so they could be broken. Driving a stagecoach and breaking wild bronchos was just part of the daily life of this pioneer woman.[190]

Sadie Orchard also opened the Ocean Grove Hotel (now the Black Range Museum) in Hillsboro and later the Orchard Hotel, which she still owned in 1936, when Clay W. Vaden (NMFWP) interviewed her:

"The stage Harry Orchard drove from Lake Valley to Kingston. It stands in front of the building in Hillsboro which his wife, Sadie Orchard, operated as the Orchard Hotel." (Erna Fergusson Collection, Special Collections, General Library, University of New Mexico. Used with permission.)

Sadie Orchard and unidentified men. (Erna Fergusson Collection, Special Collections, General Library, University of New Mexico. Used with permission.)

"I came to Kingston . . . in 1886," Mrs. Orchard said. "At that time Kingston was a mining town of about 5,000 population with a big silver boom going full sway. Dance halls and saloons did a rushing business almost day and night. Fortunes were made, and in some cases lost, overnight.

"Mr. Orchard and I drove the stage line for 14 years. We had two Concord coaches and an express wagon. . . .

"I drove four and six horses every day from Kingston to Lake Valley and sometimes as far as Nutt station. In those days we did not have the roads we can justly boast of in New Mexico today, and my trips were surely trying—especially through picturesque Box Canyon between Kingston and Hillboro.

"Many times I had for passengers some very famous people. Lillian Russell, stage star, as far as I know was never in Kingston, but members of her troupe were, and I had occasion to meet the actress. She was a guest at one time on a ranch west of Hillsboro, the Horseshoe Ranch, I believe. . . ."

Sadie, the daring stage driver of those good old days which Gene Rhodes delighted to write about so realistically, is getting older as the years slip by, but she is still the big-hearted, resourceful woman of frontier days who saw her job, tackled it heroically and did it manfully with a twinkle in her eyes.

"I'm a product of the 'Old West,'" laughed Mrs. Orchard, "and you know in those days we didn't have much chance to practice the niceties of high society."

Almost ninety when she died in Hillsboro in the early 1940s, Sadie Orchard was buried in Hot Springs (now Truth or Consequences). According to Mary Frances Beverley: "Sadie by now has faded into legend. Perhaps she didn't actually ride, Lady Godiva-style, down Main Street on a dare. Maybe she and a friend didn't intend to seriously hurt the friend's husband when they set off a charge of dynamite under his chair. Who knows the identity of the blind child she kept and cared for so lovingly?" Nevertheless, "regardless of whom you talk to in Kingston or Hillsboro about Sadie Orchard, sooner or later everyone agrees: She was a good ol' girl."[191]

Copper, as well as gold and silver, was mined in southwestern New Mexico, and Carey McWilliams calls the Santa Rita copper mine near Silver City "perhaps the most famous mine in Western America, for it was here that the techniques of copper mining were first developed in the Southwest." In 1798, an Apache Indian showed Colonel José Manuel Carrasco his copper find. In 1938, eighty-year-old prospector Celestino Carrillo of the Mimbres Valley told Ernest Prescott Morey (NMFWP) that

Colonel Carrasso [sic] of the Spanish army was stationed in the Santa Rita area. He was a very good religious man. It was said that he tried to be fair with the Indians as well as the people of his own race. An old prospector said that he was a good, as well as a handsome man. He said Carrasso was tall, well built, broad shouldered, and wore a mustache and sideburns. He had left a wonderful home in Spain, where he had been reared on a large estate, or rancho, which was owned by his father, a Don.

One morning, an Apache Indian rushed into the fort at Santa Rita having been bitten by a rattle snake. Caruso, who at the time was drilling his detachment in the cool of the morning, hastened to the Indian's side and immediately treated him for snake bite. . . . Upon the day that the Indian was able to leave the fort and go back to his tribe, he called Colonel Carrasso aside to show his gratitude and bid him good-bye. It is a common story around Santa Rita that the Indian said, "Me show you red metal you follow me."

Billy D. Walker notes: "Traditionally, the date of discovery [by white men] is given as 1800. . . . The Apache's incentive can only be imagined, but the likelihood of self-preservation as a motive is great, for the Spaniards were at that time engaged in a campaign to suppress the Indians of New Mexico to bring protection to the frontier regions of Chihuahua and Sonora."[192]

Morey claims that "the town of Santa Rita is supposed to mark the very spot where copper was first discovered" and that in 1938 "Santa Rita boasts that they possess the largest open pit copper mine in the United States, if not in the world." It was this pit that eventually brought the destruction of Santa Rita, which suffered Apache raids throughout the nineteenth century but could not withstand mining developments in the twentieth. The Chino Copper Company was formed in 1909, the first steam shovels imported in 1910, a mill erected nearby at Hurley in 1911, a smelter in 1939, a fire refinery in 1942, "and as the width of the Glory Hole expanded, so the town of Santa Rita moved back to make room for the harvest— for Copper the King—and finally at the monarch's command be gone, dissolved, live only on the pages of history."[193]

José Manuel Carrasco called a monolith standing apart from the nearby mountains the Kneeling Nun, "and he named the *criadero de cobre* 'Santa Rita' after the patron saint of stray members of a flock." In 1938, twenty-year-old Mrs. Mary Watson remembered her grandparents telling her that the formation was named for a nun who left her convent seeking the Santa Rita man who had been the convent

Santa Rita from Gold Hill, May 21, 1915. (MNM Neg. No. 65745.)

gardener and with whom she had fallen in love. "When at last she arrived at the foothills of a large mountain overlooking Santa Rita . . . she was so overcome with grief . . . that she prayed to be sacrificed as a monument to the people of this new country and her lover in Santa Rita." Morey comments that it is "strange, but true, [that] many of the present day inhabitants of this region regard the story of the Kneeling Nun as sacred and liken unto the Bible story of Lot's wife. . . . I wish to add that this Kneeling Nun Monument has furnished many persons a place of prayer and worship, in the present as well as the past generations."[194]

In 1936, Mrs. Mildred Jordan (NMFWP) noted that "perhaps no story is so dear to the people of Grant County as the legend of the Kneeling Nun," which she records as follows:

> In the early days of the Spanish Conquest of Mexico, a band of men under Coronado came through Santa Rita searching for gold. Shortly after, there came a band of Monks and Nuns, building a monastery. Times were hard not only to make a living, but there was the constant fear of Indians. Soldiers of the Coronado army were brought to the monastery wounded and dying. One of these soldiers . . . was tenderly cared for by a young nun, Sister Rita. Love came to these two although she fought and prayed against it. But, alas, they were reported by a jealous man, and Sister Rita was condemned to die.
>
> She prayed to be turned to stone and her wish was granted. A terrible earthquake shook the walls of the monastery and only the Kneeling Nun or form of Sister Rita was left alone. . . . Santa Rita is supposed to have been named from this legend.[195]

N. Howard (Jack) Thorp described five legendary, lost Spanish mines in the Placitas area not far from Albuquerque for the NMFWP. Among them was the Montezuma mine.

The Kneeling Nun formation near Santa Rita. (MNM Neg. No. 88234.

Until these mines had been rediscovered, no amount of coaxing could get the Indians to tell where they were located. While working them, the Indians lived in a village of their own near them, the remains of which now stand in Las Huertas Canyon. . . . An Indian who some years ago was chief of the Cochitis says his ancestors worked in these mines for six moons in every year, the remainder of the time being spent in raising their crops in the valley of the Rio Grande. According to this arrangement, the different pueblos must have alternated in sending workers to these mines. This Cochiti further stated that the gold and silver ornaments used in the pueblo churches were fashioned from gold extracted from these mines. He also states that the levels of one of the mines caved in, burying many Indians.

Montezuma, also known as Poseyemo, is the male god of these Indians, and it is but natural that the principal mine of this group should have received his name. Indians expect Montezuma to return to earth, to place them again in possession of all their land, and even now at sunrise you can see some of them looking toward the east for Montezuma being borne toward them by an eagle.

The tradition among the natives who now live at Ojo de la Casa is that one of these mines has no bottom. There was no pumping machinery in those days. The water was carried to the surface in earthenware vessels and rawhide buckets on the peon's back, held in place by straps around the forehead of the slaves, who climbed a notched pole, sometimes for a hundred feet or more, carrying the water and ore to the surface. If one should slip and fall with these tremendous loads, all would plunge to the bottom. These people of Ojo de la Casa also repeat the story of the Cochiti, that the crowns and statues of Saint Joseph, the Virgin Mary, and others in Saint Joseph's Church in Algodones were made from beaten gold and silver taken from these mines.[196]

In Spanish, latter-day prospectors were known as *gambusinos,* a name, Lorin W. Brown notes, "given to placer miners, who roam the hills seeking scattered pockets or deposits of gold, mostly working over country which has already been worked on a large scale, trying to retrieve what others have left or overlooked." Writing for the NMFWP in 1938, he describes *gambusinos* in the Cerrillos area, who had to sneak into the closed mines on the Ortiz Grant. "The absence of the men of the town was especially noted after a rain, for then they knew that the gold was washed down from the hillsides and slopes into the gullies and arroyos and, collecting in the pockets or depressions, gave better promise of profitable returns for their efforts. *Gambusinos* usually worked in groups of three or more, for one of their number must be posted to watch for the approach of the grant's caretaker." Brown describes the "king of the *gambusinos*" as

one old miner, who has lived all his life in that section and who has been actively connected with all the mining ups and downs of the grant, who is the only one allowed free ingress and egress to the grant at all times. The reason for this is that he possesses knowledge of the location of a rich vein of gold-bearing ore. The owners of the grant hope that some day he will lead them to the location of this vein. But he is a very crafty and wise customer, and when conscious of spying eyes he will confine himself to washing very poor paying dirt out of the arroyos or the bed of the little stream which is found close to Dolores. . . . He is still making a very good living from his hidden gold vein and as yet the company has not been able to find out its location. It was this man who conceived the idea of washing the adobes from the abandoned houses in Dolores and securing much gold from them.[197]

By 1890, turquoise mines in the Cerrillos district were also closed, including those on Turquoise Hill, which contained the ancient Castilian mine, popularly known as Tiffany mine because Tiffany's held principal interest in the North American Turquoise Company, which bought the site. According to Marc Simmons:

> All activity surrounding extraction of turquoise was shrouded in the greatest secrecy. The companies never divulged the exact location of their diggings nor the methods they used. No one was allowed to inspect the mines, photographs were forbidden, and employees were prohibited from speaking about their work to outsiders. Governor William T. Thornton (1893–1897) came down from Santa Fe to examine a turquoise property in which he hoped to invest, and even he was denied entrance. Such secrecy helped to hoodwink the tax collector, and allowed several brazen operators to declare that their claims were actually operating at a loss. Much of the blue stone left New Mexico unreported, but one gunnysack was intercepted containing $100,000 worth of turquoise. Part of the control measures of the mine owners could be justified, however. The open pits and shafts were vulnerable to thieves, and while the district was in operation, stealing remained a continuous problem.[198]

Until 1890, Pueblo Indians from Santo Domingo, Santa Ana, Cochiti, San Ildefonso, and San Felipe were accustomed to mine turquoise according to traditional needs. "The Pueblo of Santo Domingo, whose eastern reservation boundary approached the Cerrillos Hills, claimed ownership through a number of its residents who were descended from the early occupants of San Marcos and Galisteo Pueblos . . . [which] had been abandoned during Spanish times and their people scattered." In 1888, Irishman J. P. McNulty, superintendent of the Tiffany turquoise mines, had several threatening encounters with Pueblo Indians. His application to territorial officials for protection in part led to passage of a legislative act in 1890 "making it a crime for any Pueblo to enter the turquoise claims without permission of the current owners." Marc Simmons notes that, "reflecting on the episode decades later, white-haired McNulty philosophized: *'The Indians always thought they had a prior right to those old turquoise mines. And to be truthful I had a hankerin' notion they did, too.'"*[199]

Geologist and anthropologist William P. Blake made the first modern discovery of turquoise in 1858 and wrote a technical paper on it. Mount Chalchihuitl, 2.4 miles north-northeast of Cerrillos, was "site of the most extensive prehistoric mining operations known on the American continent," a pit some two hundred feet deep with about a hundred thousand tons of waste rock.[200] Stuart A. Northrop notes that "in ancient Spanish writings there are numerous references to a green stone highly prized by the Aztecs of Mexico and called by them *chalchihuitl.*" There is debate as to its mineralogical identity, some scientists claiming that in New Mexico much of it was green (not blue) turquoise and in Mexico either jade or jadeite, the latter from a Guatemalan deposit. Marc Simmons claims that the Aztec word *chalchihuitl* "was

Miners trenching for the lode, Archibeque in distance, Los Cerrillos Mining District, ca. 1880–1884. Photo by George C. Bennett. (MNM Neg. No. 14847.)

introduced by the Spaniards and their Indian servants from central Mexico" and that, "according to legend, the powerful Aztec emperor Montezuma II went about bedecked in necklace and pendants of turquoise from the remote Cerrillos deposits."[201]

Spanish explorers like Fray Marcos de Niza, Esteban, and members of the Coronado expedition saw turquoise but were not particularly interested in it. In 1629, Father Zarate Salmerón reported that the Spaniards in New Mexico were "too poor in capital . . . and are of less spirit" to mine, even though "in the country we have seen silver, copper, lead, . . . and mines of turquoise which the Indians work in their paganism, since to them it is as diamonds and precious stones." Nevertheless, a persistent legend about turquoise mining and the Pueblo Revolt developed, at least in

Herculano Montoya of Cienega in turquoise mine south of Santa Fe, ca. 1943. Photo by Bill Lippincott. (MNM Neg. No. 5237.)

the nineteenth century. In *The Land of the Pueblos,* Susan E. Wallace gives a standard version:

> The tradition is that the *chalchihuite* mines, through immemorial ages known to the primitive races, were possessed by the Spaniards in the sixteenth century. Indian slaves then worked them under the lash of the conqueror until 1680, when, by accident, a portion of the rock fell and killed thirty Pueblos. The Spaniards immediately made a requisition on the town of San Marcos for more natives to take their places; when, with a general uprising, they drove the hated oppressor from the country as far south as El Paso. I give the tale for what it is worth.[202]

Turquoise, whiteshell, abalone, jet, and native redstone (later replaced by coral, introduced by the Spanish) are considered precious stones by the Navajo. Turquoise, or *do·tłiji·,* "the-particular-one-which is blue," seems to "be the general collective term for all the precious stones, wealth, or mixed offerings, [and] good fortune is attributed to the stone." Gladys A. Reichard gives several "of the most unusual references to turquoise":

> Sun gave one of his wonderful children a pair of turquoise earstrings to enable him to win at gambling.
>
> The hair of a remarkable girl, desired by many suitors, was covered with images of coyote and birds of different kinds, all of turquoise; and she possessed a huge disk of turquoise.
>
> Four rattles of buffalo hide are important equipment in the Shooting Chant. One explanation says they symbolize Big Snakes, another that they represent Sun's turquoise rattles.
>
> Sun's son smoked a turquoise pipe, as did Frog.
>
> Perhaps the most unusual allusion is that to First Woman, who, in the first world, was intrigued by a distant fire. When she got to it she found a man, who said, "Your fire is rock crystal; mine is turquoise." This identification was cited as a reason why the two should live together.
>
> The Twins' bows and arrows are sometimes said to be of turquoise.[203]

Turquoise figures in the myth of the Male Shooting Chant recorded in 1924 by Father Berard Haile from Blue Eyes of Lukachukai. Gladys A. Reichard, who finally prepared it for publication in 1937, notes that "this myth is the description which gives the Chanter the key to the order of his rites and explains to him the why and wherefore of his action." In the following section of the myth, the Twins have been instructed to travel in various directions with two women:

> Two days later the four . . . started west in Mirage to make them invisible. Their one-day journey brought them to the edge of a body of water where they met twelve scouts of Changing Woman. Over a straight rainbow bridge they conducted the party past the guards, up through the water to the room where Changing Woman sat. Four tracks like those of a human being led to the door where a turquoise ladder stood. These were succeeded by whiteshell footprints, ladder and door, four of abalone and finally four of jet. When they had gone through the black door they saw her.
>
> This happened in the autumn when Changing Woman is old and just squats. It was dark with fog as when there is no moon. . . . The Dark Sky Man, holding a turquoise cane, went to Changing Woman. Both taking hold of it, he led her through the turquoise door at the east and returned with her, a very old woman indeed. The Water Woman handed her a whiteshell cane, and after going through the whiteshell door at the west, Changing Women returned looking middle-aged. Returning from the south after being led by an abalone cane, she was a young woman, and when the Summer People gave her a redstone cane, she went through the redstone (sic!) door of the north, and returned a young girl. She was attired in perfect garments of whiteshell, and in this ceremonial attire decreed her gifts to Earth People declaring,
>
> "Now the Sky People with the dark cloud will be your helpers, also the Water People with male rain and female rain, likewise the Sun People with vegetation pollen, and the Summer People with vegetation dew. With these your lands will

thrive....

"The Earth, Sky, Female Mountain and Female Water will do for you what you ask them. I, for my part, with vari-colored stones, horses, sheep and goods will help you.... Thus it happened."[204]

Conclusion

New Mexican place lore focuses on centers and peripheries. The Native American world is bounded by mountains and centered in ceremonials stemming from the place of emergence. Hispanos erected crosses and constructed plazas surrounded by common lands for grazing and wood gathering. Anglo ranchers and homesteaders fenced domains centered on springs, windmills, and later crossroads of commerce. Such settlements became sanctuaries, protecting and sustaining their inhabitants. Beyond their bounds were the wilds, the elemental, and the alien.

Herders, hunters, trappers, miners, and prospectors regularly ventured onto the peripheries and, upon their return from "the wilds" or "below" were often viewed as special, marked by their outside experiences. Those who, like raiders, warriors, traders, and freighters, periodically crossed and recrossed boundaries between centers

Navajo women, ca. 1933. Photo by T. Harmon Parkhurst. (MNM Neg. No. 3236.)

of people were also marked as heroic figures. Whether traveling trackless wastes, corn pollen ways, foot trails, horse and cart roads, highways, or rails, these heroes engaged in profound commerce—a communication of powerfully expressive and materially important symbols, goods, plants, and animals. Their commerce is a voluntary journeying, far different from the dislocation of captives and the conquered and encroached upon. Nevertheless, those who brave the wilds, those who communicate across boundaries, and those who are uprooted bring into focus traditional notions of settlement and centering.

These traditional notions have also been embodied in the Zia symbol on the New Mexico flag. Seen from Native American, Hispanic, and Anglo perspectives, it incorporates fundamental concepts of settlement and movement. Indians' sacred space is centered inward along corn pollen roads and surrounded by mountains, rivers, oceans, and under and upper worlds. For Hispanos, the lines form a cross, symbolic of the central Christian sacrifice, which makes sacred and establishes place and people wherever it is properly raised. Anglos view the sixteen lines as radiating outward—whether along roads and rails to homes and commercial centers elsewhere, down into mines and pits, or out into space.

6 PEOPLE OF POWER

TEXTS OF FEAR AND FASCINATION

If you get mad at a singer and tell him you are going to punish him, he will say, "You can't do anything to me. I have a power."

—Navajo informant to Clyde Kluckhohn.[1]

[Pete] Maxwell was not the only jittery man on the porch. Garrett and his deputies huddled, trying to decide whether the Kid was dead. No one was willing to try the simple expedient of re-entering the room to see whether a corpse lay on the floor. John Poe later spoke of hearing a death rattle very distinctly. Maxwell agreed that he had heard it too. He lit a candle, holding it up to the window to peer inside. He waved the tiny light around while Pat Garrett and the others stood back in the darkness and finally got a glimpse of the Kid lying on his back, staring upward, a butcher knife in one hand and a pistol in the other.

Billy the Kid was dead. But his legend was about to come alive.

—Leon C. Metz, *Pat Garrett: The Story of a Western Lawman*, 117.

Extraordinarily powerful people play important roles in New Mexican folklore. Culture heroes and heroines, healers, and witches are believed to obtain their power from divine or occult knowledge. Hermits, wanderers, beggars, and other eccentrics are thought to derive special potency from their marginal or solitary existence, while outlaws gain illusory might through their defiance of community codes. The legendary exploits of all these figures are expressed covertly in gossip, rumor, and innuendo and openly in tales, songs, and public testimonies.

Culture Heroes and Heroines

Culture heroes and heroines bring or bring about valuable teachings, rites, objects, and natural changes that make possible human survival and society. Alfred Métraux frames his definition in masculine terms, noting that culture heroes may be "human or animal, prehistoric or not," and that "all good and useful things are either given by him, invented, originated, or taught by him: the foods, arts, devices, and usages of a people."[2]

Poseyemu

One of the most complex figures in Pueblo mythology is the culture hero known as Poseyemu by the Rio Grande Tewa, as Piankettacholla by the Taos Indians, as Boshayanyi by the Keresan Pueblos, and as Poshayanki by the Zuni. In the early part of the twentieth century, Edward S. Curtis collected the following version of Poseyemu's myth, which contains important Tewa motifs associated with this culture hero:

> At Posii [*posiʔ* 'Ojo Caliente', the traditional Tewa homeland] lived an old woman and her granddaughter. They were very poor. The people despised them, and children would throw stones at their house and scatter refuse about it. When the cacique announced that it was time to move to the piñon camp, the girl said that she too would go. Her Grandmother tried to desuade [*sic*] her: "You are poor, you have only rags. Nobody likes you. Who will bring you wood and water?" Nevertheless the girl followed the others at a distance up toward Rattlesnake Mountain. At noon as she rested alone she heard a voice. She looked up and saw a handsome young man. He asked "Where are you going?" "I am going to gather piñon nuts." "Do not go," he said. "Will you take some piñons from me?" "Yes," she said. "How many rooms have you?" "Two," she answered. "Take these nuts," he said. She agreed, took the three piñon nuts, and swallowed one. She returned to the village and tossed a nut into each room and closed the door. Night came, and they slept outside. Early in the morning the girl was astir and went quickly into the house. She found both rooms full of piñons. Four days later, she bore a child. In four days he crept, in six days he walked, on the eighth day he killed a woodrat with a little bow made by the old woman. At twelve days of age he killed rabbits, at fourteen he went hunting antelope. A man spoke to him from behind a bush. "Come here, my son. What are you hunting?" "I come to hunt antelope, but my arrows are small. My bow is weak." "I have brought you a quiver full of good arrows," said the man, "a quiver of cougar-skin. With these you will kill anything. My son, you have no name. You will take this name, Poshweve. I, Sun, am your father." The boy went home, and on the way he killed an antelope. He told his grandmother what had occurred, and she said, "We will call you Poseyemo, because the woman who bore you is stronger than the Sun."[3]

The name Poseyemu is etymologically connected with scalps, mist, dew, rain, and the powerful trickster Coyote, all fundamental to the general Pueblo notion of well-being. Poseyemu is also etymologically related to Sipapu, the Tewa place of emergence, and some myths show him leading the people from the underworld. In this he

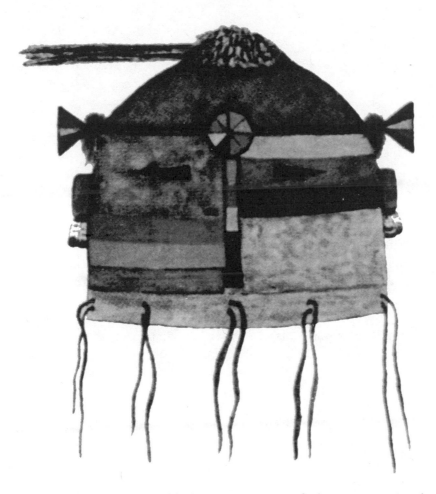

Acoma mask of Paiyatiuma (Poseyemu). From Matthew W. Stirling, *Origin Myth of Acoma and Other Records,* BAE Bulletin 135 (GPO, 1942), pl. 1.

strongly resembles various Pueblo hero twins, many of whom are associated with the underworlds as well as this world. A hunter, agriculturalist, and war leader, Poseyemu is also a creator and teacher of rituals. He teaches dances to the Tewa, orders the kachinas to dance in underground kivas safe from Spanish interference, and himself confronts the rival culture hero Jesus Christ. In a Tewa myth collected by Alfonso Ortiz, Poseyemu and Jesus met, and, "upon finding that they were both supernatural beings, they engaged in a lively discussion as to which one of them should lead the Indians. Poseyemu said, 'The Indians are my people. Therefore, I shall be their leader.' But Jesus replied, "All people are my people. It is I that should lead them.'" They then engage in contests—eating squash, growing corn, and uprooting a large tree—all of which end in Poseyemu's triumph.[4]

In these mythic confrontations Poseyemu has a historical counterpart in Popay, the Tewa leader of the 1680 Pueblo Revolt against Spanish rule. Popay was an important and highly respected religious leader who inspired the Pueblo warriors from his religious retreat in the kiva at Taos Pueblo. He invoked Poseyemu as the Pueblos' universal heroic deity. According to Alfonso Ortiz,

> when Governor Otermín questioned three particular Pueblo captives, each speaking a different language, about the causes of the rebellion and of its leaders, he received the following replies. A *Tewa* captive asserted that the leader of the Revolt was *"Po-he-yemu,"* and that he lived in the northern mountains. A *Keresan* captive

said the leader was *"Payastimo,"* and when asked where this *"Payastimo"* lived, he pointed to the mountains. A *Towa* man also said the leader was *"Paya tiabo,"* and that he lived in the mountains. The point here is that all three were referring to the same deity, and not to a real man who lived in the mountains and who led the Revolt. "Po-he-yemu," by whatever name, was and is a spiritual guide who was and is invoked by Pueblo religious leaders on behalf of their people in times of need. The Revolt was such a time of need, and so "Po-he-yemu" was invoked to justify and to guide the actions of the Pueblo leaders. The correct Tewa name for this deity is *P'ose yemu,* and it translates literally as "mist-scattering," or more freely as "he who scatters mist before him."[5]

Later Pueblo mythology assigns Poseyemu's role of religious and sociocultural confrontation to the Aztec ruler Montezuma, who was thought once to have resided in New Mexico. Isletans told stories of Montezuma's former residence in a village near Sandía Mountain. According to Elsie Clews Parsons's informants in 1925: "Montezuma or Weide used to ride on a white horse. He went down into the ground at Zia, leaving a ring of stones around the big stone where he went in with his horse. When the world is going to end or when white people fight with Indians, Montezuma will come back."[6] They also told her about confrontations between the Catholic god Kikaawei Dios and Weide, or Montezuma:

> Kikaawei Dios made a gun and a koanła (thunder stick). He said to Weide, his younger brother, to choose the one he wanted and the other would be for him, Dios. So Weide took the koanła and left Dios the gun. Then Dios fired the gun at a tree and made a little hole in it and Weide threw the thunder stick and it thundered and lightened and the lightning hit the tree and threw it down and burned it up. Then Dios said he could not use that thunder stick except in war. So Dios gave us bows and arrows to use.[7]

A similar twentieth-century legend collected by Leslie White at Santo Domingo Pueblo has God contesting with Boshayanyi-Poseyemu-Montezuma:

> Then they were going to see who could get some water from Shipap [Sipapu] first. God wrote a letter. [Boshayanyi] made a wabani (feather bunch). He got water while someone was reading God's letter. The next was to see who could make the best music. God had a horn and blew on it. [Boshayanyi] used a drum and sang. After a while God got tired and gave up. God went home on a cloud. [Boshayanyi] left on the back of a duck.[8]

Franciscans

Two Franciscan nuns, Poor Clares—Mother Luisa de Carrión (1565–1636) and Mother María de Jesús (1602–1665)—who resided in convents in Spain, were among the first to be heralded by the Spanish as New Mexican spiritual champions in the tradition of Poseyemu and Montezuma. Mother Luisa de Carrión, whose convent was at Carrión de los Condes, "enjoyed a great reputation for sanctity and, according to popular report, bore in her hands the stigmata of Christ's Passion." She was so popular, in fact, that "in 1635 the Inquisition decreed that all pictures, statues, crosses and other objects of devotion bearing the name of Mother Luisa should no longer be circulated among the faithful."[9] At the height of her popularity in the 1620s, Franciscans in New Mexico carried images of her on their missionary ventures to the Indians.

When Fray Alonso de Benavides finished his term as Custos of the Franciscan Missions of New Mexico, he submitted a 1630 Memorial report to King Philip IV of Spain in which he recounts how, "with the royal assistance and protection of Your Majesty, we have discovered such great treasures, both spiritual and temporal, which the divine Majesty has seen fit to confirm with so many wonders and miracles."[10] Among those "wonders and miracles" was the confrontation between Fray Juan de Salas and Fray Diego López and the Jumano Indians of eastern New Mexico and west-central Texas. Fray Salas had ministered to the Jumanos and other Indians in the Salines of the Estancia Valley about 1626, and the Jumanos periodically sent emissaries to Benavides requesting Salas's return.

Benavides tells what happened on one occasion when some fifty Jumano petitioners appeared at Isleta Pueblo:

> Before they left, we asked the Indians why they were so zealous in asking for Baptism and for friars to go to instruct them in Christian doctrine. They replied that a woman, similar to the one whose likeness we had there painted (which was that of Mother Luisa de Carrión), used to tell them, each in his own language, to come without delay and summon the priests that they might teach and baptize them. They said that the woman that used to preach to them was dressed just like the one painted there, but that her face was different, for she was young and beautiful. And whenever any Indians of those nations on other occasions came to look at the picture, after conferring among themselves they remarked that the dress was the same but not the face, because the face of the woman that had preached to them was of a young and beautiful person.

This young and beautiful woman's identity was not confirmed until after Fray Benavides had visited with the younger Mother María de Jesús at her convent in Agreda. Both Mother Luisa of Carrión and Mary of Agreda wore the same Franciscan nun's garb—a gray habit under a mantle of blue, but it was Mary of Agreda who became known as the Lady in Blue of New Mexico and Texas folklore.[11]

A contingent of thirty friars reached New Mexico in 1629, and Benavides was able to dispatch Fray Juan de Salas and Fray Diego López to the Jumanos. Their joyous reception, as told by Benavides, was assured by the Lady in Blue:

> At dawn the holy woman spoke to each one of them [Jumanos] separately and told them not to leave, because the friars they had sent for were already drawing near. After all of them had gathered in consultation, they sent off a dozen of their most trustworthy captains to find out if this were true. On the third day they came across the friars, and they asked to see the picture of the woman that had preached to them. The father showed them one of Mother Luisa de Carrión, and they said that

La V. M. Maria de Iesus de Agreda, Predicando á los Chichimecos del Nuebo-mexico. Antt de Castro fs.

Mary of Agreda preaching to the Indians of New Mexico. From an eighteenth-century engraving.

she was dressed like that, but that she was younger and more beautiful. Whereupon they departed in order to carry to their people the news of the arrival of the fathers.

They had been so well instructed by heaven, that they marched out to welcome the priests, carrying two large crosses at the head of the procession. After the priests and the three soldiers who accompanied them had adored the crosses, the priests also drew out their own two crucifixes which they wore about their necks, and they all came to kiss and venerate the crucifix, just as if they had been Christians for a very long time. They manifested the same devotion toward a very beautiful Infant Jesus, which the fathers had brought, touching their mouths and eyes to its feet very devoutly—a scene at which our men greatly marveled.[12]

Following the Pueblo Revolt of 1680, another Mary took over the spiritual functions of conquest for the Spanish who accompanied Don Diego de Vargas back to Santa Fe. Fray Angelico Chavez summarizes nineteenth- and twentieth-century popular tradition about this aspect of the Virgin thus: "As the Spaniards were preparing to reconquer Santa Fe in 1692, the great Captain-General, Don Diego de Vargas, solemnly vowed to build a special chapel for his own favorite statue of Our Lady of the Rosary, should he gain a quick victory, and also to hold a yearly procession in her honor; the image was carried into battle and the Spaniards gained an effective *conquista,* and thereafter this particular image came to be known as *La Conquistadora* and Santa Fe's very own little Lady."[13] De Vargas had learned of this image, which Santa Fe inhabitants fleeing the Pueblos' siege had brought with them to El Paso, when he became Governor and Captain General of New Mexico. He referred to it in a letter of January 12, 1693, in which he declares:

> It is my wish, and of those with whom I enter, including the soldiers, that they should, first and foremost, personally build the church and holy temple, setting up in it before all else the patroness of the said Kingdom and *Villa* [Santa Fe], who is the one that was saved from the fury of the savages, her title being Our Lady of the Conquest. And so, with the aid of the soldiers and settlers, the foundations will be laid and the walls of the holy temple raised.[14]

Santa Feans' devotion to la Conquistadora has continued in various forms, notably the Fiestas de Santa Fe, until the present day, and her statue is now housed in a special chapel at the Cathedral of St. Francis. Contemporary devotional songs and prayers attest "that La Conquistadora conquers the serpent, evil, doctrinal error, infidels, enemies of Jesus' peace, men's hearts, sin, and death. Many devotees condense the matter by saying simply that she conquers evil."[15]

St. Francis himself is a second, long-standing symbol of spiritual confrontation in New Mexico. When the prominent New Mexican, Don Pedro Bautista Pino, addressed a report on the condition of his homeland to the King and Spanish Cortes or constitutional congress of 1810, he lamented that the "spiritual administration in New Mexico is in a truly doleful condition" and recommended that a bishop and twelve ecclesiastics be dispatched to the region. He reasoned that:

> Since the order of Saint Francis has been, so to speak, the spiritual conqueror—
> and it has actually been unique in New Mexico—the settlers have become so

La Conquistadora procession, San Francisco Street, with Cathedral in background, Santa Fe, June 1897. Photo by Philip E. Harroun. (MNM Neg. No. 11326.)

accustomed to seeing the Franciscan gown that it is likely that any other order would not be so welcome. In view of this fact, therefore, it would be advisable for the twelve ecclesiastics and even the first bishop to belong to the Franciscan order. Through the above suggested procedure, your majesty would settle all the internal educational and religious difficulties in regard to New Mexico.[16]

One common belief about St. Francis's patronage is associated with Santa Fe. "On June 29, 1823, the City Council of Santa Fe and the secular clergy drafted a formal resolution proclaiming St. Francis of Assisi as Patron of the city, likewise proposing the annual celebration of his feast day [October 4] with the utmost

La Conquistadora procession,
Johnson Street at Grant Avenue,
Santa Fe, ca. 1890. (MNM Neg.
No. 13641.)

solemnity. This gave rise to the legend that the original full name of Santa Fe was
'The Royal City of the Holy Faith of St. Francis.'"[17]

In 1920, nearly a century after declaring St. Francis their patron, Santa Feans
erected the Cross of the Martyrs marking the death of twenty-one Franciscans
during the Pueblo Revolt of 1680. In the 1970s, Ronald Grimes notes that:

> the Franciscans have a mystique in the eyes of many Santa Fe Catholics which the
> [church] hierarchy does not have. Occasionally people refer to the Franciscan
> padres as "the real spirit of the cathedral," and they tend to regard the Franciscans
> as essentially unchanged from the days of De Vargas, whereas the archbishops are
> seen as fluctuating radically between good and bad. . . .
>
> . . . The people regard the Franciscans as defenders and interpreters of folk
> piety and are fond of contrasting them to the "foreign" French clergy, who "did
> not really understand us." Generally, the Franciscans are seen as indigenous
> whether or not they are in fact. Their coat of arms is prominently displayed in both
> La Conquistadora and Rosario chapels; it is a frequent motif in the reredos of rural
> New Mexican churches.[18]

Later Clergy

Ironically, the Santa Fe Cathedral with its Franciscan spirit was the design of Father
Jean Baptiste Lamy (1814–1888), the first of five French archbishops of Santa Fe.
Lamy first spoke of such an edifice in 1864, according to Paul Horgan:

Dedication ceremonies, Cross of the Martyrs, Santa Fe, September 1920. (MNM Neg. No. 52459.)

For he had never changed his response to the mud constructions of New Mexico—though he understood as he deplored the necessity of making them from their humble materials. But to him a chapel, a church, a cathedral above all, should give rise to the glory of God as more than a "stable of Bethlehem"; and with his own memory of the high architectural art whose tradition he had inherited, he must, whenever he could manage it, build his cathedral out of another vision than the local one. Byzantium and ancient Rome would still speak through him. There was suitable native stone to be had near Santa Fe. Ochreous limestone for the exterior could be quarried in the Arroyo Sais, and the light volcanic stone for the vaults in the Cerro Mogino within a few miles of the city; and for the interior wails, a heavy granite could be taken from the low hills in the country where the bishop's land lay seventeen miles away on the Santa Fe Trail (the site of the present railroad junction of Lamy . . .).[19]

The cathedral was built around the old adobe *parroquia,* or parish church, which was then removed from within the stone structure. The cornerstone laid on Sunday October 10, 1869, was stolen on the following Saturday and never recovered. The unfamiliar, French Midi-Romanesque edifice was never completed as envisioned by Lamy,[20] but the unfinished cathedral was blessed on March 7, 1886, and the archbishop buried there on February 16, 1888.

In setting up an American Catholic Church administration initially run by largely French clergy and sisters, Lamy often confronted important nineteenth-century culture heroes—the native-born secular clergy already working in what was the Diocese of Durango, notably Don Antonio José Martínez of Taos, and members of the growing Penitente Brotherhood, who preserved many Franciscan rites and symbols in their lay devotions. Padre Martínez (1795–1867), as he is popularly known, was born in Santa Rosa de Abiquiú and began studying reading, writing, and arithmetic at the age of five. As first-born son, he also learned agriculture, stock-raising, and management of his father's considerable estate after the family moved to Taos. On May 20, 1812, Martínez married María de la Luz Martin of Abiquiú, who died about a year later, leaving an infant daughter who died in 1825. Early in 1817, Martínez journeyed to Durango to begin studying for the secular priesthood. He excelled in his seminary studies and was ordained on February 10, 1822, less than six months after Mexican independence. Although he served briefly at Tomé and Abiquiú, from July 23, 1826, until his death on July 27, 1867, Padre Martínez was associated with the parish at Taos, which at one time included the San Luis Valley of southern Colorado.

The legends about Padre Martínez generally focus on his family, his school, his political involvements, his schism with Lamy and the official Catholic Church, and his relationship to the Penitente Brotherhood. In *Enchanted Temples of Taos*, for example, Dora Ortiz Vásquez claims Martínez as her great-grandfather, through his union with Teodorita Santistevan y Romero. Her local and family folklore comes from stories told by her father, Justo Delgado y Ortiz; her blind mother, María de la Luz Martínez; and Rosario, a Navajo slave in Padre Martínez's house, whom she and her family "called Mayayo and loved as a grandma."[21] Martínez's contemporary biographers, Ray John de Aragon and Fray Angelico Chavez, discount such claims, and Chavez carefully reviews documentation on Teodora Romero's children. He concludes that "long after Padre Martínez was dead, a slew of individuals began claiming their descent from the subsequently 'famous' Padre Martínez, as folks do elsewhere in similar situations when they have nothing else to crow about."[22]

Cleofas M. Jaramillo's primary interests are in Martínez's altercations with Bishop Lamy and especially in his learning, school, and printing press. She notes that he returned from Durango "well versed in the Latin and Spanish languages" and became an educator. "Sixteen of the young men he educated became priests," and later many in the Taos Valley remained loyal to him because, "having educated most of the young men of the prominent families in that section, he had great influence with the people." Lorin W. Brown's grandfather, Vicente Martínez, attended Padre Martínez's school, where he was exposed to astronomy, botany, Greek mythology, Virgil, and Victor Hugo, as evidenced by his children's names—Cassandra (Brown's mother), Rolando, and Horacio Hugo.[23]

Among the legends associated with Martínez's seminary is one recounting the Padre's astute reaction to the new American government. According to Fray Angelico Chavez:

> It was not in Padre Martínez to see the new American regime overturned, much less in such a savage manner which had no hope of success to start with. If certain matters had to be righted, and undesireable individuals removed from office, it had

Don Antonio José Martínez (1793–1867) of Taos, ca. 1848. (MNM Neg. No. 11262 from the original daguerreotype, with the permission of Ward A. Minge.)

to be rather in the halls of debate, and for this he foresaw native young men following his lead in the civil assemblies. As he was telling his students around this time, as worded by [Pedro] Sánchez from the recollections of some of them, and perhaps his own:

"*Muchachos,* you came to this college to study with the purpose of being ordained priests; in this regard I have done my utmost so that you might attain the desired end. But since there has been a change in government, it becomes necessary to have a change in ideas. The nature of the American government goes in complete harmony with the toleration of cults and a complete separation of Church and State. From this you can logically conclude that the clergy's razor has lost its edge."

Then, when a pupil asked him what the form of the American government was, and he answered that it was republican, he also added, "You might say that by way of comparison the American government is a burro, but on this burro ride barristers and not the clergy."[24]

Martínez and other native clergy followed this advice, and the former served as delegate and president of the group charged with preparing a territorial plan and constitution and as a member of various territorial legislatures.

Martínez's relations with his new ecclesiastical superior, Bishop Lamy, are a complicated matter of theology, politics, and administrative nuance. Whatever the substance, folk tradition sees the outcome as excommunication of a bold champion of the poor, devout, native Hispanos by an unyielding, unsympathetic, aristocratic Frenchman. Both Padre Martínez and Padre Lucero of Arroyo Hondo are linked in the excommunication proceedings, which were probably carried out with relatively little fanfare because of Lamy's uncertainty about his official power to do so. As Chavez summarizes: "Since Lamy left no official record of them, we do not know when they actually took place. This could have been in 1858 or 1859, or even as late as the Spring of 1860." In any case, Martínez died unreconciled,

on July 27, 1867, after having received the last rites from his faithful but sometimes vacillating disciple, Padre Lucero. As the latter recorded it, he buried him on the 29th inside his private oratory of Guadalupe on the Plaza of Don Fernando. When Willa Cather was preparing her now classic novel about Lamy [*Death Comes for the Archbishop,* 1927], she picked up a piece of Taos gossip of those days, to the effect that the dying Martínez had said to Lucero at his bedside: "Lucero, *cómete tu cola!*" This was a Spanish scatological profanity, the equivalent of the more curseful American-English "Go to hell!"—by which he evidently meant that Lucero should quit bothering him. On the other hand, Pedro Sánchez wrote that the good Padre Martínez had died, while surrounded by his brothers and many friends, with these words on his lips: "Lord, may your Will be done." Cather's version reflects the cynical view which had come down from the padre's foes, the one of Sánchez the wishful tradition among those who still remembered him with love and admiration. Whichever one might be authentic or false, they both fall within the province of legend and not history.[25]

Another matter for both legend and history is the attendance of some three hundred Penitente Brothers at Martínez's funeral.

Padre Martínez probably had some hand in shaping the Brotherhood,[26] which developed in the nineteenth century as a creative lay response to inadequate church ministrations by both Mexican and French-American clergy. The Mexican bishop José Antonio Laureano de Zubiría y Escalante specifically objected to the challenge to official church leadership by an *"Hermandad de Penitentes"* at Santa Cruz and elsewhere during visitations in 1835 and 1845. Lamy, and especially his successor, Archbishop Jean Baptiste Salpointe, issued various statements on the organization, which rapidly developed in Hispanic villages and, to a more limited extent, in towns.

Local chapters, called *moradas*, and increasingly widespread, organized *concilios*, or councils, of moradas grew more secretive as Catholic, Protestant, and political opposition to the almost solely Hispanic Brotherhood grew. This circumspection led to the development of legends about ghostly Penitentes. Brothers engaged in active self-discipline like flagellation and cross-bearing were thought to be revenants. Such legends kept unwanted observers at a distance and also reinforced members' commitments. A Penitente Brother from Córdova told Lorin W. Brown, New Mexico Federal Writers' Project (NMFWP), that encountering ghostly Penitentes was "of great personal significance to him, a sort of personal revelation that his quest for redemption was fruitful . . . [confirming] to him that his salvation was certain, that his life of self-denial had assured him of heaven."[27]

Although not all males in a community would become Brothers, as a rule, morada members and especially chapter officers were respected for their spiritual and social commitments. In "a definite declaration regarding the Brothers of Jesus of Nazareth (commonly called the Penitentes)" on January 28, 1947, Archbishop Edwin V. Byrne officially recognized that "these Brothers or Brethren constitute a pious association of men joined in charity to commemorate the passion and death of the Redeemer." He declared that, although the Brotherhood's "origin is obscure in history," it probably

> began somewhere in the beginnings of the last century [nineteenth] when the Franciscan padres left New Mexico by order of the new government of Mexico. No other priests were sent to take their place. Groups among the faithful tried to keep up Catholic practices without priestly guidance, and though certain excesses crept in, it is to these groups of penitential brethren that we owe, in a manner, the preservation of the faith in those hard and trying times.[28]

Many times, Brothers not only preserved the Hispanic Catholic faith in the absence of sufficient clergy and in the face of Anglo or Protestant encroachment, but they also helped assure community survival. Although there certainly were and still are tensions between Brothers and nonmember neighbors, community life was, and in some places still is, enhanced by the presence of an active, functioning morada. The morada provided setting and personnel for joyous and solemn lay community celebrations and served as an informal court, a welfare agency, and a burial society. According to Paul Kutsche and Dennis Gallegos:

> Services to individuals center on the sick and the dead. *Hermanos* take charge of the vigil for the sick, relieving the family so they can get some rest. (Note, they do not nurse the sick, as nursing takes specialized knowledge both in Hispanic and Anglo

"All santos within the church are common property and an individual or group can carry a santo home for the night returning it the next morning. These four men [probably Penitente Brothers] are borrowing santos for their chapel, three miles over the mountains." Note image of San Francisco on right of reredos. FSA photo by John Collier, Las Trampas, January 1943. (LC-USW 3-15218-C.)

traditions.) They conduct the *velorio* (wake) for the dead, prepare the body, dig the grave, and lead the procession from church to *campo santo* after the funeral mass, singing *alabados* (songs of praise). These things they do for *hermanos* or for members of the families of *hermanos* as a matter of course. They do any of them for other Catholics upon request, and the request is frequently made. Requests are rarely made by non-Catholics, but such a request is likely to be honored. *"Somos todos hijos de Dios"* (we are all the sons of God whatever sect we belong to) is a folk saying which covers this attitude.[29]

Brotherhood commitment to year-round Christian and Franciscan charitable acts and to annual lay devotions centered on the Passion contributed substantially to community life. Although rarely known as individual culture heroes like their Franciscan predecessors, the Brothers collectively benefited their faith and their society.

Healers and Witches

Culture heroes and heroines also confronted the devastating epidemics that were in large part the costly consequence of conquest, contact, and increasing population. Gladys A. Reichard cites Father Berard Haile's 1938 *Origin Legend of the Navaho Enemy Way* for an account of how the culture hero "Monster Slayer accused the Syphilis People of being the vilest of venereal diseases. He was about to burn them up when they pleaded for their lives. They said that people who catch these diseases have no sense anyhow, that telling and teaching the people does no good, but for this reason, they, not the Syphilis People, should be punished. They concluded, 'Therefore we shall be the last resort of painful instruction. If we become extinct, the major monsters which you have already killed will come into being again.' Monster Slayer thought their reasoning good and permitted them to live."[30]

In the 1880s, one of James Stevenson's Navajo informants told him how "this world had already been destroyed five times, by whirlwind, hail, smallpox, coughing, and the slaughter of the monsters."[31] The reference to smallpox and coughing is significant, for the socioeconomic and psychological consequences of the periodic epidemics that ravaged New Mexican society throughout the Spanish colonial, Mexican, territorial, and early statehood periods seriously disrupted life almost as much as drought, flood, storms, raiding, and warfare. For example, Marc Simmons claims that "apparently no decade in the eighteenth century was entirely free from a major plague of one variety or another."[32] The great smallpox epidemic of 1780–1781 started in the larger Spanish towns of the Rio Grande Valley, especially Albuquerque, and quickly spread to the pueblos, gathering new strength at Pecos Pueblo, Zuni Pueblo, and as far west as Hopi. It affected virtually all the population, and casualties were as high as 50 percent. Europeans had read the results of Edward Jenner's cowpox vaccination process in 1799, but New Mexicans did not begin to benefit from this medical advance until after August 10, 1804, when New Mexico Governor Fernando de Chacón was ordered "to send surgeon Cristóbal Larrañaga with the annual caravan at the end of the year, bringing with him six or eight children, sons of the soldiers, so that they might be vaccinated and transmit the serum to others in New Mexico from one arm to the next. . . . By November 20, 1805, Larrañaga reported the vaccination of 3,610 children in New Mexico at the cost of one *real* per person."[33]

In August 1882, Jack Sheddon's silver find near Kingston brought some 1,800 people to the town by late fall. Those who came to the "silver mecca" had to make their way to Kingston from Nutt, then the terminal of the Santa Fe Railroad. According to James A. McKenna: "At Nutt Station many pilgrims [tenderfoot prospectors] stopped to read the bill posted there: 'Ho! For The Gold and Silver Mines of New Mexico! / Fortune hunters, capitalists, poor men, / Sickly folks, all whose hearts are bowed down; / And ye who would live long, be rich, healthy, And happy: / Come to our sunny clime and see / For yourselves!'" Ironically, the pilgrims arrived to endure the coldest winter in the settlement's history.

> One cold morning in the early winter smallpox broke out in Kingston. The disease had got into the town in the furs and blankets of emigrants from Indian Territory (Oklahoma). An epidemic of black smallpox had almost wiped out an Indian tribe in that country; people had brought the furs and blankets gathered from vacant

Indian tents. Two newcomers from Indian Territory were the first to die.

Kingston was better able to deal with the wiles of the Apache than to handle smallpox. Doctor Guthrie, the only medical man in the settlement, . . . ordered the largest tent in town to be made into a pesthouse, locating it at the west end of the settlement in a grove of juniper trees. . . .

By the time the pest tent was ready, more cases of smallpox had broken out. . . . Three women from the red-light district then went to [Doctor Guthrie] and offered to look after his patients, if the doctor himself promised not to touch another drop until the disease was under control. . . .

The girls quickly changed their fine dresses for calico. Seven men had died under the first two [male] nurses, but from the moment these girls went into the pest tent the disease began to die out. Side by side they worked with Doctor Guthrie until the smallpox was a thing of the past. The youngest nurse of the three caught the disease but she pulled through. It was plain to all Kingston that the girl from Shady Lane often had her heart in the right place.[34]

The Spanish flu epidemic of 1918 probably affected one out of every five humans in the world, killing "more humans than any other disease in a period of similar duration in the history of the world."[35] In New Mexico, according to Richard Melzer:

some towns, like Tucumcari, Albuquerque, and Raton, were extremely fortunate; few of their residents contracted the flu and died. Many other towns, however, were devastated by the epidemic. By 17 October the *Gallup Independent* went so far as to write that "the disease has taken on such dangerous proportions here as to make it as serious as the Bubonic Plague." Twelve hundred cases of the flu and 150 deaths attributed to the disease were reported in the western municipality by the end of the month. Carpenters worked day and night to keep up with the demand for coffins. The situation was even worse in towns like Baldy, where the entire population of two hundred residents was ill; in Belen, where more than half the population was stricken; and in San Pedro, where forty-seven of the small town's fifty citizens were down with the flu. Church bells mourned the death of a new victim nearly every hour in Socorro. To make matters worse, New Mexico experienced its coldest autumn and winter in more than twenty-five years as temperatures dropped to as low as thirty below.

A majority of New Mexicans lost at least one family member or friend to the disease.[36]

Indian and Hispanic New Mexicans alike were especially vulnerable, and southern New Mexico towns were exceptionally hard hit because of migrant workers bringing germs from the devastating epidemic in northern Mexico.

Although epidemics were impervious to traditional methods of healing, folk healers could and did cure known dysfunctions. They provided physical, psychological, and spiritual remedies to combat local illnesses and to restore stricken individuals to full participation in the life of their group. Some malevolence is generated by witchcraft, the belief "that it is possible for human beings to cause harm to their fellows by the exercise of powers not possessed by ordinary folk, powers which operate in a manner that cannot be detected, so that the cause can

Navajo sandpainter, ca. 1935.
Photo by T. Harmon Parkhurst.
(MNM Neg. No. 8717.)

only be recognized when the damage comes to light."[37] Both healing and witchcraft are part of a system of beliefs and practices related to the human life cycle and the state of health or illness within that cycle.

The origin of sickness, healing, and death is of primary importance in most Southwest Indian origin and emergence myths. Between 1923 and 1938, for example, eight Navajos told Clyde Kluckhohn variants of the following origin myth:

> After first Man and first Woman had come out of the Big Cave and built the first sweathouse, Witchcraft Woman gave all the people some ʔanti'į [witchcraft]. She gave some to the rattlesnake too, and he didn't have any place to put it so he ate it. That is why you will die if a rattlesnake bites you.

Other Navajos said:

> Witchery started out under the ground. First Man, First Woman and Coyote—these three started it. After everybody got above ground First Woman gave it out. Snake wanted some too, but his mouth was the only place he could put it. And so his bite kills you.[38]

The Tewa myth of emergence and migration, summarized by Alfonso Ortiz from seven versions recorded between 1958 and 1965, tells how the first mothers of all the Tewa, other supernaturals, humans, and animals lived in the underworld without knowledge of death. After their emergence, the people started southward [and] many began to fall ill. The Winter and Summer chiefs decided that they were not yet complete; something else was needed. All returned once again to the home under the lake, and there the Hunt chief opened up Summer chief's corn mother. He discovered that the hollow core was filled with pebbles, ashes, and cactus spines. The Hunt chief replaced these with seeds and declared that one among the people was "of a different breath," or a witch, for the items discovered in the corn mother were recognized as items of witchcraft. This, then, marked the beginning of witchcraft and other forms of evil. In order to combat these and to make people well, the Ke (medicine man) was created as the fourth Made person. The people then started out once again.[39]

Such origin myths are part of complex systems of belief and ritual aimed at the balance and harmony that the Tewa consider to be necessary to health and well-being. According to Richard I. Ford, the winter and summer duality of Tewa social organization

permeates all aspects of Tewa thought and is part of medicinal cures as well. A distinction between "hot" and "cold" is made for both specific illnesses and their remedies. . . . A few medicines, depending upon their preparation, are "of the middle." These are usually mixtures of medicinal agents used to alleviate or prevent forms of bad luck. Following from the principle of opposition, an illness classified as hot must be cured with its opposite, a cold medicine, and vice versa for cold illnesses.[40]

In addition, the sex of the patient is also important to medicinal lore and diagnosis.

In Tewa society, those who initially diagnose and prescribe are usually the household's senior women. If the condition persists, relatives, friends, and neighbors may be consulted before seeking specialists' assistance. From Rina Swentzell and Tito Naranjo, natives of Santa Clara Pueblo, Stephen Fox learned about "a category of healers known among the Tewa as 'community mothers'" or *gias,* who "are midwives who are also expert in massage, herbal medicines, and first-aid treatment. They used to do . . . up to 80% of the healing at Tewa villages." Swentzell and Naranjo, who are brother and sister, have written a biography of their great-great-grandmother, traditional *gia* Khuun Tsawi (1870–1953), and their grandmother, "present-day" *gia* Rose Sisneros Naranjo. They explain that

the Santa Clara Tewa word "gia" in its most frequent and simple usage is synonymous with "mother." . . . It refers to a person who gives, loves, provides, protects, and assures balance and harmony—a person who gives food, life, and health. According to Pueblo thinking, the word is not exclusively used to designate female nurturers but rather is also applied to particular groups of males, or spiritual entities, and is even used in reference to the ultimate nurturer—the Earth.

Female *gias* are first biological, family mothers; then core *gias* who undertake "special roles in counseling and healing, and also in controlling resources and assets" of "a large number of the pueblo's members"; and finally initiated community *gias,* "respected for medical training, experience, and service . . . [and] treated as wise individuals who possessed capabilities and qualities that were desirable for the good of the community."[41]

Witches are frequently blamed for disorder and sickness in Southwest Indian societies. Among the very conservative Santo Domingos, a witch is "a supernatural whose function is to make Indians sick and die."[42] This is but part of a larger pattern of calamity, according to Florence Ellis, because "Pueblo witches are thought to cause wind storms during dances, alienate the affections of mates by offering one the power for new conquests, and destroy crops by bringing grasshoppers or other plagues. More important, illness (including madness) and death, except for the very old, are believed to result from one's wrongdoing or from the work of a witch."[43]

In his 1958–1959 study of Cochití Pueblo social organization and witchcraft, J. Robin Fox generalizes about pan-Pueblo beliefs:

> In Pueblo cosmology, there is an uneasy balance of forces in the universe. The forces of good—the *shiwana* and the various other deities and spirits—are only precariously in control. Even they have to be compelled by elaborate rituals into producing rain and health. The witches represent a vast conspiracy of ill defined but definitely malignant beings that seek to destroy Pueblo civilization by attacking the health of its members. They are of various types, appearing as humans, animals, and birds (especially owls) or as fireballs. Living humans can be witches by being born with two hearts, one good and one bad. Practically everyone is suspected by someone at some time of being a witch or of practicing sorcery. . . . Witchcraft mythology is riddled with inconsistencies, and it is often difficult to know whether an accused person is simply a "passive" witch, an active sorcerer, or an ordinary human in league with the witches.[44]

Because of this difficulty in identification, many elaborate precautions are taken to prevent witchery. Some practices concern the notion that the witch's good heart is represented by a kernel of corn, and "when a child is left alone, an ear of corn is placed beside him (a custom of all Pueblos), either because a witch presumably would not want to harm his own heart, or because the ear of corn symbolizes Earth or the Corn Mother and keeps witches away."[45]

Jane Kluckhohn reports that Jemez Indians modify their customary greeting patterns after sunset:

> After dark, however, greetings are not exchanged. Then no one speaks even to a close friend, for it is believed that witches may be abroad and at work. For that reason, one passes silently on the right so that the individual met will be kept as far as possible from the heart. On moonlight nights, a slight grunt of recognition is permissible—but no word.[46]

Such behavioral precautions are necessary because, as Florence H. Ellis says in "Pueblo Witchcraft and Medicine": "Anyone can be accused of witchcraft. The cases indicate that a person who happens to be in a certain place at a certain time may find himself the accused. Persons exhibiting anti-social behavior are regularly suspected of having witch power."[47] Early in this century, Father Noël Dumarest at Cochití related this uncertainty to the Pueblos' pacifism, asking rhetorically: "Why do they not even try to defend themselves in quarrels? Because from their youth their elders have taught them that nobody can know the hearts of men. There are witches everywhere."[48]

At the foundation of the Navajo system of healing and blessing is the concept called *hózhǫ́*, usually translated as "beauty" or "beautiful conditions." According to Gary Witherspoon, "the goal of Navajo life in this world is to live to maturity in the condition described as *hózhǫ́* and to die of old age, the end result of which incorporates one into the universal beauty, harmony, and happiness described as *sǫ'ah naagháii bik'eh hózhǫ́*."[49] In healing and blessing ceremonies, often called sings or chants, patients are identified with the beneficent powers of various deities, as in these lines from the Blessingway rite of restoration:

> *Earth's feet have become my feet*
> * by means of these I shall live on.*
> *Earth's legs have become my legs*
> * by means of these I shall live on.*
> *Earth's body has become my body*
> * by means of this I shall live on.*
> *Earth's mind has become my mind*
> * by means of this I shall live on.*
> *Earth's voice has become my voice*
> * by means of this I shall live on . . .*

> Sǫ'ah Naagháii Bik'eh Hózhǫ́ *I shall be,*
> *Before me it will be* hózhǫ́ *as I live on,*
> *Behind me it will be* hózhǫ́ *as I live on,*
> *Below me it will be* hózhǫ́ *as I live on,*
> *Above me it will be* hózhǫ́ *as I live on.*

> Hózhǫ́ *has been restored.*
> Hózhǫ́ *has been restored.*
> Hózhǫ́ *has been restored.*
> Hózhǫ́ *has been restored.*[50]

The beneficial identification of patient with deity is the accomplishment of the medicine man, who oversees all details of the ceremony and whose reputation depends upon his mastery of one or more of these elaborate rituals.[51]

Clyde Kluckhohn found that his Navajo sources differentiated several kinds of witchcraft and practitioners: (1) male and female *ʔádant'į*, or witches, who are associated with death, the dead, and incest; (2) *ye·na·lọ·ši·*, or were-animals, also known as skinwalkers;[52] (3) *ʔi·nzį·d*, or sorcerers, who enchant people with spells and do not need to encounter their victims directly; (4) wizards, almost exclusively old men, many of whose victims are rich, who inject a foreign substance, their wizardry or *ʔadagąš* described by the English term "bean-shooting"; (5) Frenzy Witchcraft, or the use of certain plants for "love magic" and success in trading and gambling; and (6) various less reported forms of disease and witchcraft and "evil magic."[53] Kluckhohn's findings agree with those of Mary Shepardson and Blodwin Hammond, who claim that witchcraft "is a deliberately learned, deliberately practiced ritual, aimed against a deliberately chosen victim."[54] The social organization with its chief witch and helper witches is like the medicine man and his ritual helpers. According to Clyde Kluckhohn:

English-speaking informants will describe the proceedings as "kind of like a sing" or "just like a bad sing." Most informants agreed that songs were sung and dry paintings (often described as of "colored ashes") made. Some informants specified that the paintings represented the intended victim. One interview suggests that the assembled witches spit, urinate and defecate upon the sandpictures. A few stated that the chief Witch shot a turquoise bead with a small bow at some definite part of the figure represented in the painting. Some informants assert that the bows are made of human shin bones.[55]

Throughout his study, Kluckhohn emphasizes the Navajos' circumspection in these dangerous matters, and his observations apply as well to all Southwest Indian groups.

The principal reason that so little is known of Navaho witchcraft is the extreme reluctance of the Indians to discuss the matter. As one informant remarked, "People don't tell abut these things; they keep them down here in the body." On the one hand, if other Navahos learn that a certain man or woman has discussed the subject, that person is by that very fact open to suspicion of knowing too much, i.e., of being a witch. On the other hand, if the informant relates anecdotes referring to the supposed witchcraft activities of others, he becomes liable to their hatred and revenge. In particular, if these persons "really are witches," and they learn that someone has gossiped about them, they are, it is believed, certain to witch the gossiper and get him out of the way. Over and above these two excellent reasons for caution and silence, there is the additional motive that most Navahos who are "good citizens" feel a genuine discomfort in talking about such topics which are defined for them by their culture as evil and ugly.[56]

Despite Native American belief in the prevalence of witches, witchcraft accusations were rarely leveled against Anglo neighbors and newcomers. This pattern of belief and behavior also prevailed in traditional Hispanic communities. Nevertheless, the historical record shows numerous instances where formal charges were brought against both Indian and Hispano witches in cross-cultural situations.[57]

For Hispanos, witchcraft was only one explanation for sickness, death, accidents, natural disasters, and other kinds of calamity. Individual illness, for example, might be caused by *castigo,* the direct punitive action of God on the sinner or someone close to him or her; improper exposure or overexposure to forces of nature like sunlight, air or water; natural adversities like some inherited conditions; a disturbance or imbalance of elements in one's life (excesses, sudden outside changes, or internal upset); the violation of specific taboos; and encounters with persons possessing malevolent powers, notably witches.

Hispano villagers consulted during a 1959–1960 field study of the traditional health-disease complex distinguished five stages of illness: (1) suspected or minimal *(poco bien, poco mal),* for which adults administered to themselves or consulted family and neighbors informally; (2) true illness *(mal),* for which more people within and outside the family are consulted, with males deciding about therapy and females providing the care; (3) severe illness *(muy mal),* for which a range of therapists were consulted; (4) grave illness *(grave, muy grave),* when there was still hope, and for which the priest would be called and gatherings for lay prayers convened; and (5) the final stage (*agonizando*), during which the patient and those gathered around prepared for the dying moments. Specialized therapists were the *partera,* or midwife; the *médica/-o* or *yerbera/-o,* who has herbal expertise; the *sobador/-a,* or massager, who also knows skin snapping and sometimes cupping, or *ventosa,* the use of suction to draw out pain; and the *curandera/-o,* who is more often female and who can deal with many kinds of illness, including witchcraft. *Arbolarios,* who have further specialized knowledge in fighting witchcraft, were more often males. Various doctors were also consulted.[58]

In her 1975 interviews with Jesusita Aragón, a traditional Hispanic *partera* from Las Vegas, Fran Leeper Buss found that parteras might also be *médicas* or *curanderas,* although not necessarily. *Médicas* had some advanced healing knowledge, especially herbal.[59] According to Buss:

> These Hispanic health care systems stressed the important harmonious relationship between the natural and the supernatural when dealing with human health needs. In addition, the curanderas believed that their ability to cure was a blessing given them by God, an ability they were required to use in the service of others. For these reasons, many of the curanderas' treatments of illnesses and physical misfortunes involved both specifically medical treatment and religious rites performed with the patients and the families under the curanderas' leadership. . . .
>
> Various treatments were given, such as herbal teas, massage, poultices, and different kinds of cleansings. These treatments were accompanied by prayers and appeals to saints and attempts to set right again causes of imbalances or sources of bewitchments.[60]

Fran Leeper Buss further reports that:

> The people also stated that a curandera relies more on magic and often deals with bewitchments as well as healing in general. Jesusita Aragón pointed out that today many young people considered curanderas to be old-fashioned and said, "Most of the kids now don't believe in curanderas, but years ago everybody did."

Another *curandera* and *partera,* Juanita Sedillo, eighty-six years old when Nathan Skallman and Chella Herrera interviewed her in 1981, practiced in the Cuchillo and Fairview area for much of her life. She claimed knowledge of remedies and relied on faith in God but would not treat witchcraft cases.[61]

Both the predominantly female *curanderas* and the usually male *arbolarios* who dealt with bewitchment were combating fairly well-characterized malevolent individuals. Ruth Laughlin Barker recorded New Mexico witch stories from Carlota Quintana in the early 1930s. Quintana heard them from her grandmother, who "would not tell us stories on Friday nights. Other nights she would make us all pray the rosary first and then she would begin." Among the witch stories told by Quintana's grandmother was that of Dolores la Penca's death. The grandmother prefaced this tale with her own didacticism and memories of the witch.

> Dolores la Penca was one of the witches we feared most. As you know, children, *la penca* means that she was a stray baby who was raised without her mother. Her foster mothers said that Dolores la Penca was ever a strange child. When she grew

up, she left her foster family and lived by herself in a deserted house, the last house in Santa Fe on the road to Agua Fria. She would wander away to the mountains for weeks at a time gathering herbs. She started to be a *curandera* and gave people powders to get them under her power. Most people were afraid to take the medicines she brewed from her herbs for fear they would bring evil spells. Her room was crowded with strange things—horns and hoofs of animals, bunches of herbs hanging from the *vigas,* and bagsful of leaves everywhere. She traded with the sheepherder for herbs they brought her from the high mountain pastures.

The day before I was to be married, forty-eight years ago, she came to bring me a gift. It was some highly perfumed soap she had made. My mother told me not to use it, but it smelled so nice that I washed my hair with it that night. The next day my face and arms and hands broke out with a red rash. I was frightened lest she had cast some spell on my marriage. And I was very angry at Dolores la Penca, for no bride wishes to look as though she had smallpox.[62]

Cleofas M. Jaramillo remembers similar stories from her childhood in late nineteenth-century Arroyo Hondo, north of Taos. There, she writes:

Old women who lived alone were usually suspected of being witches. La Chon was one of these women in our village. She was usually found sitting on a sheepskin in the corner of her fireplace, smoking a *cigarrito* and poking the fire with a stick to keep her pot of beans boiling. A low door, always kept covered with a ragged patch quilt, led into her storeroom. No one was allowed to enter this secret room, where bunches of dried herbs hung from the rafters of the ceiling and a pile of ripe pumpkins stood in a corner. From the pumpkin rinds, Chon made the *guejas,* into which she crawled and sailed through the air to places she wanted to visit. Once La Chon was met walking through the park in Santa Fe by a lady who knew her well. The lady asked Chon if she would take a package to her mother who lived in the same village. La Chon called for the package and delivered it to the lady's mother the next morning. In those days it took three days to make the trip from Arroyo Hondo to Santa Fe, and her neighbors could never find out who had brought the old woman to town. Many stories were told of how she was met at night in the form of a dog, cat, or some other animal.

One night the husband of a woman who was always ailing and was supposed to be *maleficiada* (bewitched) met a dog coming out of his yard. Picking up a stick, he gave the dog a good licking. The next day the old woman was found sick in bed with black and blue bruises over all her body. . . .

The wife of the foreman at our ranch told my mother another story; and when Mother looked incredulous, Andrea was ready to swear that it was the truth: Andrea and a girl friend, who lived near Chon's house, went into see the old woman one evening. Not finding her in her room, or in her usual corner by the kitchen fireplace, they tiptoed softly into the secret storeroom. There in a corner on a pumpkin sat Chon, holding her two eyes on a little cushion in her lap. Her dark eye sockets frightened the girls, and they ran out to tell their mothers.

A horseman who often rode into town on dark nights was bothered at times by different objects appearing in the middle of the road. Sometimes a black sheep fleece rolled and rolled before his horse for miles, then it would turn into a bright

"Old Spanish-American woman."
FSA photo by Russell Lee, Taos
County, September 1939. (LC-
USF 33-12423-M4.)

spark of fire, skipping before him. One night a dark shadow kept leaping at his horse's head, frightening the animal. The faster he raced, the faster raced the shadow. The man suddenly leaned over his horse's head and grabbed at the black object. When he opened his hand, he found he held only a piece of black shawl; and the black shadow had disappeared. When he entered the town, he saw the black shadow against the old woman's house. Dismounting, he went up to it and found it to be the old woman Chon, panting for breath and tired out. She cried out to him not to hurt her, promising never to bother him again.[63]

In Hispanic culture, although women were more frequently identified as witches, men too were thought to practice witchcraft, as in the following legend recounted by a Mora resident in 1954:

There once lived an old woman and a man. The woman was very unhappy because her husband became a frog at night, she claimed. She wanted to get a divorce, but before she could get it she had to make a declaration in court that this was true. She got a group of people to witness the case and they were surprised to see the frog she claimed to be her husband. Everybody was allowed to see the puddle of mud. She got her divorce.[64]

In fact, this is just one legendary account of an actual case of January 1940 that was heard before the justice of the peace in court at Precinct No. 1, Mora.

Mr. V. F. Romero, the presiding justice of the peace, told his recollections of the then nationally famous case to a student folklorist from Highlands University in 1955. Romero's "verbatim report" follows in full because it illustrates the complicated dynamics of witchcraft allegations in community and family life and shows the processes through which such beliefs are communicated and legends developed. Romero begins with a disclaimer:

I want to make it plain, first of all, to say that there never was a frog man, or for that matter, a toad man.[65] I do not believe in witchcraft or magic of any kind. The man that was called the sapo was known to me as A[velino] E[spinosa]. This was his Christian as well as his legal name. I had known this man since his infancy and never considered him to be anything other than a real human being. He was a shy, super shy, I should say, unassuming, inconspicuous, harmless human being. He was and had been a hard worker all of his life and led a rather barren existence. He was of short stature, he had a wrinkled face, and he was very thin. He was known to be a miser of a sort, and to be very stingy.

I also want it to be known that witchcraft cases cannot be heard or tried in any court in New Mexico. The case against A. E. was docketed as mayhem.

The stories surrounding this man are so numerous that I do not know of anyone who was around Mora, New Mexico, at the time of this man's hearing who has not heard at least several versions of how he turned into a toad. All these stories, I am sure, are fabrications of people's imaginations. As such they make good stories, much in the same way that fairy tales are good stories. Fairy tales are told all over the world for the sake of entertainment. People here are no different and they too tell fairy tales.

Mora County Courthouse, 1904.
(MNM Neg. No. 1617.)

Romero then proceeds to tell how the case came to him:

On Christmas eve of 1939, the entire village of Mora was preparing to celebrate *la Nochebuena* and the *misa del gallo*. The focal point of these celebrations is the parish church of Saint Gertrudis. The parish priest at this time was a Spaniard. His name is Father Peris. He had been in Mora for a number of years. He was never too surprised at the number of tales that his parishioners were always bringing him, for in Spain similar tales were also common. He would listen to these tales with an amusing attitude and considered them all to be good folklore.

The tale that Father Peris heard on this particular day of Christmas eve disturbed him very much, as it disturbed the entire village of Mora. This story came to Mora from the district of El Abuelo. The village and district of El Abuelo have always been considered as the headquarters of witches in Mora folklore. It lies at the foot of Jicarita Peak in sort of a cup-like valley. All the witches that were ever supposed to have existed in this valley of Mora came from El Abuelo. The whole village, as I have said, of Mora was held spellbound at this new tale that came from El Abuelo. This tale came to me in the form of three persons who wanted to swear out a warrant of arrest. The sheriff of Mora county at this time was Isaac Castillo. I asked these people on what charge I should issue the warrant. When I was told their story I decided it was too fantastic to believe. Frankly, I did not know what type of warrant I should make out, so I called up Mr. E. R. Cooper, the assistant district attorney at Las Vegas, New Mexico, for assistance. Mr. Cooper answered my call promptly and came to Mora immediately. Upon his arrival at the Mora courthouse he found a huge gathering of people. He had difficulty getting to my office because of this crowd which had come from all over the valley to see the toad man.

Mr. Cooper drew up a complaint. "Witchcraft cannot be a subject for trial in any court of New Mexico," he said, "but being that there was supposed to have been some kind of fight, I will draw up a complaint for mayhem." Mr. Cooper was also amazed at the story of the toad man.

A. E. was arrested and brought to jail. Upon searching him, the arresting officials found on his person a tobacco sack, Duke's Mixture, I believe, and in this tobacco sack was a huge sum of currency. There were twenty one-hundred dollar bills and other currency of large denomination, about three thousand dollars in all. This huge sum of money, as a matter of course, was put in safe keeping for A. E. A. E. was also told on what charge he was being held, but he made no comment. A. E. did not have a lawyer to defend him and one could not be readily found because of the approaching holidays. Because of this, his hearing was deferred to the early part of January, 1940.

The day for the hearing arrived. By this time the story of the sapo had circulated far and wide and I was surprised to see so many reporters from so many well known newspapers present at this hearing.[66] The hearing got under way and here are the findings.

Dr. Husted was called upon for the medical evidence. His testimony brought out the fact that on the morning of December 24, 1939, Mrs. A. E. and two other persons had come to his office. Mrs. A. E. was suffering from some wounds about the face and neck. He also stated that he had treated this woman for some puncture-like wounds about the two sides of the face. These wounds looked like wounds that could be inflicted with an ice pick. There were also deep incision-like scratches on the woman's throat.

The plaintiff was asked to show her wounds, and this she did. Her face was badly swollen and she seemed to be in ill health.

Because of the press of the big crowd present at the hearing and because of the intense curiosity of the crowd and fearing some sort of disorder in the court, I decided to hear the testimony of the plaintiff in private with only the proper authorities present.

Herewith is the plaintiff's testimony as well as I can remember. This testimony was not written in the record because of the witchcraft elements in it.

"My name is B. E. I have been married to A. E. for twenty years. I married him when I was very young and in my ignorance I did not realize I was marrying a sapo. I bore the sapo a son and as soon as my son was born I knew he was bewitched. I knew this because my son suffered horrible fits. There we something strange about my husband, because every time my son would see him my son would suffer horrible fits. My husband was *embrujado*. Of this I am sure, because I found out he was visiting with the Abuelo witches.

"Even though my son was bewitched, I loved him, for he was part of me. Early in my son's life I took measures to bewitch him, for like I said, my son suffered fits upon seeing his father and he would go into horrible spasms. My son grew up to hate his father, because he had bewitched him. I gave my son certain *remedios* to counteract my husband's witchcraft. When my son had the fits I would administer these remedios and he would get over them. Of course the sapo loved his son and he was always trying to take him from me. Fortunately my son hated him so much he would not even look at him, except with his eyes shut. When my son had the misfortune to see him, he would immediately go into fits. Then I would come and chase the sapo away and minister to my son. The fits of my son went on for years. My son got weaker and weaker until finally in a horrible fit of agony he gave up the ghost. He died on 22 December 1939 at the age of nineteen.

"We held the velorio ("wake") at the sapo's the night of the twenty-second, because the sapo's house was also mine. On December 23, in the afternoon, we buried my son. On this day it began to snow very much. After the burial I went back to the house for no other reason than to search for a hoard of money that I knew the sapo had hidden somewhere in the house. My sister and brother-in-law helped me in the search. We did not find anything, not even a nickel. I became frantic with fear. I needed the money, because I was going to leave the sapo and go to live with my own people. By now I was deathly afraid of what he was going to do to me now that my son was dead. I knew now that he was going to bewitch me and I would get the fits that my son had.

"After the search for the money failed, I decided to go to my sister's house at El Aguila which is about one and one-half miles from the sapo's house. The snow kept falling and by the time we got there, there was about six inches of snow on the ground. By nightfall it stopped snowing and a very bright moon lighted the sky and all the countryside.

"My sister and brother-in-law went to bed, as did I. Some time during the night I was awakened by a choking sensation in my throat. I screamed. At my throat was a sapo about the size of a ten-year old boy. My screams awakened my brother-in-law, who came running to my rescue. When my brother-in-law came to my rescue, I was almost unconscious. My brother-in-law got a hold of a broom and began to beat the sapo off of me. The sapo finally let go of my throat, hopped toward the window sill, hopped on to it, and jumped through the window and disappeared into the moonlit night. How he jumped through the window without breaking a single pane is a mystery to me. However, to an embrujado anything is possible when they are under the spell. The three of us, my sister, my brother-in-law, and I, went out into the night to track the sapo down. But we could find no tracks. All we found was a large circle with strange signs in the center. There were no tracks leading to this circle and no tracks anywhere. We gave up the search and went back into the house very scared.

"Soon after entering the house we heard a voice coming from the attic. I, my sister, and brother-in-law recognized the voice as my husband's voice. He spoke these words: '*Si no los logré ahora, los voy a lograr después.*' 'If I did not get you this time, I will get you later.' We went to the attic but found no one.

"That night my wounds got worse and worse until in the morning I was obliged to come to Mora to see the doctor."

This fantastic story was all the testimony I got from Mrs. A. E. The testimony of the sister and brother-in-law was in the same vein.

Romero concludes:

I could not permit these stories in court, because these stories were so obviously, so grossly fantastic and untrue that I could and would not believe them to be evidence.

Mr. A. E. could not be proved to have been anywhere near the scene of these purported weird happenings, so surely he was not guilty of any tort or crime. He was set free and the case of the toad man was discharged from the docket.[67]

Witches like Avelino Espinosa were thought to learn their malevolence at special schools. According to Wesley R. Hurt, Jr., there was a story in Bernalillo around 1940,

of a man who had the desire to become a witch. He went to a native of Mexico, who was a brujo [male witch] and a student of the ill-famed *Libro Negro,* or Black Book, to seek information. The brujo told him that if he aspired to become a witch he would have to pass three tests, to which the man willingly agreed. Suddenly developing a pair of wings, the brujo grabbed the man and flew away to a witches' party. There the brujo told him that his first test would be to kiss a magical goat which had just entered the room. This test the man passed successfully. His next test was to kiss a snake which had crawled into the room. After completing this act, the applicant learned that there would be a feast, of which he must partake as the final test. As the table was being set, the man noticed this queer fact—the servants brought in a table cover but no silverware or plates. Then four men came into the room carrying a coffin in which lay a cadaver. When the man saw the body he cried out, *"Alavado sean los dulces nombres de Jesús, María, y José."* Immediately everything disappeared from his sight and he found himself alone in the desert. For two days he staggered through the sands and finally reached home, a much wiser man.[68]

Aurelio M. Espinosa claims that a place near Peña Blanca was the site of "a school of witches [where] the apprentice first enters their cave, where the Devil and old witches preside." In his 1910 study of "New-Mexican Spanish Folk-lore" Espinosa maintains:

Los brujos ó brujas are mischievous individuals who practise evil on their neighbors, often for little or no cause. Generally, however, it is on their enemies that witches practise the evil doings which they are able to perform. No one is born a witch. Witchcraft is a science, a kind of learning which may be learned from other witches. Any one who is a witch can give his or her powers to another one; though an individual, by practising evil, may, on agreement with the Devil, become a witch. New Mexicans speak of a witch as being in agreement with the Devil (*pactado con el diablo* or *pautau con el diablo*).[69]

Cleofas M. Jaramillo identifies *ambularias* as "graduates in witchcraft" who themselves held such schools. Some came into possession of a powerful *Piedra Iman,* through which "they knew everything and could transform themselves into any shape. [It] was a fury stone which was fed needles and water, and if the stone was lost or stolen from its owner, the owner immediately lost her mind or dried up into a skeleton."[70]

Such sinister transformations contrast markedly with the memories of Luisa Torres of Guadalupita, born there in 1903 and seventy-five years old when she was interviewed by Gioia Brandi. Torres recalled the women's role in gathering and planting beneficial herbs and plants. She "wanted to know all that my grandmother knew; especially how to make use of the medicinal plants, how to prepare oregano, *osha,* fennel, amaranth, *pasote,* spearmint, peppermint, sweet basil and the many, many others that grew around our place." She told of a remarkable childhood vision:

> I watched my maternal grandparents a lot; they were the only grandparents I knew. On the day that my grandmother was seventy, I saw her open the doors of her little adobe house. It was a spring day and there were millions of orange and black butterflies around the corn plants; my grandmother ran towards the butterflies and gathered so many of them in her apron that she flew up in the air, while she laughed contentedly.

> Observaba yo mucho a mis abuelitos maternos, que son los unicos que conocí. El día que mi abuelita cumplió setenta años, yo la ví abrir las puertas de su casita de adobes; era un día de primavera y había millones de mariposas anaranjadas y negras alrededor de las plantas de maíz, corrió me abuelita hacía las mariposas y juntó tantas en el delantal que se levantó en el aire, mientras se reía contenta.[71]

Albeit of more modest social standing, Luisa Torres's grandmother resembles Fabiola Cabeza de Baca's, whom the latter describes as follows:

> Quite often, the wife of the *patrón* was well versed in plant medicine. I know that my grandmother, Doña Estéfana Delgado de Baca, although not given the name of *médica,* because it was not considered proper in her social class, was called every day by some family in the village, or by their *empleados,* to treat a child or some other person in the family. In the fall of the year, she went out to the hills and valleys to gather her supply of healing herbs. When she went to live in La Liendre, there were terrible outbreaks of smallpox and she had difficulty convincing the villagers that vaccination was a solution. Not until she had a godchild in every family was she able to control the dreaded disease. In Spanish tradition, a godmother takes the responsibility of a real mother, and in that way grandmother conquered many superstitions which the people had. At least she had the power to decide what should be done for her godchildren. . . .
>
> As did my grandmother, so all the wives of the *patrones* held a very important place in the villages and ranches on the Llano. The *patrón* ruled the *rancho,* but his wife looked after the spiritual and physical welfare of the *empleados* and their families. She was the first one called when there was death, illness, misfortune or good tidings in a family. She was a great social force in the community—more so than

her husband. She held the purse strings, and thus she was able to do as she pleased in her charitable enterprises and to help those who might seek her assistance.[72]

Such women were, as Buss points out, "counselors and advice givers for the community, as well as medical practitioners and religious leaders, and they represented a centuries-old tradition of female medical care."[73]

Anglo ranch women were also important caretakers, as May Price Mosley (NMFWP) recounts for southeastern New Mexico pioneers:

There were no doctors; and when illness or accident befell, much was endured without their aid or anesthetic. Hours of racking pain by the patient, days of haunting apprehension and worry by his companions (whether family or friends), while doing everything known or possible for them to do to aid him. Caring for the sick was a much lonelier vigil here than in rural sections not so thinly settled; unless someone was sent for help much sickness and death might come without one's neighbors knowing of it. . . .

On ranches where there were only men, about all the medicines around were axle grease and coal oil—and strychnine to kill coyotes. But most every ranch woman had a medicine box full of home remedies which she administered almost to the extent of "practicing medicine." A few had doctor books. One who could never stand seeing wounds always kept a supply of court plaster on hand and did some very effective patchwork with strips of it. Another first-aid soul kept a kit of all sorts of homeopathic or similar remedies on hand.[74]

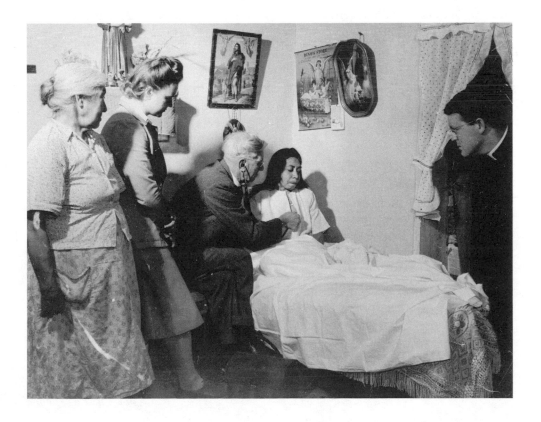

"Doctor Onstine, of the clinic operated by the Taos county co-operative health association, and Father Smith, the parish priest, at the bedside of a Tuberculosis patient." FSA photo by John Collier, Questa, January 1943. (LC-USW 3-17918-C.)

Dan McAllister's Grandma Findley, as she was known to pioneers in the Sacramento Mountains and Alamogordo area, learned her doctoring skills from experience, an Apache woman, and her copy of *Old Reliable Family Physician or What To Do Until the Doctor Comes*:

> Grandma assisted many a baby through the gates of the morning of life. She set broken bones, and upon a few occasions dug lead out of men that had been shot. When a smallpox epidemic raged in and around the sleepy village of La Luz and some houses had to be quarantined and used as "pesthouses," Grandma vaccinated dozens of people . . . [using] a vaccine that she personally extracted from calves she had inoculated with virus of the disease. Grandma's vaccinations nearly always "took" beautifully.
>
> . . . Even after 1900 our nearest drugstore was Frank Rolland's in the new town of Alamogordo, six miles away by horseback. So Grandma kept a medicine chest. . . . Some remedies that she used effectively were those old frontier standbys, quinine, turpentine, coal oil, and whiskey. (Except for medicinal purposes, Grandma abominated whiskey.)
>
> Grandma used also some old Indian remedies an Apache squaw had taught her how to prepare. . . . One such Indian remedy was an efficacious febrifuge brewed from pine needles and *yerba buena* or good herb that grows here and there on the plains. And green cactus meat beaten to a pulp made poultices that drew inflammation from and even abated infection in knife cuts, barbed wire rips, severe bruises from horsekicks, and even gunshot wounds.[75]

Some men became adept healers in the absence of women. Trappers, hunters, prospectors, and cowboys were all versed in folk medicine. According to May Price Mosley:

> On rare occasions a lone cowboy in a bachelor camp has suffered, even deliriously, the fever and pain of pneumonia or a broken limb, without aid from any person—no doctor, no medicine, no nurse, little food, and perhaps no fuel in winter—and survived. Found perhaps by some passer-by in his convalescence. . . .
>
> Some cowboys were surprisingly adept nurses. Some in an emergency have set broken limbs, pulled joints back into place. They have performed crude but effective bits of surgery such as completing the amputation of a finger with a pocketknife, sewing a lip in place with a common needle and thread (all victims without an anesthetic), and the cleansing of a woman's gunshot wound with a willow withe and white silk from the sleeve of her wedding dress.[76]

Hermits, Beggars, and Wanderers

Like their colonial predecessors, territorial New Mexicans often encountered solitary or eccentric individuals whose strangeness excited their imagination. In this respect they were no different from other colonial or frontier communities in America. Don Yoder comments: "Hermits, saintly and secular, abound in early American society. I am always amazed at the amount of material one comes upon in early American documentation on the nonconformists of this sort, whether voluntary or forced rejects of society. . . . Our roads were crowded with offbeat 'hawkers and walkers,' tramps, religious itinerants, self-appointed messiahs, and utopia builders."[77] Across New Mexico, from Raton to the Gila country, people told stories about eccentric figures like *el mal hijo,* Patches, Crazy Juan, Luardo, Bear Moore, and the Frenchman of Dog Canyon. Perhaps the most widely recognized of these characters were Giovanni María d'Agostino, the Hermit of New Mexico, and Francis Schlatter, the New Mexico Messiah.

D'Agostino, also known as Marie Agustine, Juan Bautista Agustiniani, Matteo Boccalini, Father Francesco, and Juan María Agostini, was born in Italy in 1800 or 1801. He began a lifelong pilgrimage when at the age of thirty he journeyed to Spain and arrived at the shrine of Santiago de Compostela in Galicia on February 27, 1831. From this northwestern shrine he traveled east and south, visiting sanctuaries and monasteries but always choosing solitude. Following a vision of the beckoning Virgin, d'Agostino sailed westward across the Atlantic and arrived in Caracas, Venezuela, in 1838. For twenty-one years he wandered alone through South and Central America and in 1859 set out for Mexico, where he lived in a cave and attracted many worshippers. Fearful Mexican authorities deported him to Havana, Cuba, in October 1861, and from there he sailed to French Canada. Quebec proved inhospitable, and according to his diary: "Finally, I decided to go west."[78]

In the early 1860s, d'Agostino lived in a cave in Council Grove, Kansas, before joining the wagon train of Don Manuel Romero on May 28, 1863, to walk the 550 miles to Santa Fe.[79] Romero was a prominent citizen of Las Vegas, but d'Agostino declined to accept his hospitality for long, settling instead in a cave in nearby Romeroville. According to Arthur L. Campa, who traced the Hermit's legend in the early 1950s:

> The Hermit did not tarry long at the home of Don Manuel Romero, but in the short time he was there word spread through the nearby villages that a holy man had come into town from afar. The benign aspect of the blackrobed old man leaning on a staff wherever he went, his willingness to give counsel, and the story of his travels appealed to the religious nature of the New Mexicans. . . . They saw in this anchorite the reappearance of one of the Biblical prophets, and looked to him for guidance and advice. In spite of his eccentricities the Hermit must have been a kindly man and a good man, for he has continued to live in the memory of the villages around Las Vegas for almost a century. To this day, no one has ever said anything but good about him.
>
> In the days when the healing arts were essentially nothing more than advice and the application of a few household remedies, the experienced Hermit acquired the reputation of a healer, and was sought out by countless unfortunates suffering from chronic and incurable diseases. The persistent crowds soon drove him out of Las Vegas in search of a place where he might escape the company of his fellow men. Several miles southeast of the village, where Romeroville now stands, he came to natural cave on the east wall of the canyon, and there once more he took up the anchorite life he had led for almost half a century. But here too the people from Rosiada, Gallinas, and San Geronimo discovered his retreat and came to him in increasing numbers. Not only did they call on him, but they pitched tents and windbreaks near the cave in order to enjoy the beneficent influence of "El Santo Ermitano."[80]

Giovanni María d'Agostino
(1800 or 1801–1869), the
Hermit of New Mexico.
(MNM Neg. No. 110764.)

At the summit of Hermit's
Peak, ca. 1898. (MNM Neg.
No. 77017.)

This unwelcome attention disturbed the Hermit and he abruptly left Romeroville Canyon for a more solitary abode atop Cerro del Tecolote about twenty miles northwest of Las Vegas.

> About three hundred feet below the eastern side of the Peak, the Hermit selected a hollowed cave. . . . Inside this open cave, moisture dropped into a hole he dug in the floor, providing all the water necessary for his needs. Many years after his death, the dripping from the ceiling of his abandoned cave slowed to an occasional drop, and the villagers claim that anyone able to catch three drops on the tip of the tongue will forever tell the truth. One wag insists that the reason these mountaineers can tell the truth only partially is that no one has ever caught more than two drops.[81]

Although the Hermit came down from Cerro del Tecolote to replenish his supply of corn meal and to sell crucifixes and beads he had carved, a fair number of villagers climbed the peak to seek his advice and to help him build a shelter. Some workers said that "when they ran out of water . . . the Hermit walked over to one of the rocks along the cliff and touched it with his staff, and that a spring of crystalline water gushed forth." They also claimed that "the old man insisted on feeding them a very tasty stew he had prepared . . . [and that] no matter how many servings were taken from the pot, it never gave out during the time they were with him."[82] These and other legends continued to be told in the Las Vegas area long after the Hermit had left. In later years those who had known him formed an informal "Sociedad del Ermitaño," or Society of the Hermit, and constructed a "Via Crucis" atop what came to be called Hermit's Peak. Until the 1960s, they made "pilgrimages in May and September to the Hermit's cave to commemorate the recluse's life of service."[83]

In the spring of 1867, the Hermit arrived in Old Mesilla and presented himself to Colonel Albert J. Fountain, with whom he arranged a system of signal fires like the one he had set up with Samuel B. Watrous of La Junta near Hermit's Peak. He then retired to a retreat in the Organ Mountains. In April 1869, no signal fires were seen. A search party found the anchorite's body with a dagger thrust in his back. According to Arthur L. Campa:

> In the ninety-odd years that have elapsed since the Hermit's murder numerous conjectures have been advanced, not only as to why he was killed but as to how he met his death. Some say that his body was pierced with arrows, thus suggesting an Indian attack. Others claim that he was badly mutilated by sword thrusts. The most interesting recent account is the one that appeared in the April 30, 1953, issue of the *Las Cruces Citizen:* "The murderers attacked the Holy One while he slept, as he had only his underwear clothes on his body." This story assumes that the Hermit undressed when he lay down to sleep in the barrenness of his lonely cave, a most unlikely habit for a man whose design for living was not physical comfort.
>
> The fact remains that no one has been able to determine conclusively who was responsible for the death of Juan María Agostini. There are widespread rumors that the Catholic Church was not in sympathy with his religious practices, and that the local clergy wherever he went resented his popularity among their parishioners, but it is hard to believe that even the strongest feeling against him would have led to murder.[84]

In May 1937, Marie Carter (NMFWP) interviewed Elizabeth Fountain Armendáriz, the granddaughter of Colonel Albert J. Fountain, at the family home of her parents in Old Mesilla. Mrs. Armendáriz kept the family curios which formed part of the Gadsden Museum collection. The hermit's few possessions were among the objects. She told Mrs. Carter:

> I want you to examine these articles; they were given to my grandparents by Juan María Justiniani, or the Hermit of the Organ mountains, a Cartuchian monk. This little brass bell is the same one he always carried, tied to the handle of his cane. These brown rosary beads, which he gave to my grandmother, are made from the leaves of flowers. This black rosary he gave my grandfather. Note the artistic rose design hand–carved by the Hermit. . . .
>
> The brown book is written in Spanish, and its cover is crude cowhide. The other book is written in Italian, and is covered with sheepskin. The Hermit used to walk from the Organ mountains to Mesilla to preach to the people. Here is another rosary much larger than the other two; it came from the Grotto of Our Lady of Lorades [Lourdes], (France) and he wore it around his waist. This ring with the spikes in it he used for inflicting punishment upon himself. It was his way of doing penance.
>
> The Hermit was a very religious man. The natives feared him because they believed that he could read their minds; also predict the future. . . .
>
> That . . . picture of a tall, white-bearded monk wearing the brown hooded cape of his order and leaning on a cane to which a small brass bell . . . was attached is the Hermit. My father painted him from memory. Whenever the natives wish to find something real bad, they pray to the Hermit to help them.

Mrs. Armendáriz also told Mrs. Carter a different version of the Hermit's death.

> It seems that the Hermit predicted his own death. He was in the habit of lighting a bonfire every night to say his rosary.
>
> "Tonight" he told Father Baca of Las Cruces, "there will be no fire."
>
> And when the bright flames, to which the people of Mesilla had grown accustomed, failed to appear in the eastern sky, they knew, even before they found him, that the Hermit of the Organs was dead.[85]

Late in the nineteenth century, another religious wanderer drew even wider attention in the Southwest. Francis Schlatter, a German immigrant, arrived in Denver in the fall of 1892 and began work as a shoemaker. The following year, he began peregrinations through Kansas, Arkansas, Texas, Arizona, California, and finally came to Pajarito, New Mexico, around July 9, 1895.

> Drawing on the *curandero* tradition of the little Spanish village, he began healing there in earnest. Stories of numerous cures soon reached Albuquerque and the *Albuquerque Morning Democrat* sent reporters down to investigate. There they were met with incredible tales of healing. These would have been instantly dismissed, had not hundreds of people vouched for their truth. Jesus Maria Vasques, who had been three years blind, was touched by Schlatter and now could see. Juliana Sedillo,

who for 16 years could not use her arms, was now off working in the fields, and so on. Andreas Romero, an elderly prominent citizen of nearby Peralta, confirmed the stories. "The work of this man is something inexplicable and wonderful," he said. "There is something in his touch which seems to heal the sick. What you have heard of him is true to the letter. I cannot explain it myself; no one can; yet we know some remarkable cures have been effected."

When the *Albuquerque Morning Democrat* broke the story, the issue sold out immediately. "El Sanador" ["The Healer"] became the sole topic of conversation on every street corner.[86]

The reporters also noted Schlatter's resemblance to standard pictures of Christ and quoted his often repeated pronouncements about the healing mission "The Father" had sent him on.

Schlatter was persuaded to move to Albuquerque on July 20, 1895. There he continued his miraculous cures:

Francis Schlatter, 1892. Photo by W. A. White. (MNM Neg. No. 91346.)

> Black railroad worker Charles Stamp could suddenly walk on his crushed foot; Peter Maguire found himself cured of his rheumatism; Mrs. C. J. Roentgen could now hear better; C. G. Lott could suddenly move his paralyzed arm. For those who felt no improvement, Schlatter simply said that more treatments were necessary. Moreover, he took no payment for any of his work. When money was occasionally forced on him, he later distributed it to the poor. Schlatter was always very open whenever he was questioned about his power. He was only a poor shoemaker, he said, who was simply doing the bidding of his Master. When asked to account for the cures, he replied, "My work speaks for itself." Albuquerqueans were astounded when he ended his fast by eating a gigantic meal and seemingly felt no ill aftereffects. They were even more astounded when he informed Reverend Charles Bovard that he was Jesus returned for a second life on earth. He did not volunteer this information but when asked directly, replied in the affirmative.[87]

A weakened Schlatter left Albuquerque for Denver on August 21, 1895. He rested at the home of E. L. Fox and began healing Denver crowds after September 16.

Schlatter disappeared from Fox's house on the morning of November 14, 1895, and a search was conducted throughout the western states. According to Ferenc Szasz:

> Meanwhile, Schlatter and Butte, his big white horse, were slowly riding south into New Mexico. In mid-December he was spotted in the Santa Fe area and he spent time healing in Peña Blanca, Santo Domingo, and Bernalillo. . . .
>
> Early in January Schlatter quietly appeared at the Morley ranch in Datil (near Socorro). There he met a sympathetic listener in Mrs. Ada Morley (Jarrett) who gladly housed him for the winter months. "The Father has directed me to a safe retreat," he told her. "I must restore my spiritual powers in seclusion and prayer." For three months Schlatter stayed in an upstairs room at the Morley household, venturing out only when the coast was clear. During that time he alternately rested and exercised by swinging a large copper rod over his head, as a drum major might swing a baton. He said that The Father had told him this was necessary or he would lose his power. He and Mrs. Morley had long conversations during the

winter and, with his permission, she copied them down in a book later published under the title *The Life of the Harp in the Hand of the Harper* (Denver, 1897).[88]

Schlatter left the Morley ranch in the spring of 1896 and was spotted near Silver City on April 8. He disappeared into Mexico, where he died in Chihuahua sometime in 1897. Although archeologist Edgar Lee Hewett confirmed his death in 1906, "for over twenty years afterward, imposters claiming to be Schlatter appeared intermittently across the nation [in] Chicago, New York City, Canton, Ohio, central Nebraska, Los Angeles, Long Beach, and St. Louis. . . . But there was a key difference between Schlatter and his imposters: They almost always took money."[89]

Such religious imposters appeared from time to time in New Mexico. Colonel Jack Potter wrote about Hugh Leeper, the "Sanctified Texan," a fugitive and ex-buffalo hunter who lived in the Pecos Valley.

> No matter how shady his past may have been, it was generally conceded that he was fairly well educated and was an accomplished scholar of the Bible. At least he quoted it a lot. Later he achieved real fame in the Pecos region as a prophet of sorts. Many a hazardous adventure of the early seventies was started upon assurance by the Texan that things would go all right, that "their time had not come."

Leeper prophesied Billy the Kid's demise and the destruction by flood of the adobe saloon in Fort Sumner. Afterward, "all that was left of the old saloon site was a muddy sand bar. Leeper's reputation increased till he had everyone believing that he could really foretell the future. Not that they were superstitious or anything like that. 'It was the Lord's will.'" A friend discovered a wanted poster and description of the Sanctified Texan in the coat pockets of Barney Mason, an undercover man for Pat Garrett. This friend informed Leeper, and "that old Bible-quoting feller took the news real calm like . . . [turning] to his friend and [saying], 'Well, just tell the folks that *my time has come* to move on. I'll be seeing them when the Roll is Called Up Yonder. Adios!'"[90]

During the 1870s in northern Taos County, a sheepherder named Eduardo or Luardo Gallegos began making strange claims about Ute Mountain near the Colorado border. He maintained that it was the headquarters for a secret branch of the Penitente Brotherhood whose membership included "people from the other world [and] former residents of Cerro and of the neighboring villages, long past dead." According to Reyes N. Martínez (NMFWP), who spoke with Rafael Vigil and Tomas J. Martínez:

> It was Tuesday of Holy Week, when Luardo . . . once returned to the village [of Cerro] after several days' absence, saying that he had assisted at the Penitentes on Ute Mountain. No one believed his story, as he was already held by the residents of the village as a mentally deranged person. Yet, on the three succeeding nights, when the local lodge of Penitentes performed their rites and sacrifices at Cerro, long, mysterious, double rows of bright lights were seen ascending from the foot to the summit of Ute Mountain. These unexplainable happenings caused the residents of the village to begin to place some credence in the stories told them by Luardo, and on the following Monday, several residents of the village made their way to the mountain to try to discover the cause of the strange phenomena. . . . They encountered no signs on their way up, but, upon arriving at the summit three "maderos" (large wooden

crosses, which are dragged along the ground by the Penitentes on their bare shoulders when performing their sacrifices) met their gaze, arranged resting on their crosspieces on the ground, two of them leaning against the third one, placed between them, as is the usual custom of placing them during Holy Week outside of all "moradas" (lodge houses of the order). How they came to be there was a mystery ...; there were no signs that they had been dragged up the mountain; nor was there to be seen a morada on the place. . . . Awed and mystified by the spectacle, the searching party retraced their steps and wended their way homeward to tell a waiting populace of the result of their unusual adventure, with no definite information about the phantom procession seen on the mountain the week before.

Luardo next proclaimed that he would bring three bells from the summit of Ute Mountain to Arroyo Hondo. "He claimed to be a prophet, sent . . . by God and told [the villagers] that they were ordained by God to build a church . . . [and] that he would bring them three bells . . . as proof to them."

On the seventh day following his departure from Arroyo Hondo, Luardo neared the village from the north, driving a buggy in which he said afterwards he was bringing the three bells. On the ridge, just before going down to the village, he stopped. Somehow he seemed to sense that all was not well among the residents of the village. He tied the team of horses to a tree, leaving the buggy with the bells there, and walked down to the village. There he found dissension and discord among the villagers and forthwith turned back, telling them in a rage that their lack of faith prevented him from bringing the bells down to the village. Arriving at the place where the team and buggy were, so the story is, he dug a pit on top of the ridge and buried the three bells there, the whereabouts of which has never been found to date, although several attempts have been made to locate the place.[91]

Martínez's sister, Cleofas M. Jaramillo, gives a different version of this incident and adds another episode in Luardo's legendary activities:

On another day [Luardo] was going to bring a church bell down from the Cerro. On the way he would give three rings, the last one at the top of the north ridge. As he approached the village at this last ring, the dead would rise from their graves in Padre Lucero's cemetery on the hill. A large throng of people from Taos, Arroyo Seco and San Antonio lined the road from the south ridge to the north, all expecting to see the miracle. My father's brother wrapped in a sarape borrowed from one of his *peones,* and his wife, wearing a skirt and *reboso* belonging to one of her *criadas,* went to see the crowd, thinking that Luardo would not recognize them in that garb. But Luardo spied them, and made the excuse that he could not perform the miracle because there were some unbelievers among them.

Another time he was about to perform a miracle. While a large crowd waited outside the Padre's Chapel, Luardo stretched Juan Vernal before the altar and knelt praying and making signs over him. Then in a fit of fanatic zeal he stabbed the man in the heart with his knife. Failing to revive him by prayers and signs, he dragged him out and showed him to the people. He told them, "Here, I have killed the *Antecristo* and set you free."

Legless man on burro, Railroad Avenue, Las Vegas, ca. 1900. (MNM Neg. No. 11779.)

Juan's brothers, who did not belong to *Los Luardos* became enraged at this act and called for help from a detachment of government cavalry men, who were passing to the north. The brothers led the soldiers to Luardo's hiding place. Luardo came out brandishing his knife and started running, but the soldiers overtook him and gave him a good beating with their muskets. Then they left him.[92]

Luardo was a localized religious fanatic. New Mexicans of his day were also familiar with deformed figures known as *mal hijos,* who appeared in communities from southern Colorado southward through the Rio Grande Valley. According to T. M. Pearce:

The earliest reports of *el mal hijo* are found in the mid-nineteenth century. He was usually one of the *leperos* or rabble, using his deformity to entice superstitious and charitable villagers into aiding him. . . . Whenever he had an audience, he told his story or *relación*. In some accounts this seems to have been in ballad form and was sung. Ordinarily, however, the *malhijo* preached a sermon using his narrative, or *relación,* as an *exemplum*. He must have resembled an ancient bard delivering prophetic utterance, or, by contrast, an itinerant actor entertaining while he gospelized, for he could cry, rant, and pray in one sentence. One New Mexican *relación* told how the father of the *malhijo* went one Sunday to borrow a bushel of corn of his son. The boy cursed his father and started to beat him. As he was chasing his father, the ground opened up and swallowed him all the way to his waist. After extricating himself, *el mal hijo* went to the priest seeking forgiveness. He was refused and sent to the bishop. The bishop told the bad son he must roam the "four parts" of the earth and to confess his sins to all men.[93]

In the late 1930s, Primitivo H. Metzgar and Benny Rubi told T. M. Pearce about Chavetas, a *mal hijo* whom Pearce first encountered in Albuquerque in 1936. Metzgar

told me that he knew Chavetas as a young man of twenty. He saw him once driving a burro. The youth was evil-tempered and uncontrollable. He beat his mother, dragged her on the floor, and then made an incestuous attack upon her. The woman lost her mind and was sent to an asylum where she died within three months. Before she left her home, she cursed her son. "You will crawl on the ground like a snake," she said. "You will go like a horned toad."

After his mother's death, *el mal hijo* felt his legs shriveling. They shrank until they were no longer than a broomstick and would not support him. He had to fashion a platform on roller skates on which he propelled himself with his hands. And he began the restless crawling up and down the concrete highway where, like a horned toad, he moved at the peril of motors and horses. Chavetas was disagreeable to those who offered him charity, tossing money at people who offered it to him unsolicited. He was once imprisoned for throwing rocks at drivers of cars who refused to pick him up.

Another explanation of *el mal hijo* Chavetas [according to Rubi] is that he was once a cowboy and after he dragged his mother around by the hair and abused her, his legs shriveled and he had to crawl on the ground. When water was brought to him it dried up in the glass.[94]

Other beggars were mentally defective and accorded special treatment in traditional Hispanic communities. Lorin W. Brown (NMFWP) notes that "congenital idiots, imbeciles, or mental cases of any kind . . . are regarded in the same light as an infant . . . [and] no matter how long they live they are *inocentes* or innocents, and their unquestioned assurance of a place in heaven is acknowledged by all." Brown describes the attitude toward Onésimo the deformed village idiot in Córdova, as follows:

Yet even the children from infancy became used to him and never mistreated him. This shambling figure could be expected to enter any home at any time, for he ran at large through the village. Thus it was that the children were early imbued with the idea that he was a *pobre inocente* who should be treated kindly. If he entered a home while the family was seated around the table, the children were taught to carry a piece of tortilla and a dish of food to the corner in which he sat. For he was an *inocente,* and his presence safeguarded the home village from harm and violence. Good fortune and a favorable entry in the recording angel's books were the reward for kindly acts toward Onésimo. So it was that he was made room for and accepted with good-natured tolerance wherever he appeared. He would take his place at any and all gatherings—at mass, at a wake, or with the Penitentes as they made the pilgrimages to Calvary or the village church. He would be the only male attending the vesper services of the Niñas de María during the month of May.

Soon after Onésimo died in the early 1930s,

there was a killing in the place. True, neither the man killed nor the killer were of the village, but it gave the place a bad name, linking it with its neighboring villages in Rio Arriba County which were notorious for the killings committed in them with appalling frequency. Also the crops failed for two years, and work outside in the sheep and railroad camps became very scarce. People would say, "Since Onésimo died we are having bad luck; money is scarce, work is not to be found, and now this killing in our town."

When a second killing was committed by Córdova's lame fiddler, who had taken particular care of his "lucky talisman" Onésimo, villagers concluded that "Onesimo's death had removed a kindly protection from the village and loosed a malignant spirit that bred discontent and hatred with fatal results."[95]

Not all eccentrics were viewed in a religious sense, however. Some, like Crazy Juan of Raton, were thought of as curiosities. The hapless Juan never recovered from the loss of his wife to another man and finally moved to a lean-to on the side of Hermit's or Red River Peak south of Raton. He lived by scavenging in the growing town's garbage dump. According to Kenneth Fordyce (NMFWP), after about 1910: "The old man learned that if he would receive those who curiously sought to see him that he would be rewarded with cigarettes, and he was fond of tobacco. For a package of cigarettes, visitors were even permitted to photograph Juan and his living quarters." Fordyce describes Crazy Juan as

a man about five feet ten inches tall. He was rather bright-eyed but wild-looking. He was healthy-looking considering the life he had lived and the sort of food he had eaten. His hair was dark with some gray in it and so much dirt that it was difficult to tell much about it. It hung about his face and over his shoulders and was uncombed. His beard hid most of his face. . . . Juan was crazy, of course, and it is little wonder that he did not become helplessly insane, living as he did over a period of twenty-five years. Many people stood in awe and wonder when they realized the food that Juan ate without dying of poisoning.[96]

The influenza epidemic of 1918 finally killed the unfortunate man.

Crazy Juan's solitude is extreme; others were hermits by choice. A hermit known only as "Patches" had been part of an 1870s posse chasing four bandits who held up a Wells Fargo shipment of gold in the Cimarron area. The manhunt was successful, but Kenneth Fordyce claimed that in 1938 "Patches" was still seeking the stolen gold.

He must believe it is still there, for those who know his habits tell of his working on ranches near the present town of Maxwell, New Mexico, for a few months until he gets enough for a grub stake and of his disappearance into the mountains where he stays for months at a time.

Santa Fe, ca. 1900. Photo by
Eugene J. Hall, Chicago. Prince
Collection. (MNM Neg. No.
8102.)

Anyone would recognize "Patches." His name describes him; his ragged clothes with many patches over the holes and his hermetical habits which account for his untidy and even dirty appearance brand him a strange one. Of course, his gray hair and walrus-like mustache are familiar to those who know him, but none would think when they see him nimbly start up a mountain trail that the old man was nearing his ninetieth birthday, nor can anyone explain why month after month "Patches" spends his time tramping the lonely hillsides of Tenaja and Eagle Trail.[97]

The mountains of southwestern New Mexico also harbored a fair number of prospectors and treasure seekers like "Patches." In the Gila country, prospector and hunter Bear Moore lived as a recluse following an 1892 attack by a grizzly. John Oglesby of Pinos Altos told Mrs. W. C. Totty (NMFWP) how Moore came to his house after the attack.

> Bear Moore stayed at my house several days and rested up, but poor fellow never went around people after his fight with the bear; he was so self-conscious of the condition of his face. I must admit it was the most horrible thing I ever saw. His face was half gone, and, having healed without any medical treatment, it was badly drawn, and the scars looked horrible.
>
> Mr. Moore was called Bear Moore until his death. Children would run from him if they saw him. He cut himself off from the human race, but he sure did this part of the country a favor when he killed Club-Foot [the bear].
>
> Mr. Moore was a very independent person; he always paid for everything he received. In the early days even a stranger outlaw or respected citizen was never asked to pay for anything, but Bear Moore would never accept this Western hospitality.[98]

East of the Gila, in the Tularosa Basin, François Jean Roche became a squatter in Dog Canyon in the early 1880s. C. L. Sonnichsen describes him as "the bravest man who ever came to the Tularosa country . . . , a cantankerous little Frenchman who lived a hermit's life in the wildest part of the Territory and . . . was fifty-one when he was murdered in 1894 just after Christmas—an ailing, aging foreigner who spoke broken English, dressed in rough clothes, and came only occasionally to Las Cruces. Many people recognized his stocky figure, bald head, and wind-reddened face, but hardly anyone was friendly with him or wanted to be friendly with him, and he was content to have it that way." Frenchy's solitary domain with its abundant water supply provoked the envy of his Texan neighbors, three of whom murdered him. Cowboy Dan Fitchett found his body two days later, but "there was no mourning and no thought of going after the killers. After all, Frenchy had not gone out of his way to make anybody love him, and his relatives were far away."[99]

"On the Dodge"

When William M. Emery, son of Matt Emery, an old-time northeastern New Mexico cowboy, was interviewing his father's friends for the NMFWP in 1937, he spoke with

Albert Easley. Easley prefaced his account of twenty-two-year-old Rufus Rough, "the toughest fellow that I ever saw," with the following sketch of cowboy outlaws:

I guess I've worked with a hundred or more bandits and outlaws. . . . And I found them to be the finest bunch of fellows in the country to work with. They used to come down here to the IOI Ranch and work and rest when the law was getting close to them; then all of a sudden they would pack up and leave and go back to their business again.

But they were a jolly, generous bunch. They'd do anything in the world for you if they liked you. They could take a joke better than lots of men and were always ready to play some prank on someone. Of course you couldn't ask them too many personal questions, and you didn't want to get serious when you were joking them. Some of them were pretty tough characters, too, but we never had a killing on the IOI Ranch.

I remember one man, when one of the boys came in and announced a new settler fifteen miles away, jumped up and said, "I'm leavin'. This country's getting

Hanging of Gus Mentzer, Raton, June 26, 1882. Photo by W. A. White. (MNM Neg. No. 14781.)

too d—n close for me." They had their principles too. Maybe a little less high than a lot of folks, but not broken half as often. They gambled, but not with kids. They drank whiskey, but would not give a kid a drink. Try to find somebody in those businesses now who does that way.[100]

The decorum for dealing with outlaws also appears in the work of another NMFWP field writer, cowboy Jack Thorp. Thorp devotes a chapter of his autobiography, *Pardner of the Wind,* to men and a few women "on the dodge."

Going on the dodge was one of the peculiar institutions of the old West. It corresponded with what is known in certain circles today as "taking it on the lam." There were other rangeland phrases for it, such as hiding out, riding the lone trails, hunting the high places, laying out with the dry cattle—this last referring to cattle that range a long way and come infrequently to water. The country was big, and the spirit was one of live and let live. A man who got into trouble in one place might easily light out and make good somewhere else, if he changed his name and more or less walked in the paths of righteousness henceforth. It was an unwritten rule not to bother a man on the dodge or be too inquisitive about him; but he better behave himself in his new surroundings and not be caught riding horses with the wrong brands or selling the wrong man's beef!

According to his wife, Annette Hesch Thorp, "it was the code of men like Jack, that the less talk there was about the private affairs of others, the better for all."[101] Nevertheless, such stories were common currency in New Mexican lore, and Thorp himself wrote down more than two dozen biographical sketches of New Mexican outlaws he had known or heard about in the cow camps and saloons between Folsom and the Guadalupe Mountains.

Taken together, Thorp's oral histories in his autobiography and NMFWP manuscripts serve as useful guides to the common motifs in New Mexicans' stories, songs, and talk about outlaws. Like many of his New Mexican neighbors, Thorp viewed "men on the dodge . . . as varied in character . . . ; some were brave, others were cowards; some you could trust with your last poker chip, others would steal a stakepin; some were modest, honest, quiet, others could on no account tell the truth or shut their mouths and stop the drip."[102] The truly vicious outlaws were generally portrayed as cowardly, cold-blooded killers. Their more innocent counterparts, though still outlaws, were brave lads gone astray, independent recluses, or victims. Some on the dodge were depicted as tricksters, either rogues or inept bumblers.

While Thorp does not dwell on the issue of culpability, he recognizes that all these men are criminals. Even those who committed what he terms "not very subtle" crimes against property are marked: "'Tis a curious fact, that most all the hold-ups have been crippled in one arm. Sam Ketchum died from a shot in one arm, blood poisoning having set in; Tom Ketchum, 'Black Jack,' was shot in the arm and had to have it amputated; Broncho Bill lost an arm by having it almost shot off, and the outlaw who [knew him] . . . also has a crippled arm caused by a bullet."[103] Those who committed suicide also suffered the consequences of their life of crime.

Throughout his writings on New Mexico outlaws, Thorp emphasizes the role of gangs.[104] He seems to be fascinated by these bands because they pose a greater threat to the developing frontier. In most of his collected accounts, gang members come to harsher ends than the individual outlaw.

According to Thorp, "the Black Jack gang was composed at different times of many men, but the backbone though was the two Ketchums [Sam and Tom], Bill McGinnis, and William Walters, or Broncho Bill. [Also there were] George Musgraves, Bill Carver, Kay Tolliver, two of the Christian brothers, and some others who are now either dead, or living in Old Mexico. Contrary to popular opinion, this Ketchum gang was not tied up with the Jennings, Cooks, and others of Oklahoma, but through Troy Hale, Butch Cassidy, and others, did exchange stolen stock with the Hole-in-the-wall Gang in Wyoming." Tom Ketchum took the name Black Jack from an old outlaw whose real name was Jack Gregg, "who when the law got too hot, disappeared into 'la tierra de silencio,' where so many of the old outlaws have gone." With his brother Sam, Black Jack came to New Mexico from the Texas Panhandle. According to Thorp, the Ketchums' first attempted train holdup, a few miles from Folsom in July 1899, was a complete failure. A month later, Tom Ketchum again held up the Colorado and Southern Railroad outside Folsom. He was wounded while trying to rob the train, taken to Santa Fe, tried, and eventually hanged in Clayton on April 26, 1901.[105]

One of the most famous outlaws in Black Jack's gang was Bronco Bill (alias William Walters). He was born Walter Brown, son of the sheriff after whom Brown County, Texas, was named. With Tom and Sam Ketchum, Bronco Bill held up a train at Steins Pass, netting some ten thousand dollars, and with Red Pitkin and Billy Johnson he robbed an AT&SF train between Shawnee and Grants and killed Sheriff Vigil. Bronco Bill was caught by George Scarboro and sent to the penitentiary on May 23, 1899. He was pardoned on April 17, 1917. An ex-outlaw told Thorp that "Bronco Bill brooded so over what he considered an injustice by his relatives, that he jumped off the windmill [in southern New Mexico], to end it all: this is probably true."[106]

Another member of Black Jack Ketchum's gang, Bill McGinnis, first "appeared in the limelight when, in company with Perry Tucker and Jim Lowe ('Butch Cassidy'), he appeared on the San Francisco River in western Socorro County and went to work for an outfit as broncho buster, one of the best. The average oldtime buster, or staumper, as they frequently termed themselves, were needlessly rough and cruel with the young horses they were breaking, not only cruel with their spurs, but by beating them over the head with a loaded quoit [quirt]. However, Mac, as he was called, gentled his horses without being cruel. He was a handsome young fellow—tall, dark, and well built. With a good education, it was evident he came from good people, and I believe he started in the train and other robberies through a love of excitement and adventure." After a robbery in Colfax County, he and Tom Caphart decided to return to Socorro County and get a job. "They figured it would take them a week, as they would have to cover half the width of New Mexico, dodge ranches, and water at night, and not show themselves more than necessary." However, McGinnis was surprised and subdued by a sheriff's posse searching for horse thieves.

In a few days the newspapers appeared in Alma, telling the details of the capture. It said Mac had put up a desperate fight with his bare hands against tremendous odds, and they only identified him when they saw the shirt which he was wearing was

According to J. Marvin Hunter and Noah H. Rose (*The Album of Gunfighters*, Warren Hunter, Texas, 1951, p. 112): "The above photo of William E. Walters, alias Bronco Bill, was made in prison in 1899. He was one of the notoriously bad men of Arizona, and was shot by Jeff D. Milton and posse in a fight, and for a time it was thought that he was dead, but he revived, and when brought to trial was convicted and served a term in a Federal penitentiary from November, 1899, to April, 1917, when he was pardoned because of failing health. He returned to Arizona, and later worked for the Diamond A Cattle Company near Hachita, New Mexico, and lived a straight life. A few years later he fell from a windmill tower and was killed." (Noah H. Rose Collection, Western History Collections, University of Oklahoma Library.)

covered with blood and the partly healed wounds. He was wearing the same shirt he had been shot in at the time of the train robbery.... Mac had ridden over three hundred miles with four bullet holes in his body, had been unable to change his bloody shirt for over a month, had no bandages or medicine and little to eat, and still fought the posse like a tiger, until by main force they overpowered him. Whether right or wrong, Mac, as the posse had to admit, was a brave and nervy man.[107]

Lute Wilcox, owner of the Las Vegas *Daily Optic* in 1879, gave Thorp an account of what happened when "Dutch Henry's gang of four men rode in from the Panhandle of Texas to 'get' Joe Carson." Dutch (or Tom) Henry, John Dorsey, Jim West, and Bill Randall carried a grudge against Las Vegas Town Marshal Joe Carson from an incident in Fort Worth, Texas. They killed Carson and a man named Costello and wounded many others at George Close's dance hall. Randall was killed in the gunfight, and the remaining three were captured and taken to the Old Town jail.

A few nights later they were taken out by the vigilantes and strung up to the windmill in the middle of the Old Town Plaza. Bonfires were lighted, and most of the population of old and new town were present.

Mr. Charles Ilfeld was there in person, and a few years ago stated that there were four men hung at this time. It seems that all the social events in those days, such as church events, dances, and hangings took place at Old Town. New Town felt very much slighted and quite overlooked.

But regarding this particular hanging, the merchants of the Old Town plaza seemed quite provoked and held a meeting of protest. Their report stated their windmill had cost them six hundred dollars and now, just think of it, they would have to dig up sixty dollars more to remove the infernal thing as a nuisance incompatible with the peace and dignity of the dear old plaza.

This Las Vegas quartet—who had paid the penalty—were still at the end of their respective ropes as the stage rolled in full of passengers. As the stage passed the old windmill on its way to the hotel, one of the passengers, evidently a woman, let out a shriek. The driver plied his whip and the stage dashed up to the curb with a woman struggling with a man and screaming, "Let me go! Take me home! Take me home! I will never live in this God-forsaken country."

These two were Mr. and Mrs. A. M. Conklin from Arkansas, who later settled in Albuquerque. Mr. Conklin afterwards moved to Socorro, where he was killed by Abran and Onofre Baca, but that is another story.[108]

Notorious rustlers like Joe Asque, Santiago Cooper, Celso Morales, Estevan Morales, Faustino Lopez, and Moro Saiz were members of the Farmington Gang. In the spring of 1883, "finding northern sheriffs too alert and the pickings too slim," they moved to the Black Range in Sierra County. With the help of friends and relatives they eluded the mounted New Mexico militia. Joe Asque, who had recently escaped from a sheriff's posse at Lake Valley, was camping at the Indians' water tanks on the Carrizozo Flats when he decided to steal "five head of fat saddle horses." While driving them down the wooded Nogal Canyon road to Roswell he approached a wagon driven by two men and found himself "gazing into a black hole in the end of a Winchester."

"Put them up!" one of the men called, "and don't 'Dally'." Joe did. "Get down," the men told him. Joe, who was armed with only a six-shooter, obeyed. He was disarmed, his hands tied behind him, and placed in the wagon. His own rope was slipped over his head, and the wagon was headed for the nearest tree. With the rope tied to a limb, he was forced to step off the wagon and left hanging with his toes just clear of the ground.

His saddle was put on one of the horses, which belonged to the two men, and wagon and stolen horses started back to the range from which Joe had brought them.

Joe was very small and light, and this fact probably saved his life. The knot in the rope happened to have been under his chin, so, although it was hard to breathe he did not actually choke. After some time he managed to get his hands loose, got out his pocket knife and cut the rope.

Joe said the hanging wasn't so bad, but riding his old horse bareback, for a hundred miles, back to his home range with only a rope around his neck certainly made him mad.[109]

In southwestern New Mexico, the Mesilla Gang was supposed to have numbered about twenty outlaws in Doña Ana County. Thorp focuses on one evening late in May 1882, when three members of the Mesilla Gang robbed a ranchman named Mason. They

covered him with pistols and guns, and ordered him to hold up his hands. He, of course, complied. All the members of Mason's family and the employees about the

Hanging of Black Jack Ketchum, Clayton, April 26, 1901. Photo by John Wheatley Studio. (MNM Neg. No. 128886.)

ranch were then locked up in a room, and the robbers stripped the house, taking everything of value, including the clothing of the men and women. They also carried off all the goods in Mason's store, likewise all bedding and what provisions there were in the house. They packed the plunder on Mason's horses and drove them off, together with what cattle they could gather about the ranch. They were supposed to have headed for Uba Springs about twenty miles northeast of Mason's ranch and about nine miles west of the town of Colorado, Doña Ana County.[110]

Due west, near the Arizona border, the Wild Bunch of the San Francisco River "drifted from the towns of Tombstone, Morenci, and Clifton when the Earps and other peace officers made it too hot for them. [They] rode north and east to the Blue River, following it up until they came to the San Francisco River and in a few miles crossed the line into New Mexico and arrived at the little town of Alma. . . . Many of these men—all former cowhands—went to work for the W.S. S.U. double circles [ranch, the] Lyon and Campbell and other outfits, eventually aiming to get to the Hole-in-the-Wall Gang of Wyoming."[111]

When Thorp turned his attention to individual outlaws, he identified Bad Man Moore, Marino Leyba, Joe Fowler, and Henry ("Bad Man") Coleman as truly vicious and cold-blooded. Born in eastern California, Bad Man Moore at age twenty-five killed his brother-in-law and then a stranger while on the dodge from his previous crime. In Cheyenne, Wyoming, he killed a black cowboy, then turned up in the Texas Panhandle and soon after bought a ranch in No Man's Land between Oklahoma and New Mexico,[112] where he began rustling cattle. He sold his ranch for seventy-five thousand dollars and bought another in the American Valley in northwestern New Mexico.

Here, although he was now well fixed for money, Moore got into another murdering fit and had to go on the dodge again. Adjoining his ranch was one owned by two partners, on which was a fine spring of water. In that thirsty region, such a spring controlled a big stretch of open range, and Moore was bound and determined to buy the partners out in order to get the watering. They refused to sell. At last, in a cold fury, Moore rode over and killed both of them. That did him just no good at all, for he had to hit the high places again. Under the name of Johnny Ward, he drifted south to the little town of Alma, New Mexico, and went to work for the WS outfit, which was owned by Englishmen, but was actively operated by a daring a bunch of train robbers, under the leadership of Butch Cassidy, as ever got together in one crew in the old West. Their operations extended from Alma in New Mexico to the hole-in-the-wall country in Wyoming. Moore stayed here for several months, but he moved on suddenly when detectives (Charlie Siringo was one of them) arrived at Alma.[113]

Marino Leyba was a native New Mexican outlaw who operated in the Sandía Mountains northeast of Albuquerque. Mr. Skinner, who owned a sawmill in the Sandías, was living in Old Town, Albuquerque, in the 1930s when he told Thorp about Leyba's killing of Colonel Charles Potter, a U.S. Geological Surveyor. Colonel Potter stopped into California Joe's saloon in La Madera.

As was the custom of the times, Colonel Potter invited everyone to have a drink, in settlement for which he laid a twenty-dollar gold piece on the bar. In those days, especially among a gathering of small ranchmen, one possessing twenty-dollar gold pieces and also a gold watch and chain and two handsome rings was classed as rich. . . .

Although Colonel Potter did not know it, the outlaw Marino Leyba was one of those in the barroom whom he had invited to have a drink. It seems that after Colonel Potter had retired California Joe called Marino into a back room and said: "Well, Marino! It looks as if we have a fat chicken to pluck, who has probably got lots of money, and it's up to you to do the plucking."

The next day Leyba and his men ambushed Potter and burned the body. They were observed by Vidal Mora, who was herding goats nearby. Mora retrieved Potter's ring from his charred remains and brought it to his patron, Don José Perea. Perea "took from the wall a crucifix and making the boy kneel down, told him to swear he would tell no one, until such time as his patron told him to." Skinner does not say whether Perea ever requested that information during the ensuing investigations by the military and Bernalillo County Sheriff Perfecto Armijo. Armijo and his deputies took some of Leyba's gang to the Albuquerque jail, "but a mob took them out shortly afterwards and decorated the cottonwood trees surrounding the old Plaza with their bodies." Eventually Leyba surrendered himself to Armijo.

As all the witnesses to the late crime but the goat herder had been hanged by the mob in Albuquerque, Merino got off with a light sentence. Upon his release he went to work for Mr. Skinner at the sawmill at San Antonito. Living with his family, he was leading an industrious life.

One day two men, Polito Montoya and Carlos Jacoma, rode into San Antonito from Santa Fe and, meeting Marino, stopped—apparently in a friendly way—to talk. Upon parting, Polito Montoya extended his hand, and while he was holding Marino's hand in his grip, Carlos Jacoma shot Marino through the head. This was supposed to have been done over some division of loot from a robbery they had all been mixed up in at Puerta de Luna some years before, and also to gain an old reward offered for Marino dead or alive.[114]

Accused of over twenty murders, Joe Fowler was a deputy sheriff in Socorro in 1884, allegedly kept in office through political connections. Reputed to be one of the most malicious men in central New Mexico, Fowler shot a crippled man in the leg and stabbed a defenseless drummer (traveling salesman) in a bar.

Finally the better element of Socorro stepped into the saddle and decided Fowler must go. . . . There are many causes in the west for crowds to assemble—a horse race, a fire, a fight, or a frolic "dance," but more people got together this night than probably ever before had assembled in Socorro. A thousand quickly increased to double that number. . . .

After a half hour or so the committee came out, dragging the most contemptible and miserable object imaginable. All Fowler's bravado was gone; he was howling and begging for his life, a craven and a coward, forgetting entirely that twenty-odd others he had murdered. . . .

Fowler was hustled into a wagon. The procession drove, rode and walked to the edge of the town, where a big cottonwood tree overhung the road. This tree, always afterward known as the Fowler tree, still stands.

The rope put on in jail by the mob, which was hung around his neck, was thrown over a cottonwood limb, and the wagon was driven out from underneath him. Several shots—which were supposed to be merciful—were fired into him, but they were unnecessary. By the looks of his face he was already dead from fright, before they swung him loose—a horrible sight, the face of a coward.[115]

Henry ("Bad Man") Coleman first became notorious in and around Deming, where with three companions he rustled cattle back and forth to Mexico. In Silver City he killed two ranchers who accused him of stealing their cattle. While on a trip to Chihuahua, he was caught with a herd of stolen cattle and arrested by the Mexican Federales. "Long John," his six-foot-five-inch friend from Quemado, journeyed to Juárez to free Coleman from prison. They made their escape but later had a falling out. Coleman settled at Canyon Largo Ranch and then killed a neighbor named Burbiny, but he was acquitted on self-defense and moved to Magdalena. There, the district attorney finally pursued him for jumping bond and cattle rustling.

It is a pretty well established fact that Henry Coleman had the Magdalena country officers up a tree—pretty well scared—and they were taking no chances with him. The Sheriff, a Mexican, and his deputy, went on a hunt for Coleman, and on the way picked up three Americans who all had it in for him; these the Sheriff deputized to go along. It seems they had some trouble in locating Coleman, but at last ran across him at what was called the Old Goat Ranch southwest of Salt Lake in

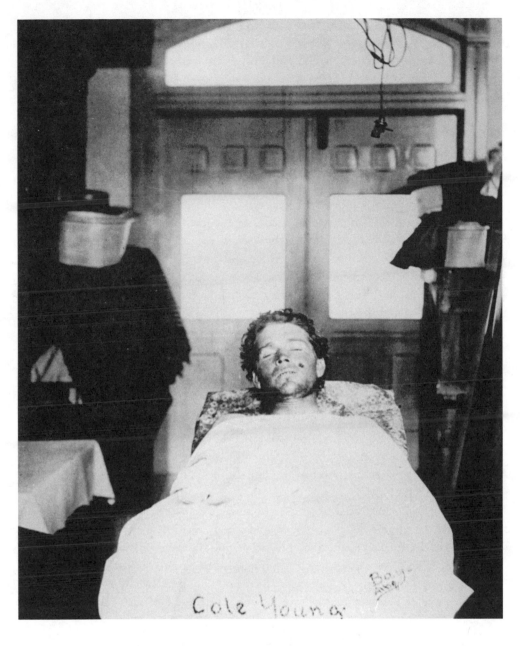

Corpse of Cole Young. (MNM Neg. No. 46194.)

the western part of Old Socorro county. As all were scared of him, as soon as the posse saw Coleman they began shooting. Coleman's horse became frightened and began bucking and fell with him in an old ditch, never giving him a chance to draw his gun. During the shooting a bullet found its way through Coleman's leg, and cut an artery. He lay out all night, and bled to death, none of the posse daring to go near him until the following morning.[116]

For Thorp, some desperados were less fierce. He seems to have had some sympathy for the penitent, the reclusive, or the unjustly accused. For years, Silent Moore "lived as lonesome as a lobo in one of the numerous canyons of the Guadalupes." Moore was thought to be "cracked but he wasn't . . . just law-shy." The reason for his reticence became known when "religion came to the cow country in the warbag of one of the best converters from Texas, who held revival meetings in a stake-and-saw-board synagogue, on the banks of the Pecos River." Silent Moore attended, came forward, and "was dipped, bathed, and had all his sins washed away, and told publicly how, years before, he had killed a man, his wife's lover, he said; and not a day had passed, he declared, that he had not relived the whole scene in his imagination." Thereafter, Silent Moore became Brother Moore, "a preacher of the gospel . . . still on the dodge." [117]

Grant Wheeler and Joe George held up a Southern Pacific train in Wilcox, Arizona, in January 1895. A month later, on February 26, Wheeler and George "came out of their hiding place in the mountains and again held up the same express train at Stein's Pass in New Mexico. They recognized the engineer and fireman with a cheery greeting of 'Well, here we are again.' In the excitement they made a blunder and only cut off the mail car, leaving the express car attached to the train. . . . The men evidently exploded their giant powder, and gave it up as a bad job." They fled to Durango, Colorado; Farmington, New Mexico; and finally to Hidden Springs, "a great resort for cattle thieves," near Cortez, Colorado. Deputy Marshal Breckenridge pursued Wheeler and discovered him "lying with his head almost in a fire he had built to cook his breakfast . . . [where] he had placed his pistol in his mouth and shot himself through the head . . . [having] told a cowboy friend, the day before, that the officers were after him, that he did not want to do any more killing, but would kill himself before surrendering." Wheeler and George had parted earlier, the latter headed for Socorro or the Sacramento Mountains, although "after he crossed the Blue River [he] must have ridden off into space, as he has never again been heard of." [118]

A man known only as Singleton was raised in either West Virginia or Kentucky and came west after avenging the murders of his three older brothers in a clan war. He hid out in a cave at the point of the Guadalupes. Thorp claimed:

> Of all the men on the dodge I knew, Singleton was perhaps the most likeable. I knew he was a thief. In the cave he used for a home, he always had a quarter of beef hung up, yet he didn't own a cow—to have plenty of grub was the main thing for a fellow riding the high places. He had a frying pan, a lard bucket for coffee, and a Dutch oven. I don't know who he "borrowed" these from. But if he was a thief, he was an affable one. In my song hunt he gave me one, "Westward Ho!" that I used in the book. [119]

Will Finn, a horse wrangler for the Block cow outfit in Eddy County, was unfairly accused of killing a man in the Seven Rivers saloon. He escaped to Navajo country and worked for a trader who was later killed.

> Finn then married the trader's widow and lived the rest of his life believing himself responsible for the crime that had caused him to change his name. Even yet, I suppose, comparatively few people know the truth. The fact is that Finn had nothing to do with the shooting. Another man did it—a man about whom there would be considerable eye-lifting if the facts ever came out. But *he* never went on the dodge. The hair grows long on some human critters, just like on cows, and you've got to look sharp to read the brands correctly. [120]

Billy The Kid

Jack Thorp devotes a chapter of his autobiography, *Pardner of the Wind,* to "Billy ('The Kid') Bonney," whom he considers "short weight for a hero" and yet whose enduring legend fascinates him.

> Actually, Billy the Kid was just a little, small-sized cow- and horse-thief who lived grubbily and missed legal hanging by only a few days. He killed, or took part in killing, several people; but his killings were more often on the order of safe butchery than stand-up-and-fight-it-out gun battles. He took part in a range war on the losing side. He died, not in a blaze of glory, but like a butchered yearling, shot down in the dead of night in his stocking feet, when he was armed with a butcher knife and, possibly, though not certainly, with a six-shooter. Yet for all that, romance does cling to his name. Half a dozen books about him have been written and published. The town of Lincoln, New Mexico, thrives on his memory. And many people regard him as a sort of super-Robin Hood of the range, a daredevil of matchless courage, haloed by smoke wreathing upward from fogging guns. He makes a fascinating study in the technique and psychology of literary and national hero creation. Many have told the "facts" about Bill. Few have agreed about them. The heavy shadow of the "hero" tradition has made unconscious liars of some; others have lied about him on purpose, loading the public with tall tales to satisfy the appetites of listeners greedy for shudders and blood.[121]

Thorp did not know Billy personally, but he was well acquainted with Pat Garrett, George Coe, Charlie Siringo, and others who did know the Kid.

When NMFWP fieldworkers during the 1930s interviewed Hispanos who personally knew or knew of Billy the Kid, they discovered a consistent pattern of admiration for "Billito" or "El Chivato," the "Infant Rascal." San Miguel County resident Guadalupe Baca de Gallegos recalled two visits the Kid made to her store in San Ilario. She told her story to Bright Lynn (NMFWP) in 1938:

> One day [she] returned to the store from a visit with one of her neighbors. Her husband was in front of the store, talking to an American cowboy in Spanish. When her husband saw her come in, he called to her and said, "Lupita, I want you to meet a friend of mine. This is Billy the Kid."
>
> Mrs. Gallegos says that she has always been a brave woman, but when she found herself actually face-to-face with Billy the Kid she almost fainted. The Kid seemed to be in a talkative mood, for he started telling Mrs. Gallegos about his adventures and for emphasis he drew his gun and shot a couple of holes in the ceiling. The neighbors all came running to find out what all the shooting was about, but upon finding it was Billy the Kid they all started running the other way.
>
> The next time Mrs. Gallegos saw Billy the Kid she was in the store by herself. He came in, bought some things, and left. Mrs. Gallegos says that he was always very courteous and that he was, in her opinion, a real gentleman.[122]

Seventy-seven-year-old Lorencita Herrera de Miranda told Edith L. Crawford (NMFWP) in 1939 about her memories of the Lincoln County War of 1878:

Unidentified New Deal Public Works of Art painting showing Pete Maxwell's old house at Fort Sumner (upper l.), with a train on a bridge with a banner reading "1907" in the background (upper r.). Recognizable figures include (counterclockwise from l.): two standing men—Pete Maxwell (r.), Lucien B. Maxwell (l.), an unidentified seated man, Deluvina Maxwell, the Kid's horse, Billy the Kid, a recumbent Tom O'Folliard, Charles Bowdre, Mrs. Charles Bowdre, and three standing men, probably Lincoln County sheriffs (l. to r.) Jim Brent, John William Poe, and Pat Garrett. The portraits are of an unidentified woman— possibly Paulita Maxwell or Celsa Gutierrez, both romantically linked with the Kid—and Pat Garrett, or maybe Susan and Alexander A. McSween. (WPA Collection, School of American Research, No. 5365, NMSRC.)

My husband and I were living on our farm just above Lincoln all during the Lincoln County War. We liked both factions so we never took any part in the war. I remember the day [July 19, 1878] the McSween home was burned. We could see the flames and smoke from our house but we stayed at home for we were scared to death to stick our heads out of the house. We could also hear some of the shooting. Billy the Kid came to our house several times and drank coffee with us. We liked him for he was always nice to the Spanish people and they all liked him.[123]

Janet Smith (NMFWP) spoke with José García y Trujillo, a former shepherd living in Albuquerque in 1936. "In broken English mixed with Spanish phrases," Mr. García told her:

"Muy generoso hombre," Billy the Keed—a very generous man. All the Mexican people, they like him. He give money, horses, drinks—what he have. To whom was good to Billy the Keed he was good to them. "Siempre muy caballero, muy señor"— always very polite, very much of a gentleman. Once lots of mens, they go together after Billy the Keed to shoot him. They pay us—we go—sure. But we don't want to shoot Billy. We always be glad he too smart for us."

Smith had shown García y Trujillo a copy of Pat Garrett's 1882 book, *The Authentic Life of Billy, the Kid, Noted Desperado of the Southwest,* and told him that Garrett had killed the Kid. He responded:

"No, *señora,*" and he shook his forefinger back and forth before his face. "You think Billy the Keed let himself be shot in the dark like that? No, *señora*—Billy the Keed?— never. I see Billy the Keed with these eyes. Many times, with these eyes. That Billy, *tenía un agilesa in su mente—in su mente aquí.*" He pointed to his forehead.
    Mr. Garcia could speak but little English, and I knew almost no Spanish, but I understood that he meant that Billy the Kid had an extraordinary quickness of mind.

Again he pointed to his forehead and then with a quick motion to the sky. *"Un función electrica,"* he said. Something that worked like lightning.

Even after Smith showed him a picture of Garrett, García y Trujillo continued to protest: "I don't want to dispute against you, Señora, but in my mind which is the picture of my soul, I know it is not true. Maybe Pat Garrett, he give Billy the Keed money to go to South America and write that story for the looks. Maybe he kill somebody else in Billy's place. Everybody like Billy the Keed—*su vista penetrava al corazón de toda la gente*—his face went to everybody's heart."[124]

In 1981, the centennial of the Kid's death, Lynda Sánchez traveled through southern New Mexico collecting "Recuerdos de Billy the Kid" from more than a dozen *viejos,* or old people. Many of them told her

> of a Catholic missionary's visit to Lincoln in the 1930s. This priest came to Billy's friends with a story about a confession of a very old man living alone in an isolated cabin in the mountains of California. He claimed that he was really Billy the Kid, that he had escaped from New Mexico, and as his last death-bed request, he wanted the priest to let his friends in Lincoln know the truth.

Sánchez supplemented her field texts with items from the NMFWP files.

> Iginio Salazar, who everyone said was as close to Billy as anyone, rarely talked about his relationship to the Kid. Until his own death he stated that the Kid's murder was a hoax. He also claimed to have received a letter from Billy telling him what happened and that he did not die; that it was 'pura mentira' (all lies). In the early 1950s, a patient in the hospital in Socorro also mentioned this letter to another resident from Lincoln. How he knew about it no one knows, but the people were surprised that it was remembered, because Iginio had died years before.[125]

These Hispanic versions of the Kid's legend attest to its enduring imaginative power in New Mexico. In *Inventing Billy the Kid: Visions of the Outlaw in America, 1881–1981,* Stephen Tatum traces how generations of New Mexicans and other Americans have reshaped the image of this outlaw hero to serve their changing psychological and social needs. He claims: "The Kid's 'golden legend,' which, as one of several observers puts it, 'has grown out of all proportion to the few sordid facts of his short, lightning-swift career,' resembles a form associated with more respected heroes such as Theseus and Heracles precisely because of the mysterious circumstances that surround his birth, parentage, and early life." No one really knows where, when, and to whom "the legendary Kid was born."[126]

Accounts of Billy's first crime vary, but, "except for the earliest dime novels' portraits of his first violent crime, the legend in whatever form tends to justify the Kid's first crime as an act of self-defense, vengeance, or honor." Forced into exile, the Kid is seen to possess "the instinctual talents for survival in the West." Tales of his "physical skills, . . . which also often suggested that the Kid led a charmed life and could not be killed by conventional means," were recounted with tales indicating that "the Kid survived in Southwest society because he also was an excellent musician, dancer, and lover."[127] Tatum continues:

Serving as what Kent Steckmesser has called "the American Robin Hood," the legendary Kid, after being forced into an outlaw's existence, was praised for legions of selfless acts. As a bandit samaritan, he delivered a small town held in thrall by one villainous Ruiz who was demanding tribute and preventing the marriage of two young lovers.[128] While one observer considered the Kid rather more of a Southwestern satan whose spiritual descendants were Lee Harvey Oswald and Sirhan Sirhan,[129] legend has it that the Kid gave firewood, money, food, and clothes to the poor—and once endowed an orphanage. Although the Kid might ravish a woman or two in some legendary accounts, he has been more characteristically seen killing Apaches, Mexicans, and Anglos who threatened Apache, Mexican, and Anglo women. If the Kid was correctly labeled the most notorious desperado in Western American history, a man who killed anywhere from four to forty-five men (not counting women and children), he paradoxically was extremely courteous to women and children loyal to his friends. For example, he would not battle a group of U.S. soldiers within shouting distance of the home of a lonely widow and her sleeping children.

Just as the legendary Kid's birth is mysterious, so the "facts" of his death remain hidden. Tatum concludes his account of "the legendary Kid" as follows:

The interesting fact remains that Billy the Kid is not *legally* dead because no original copy of the coroner's jury inquest has been filed in New Mexico. And even if the Kid were shot by Pat Garrett, or even if Garrett and the Kid buried another person or two bags of sand in the Kid's coffin,[130] the Kid's burial site has been located in Fort Stanton, Las Cruces, Old Mesilla, and—of course—Fort Sumner, where the official tombstone rests. As is the case with other cultural heroes, there is additional uncertainty about just whose remains, if any, are in the Fort Sumner site. In the first place, even the location of his grave in the old Fort Sumner military cemetery became problematic when army troopers at the end of the last century took target practice at the plain wooden marker, or when another person removed the marker from the site and took it home as one might the relics of a saint. In later years the Pecos River flooded and exposed the remains of several bodies in the abandoned cemetery, and in the following clean-up uncertainty arose about who was returned to what site. Finally, the government moved the bodies of the soldiers to the Santa Fe national military cemetery, and thus, given the confusion of sites resulting from the periodic Pecos River floods, the Kid might have accidentally made the journey to Santa Fe. The most recent addition to the legend concerning the Kid's gravesite is that when the road out of Santa Fe toward Española was improved a few years ago, it was built over some of the military cemetery—hence, the Kid's grave may be located under U.S. 285 near the Santa Fe Sheraton.

Whatever the fate of the Kid's grave and corpse, his death inaugurated the appearance of legends and rumors about his mortal and ghostly remains. Immediately after his death in July 1881, rumors about the fate of his remains (and any of its components) began circulating. A California woman claiming to be the Kid's sweetheart wrote the Las Vegas *Daily Optic* and requested that the Kid's trigger finger be sent to her; another legend circulated that the Kid's entire corpse was exhumed and "dressed" in Las Vegas and would hang there until the meat fell off.[131]

Such rumors and requests amused the *Daily Optic* so much that within two weeks of the Kid's demise the newspaper ran a column which informed the public that the tremendous rush to see the Kid's trigger finger would cause the paper to "purchase a small tent and open a side show to which complimentary tickets will be issued to our personal friends."[132] That same trigger finger was the subject of an early ballad in which the narrator attends a Chicago side show and, after paying his dime to enter the tent, sees a finger preserved in alcohol. Of course, our narrator quickly slapped leather and blew "that *thing* clar into hell."[133] Besides the persistent desire to have possession of the Kid's trigger finger or his six-shooter, even now you can walk into a certain Grants, N.M., hardware store and be told that the skull hanging over the counter is that of the Kid's horse. Other additions to the legend extend the Kid's life after death by detailing the presence of his ghost in the mountains, plains, and villages of the West. A visitor to the old courthouse from which Billy made his daring escape a little over two weeks before he was to be hanged relates that at night he could hear ghosts playing billiards; Edwin Corle reports an old man's belief that the Kid's ghost haunted the Panamint Valley country in California; and Jack Thorp recalls that native New Mexican women would scare their children into good behavior by telling them that "Bilito's ghost" would haunt them.[134] Perhaps it was because the Kid was betrayed, according to legend, by Pat Garrett and Pete Maxwell's daughter that the kid's ghost rides the range without rest, and that a lovely Spanish señorita haunts the Kid's grave.[135]

Lawmen and Mystery Murders

In 1902, Pat Garrett accompanied Western writer Emerson Hough to Billy the Kid's gravesite in Fort Sumner. Hough describes the scene as follows:

> There are no headstones in this cemetery, and no sacristan holds its records. Again Garrett had to search in the salt grass and greasewood. "Here is the place," said he, at length. "We buried them all in a row. The first grave is the Kid's, and next to him is Bowdre, and then O'Folliard."
>
> . . . In this desolate resting-place, in a wind-swept and forgotten graveyard . . . even the headboard which once stood at the Kid's grave—and which was once riddled with bullets by cowards who would not have dared to shoot that close to him had he been alive—was gone. It is not likely that the graves will be visited again by any one who knows their locality. Garrett looked at them in silence for a time, then, turning, went to the buckboard for a drink at the canteen. "Well," said he, quietly, "here's to the boys, anyway. If there is any other life, I hope they'll make better use of it than they did of the one I put them out of."[136]

By contrast, Leon C. Metz points out:

> Pat [Garrett] was laid to rest on March 5, 1908, in the shabby, overgrown northwest corner of the Las Cruces Odd Fellows Cemetery. In 1957 he and those family members who lay beside him were transferred to the Masonic Cemetery across the road. On a large granite stone is inscribed the single word: GARRETT. One can search

across all of New Mexico, and indeed the entire Southwest today, and find no other monument to his memory.[137]

The best-known traditional ballad about the Kid expresses the common motif of Sheriff Pat Garrett's betrayal of his friend. In the late 1940s and early 1950s J. D. Robb recorded this song from noted cowboy singer Ray Reed of Roswell:

1.
I'll sing you a true song
Of Billy the Kid
I'll sing of the desperate
Deeds that he did.
Way out in New Mexico
Long, long ago
When a man's only chance
Was his old fo'ty fo'.

2.
When Billy the Kid
Was a very young lad
In the Old Silver City
He went to the bad.
Way out in the West,
With a gun in his hand,
At the age of twelve years
He first killed his first man.

3.
Fair Mexican maidens
Play guitars and sing,
A song about Billy
Their boy bandit king.
Howe'er his young manhood
Had reached its sad end,
He'd a notch on his pistol
For twenty-one men.

4.
It was in Sanchez canyon
With his English friend,
A fellow named Tunstall
Who there met his end.
That Billy swore vengeance
Well down to a man,
And swore that he'd get them
All in the end.

5.
It was on the same night
That poor Billy died,
He said to his friends
"I am not satisfied,
There are twenty-one men
I have put bullets through,
And Sheriff Pat Garrett
Must make twenty-two."

6.
Now this is how Billy
Met his sad fate:
The bright moon was shining
The hour was late;
Shot down by Pat Garrett
Who once was his friend
The young outlaw's life
Had now come to its end.

7.
There's many a man
With a face fine and fair
Who starts out in life
With a chance to be square,
But just like poor Billy
He wanders astray
And loses his life
In the very same way.[138]

Andrew Jenkins and Irene Spain wrote this ballad after reading Walter Noble Burns's fictionalized 1926 *Saga of Billy the Kid*. According to Leon Metz, Burns's book became an overnight best-seller.

> Walter Noble Burns, author of the exasperatingly popular *Saga of Billy the Kid,* is credited, with considerable accuracy, with being the principal force behind the legend surrounding the life—and more particularly the death—of the incorrigible young man whose violent end brought Pat Garrett momentary fame, long-lasting rue, and a dubious distinction that can almost be compared to that of the "dirty little coward" who shot Mr. Howard and laid Jesse James in his grave. Perhaps more than any single person, other than the Kid himself, Burns, in his romanticized *Saga,* flagrant with error, distortion, and misinterpretation, became Garrett's nemesis. This vastly popular book served to haunt and cast dishonor upon the lawman long after his mutilated corpse was laid to rest in the Las Cruces cemetery.[139]

Garrett contributed to his own notoriety in his 1882 book, written with Ash Upton, *The Authentic Life of Billy, the Kid, Noted Desperado of the Southwest*. Jack Thorp thought that the book and legend troubled the sheriff. As Thorp explains in his autobiography:

> I first met Garrett at a wagon camp at the point of the White Sands, in New Mexico, when he came over to arrest a fellow. That was in 1889 or '90. . . . Garrett was a tall, slim, rawboned officer, with a black mustache and a very pleasant manner. I met him often afterwards at Santa Fe, Tularosa, Las Cruces, and elsewhere, and got to know him well. He was a rough-and-ready customer, a great lover of poker, with a good enough record in a hard line of work. He was made sheriff of Lincoln County on the theory that he would clean up Billy the Kid and other outlaws and cattle thieves; and he did that. But I have the impression that the rest of his life was haunted by ghosts from the Lincoln County War. In fact, it may have been one of these "ghosts" in the flesh that finally ended him, for he too died of a gunshot wound, under circumstances never fully explained. I think secret doubts about his own actions troubled him, and I believe he was driven to make Billy the Kid a more-than-life-size villain in order that Pat Garrett might be able to look Pat Garrett and the world straight in the eye. It's a curious and not impossible thought that he may have made the Kid a "hero," in order that he, the "hero" killer, might sleep easy at night![140]

Ironically, Garrett's alleged killer, Wayne Brazel, "himself became something of a tragic figure and, in the final analysis, a mystery also." Brazel had been acquitted of Garrett's murder on a plea of self-defense and acquired the Harrington Well homestead west of Lordsburg. He disappeared in May 1914, after litigation about the sale of this property. According to Leon C. Metz:

> Neither his son nor his many friends and relatives know exactly what happened to him. He reportedly died or was killed in one of a dozen places throughout the West.
>
> In 1935, H. L. McCune, an El Paso attorney, was hired by Brazel's son to trace his disappearance and determine the facts. McCune did a lot of checking and in his report concluded that "the probable explanation of your father's disappearance is that he went to South America to try to make a fortune in that country and was there killed by what is known as the Butch Cassidy gang."[141]

Pat Garrett's murder was an all-too-familiar instance of "high-class killings" in Territorial New Mexico. Many of these prominent victims were political figures. On December 15, 1867, for example, Chief Justice John P. Slough became such a victim when "Captain" W. L. Rynerson, a member of the Territorial Legislature representing Doña Ana County, shot him in the lobby of Santa Fe's La Fonda Americana.[142] On May 29, 1892, Santa Fe County political leader Francisco Chávez was ambushed and shot while crossing the Guadalupe bridge in Santa Fe.[143] According to Howard Lamar: "By 1893 criminal conditions in the territory were so bad that when Grover Cleveland returned to the White House he appointed William T. Thornton as Governor. A good lawyer, reputed to be honest and fearless, Thornton's job was more that of a district attorney than chief executive, for his sole task seemed to be to root out the gangs and political terrorists in the territory."[144]

Patrick Floyd Jarvis Garrett (1850–1908). (MNM Neg. No. 46217.)

Some politically motivated killings, notably those of Colonel Albert Jennings Fountain and Colonel José Francisco Chaves, remain unsolved.[145] The Republican attorney and one-time crusading newspaper editor A. J. Fountain actively opposed what he considered the lawless elements in Doña Ana County. His efforts were widely reported in the territorial press and, when he mysteriously disappeared in February 1896, *The Santa Fe New Mexican* ran daily bulletins. On February 4, the editors reported that they had received a telegram from Las Cruces.

Up to this writing, 11 A.M., only meager details are obtainable. It appears that on Friday last Col. Fountain started alone from Tularosa to drive a double team to his home at Las Cruces, a distance of some sixty-five miles. Some parties passed him on the road after he left Tularosa on Friday. On Saturday [February 2] his wagon

Albert Jennings Fountain
(1838–1896) as a major, ca. 1883.
(MNM Neg. No. 9873.)

was found in the mountains about five miles off the road, but no trace of Col. Fountain could be discovered. His team was also missing and a search instituted by friends was without result. Then a messenger was sent to Las Cruces to give the alarm and yesterday a large posse was organized to go out and scour the country. Fears are expressed that Col. Fountain has been murdered and his body buried in the soft sand of one of the numerous arroyos which abound in that locality.

The following day's paper reported that Colonel Fountain had been accompanied by his seven-year-old son Henry and that the mail carrier had encountered them about forty miles from Las Cruces. Fountain expressed concern about three mysterious horsemen following him and his son. The mail carrier, who also saw the horsemen, alerted Las Cruces residents, who formed the first search posse on Sunday, February 3. For ten days posses searched for clues without success. On February 17, *The Santa Fe New Mexican* reported that:

> Gen. E. L. Bartlett returned from a visit of a week or so at Las Cruces yesterday morning. In a conversation with a NEW MEXICAN scribe this forenoon he fully confirmed the reports that the searchers have found the spot where Col. Fountain and his son Henry were undoubtedly murdered.
>
> A pool of blood, part of what is supposed to be Col. Fountain's brains, a button from his coat, a napkin in which sandwiches were wrapped, a blood-stained sleeve from the little boy's shirt, and 15 cents in change scattered on the ground mark the place where the awful tragedy occurred. The bodies were believed to be buried near by in the white sands, but it is feared that the winds have obliterated all signs.[146]

Although three ranchers were eventually tried for the murder of Colonel Fountain's son, they were successfully defended by Albert Bacon Fall, Fountain's political rival. According to Erna Fergusson: "The trial reflected the old political and personal rivalry of Fountain and Fall. In a brilliant defense, the three accused ranchers were cleared, but popular opinion does not yet consider the case closed. Its mention is still good for a verbal row between adherents of the two old enemies."[147]

Colonel José Francisco Chaves, a New Mexican born at Los Padillas south of Albuquerque in 1833, had been a noted soldier, lawyer, and legislator. At the time of his murder in 1904, he served as superintendent of public instruction and as territorial historian. In late November 1904, Chaves was visiting his ranch holdings in the Estancia Valley of what is now Torrance County. He was dining with friends at Pinos Wells, when, as Marc Simmons tells it: "He was seated at the end of a table in a well-lighted room and was in the act of passing a platter of potatoes. Spang! A shot rang out shattering the window glass and the Colonel slumped forward. Still holding the platter in a steely grip, he died." Despite a $2,500 reward for the killers offered by the territorial legislature, no guilty party was identified, although many speculations were advanced. According to Simmons:

> This writer talked, a few years ago, with an oldtimer living near Chaves' birthplace at Los Padillas. He declared that one of his neighbors, who had died about 1950, once confessed to him that he had been the man who shot José Francisco Chaves. For the terrible act, he had been paid by certain unscrupulous politicians. After

firing the bullet, he had ridden like a demon for the Rio Grande. Fearing that a posse with dogs might come after him, the murderer sprinkled red chile powder on his trail.

This story is as likely to be true—or untrue—as the other explanations that have circulated from time to time. For the fact remains that, after a lapse of almost 75 years, no person can say with certainty who killed the unflinching José Francisco Chaves.[148]

Territorial-period killings that were not "high-class" were almost routine. Kenneth Fordyce (NMFWP) describes the situation in the Raton area as follows:

The railroad boomer, the drifting miner, and the gun-man of the cattle range were three rough types to be found mixing and mingling with the gentle people in Northern New Mexico during the first pioneer days of the 1880's. Society's restraint on the hair-trigger passions of the lawless element was unusually impotent when old Judge Lynch's court held a session, or the bad men came in contact with too much whiskey. . . . There were many killings between gun-men that worked to a double advantage, the slower on the draw passed out, and the other passed on. One heavy investor in property on first Street and the owner of a prosperous saloon killed his man and fled, never to be heard of again. Fairmont Cemetery contains the unmarked graves of many bad-men today, for whom these green pastures for an easy living had turned a sickly red. Through these tragedies of the '80's and the '90's the respectable element of those throbbing days lived blissfully on, accustomed to the occasional sight of a murdered or an injured man, yet contributing as best they could to the support of law and order.[149]

Bonito City, between Carrizozo and Ruidoso, was not so lucky. Residents of that mining town were awakened one night in 1885 to screams and gunshots. Young Martin Nelson, a permanent guest at the local hotel operated by Mr. and Mrs. John Mayberry, murdered the Mayberry family, another hotel guest, and the local saloon keeper, seven victims in all, before he himself was killed the following morning. According to Marc Simmons:

Bonito City never recovered. From then on it was a haunted place. The hotel was closed and no one dared set foot inside. Passersby reported hearing moans and muffled shots issuing from the dark interior. Children on their way to school made a wide circle to avoid it.

A newspaper reporter, according to one tale, came to investigate the story and entered the hotel to make a tour. Onlookers saw him emerge moments later on a dead run, his face pale and frightened as if he had met the Devil.

When the Southern Pacific Railroad built a dam across the creek below Bonito City, the town was submerged and the bodies from the cemetery moved to Angus. However, "to this day no one has ever been able to explain why young Martin Nelson went on his pointless shooting spree."[150]

Clay W. Vaden (NMFWP) reported on lawlessness at Magdalena during the territorial period.

In early days, and even as late as 1916, Magdalena was one of the toughest towns in the West. The branch line of the Santa Fe R.R. that ran up from Socorro carried more cattle away from Magdalena than any other town in the United States. For a hundred miles north, south, southwest, west and northwest, ranchers drove cattle in large herds to Magdalena for shipment. Cowboys, wild as the fierce wind off the ranges, stalked its streets with whiskey under their belts and looking for excitement. . . . Two other elements added to the general excitement and continuous bloodshed and warfare: the sheepmen, who were continually at odds with the cowmen, and who were sided by nearly all the Spanish-American element, and the considerable population of miners who worked at various mines in the Magdalena Mountains and at Kelly, a mining town that once boasted a population of nearly five thousand. The miners, especially on payday, loved a fight for their own propensity to indulge in battle. The fact that a large percentage of these were Irish undoubtedly softened a few skulls by shellalahs [shillelaghs].

It has been said that were all the men killed in Magdalena laid end to end, one could walk on dead men from the upper end of the business district comprising two blocks to the depot, nearly 250 yards away. The local saddlemaker, Thomas Butterfield, recounts: "When I first came to Magdalena, it was such a wild town that I was afraid to go home nights and made my bed in the saddleshop. There was always shooting and yelling after sundown, and nearly every night there was a pitched gun battle or a fight with knives, clubs or fists. Bullets sang around my saddle shop and were always smashing windows. It got to where I just left the windows broken. It didn't do any good to replace them.

"I will never forget the time when I was walking down the street with a fellow toward the saddleshop and I was talking with him about selling him a saddle. The next thing I knew, somebody shot this fellow and he dropped right in the middle of the conversation and before I could collect a down payment on the saddle. I turned around and ran so fast that provided anybody had had an airplane to keep up, they could have played cards on my coat tail."[151]

Spanish-Anglo violence was blatant when famous New Mexico lawman Elfego Baca appointed himself guardian of Socorro County in 1883. In October 1884, reports from Frisco (San Francisco Plaza, now Reserve) described atrocities against local Hispanos by Tejano cowboys. Baca, then working in Socorro, drove to Frisco and arrested a drunken cowboy named McCarty who was terrorizing the town. Cowhands working for the Slaughter outfit demanded McCarty's release, and Baca shot one of their number before retreating to a nearby *jacal*. For the next thirty-six hours Baca held off some eighty Texans who had swarmed into Frisco to quell what they supposed was a Mexican rebellion.

Elfego Baca's account of the standoff is in his eight-page campaign tract of 1944, when he was candidate for New Mexico district attorney. The frontispiece shows Baca posed with a tall statue of *Nuestra Señora Santa Ana*. Baca writes:

In the fall of 1884, Elfego Baca, then but 18, fought a lonehanded, 33 hour gun battle vs. 80 Texas Cowboys. Barricaded in an old jacal (picket hut), Elfego killed 4 and wounded 8. Santana was inside. Everything inside was shot; half the jacal was

Elfego Baca (1866–1945).
(MNM Neg. No. 128796.)

blown up; but Elfego and Santa Ana were not even touched. Elfego prepared coffee, beef stew, and made tortillas unconcerned by the continuous rat-tat-tat of bullets all around him. Court testimony after the fracas showed Texans fired over 4,000 shots; Exhibits in Court: Door, 3600 bullet holes; broomhandle, 7; spadehandle, 11.

The bullets passed over Baca, who was entrenched below the floorline. Baca was arrested and jailed in Socorro for his part in the shootout. He was tried and acquitted in Albuquerque and afterward resolved, according to his campaign tract: "From then on I made up my mind, I wanted the outlaws to hear my steps a block away from me. I always had been for law and order, and I will be till I die. Since that time, I wanted to be an 'A No.-1 peace officer, likewise a criminal lawyer."[152]

In *Heroes Without Glory; Some Goodmen of the Old West*, Jack Schaefer traces Baca's career after the Frisco episode:

With energy enough for three men and a zest for living enough for half a dozen, he was usually involved in a variety of different enterprises at one and the same time. But he moved rather steadily toward his ambition. During the next years, among many other activities, he was a deputy sheriff with a badge not of the mail-order type, then a deputy United States marshal. On occasion more shots were fired at him and he replied with his now customary efficiency. He acquired a collection of knife-cut scars and once an icepick almost did what no bullet ever did. He recovered and went on with his work. Tales of his exploits were becoming standard conversational fare through much of New Mexico. He was the man, for example, who arrested the outlaw José Chávez y Chávez who had long defied the officials of San Miguel County then made the mistake of invading Elfego's territory. He was the man who, when others had failed, went after the notorious José García. As his own latest exploit, García had killed a man in Belen and carried off the man's wife and then, tiring of her, had cut her into quarters and hung these from a tree limb like butcher's meat. Feeling ran high about him. Elfego stuck to his trail and at last plucked him from out of his stronghold in the hills, took him to the nearest town, and serenely held off a lynch mob until the next train came along and he could transport his prisoner to jail. He was coming close to being an A No. 1 peace officer.[153]

From his legendary boyhood association with Billy the Kid through his friendship and later enmity with Pancho Villa, to his civic roles as county clerk, mayor, and school superintendent, Elfego Baca personified the change in New Mexico from frontier territory to established state. He moved to Albuquerque in 1910 and died there in 1945. According to Marc Simmons: "No description of Albuquerque in the first quarter of the twentieth century would be complete without some reference to the mercurial and picturesque Elfego Baca, one of the flock of eccentric persons who lent color to the political scene. . . . Dressed in a flowing cape and trailed by a bodyguard, he stalked the downtown streets handing out business cards that read on one side, 'Elfego Baca, Attorney-at-Law, Fees Moderate,' and on the reverse, 'Private Detective; Divorce Investigations Our Specialty, Discreet Shadowing Done.'"[154]

Conclusion

Legends about people of power like those collected above are New Mexican only in their specific details. Their telling—whether in conversation, story, or song—is an important social process through which any group's members articulate significant social concerns. In focusing on extraordinary, anomalous, marginal, and deviant figures set apart by choice or circumstance, tellers and singers try to illuminate ordinary participants' social roles and interaction. Culture heroes and heroines transcend ordinary human limitations. Healers and witches can show the bounds of commonplace knowledge; hermits, wanderers, beggars, outlaws, and eccentrics, the limits of conventional society.

The social definition of illness labels the sick as "deviants," individuals legitimately unable to perform their social roles in the family or community. Those who know enough to bring the ill back to health, i.e., back to social life, must possess deep knowledge about natural, social, and spiritual matters. They learn to heal by experience, imitation, initiation, and careful attention to the inner workings of their community and its network of gossip and lore. However, the greater knowledge of healers can be perverted into the harmful powers of witches who use occult means to devastate and destroy individuals and groups.

Lawmen, outlaws, and mysterious murderers are in some respects the secular equivalent of those who fight and practice witchcraft. Those who tell their stories symbolically test the limits of community strength in the face of powerful threats. Likewise, accounts of hermits, eccentrics, and beggars suggest the limits of social tolerance and welfare. Narratives of deviance and deformity thus make clearer the changing conformity and order necessary in human affairs.

For the most part, healers and witches are insiders, and women figure prominently among them. Both women and men may be beggars or local eccentrics. Men, however, are more likely to become known in "stranger" roles as hermits, wanderers, or outlaws. Such aliens are outsiders—"on the dodge" or on the periphery, even if temporarily employed or "in town" for charity, supplies, or plunder.

Whether insider or outsider, divine or human, people of power excite strong, ambivalent feelings of fear and fascination. Like the herders, hunters, raiders, traders, and miners discussed in chapter 5, those who delve deeply within or go far beyond boundaries petrify and exhilarate those ensconced, who make the former the subject of considerable covert anecdote, speculation, and gossip, often naming them only indirectly or posthumously in story, song, and public testimony. This narrating is a process of symbolic inversion, defined by Barbara A. Babcock "as any act of expressive behavior which inverts, contradicts, abrogates, or in some fashion presents an alternative to commonly held cultural codes, values, and norms be they linguistic, literary or artistic, religious, or social and political." According to Babcock, symbolic inversion is important because

> group membership is determined not only by what members share, but by what the members recognize that "significant others" do *not* share. Thus develop the notions of stereotyping and deviance: the definition of those outsiders "on the periphery" in terms of how they depart from insiders in the direction of nature or chaos (i.e., violation of the social order). This does not mean that the deviant is simply "a bit of debris spun out by faulty social machinery" [according to Kai T. Erikson]. Rather, as Durkheim again pointed out regarding crime in *The Division of Labor in Society,* deviant forms of behavior are a natural and necessary form of social life without which social organization would be impossible.[155]

Thus, when they tell of culture heroes and heroines, healers and witches, wanderers and eccentrics, beggars and outlaws, New Mexicans participate in a significant performance process, creating images of themselves and their changing society.

7 A SENSE OF TIME

TEXTS OF COMMUNITY AND CELEBRATION

*The Southwest has so many feast days that its notable dates are days when
nothing in particular is going on. In planning the Coronado Cuarto Centennial
[for 1940], it was necessary only to make a few adjustments in the regular
sequence of gala events; to encourage every town to go on as it had been doing;
to publish a calendar of festivities, and to declare the state "in fiesta." . . .*

*Two dicta mark as celebration as they mark fun-making in the Southwest
generally. "You can't start until you're ready, can you" and "Why quit, if we're
still having fun?"*

—Erna Fergusson, *Our Southwest*, 1940, pp. 340–41.

In 1893, Charles F. Lummis dubbed New Mexico *The Land of Poco Tiempo,* arguing
that, it "is the anomaly of the Republic. It is a century older in European civilization than the rest, and several centuries older still in a happier semi-civilization of its
own." Lummis further observed that this "picturesque" land was inhabited by people
who held a different sense of time:

> Here is the land of *poco tiempo*—the home of "Pretty Soon." Why hurry with the
> hurrying world? The "Pretty Soon" of New Spain is better than the "Now! Now!"
> of the haggard States. The opiate sun soothes to rest, the adobe is made to lean
> against, the hush of day-long noon would not be broken. Let us not hasten—
> *mañana* will do. Better still, *pasado mañana.*[1]

While Lummis's remarks today appear stereotypical, they suggest important
perspectives on New Mexicans' temporal experience. Part of this experience lies in

differing notions of passing time while talking and visiting, preparing and sharing food, and contesting. A large part involves the demarcation of time in individual rites of passage and communal celebrations like ritual dances, village fiestas, and folk dramas. In more recent years, these traditional celebrations have been elaborated into self-consciously historical and commercial festivals like Old Timers Days, Santa Fe Fiesta, the Gallup Inter-Tribal Indian Ceremonial, and the Coronado Cuarto Centennial.

All these ludic and expressive occasions punctuate routine life. In an essay about the symbolic representation of time, "Time and False Noses," Edmund R. Leach argues that an important function of such gatherings is to order time because "without the festivals . . . all order would go out of social life. We talk of measuring time, as if time were a concrete thing waiting to be measured; but in fact we *create time* by creating intervals in social life. Until we have done this there is no time to be measured." Festival occasions are effective measures of time because, as Beverly J. Stoeltje points out: "Noise, smells, food, costume, rhythm, and action bombard the senses, using every semiotic code. These are expressed in local genres of music and dance, drama, feasts, verbal art, and display forms, and presented in multiple scenes, both scheduled and spontaneous, many of which occur simultaneously."[2] The contrasts between routine or daily life and visits, feasts, contests, and celebrations thus create occasional or periodic changes in people's sense of time as ordinary or special, imperceptible or heightened by communal activity.

On all the informal and formal occasions described in this chapter, New Mexicans consciously or unconsciously generate what Victor Turner calls celebratory symbols, which "usually stand for many things and thoughts at once." He notes that

> when a social group, whether it be a family, clan, village, nation, congregation, or church, celebrates a particular event or occasion, such as birth, harvest, or national independence, it also "celebrates itself." In other words, it attempts to manifest, in symbolic form, what it conceives to be its essential life, at once the distillation and typification of its corporate experience. The word *celebration* is derived from the Latin *celeber,* "numerous, much frequented," and relates to the vivacity—akin to what the great French sociologist Durkheim called "effervesence"—generated by a crowd of people with shared purposes and common values.

Any celebratory performance "rejoices in the key values and virtues of the society that produces it, and in a history whose high points of success and conquest (or even noble failure) exemplify qualities of moral and aesthetic excellence."[3]

Passing Time: Occasional Encounters and Gatherings

May Price Mosley, New Mexico Federal Writers' Project (NMFWP), evokes the sense of time on eastern New Mexico ranches:

> The monotony of the prairies and the sameness of the days were either beyond endurance or tranquilly serene, according to the temperament of the person. If one were of a lonely or pessimistic nature—or dependent on others for entertainment, he usually did not stay. But if he were of a contented, naturally happy disposition,

there was certainly little to disturb such content or interrupt his happiness. Occasionally one lost the day of the week; some rode miles to be set right again, while others made no pretense at knowing the day or date—nor cared. One ranch housewife was shocked and shaken when she learned that she had unwittingly made over a mattress on the Sabbath.

Ranch women especially suffered their solitude, which could be alleviated and "quickened" by occasional companionship.

> The aloneness of her situation is hard to imagine. There were weeks at a time— often months—when she saw no other woman, in fact, almost forgot there were other women. Many such women will tell you that the most boresome factor in such existence was having to hear nothing but cow-and-horse, boots-and-saddle, riding-and-roping conversations of the men about the ranch—who seemingly knew no other topic. Ranch wives sometimes made a house guest welcome for months just for feminine companionship.

Male ranchers were able to respond more actively to monotony and isolation. "When the smaller rancher was pretty well up with his work or felt the need of a holiday (seldom though this might be) he just turned out the milk-pen calves—if there was no one to leave at the ranch—and took the two or three days off necessary for him and his family to properly visit some neighbor—possibly without any especial invitation other than the general understanding that since visitors were so scarce and came so far, they were always welcome."[4]

Visits are occasions for talk and often for sharing food. Talk during encounters and gatherings may take the artistic form of what Georg Simmel defines as sociable conversation. According to Sally Yerkovich, who applies Simmel's concept to conversational genres of folklore:

> Sociability is the pure form of conversation: one in which the flow of the exchange—the conversing—is an end in itself. The speaker changes frequently and in spite of the momentary dominance of each participant, no one person controls the overall interchange. Everyone participates as if they were equals in order to maintain the sociability of the situation. At this level, our way of conversing becomes a kind of performance, one in which each individual accepts the responsibility not for his own aesthetic presentation but for maintaining the ambiance of artful conversational interplay. . . .
>
> . . . There is no such thing as useless prattle. When we tuck up our sleeves and loosen our talktapes, we participate in a process of association, the need for which is at the core of our humanness.[5]

This process of association carries cosmic significance for the Navajo, as Gary Witherspoon explains:

> Without language man is impotent, ignorant, isolated, and static. He is, in fact, an inactive part of a cosmos in which he cannot find any meaning for his being. With language man is an active, creative, and powerful part of his universe. Through

Trader's store, Jemez, ca. 1919.
(MNM Neg. No. 36224.)

language, the meaning that he finds in his being and that he creates and expresses through his being is fused with omniscience, omnipotence, and omnipresence of air, the source of all life, beauty, and harmony.[6]

Sharing food, like sharing talk, is also a profoundly important form of human communication. Soviet folklorist Sergeij Aleksandrovic Tokarev claims that "the sharing of meals . . . has been and remains one of the most important forms of domestic interaction among people." According to him, "the very act of sharing food or drink is often not only an expression of friendship or kinship among people, but in many instances itself creates such attitudes." Thus, "all sorts of customs connected with food and with the methods of its preparation and consumption . . . [are] engendered not by the material properties of food substances, but by their symbolic meaning as forms of human integration or estrangement."[7]

The human values of sharing food and talk are seen in Henry Glassie's folklife account of the Ulster community of Ballymenone. There,

> Quiet work—weeding the spuds in the garden, drawing tea at the hearth—produces food, then food is given as a sign of goodness. The gift of food is called "entertainment."
>
> Entertainment is also a name for speech—not all speech, but that which does the work of food: gathering personal energy into a gift to others which pleases them in the moment, then carries them on to further life.

Central to this Irish district is the notion of "passing the time," and "passing the time is what the people who live there say they are doing when they work by day—

(Above). Store in Las Trampas, January 1943. FSA photo by John Collier. (LC–USW 3-15246-C.)

(Left). "Group of farmers, homesteaders, and their families visiting all day Sunday to celebrate a birthday." FSA photo by Russell Lee, Pie Town, June 1940. (LC–USF 33-12736-M3.)

following the cows up the grassy damp slopes, sweeping their kitchens clean—and it is what they say they are doing when they fill the night's length with stories that hold the mind away from danger." Entertainment sometimes "accelerates into 'sport, [and] conversation rises to song. Tea gives way to stout." In turn, "sport can break frail limits into 'fight.'"[8]

"Passing the time" is unique to Ballymenone only in the particulars of its expression. Talking, visiting, preparing and sharing food, and contesting are the stuff of social life, and the New Mexican examples assembled in the portfolios that follow are fundamental to the state's lore. Passing time in occasional encounters and gatherings is not mere pastime, but the active creation of meaningful time in human communities.

Talking and Visiting

At the Navajo Trader's . . .

The Navajo does not hurry his shopping. The store is the focal point of the community; it is a place to chat with friends, catch up on the news. . . . Even in these times of pick-up trucks or automobiles, a trip to the store is seldom short. A half-day seems to be the least time one spends in chatting, bargaining, and buying, no matter how small the purchase.

—James F. Downs on 1960s Navajo communities.[9]

News Comes to Roswell . . .

All mail—letter, post card, newspaper or magazine—was greatly appreciated, and the news was discussed with as much relish as if it had been fresh off the wire.

On mail days it was the favorite afternoon sport to climb to the tops of the houses on Main Street—there were none elsewhere—and, through field glasses, watch the buckboard come over six-mile hill. If there chanced to be a passenger with the driver, speculation was rife as to who it might be. A stranger, always welcome, was a rarity.

—Lucius Dills on nineteenth-century Roswell.[10]

Entertaining on the Llano . . .

People were so few on the Staked Plains, and the early rancher so eager for conversation and news of the outside world that anyone passing his way was made welcome. Even the stranger was asked to come in, stay awhile, eat dinner, spend the night—or several days if he chose. No one was ever too busy to extend the common courtesy of entertaining those passersby who stopped for their own convenience as considerately as if they had been specially invited guests. Where one man met another on the prairie there was visiting—for probably an hour or two. To have passed on by with only a greeting would have been something demanding investigation or an apology.

. . . When "woman company" came the way of the lonely ranch wife, though they might be strangers, she dropped all work save that of entertaining and extending courteous consideration to her uninvited guest. Larders were raided, beds were made down; and men marvelled at their conversation and enjoyment.

—May Price Mosley on Lea County, 1930s.[11]

Socials in Union County . . .

Minnie [Crisp, of Thomas, Union County] liked to remember the good times and the good neighbors. "Everybody was your friend, your neighbor. Everybody was an equal. Everybody enjoyed life. I said I'd like to live those old days over, 'course some of them was pretty hard, but there's one thing, you had real good neighbors. Used to be your neighbor would come and stay all day with you. Come over drink a cup of coffee with you; have a sandwich with you. If you was a-canning during the canning season the women all got together. They'd be five or six of them go together and can at one house one day and another house the next day. They'd stay up all night a-canning.

"We met at the school house for all of our social gatherings. We had pie suppers and box suppers and spelling bees and things like that. Women would make their pretty boxes, take them over there with their food in it and sell it to the highest bidder. They had a cake that they'd give away to the most popular girl and we had one girl in the community that always got it. Laura Stephenson, she always got the cake, but she earned it because she was the most popular girl in the community. She was a beautiful girl and a good girl."

Church was also a social gathering. After church everyone would gather and visit and socialize. "Sunday school in the morning was over at the Snyder school house. In the evening we had it over at the Thomas school house. We all went to both. We had Baptists, we had Methodists, we had Church of Christ. All different denominations."

—Ruleen Lazzell, "Life on a Homestead: Memories of Minnie A. Crisp," 1979.[12]

Preparing and Sharing Food

Corn Harvesting at San Ildefonso Pueblo . . .

At harvest time families usually helped one another. At the San Ildefonso pueblo all the inhabitants got together to sweep the plaza before the corn was brought home "because corn is just the same as people and we must have the plaza clean, so that the corn will be glad when we bring it in." The Tewa men would bring in the corn from the fields and the women would shuck it and stack it, selecting the very best ears to be put away for seed corn. Enough seed was put away for two years so that if next year's corn should fail they would have enough seed left to preserve that pueblo's particular strain of corn. This was very important, as it was believed that the corn of a pueblo was the same as the people. When the women had finished shucking at one household they went to help other relations. Widows, orphans, and needy persons helped at as many huskings as possible, receiving a present of corn at each.

—Carolyn Niethammer, *American Indian Food and Lore,* 1974.[13]

Waffle garden, Zuni Pueblo, 1911. Photo by Jesse Nusbaum. (MNM Neg. No. 43170.)

San Juan Pueblo. Photo by T. Harmon Parkhurst. (MNM Neg. No. 3975.)

Corn Grinding Parties at Acoma Pueblo . . .

In Acoma, such grinding operations are affairs in which a group of clan related families cooperate, like a knitting bee, or log raising. There is in fact, a general tendency among these people to make all such work as will lend itself to group effort, spirited and pleasurable. There are as a rule, two or three relays of grinders and since three women are required to grind simultaneously, it takes from six to nine women to make a grinding party. In addition to the grinders, it takes at least two women to parch the corn, which is to be ground. The corn parchers are usually elderly women, who are no longer able to endure the heavy work of grinding. Two women are required to prepare the meals for the party and as a rule, the singing choir is composed of three men, however, when men are not available the singing is done by one of the relays of women grinders. A grinding party, therefore, may consist of from ten to twenty people. . . .

The singers for such an event must be men or women who have learned, and know how to sing grinding songs, that centuries ago were composed for that purpose. In grindings that I have witnessed the choir consisted of three men. All three of the men sang while one of their number beat a drum that looked more like a seat cushion than a drum.

When the singing starts a large bowl of parched corn is placed at the left side of the kneeling pad of grinder No. one who works on the coarse stone on the left side of the set. When grinder No. one has crushed enough corn into the consistency of fine chops so that she can scoop it out by the handful she very deftly passes it over the partition between her compartment into the compartment of the rock to her right and grinder No. two who grinds it to a finer meal and who in turn passes the meal on to grinder No. three who grinds it still finer. The grinding is done with considerable vigor as the strokes of the mano in the hands of the operators must be kept moving to the rhythm of the songs and keep time to the singing and drumming of the choir.

The next day the company meets at another house, taking the meal ground on the previous day with them, and puts the meal to another triple grinding into a very fine meal. One of their Indian women told me that they ground it so fine, that the meal just flowed, and in the last stage of the grinding they had to moisten it slightly or it would fly about the room and could not be handled.

—Collected at Acoma Pueblo in the 1920s by B. A. Reuter.[14]

The Art and Ritual of Making Piki Bread . . .

Piki is the original Indian bread. It is of Hopi origin but it is made in all the pueblos—the Zunis call it hewe, the Tewa tribes along the Rio Grande call it mowa, and at San Ildefonso it is called bowahejahui, which translates "put it on, take it off." . . .

Essentially it is all the same thing: blue cornmeal batter that is baked in large tissue-thin sheets, which are rolled up like a newspaper. Occasionally white or pink piki is made for special dances.

Piki-making is an art and a ritual. It takes years of practice to become a good piki baker. Years ago a young woman was required to demonstrate that she had mas-

San Juan Pueblo. Photo by T. Harmon Parkhurst. (MNM Neg. No. 3971.)

tered the art of piki-baking before she was considered a suitable bride. But today few young women have the patience to spend long, hot hours in front of the piki stone, and the number of those who excel in this art is dwindling.

—Carolyn Niethammer, *American Indian Food and Lore,* 1974.[15]

The Miller of Arroyo Hondo . . .

In the early days one-room flour mills, built of heavy logs, dotted the length of the [Arroyo Hondo] villages . . . in close proximity to the river. Here most of the wheat and corn raised in the locality was milled into flour and meal.

All day long and far into the night the miller, usually a man of advanced years, honest and devout, his face, hair and clothes white with flour-dust, sat on his low wooden bench by the grindstones, lengthening or shortening the string of his plumbline, as required, to adjust the flow of grain from the hopper to the grind-stones. The monotonous hum of the grinding stones put the miller in a pensive mood. His thoughts would wander to the past, to his beloved departed or some absent son, till he would join in the humming of the mill, breaking into a hymn now and then, and finally taking up his rosary to pray. This was his daily custom till the late hours when he shook the dust off his clothing and locked the mill for the night—just monotony, hymns, prayer and flour-dust.

—Reyes N. Martínez on nineteenth-century Arroyo Hondo.[16]

A Legend about the Devil and the Miller . . .

Once there was a miller who ground corn for rich farmers, and farmers who made barely enough to eat. He always carried on conversation with the devil, who stood behind his shoulder, as to whether or not he should play fair with his customers. One day a little before noon there drove up to the mill a very rich farmer with fifty wagon loads of corn. The miller began to grind, and as he ground he turned his head over his shoulder and said, "Devil, he's rich. Must I toll him heavy or toll him light?"

The devil said, "Toll him heavy!" And the miller tolled him heavy.

A little before sundown there came to the mill another farmer. He had one sack of corn on his back, about a bushel, perhaps. He was tired of walking and hungry. And the miller put his corn into the mill and began to grind it. And as he ground he turned once more to the devil and said, "Devil, this fellow certainly is poor. He's tired. What must I do with him, toll him heavy or toll him light?"

The devil answered, "He's poor, damn him! Keep him poor! Toll him heavy!" And the miller tolled him heavy.

> —Legend from "a long time ago," collected in 1955
> from the student folklorist's grandfather, of Anton Chico.[17]

Putting Up Food in Los Padillas . . .

At the end of every summer my mother would can the fruits and the vegetables for the next year. She had this extra wood stove that she put outside because it got so hot. She'd build up a big hot fire, and then she'd take the corn, the *chiles,* the peaches, and the tomatoes and she'd put them in jars and boil them in a big kettle. My sister and I, we used to help her. But *hijo!* that was hard work! My mother would can from morning to evening—one week, two weeks, however long it took. Sometimes two women would come together and help each other, to make it easier. They'd let the housework go and just can until they were done—because if they didn't do that, then how in the world were we going to eat?

> —Ida Gutierrez remembers Los Padillas of the 1930s.[18]

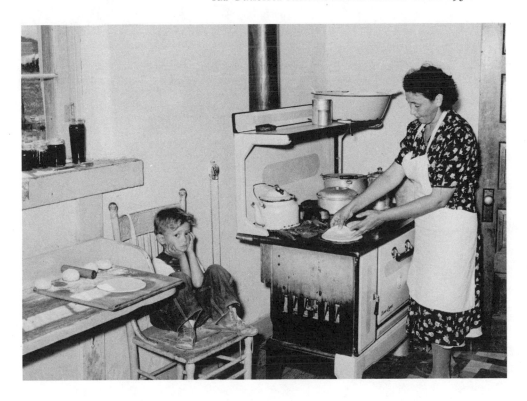

"Kitchen scene in Spanish-American home. Making tortillas." FSA photo by Russell Lee, vicinity of Taos, September 1939. (LC-USF 34-34220-D.)

"Spanish-American woman removing freshly baked bread from outdoor earthen oven." FSA photo by Russell Lee, vicinity of Taos, September 1939. (LC-USF 34-34213-D.)

Chicharrones, the Best of the Hog Rendering . . .

. . . The slaughtering of a pig specially fed for the occasion was usually referred to as *la matanza del cochino* or *del puerco,* depending on the region. In New Mexico and west Texas slaughtering took place in the fall. Friends and neighbors were invited after the "preliminaries" were over and the *chicharrones* or cracklings were ready to come out. . . .

The most popular product of pork was *chicharrones.* . . . The *chicharrones* could be a gourmet's dish when properly prepared. The *lonjas,* or thick strips of fat removed from the meat, were cut into small cubes and fried in *cazos.* The rendered fat was removed and poured into large cans. The cubes were pressed to release the fat, and removed to a large skillet, where they were browned further until they

released most of the fat. If the host of the *matanza* was well versed in making *chicharrones,* he would add cream and salt as they browned. In preparation for the occasion a couple of *tortilleras,* or tortilla makers, had been summoned to pass out hot, fresh corn tortillas to the guests. They made *burritos* with the hot *chicharrones* and added a bit of Mexican sauce made from fresh tomatoes, green chile, and fine-cut onion spiced with garlic. That was the moment they were all waiting for. If the host knew how to prepare golden brown *chicharrones,* it was worth being invited to *la matanza del cochino.*
　　　　—Arthur L. Campa, *Hispanic Culture in the Southwest,* 1979.[19]

Syrup Boiling in Agua Fria . . .

I used to like to come home [to Agua Fria, from the sheep camp] when the folks were boiling out syrup from the sugar cane. There used to be two mills here. Everybody would bring their cane to the presses, and while the syrup was boiling or while the cane was being crushed there would be dancing in the patio. Our musician was an Indian captive, Antonio Domínguez, who was very good on the violin. We had very good times then, dancing nearly all night and telling tales while the syrup boiled out. The children enjoyed it too because they were the ones who rode the cross beam which operated the pestle. There, high up in the air, they would rock back and forth shouting and laughing and fighting for their turn to ride.

"Spanish-American farmers peeling off layer of fat from a slaughtered hog." FSA photo by Russell Lee, Chamisal, July 1940. (LC-USF 33-12839-M1.)

Those were great times and I was always glad to get back at those times and I would try to stay as long as I would, enjoying myself, eating too much syrup and candy because in camp I tasted no sweets except when I could find wild honey.

—Don Nicolás López to Lorin W. Brown, Agua Fria, 1937.[20]

Gathering Piñon Nuts . . .

Late in the fall came a richer crop.

Half the village's population would go to the thickly-wooded forests between Arroyo Hondo, San Cristobal and Cerro to gather the brown *piñon* nuts. The forests rang with gay talk and laughter, for this God-sent gift meant not only a prosperous winter for the *pobres* but a vacation of a one or two weeks' camping trip as well. Periodically, every three or six years a full crop was yielded.

Flocks of bluejays added their cries of *"pi-ñon-es"* to those of gleeful children making a lucky find of a *ratonera,* a rat or squirrel hole packed full of *piñones.*

Red flames and blue smoke leaped up through the trees as the fires were started for supper. Later the people visited their neighbors' camps and sang and danced in the silver moonlight. When tired, they stopped to sit around the camp fires and hear the stories of the elders; the children always listened attentively.

—Cleofas M. Jaramillo, on nineteenth-century Taos County.[21]

The Chuck-Wagon Cook . . .

The cook digs a pit behind the chuck-wagon so that when a fire is built the wind will not blow sparks over the camp and the punchers surrounding it. . . . Having driven the two sharpened irons into the ground above the pit, the long iron is slipped through the eyes of the two iron uprights and this completes the "pot-rack," or stove. *Cosi,* as the cook is usually called, which is an abbreviation of the Spanish word *cosinero,* hangs a half dozen or more S hooks of iron above six inches long on the suspended bar and to these are hooked coffee pot, stew pots and kettles for hot water.

The chuck-wagon is always stopped with the wagon tongue facing the wind so that the fire will be protected by wagon and chuck-box. The rear end of the wagon contains the chuck-box which is securely fastened to the wagon-box proper. The chuck-box cover swings down on hinges making a table for the Cosi to mix his bread, cut the meat upon and make anything which may suit his fancy.

There is an unwritten law that no cow-puncher may ride his horse on the windward side of the chuck-box or fire. If he does the Cosi is liable to run him off with pot-hook or axe. This breach of manner would only be committed by some green hand or "cotton picker," as the Cosi would probably call him. This rule is observed so that no trash or dirt will be stirred up and blown into the skillets. . . .

Along in the evening as the men are through with the day's round-up or drive, tired horses are turned into the remuda and the Cosi hollers, "Come and get it, or I'll throw it out!"

The punchers in their chaps, boots and spurs flock to the chuck-wagon and out of the drawer get knives, forks and spoons and from the lid of the chuck-box a plate and cup which have been laid out by the Cosi. Then they go to the different bake ovens and fill their plates which, like the cups, are made of tin.

Lots of banter usually passes between the punchers and the Cosi, though he generally gives as good as he receives. Plates filled, the boys sit around on the different rolls of bedding, on the wagon tongue or on the ground with their backs against a wagon wheel.

As the boys finish their meal, plates, cups, knives, forks and spoons are thrown into a large dish-pan placed on the ground underneath the chuck-box lid. If some luckless puncher should place his "eating tools" on top of the lid, he would be sure to be bawled out by the Cosi. All the eating tools when washed are put on shelves or in drawers of the chuck-box, while the heavy Dutch ovens, coffee pot, etc., are put into a box bolted underneath the wagon bed at its rear end.

This is the real chuck-wagon and way of eating as found in New Mexico though some of the northern outfits have a different lay. From the Cimarron River north as far as grass grows many outfits have quite elaborate lays. Those that have a large tent or tarp spread over the wagon extending out on both sides are called by real punchers "Pullman outfits," and old hands will inform you that they are used so that the punchers won't get sun-burned and usually add, "bless their little hearts," further explaining, with a very straight face, that these Pullman boys usually wear white shirts and are obliged to shave and shine their boots every morning before starting work.

—N. Howard (Jack) Thorp, "Chuck-Wagon Supper," 1937.[22]

Photo by Dana B. Chase. (MNM Neg. No. 56991.)

"Farm folks, mostly homesteaders, at dinner during the all-day community sing." FSA photo by Russell Lee, Pie Town, June 1940. (LC-USF 33-12785-M3.)

Son-of-a-Gun Stew . . .

Wherever fat calves or suckling yearlings are range butchered in the cattle country of the Southwest one hears of or eats the *rascal* or *son-of-a-gun*. Some say the custom of making their rather huge stew from the combined beef "giblets" originally came from Texas—along with the expanding cattle industry. Others insist that the white cow-hunters of early cow-camping days first adopted from the Plains Indians the practice of eating the "innards." . . .

The ingredients—often referred to collectively as "the rascal"—are gathered up at the scene of the kill, and are almost always the first part of the beef to be utilized. . . . When this mass of stuff is cut rather small and stewed to tenderness, it is practically impossible to tell what the stew is made of—hence its ribald naming. Hence, also, the jocose tradition that it is made of one's chief or current enemy, political or personal. Eating him—with one's friends—is something of a celebration. . . .

Far from being a routine dish, *son-of-a-gun* was and is always a special treat. The writer recently mentioned *son-of-a-gun* in the company of an Albuquerque woman who grew up in the southwestern part of . . . New Mexico. "Oh," she exclaimed, her eyes glowing bright, "I haven't had any *son-of-a-gun* in ages! We used to make it every time we'd kill a calf, and invite the neighbors—young and old— over for a dance. All we'd want, or serve, was a pot of *son-of-a-gun* and cake and coffee." She wished she had some "right now," and finished with, "I could make it, too, if I had all the stuff." She failed to say who their *sons-o'-guns* were in that part of the state, however.

—May Mosley, then of Estancia, 1948–49.[23]

Good Times in Anthony . . .

They had good times in the old days [in Anthony]. "Innocent fun," Mr. Geck called it. "We had picnics, barbecues, dances, chuck wagon suppers and rodeos. The last rodeo was staged about eight years ago by a group of old timers, and the last chuck wagon supper ten or eleven. The good old days when we took our guitars and sang love songs to the girl of our dreams will never return. Pretty soon the mothers will be like the girls and buy all of our native dishes in tin cans."

—Charles C. Geck to Marie Carter, Anthony, 1937.[24]

Contesting

Winter Gatherings in the Hogan . . .

During the long, cold months of January and February not many ceremonies were held, but groups gathered in the larger hogans to listen to long legends as related by some elderly person who had gained a reputation as a storyteller. And sometimes a group of men would gather to chant ceremonial songs so the younger men and boys could learn the old chants. But most frequent of all were the groups who met to play games. . . .

. . . There seemed to be no hurry about getting on with the [moccasin] game. . . . After a time of visiting, with many jokes and much laughter, the shoes were buried in the long mound of sand and a blanket was held in front of them while one group placed the ball well down in a toe, then filled all of the shoes with sand. As soon as the man started to hide the ball, the chant began, as the Navahos do not enjoy carrying on any community labor or entertainment in silence and all activities have prayer chants to accompany them. There are more than forty-eight chants that may be sung while the moccasin game is in progress. Most of these are dedicated to the spirits of the bird-people who originated the game and are supplications for luck to attend the side that is doing the chanting.

—Franc Johnson Newcomb on 1920s Navajo life near Shiprock.[25]

Wintertime Diversions in Taos County . . .

The season of repose had come; and while the land rested under a blanket of snow, the farmers sought diversion in sports and games. . . .

On a large level field across the river, on bright Sunday afternoons, the more active men played *El Juego de Pelota*. When the upper town men played against the lower town team, the ball was brought down through the fields, a distance of two miles. A hot struggle carried the ball back and forth until one of the sides succeeded in hitting the fence marked as the winning goal. The losers paid by giving a dance.

Horse races took place out on the level *Llanito*. The men bet money, the women *sudarios* and *rosarios*.

In sunny *placitas* men gathered to witness cock fights. For weeks before the fight, the roosters were fed and given special care. Heavy wagers made the sport exciting. . . .

Through the long, winter evening, neighbors gathered before warm fireplaces to play *canute,* card games, and to tell interesting stories....

—Cleofas M. Jaramillo on nineteenth-century Arroyo Hondo.[26]

Hispanic Canuto . . .

The favorite and most often played game was Canuto (Pipe or Flute). For this game a pile of sand was placed in two corners of the room diagonally opposite and upon the mud floor. Navajo blankets were hung as drapes to conceal these corners. The game was played with four hollow sticks or reeds and a slender stick which could be inserted in the hollows; all the sticks being about eight inches long.... Two leaders chose sides; each side had four players and each side possessed one of the corners. When the game was on everybody in the village who could leave his house was there to watch and bet on the side that would score the most points during the evening's game. The side that was to start the game repaired behind the blanket in their corner. The slender stick was inserted into one of the reeds and

Horse racing, El Cerrito, April 1941. Bureau of Agricultural Economics photo by Irving Rusinow. (Neg. No. 83-G-37878, National Archives.)

the four sticks buried in the sand pile. The drape was pulled aside and the other four rushed in to the draw. They had but one draw. If the reed pulled from the sand pile contained the slender stick they were entitled to a second draw, if not they retired with the score given them by the one reed they did draw, and with all the reeds which were now to be hidden in their own sand pile. And so it went, with betting and drinking on the outside. Each time the players rushed to the draw everybody sang:

Paloma Lucida	*Beautiful Dove*
Lucido Palomar,	*From beautiful Dove house,*
Vengan atinados	*Come ready to win*
Vengan a jerrar.	*Come ready to lose.*

—Lou Sage Batchen, on nineteenth-century Las Placitas.[27]

Tewa Cañute . . .

Katc'e·p'e·e· [canute] is played by males only. The game is played for the most part in winter, when the Indians have little else to do, although they have no objections to playing it in the summer time. At the Tewa pueblo of San Juan it is invariably played on All Saints' eve (the eve of the first of November), when it forms the chief amusement and means of celebration. This year it was played only once at San Ildefonso previous to Christmas. It is played most in January, February, and March. At present it is more likely to be played on Saturday nights or Sundays than at other times.

The game is frequently played continuously for hours. In ancient times, it is said, the gaming often lasted an evening and a day.

—John Peabody Harrington, "Tewa Indian Game of 'Cañute,'" 1912.[28]

Playing the Hispanic Card Game, Cunquián . . .

Love of gambling is an inherent trait with the native of New Mexico; every form of gambling attracts them with *Monte* . . . the favorite of the card games. Equally popular, yet one which can be played by only two players is *cunquián;* coon-can in English, spelled conquian by Webster's Dictionary which gives its origin as coming from the interrogation in Spanish; *con quien* (with whom?). Perhaps its origin being Spanish explains the fascination it has for these descendants of the Spanish colonizers of New Mexico; a fascination which will induce two players to sit opposite each other for a whole day and still continue through the following night, completely lost to the passing of time and heedless to the call of more imperative duties. To an addict, this game is as enthralling as is chess to one of its devotees. Indians have learned this game from their Spanish neighbors; some tribes, notably the Apaches and Navahos, will stake ponies, blankets and some say even their wives on the outcome of one hand or a series of hands of this game. . . .

The fact that the loser must deal as long as he is losing gave rise to a story of a woman who took advantage of this rule to keep check on the course of a game of *cunquián* which had kept her husband away from home for many long hours.

This wife would send her little boy to look on at the game and report back to her as to which of the two players was dealing. The boy returned from several such errands with the assuring news that the other fellow was doing all the dealing, so that the housewife was content and made no attempt to break up the game. This continued throughout a day and part of the following night. The last trip the boy made occurred rather late in the night, and he tarried so long that his mother was about to go and see for herself what could be keeping him, when he burst into the room, with these words: *Mamá, mamá! Papa está dalas y dalas y en calzoncillos blancos!* (Father is dealing and dealing, clad only in his drawers!) By this time, the anxious housewife knew that not only had her husband lost the proverbial shirt off his back but that he was in a fair way of losing everything else as well, and that she must hasten to break into the game and bring her husband home, wrapped in the *sarape* (blanket), which she took along for that purpose. The phrase, *dalas y dalas,* above, is used also with a loser at this game to taunt him for being such a poor player and to remind him to what state he will be reduced if he persists in playing against an opponent who is so much better than he is.

—Lorin W. Brown, on Taos and Córdova, 1920s and 1930s.[29]

Apaches Playing Cards . . .

Dr. M. R. Harrington, Curator of the Southwest Museum, has some hand-written notes of Charles Lummis . . . [who] in 1886, was visiting army posts in the Southwest and he describes the Apache men, women and children who were being held at one fort. . . . He writes: "Squatting around some blanket spread upon the sand, they deftly dealt coon-kan (Mexican Monte) with very rare inconsistencies. Their 'chips' were sometimes coffeebeans, sometimes cartridges,

Julian Martínez playing cañute, San Ildefonso Pueblo, ca. 1925. (MNM Neg. No. 82140.)

sometimes neat slivers of bear-grass, cleverly bundled, and sometimes mere twigs snapped from a handy bush. The stakes were money, cartridges, blankets, ponies and everything else that was bettable. It was notable that they slapped down their plays with that indispensible vehemence of whack without which cards wouldn't act right in any game."

—Virginia Wayland, on Apache playing cards, 1961.[30]

Cowboys' Card-Playing . . .

Most ranch owners frowned upon card-playing, and with good reason. Horses would stand all night with their *morrales* on, gates would be left open when they should have been shut, and even meals would be neglected if a good stiff poker game was in progress.

So the better-organized ranches forbade cards entirely and the smaller ones struggled with the problem. . . . We never forbade card-playing on our place in the long winter evenings. We tried to make life as tolerable as possible. I remember how pleased I was to discover that ours was sometimes referred to as the "ranch of the popping matches," because we supplied the present type of tipped match instead of the blocks of sulphur-headed matches the fumes of which gave them their local name of "hell-sticks" and "choked a fellow to death before he could get his cigareet lighted." Most ranches supplied "hell-sticks." But we didn't like gambling. . . . It was a nice problem, this fine line between entertainment and vice.

—Agnes Morley Cleaveland, on ranch life in
Catron County, early twentieth century.[31]

Gambling Cowhands . . .

There was always a horse race brewing or in prospect when cowhands got together. The usual kind, which was for a short distance, such as a half mile or less, could be gotten up almost anywhere, in a few minutes, impromptu, with no jockey club rules to worry about. The boys would go to a level place, step off the distance, strip their ponies to save weight, and ride. Whoever had money bet on the outcome. Lacking money, almost anything else of value would do for what our English highness, Lord Lincoln, usually called a wager. . . .

[Cowboys also played] the game of fuzzy-guzzy . . . with a small top with four sides on which are marked the letters A, N, W, and L—meaning all, nothing, win, lose.

—N. H. (Jack) Thorp, *Pardner of the Wind,* 1941.[32]

Top Contests in Taos . . .

Taking a top string from his pocket, [topmaker] Juan S— wound the top tightly, then flung it forcibly to the ground with the practiced throw of an expert. Whipping the cord back and away, he gave the top the needed impetus to set it spinning. Critically he watched it as it rotated . . . giving off a quite audible hum. So truly was it shaped that at the peak of its spin it appeared to be entirely motionless—only a faint blur encircled its spinning form.

"*¡Se durmió!* ('It has gone to sleep')" came the admiring cry from several onlookers. A tribute to the skill of this topmaker, for only a well-balanced top will achieve that state of seeming immobility. . . .

The favored form [of top contest] was one which promised a quicker turnover for the gamblers. A *babita* ["large gob of spittle"] was enclosed in a circle drawn with a sharp stick approximately five feet in diameter. Spike throws at the *babita* fixed the order in which each player took his turn. Each player deposited a top within the circle. The object of the game was to drive tops out of the enclosure. Tops driven out became the property of the successful player, who could continue as long as he drove a top out with each successive throw. Losers could redeem their tops at a predetermined price. . . .

This game was called *El Corte*, perhaps derived from the practice of cutting individual animals from a herd or flock. Players became so adept at this game that many tops were split. All of this brought a thriving business to the shrewd woodcarver.

El Aguante consisted in simply pitting spinning tops against each other. At a given signal all participants spun their tops. . . . Each one then had to pick up his top and hold it spinning in his outstretched palm. The last top to waver and fall won for its owner all of the other tops or a sum agreed upon beforehand. *El Aguante* roughly denotes an endurance test.

One top contest was an unusually boisterous one with lots of action and a fair chance for bruises or for being spiked by a thrown top. This fast game was called *La Arriada* ("The Drive"). This term was also applied to a round wooden ball whittled out of piñon wood. It was about the size of a golf ball and in due course became as pitted as one. Goals were established and teams of players chosen, usually the same number on each side. A purse was made up by each side, both sums being left with some onlooker as stake holder.

The wooden ball or *la arriada* was placed midway between the two goals. The leader of each team stood on either side of it. At a given signal each launched his top with a sideways motion, striving to strike the ball and send it toward his goal. Teammates stood poised with wound tops, ready to further the ball on its initial course or to turn it in the opposite direction. In this exciting drive the pace was fast and furious; the ball was driven hither and yon. Tops and their humming filled the air.

Shouts of encouragement and jeers for a bad throw came from the spectators, who greatly enjoyed this test of skill and team work. As usual, much betting went on. If not cash, . . . beans, piñons, corn flour, chickens, *cabritos* ("kids"), or whatever were wagered on the outcome. The women of the town were enthusiastic viewers and backed their men's efforts with wagers as those above. They were as vocal in their shouts of encouragement as were the small fry.

—Lorin W. Brown, on nineteenth-century Taos.[33]

A Navajo Myth of the Great Gambler . . .

When the young man [son of the Sun and a poor woman called She Goes Around Gathering Seeds or Rock Woman] had learned all these [eight] games the Sun sent him back to Tse be'na y i [his home]. At once he started to gamble. For a time the

"Shooting for drinks in a gold mining town barroom." FSA photo by Russell Lee, Mogollon, June 1940. (LC-USF 34-36811-D.)

Navajo gamblers, 1901. Photo by Carl N. Werntz. (MNM Neg. No. 37596.)

people tried to buy his turquoise earrings [given him by the Sun], they were so pretty. But he would always say: "If you can win them you can have them." When he chanted the people came to him. Soon he was called the Great Gambler, for he won all their corn and goods. He even won the children and the women and the men for his slaves. They worked for him and they built a great house [Pueblo Bonito] for him. He had a great many wives and the men built homes for him. Everyone worked for him. He won the Male Rain, the Female Rain, the Rainbow, the rivers, the mountains, and all the earth. The rest of the land went dry for it only rained where he lived. He had good corn and beautiful flowers. He even won the wife of the chief and the chief himself, together with his prayer sticks and his beads. There was also a big, round turquoise that stood as high as a man, and it had 12 feathers standing around it. The Sun told his son that when he should win the great turquoise it should be his. It was the most precious of all. It was the last thing that the Gambler won from the people.

Then the Sun came down, and he said: "My son, this is what I want. This is the only thing that I want. Now give it to me." But the Gambler had grown to be a very strong man, and instead of turning the great turquoise over to his father, he said: "You will be the next I will gamble with. Come on."

—Old Man Buffalo Grass, a Navajo, to
Aileen O'Bryan (Nusbaum), 1928, at Mesa Verde.[34]

Rites of Passage

Since the 1908 publication of Arnold van Gennep's *Les rites de passage,* anthropologists and folklorists have classified individual "life crises" as "a series of passages from one age to another and from one occupation to another." According to van Gennep, "birth, social puberty, marriage, fatherhood, advancement to a higher class, occupational specialization, and death" are accompanied by "ceremonies whose essential purpose is to enable the individual to pass from one defined position to another."[35] These ceremonies help assure the collective well-being in the face of individual uncertainty and change. Baptisms, initiations, marriages, and funerals are as much for the families and communities as a group as for the individuals upon whom the ritual is focused. The following New Mexican texts of marriage and funeral rites make clear both the individual and the communal responsibilities in union and separation.

Marriage Rites

Chivarees on Eastern Ranches . . .

In the early 1900s, ranch couples in eastern New Mexico were customarily married in the bride's home, where they remained for the night. Sometimes a chivaree was nothing more than cowboys circling the house while they shouted and shot pistols into the air. Agnes Foreman Coplen, a Roosevelt County homesteader, related that the chivareers would drive wagons a short distance from the house, wait patiently for the bedroom light to go out, then stealthily surround the place. Upon signal they would burst forth with a mighty blast like Joshua at the walls of Jericho. This kept up until the bride and groom hastily dressed and invited both boys and girls in for refreshments, which the bride's mother usually had already set on the table in anticipation of their arrival. . . .

After the Model-T Fords replaced cow ponies, older bachelors of Tatum joined the young blades to add rougher tactics to former mild practical jokes. W. O. Dunlap, Jr., stated that physically taxing and emotionally upsetting pranks were the order of the day in the early 1920s. Bridegrooms were forcibly kidnapped and thrown in a dirt-walled water tank on Main Street, often in bitter cold weather. Or the hapless groom was driven miles away, where he was dumped, often without shoes and trousers. Men sometimes spent their entire wedding night wandering over the dark prairie. The practice became so unruly that the sheriff of Lea County finally had to break up this type of chivaree. . . .

—Jean M. Burroughs, "Courtships, Weddings and Chivarees," 1980.[36]

Hispanic Wedding Customs . . .

The *Prendorio,* or the giving-away of the bride ceremony, was held at her home, eight days before the date of the wedding. The prendorio was the occasion for the giving of presents or gifts to the bride, as tokens of love and friendship. Prendorio is a word [derived from] *prenda*, meaning a jewel, or some other highly prized object. At this ceremony, the bride was introduced to the bride-groom's relatives, and, after a banquet, everyone enjoyed dancing throughout the day. . . .

Cordova wedding procession, February 15, 1939. Bride Marcelina Romero and groom Milton Trujillo are led by guitarist and fiddler and followed by the guests. Photo by B. Brixner. Nina Warren Collection. (MNM Neg. No. 12034.)

The marriage ritual took place at the village church. The parents remained at the home of the bride to await the return of the bridal party which was a spectacular affair. Headed by the *músicos,* usually two violin and guitar players, and to the tune of a wedding march, amid shouts and gun shots fired into the air, the wedded couple were met by their parents and other relatives and friends a short distance from the house. Hearty hugging, kissing, and crying took place, then the march was resumed, the parents falling in line behind the bride and the groom. In the house a banquet awaited them. First came the refreshments. When all had partaken, the regular meal was served. It was considered a slight to the well-meaning hosts not to eat heartily, and, as that morning they had eaten only a very sparing breakfast, in anticipation of the banquet, the guests did real justice to everything placed before them. Liquor flowed freely, wine for the women, stronger drink for the men. Hilarity reigned supreme. Dancing and singing were enjoyed throughout the rest of the afternoon, till the guests went home to get ready for the wedding dance at the hall.

Immediately after supper, the wedding march wended its way towards the dance hall, in the same order of formation as before, and to the same noisy accompaniment. The walls, decorated with as many mirrors as could be procured, gave the hall an elegant appearance, considered indispencable [*sic*] for a wedding dance. The entry into the hall focused all eyes on the bridal couple. The look of modesty of the bride, in contrast with the look of pride of the bridegroom, was a sight to be remembered long afterwards. They marched two or three times around the hall, then all were seated, the bridal party taking their place at the head of the hall, opposite the entrance, in front of the musicians, who were seated on chairs placed upon a table. . . .

Laughter and gaiety reigned until dawn, when the novios and the padrinos would retire to the home of the bride. There the *Entriega* [*sic*], or delivery, of the wedded couple took place. A special verse, indicative of the responsibilities of wedded life, separation from parental care, and a final farewell to bachelorhood, was sung to the accompaniment of the guitar. The young couple then knelt to receive the blessing of their parents and older relatives, reverently kissing their hands. A few refreshments were served and thus the final curtain was drawn on the first episode ushering two young souls into a journey of matrimonial adventure. Quiet again descended upon the village that had celebrated so gaily and so fully.

—Reyes N. Martínez, "Rural Weddings," 1936.[37]

Entrega de novios, *the Delivery of the Newlyweds* . . .

Of all the ceremonies that take place during the typical New Mexican Spanish wedding, the *entrega de novios* is perhaps the most genuinely New Mexican. This ceremony, which marks the climax to all the other wedding observances, generally takes place after the wedding dance, upon the arrival of the newly wedded pair and the guests at the home of the bride's parents. It is so called because the bride and groom are returned once more to their parents and placed under their guidance. When all the guests have crowded around the bride and groom, a singer or *pueta (poeta),* as he is often called, begins to sing to the accompaniment of a violin and a guitar. The name *entrega de novios* refers both to the ceremony itself as well as to the series of *coplas* or stanzas sung on such an occasion. In the first two or three stanzas of his song, the singer generally requests the attention of the audience and sometimes apologizes for not being a more gifted singer than he is. Then he summarizes the Bible's story of the creation of man, reminding those present of how God created man out of clay in his image and likeness and how the first woman was formed out of one of Adam's ribs. He also passes in review the marriage ceremonies before the altar. The wedded pair is then admonished regarding the sacredness of marriage and its indissolubility, and they are told of their responsibilities and their duties to each other. Even the *padrinos* or best man and bride's maid are reminded of their obligation, which, according to the singer, consists in bestowing their blessings upon the newly wedded couple and placing the latter in the hands of their parents (two formalities never carried out). The parents are then advised of the need of guiding their children in their new life. That, in brief, is what the typical *entrega de novios* tells.

—Juan B. Rael, "New Mexican Wedding Songs," 1940.[38]

Navajo Wedding Speeches . . .

The relationship between male and female in the roles of husband and wife is defined both through myth and ritual and through the public expression of the norms governing the relationship. . . . The Navajo pantheon contains many pairs of male and female supernaturals (e.g., Holy Man and Holy Woman, Holy Boy and Holy Girl). Their exploits are described in Navajo myths, each of which provides a charter for one of the sings. The sexual and procreative aspects of the male-female relationship are the topic of many myth episodes. . . .

In contrast to curing rituals, which stress male-female symbolism, and myth, which treats the sexual aspects of the male-female relationship, domestic aspects are publicly acknowledged as part of the Navajo wedding ceremony. The roles of husband and wife entail certain rights and duties of coresidence and the pooling of goods and services. These obligations are the subject of speeches that follow the wedding feast provided by the bride's relatives.

As one Copper Canyon woman described the content of the speeches, "They tell the man to take care of the wife, to think of the home—how to build it—and to think about the food and getting wood and water. Later they say he should never take his hand to his wife (i.e., beat her). For the woman, she is told to cook, cash, iron, take care of the house, fix the bed, and keep care of the children."

—Louise Lamphere on the Eastern Navajo Reservation, 1960s.[39]

A Cochiti Pueblo Folktale about Marriage . . .

In the beginning the [Cochiti] people stopped at Frijoles, and settled at White House and at the village of the Stone Lions. An old man and an old woman had four sons. . . .

The next day the eldest son said to his father and mother, "Tomorrow morning I am going to the Village of the Stone Lions to see if I can get a girl to marry me. I will bring her back to White House." He said to his mother, "You are old and not able to work any more and you need some one to help you with the grinding. If I find her I will bring her back." The boy went to the village of the Stone Lions and stayed for two days. He found a girl and he said to her, "Are you willing to come to my village and marry me? My mother and father are very old and I have three brothers." The girl said, "Yes; I shall be glad to go with you to your village and marry you. first you must tell my mother and father what it is that you want." "I will go and ask them." He said to the girl's parents, "Your daughter is willing to go with me and live in my village." They answered, "Yes, it is as she says. She may go with you if she is willing." The girl's father said to the boy, "Bring your father and mother to this village so that we may know who they are." "My father and mother are too old, they can not walk so far." The boy took the girl home to his village. She took wafer bread with her to give to his mother and father.

They came into White House and the people watched them. The boy was a poor boy but the girl was very beautiful. He said to the girl, "Here is our home. Wait here a moment and I will go in and tell them." His mother and father were sitting side by side at the fireplace. He said, "Where are my brothers?" They answered, "They went out to gather the fruit of the giant cactus. They will be back soon." "Mother and father, I am bringing a girl home." "Where is she?" "She is waiting outside. I will get her." He went out and brought her in. His father and mother were glad to see her and she gave them the paper bread she had brought. His mother began to prepare food. She cooked venison and gave them the fruit of the giant cactus. The brothers came home. They were glad to see the girl and they made bows and arrows to go hunting every day. After that they were great hunters and never came home without bringing a deer.

—Collected in the summer of 1924 by Ruth Benedict from a Cochiti Pueblo woman, who held an important ceremonial position.[40]

Funeral Rites

Apache Funerary Customs and Beliefs . . .

As soon as a death occurred, close relatives went into mourning. Men wept, women wailed, and both sexes cut the ends of the hair and donned old clothing. One or two elderly relatives (death was particularly contaminating to the young) washed the body, combed the hair, and dressed the deceased in his finest clothes. Burial took place during the daytime and as soon as possible. The deceased was placed on his favorite horse with as many of his personal possessions as could be carried and taken far from the habitations of the people, into hilly or mountainous country, if possible. Because of the risk of contamination, the burial party was small. It proceeded silently, and tribesmen it encountered turned away. A crevice in the rocks that could be covered with earth, brush, and stones was sought as a grave. Some personal possessions were buried with the corpse; the rest were broken and left at the burial site. The horse was killed at the graveside, for the dead person needed his mount as well as his belongings in the afterworld. The burial party returned by a different route, and its members refrained from looking back toward the grave or discussing its location with others. Upon their return they discarded the clothes they had worn and thoroughly washed themselves. They and the other mourners burned sage, juniper, or some pungent plant considered to be "ghost medicine" and bathed themselves in the smoke. Ashes, too, were liberally used on their persons and around the camp to discourage any lingering or returning ghost.

While the burial was in progress, other relatives carried out requirements at home. Personal possessions of the dead that had not been taken to the grave were broken or burned. Even possessions of others that the dead person had lately used or handled a great deal were destroyed. Nothing that would constantly remind the living of their dead relative was retained, for to think of the dead was to attract the ghost. As a precaution, the name of the deceased was not uttered; if it was absolutely necessary to refer to him, a circumlocution was used. Since ghosts strove to return to their former homes, the encampment in which a death occurred was moved, even though sometimes the shift was to a nearby location and was more symbolic than substantial. The mourning relatives remained isolated for a time, shunning social events.

—Morris E. Opler, "The Apachean Culture Pattern and Its Origins," 1983.[41]

Navajo tree burial near Fort Wingate, ca. 1890. Photo by Ben Wittick. (MNM Neg. No. 16306.)

Funeral procession, Isleta Pueblo, ca. 1915. (MNM Neg. No. 46204.)

Isleta Pueblo Practices at Death . . .

A kinsman, the son of the deceased, or other relative, goes to the chief of the Corn group of the deceased, who will send an assistant to the house to sprinkle meal from the feet of the corpse to the door. (There is no orientation of the corpse. Formerly the head was placed on a block of adobe.) The aunt (ky'uu) of the deceased is also summoned. (If the deceased have no kyunin the Corn chief will appoint a woman assistant to perform the proper functions.) With her she brings a bowl of water and cotton and a twig brush. She brushes the hair of the deceased, washes and dries the face. The water she has used may not be thrown outside the door. She throws it within the threshold where she also breaks the bowl, leaving the pieces, that the people coming in may step on them. The hands of the dead are placed clasped together, and between the middle fingers is placed a small cross of perliu [a high brush with a white bloom which grows in the mountain arroyos]. The aunt covers the corpse with a black blanket (manta) which is sewn together. Four men volunteer to carry the body first to the church, then to the cemetery.
—Elsie Clews Parsons on Isleta Pueblo in 1925.[42]

Funerals at Villanueva . . .

At the time of a death in Villanueva the church bell tolls solemnly for about ten minutes to announce to all the villagers that one of their company has died. The friends of the deceased then hurry to the side of his bed, to find the family in tears and unrestrained grief. The close relatives prepare the dead man for burial. If the relatives can afford it, a casket is purchased from Las Vegas, but usually one made locally of crude lumber is used. It is covered with gray muslin and a small cross is placed on top of the lid. A large dish of chopped onions is put under the casket in order that the odor of the body be modified. Rarely has a dead person in Villanueva been embalmed. In summer the casket is left out in the yard and buried within twenty-four hours after death. If the priest is not at some mission saying mass, he conducts the requiem burial. Because the priest is out on mission so frequently, most bodies are buried within a day after death, and the mass for the dead is said later.

—New Mexico Rural Council study of Villanueva, February 1938.[43]

Wakes for the Dead in Hispanic Villages . . .

The corpse, having been laid out, occupies a central position in the largest room, surrounded by lighted tapers. As is the custom, all looking-glasses in the house have been covered or turned face to the wall. Vanity will have no place in that home until a certain period of mourning is over.

People begin to arrive in family groups, all the women wearing long-fringed black shawls. Entering the presence of the corpse, everyone kneels beside it and offers prayers for the soul's welfare and repose. There is a bowl or vessel nearby to receive the contributions of those who feel so inclined. When next the *padre* from Santa Cruz visits, the sum will help pay for a mass.

Each group passes from this room to an inner one where the bereaved family is gathered. The women burst into loud wails while the men stand by rather self-consciously. When the wailing dies down, there are murmured expressions of sympathy, after which the menfolk leave the room and join those watching the dead.

Around the body, the watchers join in the responses to the *alabados* or mournful funeral hymns. The verses to these hymns are sung by a select group huddled around a notebook in which the words are painfully written down. The rest of the mourners join in the choruses, which are well known to all.

Between hymns there are scattered conversations and interchanges of remarks. At first all speech is rather strained, and voices are carefully modulated. As the night lengthens, the restraint lifts; witty stories and spicy comments go the rounds, punctuated by bursts of laughter.

Outside in the patio, several bonfires have been lit for warmth and light. Here, the younger men and less serious elders gather to tell lies and play practical jokes, with not a little drinking of *mula* or wine. Flirtations take place at windows and around the bake-ovens where the aroma of fresh bread provokes hunger. The kitchen is full of cooks attracted there by the wonderful chance for gossip, as well as to hear the sickness and last moments of the deceased discussed in detail.

At intervals, the chanting of *alabados* breaks in on all conversations, and fresh arrivals are announced by renewed outbursts of weeping. Around midnight, the rosary is prayed, and everybody takes part. If the deceased is a Penitente or one of the immediate family of a member of that Order, the song and prayer service is conducted by the Brothers. The wake of a dead Penitente will usually be visited by a procession from the *morada*. This procession will include several flagellants.

After the *rosario,* there will be some departures—very few, however, nearly everybody electing to stay. Visiting becomes more general, and there is continuous going in and out of doors and from room to room. Singing of the *alabados* never stops for long, with volunteer groups spelling the regular singer and leading out their favorite hymns. In fact, there is quite a bit of rivalry amongst the younger and older men, and the outsiders and the home guard in the rendition of these hymns.

Shortly after the *rosario,* several men, close friends of the mourning family,

Funeral procession, Mora, ca. 1895. Photo by Tom Walton. (MNM Neg. No. 14757. Historical Society of New Mexico Collection in the Museum of New Mexico.)

begin to summon the mourners to the supper table. There is a certain rule of etiquette followed in the order in which guests are served. Close relatives and friends from a distance eat at the first table with the regular singers and prayer leaders. After these folks have eaten supper, the next table is served. To this will be called the older and more respectable home folks and neighbors. The last table is the most lively, surrounded as it is by the younger fellows and the cooks. Much banter and flirting takes place. This happens in spite of the shocked and angry glances of the inevitable watchful old ladies.

—Lorin W. Brown, on Córdova and Taos, 1937.[44]

Ranch Country Burials . . .

No ministers were at hand for many years to conduct the funerals of those who died out in this ranch country. Such burials—there were not many—were made by a handful of ranch friends and cowboy comrades. A hymn might be sung; more often only an awed silence and bowed heads marked the interment. But no words could have been more eloquent nor rites more reverent.

—May Price Mosley on Lea County, 1936.[45]

Not many of our women neighbors got about as did my mother and her daughters. Not many had reason to, with their menfolks to carry the responsibility of looking after their cattle. It was this deadly staying at home month in and month out, keeping a place of refuge ready for their men when they returned from their farings-forth, that called for the greater courage, I think. Men walked in a sort of perpetual adventure, but women waited—until perhaps the lightning struck. One mother, carrying the body of her three-months-old baby, which had died suddenly of some infantile disorder, was being driven to town by a neighbor, her husband not being home at the time. Halfway across the plains, one of the team dropped dead from overdriving. All night the mother sat with the dead child in her arms while the man, riding the other horse bareback, went into Magdalena to fetch back a fresh team. For him, that last ten miles was undoubtedly a longer stretch than a mere ten miles; for the woman, it must have seemed the long road to eternity. Again, coyotes played their part. We used to say they detected the presence of death with some macabre instinct. This night they sat close to the buckboard, with the dead horse lying in the harness and the dead child in the mother's lap, and howled the night through.

> —Agnes Morley Cleaveland, *No Life for a Lady*, 1941.[46]

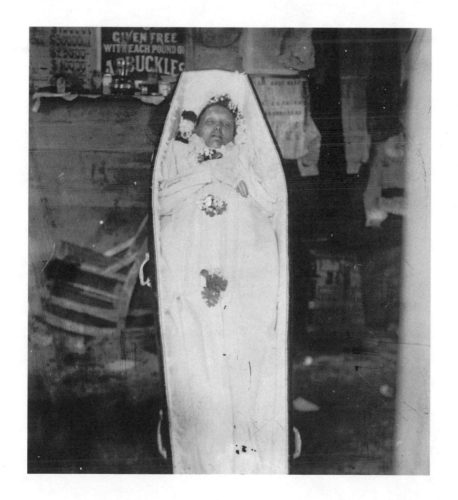

Corpse in casket in storeroom, ca. 1890–1905. Black Range Museum Collection. (MNM Neg. No. 76943.)

Corpus Christi, Pecos, ca. 1905.
(MNM Neg. No. 87047.)

Seasonal and Liturgical Celebrations

Cyclical notions of time are endowed with meaning from natural, solar, lunar, and seasonal periodicities. The annual cycle of the Tewa Pueblos, for example, "is tied to nature's basic rhythm and to the Tewa's attempts to influence that rhythm for his well-being."[47] Ritual dances are a major influence. Gertrude Kurath and Antonio Garcia explain the complex relationship between dance, direction, diurnal cycle, and season:

> The dances express the Tewa equation of the east with sunrise and spring, the south with noon and summer, the west with evening and fall, the north with night and winter. . . .
>
> . . . The fullest dance season extends from the winter solstice to the spring equinox. As winter struggles with spring, cold days and bright days appear sporadically during the midwinter holiday period and before Lent. At this time Animal Dances predominate, because the people formerly depended on game during the winter season and they still hunt at this time. With the lengthening of the days the people turn their thoughts to the cleaning of irrigation ditches, planting corn and other vegetables. With the growth and harvesting of crops, the late spring, summer, and early fall are times for rain, corn, and harvest dances. Then comes the hunting season, with private ceremonies but not many plaza dances, and the cycle starts all over again.[48]

Both the extended Christmas season and a Lenten period culminating in intense observance of Holy Week are the heightened times of Hispanic folk Catholicism in New Mexico. Indians and Hispanos also observe saint's and holy days from the Roman Catholic liturgical calendar. For the Pueblo Indians, however, "although certain portions of these activities are tied to the Catholic Church, the basic underlying power is directed toward the native religion."[49] In Spanish villages, by contrast, Christmas, Holy Week, and the annual saint's day are profoundly significant. Thomas J. Steele, S.J., explains villagers' belief that

> the village is centered on the church and inserted into one kind of sacred time—the solar cycle of the feast days of the saints—by the annual fiesta of the patron saint of the village. . . . The name of the chapel would be its great strength, for it would summon a power from outside into a profane world and would thereby establish an intelligible center within the warm glow of which the entire community of villagers could feel secure. So in New Mexico the villages, one by one, were centered and inserted into the sacred calendar by naming the chapel and in many cases the village itself with the name of a sacred personage.[50]

Traditionally, wakes for the saints, *bailes,* and folk dramas, which also were especially important at Christmas time, were among the observances at Hispanic fiestas.

Ritual Dance and Drama

Kachinas

> Kachinas are benevolent, anthropomorphic beings who live in mountains, lakes, and springs. They bring blessings, among which are included rain, crops, and, especially among the Eastern Pueblos, healing. While they are essentially benevolent, they can be dangerous if not treated properly. They visit the various villages at certain seasons of the year and dance publicly. There is a widespread belief that in times past, the kachinas danced in their own forms. Nowadays they simply invest their impersonators with their spirit. . . . Due to this, the masked dancer becomes the kachina after a period of suitable preparation. A Tewa male, for example, "tries out" for a kachina role in front of the elders of his moiety. If he is successful after an exacting, two-day session, "the elders call out in unison: 'He has become! He has become! . . .'" He then undergoes a four-day retreat during which he is immersed in all the sacred narratives of the Tewa, involving the creation of the cosmos and the emergence and migrations of the Tewa. "After four days of this retreat, also accompanied by continence, reflection, and fasting, and regaled with—yes, immersed in—the process of creation, he is indeed become a god. . . . The Tewa say that such a person 'has been placed upon cloud blossom. . . .'"
>
> [For the Zuni,] before participating in any masked ritual, in fact, before any participation in ceremony, the head must be washed in yucca suds. Even impersonators of katcina priests, who have been in retreat before their public ceremonies, return to their houses before dressing long enough to have their heads bathed by their wives or mothers. No man ever washes his own hair. In dressing

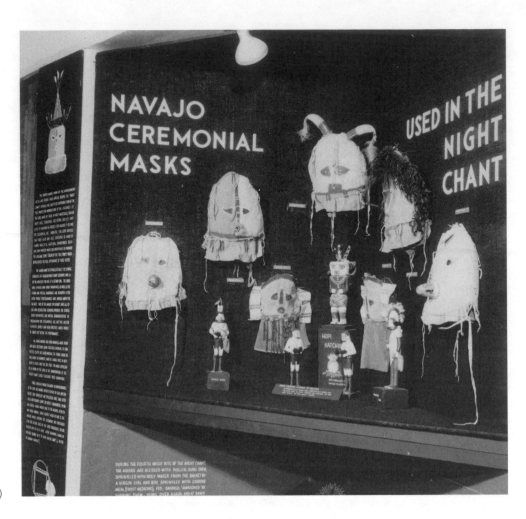

Exhibit at (Wheelwright) Museum of Navajo Ceremonial Art, Santa Fe. Photo by Tyler Dingee. (MNM Neg. No. 120185.)

the order is, first the body paint, then the costume, and last of all the mask. There are probably more elaborate rituals of dressing for all the katcina priests. When all the men are ready to go out, as the line of dancers leaves the kiva the chief spits medicine on each one of them. "It is called utea'owe (flower meal) or Paiyatamu medicine. It is made by medicine men in the society houses, and only society people have it. If the kiva chief does not belong to a society he must get this medicine from someone who has it. It is made from the petals of yellow and purple flowers." All the butterflies go to the bright-colored flowers and people like to pick them. Therefore they make this medicine from the bright flowers. They mix it with the paint they use on the masks and body, to make the dancers beautiful. Only the headmen know about this medicine. They take a little of it and as the dancers come out of the kiva to go to the plaza the kiva chief puts the medicine in his mouth and prays: "Now my father sun, you make the day beautiful. You send light and the clouds of all directions to make the world beautiful. You make the days beautiful in all directions. Therefore, we have made this paiyatamu medicine from the bright flowers." So he says and takes the medicine in his mouth and spits a little of it on each of the dancers as they come out.

—Ruth L. Bunzel, "Zuñi Katcinas," 1932.[51]

The mask is the focal aspect of the regalia of the kachina and indeed has a sacredness and power of its own. Masks are treated with reverence and periodically fed with cornmeal and other sacred substances. It is the placement of the mask upon the head of the individual that completes the transformation from a man into something much greater, removed from the specific time and space of the village and in touch with the truths and powers of the cosmos. Knowing this, it will be more readily understood that the use of masks as art objects in a Western sense is repugnant to many Pueblo Indians. In addition to this, in all villages there are social groups usually including small, uninitiated children, who are not supposed to know that the kachinas are, in fact, masked impersonators. In many of the Eastern Pueblos the very existence of the kachinas is kept a secret from outsiders.

—James Seavey Griffith, "Kachinas and Masking," 1983.[52]

Matachines

This dance, performed in San Juan each year on December 24 and 25, is believed to be of Spanish and Christian origins, taught to the Indians by the early Franciscan missionaries. Its movements and accompaniment are not typical of

Cochiti Pueblo Matachines Dance, showing Malinche in center, Santa Fe Fiesta, September 1920. Photo by H. C. Tibbitts. (MNM Neg. No. 13462.)

Tewa dance and music. The dancers execute skips, hops, swing kicks, and polka steps in many intricate choreographic patterns, while visiting Hispanic musicians play [some] tunes traceable to sixteenth-century Europe on the violin and guitar.

The matachines dancers include men who wear black pants and vests trimmed in beadwork, beaded moccasins, scarves over their mouths, and black fringe over their eyes. On their heads they wear miters from which long colorful streamers flow down their backs. . . . One young girl, called *Malinche,* dressed in a white sweater over a white or solid-color dress, dances among the matachines or with the male soloist called *Monarca.* He is distinguished from the matachines by his conical crown topped with a small crucifix. A small boy wearing a bull hide and carrying two sticks as forelegs takes the role of *el toro,* the bull. There are also two clowns or *abuelos* ("grandfathers") who wear masks and carry whips.

San Ildefonso also holds a matchines dance on December 25, similar to the San Juan version. Santa Clara's summer moiety performs its version on the same day. The Santa Clara Malinche wears a tan-colored manta decorated with Tewa symbols, and the accompaniment is provided by drummers and a male chorus. Versions of this dance are performed at other Pueblo and Hispanic villages throughout New Mexico, as well as in some Mexican communities.

—Jill Sweet, *Dances of the Tewa Pueblo Indians,* 1985.[53]

I remember the [Arroyo Hondo Matachine] dancers' fantastic costumes: purple shirts trimmed in pink, green ones in yellow—all in bright, contrasting colors. Bunches of bright-colored ribbons hung down their backs from the fancy, bishop-like caps; jewels, laces, and fringes half-covered their faces. Gay silk handkerchiefs floated from their shoulders and waists. This costume made a wave of color as each dancer took his turn, and with a stamping step to the tune of the one fiddle danced in and out around the single file of dancers, facing forward in two lines. Each participant held stiffly in one hand a fan-like wooden *palma* made of gayly-painted sticks. Each dancer went through different *danzas, la corrida, la palma* and other figures. *El Monarca* and the *Malinche* (a girl dressed in white, with her hair hanging loosely down her back) also took part. Then came the *abuelo,* a man dressed in shabby clothes, carrying a long whip; he acted as a clown—hitting the dancers on their heels with his whip or mimicking their dancing. At the end, the *abuelo* fought and killed the *toro* (wild bull), represented by a man wearing a bull's head. The dancers made their exit dragging out the dead bull.

—Cleofas M. Jaramillo, on nineteenth-century Arroyo Hondo.[54]

Another reason for the preservation of these dances is that many of them have religious connotations. The matachines dance, for instance, is danced in honor of the patron saints of the Catholic villages of New Mexico. Still another reason for their preservation is the common practice of swearing oaths to preserve them. . . . A young man, a war veteran from San Antonio, Bernalillo County, New Mexico, told me that his mother had sworn during the Second World War that if he were spared she would see that he danced the matachines dance every year in honor of the patron saint of the village, Saint Anthony.

A charming legend of this same village of San Antonio relates that many years ago during a battle between the villagers and Indian raiders a little boy in blue was seen fighting beside the villagers. They knew at once that this was Saint Anthony, come in this form to help them and they then and there swore that if he brought them victory they would dance the matachines dance every year on his name day, June 13. This promise was carried out year after year. During the performance the villagers dance all the way to the village spring on the mountainside and back. One year, however, the dance was omitted and shortly thereafter the spring dried up, a calamity in that dry country. The dance, it is said, has been performed faithfully on June 13 each year since then.

—J. D. Robb, "The Matachines Dance—
a Ritual Folk Dance," 1961.[55]

According to J. D. Robb, the following corrido, "composed as a poem without music, is a tribute to José Apodaca, *Monarca* (leader) of the *matachines* dancers of San Antonio, Bernalillo County, New Mexico."

1

Gentlemen, I am going to sing
That which I carry in my memory
About a man who was notable.
I am going to sing you the story.

2

In the village of San Antonio
Was born a very brilliant man,
And with the passage of time
He came to be the best dancer.

1

Señores, voy a cantar
lo que traigo en mi memoria
de un hombre que fué notable.
Voy a cantarles la historia.

2

Del pueblo de San Antonio
nació un hombre muy brillante
y con el tiempo llegó
a ser el mejor danzante.

3

This distinguished career
Was favored by circumstances,
And with the passage of time
He came to be the best Monarca.

4

José Apodaca was a man
With a very great heart.
Always he carried in his mind
The thought of serving his Lord.

5

With his guajito [rattle] and his palma
    [three-forked stick]
And his headdress of diamonds
He presented himself before San Antonio
With a group of dancers.

6

With this gilded headdress
He touched his heart
And the Malinche at his side,
He danced before his patron.

7

Dressed in a thousand colors
In our church he danced,
And the entire village rejoiced
When Apodaca danced.

8

San Antonio was left sad
And appeared in deep mourning;
As pale and serene
As the dawn of the day.

9

On his tomb is engraved
In interesting letters
An inscription which says:
"Long live the king of the dancers."

10

Now farewell, gentlemen.
This is the end of the story.
And Apodaca is in heaven
Rejoicing with God in his glory.

3

Esta dichosa carrera
circunstancia mucho abarca,
y con el tiempo llegó
a ser el mejor Monarca.

4

José Apodaca era el hombre
de tan grande corazón.
Siempre lleva en su mente
de servirle a su patrón.

5

Con su guajito y su palma
y aquel cupil de diamantes
se enfrentaba de San Antonio
con un grupo de danzantes.

6

Con aquel cupil dorado
le nació del corazón.
y la Malinche a su lado
bailándole a su patrón.

7

Vestido de mil colores
en nuestra iglesia se alegraba,
y el pueblo llenó de gusto
cuando Apodaca bailaba.

8

Quedó triste San Antonio
con grande luto se vía;
tan pálido y tan sereno
como un aurora del día.

9

En su tumba está grabado
con letras interesantes
con un letrero que dice:
—viva el rey de los danzantes.

10

Nos despedimos, señores.
Aquí termina la historia.
Y Apodaca está en el cielo
gozando de Dios y gloria.[56]

Penitente Brotherhood rite, Holy Week, San Rafael, ca. 1908. Note Veronica in center. From Laurence F. Lee, "Los Hermanos Penitentes," B.A. thesis, University of New Mexico, 1910. Courtesy Zimmerman Library, University of New Mexico.

Passion Plays

Good Friday Afternoon, Ranchos de Taos . . .

In front of the half square which the building [Ranchos de Taos morada] makes, was run a rope, supporting a sheet curtain, which did not hide from view the workers who brought out of the *morada* and placed in position, a black cross, about seven feet high. On this they hung an old wooden figure of the Christ about the waist of which fluttered two aprons, pink beneath and white on top. On the head was the crown of thorns which was secured by corn-colored ribbon caught under the wooden beard. By his side stood a barefooted centurion, dressed in white and wearing over his cross-marked forehead, a colored turban into which was thrust a tiny American flag. He carried a spear, a pole topped with an old bayonet, with which he struck the figure in the side at the proper time in the reading. Again, this was the only effort at dramatization during the whole "play" which is in reality a service.

When the reading was done, the figure was tenderly lifted from the cross and carried to the shrine of Mary—an image placed on a table nearby covered with white oil-cloth. It was carried past the three little girls, all in black, save for orange-blossom wreathes over their flowing hair. They held a long cloth on which were three impressions of the thorn-crowned Christ head. Then the wooden figure of the Crucified One was laid in a coffin lined with artificial flowers and decorated on the outside with strips of white embroidery which, against the black, suggested carving. When the peaked rooflike top was closed, the men lifted the coffin. Out from the *morada* came a young man who carried a crucifix on his shoulder. He led the whole procession. He . . . wore a regulation khaki army overcoat. Behind the coffin, held high on the shoulders of the bearers, followed and well-nigh staggered, the fellows who had been inside the church and on whose bleeding backs we had heard the swish of the lash fall during the service. They wore their coats and bandaged their heads with colored kerchiefs. We followed after, stopped too at the cross and then watched the procession turn and wind its way back to the *morada,* singing as they went.

—Blanche C. Grant, on Ranchos de Taos, after World War I.[57]

Tomé's Passion Play . . .

In Tomé, it is known that Fr. Jean-Baptiste Rallière, pastor from 1858 to 1911, contrived to separate the Penitentes from the passion play, allowing them only to prostrate themselves at the doorway of the church on Wednesday evening of Holy Week, humbly permitting the faithful to tread on them when entering.

As it eventually developed under Rallière's direction and in succeeding years down to 1955, when it was last performed, the Tomé passion play began with this Wednesday evening Tinieblas ceremony and the capture and imprisonment of Jesus on Thursday. The *Procesión de Las Tres Caídas* on Friday morning dramatized stations one to nine of the Way of the Cross, *El Sermón del Descendimiento* in the afternoon dramatized stations ten to fourteen, and *El Sermón de la Soledad* commemorated the bereaved mother with a sermon and procession in the evening. After a very brief enactment on Holy Saturday at the time of the Gloria of the mass, the ceremonies ended with a procession of the Risen Christ meeting his mother on Easter Sunday morning; this last ceremony is found in New Mexico only in Tomé and San Miguel, and may be assumed to be an addition of the French priests Rallière and Fayet to the passion-centered spirituality of the New Mexico Spanish. . . .

For a few years after the complete Tomé play was suspended, attempts to continue at least the stations of the cross on the *Cerro de Tomé,* a volcanic cone in the vicinity of the village; this service lapsed after a few years, to be revived in 1975, enlarged for the Bicentennial, and continued in 1977 and 1978 because "it proved to be a good thing and the people liked it." In these latter years the *"piadosa práctica"* became even more ambitious, with the parts of Christ, Mary, the *esposas benignas* (who help "embalm" the body), and the other participants taken by various persons of the vicinity, except that the venerable *"Sangre de Cristo"* crucifix took over for the twelfth and following stations. Following the capture, the action closely followed the fourteen stations, repeating in our own day the probable origin of the New Mexican passion play more than two centuries ago.

—Thomas J. Steele, S.J., "The Passion Play in New Mexico and Colorado," 1978.[58]

Village Fiestas

Laguna Pueblo Fiesta . . .

Fiestas, with Catholic masses and processions, markets, carnivals and/or native dances, honoring the patron saint of the community, are found throughout the Catholic countries of Latin America. This fiesta pattern extends northward into the area of early Spanish occupation in the North American Southwest where it still appears in the annual calendar both in Spanish-American and in Indian villages, notably among the Eastern Pueblos in New Mexico. . . .

Unlike the more famous Southwestern "fiestas" [Santa Fe] or "ceremonials" [Gallup], which were initiated, or are now promoted, by Anglo-American business-men, the village fiestas are predominately "native" affairs. . . . The village fiestas . . . have deep roots in history and important relationships to the Catholic religious calendar and the annual cycle of tribal ceremonies. The Laguna [Pueblo] Fiesta exemplifies this village-type fiesta, for it is controlled and participated in by "native" Southwestern peoples, with Anglo businessmen and tourists playing relatively minor roles. . . .

An observer's first impression of the [Laguna] fiesta is that thousands of people move rather aimlessly through a welter of activities during the two days of festivities. But after continued observation and systematic interviewing . . . , the initial impression gives way to an understanding of the fiesta situation as a highly structured series of events. The fiesta is at one and the same time: (a) a religious ceremonial which combines Catholic vespers, masses, and processions honoring St. Joseph, with a Laguna Harvest Dance in the plaza; (b) an enormous "native" market for the exchange of economic goods; and (c) a carnival with merry-go-rounds, tent dances, bingo and other games of chance, hot dog and hamburger stands, etc.

—Evon Z. Vogt, "A Study of the Southwestern Fiesta System as Exemplified by the Laguna Fiesta," 1955.[59]

Hispanic Village Fiestas . . .

Each year *mayordomos* (fiesta councilors) are appointed to take charge of the preparations for the year's fiesta. Among other things they take up a collection for the purpose. If the amount raised does not come up to expectations, the councilors have to make up the deficit out of their own pockets. This is a very nice custom as it insures not only the success but the continuance of the fiesta.

The *mayordomos* are charged, in addition, with the duty of repairing and cleaning the village church. . . . Altar cloths are washed and mended; the old paper flowers discarded for gay new ones, and the *Santos* are dressed in their fiesta finery.

If there is no resident priest, the home of one of the councilors is chosen to serve the fiesta dinner and to furnish quarters for the *padre* and members of his party. The house, too, undergoes the same thorough cleaning and scrubbing as the chapel. . . .

Vespers are held in the village chapel the evening before the fiesta. *Luminarias,* pitch wood fires, are built around the church and throughout the village. *Salves* (gun fire salutes) are fired at intervals just before and during the service, but there is no merry-making on the night of the vespers, as every one has gone to confession in order to receive communion the next day at mass. The whole *placita* (village) takes on a holiday air during the fiesta. Those who can afford it deck themselves out in new raiment, the rest make the best of old clothes, adding a ribbon here, a colored kerchief there, so as not to be completely outdone. . . .

If the members of the choir have accompanied the priest, high mass is said. . . . After mass, the fiesta dinner is served. Local musicians provide the entertainment, playing, now old ballads, now modern jazz tunes. In olden days the *cantador* (singer) occupied a prominent part during fiesta but now he is being relegated to the scrap heap, the young people no longer being interested in the traditional *cantadas,* or even in the more modern *corridos,* which deal with episodes of love, politics, or crimes.

After dinner there is a full schedule—dancing goes on in all the halls, or at least in as many as there are dance orchestras to provide the music. Very often there are *caballitos* (merry-go-rounds) for the children, the *corrida de gallo* (rooster race) and sometimes *carreras de caballos* (horse races) for the elders. All the stores carry on a lively business, and in addition booths are set up where *comestibles* are sold, consisting of candy, ice cream, hamburgers, peanuts, popcorn, and souvenirs. The *rancheros* who have no relations in the village camp out and eat at the booths. . . .

—NMFWP files, 1930s.[60]

San Ysidro Is Honored in Córdova . . .

[In Córdova,] the wake [for San Ysidro] began after vespers on May 14, the eve of the saint's day. All the villagers would gather at the community chapel, where Saint Isidore's image was placed on a freshly decorated processional platform. Saint Anthony of Padua, the patron of both chapel and community, was similarly honored. A procession then formed, and the group descended the hillside, crossed the Quemado valley, and ascended approximately three miles to the upland dry farms at Las Joyas. The journey was punctuated by the rhythm of chanted prayers and of the melodious hymn for Saint Isidore.

Upon reaching Las Joyas, the image was taken from the platform and laid in a green bower. Córdovans who owned fields at Las Joyas would take turns preparing the bower and hosting the wake on their land. The normally early-retiring farmers then began an all-night vigil. The darkness around the image was broken only by a line of candles. Two or more rezadores sang the many stanzas of the hymns, and the people intoned the chorus. This devotional concentration was broken only by a communal meal served at midnight.

The end of the wake was signaled when the face of Saint Isidore's image was illuminated by the first rays of direct sunlight. A procession immediately formed around the image, and the saint was carried on the platform at the head of the crowd across all of the Las Joyas fields, down the trail to the beginning of the Quemado valley and through each of the valley fields. Upon reaching the plaza the image was returned to its place in the chapel, and the populace dispersed. Most would reassemble at nightfall for an all-night dance.

The wake thus unified the villagers through their faith in God, their respect for Saint Isidore, and their desire to obtain an abundant harvest. Manuel [a village elder] notes that Saint Isidore responded quickly to the villagers' petitions, since "if the rain didn't come that day, [it came] the next day." An additional sign of faith was provided by the farmers' willingness to allow the procession to trample the young plants, believing God would renew them.

—Charles L. Briggs, "A Conversation with Saint Isidore:
The Teachings of the Elders," 1983.[61]

"Procession of Spanish-American Catholics in honor of a saint." FSA photo by Russell Lee, Peñasco, July 1940. (LC-USF 33-12802-M4.)

San Juan Day in Taos County . . .

The women of the village [of Arroyo Hondo] were up early on the twenty-fourth of June. At six o'clock they were bathing in the river or in the *acequias*. Later in the morning the small children were seen also in the river and ditches, splashing cold water at each other, for on this day the waters in the streams were believed to be holy. Better health awaited those who rose early to bathe at least their faces and feet in the holy water. For was it not St. John who baptized Jesus in the river Jordan and blessed the waters?

—Cleofas M. Jaramillo, *Shadows of the Past*, 1941.[62]

Rooster Races in Mora . . .

The rooster race is perhaps the most picturesque survival of fiesta folk customs and it is still engaged in with the same gusto as of old . . . as [in] the following description of a *corrida* held at a village fiesta in Mora, Mora County. . . .

Riders in the races may come from several villages in cavalcades. They place themselves seventy-five yards or so on either side of the chicken. The signal is given, *"al gallo!"* From one group or both springs a galloping pony. Straight for the buried rooster he runs. As he nears the buried *gallo*, the rider leans lower, then sweeps past the rooster with one swift grab. If he misses, the next rider is signalled, and so on until some one succeeds in yanking the *gallo* from his living grave. If excitement is high the run is made *en masse* by half a dozen riders from both sides. The successful *gallero* swings the bird in the air and shouts his challenge, then the fun begins. The *gallero* flees and the other rivals swoop after him. His own *compañeros* swing into action and "run interference." They charge into the path of their rivals.

Chicken pull, Agua Fria, ca. 1920.
Photo by T. Harmon Parkhurst.
(MNM Neg. No. 57659.)

Chicken pull, Agua Fria.
(MNM Neg. No. 50679.)

Sometimes the victor gallops home with the bird; other times the battle rages until all that is left is scattered feathers. Getting away with the rooster is not the principal aim. The rider must stop, circle and taunt his enemies, even if to do so he has to pass the *gallo* to a friend. If after all this anything is left of the poor bird, it is passed to the women to be cooked for supper. The *corrida* goes on while there is some one to furnish a fowl. As many as two dozen may be pulled in a day.

—NMFWP files, 1930s.[63]

The chicken, an Old World bird, was brought from Spain to Mexico, and eventually to the upper Rio Grande Valley. With it came the *corrida de gallo*. Soon the Pueblo Indians adopted the rooster pull. And, as a matter of fact, they are the only ones who still occasionally do it, the custom having died out in Hispanic communities during the 1940s.

The entire affair can be fairly dangerous. . . . In a number of places, the *corrida de gallo* was abandoned after someone was killed.

That happened at the village of Manzano, east of Albuquerque, in 1898. A teenager, Antonio Sanchez, fell from his horse and died. I saw a serious accident during a pull at Cochiti Indian Pueblo in the 1950s. There, a young man caught a hoof in the face as he tumbled from the saddle. . . .

In most cases, the rooster pull was conducted on the feast day of San Juan. . . . In part, the rooster pull was regarded as a manly art . . . in which youths showed off their riding skill in front of the ladies. But it also had a deeper, almost unconscious, religious meaning dating back to the pre-Christian pagan rites of Europe.

In ancient Spanish symbolism, drops of blood were closely identified with drops of water. . . . The shedding of blood, as in the rooster pull, helped bring rain because the spattering of red drops was powerful magic.

Nor is it a coincidence that the *corrida de gallo* was scheduled for the feast of St. John the Baptist . . . [who] is closely identified with water. . . . Also, like the rooster, he lost his head. . . .

St. John's feast day falls on June 24, which in New Mexico is just about the beginning of the rainy season. Those rains in colonial days were essential to replenish the irrigation waters that started to grow short after the spring run off of snow melt. So the rooster pull, closely tied to the bringing of rain, may have been more a "religious event" than a sport.

The Pueblo Indians had something of the same notion. A resident of Acoma told an anthropologist that "rooster blood is good for rain." And at Santo Domingo Pueblo a religious leader said of the *corrida de gallo:* "When the horses and men get sweaty, that is a prayer to God and the King for rain."

To the Indian mind, the beads of sweat represented raindrops and white, foamy lather on the animals symbolized clouds. Similarly, the splashing of rooster blood during the pull has the magical power to bring rain.

. . . This age-old custom has disappeared in most parts of New Mexico. The danger associated with it as well as the declining number of horses available to villagers provide a partial explanation.

But the late Arthur L. Campa of the University of Denver also cited another reason. He claimed the Society for Prevention of Cruelty to Animals waged a campaign against rooster pulls. As a result, the few that remain are performed quietly, without fanfare.

—Marc Simmons, "Pity the Poor Rooster," 1983.[64]

"Dia de San Geronimo," a foursome of words that up to the year nineteen hundred always awoke pleasant memories and brought joyous anticipation to the hearts of both young and old, of a most enjoyable time always to be had at the Indian pueblo of Taos and La Plaza de Don Fernando on September thirtieth. San Geronimo Day was the most famous celebration, at that time, in northern New Mexico. Not even the old capital of the territory, Santa Fe, had anything to equal it for romantic lure, in those years; so the Indian feast day of the Taos Indian pueblo and its companion festivities at the village of Taos became famous throughout a wide area of New Mexico and Colorado. There were no automobiles or first-class highways in this section of the country then, to provide rapid and easy travel to the celebration, as now, and few easterners attended; but hardly a native missed attending. Romance and Taos were synonymous words and many a young man from distant parts made the journey to Taos, each year, to meet the damsels of the Taos Valley—and the young women of Taos were famous, far and wide, for their beauty.

Long before the date of the feast, preparation of new dresses and hats, or the altering of old ones, were in progress at almost every home within a distance of fifty miles from Taos (in those days dresses and women's hats were made to serve for years, by making a few alterations in them every now and then), and when the day arrived the display of colors in wearing apparel was truly dazzling. Bright red, pink, purple and similar shades, including white, were the predominant colors.

The Apaches, from their reservation to the west, on their customary annual visit, on this date, to the Taos Indians, were the first arrivals at the pueblo, several days before the feast day. Scores of them, in groups, on their pinto ponies, crossed the Rio Grande by way of Wamsley's toll road. Big, husky fellows were most of them, who had already discarded the Indian garb for the . . . apparel of the white man, yet wore high-peak hats (these probably imported from Old Mexico), fancy beaded chamois or calf-skin vests, brightly colored shirts, and their tightly braided hair hanging down in front in two thick strands, one on each side and bound by bands of varicolored beads. People from the farther villages started the journey two and three days before the feast day, stopping enroute at night at the houses of relatives.

The early hours of September thirtieth found the roads that led to Taos, from the north and from the south, outlined by thick clouds of dust, for at least ten miles in each direction, as the long strings of wagons, buggies, and people on horse-back made their way in the direction of the pueblo. Every now and then some spirited team of horses, frightened, got out of control of the driver and raced out, away from the road, over the sage brush of the prairie, furnishing moments of excitement on the way. Those on the buggies considered it smart to race past the slower-moving wagons, every now and then; and those on horseback (they were mostly young men) zig-zagged across the road, from side to side, on their especially well-groomed horses, as if showing off their mounts and in coquetry with the girls in the wagons and buggies.

Nine o'clock that morning found the pueblo a dense mass of people. Wagons and buggies lined thickly the whole length of the east side. People climbed and stood upon the receding terraces of the north pyramid of the pueblo, which lies at the west end of the race track. Several Indians, in their gaily colored blankets,

"Resting in the shade on the fiesta day." FSA photo by Russell Lee, Taos, July 1940. (LC-USF 33-12847-M4.)

"Old merry-go-round during the fiesta. This is reputed to be the oldest merry-go-round in America." Known as Tio Vivo, it was discovered at the Peñasco home of "El Doctorcito Martinez" and purchased by the Lions Club in 1937. It appeared in the 1947 movie "Ride the Pink Horse," based on a mystery story by Santa Fe writer Dorothy B. Hughes. An electric motor was installed in 1954. FSA photo by Russell Lee, Taos, July 1940. (LC-USF 33-12869-M2.)

intermingled with them, making of the whole an interesting, multi-colored spectacle in the bright sunlight. Presently the runners were seen emerging from their respective kivas, on each side of the river, their coppery-red color of their skin showing through the white paint smeared over their bodies. The peculiar shout of the Indians went up all around, as the runners took their places, one half of their number at each end of the race course, each group divided into an equal number of contending opponents. (The race track runs east and west and is about two hundred yards in length.) Augmented shouting indicated that the famous relay-race, that yearly decides the election of the governor and his council, had started, as the first pair of runners raced down the track. Back and forth the racers speeded. Within a few minutes the advantage of one or the other side became apparent, as the distance between the runners increased, although this advantage was sometimes recovered by an extra fleet racer of the other side. The coaches, on both sides of the track, by words and gentle strokes with their aspen branches to the backs of the runners, exhorted them to a faster pace. . . .

The sound of the tom tom and chanting and dancing marked the conclusion of the race and the spectators made ready to make their way to the village of Don Fernando. In the few minutes following, the two roads that led from the pueblo to the village of Taos were marked by clouds of dust as every one scurried along towards the old village.

At the pueblo, even before the races were over, several boys and young men had already been busy, selling tickets among the throngs of people, on commission for a ride on "Los Caballitos" (Spanish—little horses), the merry-go-round, which made the main attraction during the day in the old plaza. The arrivals at the plaza were greeted by the music of the cornet band-box of the merry-go-round, as it revolved with the circular platform and the merry riders that rode the wooden horses and the seats. The merry-go-round was put up on some vacant lot in the vicinity of the park. Ten cents each, three for a quarter, was the price for adults, and five cents each, or six for a quarter, the children's fare. . . .

The San Geronimo dances at Taos hall and at the old court house concluded the San Geronimo celebrations. At the Taos hall the elite of Society of the region attended; those in the lower category, at the court house. This was the one occasion of the year for an extra-special display of finery in dress and jewelry, also for the time of their lives for the young people that had come from afar. Taos hall was especially famous all over New Mexico and southern Colorado.

—Reyes N. Martínez, "San Geronimo
Celebrations during the Nineties," 1937.[65]

Folk Dramas

Itinerant Entertainers . . .

As late as World War I it was customary for troupes of *maromeros,* trapeze artists, actors, singers, troubadours, and clowns to come up the old Camino Real, stopping at every village along the way to perform. During viceregal days these performances were known as *volantines,* but soon thereafter they became known as *maroma,* and under this name they came into the Southwest. In addition to trapeze artists and clowns, companies of comedians traveled as part of itinerant troupes. Many of the plays presented by these traveling companies have found their way into the repertoire of the folk and circulated for decades as folk plays, because people were more interested in the play than in preservation of the author's name. Singers composed and sang their own songs or those popular in their day. Many of the folk songs of the Southwest arrived from the south by way of these itinerant artists. They sold their wares in broadsides, which the folk learned by heart and incorporated into their own traditional repertoire.

Because very little coin circulated in the Southwest, traveling troupes had to resort to barter by charging admissions in kind: a chicken, a dozen eggs, wine, cheese, or whatever else was available. The artists used these supplies for their own consumption, and the populace, short of money, was happy to be entertained in exchange for produce.

—Arthur L. Campa, *Hispanic Culture in the Southwest,* 1979.[66]

Puppet Shows in Arroyo Hondo . . .

Although there were numerous feast days and games that served to break the monotony of the humdrum, everyday life of the residents of the villages of this section, there was no occasion that furnished them more pleasure and entertainment than "Los Titeres" (puppet show), those little marionettes that were so skillfully handled by their manager as to make them look and act like real living manikins.

The arrival of the "Tirititero," or manager of the puppet show at a small village was usually cause for much excitement. The news of his arrival soon spread

"Spanish–American clowns at a travelling show." FSA photo by Russell Lee, Peñasco, July 1940. (LC-USF 34-37099.)

all over the village. He usually came in the afternoon. Hurried preparations of the evening meal were soon in progress in every home, so as not to be late for the show. People, in those days, as for any other celebration, put on their best clothes. The show-man usually rented the most spacious hall in the village. . . . The halls, in those days, had no regular seats, and the husbands and the older boys of the family had to carry chairs from their homes to the hall, on which to sit during the show. The chairs were arranged about three sides of the hall, the other side was occupied by the impromptu stage put up by the showman. The usual admission fee was twenty-five cents for adults and ten cents for children.

Early in the evening most of the residents of the village had arrived at the hall. . . . At about seven o'clock the curtain would rise for the first act. . . . The stage . . . consisted of screens about six feet in height. Several oil lamps, placed on the floor, at the sides, furnished good illumination for the stage. . . .

The first act was a speech of welcome to the audience, by one of the marionettes. The manager stood behind the screen, back of the stage, from which position he manipulated the strings, uttered the words, etc., for the diminutive actors. For talking and singing for the marionettes, he used a whistle made of two narrow pieces of wood, about one inch in length, each piece concaved on one side, both joined together with the concave sides facing each other and a piece of rubber between them. He held the whistle between his teeth and let the sound of his voice pass through it, forming the words in the usual way, with his tongue and lips. It was marvelous, the way he handled the marionettes by the strings that led from his fingers and thumbs to each of them . . . a feat that only a past master of the art could perform, and even he required constant practice to do so. Such a feat as the throwing of a rubber ball by one marionette and the catching of it in mid-air by another one, and others similarly difficult, were among those in the regular run of the show.
—Reyes N. Martínez, on Arroyo Hondo, 1937.[67]

A Puppet Show in San José . . .

Eighty-year-old Samuel Lucero of San José on the Pecos saw his last performance of *los titeres* in 1910. He vividly remembers the colorful figures stepping onto the stage, each one introducing himself to the audience. They wore a variety of dress, representing different occupations and social classes. A number of the puppets sported large sombreros and carried machetes in the Mexican style. Samuel recalls his favorite part of the production. A baker died and the other puppets conducted a funeral. Lined up for a procession to the graveyard, they played reed flutes, called *pitos,* the same instrument used by the religious sect of Penitentes. The success of this little drama brought cheers from the floor.
—Marc Simmons, "The Southwest's Traveling Puppet Shows," 1978.[68]

Religious Folk Drama

Folk Dramas at Fiestas . . .

Formerly each *placita* had its own troupe of entertainers and *danzantes* who performed *autos* (plays) and gave *danzas* (dances) during church fiestas. Parts were usually handed down from father to son. The whole village attended the rehearsals, hence the performance became a community enterprise. The night of the play, should an actor develop stage fright, the audience took on the role of prompter. Village women made the costumes, gathered the properties, decorated the hall, or church, as the case might be. No fee of admission was charged for the performance and the only remuneration received by the director and actors was the silver offering taken up the night of the play. Of course expenses were reduced to a minimum, the community sharing in the cost of production. The owner of the hall made no charge; the kerosene lamps and chairs were loaned by the neighbors; in winter each family contributed a few sticks of wood for the rehearsals and again for the play. Each actor furnished his own costume.

Plays were nearly always given during the Christmas season, and in the villages where there was no resident priest, the performance took on the importance of the corresponding church service.

—NMFWP writers, 1930s.[69]

Adán y Eva, or Adam and Eve

"Adam and Eve" is still presented in a quiet, golden-walled placita not far from Albuquerque to the delight of the numerous family of Candelarias who make up the entire citizenry of that village. Children are chosen from birth for the roles of Adam and Eve and play them until they marry. The Garden of Eden is a simple stage with the apple and fig trees resembling small, tapering piñones. The serpent tempts Eve, and she munches the apple con tanto gusto that Adam snatches the forbidden fruit away from her after the first juicy bite. Then God appears and scolds them in a terrible booming voice. He shames them for their nakedness, though Adam and Eve appear to be fully clothed in overalls and a cotton dress. A little boy hangs two aprons on the piñon branches and the first Man and Woman shamefacedly pick the aprons off the "fig tree" and tie them around their waists.

—Ruth Laughlin, Caballeros, 1931.[70]

Las Posadas, or The Inns:

The Christmas season in the Hispanic Southwest was never a one-day affair, either socially or religiously. It began on December 15 and continued through the Epiphany, January 6. An important folk presentation of the season was Las Posadas (The Inns), which tells the story of Mary and Joseph and their unsuccessful effort to find lodging at one of the inns of Bethlehem. Las Posadas was more like a miracle play than a mystery play, because emphasis was placed on the devil's design to turn Joseph and Mary away from the inns.

Originally Las Posadas was presented on nine evenings, culminating on Christmas Eve. Gradually, the custom was modified, and the play was presented on any evening before Christmas. In California, where the December weather is benign, they celebrated on all nine evenings, but in the mountain villages of New Mexico the participants compromised by holding the Posadas celebration on Christmas Eve, stopping at nine different homes on the way to the manger.

—Arthur L. Campa, Hispanic Culture in the Southwest, 1979.[71]

Los Pastores, or The Shepherds:

The *pastores* play constitutes the core of the New Mexican Spanish folk theater. It is, furthermore, the only play that is common to the entire American Southwest from California to the lower Texas-Mexican border and from the border to Spanish-speaking pockets scattered over the mid-Rocky Mountain area. Outside of New Mexico, instances of the performance of other plays in the Southwest are rare. . . . Only New Mexico . . . can claim so rich a repertoire . . . , and no other sharply defined area north of the border can boast of so heavy a concentration of manuscripts of plays among the folk. . . . The majority of New Mexican plays can be dated and identified with far more accuracy and ease than we have been given to believe. That the dating and identification of the *pastores* play becomes, by contrast, a more complicated matter is evident from statistics alone. I personally have examined some sixty-three New Mexican manuscripts of the play in the possession of the folk and know of the existence of some fifty-six others. . . . Against this total of approximately one hundred nineteen copies, I have seen, or know of, only some thirty-odd manuscripts of all the other religious pieces exclusive of the Guadalupe play, *La Pasión,* and the two dance dramas [Matachines, "Moors and Christians"].

—John E. Englekirk, "The Source and Dating
of New Mexican Spanish Folk Plays," 1957.[72]

In the first *coloquio* of the *Coloquios de los Pastores* (there are two), besides the Angel and Lucifer, the persons in the play are the shepherds Teután, Tubero, Rotín, Tubal, Aquías, Cerecías, Heras, Afrón, Martín and Martiniaco. Celestial voices sing the song, *Cuando por el Oriente;* the Hidden Voice tells of the birth and extends an invitation to all to journey thither. The Angel appears and says that his mission is to advise the shepherds. He proceeds to do so, whereupon the shepherd Teután hears the celestial voice and decides to follow its bidding, after advising the other shepherds. A colloquy ensues among them, then they sing the beloved lullaby which begins, *"O duérmete Niño lindo."* They arrive at the portal and there render homage, each one presenting his humble offering. The Devil appears, wondering if the day of the birth has arrived. The Angel comes to him and tells him that this is indeed so—and the first *coloquio* ends.

In the second of the *Coloquios de los Pastores,* the shepherds change names. Now they are Bato, Tebano, Lépido, Gil, Lipio, Tubal, Bacirio, Cojo and Bartolo. Gila is a shepherdess. The Angel and Lucifer continue to be the central characters and a Hermit puts in his appearance. Celestial voices sing a song. The shepherds then sing one of their marching songs, going back and forth to indicate the passing of time. A colloquy ensues whereupon they decide to stop and rest. Again they take up the journeying, singing the second of the marching songs. They stop to sup and engage in a second colloquy, then retire for the night. The Hermit tries to tell his beads but can hardly keep awake. Lucifer appears on the scene and delivers one of his long-winded speeches. He approaches the Hermit and suggests that he take himself off, carrying the girl Gila. The Hermit consents and is about to carry out the diabolical plan when the girl awakens the shepherds with her screams. A

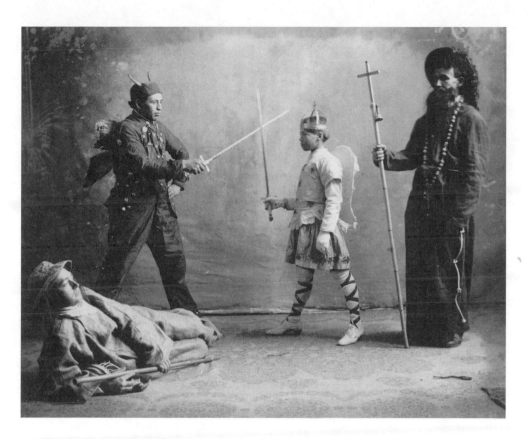

Los Pastores, ca. 1915. L. to r.: Abran Sena, Felipe Perea, Perfecto Baca, Frank Montoya. Photo by Aaron B. Craycraft. (MNM Neg. No. 13695.)

beating is administered to the old man for his attempted foolishness. Celestial music is heard. Tubal, who had been on vigil, appears and tells of his encounter with the Angel. The Hermit quotes from the scriptures in order to convince the confused shepherds. The Devil reappears, ranting and panting, wary as the end of his earthly kingdom seems about to be at hand. The Angel comes forth; a duel ensues in which Lucifer is vanquished. The shepherds prepare for their journey; each makes mention of the gift he will give the Child. The Devil appears, to make one last sally before his final disappearance, when the Hermit thrusts him into the mouth of Hell. The shepherds resume their journeyings. They arrive at the Portal where they render homage and adoration to the New-born One. They sing to express their joy and finally depart, singing the last of the marching songs.

—Aurora Lucero-White Lea, *Literary Folklore of the Hispanic Southwest,* 1953.[73]

Los Reyes Magos, or The Wise Kings:

Spanish Christmas is celebrated on the sixth of January. Instead of Santa Claus, the wisemen, the Magi mounted on camels ride past the balconies. This event is celebrated by *Los Reyes Magos,* a much shorter play than most of the others. The three kings guided by the traditional star are on their way to the manger of Bethlehem. They stop at the court of King Herod who receives them very cordially and asks them to stop on their return in order that he too may know where the Messiah has been born. The Magi kings fearing that Herod will harm the babe, return by a different route, whereupon Herod orders the slaughter of the innocents in hopes that he will find Christ. This scene is particularly realistic and a bit gruesome. Herod has his own child killed as an example to the soldiers. The last scene enacts the flight to Egypt and Herod's deception by a group of rustics.

–Arthur L. Campa, *Spanish Religious
Folktheatre in the Southwest,* 1934.[74]

On July 17, 1941, on the occasion of the Fiesta de Taos, the seventeenth-century mystery play of *Los Tres Reyes* was presented at Taos, New Mexico. The play was directed by Judge Samuel Martínez y Labadie, who—carrying on in the footsteps of his father, the Grand Old Man of the Spanish religious folk theatre—had committed the whole to memory and was capable of playing any of the roles with pantomime and gestures. At this particular presentation, other players also were descendants of persons who had inherited their roles traditionally, and who not only knew their own lines but the whole play from memory.

On this occasion the play was presented on a raised platform in the plaza. Multitudes of persons—men, women and children—stood entranced below, during this July evening, as they watched Judge Labadie with his manuscript, moving about the stage, directing, prompting, even acting when things did not go to his liking.

—Aurora Lucero-White Lea, *Literary Folklore
of the Hispanic Southwest,* 1953.[75]

El Niño Perdido, or The Lost Child:

In February, early in Lent of 1933, it was produced in a suburb of Taos about a mile from the plaza. The stage was a large vacant corner lot, dozens of pine trees about six feet high having been set up in rows across the lot to represent a forest. At one end of this long narrow lot was hung a white sheet for a back, or side, drop, and the actors went behind this when they left the stage. The top of a barn covered with hay in an adjoining lot was the gallery where a large part of the audience sat, and along the side of the barn two immense logs were the reserved seats. Opposite this barn were parked cars on the running boards of which people sat, some standing on the fence to get a better view.

At about two o'clock the official prompter came from behind the curtain and announced the play with a summary of the story—that of the Child Jesus when he was twelve years old having been lost for three days and finally found in the temple talking with the "Doctors." Then from behind the curtain came the sound of the Penitente flute, and a chorus of men's voices in the first *letra*. At every change of scene throughout the play a *letra* was sung by the chorus, accompanied by the flute. The wandering of Mary and Joseph through the forest searching for the Child filled up most of the first act, but the Rich Man and his conversations with his clownish servant gave the necessary touch of comedy. The Rich Man was seated at a small table near the curtain at one end of the "stage" and at the other end sat the six Doctors around a larger table, all dressed in black cassocks such as are worn by choristers. In the middle of the stage sat three men in black dresses and long black veils who comforted Mary and Joseph, and later on the Child in their sad wanderings. After the feasts by the Rich Man on much wine (pink soda-pop) and after the lamentations of Mary and Joseph, came an intermission, when the chorus sang a long "Miserere," accompanied by the flute. This was undoubtedly one of the Penitente songs to be heard during Lent.

In the second act, after a short *letra* by the chorus, the Child appeared wandering through the forest, telling of the agonies to come and of the cruel punishments predicted for him. The part was enacted by a small boy not over twelve years old, who had a lovely face and wore a long black wig. He had a remarkable memory, his lines filling several pages of the manuscript, which we followed closely. The prompter repeated or sang the lines along with all the actors, seemingly not disconcerting them in the least. The Angel appeared at the end, over the top of the curtain, where he sat perched on a ladder, apparently. He was dressed in a white lace dress, with crown and wings. Mary was dressed in a light blue evening dress in the latest style, with high-heeled slippers and a long blue veil. She did not look cold, but the Child's teeth chattered so that they had to put a coat over his white robes. The childlike sincerity of the people was evident in every line they spoke and listened to, and the action was at all times dignified and in keeping with the religious character of the play.

—Mary R. Van Stone and E. R. Sims, "Canto del Niño Perdido," 1933.[76]

Las cuatro apariciones de la Virgen de Guadalupe, or The Four Apparitions of the Virgin of Guadalupe:

According to the legend upon which the play is founded, the Virgin first appeared as an apparition to the Indian, Juan Diego, on December 9, 1531. There were four such apparitions on each of four succeeding days—the last having occurred on December 12, when the diocesan Archbishop became convinced that a miracle had been effected. On this date, an impression of the Virgin, that had appeared on the Indian's blanket, was put into a frame and was placed on the main altar in the Cathedral in Mexico. On February 7, 1532—a few weeks later—the picture then was removed to the Sanctuary of Guadalupe, ordered built by the apparition, where it has remained to this day.

—Aurora Lucero-White Lea, *Literary Folklore of the Hispanic Southwest*, 1953.[77]

Historical Folk Drama

Los Moros y los Cristianos, or The Moors and the Christians:

After the Spanish colonists' arrival at the Tewa Pueblo they named "San Juan de los Caballeros," the settlers under Don Juan de Oñate encountered internal dissension. In his 1610 epic, Gaspar Pérez de Villagrá notes that: "a mutiny occurred among some of our soldiers, among whom was [Captain Pablo de] Aguilar [Hinojosa]. The general wished to punish the evildoers severely, as an example, but so many persons begged him, even with tears, that he show mercy toward them; consequently he pardoned them all. In honor of this event a week of celebration and festivities was ordered. There were tilting matches, bullfights, and a comedy which was especially composed for the occasion, together with many Moorish and Christian games."[78]

According to Aurora Lucero-White Lea:

> Until recently, the play has been reënacted in New Mexico at the village of Santa Cruz de la Cañada, twelve miles from the original camp site of Oñate.... A cavalcade of men wearing red bands on their hats represents the Moors; a cavalcade wearing white, the Christians. The spectacle is performed in the village *plaza* or square. Here, mounted on New Mexico ponies, the Moors clash swords with the Christians; the Christians, with the Moors. A dialogue goes on between the two and, if one understands Spanish, it is possible to follow the lines. There are no props of any kind, other than a wooden cross set in the center of the square. Nothing out of the ordinary happens, and the piece ends almost as unostentatiously as it began.[79]

> At the Alcalde performance there was no costuming except the use of white sashes and bandas and banners for the Christians, and crimson for the Moors, though it is known that there are still preserved in ancient chests many handsome relics of the colonial period. There were swords, however, ancient Spanish blades, slender buffalo stickers, rusty cavalry sabers of the period of the American occupation and beautiful, free sword-swinging gestures. . . .

> The stage setting was of the simplest; a white covered altar topped with a white cross for the camp of the Christians, set in the open plaza, and a smaller rosy cross for the Moors to steal and race away with to their own camp under a cottonwood tree. During the play the prompter leaned against the altar and not infrequently lost his place in the excitement of the action, thus holding up the play, as unselfconsciously as the property man in a Chinese theater. The audience was about equally divided between black-shawled and wide-hatted descendants of the Spanish colonial families and modern American spectators. The note of formality was given—for this was on the thirtieth of May—by the truck load of the local members of the American Legion, with *their* banners over them. Half a dozen guitars and violins made a strange half-Spanish, half-jazz accompaniment. Over all was the wide New Mexican day.

> It is necessary to witness one of these naive folk plays to realize their charm. . . . You may not care for what the Cross symbolizes; you may think war too awful for this mimic play; you may be quite indifferent to the conversion of the Moors. But if you happen to stray into the plaza of one of these little Rio Arriba towns when they are playing "The Moors," you will not leave it until the last Christian has led captive the last infidel, and the audience, with a long sigh of satisfaction, follows after.

> —Mary Austin, "A Drama Played on Horseback," 1928.[80]

Los Comanches, or The Comanches; and Los Tejanos, or The Texans:

According to Aurelio M. Espinosa and J. Manuel Espinosa: "There also exist in New Mexico, as in other parts of the Western Hemisphere where Spanish is spoken, historical Spanish folk plays of American origin and setting. Thus far [1943], the manuscripts of two such plays have been found in New Mexico: *Los Comanches,* a play composed in the latter part of the eighteenth century, depicting a decisive New

Mexican Spanish victory of the warlike Comanche Indians, and *Los Tejanos* (The Texans), a folk play of the middle of the last century describing the 'capture' of the Texan expedition to New Mexico of 1841 by General Manuel Armijo's men."[81]

> *Los Comanches* as put on in El Rancho under the direction of Sr. Martín Roybal is a play full of action, interesting and diverting. This play of all the many plays produced by troupes of players among the early Spanish settlers is one of the few which does not treat of a moral or religious theme. It treats of an encounter between a band of Comanche Indians under the command of their chief, Cuerno Verde ("Green Horn"), and a troop of Spaniards commanded by their captain Don Carlos Fernández. These two with Barriga Dulce, the comedian of the piece, are the principal characters of the play.
>
> As staged in El Rancho, December 28, 1938, the two forces mounted on the pick of the saddle horses of the valley, meet on the sandy bottom of an arroyo close by the village church. The sloping banks of the arroyo make ideal vantage points from which the spectators can enjoy and follow the action of the play.
>
> Previous to the enactment of the play, mass is said in the church, for this day is also the feast day of the patron saint of the village, San Antonio de Padua. While the devout villagers, with not a few Indians from the nearby pueblo of San Ildefonso, are listening to the service of the mass and the sermon which follows, the jingling of sleigh bells is heard through the open church door. Many knowing smiles are exchanged by those who are aware of the scene taking place outside of the church, for the actors who take the part of Comanches do not attend mass but are quite busy in the pursuit of a custom in which tradition grants them full liberty and protection. In their fringed buckskin garb, beaded vests, and plumed bonnets, they are busily engaged in pilfering articles of various kinds from the automobiles, buggies, and wagons which are parked here and there near the church. Individuals are not exempt, and every now and then a victim is surrounded by three or four of the Comanches or perhaps by all the band; they perform a brief dance of exultation around him, for he is now their captive and must pay a ransom in order to be set at liberty. The usual ransom is delivered to the captors in the nearby *cantina* and is usually a quart of wine.
>
> In like manner the owners of the different articles pilfered from car, wagon, or buggy must redeem them when mass is over. This is the only source of revenue for the players who take part in the play. The most welcome form of payment is a quart of wine, but the victim may pay off with money, and many a quarter, dime, and nickel are collected and turned over to *el director* to be divided later.
>
> —Described by Lorin W. Brown, 1939.[82]

Los Comanches, unlike the religious plays, was staged in the open spaces, where a battle on horseback could be enacted, and the plains of Galisteo and the high mesas around Taos were favorite sites where both audiences and participants could enjoy the drama. Real Indians often took the parts of the Comanche braves, and as the battle that is the climax of the play opened, both sides became caught up in the action. When the summer tourists visiting Taos in 1929 witnessed the drama on the mesa between Taos village and Ranchos de Taos to the south, hundreds of warriors and soldiers took part on both sides. They presented such a realistic scene, to the accompaniment of rifle shots and arrows, that the visitors took cover, thinking that real warfare had broken out.

—Arthur L. Campa, *Hispanic Culture in the Southwest,* 1979.[83]

Invented Festivals

By the turn of the century and during the period immediately following statehood in 1912, in attempting to establish an official "lore" and "life" that would foster political and economic growth, New Mexicans began to assess the state's peoples, their past, and their traditional forms of community and folklore. They sought to devise new "old" traditions, which would include the whole of the fledgling state and its "tri-cultural" citizens. Invented festivals figured prominently in this campaign.

British historian Eric Hobsbawm defines "invented tradition" as "a set of practices, normally governed by overtly or tacitly accepted rules and of a ritual or symbolic nature, which seek to inculcate certain values and norms of behaviour by repetition, which automatically implies continuity with the past. In fact, where possible, they normally attempt to establish continuity with a suitable historic past." According to Hobsbawm, "Inventing traditions . . . is essentially a process of formalization and ritualization, characterized by reference to the past, if only by imposing repetition."[84] In this way twentieth-century Old Timers Day organizers in Deming, Roswell, Clovis, and elsewhere decree their town's identity by deciding who is to be considered a pioneer and how their "old" way of life is to be celebrated. Santa Feans proclaim a municipal ethos by increasingly coming to focus on De Vargas's 1692 Entrada in the revived Santa Fe Fiesta after 1919. Trader Mike Kirk and other Gallup businessmen create an "Indian" spiritual and aesthetic inheritance for the Inter-Tribal Indian Ceremonial they started in 1922. Two commissions, one headed by the University of New Mexico president, Dr. James F. Zimmerman, the other by U.S. Vice-President James N. Garner, establish a statewide celebration marking the four-hundredth anniversary of Coronado's 1540 expedition.

Old Timers Days

In Deming . . .

Deming's Old Timer's Day has for many years been celebrated and many visitors, and native sons of Deming, from all parts of the Southwest have gathered here to meet old friends.

Julius Rosch arrived in Deming March 13, 1883. Thirty years later his wife conceived the idea of an anniversary party commemorating the occasion and a number of old timers gathered at the Rosch home on the evening of March 7, 1913, to help celebrate the anniversary of Mr. Rosch's choice of a home. The evening of reminiscence proved so enjoyable that it was there decided to establish the custom of meeting once a year to hob-nob on events past, present and future; and the Old Timer's association was formed with Joseph P. McGrorty as president

William Kit Carson (1857–1957), nephew of Kit Carson, leading a Roswell parade as the oldest citizen, ca. 1955. Photo by Ken Cobean. (MNM Neg. No. 135152.)

and Edward Pennington as secretary, a position which he held until his death on March 30, 1930.

As the years have gone by, the attendance at these reunions has increased until, coming from all over the state, there are gathered seldom less than 150 old timers and their guests. A picnic at Palomas, Chihuahua, Mexico, 35 miles south of Deming was one of the features of Old Timer's Day that was especially popular during those years of "Prohibition."

The celebration was usually held in March or April, but this year the annual Old Timers Reunion and dedication of Deming's new underpass will be celebrated jointly in Deming July 17 with an all-day fiesta. Old timers from West Texas, New Mexico and Arizona are invited to attend. Prizes will be given to the oldest couple living in New Mexico the greatest number of years, to the oldest couple

Old Timers picnic, Roswell, ca.
1950. Three men seated (r. to l.)
are identified as former governors
George Curry and James F.
Hinkle and peace officer Dee
Harkey. Photo by Redmon.
(MNM Neg. No. 111674.)

traveling the greatest distance to the celebration, and to the couple driving the
oldest car the most miles to be present at the festivities.
          —Robert Athon of Deming, to Betty Reich, 1937.[85]

In Roswell . . .

Inaugurated in 1924 as an honor to Roswell Old Timers—a third day feature of the
Chaves County Cotton Carnival, this annual reunion and celebration has grown to
be a state wide home coming day, for the pioneers and builders of southeast New
Mexico. Those who have lived in this district thirty years or longer, came from all
parts of New Mexico and some from distant states for this year's [1936] reunion.
          Elizabeth Garrett introduced by Cecil Bonney (Master of Ceremonies) at 9
A.M. opened the day's program at Main and Third Streets by singing the state
song—"Oh Fair New Mexico" [1915]. This is one of Miss Garrett's own compo-
sitions on the Sunshine State, where she is known and loved as a composer and
musician of unusual talent who all her life has lived in New Mexico.

Mrs. Pat Garrett, mother of Elizabeth Garrett, shared honors of the day with her daughter. Mrs. Garrett is the widow of the Roswell pioneer sheriff, Pat Garrett, who helped make the Pecos Valley a peaceful and safe place to live. . . .

The parade started after the opening program at 10 A.M. was led by J. F. Hinkle, president of the Old Timers' Association, followed by all the men and women horseback riders who had ridden over the old trails fifty years or longer.

The pioneer women of fifty years' residence in New Mexico rode in the old stage coach, operated in '49 between Roswell, Socorro and Carrizozo.

—Georgia B. Redfield, 1936.[86]

A Chuck Wagon Dinner is served to the [Roswell] old-timers (exclusively) after the parade has disbanded. . . .

For entertainment at the barbecue there are old-fashioned dances, quadrillas and Virginia reels, cowboy and cattle trail songs and speeches by the pioneers. Many of the guests wear old-time costumes—clothes worn by them in the pioneer days. Before dinner is served there is a pleasant hour for greetings of old friends and reminiscences of the early years, when just such round-up dinners as this were given at the Chisum Ranch, when ranchers and cowboys, clad in chaps and sombreros, came from all parts of the country in southeast New Mexico.

At noon the chuck-wagon meal is served from a long table loaded with barbecue meat, frijoles, and "son-of-a-gun" (a special cowboy's favorite dish made of parts of beef not barbecued—the liver, heart, farrigut, sweet-bread, brains, suet and kidney stewed with onion) all of which is served on paper plates to the old-timers who are seated at small tables around the picnic grounds. . . .

The boy and girl scouts of Roswell do the serving and every effort is made to make the day a happy event for the honored guests—the Old-Timers' of Southeast New Mexico.

—Georgia B. Redfield, 1937.[87]

In Clovis . . .

In the early spring months of 1935 the city officers, business men and old timers discussed the celebration of the birthday of Clovis' 28th anniversary which occurs in March. On April 12, 1935, a meeting of officers of the city, members of the chamber of commerce, different clubs of the city and business men, including old timers, of course, was called for 7:30 o'clock at the city hall, when preliminary arrangements were discussed concerning the celebration. . . .

If you were in Curry County before statehood in January 1912, you were a pioneer, it was decided last night at the preliminary meeting at the city hall. It is recognized that the territorial days will admit a great number of people to the pioneer classification, but this number will be reduced each year and the event is being planned as a permanent Clovis celebration. . . .

Two types of pioneers have blazed the way in this country, it was pointed out by an old timer of this region. . . . The first type is that of the man who rode the cowtrails 30, 40 and 50 years ago, whose home was the great open spaces, and whose bed was his saddle and its blanket. His law hung in a loose dangling holster or two and its enforcement was deadly as the unerring aim of the man behind the gun. His shelter was the starlit sky and his domain as limitless as the prairies.

Then there followed the farmer pioneer, the man who saw in the soil the possibility of a livelihood and he turned to the far from romantic task of making it yield that livelihood. His type is brave of heart, sturdy of purpose and stubborn to adversity. His pursuits were arduous and his labor long and difficult. A glowing tribute to the pioneer of this region among the agricultural development of this country.

Then hand in hand with the farmer we have the business man and the town dweller, who by their strength and determination have built a city and all that is implied in its comforts and conveniences. All these were hardy frontiersmen whose place in the sun is gloriously written in the pages of the past. . . .

June 5, 1935: The biggest crowd that ever hit town was here today for Pioneer Day and to help Clovis celebrate the 28th anniversary of the day when the "magic city" changed over night from Riley Switch to a budding metropolis of the plains.

Conservative estimates were that 15,000 people jammed the business districts this morning to witness a parade so long that it ran into itself again when the leaders came back to the starting point. The extravaganza of beautiful floats, cowboys, freaks, stunts and commercial display was two miles long and it would have been twice that long if the entries had been spaced as far apart as in conventional parades.

—Belle Kilgore, of Clovis, 1937.[88]

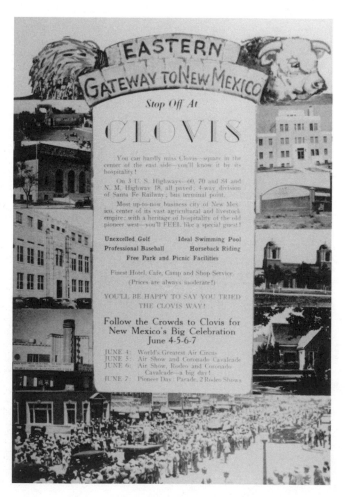

From *Coronado Magazine: The Official Program of the Coronado Cuarto Centennial*, 1940. (Private Collection.)

Santa Clara Pueblo racers in front of Palace of the Governors, Santa Fe Fiesta, 1919. (MNM Neg. No. 52368.)

Santa Fe Fiesta

The "Revived" Fiesta of 1919 . . .

As far back as 1712 the people of La Villa Real de Santa Fe de San Francisco de Assisi, the three hundred and more years old capital of New Mexico, were directed by the Marquis de la Penuela to hold an annual celebration in the month of September to commemorate the Reconquest of the Southwest from the Pueblo Indians by Don Diego de Vargas on September 13, 1692. Annually since then, it is presumed, that the church procession on the Sunday after Corpus Christi Sunday has taken place in memory of the victory that gave New Mexico back to Spain. Periodically too, of late years, there have been secular pageants and fiestas in Santa Fe, notably during the socalled [sic] "Tertio-Millenial" celebration more than 45 years ago [before 1919], and again in 1913 and 1914. Plans for a pageant during 1919 were discussed at length and in detail, but on final analysis it was deemed too great a tax upon the financial resources of the comparatively small business community to stage a pageant worthy of the traditions of the Capital.

It remained for Director Edgar L. Hewett of the School of American Research and of the Museum of New Mexico, to point out Santa Fe's resources and facilities for giving a "Fiesta" at nominal cost and on short notice. A pageant is after all, more or less theatrical and lacks the distinctive qualities which would emphasize Santa Fe's unique place in history or her attractiveness and quaintness from the standpoint of ethnology, folk-lore and scenic setting. In a pageant, a certain select number of actors present scenes from history and folk-lore; in a Fiesta, the entire populace is a part of the celebration, and when a populace is as varied, as picturesque, as that of Santa Fe, that in itself furnishes the substantial basis for a colorful, distinctive and noteworthy event. . . .

De Vargas and Franciscans, Fine Arts Museum at right, Santa Fe Fiesta, 1919. Photo by T. Harmon Parkhurst. (MNM Neg. No. 52375.)

The civic organizations took Dr. Hewett's view, out-lined plans for the three days' "Fiesta," the first day to be given to the Indians or to the days "Before Santa Fe Was," the second day to the Spanish culture transplanted to New Mexico or "Santa Fe Antigua," while the third day was to be given to "Santa Fe Moderna," with a formal welcome to the 17,000 and more men from New Mexico who served in the Great War. . . .

—*El Palacio,* 1919.[89]

A Proclamation of July 7, 1925:

Whereas, At a meeting of the Illustrious Cabildo of Justice and Government, held in the Villa of Santa Fe on the 16th day of September, 1712, it was ordered that in honor of the redemption of this ancient capital from the possession of the Indians, a Fiesta season be established and observed annually for all time to come, said order being in the following language:

"It is our desire that a Fiesta be celebrated forever in honor of the elevation of the Holy Cross, and we obligate in so far as we are able upon all who may succeed to places in said Illustrious Cabildo, the charge of gathering the contributions, also of assigning the sermon to the person who may be fitting, to whom shall be given a gratuity of 25 pesos; that of the balance which may be collected, 30 pesos shall be paid for the vespers, mass and procession—to all of which we, those present, obligate ourselves, and we obligate those who may succeed us, as we also obligate ourselves, to provide the candies that may be necessary, and if perhaps in the course of time, this Villa should have some sources of income, a portion of them shall be designated for said festivity, all of which as already said we swear in due and rightful form."

Therefore, be it Resolved by the Mayor and Council of the City of Santa Fe, successors to the Illustrious Cabildo above mentioned, that the Fiesta above established shall be held from the 2nd to the 8th of August of the year 1925, in and about the ancient plaza of this capital. . . .

Likewise, we obligate ourselves, as did our illustrious predecessors, to attend the exercises of Fiesta week and take part therein as we may be called upon, and this writing and obligation we sign and proclaim on this 7th day of July of the year 1925.

Nathan Jaffa, Mayor.
Attest: Joe T. Conklin, Clerk.[90]

Dr. Edgar Lee Hewett's Announcement for the 1925 Fiesta . . .

THE FIESTA OF SANTA FE
THE EPIC OF THE SOUTHWEST

Inaugurated Two Hundred Thirteen Years Ago

August 4th to 8th, Inclusive, 1925

Announcement

The Fiesta Council announces the date of the Fiesta of Santa Fe from the 4th to the 8th of August inclusive. The advance to a month earlier than heretofore is in response to a general demand for a Fiesta week that will not conflict with the opening of the schools and colleges; that will enable the pupils of the State to witness and participate in the educational pageants that portray the history of New Mexico and that will accommodate the great number of vacation visitors that are in the Southwest in midsummer.

The Fiesta is under the auspices of the School of American Research, which aims to make it an exposition of the history and civilization of the Southwest throughout the ages.

THE SOUTHWEST of Two Thousand Years Ago: Land of the Cliff Dwellers and Pueblos.

THE SOUTHWEST of the Conquistadores and Soldiers of the Cross.

THE SOUTHWEST of Today Where the Glories of Old Spain, the Romance of Old Mexico, the Life of Ancient America Survive in the Pageantry, Drama, Music and Art of Old Santa Fe.

In their annual Fiesta, the people of Santa Fe and surrounding country are celebrating a heroic past; are reviving the memory of romantic days, and voicing their love for the land of opportunities. They welcome the participation of all who believe with them that "Tomorrow is the flower of all its Yesterdays."

GENERAL PROGRAM

Tuesday, August 4th. Excursion to the Green Corn Dance at Santo Domingo, Greatest of all Indian Festivals.

Wednesday, August 5th. La Villa Real de Santa Fe de San Francisco: Memorial to the Franciscan Missionaries and Martyrs: Pilgrimages to Historic Monuments.

Thursday, August 6th. The Day of the Conquerors: Cabeza de Vaca, Coronado, De Vargas, Villasur, Kearny. The Southwest in Historic Pageantry.

Friday, August 7th. The day of Spanish Romance: Old Santa Fe in Spanish Drama, Dance and Song.

Saturday, August 8th. Indian Day: Grand Cycle of Dramatic Ceremonies of the Pueblos—The Children of the Sun. (Tan Sando.)

DAILY FEATURES

1. El Pasatiempo: an organization of fun features that has never been equaled.

2. Indian artists who have won distinction throughout the world in song, painting and drama.

3. Spanish dances and songs that bring back Old Spain and Mexico in the days of their glory.

4. The Indian Fair: Showing what the Indian race is doing through the revival of its unique industries and arts to make itself independent and self-reliant.

5. Exhibition of Southwestern Art: the artists of Santa Fe and Taos in a Grand Exhibition which can never be seen elsewhere.

6. The Museum of Southwestern Archaeology, Ethnology and History in the Historic Palace of the Governors.

7. The entire population of Santa Fe in Fiesta attire: Spanish, Moorish, Mexican, Indian.[91]

The first Zozobras . . .

In 1924 artist Will Shuster built a little figure to burn in his backyard during Fiesta. The following year Shuster and E. Dana Johnson, editor of *The Santa Fe New Mexican,* created an eighteen-foot-high paper puppet based on a similar effigy they saw in Mexico and named it Zozobra which they said meant "the gloomy one" in Spanish, which is close to the real meaning: "afflicted" or "anguished." In 1926, they presented Zozobra to the public for the first time, in a program sponsored by the Old Santa Fe Association called *El Pasatiempo.* That initial public burning behind the old courthouse on Washington Avenue began a Fiesta tradition Santa Fe could hardly do without now.

—Thomas E. Chávez, "Santa Fe's Own: A History of Fiesta," 1985.[92]

Burning Zozobra and Processing to the Cross of the Martyrs . . .

Patriotic observances, on the Plaza, Santa Fe Fiesta, 1919. Photo by Wesley Bradfield. (MNM Neg. No. 52394.)

Tsianina giving sunrise call, Palace of the Governors behind, Santa Fe Fiesta, August 1925. (MNM Neg. No. 117766.)

De Vargas Entrada, Palace of the
Governors to right, Fine Arts
Museum beyond at right, Santa
Fe Fiesta, August 1925. (MNM
Neg. No. 117869.)

"Los Trovadores" in fiesta attire,
patio, Palace of the Governors,
Santa Fe Fiesta, August 1925.
(MNM Neg. No. 44429.)

Zozobra is a puppet made of chicken wire, wood, cloth, and paper. . . . Copyright and responsibility for the event now belong to the Kiwanis Club, which inherited the project from Shuster. Many fiesta goers regard this ritualistic burning, rather than the De Vargas Mass, as the beginning of the fiesta. . . .

Zozobra looks a bit different each year, but his basic features communicate terror, destructiveness, and gloom. During World War II he was designed with slanted eyes and nicknamed "Hirohitlmus." He is hung from a tall pole on a hill so he can be seen by the thousands who watch his destruction. And his eyes, mouth, and arms are manipulated by persons hidden. . . .

Long lines of bonfire and torches are lit as the Fire Spirit dressed in red begins his taunting dance at Zozobra's feet. The death of Zozobra, which is eventually induced by the Fire Spirit, who puts a flaming torch to Zozobra's highly inflammable gown, is supposed to symbolize the death of gloom and the resurrection of gaiety and happiness sufficient to provide enough fiesta spirit for four days. One writer speaks of the rite as "a pagan ritual with overtones of religious cult." . . . Another writer observes, "As Christ died for man's sins, Zozobra dies for man's sadness year in and year out." . . . Santa Feans, of course, have not overlooked the archetypal possibilities of this "modern mythical battle" between the spirits of gloom and fire. The Spanish term *zozobra* has religious overtones; it connotes moral pollution or guilt and does not merely mean "spoil sport" or "party pooper" as some current suggestions imply. . . .

. . . It is perhaps significant that the two events participants seem to consider most moving, the burning of Zozobra and the procession to the Cross of the Martyrs, both occur at night and involve the use of fire.

The procession, on the penultimate day of the fiesta, follows a Mass which commemorates the death of twenty-one Franciscan martyrs. It begins at the cathedral, where participants are given lit candles. Then the procession, which is usually quite long, winds its way to the top of a hill overlooking Santa Fe. At the top of the hill is a large cross beneath which a Franciscan priest delivers a sermon, usually related to the theme of death by martyrdom. The path is lit with bonfires and the cross is illuminated with large spotlights, thus creating a patchwork of strangely shaped shadows and winding rows of candles and bonfires.

In both the procession and the burning of Zozobra the normal sounds of everyday life are radically altered. During the Zozobra drama-rite the noises are chaotic and bombastic; during the procession and subsequent sermon an awesome silence dominates. The usual organ and mariachi-style guitar music are minimized or missing from both, except as preludes. Instead, one hears drums at the Zozobra burning and hand bells at the sermon of the martyrs. Both events occur on the edge of the city removed from the central plaza, and both involve unusual physical heights. Whereas the Zozobra burning is considered pagan, the procession and sermon are considered normatively Christian. . . . Both events touch the emotional centers of most participants in a way unmatched by any of the other events. Both are concerned with the theme of death. . . . In both rites some form of renewed life comes from the ritualized contemplation or enactment of death.

—Ronald L. Grimes, *Symbol and Conquest: Public Ritual and Drama in Santa Fe, New Mexico,* 1976.[93]

Burning of Zozobra, Santa Fe
Fiesta, ca. 1942. (MNM Neg. No.
47328.)

Gallup Inter-Tribal Indian Ceremonial

The Ceremonial's Beginnings . . .

Gallup was looking for business from the venturesome motorists who were blazing highways across the continent. Gallup was on the route then designated as the National Old Trails Highway which followed the old Santa Fe trail eastward across Kansas. The issue [of *Carbon City News*] which carried Mike Kirk's suggestion for an Indian day also carried the brief comment, "Ten auto loads of tourists, all eastward bound, passed through the city Friday. The camp grounds were made ready none too soon." . . .

The Gallup Tourist Travel Association hired boosters and stationed them in Los Lunas and Holbrook so they might proclaim the virtues of the route through Gallup in competition with Springerville, Ariz., boosters who advocated the southern route. Meanwhile the "Indian day" talk among Gallup Kiwanians had progressed to the stage where an "Indian Pageant and Exposition" was being considered. Later this grew into the Inter-Tribal Indian Ceremonial organized at a public meeting held at the McKinley County courthouse on August 3, 1922, when papers of incorporation were drawn up. Mike Kirk was made president and placed in charge of Indians. . . .

Back of Gallup Chamber of Commerce stationery, 1940s. (WPA#215, NMSRC.)

The Ceremonial association started out with 40 memberships at $10 each and raised it to 168 by Ceremonial time. The Kiwanis Club scheduled its district convention on the Ceremonial dates, Sept. 28–30, thus guaranteeing a nucleus crowd. Directors scrounged a tractor to fill in the ditches cut in the fair grounds, and William Fox promised to send a cameraman to film the dances. Zane Gray, famous author of western stories, put in an appearance and declared the Ceremonial a great success. The directors were pleased . . . and talked of building a double-deck grandstand to accommodate the crowds which were sure to increase each year. In December of 1922 the Fred Harvey system announced it would spend $750,000 on a hotel in Gallup and the Santa Fe railroad made the town a hub for tourist trips to Mesa Verde, Canyon de Chelly and Zuni. The Kiwanis Club continued to boast the Ceremonial and Gallup was set up in the tourist business almost before there were roads.

Ray Aldrich and Mike Kirk lined up the Indians for that first Ceremonial which included "exhibits, educational lectures on sandpaintings, etc., two side shows with the big dances pulled off at night around the campfires." One of the major attractions was a marathon race from the Ceremonial grounds to Allison, Navajo, Gibson, Heaton and finishing with five laps around the fair grounds track. Four Kiwanis club baseball teams played a series for the district championship.

The new Harvey House was completed and dedicated with Indian ceremonies on May 25. Railroad officials here for the opening of the new hotel were told of the Ceremonial at a meeting in the courthouse on May 24 and promised to distribute publicity. Mike Kirk wrote a story about the Navajos and Evon Z. Vogt compiled Zuni lore and legends for the first Ceremonial publicity pamphlet issued in July by J. W. Chapman. Kirk, Vogt and Homer Powers spent long tedious days in the councils of the Pueblos and at Navajo pow-wows while the Indians argued whether they should permit their young men to dance at the Ceremonial. Days and weeks ran into months and their families despaired of ever seeing them again. But they got the Indians out to the Ceremonial in such numbers that now the Ceremonial is considered by the Indians of the Southwest to be their official annual reunion.

—J. Wesley Huff, "A Quarter Century of Ceremonials," 1946.[94]

The 1936 Gallup Ceremonial . . .

The largest Ceremonial to be seen anywhere in the United States is the Inter-Tribal Indian Ceremonial held annually at Gallup, New Mexico, the last Wednesday, Thursday and Friday in August. The dates this year [1936] are Aug. 26, 27, and 28. At this great tribal conclave more than seven thousand Indians of thirty tribes gather to dance, chant, compete in races, sports and games, and to exhibit their finest arts and crafts.

For the tenderfeet who do not wish to endure the hardships of reservation travel, and for the traveler whose time is limited, the Gallup Ceremonial offers more in three days than can be seen at any other time or place in the United States.

During the months preceding the Gallup Ceremonial [Indians] make elaborate preparations. Dancers brighten up their costumes and practice frequently; athletes train arduously; craftsmen work hard to produce their finest handicrafts. The Ceremonial is a great competition, there being cash prizes for excellence in everything typically Indian.

When all the hundreds of Indian competitors and the thousands of Indians who attend as spectators swarm Gallup for their Ceremonial that little western frontier town becomes more Indian than any town in the country. Hordes of Indians roam the streets, all in their tribal costumes of great variety. Their camps are set up in and around the town at every available spot. Hundreds of their camp fires pierce night's darkness. This horde of Indians makes a panorama of Indian tribes and Indian life that cannot be duplicated. Enough pictures, both motion and still, are taken to consume a teepee full of films.

—Unidentified newspaper clipping, August 22, 1936.[95]

Zuni parade, Gallup Ceremonial. Photo by Mullarky. (MNM Neg. No. 47920.)

Zuni women, Gallup Ceremonial, August 19, 1939. Photo by Anne Edna Buvens. (MNM Neg. No. 101375.)

Navajo wagons at Gallup
Ceremonial, ca. 1946–1952. Photo
by Ferenz Fedor. (MNM Neg. No.
101689.)

The Ceremonial by 1946 . . .

The prophecy of the writer in the Gallup *Independent* on August 31, 1928, has
become true in the ensuing years: "Without a discordant note the Ceremonial will
continue to live, a pulsating, throbbing spectacle typifying all that is best in this
Land of Enchantment."

The all–Indian show remains much the same today [1946] as it was in those
earlier days, except that it operates more smoothly and rapidly. The experience of
years has given the Ceremonial staff the know-how so that the show is organized
and follows its schedule with the efficiency of a big circus.

—J. Wesley Huff, "A Quarter Century of Ceremonials," 1946.[96]

The Governor Speaks . . .

Governor John J. Dempsey expressed the spirit of the Ceremonial when he said
last year [1945]: "If the Ceremonial were to be presented without a single white

The ceremonial dances of Southwestern Indians are probably the most interesting survival of pagan rites in America. The opening of the ditches in the spring, the planting of the fields, and particularly the harvesting of the crops, are all occasions for solemn ceremonial dancing. Navajo ceremonies are best seen at Gallup in the Inter-tribal Indian Ceremonial, held in 1940 on August 14-15-16 and 17. Good photographs of dances are rare, for the Indians do not permit cameras on dance days. Shown here are typical Pueblo dances and Apache Devil Dancers.

From *Coronado Magazine: The Official Program of the Coronado Cuarto Centennial*, 1940. (Private collection.)

visitor, I believe it still should go on. For primarily it is for, as well as of, the Indians. It is their show and it is a recognition of their contribution to our American way of life. Its presentation will not detract one whit from our war effort, and it will be a real contribution to morale for those tribesmen whose sons are making so fine a record in the Pacific area."

—J. Wesley Huff, "A Quarter Century of Ceremonials," 1946.[97]

Coronado Cuarto Centennial

A 1938 Declaration by University of New Mexico President James F. Zimmerman . . .

Recognizing the priceless heritage of four hundred years of history under the flags of Spain, Mexico, and the United States, we are planning to commemorate our four hundredth anniversary with a statewide celebration embracing almost the entire year of 1940.

During the past five years, the people of the United States, led by President Franklin Delano Roosevelt, have sought to bring about a closer relationship among the Americas. New Mexico, with its essentially Hispanic background, still preserves much of the tradition as well as the language of the *Conquistadores,* who, four centuries ago, brought European culture to both North and South America. With the celebration of her four hundredth birthday, New Mexico will have an unprecedented opportunity to further the cultural relations between the United States of America and those countries lying to the South, whose historic background is so linked with ours. To this day a large portion of New Mexico is Spanish in blood and thinking. Through the Coronado celebration, we shall unite our colorful past with the realities of the present, and in so doing lay new foundations of spiritual relationship with our sister nations in this hemisphere.[98]

Erna Fergusson Reviews the Coronado Cuarto Centennial in 1940 . . .

The first problem was how to make the uninformed aware of Coronado and of his importance. One of hundreds of explorers whom Spain sent out from her first American capital at Mexico, he is not well known even there. And the United States, growing westward on a lengthening English apron string, has just begun to appreciate that some Americans are of Spanish blood. . . .

. . . To attract people to New Mexico, to present the story as a living thing, some sort of dramatic presentation seemed the best way. Hence the Coronado Entradas. Nothing makeshift would do. The drama must be written with distinction, with truth to the high spirit of the Spanish conquerors; it must be presented on a scale large enough to suggest the enormous country Coronado covered, the number of men involved, the difficulties they overcame; and it must be staged with technical skill equal to the best. Only a few people in the United States could qualify for such a job. One of them, happily, is a citizen of New Mexico. Thomas Wood Stevens, acknowledged master of pageantry, wrote the script which is presented by a cast of hundreds, many mounted, all costumed, armored, and accoutred with absolute historical accuracy. . . .

But New Mexico . . . has its simpler phases too. Most of us live in small towns, making a living from farms or herds or unimportant jobs; most of our towns did not care for anything as elaborate or as costly as the Coronado Entrada. Many of our people can claim no descent from the conquerors. New Mexico has been made, too, by later comers of many stocks with a history and traditions quite as interesting if not quite as picturesque as the story of the conquerors. A Cuarto Centennial which did not take account of all this would fail of its intent to be an all-New Mexican fiesta. Every town, however small, should have a chance to present its history, to stage its typical show—rodeo, fair, religious feast, or celebration of legendary hero. Folk festivals were proposed as the second phase of the Coronado Cuarto Centennial. New Mexico people accepted the idea with almost perfect unanimity; for we have a habit of making and enjoying our own fiestas. Hundreds of club, school, and church affairs have taken on a Coronado tinge. More than fifty small towns have received aid from the Cuarto Centennial Commission in putting on Coronado fiestas which vary from old Spanish morality plays to ballad contests, old fiddlers' tournaments, and revivals of forgotten dances. Generally these folk festivals are what has always been done. The effort has been to assist the townsfolk in making them better, in reviving old customs, and in advertising them for the benefit of visitors to New Mexico.

A curious problem was presented by our Indians. Of all the original Americans the Indians of New Mexico and Arizona have been retained their primitive customs; their ceremonies are of unexcelled beauty and of the impressiveness that comes of ancient forms reverently preserved. Nothing white men might suggest to Indians could be as worthy a contribution to a New Mexico program as what Indians do every year at their own time and in their own way. To list such dances as Indians are willing for visitors to see, to point visitors the way to see them, and to indicate the manners which make visitors welcome seemed all that the Coronado Cuarto Centennial Commission might do. In only one case— the dedication of the Coronado Museum at Kuaua, near if not the actual place where Coronado wintered in 1540–41—have Indians been asked to do something in the white man's way. Even there the unveiling of copies of the original kiva murals will be done by Indians according to a ceremonial worked out by the Inter-Pueblo Council.

— Erna Fergusson, "The Coronado Cuarto Centennial," 1940.[99]

Pablo Abeyta Speaks at the Dedication of the Coronado Monument, Bernalillo, May 29, 1940 . . .

Those who attended the dedication ceremonies of the Coronado Monument at Bernalillo on May 29 are still smiling occasionally at the way Pablo Abeyta, Isleta Pueblo Indian, completely captured the spotlight from the Spanish ambassador and assorted officialdom. Dedication of the monument and museum, the construction of which was directed by Dr. [Edgar Lee] Hewett and Dr. [Reginald] Fisher, marked the opening of the Coronado celebration. Ambassador Cardenas had flown here from Washington; Dr. [Aurelio M.] Espinosa had flown from Stanford; Governor Miles, President Zimmerman, Director Anderson, and others joined them in making speeches extolling the conquistador Coronado and his exploits in

Coronado's Entrada, Coronado Cuarto Centennial, 1940. Photo by Harold D. Walter. (MNM Neg. No. 135147.)

the typical American manner of such occasions. At the very end, the crowd, which had grown bored sitting in the hot sun listening to speech after speech of compliments and praise, was electrified as Pablo Abeyta arose, as scheduled, to reply hospitably to the ambassador, and said, calmly but with great force, "I am afraid I will have to contradict some of the things you gentlemen have said. Coronado came by Isleta, and as you who have read his chronicles know, was given food and royally received. He came on up the valley, and what did he do? Well, we had better say no more about it, for his record isn't good and you know it." With that the crowd, aware of the cruelties and depradations of the entrada, broke into the heartiest applause of the afternoon, and did so again at every pause, as the respected Isletan continued a short and cutting debunking of white man's history, which he said is 90 percent wrong.

When he finished the applause continued so long that the chairman had to motion him to his feet again for a bow. In all fairness it must be said that the official speechmakers enjoyed the debunking as much as the crowd did, and everyone apparently came away with the feeling that a little blunt truth telling had added to the occasion, rather than detracted.[100]

An Indian's Song to Coronado, From an Unidentified Newspaper of October 7, 1936 . . .

"Navajo, 106, Former Mexican Slave, Sings Old Song of Coronado"

Caught by Mexicans when she was 8 years old and held as a house slave for many years, a full-blooded Navajo, Señora Gertrude S. de Garcia, now 106 years of age, has given to the world the first song in which the name of Coronado is mentioned.

Stopping her work while plastering a wall in her adobe hut in Las Cruces, and muttering her anger at God because He made her so poor and placed so much work on her aged shoulders, the old woman sang the following:

> *Coronado se paseaba por toda la tierra afuera,*
> *Y huba quien la pisara el paso de su bandera.*
> *Por aqui, por alli que, bueno va!*
> *Por aqui, por alli que, bueno va!*

Translated by Dr. Arthur Campa, professor of Spanish at the University of New Mexico, and one of the 1936 Conquistadores who are working for the success of the Coronado Quarto Centennial, the words are:

> *Proudly rode brave Coronado through the confines o*
> > *the land,*
> *And but few had dared to question the bold*
> > *conquest of the band.*
> *Hither and yon, heigh ho, he rides!*
> *Hither and yon, heigh ho, he rides!*

This song was considered to be of exceptional historic value as none other has been yet unearthed that definitely referred to the conqueror of 400 years ago by name.[101]

The Coronado Cuarto Centennial, according to New Mexico Magazine's *Edmund Sherman, June 1940 . . .*

Colorful New Mexico will be more colorful than ever. To the regular summer events and celebrations that attract visitors from throughout the world be the *Entradas* and the nearly two hundred folk festivals scattered throughout the State all during the summer.

No central celebration point has been established, but the *Entradas,* pageants on a tremendous scale, and the folk festivals have been so arranged that there will be celebration interest for visitors at some point in the State on almost every day during summer and fall months. . . .

In all, seventeen New Mexico, West Texas and Arizona cities will present feature *entradas* during 1940, in which approximately 20,000 persons will appear. . . .

Every town in the State, too, will have some added interest. Those not listed for *Entradas* or folk festivals will have other types of celebrations such as rodeos, frontier days, old Trail days, local *fiestas,* county or local fairs, pageantry or cavalcades.

And, as always, at every Indian *pueblo* there will be dances on stated occasions. The holiday mood will prevail. Towns will be gaily decorated, and no village will be too small for a special celebration that will bring out the old time costumes and the native musicians with their fiddles and guitars to play the traditional dances *La Varsoviana* and *La Raspa* that today are as popular in the ball room as in the most isolated mountain village. There will be the folk plays, *Los Pastores, El Niño Perdido, Moros y Cristianos, Adán and Eva* which have been handed down orally from generation to generation. Coronado arts and crafts exhibits have been arranged at several points in the State. Virtually every activity of the summer, regular or special, will have some sort of tie-up with the Coronado celebration, whether it's conventions, coiffures, costumes, styles, sports, foods. Even tourists crossing the State in a few hours can hardly miss contact some way or other with the 400th anniversary celebration.[102]

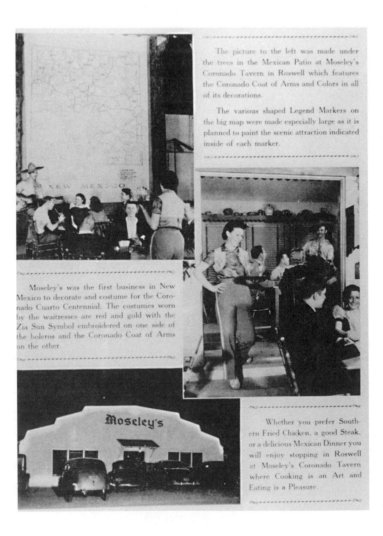

Ad from *Coronado Magazine: The Official Program of the Coronado Cuarto Centennial,* 1940. (Private collection.)

Conclusion

Invented traditions like Old Timers Days, the Santa Fe Fiesta, the Gallup Inter-Tribal Indian Ceremonial, and the Coronado Cuarto Centennial may not be completely new creations, as Eric Hobsbawm observes, but adaptations "for old uses in new conditions and by using old models for new purposes." However, "in all such cases novelty is no less novel for being able to dress up easily as antiquity."[103]

Fourth of July observances, informal rodeos and working cowboy contests, picnics, family reunions, and the like were characteristic of the Anglo culture imposed by New Mexico immigrants. Gallup had been a typical mining town before the first Indian Ceremonial in 1922. According to Terry Lee Carroll, the small town

> had had other attractions. One of these was an especially noisy Fourth of July that was held each year on the street that is now US 66 and was then, as now, called Front Street or Railroad Avenue. There were foot races and all kinds of festivities. E. P. Sellard, an optometrist in town, often ran races with local citizens and Indians who happened to be in town. He told once of racing in these celebrations on the dust filled street that was Front Street. The spectators would sit on flat cars that the Santa Fe Railroad would pull up on the siding. This fronted all along the street and the railroad would put seats on the flatcars for spectators.
>
> The Fourth of July celebrations were wild affairs when most of the visitors used to be coal miners. They had the day off and there was much activity in town. Many of the Fourth's rodeo events were incorporated in the afternoon program of the Ceremonials.[104]

Santa Fe traces its fiesta to 1712. Eighteenth- and nineteenth-century observances had been strictly Hispanic and religious, centered around Our Lady of the Conquest, as described by Thomas E. Chávez:

> Early processions differed from the present in that they had *descansos* (rest stops) where the statue [of La Conquistadora] was put on a temporary pedestal and prayers were offered. . . .
>
> Another early-day difference was the use of evergreens to line the route. The role of women in the procession is probably the most obvious change. Until relatively recently, women of the Cofradia had the honor of carrying La Conquistadora. Now members of the Caballeros de Vargas perform the duty.[105]

The present historical emphasis of the Santa Fe Fiesta was largely a late-nineteenth-century Anglo invention. In an interview with Beatrice Chauvenet, "Ruth Seligman, wife of plaza merchant James Seligman, . . . gave her recollections of how the revival of a civic celebration honoring the reconquest came about in the years after 1896 when she arrived in Santa Fe":

> The real idea of a town fiesta came from the Episcopal minister named James Mythen. . . . A day or two before he was leaving my husband and I . . . stopped in the old Santa Fe Club. . . . Mr. Mythen got to talking to us and he said, "You

know, I don't see why Santa Fe doesn't have some yearly historical event as they do in New Orleans at Mardi Gras. Santa Fe is so full of history."

So Jim and I were very much interested, and a few days after Mr. Mythen left, Jim asked a few men to come up to the house. We sat around our dining table, and Jim suggested that one of the best things to start with would be the reconquest by De Vargas. . . .

That's the way it started, right there in our house. In those days all the little towns had fiestas. They used to have cock fights in Agua Fria and things like that, but in Santa Fe they had had only a small religious remembrance each year. For a few years we just had the De Vargas parade. It was in September because we thought the rains would be over then. They knew De Vargas had taken a vow, as in the religious processions, but they never combined the two—the religious and the military conquest in those days. . . .

It was Jimmy Mythen's idea to have some historical event and Jim Seligman's idea to have De Vargas. After a few years it was Mr. Twitchell's idea to have a fiesta—they called it the 300th or whatever year it was, but in all the years I'd lived here we'd never before had one. It had probably been dropped in the early days.

Then Dr. Hewett got interested in it and Mr. Twitchell. They decided to have a candlelight procession. It had nothing to do with the De Vargas parade which we had several years all by itself.

Although Twitchell directed the revived Santa Fe Fiesta in 1919 and 1921, and Paul A. F. Walter that of 1920, Chauvenet claims the early festival bore the stamp of Museum of New Mexico director Edgar Lee Hewett.

Hewett kept in mind that [the 1915] San Diego [Panama-California Exposition] had provided something for everybody, highbrow and lowbrow—a happy commingling of a street carnival with the best cultural features of a Chautauqua, a form of entertainment that was at the height of its popularity during the years the Exposition promoters were planning their show. Chautauquas took their name from the town in New York State where they originated. In the early years of the twentieth century the Chautauqua movement brought cultural recreation to hundreds of American communities where people could not otherwise see good theater, listen to good music, or hear outstanding lecturers. . . . Chautauqua was big business for entertainers until World War I interrupted it and the postwar development of radio made it unprofitable. As developed by Twitchell, [Jesse] Nusbaum, Walter, and Hewett, the Santa Fe Fiesta carried out a similar concept, with emphasis on the special features of the Southwestern community.[106]

The impetus for the Coronado Cuarto Centennial was entirely "historical" and "Chautauqua cultural." When Roswell school teacher Charles M. Martin conceived of the idea to give national currency to New Mexico history in 1930, it was, as he said, "just one of those inspirations a man is glad to have to give to his state." He took a resolution to the Roswell chapter of the New Mexico Archaeological and Historical Society on February 19, 1931, declaring: "Other states have held elaborate ceremonies at their Hundredth Anniversaries. We are entitled to hold an even greater celebration at our Four Hundredth Anniversary."[107]

Photo by Harold D. Walter.
(MNM Neg. No. 58036.)

In 1935, Governor Clyde Tingley signed a legislative act creating the Coronado Cuarto Centennial Commission with University of New Mexico president Dr. James F. Zimmerman as president, Albuquerque writer Erna Fergusson as vice president, Albuquerque lawyer Gilberto Espinosa as secretary, and Santa Fe businessman Henry Dendahl as treasurer. By adding Arizona, Texas, Colorado, Kansas, and Oklahoma to the plans, they were able to obtain two hundred thousand dollars in federal funds in 1939, when a United States Coronado Exposition Committee was established. It included Vice-President John N. Garner, Speaker of the House of Representatives William H. Bankhead, Secretary of the Interior Harold L. Ickes, Secretary of Commerce Harry L. Hopkins, and Clinton P. Anderson as managing director.[108] This sets the Coronado Cuarto Centennial apart from the Gallup Inter-Tribal Indian Ceremonial, which was first supported locally and in 1939 officially began receiving state support, and from the Santa Fe Fiesta and Old Timers Days, which were carried out with municipal support.

All the invented festivals discussed in this chapter came into being and flourished during times of social and economic distress, notably World War I and the drought and depression of the 1920s. As Eric Hobsbawm notes: "There is probably no time and place with which historians are concerned which has not seen the 'invention' of tradition in this sense. However, we should expect it to occur more frequently when a rapid transformation of society weakens or destroys the social patterns for which 'old' traditions had been designed."[109] The automobile was prime among those transformations.

The key to this change in celebration patterns is found in Mrs. R. S. Hamilton's 1933 reminiscences about Roswell's Alfalfa Palace built for the Eastern New Mexico Fair: "In the early fall of 1892 there was a general opinion expressed by the citizens of Roswell and by stockmen and the farmers, especially those with orchards, that the time had come when something must be done to advertise Roswell and Chaves County that would 'put us on the map'—a rather new phrase at that time."[110] At first this "map" was generated by foot, horse, cart, and wagon trails, so celebrations involved more local people.

After 1900, New Mexico's place on railroad maps was secured and more tourists were attracted. Not until the 1920s did the New Mexico Highway Department and New Mexico Tourist Bureau begin to help define a road map for potential in-state and out-of-state festival participants and spectators driving cars, trailers, and trucks. The culmination of this campaign is suggested in the conclusion to a 1938 booklet entitled "What the Coronado Cuarto Centennial Means to New Mexico," in which the anonymous author claims: "If our many local celebrations are responsible for one car out of twenty remaining in the state one extra day, then the total increase in income from tourists should be between SEVEN AND EIGHT MILLION DOLLARS."[111]

One effect of these campaigns to "put New Mexico on the map" as a quintessentially "folk" or "fiesta" state is highlighted in John DeWitt McKee's caustic 1957 observation that in "The Unrelenting Land" of New Mexico

> they place a tradition in an iron lung and will not let it die a decent death. They build an association around it to give pneumatic similitude of life to the tradition, and busyness to minds besieged by boredom. They do not realize that when it is pumped up and preserved in associations and annual meetings, it is as false as the seeming blush of life on the rouged face of a corpse. They fail to see, for instance, that the strength of aesthetic pleasure in folk arts is rooted in the absolute material and spiritual necessity of those arts. . . . These things can become and remain traditions because they grow out of the needs of the people on the land and out of the land itself.[112]

In *Our Southwest* Erna Fergusson maintains that "there is no surer way to get at the real nature of a people than to observe them on their feast days and bonfire nights." These celebrations she identifies as traditional "Dances, Fiestas, Fairs, and Rodeos." In the post–World War I Southwest, the "money-making show" came into its own. By 1940, Fergusson observes,

> a genial climate, millions of tourists to be amused, and a wide choice of merry-making customs have brought every crossroads town out with its special stunt day: Fair, Fat Stock Show, Pioneer's Day, Cotton Carnival, Old Timers Week, Rodeo, Fiesta. Every such affair is boosted by the Chamber of Commerce, "sold" to merchants, who hope to take in more eventually than their public spirit puts up,

and widely advertised. Lately every town has cannily flavored its offering with something designed to catch the traveling public as well as the country cousins.

This highjacking of one people's practice by another has speeded up the interfusion which was going on anyway. Doubtless it will hasten the coming of something that may, in time, become a true Southwestern culture; except that by then it will be on the way to transforming itself into something else. Nothing is surer than change, nothing more futile than to mourn it; nothing more instructive, really, than to watch it. And, in this case, we may watch the lumps of various widely different types and stages of culture bobbing, still undigested, in a sort of sunny stew.[113]

 NOTES

Abbreviations

AA	*American Anthropologist.*
BAE	Bureau of American Ethnology (Bureau of Ethnology, 1879–1894).
EP	*El Palacio.*
II-MNM	History Library, Museum of New Mexico, Santa Fe.
Handbook 9	*Handbook of North American Indians,* Volume 9: *Southwest,* William C. Sturtevant, general editor; Alfonso Ortiz, volume editor. Washington, D.C.: Smithsonian Institution, 1979.
Handbook 10	*Handbook of North American Indians,* Volume 10: *Southwest,* William C. Sturtevant, general editor; Alfonso Ortiz, volume editor. Washington, D.C.: Smithsonian Institution, 1983.
JAF	*Journal of American Folklore.*
MNM	Museum of New Mexico, Santa Fe.
NM	*New Mexico Magazine.*
NMFR	*New Mexico Folklore Record.*
NMFWP	New Mexico Federal Writers' Project, Works Progress Administration.
NMHR	*New Mexico Historical Review.*
NMSRC	New Mexico State Records Center and Archives, Santa Fe.
Robb	J. D. Robb Collection, John Donald Robb Archives of Southwestern Music, Fine Arts Library, University of New Mexico.

SAR   School of American Research, Santa Fe.

WF   *Western Folklore.*

WP: Writers' Program, Work Projects Administration.

A#:   As of July 18, 1983, the Works Progress Administration (WPA) Files at the NMSRC have been indexed by folder number in a list of 268 folders (30 expandable files) prepared by archivist Louellen N. Martínez.

BC: Number assigned in a preliminary compilation by Gilberto Benito Córdova, *Bibliography of Unpublished Materials Pertaining to Hispanic Culture in the New Mexico WPA Writers' Files* (Santa Fe: New Mexico State Department of Education, December 1972). Some of the NMSRC documents are filed by BC numbers.

HC: The alphabetical city files at the History Library, Museum of New Mexico, Santa Fe.

H#:   Materials at the History Library, Museum of New Mexico, Santa Fe, were originally filed by file cabinet, drawer, and folder numbers, and many remain so. A card file of most of these documents was assembled in the 1970s, but it has not been updated to accommodate new discoveries from other vertical files or the extensive city files.

LC: In 1980, the Federal Writers' Project files were under the care of the Folksong Archive at the Library of Congress. Ann Banks of the American Studies Center, Boston College, compiled a "Survey of Federal Writers' Project Manuscript Holdings in the Archive of Folk Song, Library of Congress," dated December 28, 1979. Manuscripts are numbered by file and drawer, from 36.2 to 48.4, as they are herein. These holdings are now in the Manuscript Division of the Library of Congress, where another group of FWP documents was released from the Library's Landover warehouse. Those holdings were examined in June 1981 and are listed here as LCms#, indicating file boxes but not individual folder names.

Chapter 1. Sky Looms: Texts of Transformation and Sacred Worlds

1. Herbert Joseph Spinden, trans., *Songs of the Tewa* (1933; reprint, Santa Fe: Sunstone Press, 1976), 94, 9, 120.

2. Erna Fergusson, *Our Southwest* (New York: Alfred A. Knopf, 1940), 18–19.

3. Matthew W. Stirling, *Origin Myth of Acoma and Other Records,* BAE Bulletin 135 (Washington, D.C.: Government Printing Office, 1942), 1, 3–4. Stirling explains that this version "was learned by the chief informant during his initiation in youth into the Koshari, the group of sacred clowns to whom theoretically all religious secrets are divulged. . . . The tradition is couched in archaic language so that in many places the younger interpreters were unable to translate and the elderly informant would have to explain in modern Acoma phraseology. . . . Other paraphrases may have been made for the benefit of the White man or as interpretation of Acoma religion by one who is an exceptionally good Catholic and no longer a participant in the ceremonial life of Acoma" (vii). C. Daryll Forde worked with Stirling in the early stages of recording this myth and published a version of it, "A Creation Myth from Acoma," in *Folk-Lore* 41 (1930): 370–87. Paula Gunn Allen frames her novel, *The Woman Who Owned the Shadows* (San Francisco: Spinsters, Ink, 1983), with a literary version of this Keres Pueblo emergence myth. See also Allen, *The Sacred Hoop: Recovering the Feminine in American Indian Traditions* (Boston: Beacon Press, 1986), 13–29.

4. Sam D. Gill, "Navajo Views of Their Origin," in *Handbook 10,* 502–5. See also Washington Matthews's dated paper on Navajo and other emergence myths, "Myths of Gestation and Parturition," *AA* 4 (1902):737–42; and Erminie Wheeler-Voegelin and Remedios W. Moore, "The Emergence Myth in Native North America," in *Studies in Folklore,* ed. W. Edson Richmond, Indiana University Publications in Folklore 9 (Bloomington: Indiana University Press, 1957), 66–91.

5. Gladys A. Reichard, *Navaho Religion: A Study of Symbolism,* Bollingen Series 18, 2d ed. in 1 vol. (Princeton, N.J.: Princeton University Press, 1974), 17.

6. Leland C. Wyman, *The Windways of the Navaho* (Colorado Springs, Colorado: Taylor Museum of the Colorado Springs Fine Arts Center, 1962), 106–7.

7. Reyes N. Martínez, coll. and trans., "Venid Pecadores (Come, Ye Sinners)," n.d., NMFWP, 5-5-5#125, H-MNM. Diacritical marks added. See also *"Venir, pecadores,"* the five versions collected by Juan B. Rael, *The New Mexican 'Alabado',* with transcription of music by Eleanor Hague, Stanford University Publications University Series, Language and Literature vol. 9, no. 3 (Stanford, Calif., 1951), 44–48, 142.

8. Alice Corbin Henderson, *Brothers of Light: The Penitentes of the Southwest* (New York: Harcourt, Brace, 1937), 46–49.

9. Reyes N. Martínez, "Salve de Dolores (Hail, Lady of Sorrows)," coll. from Mrs. Alcaria R. Medina, Arroyo Hondo, March 18, 1940, NMFWP, 5-5-5#29, H-MNM. Diacritical marks added.

10. Lorin W. Brown, "Lent in Córdova," n.d., NMFWP, revised version reprinted in Lorenzo de Córdova, *Echoes of the Flute* (Santa Fe: Ancient City Press, 1972), 43.

11. Marta Weigle and Thomas R. Lyons, "Brothers and Neighbors: The Celebration of Community in Penitente Villages," in *Celebration: Studies in Festivity and Ritual,* ed. Victor Turner (Washington, D.C.: Smithsonian Institution Press, 1982), 246–47.

12. Lorin W. Brown, "Manuel Maes," October 11, 1937, NMFWP, 5-5-50#14, H-MNM (diacritical marks added); intro. only in Brown with Charles L. Briggs and Marta Weigle, *Hispano Folklife of New Mexico: The Lorin W Brown Federal Writers' Project Manuscripts* (Albuquerque: University of New Mexico Press, 1978), 49.

13. Jim Bob Tinsley, *He Was Singin' This Song* (Orlando: University Presses of Florida, 1981), 86; Austin E. Fife and Alta S. Fife, eds., *Songs of the Cowboys* by N. Howard ("Jack") Thorp (New York: Bramhall House, 1966), 28.

14. The text is from pp. 10–11 in the facsimile of the 1908 ed., reprinted in the Fifes' book following p. 257.

15. May Price (Mrs. Benton) Mosley, "Desert Water (Lea County)," NMFWP, October 12, 1936, in her *"Little Texas" Beginnings in Southeastern New Mexico,* ed. Martha Downer Ellis (Roswell, New Mexico: Hall-Poorbaugh Press, 1973), 6.

16. Roland F. Dickey, "Chronicles of Neglected Time: Windscapes," *Century Magazine,* March 16, 1983, 10.

17. Lena S. Maxwell, "As It Happened in Curry County," NMFWP, 1938, reprinted in *New Mexicans in Cameo and Camera: New Deal Documentation of Twentieth-Century Lives,* ed. Marta Weigle (Albuquerque: University of New Mexico Press, 1985), 158–59; Mrs. Belle Kilgore, "Mrs. Lena Kempf Maxwell, School Teacher & Museum Manager, Clovis, New Mexico," NMFWP, June 26, 1937, reprinted in Weigle, ibid., 169–70.

18. Lansing Lamont, *Day of Trinity* (New York: Atheneum, 1965), 235. See also Ferenc Morton Szasz, *The Day The Sun Rose Twice: The Story of the Trinity Site Nuclear Explosion, July 16, 1945* (Albuquerque: University of New Mexico Press, 1984), 83–91. Szasz quotes William L. Laurence: "One felt as though he had been privileged to witness the Birth of the World—to be present at the moment of Creation when the Lord said: 'Let There Be Light'" (p. 89).

19. Lamont, ibid, 238–39.

20. Mircea Eliade, *The Sacred and the Profane: The Nature of Religion,* trans. Willard R. Trask (New York: Harper & Row, 1961), 9.

Focal Place One: Shiprock and Four Corners

1. Paige W. Christiansen and Frank E. Kottlowski, eds., *Mosaic of New Mexico's Scenery, Rocks, and History,* Scenic Trips to the Geologic Past No. 8 (Socorro: New Mexico State Bureau of Mines and Mineral Resources, 1972), 49, 51.

2. Ibid., 36–37.

3. Ibid., 164.

4. Aileen O'Bryan, *The Díné: Origin Myths of the Navaho Indians,* BAE Bulletin 163 (Washington, D.C.: Government Printing Office, 1956), 23, 26.

5. Ibid., 87. O'Bryan refers to Washington Matthews, *Navaho Legends,* Memoirs of the American Folk-Lore Society, vol. 5 (Boston and New York: Houghton, Mifflin and Company, 1897), 119, 235; Franciscan Fathers, *An Ethnologic Dictionary of the Navaho Language* (Saint Michaels, Arizona, 1910), 357.

6. Gladys A. Reichard, *Navaho Religion: A Study of Symbolism,* Bollingen Series 18, 2d ed. in 1 vol. (Princeton, N.J.: Princeton University Press, 1974), 420–21.

7. T. M. Pearce, ed., with Ina Sizer Cassidy and Helen S. Pearce, *New Mexico Place Names: A Geographical Dictionary* (Albuquerque: University of New Mexico Press, 1965), 154–55. The source of these "myths" is George B. Anderson, *History of New Mexico* (1907), vol. 1, p. 395, according to Mary Hudson Brothers, who notes: "The huge pile of masonry does resemble a giant ship. . . . but such imagery is closer to the white man's world than that of the Navajo" ("Place Names of the San Juan Basin, New Mexico," *WF* 10 [1951]: 166).

8. Lance Chilton et al., *New Mexico: A New Guide to the Colorful State* (Albuquerque: University of New Mexico Press, 1984), 317.

9. Ibid., 583–84.

10. Ibid., 585–86.

11. Ibid., 316. Four Corners is not mentioned in the 1940 New Mexico guide. Harold F. Thatcher and Mary Hudson Brothers note that "at the lofty summit of the La Platas [Mountains], a raindrop splits four ways going to four rivers, the La Plata, the Animas, the Mancos, and the Dolores. This four-way split of the raindrop is symbolic of the four corners near by where the four states . . . can all be touched by a pin point" ("Fabulous La Plata River," *WF* 10 [1951]: 167).

Chapter 2. Royal Roads: Texts of Migration, Adventure, and Commerce

1. Hubert Howe Bancroft, *History of Arizona and New Mexico, 1530–1888* (San Francisco: The History Company, 1889), 114, 113. See also Gaspar Pérez de Villagrá, *History of New Mexico* (Alcalá, 1610), trans. Gilberto Espinosa and ed. F. W. Hodge (Los Angeles: Quivira Society, 1933).

2. Herbert J. Spinden, trans., *Songs of the Tewa* (1933; reprint, Santa Fe: Sunstone Press, 1976), 97.

3. Ruth Benedict, *Tales of the Cochiti Indians,* BAE Bulletin 98 (1931; reprint, Albuquerque: University of New Mexico Press, 1981), 15. The man who told Benedict the story "was a priest of importance, and except for the taboo against imparting esoteric information to the whites, which both Professor [Franz] Boas and I found very strong in Cochiti, . . . he . . . could, I think, have given a great body of such lore. As it is, such references are slurred or appear in obviously abbreviated accounts" (xiii).

4. Matilda Coxe Stevenson, *The Zuñi Indians,* BAE 23d Annual Report (1904; reprint, Glorieta, New Mexico: Rio Grande Press, 1970), 78–79.

5. Dennis Tedlock, "The Spoken Word and the Work of Interpretation in American Indian Religion," in idem, *The Spoken Word and the Work of Interpretation* (Philadelphia: University of Pennsylvania Press, 1983), 234–35.

6. Peter Nabokov, *Indian Running* (1981; reprint, Santa Fe: Ancient City Press, 1987), 23.

7. Morris Edward Opler, "The Jicarilla Apache Ceremonial Relay Race," *AA* 46 (1944): 77. For photographs taken by Marguerite Rymes at September 14th and 15th footraces near Dulce, see Joanne Rijmes, "Jicarilla Apaches—Stone Lake in the 1930s," *NM,* September 1984, 40–43.

8. Bernhardt A. Reuter, "Acoma Trails," NMFWP, November 19, 1938, WPA#62, NMSRC; 5-4-15#2, H-MNM.

9. George P. Hammond, "The Search for the Fabulous in the Settlement of the Southwest," in *New Spain's Far Northern Frontier: Essays on Spain in the American West, 1540–1821,* ed. David J. Weber (Albuquerque: University of New Mexico Press, 1979), 20. Weber also notes Herbert Eugene Bolton's presentation of Spanish myths throughout North America, including the belief that "somewhere beyond the Colorado were people who lived under water; another tribe who sat in the shade of their own generous-sized ears; and still other people who did not eat their food, but lived on smells." Bolton, "Defensive Spanish Expansion and the Significance of the Borderlands," 1930, in *Bolton and the Spanish Borderlands,* ed. John Francis Bannon (Norman: University of Oklahoma Press, 1964), 40–41.

10. Cabeza de Vaca, *Adventures in the Unknown Interior of America,* trans. and ed. Cyclone Covey (New York: Collier Books, 1961), 111–12.

11. John Francis Bannon, *The Spanish Borderlands Frontier, 1513–1821* (New York: Holt, Rinehart and Winston, 1970), 12.

12. Hammond, "Search for the Fabulous," 21. For the quote, see "Report of Fray Marcos de Niza," in *Narratives of the Coronado Expedition, 1540–1542,* ed. and trans. Hammond and Agapito Rey (Albuquerque: University of New Mexico Press, 1940), 65–66.

13. Bannon, *Spanish Borderlands,* 20.

14. Hammond and Rey, *Narratives of Coronado,* 221.

15. William B. Conroy, "The Llano Estacado in 1541: Spanish Perception of a Distinctive Physical Setting," in *The Spanish Borderlands—A First Reader,* ed. Oakah L. Jones, Jr. (Los Angeles: Lorrin L. Morrison, 1974), 27.

16. Quoted in Conroy, "The Llano Estacado in 1541," 28; source, Hammond and Rey, *Narratives of Coronado,* 241.

17. Quoted in Conroy, "The Llano Estacado in 1541," 28; source, Hammond and Rey, ibid., 279.

18. Hammond, "Search for the Fabulous," 22.

19. Ibid., 26.

20. Ibid., 27.

21. Castañeda, in Hammond and Rey, *Narratives of Coronado,* 218.

22. Hartley B. Alexander, "The Horse in American Indian Culture," in *So Live the Works of Men,* ed. Donald D. Brand and Fred E. Harvey (Albuquerque: University of New Mexico Press, 1939), 67.

23. Michel Pijoán, M.D., "The Horses of Oñate," *EP* 81, 3 (Fall 1975): 13 (special issue on "The Horse in the Southwest").

24. Ibid., 14.

25. LaVerne Harrell Clark, *They Sang for Horses: The Impact of the Horse on Navajo and Apache Folklore* (Tucson: University of Arizona Press, 1966), 8.

26. Ibid., 12.

27. "The War God's Horse Song," words by Tall Kia ah'ni, interpreted by Louis Watchman, in Dane Coolidge and Mary Roberts Coolidge, *The Navajo Indians*

(Boston: Houghton Mifflin, 1930), 2. The Coolidges claim that "for many years, since 1913, the authors have traveled the length and breadth of the Reservation, learning from trader and Indian and Government official alike the story of the Dineh" (p. vi), and that "when the book was in final form, it was read back, word for word, to the Indians" (p. v).

28. Ramon F. Adams, *Western Words: A Dictionary of the Range, Cow Camp and Trail* (Norman: University of Oklahoma Press, 1944), 3.

29. N. Howard (Jack) Thorp with Neil M. Clark, *Pardner of the Wind* (1941; reprint, Lincoln: University of Nebraska Press, 1977), 46.

30. Margaret Larkin, *The Singing Cowboy: A Book of Western Songs* (New York: Alfred A. Knopf, 1931), 111. According to Jim Bob Tinsley: "Larkin was born in 1899 in Mesilla Park, New Mexico, 'with a guitar in her lap,' to use her own expression. During her illustrious career she was a poet, trade union activist, folksinger, writer of nonfiction, and theater personality. She died in Mexico City in 1967" (*He Was Singin' This Song* [Orlando: University Presses of Florida, 1981], 127).

31. Richard I. Ford, "Inter-Indian Exchange in the Southwest," in *Handbook 10,* 711.

32. J. J. Brody, *The Chaco Phenomenon* (Albuquerque: Maxwell Museum of Anthropology, University of New Mexico, 1983), 23–24.

33. Linda S. Cordell, *Prehistory of the Southwest* (Orlando, Florida: Academic Press, 1984), 257.

34. Robert H. Lister and Florence C. Lister, *Chaco Canyon: Archaeology and Archaeologists* (Albuquerque: University of New Mexico Press, 1981), 147.

35. Linda S. Cordell, "Prehistory: Eastern Anasazi," in *Handbook 9,* 141.

36. Ford, "Inter-Indian Exchange," 713.

37. Elsie Clews Parsons, *Taos Tales,* Memoirs of the American Folk-Lore Society, vol. 34 (New York: J. J. Augustin, 1940), 32–33.

38. Leslie A. White, *The Acoma Indians,* BAE 47th Annual Report (1932; reprint, Glorieta, New Mexico: Rio Grande Press, 1973), 139.

39. Paul M. Kraemer, "New Mexico's Ancient Salt Trade," *EP* 82, 1 (Spring 1976): 24.

40. Marc Simmons, "Carros y Carretas: Vehicular Traffic on the Camino Real," in *Hispanic Arts and Ethnohistory in the Southwest: New Papers in Honor of E. Boyd,* ed. Marta Weigle with Claudia Larcombe and Samuel Larcombe (Santa Fe: Ancient City Press; Albuquerque: University of New Mexico Press, 1983), 325.

41. Marc Simmons, "Colonial New Mexico and Mexico: The Historical Relationship," in *Colonial Frontiers: Art and Life in Spanish New Mexico, The Fred Harvey Collection,* ed. Christine Mather (Santa Fe: Ancient City Press, 1983), 77–78.

42. Ibid., 85; Arthur L. Campa, *Hispanic Culture in the Southwest* (Norman: University of Oklahoma Press, 1979), 45.

43. Marc Simmons, *Taos to Tomé: True Tales of Hispanic New Mexico* (Albuquerque: Adobe Press, 1978), 10–11.

44. Arthur Leon Campa, *Spanish Folk-Poetry in New Mexico* (Albuquerque: University of New Mexico Press, 1946), 18–19.

45. "Santa Fee Trail," coll. by J. D. Robb from Doughbelly Price, Taos, 10 December 1950, Robb R-399.

46. Max L. Moorhead, ed., *Commerce of the Prairies,* by Josiah Gregg (Norman: University of Oklahoma Press, 1954), ix. On the social and economic consequences of extending the Chihuahua Trail into Missouri after 1821, see idem, *New Mexico's Royal Road: Trade and Travel on the Chihuahua Trail* (Norman: University of Oklahoma Press, 1958), 182–204.

47. Gregg, *Commerce of the Prairies,* 77–78.

48. Ibid., 69, 71–72.

49. Marian Sloan Russell, *Land of Enchantment: Memoirs of Marian Russell along the Santa Fe Trail,* as dictated to Mrs. Hal Russell, ed. Garnet M. Brayer (1954; reprint, Albuquerque: University of New Mexico Press, 1981), 15, 18–19.

50. Ibid., 19, 26–27.

51. Bertha S. Dodge, *The Story of Inscription Rock* (Canaan, New Hampshire: Phoenix Publishing, 1975), 29. See also David J. Weber, *Richard Kern: Expeditionary Artist in the Far Southwest, 1848–1853* (Albuquerque: University of New Mexico Press, 1985).

52. *El Morro Trails: El Morro National Monument, New Mexico* (Globe, Arizona: Southwest Parks and Monuments Association, 1982), 4, 8–9.

53. Gerald Thompson, *Edward F. Beale & The American West* (Albuquerque: University of New Mexico Press, 1983), 114.

54. A. Irving Hallowell, "Cultural Factors in Spatial Orientation," in his *Culture and Experience* (1955; reprint, New York: Schocken Books, 1967), 196. Hallowell observes of the Saulteaux that "in principle, this step by step procedure emerges in certain mythological narratives where it takes the following form: The protagonist is directed from point to point in a strange country by a series of old women. . . . The analogy to actual travel should be clear. Familiar landmarks in a journey correspond to the old women; they mark the nodal points in a geographic progression in space" (p. 196).

55. Norman O. Brown, *Hermes the Thief: The Evolution of a Myth* (1947; reprint, New York: Vintage Books, 1969), 39–40.

56. Russell, *Land of Enchantment,* 53, 55–56.

Focal Place Two: El Santuario de Chimayó

1. John Peabody Harrington, "The Ethnogeography of the Tewa Indians," in BAE 29th Annual Report (Washington, D.C.: Government Printing Office, 1916), 341–42.

2. Alfonso Ortiz, *The Tewa World: Space, Time, Being, and Becoming in a Pueblo Society* (Chicago: University of Chicago Press, 1969), 19.

3. Stephen F. de Borhegyi, "The Miraculous Shrines of Our Lord of Esquípulas in Guatemala and Chimayó, New Mexico," in *El Santuario de Chimayo,* The Spanish Colonial Arts Society (1956; Santa Fe: Ancient City Press, 1982), 8. Borhegyi's article originally appeared in *EP* 60 (1953): 83–111. See also Elizabeth Kay, *Chimayo Valley Traditions* (Santa Fe: Ancient City Press, 1987).

4. Quoted in Samuel Larcombe, "Plaza del Cerro, Chimayó, New Mexico: An Old Place Not Quite on the Highway," in *Hispanic Arts and Ethnohistory in the Southwest: New Papers in Honor of E. Boyd,* ed. Marta Weigle with Claudia Larcombe and Samuel Larcombe (Santa Fe: Ancient City Press; Albuquerque: University of New

Mexico Press, 1983), 171–73. Boyd's account originally appeared in *Historic Preservation: A Plan for New Mexico* (Santa Fe: New Mexico State Planning Office, 1971), 79–81.

5. "Tewa Basin Study, Volume II: The Spanish-American Villages," 1935, reprinted in *Hispanic Villages of Northern New Mexico: A Reprint of Volume II of The 1935 Tewa Basin Study, with Supplementary Materials,* ed. Marta Weigle (Santa Fe: The Lightning Tree, 1975), 85–86.

6. Paul A. F. Walter, "A New Mexico Lourdes," *EP* 3, (2 January 1916): 3. On the 1837 Chimayó rebellion, see Janet Lecomte, *Rebellion in Rio Arriba 1837* (Albuquerque: University of New Mexico Press in cooperation with the Historical Society of New Mexico, 1985).

7. Quoted in Marta Weigle, "The First Twenty-Five Years of the Spanish Colonial Arts Society," in Weigle et al., eds., *Hispanic Arts,* 185. See also Beatrice Chauvenet, *John Gaw Meem: Pioneer in Historic Preservation* (Santa Fe: Historic Santa Fe Foundation/Museum of New Mexico Press, 1985), 61–71.

8. William Wroth, *Christian Images in Hispanic New Mexico: The Taylor Museum Collection of Santos* (Colorado Springs, Colorado: Taylor Museum of the Colorado Springs Fine Arts Center, 1982), 203. For an account of the Guatemalan pilgrimage, see Erna Fergusson, "The Shrine of the Black Christ," in her *Guatemala* (New York: Alfred A. Knopf, 1937), 48–61.

9. Stephen F. de Borhegyi, "The Cult of Our Lord of Esquípulas in Middle America and New Mexico," *EP* 61 (1954): 397. On Bernardo Abeyta, see Thomas J. Steele, S.J., and Rowena Rivera, *Penitente Self-Government: Brotherhoods and Councils, 1797–1947* (Santa Fe: Ancient City Press, 1985), 16–19.

10. Elizabeth Willis DeHuff, "The Santuario at Chimayo," *NM,* June 1931, 16–17. See also a version of this, "The Shrine at Chimayo," in DeHuff, *Say the Bells of Old Missions: Legends of Old New Mexico Churches* (St. Louis, Missouri: B. Herder Book Company, 1943), 64–68.

11. Elsie Clews Parsons, *Isleta, New Mexico,* BAE 47th Annual Report (1932; reprint, Albuquerque: Calvin Horn Publisher, 1974), 415 16. Both Parsons and Esther Schiff Goldfrank collected from Juan Abeita, whom the former calls "shrewd . . . [but] also exceedingly credulous" and given to "emotional irresponsibility" (201, 202). See Goldfrank, "Isleta Variants: A Study in Flexibility," *JAF* 39 (1926): 70–78.

12. Borhegyi, "Miraculous Shrines," 17–18. For a comparative perspective on these legends, see Victor Turner and Edith Turner's summary of the Spanish "shepherds' cycle"—"a body of legends, current between the ninth and thirteenth centuries, which describe the miraculous discovery of images of the Virgin Mary, mainly by shepherds, cowherds, and farmers. . . . Very often the shepherd is led to his discovery by a miraculous happening. . . . This narrative genre had a very wide distribution in medieval Europe" (*Image and Pilgrimage in Christian Culture: Anthropological Perspectives* [New York: Columbia University Press, 1978], 41).

13. Borhegyi, ibid., 21–22.

14. E. Boyd, *Saints and Saint Makers of New Mexico* (Santa Fe: Laboratory of Anthropology, 1946), 127. See also Yvonne Lange, "Santo Niño de Atocha: A Mexican Cult Is Transplanted to Spain," *EP* 84, 4 (Winter 1978): 2–7; Thomas J. Steele, S.J., *Santos and Saints: The Religious Folk Art of Hispanic New Mexico* (1974; rev. ed., Santa Fe: Ancient City Press, 1982), 109–10, 170.

15. Nina Otero (Warren), *Old Spain in Our Southwest* (New York: Harcourt, Brace, 1936), 151; Stanley L. Robe, ed., *Hispanic Legends from New Mexico: Narratives from the R. D. Jameson Collection,* Folklore and Mythology Studies, 31 (Berkeley: University of California Press, 1980), 514. Jameson's students also collected other legends about Chimayó (pp. 511–15).

16. David Roybal, "Legends abound about Chimayo's 'other' church," *The Santa Fe New Mexican,* 18 March 1979, B-3.

17. Walter, "New Mexico Lourdes," 3, 5; Robe, *Hispanic Legends,* 514; Amy Passmore Hurt, "Chimayo: The Village Time Has Blest," *NM,* November 1934, 11.

18. Alice Marriott, *María: The Potter of San Ildefonso* (Norman: University of Oklahoma Press, 1948), 36, 37.

Chapter 3. Steel Rails: Texts of Health-Seeking and Tourism

1. The New Mexico Bureau of Immigration had been established on February 15, 1880. According to Herbert H. Lang: "The primary purpose of the bureau was to break the restricting chains of history so that the territory might assume its proper role as a fully integrated component of the national economy. What was deliberately left unsaid (but what was also clearly implied) in the legal verbiage that breathed life into the bureau was a desire to attract large numbers of American farmers and business men. A predominately, or at least substantial, Anglo-American population was the key to long-desired statehood, and statehood was inseparably intertwined with economic progress. In the final analysis, then, the Bureau of Immigration was designed to serve as the catalyst that would enable an underdeveloped community of shepherds and subsistence farmers to evolve into a thriving, viable state in the American Union" ("The New Mexico Bureau of Immigration, 1880–1912," *NMHR* 51 [1976]: 195).

2. Karen D. Shane, "New Mexico: Salubrious El Dorado," *NMHR* 56 (1981): 389; R. W. Wiley, *Albuquerque: In the Heart of the Well Country,* for the Health Department of the Albuquerque Commercial Club (Albuquerque: Anderson & Anderson, n.d.), 3.

3. *Nature's Sanitarium: Las Vegas Hot Springs, Las Vegas, New Mexico, on the Line of the Atchison Topeka and Santa Fe Railroad* (Chicago: Rand, McNally, January 9, 1883), 15.

4. *The Phoenix (formerly Montezuma), Las Vegas Hot Springs New Mexico* (n.d.; reprint, Las Vegas, New Mexico: La Galeria de los Artesanos, October 1982).

5. Stephen D. Fox, "Healing, Imagination, and New Mexico," *NMHR* 58 (1983): 213.

6. F. C. Nims, *Health, Wealth and Pleasure in Colorado and New Mexico* (1881; reprint, Santa Fe: Museum of New Mexico Press, 1980), 15.

7. Billy M. Jones, *Health-Seeking in the Southwest, 1817–1900* (Norman: University of Oklahoma Press, 1967), 126–33; Fox, "Healing and New Mexico," 218, 219.

8. Wiley, *Albuquerque,* 3–4, 6.

9. See, e.g., James Marshall, *Santa Fe: The Railroad That Built an Empire* (New York: Random House, 1945); L. L. Waters, *Steel Rails to Santa Fe* (Lawrence: University of Kansas Press, 1950); Keith L. Bryant, Jr., *History of the Atchison, Topeka and Santa Fe Railway* (New York: Macmillan, 1974). On Edmund G. Ross's career in Kansas and New Mexico, see Marc Simmons, "The Man Who Saved a President [Andrew

Johnson]," in his *Ranchers, Ramblers and Renegades: True Tales of Territorial New Mexico* (Santa Fe: Ancient City Press, 1984), 89–92. Will Rogers is quoted in Dale Bullock, "The Most Interesting 100 Square Mile in America and Its Impact on Santa Fe," *La Gaceta* (El Corral de Santa Fe Westerners) 7, 1 (1981): 7.

10. James David Henderson, *"Meals by Fred Harvey": A Phenomenon of the American West* (Fort Worth: Texas Christian University Press, 1969), 11. According to Henderson: "Service was excellent, and for thirty-five cents patrons received ample portions of well-prepared food. A typical breakfast consisted of steak with eggs, hashed brown potatoes, a six-high stack of pan-sized wheat cakes with maple syrup, and apple pie with coffee for dessert" (ibid).

11. Ibid., 45.

12. Otero quoted in Lynn Perrigo, *Gateway to Glorieta: A History of Las Vegas, New Mexico* (Boulder, Colorado: Pruett Publishing, 1982), 23; Henderson, *"Meals by Fred Harvey,"* 23. Perrigo draws on Miguel A. Otero, *My Life on the Frontier, 1864–1882* (New York: Press of the Pioneers, 1935), 260.

13. Frank Waters, *Masked Gods: Navaho and Pueblo Ceremonialism* (Chicago: Swallow Press, 1950), 109.

14. Marc Simmons, *Albuquerque: A Narrative History* (Albuquerque: University of New Mexico Press, 1982), 329, 330. See also David Gebhard, "Architecture and the Fred Harvey House: The Alvarado and La Fonda," *New Mexico Architecture,* January–February 1964, 18–25.

15. Lawrence Clark Powell, *Southwestern Book Trails: A Reader's Guide to the Heartlands of New Mexico & Arizona* (Albuquerque: Horn & Wallace, Publishers, 1963), 3, 2. According to Susan Dewitt, who quotes Powell: "Where the Alvarado once stood, there is now a parking lot. The loss of the hotel in 1969 [*sic*], because the Santa Fe was unwilling to delay demolition while funds for purchase were sought, was the most serious loss of a landmark the city has sustained" (*Historic Albuquerque Today: An Overview Survey of Historic Buildings and Districts,* Historic Landmarks Survey of Albuquerque, 1978, 73; photo, 126). See also the account of the last days (February 2–March 15, 1970) in John Conron, "The Alvarado Hotel," *New Mexico Architecture,* May–June 1970, 16–19.

16. Toby Smith, "Those Harvey Girls," *Impact: Albuquerque Journal Magazine,* August 11, 1981, 8–9. For a good account of this lore and other topics in this section, see Erna Fergusson, "Fred Harvey, Civilizer," in her *Our Southwest* (New York: Alfred A. Knopf, 1940), 190–206. See also the novel by Samuel Hopkins Adams, *The Harvey Girls* (Cleveland, Ohio: World Publishing, 1942).

17. Jan Hartnett, "Harvey Chain Grows Longer But Rail Station Restaurants Fade," *Albuquerque Journal,* November 17, 1968, C-15, based on Henderson, *"Meals by Fred Harvey,"* 25. After an incident on September 9, 1921, the Harvey Company rule was challenged in Oklahoma courts. Justice Lydick of the Oklahoma Supreme Court later pronounced: "Society in America has for years assumed jurisdiction to a great extent to dictate certain regulations of dress in first-class dining rooms. . . . To permit the coatless to enter would bring in those with the sleeveless shirt, and even the shirtless garb that we frequently see where no formality is required. Man's coat is usually the cleanest of his garments, and the fact that he is required to wear a coat serves notice that decorum is expected and creates a wholesome psychological effect" (Henderson, pp. 51–52).

18. Marshall, *Santa Fe,* 105. Henderson gives another version, based on the *New Mexico Sentinel,* October 27, 1937 (*"Meals by Fred Harvey,"* 23). Bryant places the incident at the Montezuma and cites William E. Curtis, "Hotels in West Owe Excellence to Fred Harvey," *Chicago Record-Herald,* April 27, 1911 (*History of AT&SFRR,* 112–13).

19. Henderson, *"Meals by Fred Harvey,"* 14. See also Carla Kelly, "Fred Harvey's Railroad Cuisines," *American West,* September–October 1982, 14.

20. John Adair, *The Navajo and Pueblo Silversmiths* (Norman: University of Oklahoma Press, 1944), 25–26. See also *White Metal Universe: Navajo Silver from the Fred Harvey Collection* (Phoenix, Arizona: Heard Museum, 1981).

21. On the Fred Harvey Fine Arts Collection, see two recent exhibition catalogues: *Fred Harvey Fine Arts Collection: An Exhibition Organized by the Heard Museum* (Phoenix, Arizona, 1976); Christine Mather, ed., *Colonial Frontiers: Art and Life in Spanish New Mexico, The Fred Harvey Collection,* Museum of International Folk Art Publication (Santa Fe: Ancient City Press, 1983).

22. Virginia L. Grattan, *Mary Colter: Builder Upon the Red Earth* (Flagstaff, Arizona: Northland Press, 1980), 8–13.

23. "Santa Fe and the Santa Fe Railroad," *La Cronica de Nuevo Mexico* (Historical Society of New Mexico), ed. John P. Conron, August 1984, 2.

24. Quoted in Grattan, *Mary Colter,* 25.

25. *La Fonda: The Inn at the End of the Trail In Old Santa Fe, New Mexico* (Rand McNally, July 1929), 1–2.

26. Bainbridge Bunting, *John Gaw Meem: Southwestern Architect* (Albuquerque: University of New Mexico Press, SAR Book, 1983), 74.

27. Grattan, *Mary Colter,* 54.

28. Quoted in D. H. Thomas, *The Southwestern Indian Detours: The story of the Fred Harvey/Santa Fe Railway experiment in 'detourism'* (Phoenix, Arizona: Hunter Publishing, 1978), 65.

29. Ibid., 77, 46–47.

30. *Harveycar Motor Cruises off the beaten path in the Great Southwest* (Rand McNally, January 1, 1929), 12. For more on the Couriers' costume, see Nancy Fox, "Margaret Moses: Collector and Courier," *EP* 90, 3 (Fall/Winter 1984): 29–31. See also Emily Hahn, *Times and Places* (New York: Pinnacle Books, 1971), 87–100.

31. Thomas, *Indian Detours,* 62.

32. Albert D. Manchester, "Couriers, Dudes, and Touring Cars: The Legend of Indian Detours," *NM,* June 1982, 46; *Indian-detours: Most distinctive Motor Cruise service in the world* (Chicago: Rand McNally, November 1930), 7.

33. *Harveycar Motor Cruises,* 1929, 11.

34. Dickson Hartwell, "Let's Eat With The Harvey Boys," *Collier's,* April 9, 1949, 30, 32.

35. "What Fred Harvey Means to the Hotel Business," *The Hotel Monthly,* December 1951, 52; "Elbert Hubbard's Eulogy on Fred Harvey," ca. 1907, in Henderson, *"Meals by Fred Harvey,"* 53–54.

36. Cf. Earl Pomeroy, "Palace Cars and Pleasure Domes," in his *In Search of the Golden West: The Tourist in Western America* (New York: Alfred A. Knopf, 1957), 3–30. See also Richard A. Van Orman, *A Room for the Night: Hotels of the Old West* (Bloomington: Indiana University Press, 1966).

37. Nelson H. H. Graburn, "Tourism: The Sacred Journey," in *Hosts and Guests: The Anthropology of Tourism,* ed. Valene L. Smith (Philadelphia: University of Pennsylvania Press, 1977), 25. See also Maxine Feifer, *Tourism in History: From Imperial Rome to the Present* (New York: Stein and Day, 1985), 95–134.

38. Pomeroy, *In Search of Golden West,* 39; T. C. McLuhan, *Dream Tracks: The Railroad and the American Indian, 1890–1930,* with photographs from the William E. Kopplin Collection (New York: Harry N. Abrams, 1985), 49. See also Keith L. Bryant, Jr., "The Atchison, Topeka and Santa Fe Railway and the Development of the Taos and Santa Fe Art Colonies," *Western Historical Quarterly* 9 (1978): 437–53.

39. Quoted in Thomas, *Indian Detours,* 52–53.

40. Graburn, "Tourism," 25.

41. Daniel J. Boorstin, *The Image: A Guide to Pseudo-Events in America* (1961; reprint, New York: Atheneum, 1982), 3–4.

42. Manchester, "Couriers, Dudes, and Touring Cars," 41; Marta Weigle, *Brothers of Light, Brothers of Blood: The Penitentes of the Southwest* (Albuquerque: University of New Mexico Press, 1976), 114.

Focal Place Three: Pecos Pueblo and Mission

1. Alden C. Hayes, *The Four Churches of Pecos* (Albuquerque: University of New Mexico Press in cooperation with Southwest Parks and Monuments Association, 1974).

2. On the pre-Columbian Mexican culture hero Quetzalcoatl, see David Carrasco, *Quetzalcoatl and the Irony of Empire: Myths and Prophecies in the Aztec Tradition* (Chicago: University of Chicago Press, 1982).

3. John L. Kessell, *Kiva, Cross, and Crown: The Pecos Indians and New Mexico, 1540–1840* (Washington, D.C.: National Park Service, U.S. Department of the Interior, 1979), 463, 471–73.

4. Marc Simmons, "Pecos Pueblo on the Santa Fe Trail," *Exploration: Annual Bulletin of the School of American Research,* 1981, 4.

5. Marc Simmons, *Following the Santa Fe Trail: A Guide for Modern Travelers,* 2d ed. (Santa Fe: Ancient City Press, 1986), 184. Most sources give Kozlowski's first name as Andrew; Simmons first identified him as Napoleon, but he has since determined Martin to be the proper designation.

6. Kessell, *Kiva, Cross, Crown,* 476–77. See also Beatrice Chauvenet, "Hewett Takes on the San Diego Exposition," in her *Hewett and Friends: A Biography of Santa Fe's Vibrant Era* (Santa Fe: Museum of New Mexico Press, 1983), 97–108; Michael Miller, "New Mexico's Role in the Panama-California Exposition of 1915," *EP* 91, 2 (Fall 1985): 13–17.

7. Albert H. Schroeder, "Pecos Pueblo," in *Handbook 9,* 432. See also G. Emlen Hall, *Four Leagues of Pecos: A Legal History of the Pecos Grant, 1800–1933,* New Mexico Land Grant Series (Albuquerque: University of New Mexico Press, 1984).

8. Kessell, *Kiva, Cross, Crown,* 472; *Lieutenant Emory Reports: A Reprint of Lieutenant W. H. Emory's 'Notes of a Military Reconnaissance',* ed. Ross Calvin (Albuquerque:

University of New Mexico Press, 1951), 53–54. Calvin notes that *estuffa* "is correctly spelled estufa (Span. stove, hothouse). It signifies the subterranean chamber (now more commonly called the *kiva*) in which the secret religious ceremonies of the pueblo are performed" (p. 198).

9. William G. Ritch, "Introductory. New Mexico. A Sketch of Its History and Review of Its Resources," 8–9, in *New Mexico Blue Book, 1882* (facsimile ed., Albuquerque: University of New Mexico Press, 1968).

10. The complicated history of the Great Seal of the State of New Mexico is described in *New Mexico Blue Book, 1965–1966,* comp. Alberta Miller (n.d.), 51–52. There are various differences in the design from the time of the first seal (now lost), presented to the Historical Society of New Mexico in May 1860. In 1965, "the seal imprint still used by the Secretary of State is the same as that used by the first Secretary of State, Antonio Lucero. . . . At least four slightly different impressions have been used on printed materials since 1912. . . . Legally, however, the design of the Great Seal of New Mexico is still that described in the 1915 codification. In colored versions, the larger eagle should be depicted as the American Bald Eagle, dark brown in body with white head and tail, while the smaller Mexican eagle should be the Harpy Eagle, with brown body, shading to a lighter tone at the breast and head" (p. 52).

11. Matthew C. Field, in Kessell, *Kiva, Cross, Crown,* 459–62.

12. Josiah Gregg, *Commerce of the Prairies,* ed. Max L. Moorhead (Norman: University of Oklahoma Press, 1954), 188–89.

13. Susan Shelby Magoffin, *Down the Santa Fe Trail and into Mexico: Diary of Susan Shelby Magoffin, 1846–1847,* ed. Stella M. Drumm (1926; reprint, New Haven: Yale University Press, 1962), 99–100.

14. Willa Cather, *Death Comes for the Archbishop* (1927; New York: Vintage Books, 1971), 127, 130, 133, 134. James M. Dinn interprets Cather's use of this incident mythically as "fundamentally, . . . the Perilous Chapel experience, summarized by Jessie Weston [*From Ritual to Romance,* 1957]. The questing knight [Latour, according to Dinn] seeks shelter from a storm in a strange chapel where he undergoes an adventure 'in which supernatural, and evil forces are engaged.' In one version a Black Hand comes through a window, extinguishes the candle and rocks the building with its cries" ("A Novelist's Miracle: Structure and Myth in *Death Comes For The Archbishop,*" *Western American Literature* 7 [1972]: 42).

15. Frank G. Applegate, "The Twelve Virgins of Pecos," in his *Indian Stories from the Pueblos* (Philadelphia: J. B. Lippincott, 1929), 177–78.

16. Bandelier, *The Southwestern Journals of Adolph F. Bandelier, 1880–1882,* ed. Charles H. Lange and Carroll L. Riley (Albuquerque: University of New Mexico Press; Santa Fe: School of American Research Press, Museum of New Mexico Press, 1966), 78, 79–80.

17. Quoted in Kessell, *Kiva, Cross, Crown,* 473; from Edward S. Curtis, *The Native American Indians,* vol. 17 (Norwood, Massachusetts: Plimpton Press, 1926).

18. Helen H. Roberts, "The Reason for the Departure of the Pecos Indians for Jemez Pueblo," *AA* 34 (1932): 359–60. Some themes in this version are suggested in Aurelio M. Espinosa, "The Monster Viper": "This is a Spanish-Indian myth. The belief is that the Pueblo Indians of New Mexico have in each pueblo a monster viper *(el viborón)* in a large subterranean cave, which is nourished with seven living children each year. . . . I am inclined to believe that this is a pure Indian myth, probably of Aztec

origin. The interesting thing about it is, that the Indians themselves have very vague ideas concerning it, some even denying it. The belief among the [Hispanic] New Mexicans of this Indian myth is widespread, and the gradual disappearance of the New Mexico Pueblo Indians is explained by the myth in question. In the pueblo of Taos it is said that an Indian woman, when her turn came to deliver her child to the monster viper, fled to her Mexican neighbors, and thus saved her child." Espinosa also notes: "This myth may have something to do with some old sacrificial rites of the Pueblo Indians" ("New-Mexican Spanish Folk-Lore," *JAF* 23 [1910]: 403).

19. B. A. Reuter, "Pecos Indian Caves," NMFWP, May 27, 1939, WPA#57, NMSRC. Reuter refers to J. Frank Dobie's account of José Vaca, "In the Sunshine of Pecos," in his *Coronado's Children: Tales of Lost Mines and Buried Treasures of the Southwest* (1930; reprint, New York: Literary Guild of America, 1931), 222–38.

Chapter 4. Land of Enchantment: Texts of Color and Spectacle

1. D. H. Lawrence, "Just Back from the Snake Dance," *Laughing Horse,* September 1924, reprinted in *D. H. Lawrence and New Mexico,* ed. Keith Sagar (Salt Lake City, Utah: Gibbs M. Smith, 1982), 64.

2. Mary Irene Severns, "Tourism in New Mexico: The Promotional Activities of the New Mexico State Tourist Bureau, 1935–1950" (Master's thesis, University of New Mexico, 1951), 11–12. See also Julie Dunleavy, "New Mexico: A Pioneer in Southwestern Tourism," *NM,* November 1984, 61–65; Stanley M. Hordes and Carol Joiner, comps. and eds., *Historical Markers in New Mexico* (Santa Fe: Delgado Studios, 1984), a record of the texts on current markers from the program begun in 1935.

3. Lilian Whiting, *The Land of Enchantment: From Pike's Peak to the Pacific* (Boston: Little, Brown, 1906), 3–4; Eugene Manlove Rhodes, "A Number of Things," *Saturday Evening Post,* April 8, 1911, reprinted in *The Rhodes Reader: Stories of Virgins, Villains, and Varmints,* selected by W. H. Hutchinson, 2d ed. (Norman: University of Oklahoma Press, 1975), 82.

4. Ina Sizer Cassidy, "Works Progress Administration Handbook, Federal Writers' Project, State of New Mexico," 1938, WPA#71, NMSRC.

5. John A. Jakle, *The Tourist: Travel in Twentieth-Century North America* (Lincoln: University of Nebraska Press, 1985), 126, 121. Jakle refers to Foster R. Dulles, *America Learns to Play: A History of Recreation* (New York: Appleton-Century-Crofts, 1965).

6. Monty Noam Penkower, *The Federal Writers' Project: A Study in Government Patronage of the Arts* (Urbana: University of Illinois Press, 1977); 84–85, 86; National Archives, Record Group 69.

7. Quoted in Marta Weigle, ed., *New Mexicans in Cameo and Camera: New Deal Documentation of Twentieth-Century Lives* (Albuquerque: University of New Mexico Press, 1985), xvii–xviii.

8. Charles Ethrige Minton to John D. Newsom, May 20, 1940, National Archives, Washington, D.C. Quoted in notes to a commentary on the literary side of the NMFWP/WP in Marta Weigle and Kyle Fiore, *Santa Fe and Taos: The Writer's Era, 1916–1941* (Santa Fe: Ancient City Press, 1982), 70.

9. This material is drawn from Arthur Scharf's bibliography, "Selected Publications of the WPA Federal Writers' Project and the Writers' Program," in Jerre Mangione, *The Dream and the Deal: The Federal Writers' Project, 1935–1943* (Boston: Little, Brown, 1972), 375–96. States without epithets in their guide's subtitle and their guides' first publication dates are: Arizona (1940), Arkansas (1941), Connecticut (1938), Georgia (1940), Idaho (1937), Illinois (1939), Louisiana (1941), Massachusetts (1937), Minnesota (1938), Montana (1939), New Jersey (1939), Ohio (1940), South Dakota (1938), Tennessee (1939), Utah (1941), and Wyoming (1941); those with epithets: Alabama—Deep South (1941), California—Golden (1941), Colorado—Highest (1941), Delaware—First (1938), Florida—Southern-most (1939), Indiana—Hoosier (1941), Iowa—Hawkeye (1938), Kansas—Sunflower (1939), Kentucky—Bluegrass (1939), Maine—"Down East" (1937), Maryland—Old Line (1940), Michigan—Wolverine (1941), Mississippi—Magnolia (1938), Missouri—"Show Me" (1941), Nebraska—Cornhusker (1939), Nevada—Silver (1940), New Hampshire—Granite (1938), New Mexico—Colorful (1940), New York—Empire (1940), North Carolina—Old North (1939), North Dakota—Northern Prairie (1938), Oklahoma—Sooner (1942), Oregon—End of the Trail (1940), Pennsylvania—Keystone (1940), Rhode Island—Smallest (1937), South Carolina—Palmetto (1941), Texas—Lone Star (1940), Vermont—Green Mountain (1941), Virginia—Old Dominion (1940), Washington—Evergreen (1941), West Virginia—Mountain (1941), and Wisconsin—Badger (1941).

10. *New Mexico: A Guide to the Colorful State,* comp. Workers of the Writers' Program of the Work Projects Administration in the State of New Mexico (New York: Hastings House, 1940), 4, 3.

11. Edmund Sherman, "New Mexico Celebrates," *NM,* June 1940, 12, 11, 13. See also chap. 7 below.

12. Daniel J. Boorstin, *The Image: A Guide to Pseudo-Events in America* (1961; reprint, New York: Atheneum, 1982), 84.

13. May Price Mosley, "Customs and Conditions of Early Ranch Life (Lea County)," NMFWP, December 7, 1936, in her *"Little Texas" Beginnings in Southeastern New Mexico,* ed. Martha Downer Ellis (Roswell, New Mexico: Hall-Poorbaugh Press, 1973), 29, 30.

14. Boorstin, *The Image,* 85.

15. Cf. Eric Hobsbawm and Terence Ranger, eds., *The Invention of Tradition* (Cambridge: Cambridge University Press, 1983); Dean MacCannell, "Staged Authenticity," in his *The Tourist: A New Theory of the Leisure Class* (New York: Schocken Books, 1976), 91–107; MacCannell, "Reconstructed Ethnicity: Tourism and Cultural Identity in Third World Communities," *Annals of Tourism Research* 11 (1984): 375–91.

16. T. C. McLuhan, *Dream Tracks: The Railroad and the American Indian, 1890–1930,* with photographs from the William E. Kopplin Collection (New York: Harry N. Abrams, 1985), 37.

17. Nelson H. H. Graburn, "Tourism: The Sacred Journey," in *Hosts and Guests: The Anthropology of Tourism,* ed. Valene L. Smith (Philadelphia: University of Pennsylvania Press, 1977), 28.

18. D. H. Lawrence, "New Mexico," *Survey Graphic,* May 1, 1931, reprinted in Sagar, *Lawrence and New Mexico,* 95–96.

Focal Place Four: Carlsbad Caverns

1. T. M. Pearce, ed., with Ina Sizer Cassidy and Helen S. Pearce, *New Mexico Place Names: A Geographical Dictionary* (Albuquerque: University of New Mexico Press, 1965), 27.

2. Stevens quoted in Billy M. Jones, *Health-Seekers in the Southwest, 1817–1900* (Norman: University of Oklahoma Press, 1967), 115.

3. Paige W. Christiansen and Frank E. Kottlowski, eds., *Mosaic of New Mexico's Scenery, Rocks, and History,* Scenic Trips to the Geologic Past No. 8 (Socorro: New Mexico State Bureau of Mines and Mineral Resources, 1972), 77–78.

4. Blanche C. Grant, *Cavern Guide Book: Carlsbad Caverns, Carlsbad, N.M.* (Topeka, Kansas: Crane & Company, 1928), 27, 28–29.

5. Robert A. Holley, quoted in *Carlsbad Caverns National Park New Mexico: Its Early Explorations as told by Jim White* (Ireland, 1951).

6. John Barnett, *Carlsbad Caverns National Park New Mexico* (Carlsbad, New Mexico: Carlsbad Caverns Natural History Association, 1979), 34.

7. Grant, *Cavern Guide Book,* 33–34.

8. Haniel Long, *Piñon Country* (New York: Duell, Sloan & Pearce, 1941), 218–19.

9. *New Mexico: A Guide to the Colorful State,* comp. Workers of the Writers' Program of the Work Projects Administration in the State of New Mexico (New York: Hastings House, 1940), 406, 407, 411.

Chapter 5. A Sense of Place: Texts of Settlement, Communication, and Confrontation

1. Frances Densmore, *Music of Acoma, Isleta, Cochiti and Zuñi Pueblos,* BAE Bulletin 165 (Washington, D.C.: Government Printing Office, 1957), 43, 4. The song is part of the Situi, "danced by men who belong to a certain society. This dance is understood only by members of this society but is a source of pleasure to the people. It may be given at any time, winter or summer, either in the plaza during the day or in the kiva at night, and it continues for 1 or 2 days. The songs are accompanied by scraping sticks with squash resonators, played by about 18 women whose faces are covered by yellow masks, like those of the raingods. . . . The scraping sticks are used with no other sacred dance and with only one secular dance. . . . The men are in a line and face alternately toward the right and left while the women musicians, seated in a line on their blankets, face the dancers. In the words . . . we find a belief that abundant rain is due to the power of a new chief in an eastern village" (pp. 41–42).

2. Lorin W. Brown, "San Ysidro Labrador," NMFWP, n.d., reprinted in Brown, with Charles L. Briggs and Marta Weigle, *Hispano Folklife of New Mexico: The Lorin W. Brown Federal Writers' Project Manuscripts* (Albuquerque: University of New Mexico Press, 1978), 186–87. See also a version of the *alabado* collected in Córdova during the early 1970s by Charles L. Briggs, in "A Conversation with Saint Isidore: The Teachings of the Elders," in *Hispanic Arts and Ethnohistory in the Southwest,* ed. Marta Weigle with Claudia Larcombe and Samuel Larcombe (Santa Fe: Ancient City Press; Albuquerque: University of New Mexico Press, 1983), 103–9.

3. This rendering comes from the words and music reprinted in Ruth K. Hall, *A Place of Her Own: The Story of Elizabeth Garrett* (Santa Fe: Sunstone Press, 1983), 94–96. According to Leon C. Metz, Garrett was particularly attentive to his blind daughter Elizabeth (1885–1947). "The reasons behind her blindness, and whether or not she was blind at birth or became so shortly afterward, are and will always remain a mystery. It is also a mystery why such a rash of incredible rumors have become a part of Garrett's tradition and legend. . . . The most common story is that Elizabeth was blind at birth because her father had syphilis. Pat Garrett had a yen for women outside the family circle, but there is no evidence that he had venereal disease. Another grisly tale is that he blinded her with his thumbs during a drunken rage. This is too ridiculous even to consider. And, finally, there is the charge that Elizabeth lost her sight as a result of improper medicine administered to her eyes when she was an infant. This is a possible, even probable, explanation. . . . If Elizabeth ever blamed her father for her condition she never mentioned it. On the contrary, all of the evidence indicates that she adored him. . . . She was a credit to her father and an asset to New Mexico" (Metz, *Pat Garrett: The Story of a Western Lawman* [Norman: University of Oklahoma Press, 1974], 157).

   A Spanish language state song, "Así Es Nuevo Méjico," by Amadeo Lucero, was adopted by Senate Bill 182, April 1, 1971. The chorus reads: "Así es Nuevo Méjico / Así es esta tierra del sol / De sierras y valles de tierras frutales / Así es Nuevo Méjico."

4. Robert W. Larson, *New Mexico's Quest for Statehood, 1846–1912* (Albuquerque: University of New Mexico Press, 1968), 304. See also the text of the proclamation in *New Mexico Historic Documents,* ed. Richard N. Ellis (Albuquerque: University of New Mexico Press, 1975), 90–91.

5. Richard L. Polese, "The Zia Sun Symbol: Variations on a Theme," *EP* 75, 2 (summer 1968): 30.

6. Ibid., 32–33; with additional notes from *New Mexico Blue Book, 1965–1966,* comp. Alberta Miller (n.d.), 47.

7. Densmore, *Music of Pueblos,* 60, 62. Densmore notes that "the native name of Isleta Pueblo is 'Shiewhibak'" (p. 62).

8. Edmund J. Ladd, "Zuni Religion and Philosophy," *Exploration: Annual Bulletin of the School of American Research,* 1983, 31.

9. Aniela Jaffé, ed., *C. G. Jung: Word and Image,* Bollingen Series 97:2 (Princeton, New Jersey: Princeton University Press, 1979), 155; C. G. Jung, *Memories, Dreams, Reflections,* ed. Aniela Jaffé and trans. Richard and Clara Winston (New York: Pantheon Books, 1963), 252, 253; also reprinted in Tony H. Hillerman, ed., *The Spell of New Mexico* (Albuquerque: University of New Mexico Press, 1976), 42–43.

10. Gary Witherspoon, *Language and Art in the Navajo Universe* (Ann Arbor: University of Michigan Press, 1977), 146, 144–45. See also Sam D. Gill, "The Color of Navajo Ritual Symbolism: An Evaluation of Methods," *Journal of Anthropological Research* 4 (1975): 350–63.

11. Aurelio M. Espinosa, "New-Mexican Spanish Folk-Lore," *JAF* 23 (1910): 413.

12. Cleofas M. Jaramillo, *Shadows of the Past (Sombras del Pasado)* (1941; reprint, Santa Fe: Ancient City Press, 1980), 24.

13. Juan B. Rael, *The New Mexican 'Alabado',* with transcriptions of music by Eleanor Hague, Stanford University Publications, University Series, Language and Literature, vol. 9, no. 3 (Stanford, California, 1951), 94–98.

14. John Donald Robb, *Hispanic Folk Music of New Mexico and the Southwest: A Self-Portrait of a People* (Norman: University of Oklahoma Press, 1980), 647–48.

15. Winfield Townley Scott, "A Calendar of Santa Fe," in his *Exiles and Fabrications* (1957), reprinted in Hillerman, *Spell of New Mexico,* 48.

16. Elizabeth A. Brandt, "Sandia Pueblo," in *Handbook 9,* 349. Brandt notes: "The native name of the community is *napʰiʔad* 'at the dusty place', a local derivation of *napʰi* 'dust'. . . . The Taos name *nàʔpʰẹtho* has been explained as 'place of the cloud hills' . . . a presumed reference to the sand dunes in the area; it probably reflects a Taos folk etymology of the Sandia name." See also James A. Morris, *Oku Pin: The Sandia Mountains of New Mexico* (Albuquerque: Seven Goats Editions, 1980).

17. Willa Cather, *Death Comes for the Archbishop,* Book 9, 2 (1927; reprint, New York: Vintage Books, 1971), 273.

18. Clara D. True, "A Legend of Sangre de Cristo," *EP* 4 (1917): 4; William Wroth, "La Sangre de Cristo: History and Symbolism," in Weigle et al., *Hispanic Arts,* 283–88. A legend in the 1950 "New Mexico Place-Name Dictionary" tells how "a priest was riding his burro through this region with his head bowed. It was sunset and the mountains were red with the light. The priest raised his head, beheld the brilliant color, and murmured, 'Blessed be God for the Blood of Christ'" (T. M. Pearce, "Names on the Land," *WF* 9 [1950]: 377).

19. Jill Warren, "New Mexico's Famous Light: Perspective from Artists and Scientists," *NM,* February 1984, 45, 46–47.

20. Haniel Long, *Piñon Country* (New York: Duell, Sloan & Pearce, 1941), 4–5.

21. Emlen Hall, "Water—New Mexico's Delicate Balance," *NM,* May 1983, 16–17.

22. Mrs. Benton (May Price) Mosley, "Desert Water (Lea County)," NMFWP, October 12, 1936, reprinted in her *"Little Texas" Beginnings in Southeastern New Mexico,* ed. Martha Downer Ellis (Roswell, New Mexico: Hall-Poorbaugh Press, 1973), 5.

23. J. Vernon Smithson, "Old Timer's Tales," NMFWP, October 26, 1936, reprinted in *New Mexicans in Cameo and Camera: New Deal Documentation of Twentieth-Century Lives,* ed. Marta Weigle (Albuquerque: University of New Mexico Press, 1985), 163.

24. Mrs. Lena S. Maxwell, "Told by Uncle Charlie Smith (Relation of Mr. C. C. Smith)," NMFWP, n.d., reprinted in Weigle, *New Mexicans,* 160, 162.

25. W. M. Emery, "Digging for Water in New Mexico," as told by Mrs. Al Baker, Clayton, NMFWP, April 9, 1937, WPA#296, NMSRC.

26. Evon Z. Vogt, "Water Witching: An Interpretation of a Ritual Pattern in a Rural American Community," *Scientific Monthly* 75 (September 1952), reprinted in *Reader in Comparative Religion: An Anthropological Approach,* ed. William A. Lessa and Evon Z. Vogt, 3d ed. (New York: Harper & Row, 1972), 454. Clee Woods describes dowser Ben Floersheim, a rancher near Springer, in "The Magic Witching Stick," *NM,* February 1959, 16, 45–46; Beth Morgan reports interviews with contemporary dowsers W. B. Hendricks and Joe Daniels in "Finding water the old way," *Santa Fe New Mexican,* August 28, 1983, B-1, B-7.

27. Hall, "Water," 19.

28. Michael C. Meyer, *Water in the Hispanic Southwest: A Social and Legal History, 1550–1850* (Tucson: University of Arizona Press, 1984), 20–21.

29. Marc Simmons, "Spanish Irrigation Practices in New Mexico," *NMHR* 47 (1972): 140, 141.

30. Arthur L. Campa, *Hispanic Culture in the Southwest* (Norman: University of Oklahoma Press, 1979), 189; Orlando Romero, "Las Acequias, " *NM,* March 1979, 33. See also "The Irrigation Ditch," a photographic essay by Nancy Hunter Warren, *EP* 86, 1 (Spring 1980): 21–28.

31. Simmons, "Spanish Irrigation," 143; Wroth, "La Sangre de Cristo," 290, 291. Note too the belief recorded by Espinosa in 1910: "The waters of lakes and rivers are said to sting *(pican)* during the month of May; and those who bathe therein always say before entering into the water, to cure it, *'Jesús y cruz,'*—a formula similar to the one used in applying any remedy." ("New-Mexican Folk-Lore," 415).

32. Alfonso Ortiz, *The Tewa World: Space, Time, Being, and Becoming in a Pueblo Society* (Chicago: University of Chicago Press, 1969), 117, 115. In February or March, a few days before beginning spring ditch-cleaning, all three medicine societies at Cochiti Pueblo annually plant prayer sticks in each of the two ditches—the Flint Society at the head; the Giant, in the middle; and the Shí'kame, at the foot. Charles H. Lange, *Cochiti: A New Mexico Pueblo, Past and Present* (Carbondale: Southern Illinois Press, 1959), 261, 330.

33. S. F. Hassell, "Grazing: Water," WP, September 25, 1940, WPA#104, NMSRC.

34. Ernest W. Baughman, ed., "Folk Sayings and Beliefs," *NMFR* 9 (1954–55): 24.

35. Lou Sage Batchen, "The Wise Donkey," WP, January 26, 1940, WPA 5-5-49#35, H-MNM. Batchen collected versions from Ramon Nieto, age 75, of Placitas; José Garcia, age 92, of Albuquerque; Patricio Gallegos, age 60, of Ojo de la Casa; and Magdalena Gallegos, age 59, born in Tomé and married to Patricio.

36. Barre Toelken, "Prairie Dogs Cry for Rain," *Quest,* September–October 1978, 115.

37. Jaramillo, *Shadows of the Past,* 105–6; Reyes Nicanor Martínez, "A Sheepherd at Work in Taos County, New Mexico," WP, December 1940, WPA#233, NMSRC. Shepherd Basílico Garduño told Lorin Brown about *las cabañuelas,* predicting the year's weather by observing the first twenty-five days of January (*Hispano Folklife,* 163). According to Steve Winston: "Each day of the first 24 in January represents two weeks of the coming year. If the period is snowy, it means a wet year. The first 12 days represent the first 24 weeks from Jan. 1 through June. The progression reverses beginning Jan. 13. This day represents the last two weeks of the year, and successive days represent two week periods all the way to July. On Jan. 25, the 24 hours of this day follow the same progression as the 24 days of January. The first two weeks of the year; the 13th hour represents the last two weeks, etc. Thus, the weather Jan. 1 indicates the weather during the period from Jan. 1–13. The weather the first hour of the 15th indicates the same period even more accurately according to folklore. It was once a tradition for village weathermen to stay awake the entire 24 hours of Jan. 25 observing the weather" ("Cabañuelas predict dry year," *The Taos News,* January 6, 1983, A16). See also Josephine M. Córdova, "Las Cavañuelas," in her *No Lloro Pero Me Acuerdo* (Dallas, Texas: Taylor Publishing, 1976), 17; Michael Miller, "Las Cabañuelas," *NM,* January 1986, 16.

38. Lorin W. Brown, "Día de herejes," NMFWP, January 9, 1939, reprinted in Brown, *Hispano Folklife,* 40.

39. Kenneth Fordyce, "100 Days of Wind," NMFWP, July 30, 1938, WPA#189, NMSRC; Roland F. Dickey, "Chronicles of Neglected Time: Windscapes," *Century Magazine,* March 16, 1983, 9.

40. Simmons, "Colonial Agriculture," 6. See also Nels Winkless, III, and Iben Browning, "Whither Our Weather?" *NM,* May 1976, 13–19.

41. Louise Lamphere, "Southwestern Ceremonialism," in *Handbook 10,* 758. In the early 1900s, John Peabody Harrington reported that Tewa Indians "tell of a pueblo in the sky above the clouds" and say "the mythological serpents, *'Aḇan pu,* and cachinas, *ʔokʼuwa,* are supposed to live in the clouds and to be seen sometimes by people when looking upward" (*The Ethnogeography of the Tewa Indians,* BAE 29th Annual Report [Washington, D.C.: Government Printing Office, 1916], 56). This suggests a "common [Hispanic] belief" recorded by Aurelio M. Espinosa: "that the clouds descend to the ocean or to large lakes for rain, [so] water-lizards and the like, which appear after heavy rains, are said to come from the clouds, having been picked up by them from the sea or lakes" ("New-Mexican Folk-Lore," 415).

42. Joe S. Sando, *The Pueblo Indians,* 2d ed. (San Francisco: Indian Historian Press, 1982), 84, 85.

43. Severino Martínez, as quoted in *The Blue Lake Area . . . an appeal from Taos Pueblo,* n.d., but published after the Indian Claims Commission decision of September 8, 1965, establishing Taos Pueblo's title to the land and stating that the United States "took said lands from the petitioner without compensation" on November 7, 1906, to make them a part of Carson National Forest. The Taos Pueblo Council, which sponsored publication of the booklet, states at its beginning: "Our tribal government is responsible to the land and its people. We have lived upon this land from days beyond history's records, far past any living memory, deep into the time of legend. The story of our people and the story of this place are one single story. No man can think of us without also thinking of this place, we are always joined together."

44. Ladd, "Zuni Religion," 31.

45. The Pueblo of Zuni, *The Zunis: Experiences and Descriptions* (Zuni, New Mexico, 1973), 17. For a contemporary account of this trip see Sylvester Baxter, "An Aboriginal Pilgrimage," *Century Illustrated Monthly Magazine* 24 (1882): 526–36.

46. Luke Lyon, "The Zuni Journey to the East—1882," *NM,* July 1982, 18, 22, 23. For an account of a second Zuni visit to the east, in 1886, see Jesse Green, ed., *Zuñi: Selected Writings of Frank Hamilton Cushing* (Lincoln: University of Nebraska Press, 1979), 407–25.

47. Frank Hamilton Cushing, *Zuñi Fetishes,* BAE 2d Annual Report (1883; reprint, Las Vegas, Nevada: K C Publications, 1972), 17; Dennis Tedlock, "Zuni Religion and World View," in *Handbook 9,* 499–500, 501.

48. Alfonso Ortiz, "The Tewa World View," in *Teachings from the American Earth: Indian Religion and Philosophy,* ed. Dennis Tedlock and Barbara Tedlock (New York: Liveright, 1975), 185, 182. See also the account by Rina Swentzell of Santa Clara Pueblo, "An Understated Sacredness," *Mass: Journal of the School of Architecture and Planning,* University of New Mexico, 3 (fall 1985): 24–25.

49. Alfonso Ortiz, "San Juan Pueblo," in *Handbook 9,* 283–84.

50. Ortiz, "Tewa World View," 181–82.

51. Lamphere, "Southwestern Ceremonialism," 747, 751. On the Jicarilla, Lamphere cites Morris E. Opler, "Jicarilla Apache Territory, Economy, and Society in 1850," *Southwestern Journal of Anthropology* 27 (1971): 309–29. See also the emergence text collected in November 1897 by James Mooney, "The Jicarilla Genesis," *AA* 2 (1898): 197–209.

52. Washington Matthews, *Navaho Legends,* Memoirs of the American Folk-Lore Society, vol. 5 (Boston: Houghton, Mifflin and Company, 1897), 78–79. See also

Leland Wyman, *The Sacred Mountains of the Navajo in Four Paintings by Harrison Begay* (Flagstaff: Museum of Northern Arizona, 1967); *Between Sacred Mountains: Stories and Lessons from the Land* (Chinle, Arizona: Rock Point Community School, 1982), 2–3; Paul G. Zolbrod, *Diné bahane': The Navajo Creation Story* (Albuquerque: University of New Mexico Press, 1984).

53. Robert A. Roessel, Jr., "Navajo History, 1850–1923," in *Handbook 10,* 510–19.

54. Ibid., 518–19. See *Navajo Stories of the Long Walk Period* (Tsaile, Arizona: Navajo Community College Press, 1973), which editor Ruth Roessel notes as "a very significant study made by the Navajo people. For the first time one of the great tragedies of our country's history—one in which the Navajos were the victims—is being presented from the Navajo point of view and by the Navajos themselves" (p. ix).

55. *Treaty between the United States of America and the Navajo Tribe of Indians: With a record of the discussions that led to its signing,* intro. by Martin A. Link (Las Vegas, Nevada: K C Publications in cooperation with the Navajo Tribe, 1968), 1–2, 8. For official Navajo and English versions, see Ellis, *New Mexico Historic Documents,* 56–71.

56. Gladys A. Reichard, *Navaho Religion: A Study of Symbolism,* Bollingen Series 18, 2d ed. in 1 vol. (Princeton, New Jersey: Princeton University Press, 1974), 541.

57. Claire R. Farrer, "Singing for Life: The Mescalero Apache Girls' Puberty Ceremony," in *Southwestern Indian Ritual Drama,* ed. Charlotte J. Frisbie (Albuquerque: University of New Mexico Press, SAR Book, 1980), 132–33.

58. L. S. M. Curtin, "Preparation of Sacred Corn Meal in the Rio Grande Pueblos," *Southwest Museum Leaflets,* no. 32 (1968), 4–5.

59. Elsie Clews Parsons, *Isleta, New Mexico,* BAE 47th Annual Report (1932; reprint, Albuquerque: Calvin Horn Publisher, 1974), 275–76.

60. J. Manuel Espinosa, *Crusaders of the Río Grande: The Story of Don Diego de Vargas and the Reconquest and Refounding of New Mexico* (Chicago: Institute of Jesuit History, 1942), 65–66.

61. Myra Ellen Jenkins, "The Baltasar Baca 'Grant': History of an Encroachment," *EP* 68 (Spring 1961): 50.

62. William A. Keleher, "Law of the New Mexican Land Grant," *NMHR* 4 (1929): 354; Thomas J. Steele, S.J., *Santos and Saints: The Religious Folk Art of Hispanic New Mexico* (1974; rev. ed., Santa Fe: Ancient City Press, 1982), 145–46. See also G. Emlen Hall, *Four Leagues of Pecos: A Legal History of the Pecos Grant, 1800–1933,* New Mexico Land Grant Series (Albuquerque: University of New Mexico Press, 1984).

63. Victor Westphall, *Mercedes Reales: Hispanic Land Grants of the Upper Rio Grande Region,* New Mexico Land Grant Series (Albuquerque: University of New Mexico Press, 1983), 9–10.

64. Marc Simmons, "Settlement Patterns and Village Plans in Colonial New Mexico," *Journal of the West* 8 (1969): 10, 12–13; Westphall, *Mercedes Reales,* 8–9. See also an account and photos from the Aerial Historic Survey Project for the State Historic Preservation District, Office of Cultural Affairs, in Betsy Swanson, "Patterns of History," *NM,* November 1984, 67–70; Linda M. Christensen, "Historic Influences on New Mexico Settlements," *Mass: Journal of the School of Architecture and Planning,* University of New Mexico 4 (Fall 1986): 2–8.

65. J. B. Jackson, "Pueblo Architecture and Our Own," *Landscape* 3, 2 (Winter 1953–54): 24. He refers to Victor Mindeleff, "A Study of Pueblo Architecture: Tusayan and

Cibola," BAE 8th Annual Report (Washington, D.C.: Government Printing Office, 1891), 3–228.

66. George Kubler, *The Religious Architecture of New Mexico in the Colonial Period and Since the American Occupation* (Colorado Springs, Colo.: Taylor Museum, 1940), 23, vii.

67. Ibid., viii; E. Boyd, *Popular Arts of Spanish New Mexico* (Santa Fe: Museum of New Mexico Press, 1974), 30–36; Bainbridge Bunting, Thomas R. Lyons, and Margil Lyons, "Penitente Brotherhood Moradas and Their Architecture," in Weigle et al., *Hispanic Arts,* 31–79.

68. Roland F. Dickey, *New Mexico Village Arts* (Albuquerque: University of New Mexico Press, 1949, 1970), 5; Simmons, "Settlement Patterns," 17, 19.

69. Thomas J. Steele, S.J., "Naming of Places in Spanish New Mexico," in Weigle et al., *Hispanic Arts,* 300, 302; Steele interviewed in Denise Tessler, "Chapels Gave 'Sense of Place,'" *Albuquerque Journal,* December 26, 1984, C-2.

70. Boyd, *Popular Arts,* 446.

71. E. Boyd, "Crosses and Camposantos of New Mexico," in *Camposantos,* photographic essay by Dorothy Benrimo, commentary by Rebecca Salsbury James (Fort Worth, Texas: Amon Carter Museum of Western Art, 1966), 3.

72. Lorin W. Brown, "Descansos," NMFWP, October 29, 1938, reprinted in *Hispano Folklife,* 235. See also Boyd, *Popular Arts,* 448; Marta Weigle, *Brothers of Light, Brothers of Blood: The Penitentes of the Southwest* (Albuquerque: University of New Mexico Press, 1976), 176–77.

73. Fray Angelico Chavez, "La Jornada del Muerto," *NM,* September–October 1974, 34–35; Marc Simmons, *Taos to Tomé—True Tales of Hispanic New Mexico* (Albuquerque: Adobe Press, 1978), 28. See also Joseph P. Sanchez, "Bernardo Gruber and the New Mexican Inquisition," *Exploration: Annual Bulletin of the School of American Research,* 1982, 27–31; Jay W. Sharp, "Jornada del Muerto," *NM,* January 1985, 18–20.

74. Josiah Gregg, *Commerce of the Prairies,* ed. Max L. Moorhead (Norman: University of Oklahoma Press, 1954), 62–63.

75. J. B. Jackson, "High Plains Country: A Sketch of the Geography, Physical and Human, of Union County, New Mexico," *Landscape* 3, 3 (Spring 1954): 2 1.

76. Lula Collins Daudet and Ruth Collins Roberts, *Pinto Beans and a Silver Spoon* (Ardmore, Pennsylvania: Dorrance & Co., 1980), 7.

77. Walter Prescott Webb, *The Great Plains* (1931; reprint, New York: Grosser & Dunlap, n.d.), 295; Goodnight, in Henry D. and Frances T. McCallum, *The Wire That Fenced the West* (Norman: University of Oklahoma Press, 1965), 203–4.

78. Steele, *Santos and Saints,* 153, 148–49, 147.

79. Victor Westphall, *The Public Domain in New Mexico, 1854–1891* (Albuquerque: University of New Mexico Press, 1965), 94–95, 93–94; A. W. Conway, "Village Types in the Southwest: Railroad Town," *Landscape* 2, 1 (Spring 1952): 18.

80. Don McAlavy, "Curry County: Crafty Creation of Charles Scheurich," *EP* 84, 1 (Spring 1978): 22–23; Tom Pendergrass, "Prodigy on the Plains: The Founding of Clovis, New Mexico, 1906–1908," *Rio Grande History* 2, 1 & 2 (Summer 1974): 6. T. M. Pearce records a legend from the *Clovis Evening News Journal,* June 3, 1935, that "the daughter of a Santa Fe Railroad official was reading early French history and

she was much attracted to the character of Clovis, King of the Franks, who was converted to Christianity in 496. . . . When it was suggested that she be given the honor of naming the new town in the Southwest, she immediately formed expression of her admiration of King Clovis by passing the name on to the new town" (*New Mexico Place Names* [Albuquerque: University of New Mexico Press, 1965], 37).

81. Pendergrass, "Prodigy on the Plains," 8; J. B. Jackson, "The Almost Perfect Town," *Landscape* 2, 1 (Spring 1952): 6. See also Donald W. Whisenhunt's study of *New Mexico Courthouses*, Southwestern Studies Monograph No. 57 (Texas Western Press, University of Texas at El Paso, 1979), as "symbol of local government" (p. 6).

82. May Price Mosley, "Lea County," NMFWP, n.d., reprinted in *"Little Texas" Beginnings*, 49—50. Mosley also notes that: "Bringing out the mail for all ranches along one's way and for those still farther out constituted a most sacred obligation which no rancher dared forget or neglect. . . . Letters were generally posted by the 'first passing.' If one . . . did not have his letter written, the 'first passing' customarily waited until the correspondence was . . . completed. It was customary, too, for the party mailing all such letters to see they were properly stamped—gratis" (p. 33). Naomi LaVerne Hogue recounts the situation at Knowles, "founded in 1903 and named for Rube Knowles who, without asking pay for his services, volunteered to carry the mail via horseback to and from the little community, which otherwise would have been without postal service. For about a year he made regular trips to the post office at Monument Springs and returned loaded with mail, papers, and parcels, and also articles which he purchased at the request of various housewives. Finally, the petitions sent to Washington by the Knowles citizens resulted in the establishing of a branch post office and Rube continued carrying the mail, with pay, for a number of years. This first post office was housed in a structure half dugout and half frame which was more pretentious than its neighbors for it boasted a lean-to- on one side and a hog-house on the other" ("The Ghost Town of Knowles," *NMFR* 4 [1949–50]: 31). On mail service in Spanish colonial New Mexico, see Simmons, *Taos to Tomé*, 17—18; Oakah L. Jones, Jr., *Los Paisanos: Spanish Settlers on the Northern Frontier of New Spain* (Norman: University of Oklahoma Press, 1979), 145—46.

83. Ruth Kessler Rice, *Letters from New Mexico, 1899–1904*, ed. Margaret W. Reid (Albuquerque: Adobe Press, 1981), vii.

84. Richard W. Helbock, *Post Offices of New Mexico* (Las Cruces, New Mexico: Author, 1981), 3–4. According to T. M. Pearce: "Postmasters played their part in the naming of settlements: Claude was named for the town's first postmaster, who in 1906 owned a mercantile shop there, in which was the town's post office; he is now an insurance agent in Clovis. Forrest owes its name to Forrest Farr, son of its oldest citizen, first postmaster, and first storekeeper, Watt Farr, who with his family moved there from Missouri in 1907. . . . The name of the town dates from 1908, when the post office was established. The name of Floyd was selected by the first postmaster, Simon Lane, who denies that he chose the name for a friend. Tinnie was originally named Analla, for a first settler, but it was renamed for the daughter of the first postmaster" ("Names on the Land," *WF* 8 [1949]: 258).

85. Helbock, *Post Offices*, 1.

86. Pearce, *New Mexico Place Names*, 171. T. M. Pearce gives a more extended account in "The New Mexico Place Name Dictionary: A Polyglot in Six Languages," *Names* 6 (1958): 223–24. See also Elsie Ruth Chant, "Naming Tucumcari," *NMFR* 3 (1948–49): 36–37.

87. Conway, "Village Types," 18–19.

88. Gaspar Pérez de Villagrá, *History of New Mexico* (Alcalí, 1610), trans. Gilberto Espinosa (Los Angeles: Quivira Society, 1933), 99, 103.

89. Ibid., 99–100, 101. See also Lansing B. Bloom, "Early Bridges in New Mexico," Papers of the School of American Research, n.s., no. 7 (Santa Fe: Archaeological Institute of America, 1925).

90. Doyle Kline, "New Mexico's Golden Fleece," *NM,* January 1978, 16.

91. James F. Downs, *The Navajo,* Case Studies in Cultural Anthropology (New York: Holt, Rinehart and Winston, 1972), 57, 59. See also Louise Lamphere, *To Run After Them: Cultural and Social Bases of Cooperation in a Navajo Community* (Tucson: University of Arizona Press, 1977), 111–13.

92. Fray Angelico Chavez, *My Penitente Land: Reflections on Spanish New Mexico* (Albuquerque: University of New Mexico Press, 1974), 8, xii–xiv.

93. Reyes N. Martínez, "A Sheepherd at Work." See also Lorin W. Brown, "Basílico Garduño, New Mexico Sheepherder," NMFWP, n.d., reprinted in *Hispano Folklife,* 158–73.

94. Fabiola Cabeza de Baca, *We Fed Them Cactus* (Albuquerque: University of New Mexico Press, 1954), 7.

95. J. D. Robb, "'Whereof I Speak' or Songs of the Western Sheep Camps," *NMFR* 12 (1969–70): 19, 18. See also Robb, *Hispanic Folk Music,* 489–502.

96. Dan Scurlock, "Pastors of the Valles Caldera: Documenting a Vanishing Way of Life," *EP* 88, 1 (Spring 1982): 4, 7, 8. Brown describes pastor Basílico Garduño's leather-working ability: "I had seen *teguas* worn by other *pastores,* but they were hybrid affairs with handmade soles and uppers salvaged from some pair of store shoes or boots. Basílico's were his own handiwork throughout, being made of cowhide with the neatest of stitching, close fitting, and undoubtedly very comfortable; he wore no other kind. He was a master in working leather. He could braid quirts, belts, hat bands, *reatas . . . ,* and those long, braided, tapering whips known as blacksnakes. His neatest job, next to the *teguas,* was the *hondas* ('slings') he made. . . . They were shorter than those I had when a boy. The egg-shaped piece that carried the stone was larger also, and on the end of each swinging string was a lash which cracked like a pistol shot after each throw. He was amazingly accurate with it: he would never hit a sheep or goat, but would sling a stone to strike in the vicinity of a straggler and thus startle it back to the flock" (*Hispano Folklife,* 167).

97. James B. DeKorne, *Aspen Art in the New Mexico Highlands* (Santa Fe: Museum of New Mexico Press, 1970), 11–12. De Korne cites Edward Norris, *America's Sheep Trails: History, Personalities* (Ames: Iowa State College, 1948).

98. Edward N. Wentworth, "Early Phases of the Sheep Industry in New Mexico," *New Mexico Stockman* 4, 11 (November 1939): 21.

99. Diana Ortega-DeSantis, "The Hispanic Shepherd of New Mexico's Eastern Plains," *EP* 88, 1 (Spring 1982): 12, 13. See also Julián Josué Vigil, *"Vamos a La Borrega": La Vereda—The Sheeptrail* (Las Vegas, New Mexico: New Mexico Highlands Print Shop, 1980).

100. N. Howard Thorp, "The New Mexico Cattle Industry," NMFWP, October 30, 1936, WPA#104, NMSRC. (There is also a version of this dated April 22, 1937 in WPA#104.)

101. Vernon Smithson, "The Last Great Roundup of the Llano Estacado," NMFWP, July 17, 1937, WPA#97, NMSRC.

102. Col. Jack Potter, "Lead Steers," in *On the Trail: The Life and Tales of "Lead Steer" Potter,* ed. Jean M. Burroughs (Santa Fe: Museum of New Mexico Press, 1980), 69.

103. Kenneth Fordyce, "Pioneer: 'A Remarkable White Steer,'" NMFWP, February 19, 1937, WPA#189, NMSRC.

104. Pioneers' Foundation Oral History Project and Collection, Anderson Room, Zimmerman Library, University of New Mexico. The quotes are from typed transcriptions by Mrs. Mary Blumenthal. The first two are #102, the last in the paragraph from #97.

105. Pioneers' Foundation #93.

106. Ibid., #102.

107. Ibid.

108. Ibid.

109. Leslie A. White, *The Pueblo of Sia, New Mexico,* BAE Bulletin 184 (Washington, D.C.: Government Printing Office, 1962), 49. For a photo by John K. Hillers of the South Plaza in 1879, see *Handbook 9,* 413.

110. E. Adamson Hoebel, "Zia Pueblo," in *Handbook 9,* 415.

111. L. Bradford Prince, *The Stone Lions of Cochiti* (Santa Fe: The New Mexican Printing Company, 1903), 17, 19, 21; Lange, *Cochiti,* 132.

112. Sam D. Gill, *Native American Traditions: Sources and Interpretations* (Belmont, Calif.: Wadsworth Publishing, 1983), 121. See also Jonathan Z. Smith, "The Bare Facts of Ritual," *History of Religions* 20 (1980): 112–27, esp. 119–23 on hunting rituals.

113. Gary Witherspoon, "Navajo Social Organization," in *Handbook 10,* 533; Veronica E. Tiller, "Jicarilla Apache," in *Handbook 10,* 442. See also Karl W. Luckert, *The Navajo Hunter Tradition* (Tucson: University of Arizona Press, 1975).

114. Nancy S. Amon and W. W. Hill, "Santa Clara Pueblo," in *Handbook 9,* 303.

115. Simmons, *Taos to Tomé,* 53. See also Marc Simmons, "Footwear on New Mexico's Hispanic Frontier," in *Southwestern Culture History: Collected Papers in Honor of Albert H. Schroeder,* Archaeological Society of New Mexico, 10, ed. Charles H. Lange (Santa Fe: Ancient City Press, 1985), 223–31.

116. Cabeza de Baca, *We Fed Them Cactus,* 42. See also James D. Shinkle, *New Mexican Ciboleros of the Llano Estacado* (Roswell, New Mexico: Hall-Poorbaugh Press, n.d.).

117. Lester Raines, "Buffalo Hunting," NMFWP, June 1, 1936, WPA#97, NMSRC.

118. Genevieve Chapin, "Folktales: 'Tom Thumb or Tomacito,'" NMFWP, May 13, 1936, WPA#279, NMSRC WPA55-26# 15, H-MNM.

119. Jean M. Burroughs, "The Last of the Buffalo Hunters, George Causey: Hunter, Trader, Rancher," *EP* 80, 4 (Winter 1974): 15, 18.

120. Belle Kilgore, "Buster Degraftenreid as Buffalo Hunter," NMFWP, July 3, 1937, WPA#192, NMSRC. Kenneth Fordyce interviewed Robert Tomlinson of Raton in December 1936 about N. Martínez, who had died in Raton in 1931, "the first man to work for the Santa Fe [Railroad] in New Mexico . . . (and) to hunt buffalos and get their skins for the company" ("Pioneer: 'Buffalo Hides,'" NMFWP, February 5, 1937, WPA#188, NMSRC).

121. Marc Simmons, *Ranchers, Ramblers, and Renegades: True Tales of Territorial New Mexico* (Santa Fe: Ancient City Press, 1984), 75. See also Montague Stevens, *Meet Mr.*

Grizzly: A Saga on the Passing of the Grizzly (Albuquerque: University of New Mexico Press, 1943); Sharman Apt Russell, "Dan Catlin and Montague Stevens: A Friendship of the Old West," *NM,* January 1984, 63, 69–71.

122. Bill Rakocy and Rosamond Shannon Jones, *Mogollon Diary, 1877–1977* (El Paso, Texas: Rio Bravo Press, 1977), 119. See also Irma Fuehr, "The Lilly Legend," *NM,* January 1943, 10, 30–31; J. Frank Dobie, *The Ben Lilly Legend* (New York: Curtis Publishing, 1950); H. A. Hoover, *Early Days in the Mogollons (Muggy-Yones): Tales from the Bloated Goat,* ed. Francis L. Fulgate (El Paso, Texas: Western Press, 1958), 57–58.

123. M. H. Salmon, "Ben Lilly the Toughest of Them All," *Albuquerque Journal,* December 30, 1984, C-1.

124. Jack K. Boyer, "Kit Carson, the Mountain Man," *La Gaceta: El Boletin del Corral de Santa Fe Westerners* 5, 2 (1970): 7.

125. Ibid., 11.

126. Kent Ladd Steckmesser, *The Western Hero in History and Legend* (Norman: University of Oklahoma Press, 1965), 13, 23.

127. Ibid., 50–51.

128. Ibid., 52, 53.

129. Simmons, *Ranchers, Ramblers, Renegades,* 29–32. Steckmesser (*The Western Hero in History and Legend,* 22) claims the dime novel was probably Charles Averill, *Kit Carson, Prince of Gold Hunters* (Boston: G. H. Williams, 1849). See also Marion Estergreen, "Kit Carson to the Rescue," *NM,* August 1955, 23, 59.

130. Morris E. Opler, "The Apachean Culture Pattern and Its Origin," in *Handbook 10,* 373; LaVerne Harrell Clark, *They Sang for Horses: The Impact of the Horse on Navajo and Apache Folklore* (Tucson: University of Arizona Press, 1966), 85–86.

131. Marc Simmons, *Albuquerque* (Albuquerque: University of New Mexico Press, 1982), 149–50; Elsie Clews Parsons, *Tewa Tales,* Memoirs of the American Folk-Lore Society, vol. 19 (New York: G. E. Stechert, 1926), 166; Washington Matthews, *Navaho Legends,* 149. Clark cites various characteristics of Bear and Big Snake: both can travel invisibly; the former is able to transform himself at will, one of the Navajo words for bear meaning "turning into anything"; and the latter can "suck" his captives into his hole, drawing "them closer and closer until they go faster and finally run" to him (*They Sang for Horses,* 93–94).

132. Clark, *They Sang for Horses,* 102–3.

133. Marc Simmons, *The Little Lion of the Southwest: A Life of Manuel Antonio Chaves* (Chicago: Swallow Press, 1973), 34–35.

134. Ruth Roessel, *Navajo Stories of Long Walk,* xv–xvi. Dora Ortiz Vásquez describes Padre Martínez's Navajo slave Rosario, whom she called Mayayo, in *Enchanted Temples of Taos: My Story of Rosario* (Santa Fe: Rydal Press, 1975). See also Richard Slotkin, "Israel in Babylon: The Archetype of the Captivity Narratives (1682–1700)," in his *Regeneration through Violence: The Mythology of the American Frontier, 1600–1860* (Middletown, Connecticut: Wesleyan University Press, 1973), 94–115.

135. Quoted in Simmons, *Albuquerque,* 151.

136. Clay W. Vaden, "A True Indian Story: Stranger than Fiction," NMFWP, July 23, 1936, WPA#230, NMSRC; WPA5-5-27#1, H-MNM.

137. Simmons, *Ranchers, Ramblers, Renegades,* 66, 68.

138. Ibid., 63. Mrs. W. C. (Frances E.) Totty of Silver City collected three reminiscences of the McComas incident for the NMFWP: "The Murder of judge and Mrs. McComas," from Nora Dunby, July 29, 1937; "Judge and Mrs. McComas' Massacre," from Lillian Neff, October 9, 1937; "Death of Judge McComas and Wife," from C. J. Brock, February 25, 1938—all WPA#203, NMSRC.

139. Morris E. Opler, "Chiricahua Apache," in *Handbook 10*, 404.

140. Robert M. Utley, "The Buffalo Soldiers and Victorio," *NM*, March 1984, 54; Eve Ball, *In the Days of Victorio: Recollections of a Warm Springs Apache* (Tucson: University of Arizona Press, 1970), 100.

141. Frances E. Totty, "Early Days around Deming," NMFWP, August 9, 1938, WPA#213, NMSRC.

142. Porter A. Stratton, *The Territorial Press of New Mexico, 1834–1912* (Albuquerque: University of New Mexico Press, 1969), 121.

143. Simmons, *Ranchers, Ramblers, Renegades*, 69–72.

144. W. M. Emery, "A Night of Terror," NMFWP, October 12, 1936, WPA#90, NMSRC.

145. W. M. Emery, "The Last Indian Raid," NMFWP, September 9, 1936, WPA#238, NMSRC; WPA5-4-20#3, H-MNM.

146. Robert J. Rosenbaum, *"Las Gorras Blancas* of San Miguel County, 1889–1890," in *Chicano: The Evolution of a People*, ed. Renato Rosaldo, Robert A. Calvert, Gustav L. Seligmann (San Francisco: Rinehart Press, 1973), 128, 133. See also Andrew Bancroft Schlesinger, "Las Gorras Blancas, 1889–1891," *Journal of Mexican American History* 1 (1971): 87–143; Robert W. Larson, "The White Caps of New Mexico: A Study of Ethnic Militancy in the Southwest," *Pacific Historical Review* 44 (1975): 171–85; Rosenbaum, *Mexicano Resistance in the Southwest* (Austin: University of Texas Press, 1981).

147. Lynn Perrigo, *Gateway to Glorieta: A History of Las Vegas, New Mexico* (Boulder, Colorado: Pruett Publishing, 1982), 85–86. Perrigo says that when the Rough Riders assembled in 1952, "they designated this city as their permanent reunion headquarters 'to the last man,' who came alone in 1967 and 1968" (p. 86). See also Phyllis A. Mingus and Richard Melzer, "Letters Home: The Personal Observations of the New Mexico Rough Riders in the Spanish-American War," *EP* 91, 2 (Fall 1985): 27–35.

148. Haldeen Braddy, "Dorotello Arango, alias Pancho Villa," *NMFR* 5 (1950–51): 4.

149. Ibid., 8.

150. Haldeen Braddy, *Pancho Villa at Columbus: The Raid of 1916*, Southwestern Studies Monograph No. 9, vol. 3, no. 1 (El Paso: Texas Western College, 1965), 4; John V. Young, *The State Parks of New Mexico* (Albuquerque: University of New Mexico Press, 1984), 100.

151. Braddy, Southwestern Studies, 29–30, 16; Betty Reich, [untitled], from L. L. Burkhead of Columbus, NMFWP, April 30, 1937, WPA#102, NMSRC. See also Bill Rakocy, *Villa Raids Columbus, New Mexico, Mar. 9, 1916* (El Paso, Texas: Bravo Press, n.d.).

152. Reich, [untitled]; Braddy, Southwestern Studies, 26.

153. Howard Bryan, "The Night of the Raid," *NM*, March 1976, 29; Betty Reich, "Villa Raid," NMFWP, May 14, 1937, WPA#102, NMSRC; idem, [untitled], from Mr. and Mrs. A. J. Evans of Columbus, NMFWP, May 7, 1937, WPA#102, NMSRC.

154. Young, *State Parks,* 100; Braddy, Southwestern Studies, 33–34.

155. Charles H. Harris, III, and Louis R. Sadler, "Pancho Villa and the Columbus Raid," *NMHR* 50 (1975): 343; Young, *State Parks,* 101–2, 99.

156. Charles Kenner, "The Eastern New Mexico Frontier during the 1850s," in Rosaldo et al., *Chicano,* 115. See also Marc Simmons, "On the Trail of the Comancheros," *NM,* May 1961, 30–33, 39.

157. Lorin W. Brown, "Los Comanches," NMFWP, April 8, 1937, reprinted in *Hispano Folklife,* 43, 44–45.

158. Morris E. Opler, *An Apache Life-way: The Economic, Social, and Religious Institutions of the Chiricahua Indians* (Chicago: University of Chicago Press, 1941), 399; Richard I. Ford, "Inter-Indian Exchange in the Southwest," in *Handbook 10,* 717.

159. Ford, "Inter-Indian Exchange in the Southwest," 719, 717, 719.

160. Ibid., 720.

161. Campa, *Hispanic Culture,* 49; Lorin W. Brown, "The Golden Image," NMFWP, n.d., in *Hispano Folklife,* 93.

162. Simmons, *Ranchers, Ramblers, Renegades,* 25, 26.

163. Mosley, *"Little Texas" Beginnings,* 44, 21.

164. Beatrice Ilfeld Meyer, *Don Luis Ilfeld* (Albuquerque: Albuquerque Historical Society, 1973), 3, 15. However, the first National Bank did close on April 15, 1933, severely affecting business and finance in central New Mexico and northern Arizona (Simmons, *Albuquerque,* 359).

165. William J. Parish, "The German Jew and the Commercial Revolution in Territorial New Mexico, 1850–1900," *NMHR* 35 (1960): 13,1–32. See also Reyes N. Martínez, "A Knight of the Grip," NMFWP, June 12, 1937, WPA5-560#6, H-MNM; Marc Simmons's account of the nineteenth-century New Mexico adventures of peddler Campbell Hardy, in *Ranchers, Ramblers, Renegades,* 77–78; and Harvey Fergusson's fictional account of a Rio Abajo drummer, *The Conquest of Don Pedro* (New York: William Morrow, 1954).

166. Campa, *Hispanic Culture,* 53, 54, 55.

167. Reyes N. Martínez, "Arabs and Dancing Bears," NMFWP, May 1, 1937, WPA5-5-47#1, H-MNM; Parish, "German Jew," 132. Lorenzo de Córdova (Lorin W. Brown) notes "Amada, a Persian woman who had deserted her band of nomad peddlers to marry in Ranchitos," in the Taos area (*Echoes of the Flute* [Santa Fe: Ancient City Press, 1972], 14).

168. Reyes N. Martínez, "Gypsy Caravans," NMFWP, May 7, 1937, WPA5-5-2#19, H-MNM; Marc Simmons, "Our Grandparents Got Gypped by the Gypsies," *Santa Fe Reporter,* November 28, 1982, 7.

169. James A. Burns, "James [John] H. Dunn," NMFWP, September 26, 1936, WPA#234, NMSRC.

170. Ibid. On James A. Burns (1875–1951), who was a Taos Plaza character for twenty-five years, see Weigle, *New Mexicans,* 185.

171. Max West, *Long John Dunn of Taos* (Los Angeles: Westernlore Press, 1959), 142, 143.

172. Den Galbraith, *Turbulent Taos,* Western Americana Series No. 18 (Santa Fe: Press of the Territorian, 1970), 47.

173. James A. Burns, "Pioneers of Taos County: A. R. Manby," NMFWP, November 21, 1936, WPA#234, NMSRC.

174. Ibid.; Reyes N. Martínez, "The Manby Hot Springs," NMFWP, May 13, 1936, WPA5-4-22#11, H-MNM.

175. In Frank Waters, *To Possess the Land: A Biography of Arthur Rochford Manby* (Chicago: Swallow Press, 1973), 178–79.

176. Ibid., 193.

177. Ibid., 218, 244–45.

178. Steve Peters, *Headless in Taos: Arthur Rochford Manby* (Santa Fe, New Mexico: Author, 1972), 1.

179. Waters, *To Possess The Land,* 223.

180. Ibid., 59.

181. James A. Burns, "Humorous Incidents of Early Mining Days: A Self Made Reputation," NMFWP, July 18, 1936, WPA#129, NMSRC; WPA5-5-52#15, H-MNM.

182. Ralph Looney, *Haunted Highways: The Ghost Towns of New Mexico* (Albuquerque: University of New Mexico Press, 1968), 91–95; Paige W. Christiansen, *The Story of Mining in New Mexico,* Scenic Trips to the Geologic Past no. 12 (Socorro: New Mexico Bureau of Mines & Mineral Resources, 1974), 37–38.

183. Philip Varney, *New Mexico's Best Ghost Towns: A Practical Guide* (Flagstaff, Arizona: Northland Press, 1981), 41. Willa Cather gives a fictional version of Kennedy's legend in "Missionary Journeys, 2: The Lonely Road to Mora," *Death Comes for the Archbishop,* 64–77.

184. Christiansen, *Story of Mining in New Mexico,* 38. See also R. S. Allen, "Pinos Altos, New Mexico," *NMHR* 23 (1948): 302–32.

185. James A. McKenna, *Black Range Tales Chronicling Sixty Years of Life and Adventure in the Southwest* (New York: Wilson-Erickson, 1936), 13. On the legendary themes of "Prospectors and Their Gold," see Bruce A. Rosenberg, *The Code of the West* (Bloomington: Indiana University Press, 1982), 34–56. On the prospector's constant companion, the burro, and its lore, see, e.g.: N. Howard Thorp, "The American Ass, Burro or Donkey," NMFWP, June 18, 1937, WPA#111, NMSRC; Frank Brookshier, *The Burro* (Norman: University of Oklahoma Press, 1974); Richard Rudisill and Marcus Zafarand, comps., *The Burro* (Santa Fe: Museum of New Mexico Press, 1979); April Kopp, "From Babylon to Burro Alley," *NM,* March 1985, 38–41.

186. McKenna, *Black Range Tales,* 11.

187. Ibid., 5, 10.

188. C. P. Crawford to William G. Ritch, September 25, 1876, Territorial Archives of New Mexico, Letters Received by the Secretary of the Territory, NMSRC; Pearce, *New Mexico Place Names,* 156.

189. Mary Frances Beverley, "Sadie Orchard Was a Good Ol' Girl," *NM,* July 1983, 40, 41. See also John Sinclair, "Trail of the Mountain Pride," in his *New Mexico: The Shining Land* (Albuquerque: University of New Mexico Press, 1980), 133–45; Bill Rakocy, comp. and ed., *Ghosts of Kingston & Hillsboro, N. Mex.* (El Paso, Texas: Bravo Press, 1983).

190. Betty Reich, "Stagecoach Days," NMFWP, March 27, 1937, WPA#127, NMSRC.

191. Clay W. Vaden, "Sadie Orchard, One of Few New Mexico Women Stage Drivers," NMFWP, August 10, 1936, WPA 5-4-1#23, H-MNM; Beverley, "Sadie Orchard," 42.

192. Carey McWilliams, *North from Mexico: The Spanish-Speaking People of the United States* (1948; reprint, New York: Greenwood Press, 1968), 142; Ernest Prescott Morey, "Reminiscences of an Old Prospector," NMFWP, August 15, 1938, WPA#129, NMSRC; Billy D. Walker, "Copper Genesis: The Early Years of Santa Rita del Cobre," *NMHR* 54 (1979): 7.

193. Morey, "Reminiscences"; John L. Sinclair, "Santa Rita del Cobre," *NM,* March 1985, 29. See also Paul M. Jones, *Memories of Santa Rita* (Silver City, New Mexico: Southwest Offset, 1985).

194. Walker, "Copper Genesis," 9; Ernest P. Morey, "Mountains Listed Under Groups: The Kneeling Nun Mountain," NMFWP, n.d., WPA#202, NMSRC.

195. Mrs. Mildred Jordan, "The Kneeling Nun," NMFWP, May 15, 1936, WPA#204, NMSRC. See also Alice Bullock, "The Kneeling Nun," in her *Squaw Tree: Ghosts, Mysteries, and Miracles of New Mexico* (Santa Fe: The Lightning Tree, 1978), 59–61.

196. N. Howard Thorp, "The Old Mines Near Las Placitas," NMFWP, n.d., WPA#159, NMSRC. Lou Sage Batchen collected the following legend of the Montezuma Mine from Las Placitas: "The old mine was known to the Indians long before the Spaniards set foot on American soil. When Coronado wintered at the pueblo near Bernalillo he visited the mine, which was worked by the Spaniards and the enslaved Indians who were compelled to work long hours with the crudest tools to dig out and smelt the ore for their cruel masters. The gold they dug from the mine was sent on the back of burros to Mexico. When the Indians revolted and drove out the Spaniards in 1680, they filled up all the pits and shafts of the mine. They carried new soil and spread it deeply over all the places they had covered, so that weeds and other vegetation might grow over them and destroy forever all traces of the workings. They carried all the rock and ore on the dumps to arroyos and rivers where it would be washed away, so there would be no signs left of the mines where they had been compelled to slave" (reprinted in Batchen, *Las Placitas: Historical Facts and Legends* [Placitas, New Mexico: Tumbleweed Press, 1972], 36).

197. Lorin W. Brown, "Gambusinos," NMFWP, December 2, 1938, reprinted in *Hispano Folklife,* 113, 114–15.

198. Marc Simmons, *Turquoise and Six-Guns: The Story of Cerrillos, New Mexico,* revised ed. (Santa Fe: Sunstone Press, 1974), 27. Despite the large operations, prospectors occasionally made a lucky "find," like the man named Simmons who discovered "Jumbo," the largest rough turquoise—"a sky blue stone as large as a pigeon's egg"—ever found in the district (p. 26).

199. Ibid., 28–29.

200. Joseph E. Pogue, *The Turquois: A Study of Its History, Mineralogy, Geology, Ethnology, Archaeology, Mythology, Folklore, and Technology,* National Academy of Sciences, vol. 12, 3d Memoir (1915; reprint, Glorieta, New Mexico: Rio Grande Press, 1974), 52. Archeologists A. Helen Warren and Frances Joan Mathien have analyzed artifacts from nine turquoise mining areas around Cerrillos and suggest two major periods of prehistoric mining: A.D. 1000–1150 or 1000–1200, and A.D. 1350–1680 or 1375–1680. The first turquoise in Chaco Canyon sites dates from A.D. 500, but, "while Cerrillos was the closest source of turquoise found in Chaco Canyon, the data have not supported the proposition that turquoise found in Chaco necessarily came from Cerrillos." They suggest that "it is likely, too, that the Chacoans, as well as other

Anasazi, used a number of sources and trade networks from A.D. 500–1700 and did not rely on Cerrillos alone. And it is most likely that people living in the mining area were the major users of the mines" ("Prehistoric and Historic Turquoise Mining in the Cerrillos District: Time and Place," in Lange, *Southwestern Culture History,* 122).

201. Stuart A. Northrop, *Turquois and Spanish Mines in New Mexico* (Albuquerque: University of New Mexico Press, 1975), 51; Simmons, *Turquoise and Six-Guns,* 24. Also note Northrop's definition that "the name *turquois* comes from the French, meaning *Turkish stone,* and apparently was applied not because the mineral came from Turkey but because it was introduced into Europe from Persia by way of Turkey" (p. 40).

202. Simmons, *Turquoise and Six-Guns,* 25. He quotes Susan E. Wallace, *The Land of the Pueblos* (Troy, New York: Nims and Knight, 1889).

203. Reichard, *Navaho Religion,* 209.

204. Franc J. Newcomb, with text by Gladys A. Reichard, *Sandpaintings of the Navajo Shooting Chant* (New York: J. J. Augustin, 1937), 36–37.

Chapter 6. People of Power: Texts of Fear and Fascination

1. Clyde Kluckhohn, *Navaho Witchcraft* (1944; reprint, Boston: Beacon Press, 1967), 205.

2. Alfred Métraux, s.v. "culture hero," *Funk & Wagnalls Standard Dictionary of Folklore, Mythology, and Legend,* ed. Maria Leach, 1 vol. (New York: Funk & Wagnalls, 1972), 268.

3. Edward S. Curtis, *The North American Indian,* vol. 17 (Norwood, Massachusetts: Plimpton Press, 1926), 170.

4. Alfonso Ortiz, unpublished manuscript cited in Richard J. Parmentier, "The Mythological Triangle: Poseyemu, Montezuma, and Jesus in the Pueblos," in *Handbook 9,* 6 14.

5. Alfonso Ortiz, "Popay's Leadership: A Pueblo Perspective," *EP* 86, 4 (Winter 1980–81): 21.

6. Elsie Clews Parsons, *Isleta, New Mexico,* BAE 47th Annual Report (1932; reprint, Albuquerque: Calvin Horn Publisher, 1974), 415.

7. Ibid., 412–13. According to Parsons's note: "When my [the informant's] father was 20 years old, the Navaho stole an Isletan boy. They used the thunderstick as medicine and brought thunder against the Navaho. They recovered the boy, but the Navaho had cut off one of his testicles and the boy died."

8. Leslie A. White, *The Pueblo of Santo Domingo, New Mexico,* Memoirs of the American Anthropological Association 38 (Menasha, Wisconsin, 1935), 179. See also Adolph F. Bandelier, "The 'Montezuma' of the Pueblo Indians," *AA* 5 (1892): 319–26.

9. *Benavides' Memorial of 1630,* trans. Peter P. Forrestal, C.S.C., ed. Cyprian J. Lynch, O.F.M. (Washington, D.C.: Academy of American Franciscan History, 1954), 33.

10. Ibid., 8.

11. Ibid., 58. In 1689, Don Damian Manzanet wrote Don Carlos de Siguenza y Gongora about his Texas missionary experiences: "While we were at the Tejas

(Hasinai) village after we had distributed clothing to the Indians and to the Governor of the Tejas, that governor asked me one evening for a piece of blue baize in which to make a burial shroud for his mother when she died. I told him that cloth would be more suitable and he answered that he did not want any color, particularly for burial clothes because in times past they had frequently been visited by a very beautiful woman who used to come down from the hills dressed in blue garments and they wished to do as the woman had done. On my asking whether that had been a long time since, the governor said that it had been before his time, but his mother who was aged had seen that woman as had the other older people. From this it is easily to be seen that they referred to Madre Maria de Jesus de Agreda, who was frequently in these regions," as trans. Julia M. Keleher, "The Legend of the Lady in Blue," *NMFR* 11 (1963–64): 32. In 1699, Captain Mange recorded discoveries of a northwestern expedition led by Jesuits Eusebio Francisco Kino and Adamo Gil. They encountered old Indians who claimed "that when they were children there came to their land a beautiful white woman, robed to the feet in white, brown, and blue, with a cloth or veil covering her head. She had spoken, shouted, and harangued them in a language they did not understand, showed them a cross. The nations of the Rio Colorado shot her with arrows, leaving her for dead on two occasions. Reviving, she disappeared into the air. . . . After a few days she returned many times to harangue them," as trans. William H. Donahue, C.S.C., "Mary of Agreda and the Southwest United States," *The Americas* 9 (1952–53): 311. See also Cleve Hallenbeck, "The Blue Lady," *NM,* February 1945, 17, 29, 31, 33, 35; May Raizizun (sister of Cleofas M. Jaramillo and Reyes N. Martínez), "The Blue Lady," *NM,* February 1962, 22–23, 38; Alice Bullock, *Monumental Ghosts* (Santa Fe: Sunstone Press, 1987), 31–33.

12. *Benavides' Memorial,* ibid., 59–60.

13. Fray Angelico Chavez, *Our Lady of the Conquest* (Santa Fe: Historical Society of New Mexico, 1948), 2.

14. Ibid., 22.

15. Ronald L. Grimes, *Symbol and Conquest: Public Ritual and Drama in Santa Fe, New Mexico* (Ithaca, New York.: Cornell University Press, 1976), 222.

16. *Three New Mexico Chronicles: The* Exposición *of Don Pedro Bautista Pino, 1812; the* Ojeada *of Lic. Antonio Barreiro, 1832; and the additions by Don José Agustín de Escudero, 1849,* trans. and ed. H. Bailey Carroll and J. Villasana Haggard (Albuquerque: Quivira Society, 1942), 52–53.

17. *The Santa Fe Cathedral of St. Francis of Assisi* (Santa Fe: Schifani Bros. Printing, n.d., but rev. ed. of 1947 ed.).

18. Grimes, *Symbol and Conquest,* 114–15.

19. Paul Horgan, *Lamy of Santa Fe: His Life and Times* (New York: Farrar, Straus & Giroux, 1975), 358–59. See also Bruce Ellis, *Bishop Lamy's Santa Fe Cathedral* (Albuquerque: University of New Mexico Press with Historical Society of New Mexico, 1985).

20. By contrast, the nearby Loretto Chapel, for which stone was cut beginning January 19, 1874, and which was blessed on April 25, 1878, was miraculously finished. According to the Historic Santa Fe Foundation account: "When the chapel was completed, there was no means of ascending to the choir loft, since the workmen felt that there was insufficient room to build a safe staircase. The sisters [of Loretto] sought for someone who could devise a stairway. Shortly thereafter, a carpenter

appeared and constructed the famous circular staircase, built without nails or other visible means of support. He then disappeared without waiting to be paid. Legend has persisted that it was the work of St. Joseph, the carpenter saint. One of several European-born artisans living in Santa Fe at the time may have been the unknown carpenter, but recent information strongly suggests the possibility that the craftsman was Johann Hadwiger, an Austrian immigrant who had heard of the sisters' quest while visiting his son in a Colorado mining camp. The 'miraculous' nature of the staircase is in no way dimmed by the probability of human construction" (*Old Santa Fe Today,* revised ed. [Albuquerque: University of New Mexico Press for the Historic Santa Fe Foundation, 1972], 61). According to Alice Bullock: "Legend differs here as to the time the carpenter worked. Some say very swiftly, others say six or eight months. Surely it was that a double helix—two complete turns of 360 degrees each—reached the choir loft with no central support of any kind, nor is there a single nail in the whole structure. There are thirty-three steps, one for each year in the earthly life of Jesus" (*Living Legends of the Santa Fe Community,* rev. ed. [Santa Fe: Sunstone Press, 1972], 113, 116). See also Bullock, *Loretto and the Miraculous Staircase* (Santa Fe: Sunstone Press, 1978).

21. Dora Ortiz Vásquez, *Enchanted Temples of Taos: My Story of Rosario* (Santa Fe: Rydal Press, 1975), xi.

22. Fray Angelico Chavez, *But Time and Chance: The Story of Padre Martínez of Taos, 1793–1867* (Santa Fe: Sunstone Press, 1981), 40. Ray John de Aragon also notes: "In 1857, Bishop Lamy brought his niece, Marie Lamy, to Santa Fe to join him. Many later falsely claimed that she was in reality his illegitimate daughter. The sensational stories, enlarged by others, hurt the integrity of both men and twisted the truth of the excommunication of Padre Martínez out of proportion" (*Padre Martínez and Bishop Lamy* [Las Vegas, New Mexico: Pan-American Publishing, 1978), 112]. Aragon, like Chavez, notes the influence of Willa Cather's *Death Comes for the Archbishop* (1927) on the notion of Martínez's villainy and promiscuity. See also Ralph H. Vigil, "Willa Cather and Historical Reality," *NMHR* 50 (1975): 123–34; E. A. Mares, "Padre Martínez, Defender of the People," *NM,* June 1985, 57–60.

23. Cleofas M. Jaramillo, *Shadows of the Past (Sombras del pasado)* (1941; reprint, Santa Fe: Ancient City Press, 1980), 111; Lorin W. Brown, "Padre Martínez and the first College in New Mexico," NMFWP, March 3, 1939, in Brown, with Charles L. Briggs and Marta Weigle, *Hispano Folklife of New Mexico: The Lorin W. Brown Federal Writers' Project Manuscripts* (Albuquerque: University of New Mexico Press, 1978), 6. Martínez printed textbooks for his school on New Mexico's first printing press, which had been operational since August 1834 and which he had purchased from Ramon Abréu's widow in 1837 (E. Boyd, "The first New Mexico Imprint," *Princeton University Library Chronicle* 33, 1 [Autumn 1971]: 30–40).

24. Chavez, *But Time and Chance,* 86. Pedro Sánchez, *Memorias sobre la vida del Presbítero Don Antonio José Martínez* (Santa Fe: Compañia Impresora del Nuevo Mexicano, 1903), has been reprinted in a bilingual ed. by Ray John de Aragon (Santa Fe: The Lightning Tree, 1978) and in a facsimile ed. with trans. by Guadalupe Baca-Vaughn, *Memories of Antonio José Martínez* (Santa Fe: Rydal Press/Printworks, 1978).

25. Chavez, *But Time and Chance,* 150, 158. For a good review of the official ecclesiastical position, see E. K. Francis, "Padre Martínez: A New Mexican Myth," *NMHR* 31 (1956): 265–89.

26. Marta Weigle, *Brothers of Light, Brothers of Blood: The Penitentes of the Southwest* (Albuquerque: University of New Mexico Press, 1976), 48–49; Thomas J. Steele, S.J.,

and Rowena A. Rivera, *Penitente Self-Government: Brotherhoods and Councils, 1797–1947* (Santa Fe: Ancient City Press, 1985), 19–23.

27. Marta Weigle, "Ghostly Flagellants and Doña Sebastiana: Two Legends of the Penitente Brotherhood," *WF* 36 (1977): 135–47; Lorenzo de Córdova [Lorin W. Brown], *Echoes of the Flute* (Santa Fe: Ancient City Press, 1972), 33.

28. In Weigle, *Brothers of Light,* 216. See also Steele and Rivera, *Penitente Self-Government,* 71–73; Robert Sprott, O.F.M., "Making Up What Is Lacking: Towards an Interpretation of the Penitentes," Working Paper #110, Southwest Hispanic Research Institute, University of New Mexico, Fall 1984.

29. Paul Kutsche and Dennis Gallegos, "Community Functions of the *Cofradía de Nuestro Padre Jesús Nazareno,*" in *The Survival of Spanish American Villages,* ed. Kutsche, The Colorado College Studies No. 15 (Colorado Springs, Colorado, Spring 1979), 92.

30. Gladys A. Reichard, *Navaho Religion: A Study of Symbolism,* Bollingen Series 18, 2d ed. in 1 vol. (Princeton, New Jersey: Princeton University Press, 1974), 475–76.

31. Ibid., 24.

32. Marc Simmons, "New Mexico's Smallpox Epidemic of 1780–1781," *NMHR* 41 (1966): 319.

33. Oakah L. Jones, Jr., *Los Paisanos: Spanish Settlers on the Northern Frontier of New Spain* (Norman: University of Oklahoma Press, 1979), 140.

34. James A. McKenna, *Black Range Tales: Chronicling Sixty Years of Life and Adventure in the Southwest* (New York: Wilson-Erickson, 1936), 89, 90–91.

35. Alfred W. Crosby, Jr., *Epidemic and Plague, 1918* (Westport, Connecticut: Greenwood Press, 1976), 215.

36. Richard Melzer, "A Dark and Terrible Moment: The Spanish Flu Epidemic of 1918 in New Mexico," *NMHR* 57 (1982): 221.

37. Lucy Mair, *Witchcraft* (New York: McGraw-Hill, 1969), 7.

38. Kluckhohn, *Navaho Witchcraft,* 133.

39. Alfonso Ortiz, *The Tewa World: Space, Time, Being, and Becoming in a Pueblo Society* (Chicago: University of Chicago Press, 1969), 15, 16.

40. Richard I. Ford, "Communication Networks and Information Hierarchy in Native American Folk Medicine: Tewa Pueblos, New Mexico," in *American Folk Medicine: A Symposium,* ed. Wayland D. Hand (Berkeley: University of California Press, 1976), 147–48, 149–50.

41. Stephen Fox, "Consciousness and Healing in New Mexico Indian, Hispanic, and Anglo Groups," Master's thesis, University of New Mexico, 1984, 16; Rina Swentzell and Tito Naranjo, "Nurturing: The *Gia* at Santa Clara Pueblo," *EP* 92, 1 (summer–fall 1986): 36, 37, 38.

42. White, *Pueblo of Santo Domingo,* 120.

43. Florence H. Ellis, "Pueblo Witchcraft and Medicine," in *Systems of North American Witchcraft and Sorcery,* ed. Deward E. Walker, Jr., Anthropological Monographs of The University of Idaho (Moscow, Idaho: University of Idaho, 1970), 39.

44. J. Robin Fox, "Witchcraft and Clanship in Cochiti Therapy," in *Magic, Faith, and Healing: Studies in Primitive Psychiatry Today,* ed. Ari Kiev (New York: Free Press, 1964), 182.

45. Ellis, "Pueblo Witchcraft," 43.

46. Jane Kluckhohn, "Traditional Forms of Greeting in Jemez Pueblo," *NMFR* 3 (1948–49): 31.

47. Ellis, "Pueblo Witchcraft," 44.

48. Father Noël Dumarest, *Notes on Cochiti, New Mexico,* ed. Elsie C. Parsons, Memoirs of the American Anthropological Association 6, 3 (Lancaster, Pennsylvania, 1919), 162.

49. Gary Witherspoon, *Language and Art in the Navajo Universe* (Ann Arbor: University of Michigan Press, 1977), 25.

50. As rendered in Witherspoon, ibid., 26–27, from Leland C. Wyman, *Blessingway* (Tucson: University of Arizona Press, 1970), 134–36.

51. See, e.g., Gladys A. Reichard, *Navajo Medicine Man* (New York: J. J. Augustin, 1939), a study of medicine man Miguelito, who worked for the Fred Harvey Indian Department in Albuquerque; Louise Lamphere, "Symbolic Elements in Navajo Ritual," *Southwestern Journal of Anthropology* 25 (1969): 279–305; Leland C. Wyman, "Navajo Ceremonial System," in *Handbook 10,* 536–57.

52. See Margaret K. Brady's analysis of "The Anomalous Navajo Skinwalker," in her *"Some Kind of Power": Navajo Children's Skinwalker Narratives* (Salt Lake City: University of Utah Press, 1984), 19–58.

53. Kluckhohn, *Navaho Witchcraft,* 22–45.

54. Mary Shepardson and Blodwin Hammond, *The Navajo Mountain Community* (Berkeley: University of California Press, 1970), 144.

55. Kluckhohn, *Navaho Witchcraft,* 27.

56. Ibid., 13.

57. Marc Simmons, *Witchcraft in the Southwest: Spanish and Indian Supernaturalism on the Rio Grande* (1974; reprint, Lincoln: University of Nebraska Press, 1980). For an account of intimations of witchcraft in the 1952 murder of Hispano state trooper Nash Garcia by Acoma Indians Willie and Gabriel Felipe, see Lawrence J. Evers, "The Killing of a New Mexican State Trooper: Ways of Telling an Historical Event," in *Critical Essays on Native American Literature,* ed. Andrew Wiget (Boston: G. K. Hall, 1985), 246–61.

58. Sam Schulman and Anne M. Smith, *Health and Disease in Northern New Mexico: A Research Report* (Boulder: University of Colorado, Institute of Behavioral Research, 1962). See also idem, "The Concept of 'Health' among Spanish-Speaking Villagers of New Mexico and Colorado," *Journal of Health and Human Behavior* 4 (1963): 226–34; Schulman, "Rural Healthways in New Mexico," *Annals of the New York Academy of Science* 84 (December 8, 1960): 950–58.

59. For good studies of the *médica/-o's* herbalism see L. S. M. Curtin, *Healing Herbs of the Upper Rio Grande* (Los Angeles: Southwest Museum, 1965), and Tibo J. Chavez, "Herbal Medicines of the Lower Rio Grande, also known as Remedios of the Rio Abajo," in his *New Mexican Folklore of the Rio Abajo* (Portales, New Mexico: Bishop Printing, 1972), 1–40. Alfonso Griego mentions another skill: "For a broken bone of the arm or leg, the *médico* would set the bone in place, then a layer of *istiercol,* cow droppings, was placed over the break and bandaged with strips of muslin. This was repeated for several layers. When it dried, it served as a cast which was light in weight. After this, the limb could be moved without getting the bone out of place" (*Good-bye My Land of Enchantment: A true story of some of the first Spanish-speaking natives and early settlers of San Miguel County, Territory of New Mexico* [n.p., 1981], 6).

60. Fran Leeper Buss, *La Partera: Story of a Midwife* (Ann Arbor: University of Michigan Press, 1980), 5.

61. Nathan Skallman and Chella Herrera, "A Conversation with Juanita Sedillo," *NM,* April 1982, 14, 50, 58; Buss, *La Partera,* 6.

62. Ruth Laughlin Barker, "New Mexico Witch Tales," in *Tone the Bell Easy,* ed. J. Frank Dobie, Texas Folklore Society Publication no. 10 (1932; reprint, Dallas, Texas: Southern Methodist University Press, 1965), 62, 64.

63. Jaramillo, *Shadows of the Past,* 99–100. For a discussion of why "in nearly every society that believes in witches . . . the vast majority of suspected individuals [are] women," see Clarke Garrett, "Women and Witches: Patterns of Analysis," *Signs* 3 (1977): 461–70.

64. Stanley L. Robe, ed., *Hispanic Legends from New Mexico: Narratives from the R. D. Jameson Collection,* Folklore and Mythology Studies, 31 (Berkeley: University of California Press, 1980), 436.

65. Robe notes that "reporters present at the hearing misunderstood the meaning of the word *sapo* (in Spanish meaning 'toad') to mean 'frog.' Thus it came about that the stories printed in those newspapers in the early part of 1940 came to be reported as 'the frog man case.' The main character in this story, erroneously called the 'frog man,' should have correctly been called the 'toad man'" (ibid., 437).

66. According to Robe, Associated Press correspondents were among the reporters, and the story appeared in papers like *The Denver Post, The Kansas City Star, The Santa Fe New Mexican, The Louisville Courier Journal, The Las Vegas Daily Optic,* and *The Albuquerque Journal.* Edmundo Delgado draws on contemporary Spanish newspapers to describe the trial of Abelino Espinosa, accused of mutilating his wife, Genoveva, and niece, Mrs. Amadeo Cisneros, who were treated by Dr. C. M. Hussett of Mora, and indirectly of hexing his nineteen-year-old son Samuel ("'Frog Man' of Mora—His Case Decided in JP Court," *Albuquerque Journal North,* October 30, 1985, 3–4).

67. Robe, *Hispanic Legends from New Mexico,* 438–44.

68. Wesley R. Hurt, Jr., "Witchcraft in New Mexico," *EP* 80, 2 (1974): 17–18, reprinted from *EP* 47, 4 (April 1940).

69. Aurelio M. Espinosa, "New-Mexican Spanish Folk-Lore," *JAF* 23 (1910): 396.

70. Jaramillo, *Shadows of the Past,* 98.

71. Gioia Brandi, "Palabras de una viejita," *EP* 84, 3 (Fall 1978): 12.

72. Fabiola Cabeza de Baca, *We Fed Them Cactus* (Albuquerque: University of New Mexico Press, 1954), 59–60. See also Lorin W. Brown's account of his grandmother, Juanita Montoya de Martínez (called "Mana Juanita"), a well-known *curandera* and *partera* in the Taos area (*Hispano Folklife,* 7, 73, 75).

73. Buss, *La Partera,* 6. See also Nancy Scheper-Hughes and David Stewart, "*Curanderismo* in Taos County, New Mexico—A Possible Case of Anthropological Romanticism?" *Western Journal of Medicine,* 139, 6 (December 1983): 875–84.

74. Mrs. Benton (May Price) Mosley, "Customs and Conditions of Early Ranch Life (cont'd) (Lea County)," NMFWP, December 21, 1936, reprinted in her *"Little Texas" Beginnings in Southeastern New Mexico,* ed. Martha Downer Ellis (Roswell, New Mexico: Hall-Poorbaugh Press, 1973), 23–24.

75. Dan McAllister, "Pioneer Woman," *NMHR* 34 (1959): 161–62. In western New Mexico, Luna resident Emmitt Reynolds recalls his pioneer mother, Aunt Nomie, as:

"without having any degree in nursing or anything else, . . . the best doctor in the country. I can say this without bragging too much because everyone thought so. Most of the old pioneer women were pretty good nurses. They had to be. I guess one reason my mother was so good was because she had so much experience. (The family lost two young girls to pneumonia and a boy to blood poisoning). Not only did Mother raise a big family of her own, but she would always drop her work, no matter how busy, and go to help the sick." In *Do You Remember Luna: 100 Years of Pioneer History, 1883–1983* (Albuquerque: Adobe Press for the Luna Ward, Church of Jesus Christ of Latter-Day Saints, 1983), 49.

76. Mosley, *"Little Texas" Beginnings,* 24.

77. Don Yoder, "The Saint's Legend in the Pennsylvania German Folk-Culture," in *American Folk Legend: A Symposium,* ed. Wayland D. Hand (Berkeley: University of California Press, 1971), 173. Oakah L. Jones, Jr., notes: "One of the growing problems of the New Mexico frontier, as elsewhere, was the increasing number of vagabonds in the last two decades of the eighteenth century and continuing until the end of the colonial era. Authorities at all levels issued a series of regulations to control this menace by requiring all people when away from their homes or communities to carry a property issued passport. . . . These repeated orders and regulations from 1783 to 1791, and even thereafter, are indicative of the continuing lawlessness and the concern of government officials with the growing problem of controlling the populace" (*Los Paisanos,* 163).

78. Arthur L. Campa, *Treasure of the Sangre de Cristos: Tales and Traditions of the Spanish Southwest* (Norman: University of Oklahoma Press, 1963), 178.

79. Marc Simmons, *Following the Santa Fe Trail: A Guide for Modern Travelers,* 2d ed. (Santa Fe: Ancient City Press, 1986), 83.

80. Campa, *Treasure of the Sangre de Cristos,* 183–84.

81. Ibid., 186.

82. Ibid., 188. On Hermit memories and legends from San Ignacio, near Hermit's Peak, see Alice Bullock, *Mountain Villages* (Santa Fe: Sunstone Press, 1973), 66–69. See also Elba C. DeBaca, *Legends of a Hermit* (Las Vegas, New Mexico: Author, n.d.).

83. Campa, *Treasure of the Sangre de Cristos,* 189. Campa clearly distinguishes the Society of the Hermit from the Penitente Brotherhood, a distinction not always clear in, e.g., S. Omar Barker, "Pictures from Outlook Readers," *Outlook* 125 (1920): 538; Elsa Barker, "Hermit of the Mountain," in *Legends and Tales of the Old West: By Members of the Western Writers of America,* ed. S. Omar Barker (Garden City, New York: Doubleday, 1962), 199–206; Milton W. Callon, *Las Vegas, New Mexico . . . The Town That Wouldn't Gamble* (Las Vegas, New Mexico: Las Vegas Daily Optic Publishing, 1962), 317–22. For a contemporary account, see William deBuys, *Enchantment and Exploitation: The Life and Hard Times of a New Mexico Mountain Range* (Albuquerque: University of New Mexico Press, 1985), 141–45.

84. Campa, *Treasure of the Sangre de Cristos,* 194–95.

85. Marie Carter, "Old Timers Stories: Elizabeth Fountain Armendáriz (Mrs. Aureliano Armendáriz)," NMFWP, May 3, 1937; WPA#197, NMSRC. See also Constance C. Modrall, *The Centennial of the Italian Hermit in New Mexico* (n.p., November 1969), who reports that in the 1960s the Gadsden Museum Hermit artifacts "are kept locked away for safe keeping, no longer for public viewing" (p. 6).

86. Ferenc M. Szasz, "Francis Schlatter: The Healer of the Southwest," *NMHR* 54

(1979): 90–91. Reyes N. Martínez combines personal knowledge with information from Antonio María Cortez of Taos and Alberto Suazo and Pablo Gomez of Ranchito to describe an 1899 [*sic*] visit by Schlatter to Taos in "El Sanador (The Healer)," NMFWP, August 22, 1936; WPA 462, NMSRC; WPA5-5-18#5, H-MNM.

87. Szasz, "Francis Schlatter," 91–92. See also Thomas J. Steele, S.J., *Works and Days: A History of San Felipe Neri Church, 1867–1895* (Albuquerque: The Albuquerque Museum, 1983), 107–9.

88. Szasz, "Francis Schlatter," 94. See also Agnes Morley Cleaveland, "'The Healer' Comes to Datil," in her *No Life for a Lady* (Boston: Houghton Mifflin, 1941), 220–25. The thirty-five-inch-long rod, which weighs over twenty-seven pounds, is now in the Museum of New Mexico (Alice Bullock, "The Healer and the Cross," in her *The Squaw Tree: Ghosts, Mysteries and Miracles of New Mexico* [Santa Fe: The Lightning Tree, 1978], 62).

89. Szasz, "Francis Schlatter," 95. See also Edgar L. Hewett, *Campfire and Trail* (Albuquerque: University of New Mexico Press, 1942), 69–75; William Jones Wallrich, "'Christ Man' Schlatter," *NMFR* 4 (1949–50): 28–30; Larry Cantwell, "The Healer in Denver," *Denver Westerners' Brand Book* 27 (1972): 162–67; Alice Bullock, "Francis Schlatter: A Fool for God," *EP* 81, 1 (Spring 1975): 38–43; Thomas J. Steele, S.J., "The Brief Career of the 'Healer,'" *Impact: The Albuquerque Journal Magazine*, November 11, 1980, 10–13.

90. Col. Jack Potter, "The Sanctified Texan," in Jean M. Burroughs, *On the Trail: The Life and Tales of "Lead Steer" Potter* (Santa Fe: Museum of New Mexico Press, 1980), 105, 106, 107.

91. Reyes N. Martínez, "The Bells on Ute Mountain," NMFWP, July 12, 1937, WPA5-5-9#3, H-MNM.

92. Jaramillo, *Shadows of the Past,* 112–13. See also Vásquez, *Enchanted Temples of Taos,* 71–74.

93. T. M. Pearce, "The Bad Son *(El Mal Hijo)* in Southwestern Spanish Folklore," *WF* 9 (1950): 295–96. See also Raymond R. MacCurdy, "Notes on the Fateful Curse in Golden Age Drama," *Kentucky Romance Quarterly* 21 (1974): 317–34.

94. Pearce, "The Bad Son," 299. Pearce interviewed Primitivo H. Metzgar on April 15, 1936; Benny Rubi, May 12, 1939. Chavetas was said to have come from Quemado, 170 miles southwest of Albuquerque, or Peralta, about 10 miles south of the city. Pearce also quotes Reyes N. Martínez, "El Mal Hijo," NMFWP, August 10, 1936, on Reyes Castillo of Santa Cruz, whose visit to Arroyo Hondo about 1870 is also described by Martínez's sister, Cleofas M. Jaramillo (*Shadows of the Past,* 30). Jaramillo notes Santa Fe's *mal hijo,* a half-paralyzed, one-armed beggar known as El Mum-ma-ma (p. 95).

95. Brown, *Hispano Folklife,* 120, 121, 123–24.

96. Kenneth Fordyce, "Hermit's Peak: 'The Story of Crazy Juan,'" NMFWP, February 19, 1937, WPA#188, NMSRC. Robert Campbell of South Second St., Raton, told Fordyce the story on February 4, 1937.

97. Kenneth Fordyce, "Pioneer Story: 'Patches,'" NMFWP, June 13, 1938, WPA#127, NMSRC.

98. Mrs. W. C. Totty, "Bear Moore," NMFWP, November 17, 1937, reprinted in *New Mexicans in Cameo and Camera: New Deal Documentation of Twentieth-Century Lives,* ed. Marta Weigle (Albuquerque: University of New Mexico Press, 1985), 51.

According to Howard Bryan: "Raw Meat Creek in Catron County, it is said, was named by the famous old hunter, Bear Moore, after he discovered a man eating his meat raw there because he did not have matches to make a fire" ("Some Colorful Place Names in New Mexico," *WF* 15 [1956]: 286). Also note Totty on "Wild East Joe" Griggs, a hermit who lived north of Silver City (Weigle, *New Mexicans*, 49).

99. C. L. Sonnichsen, *Tularosa: Last of the Frontier West* (1960; reprint, Albuquerque: University of New Mexico Press, 1980), 98, 105. See also Kate McGraw, "Dog Canyon's Gritty Frenchman," *NM,* March 1975, 10–12, 31.

100. W. M. Emery, "A Tough One," NMFWP, July 2, 1937, WPA#239, NMSRC.

101. N. Howard (Jack) Thorp, with Neil M. Clark, *Pardner of the Wind* (1941; reprint, Lincoln: University of Nebraska Press, 1977), 136, 138.

102. Ibid., 137. For a useful alphabetical listing with minimal annotations and a short bibliography, see Peter Hertzog, comp., *Outlaws of New Mexico* (Santa Fe: Sunstone Press, 1984).

103. N. Howard Thorp, "Broncho Bill, 'Train Robber,'" NMFWP, April 9, 1938, WPA#88, NMSRC.

104. Thorp gives relatively little attention to the famous Las Vegas–area gang of Vicente Silva, whom he seems to confuse with *Las Gorras Blancas* (see chap. 5 above) by characterizing *"Vicente Silva y sus Quarenta Bandidos"* as "night riders who wore long white sheets with red daggers embroidered on the back, and who, when they rode into a town four abreast and a hundred strong, always left behind some victim of their vengeance, his corpse perhaps not being found for months" (*Pardner of the Wind,* 171). Silva's biography, *Historia de Vicente Silva y sus cuarenta bandidos* (Las Vegas, New Mexico: La Voz del Pueblo, 1896), by Manuel C. de Baca, has been translated twice. See also, e.g., Tom McGrath, *Vicente Silva and His Forty Thieves* (n.p., 1960); Alice Bullock, "Vicente Silva and the Bandidos," *NM,* August 1984, 37–39; and especially Doris L. Meyer, "Banditry and Poetry: Verses by Two Outlaws of Old Las Vegas," *NMHR* 50 (1975): 277–90.

105. N. Howard Thorp, "Black Jack Ketchum," NMFWP, October 22, 1937, WPA#88, NMSRC. Black Jack Ketchum is often confused with William T. ("Black Jack") Christian, head of a southwestern New Mexico gang called the High Fives (Marc Simmons, *Ranchers, Ramblers, and Renegades: True Tales of Territorial New Mexico* [Santa Fe: Ancient City Press, 1984], 99).

106. Thorp, "Broncho Bill"; idem, *Pardner of the Wind,* 148–49.

107. N. Howard Thorp, "Bill McGinnis: The Nerviest Outlaw of Them All," NMFWP, January 13, 1938, WPA#88, NMSRC.

108. N. Howard Thorp, "Old Days in Las Vegas, New Mexico," NMFWP, February 4, 1937, WPA#88, NMSRC. See also Lynn Perrigo, *Gateway to Glorieta: A History of Las Vegas, New Mexico* (Boulder, Colorado: Pruett Publishing, 1982), 71–73.

109. N. Howard Thorp, "Aztlan (New Mexico) Outlaws," NMFWP, January 6, 1938, WPA#88, NMSRC.

110. Ibid.

111. N. Howard Thorp, "The Wild Bunch of the San Francisco River, New Mexico," NMFWP, March 11, 1937, WPA#88, NMSRC.

112. Burroughs, *On the Trail,* 34.

113. Thorp, *Pardner of the Wind,* 155–56.

114. N. Howard Thorp, "Marino Leyba, (Outlaw) As told to me, by Mr. Skinner, of Old Town, Albuquerque, New Mexico," NMFWP, n.d., WPA#88, NMSRC. See also Simmons, "Badman Leyba," in *Ranchers, Ramblers, Renegades,* 41–43.

115. N. Howard Thorp, "Joe Fowler Hold-up-man and Criminal," NMFWP, November 26, 1937, WPA#88, NMSRC. See also Allen A. Carter, "Joe Fowler, Notorious Bad Man, Socorro County, New Mexico," NMFWP, March 20, 1937, WPA#88, NMSRC.

116. N. Howard Thorp, "Henry Coleman, 'Bad Man,'" NMFWP, April 16, 1938, WPA#88, NMSRC.

117. Thorp, *Pardner of the Wind,* 140–41.

118. N. Howard Thorp, "Grant Wheeler and Joe George, New Mexico Train Robbers," NMFWP, December 16, 1937, WPA#88, NMSRC. See also idem, *Pardner of the Wind,* 157–60.

119. Thorp, *Pardner of the Wind,* 145.

120. Ibid., 140.

121. Ibid., 169.

122. Bright Lynn, "Corrected Copy of the Biography of Guadalupe Lupita Gallegos which was sent in Nov. 8, 1938," NMFWP, December 30, 1938, reprinted in Weigle, *New Mexicans,* 21. See also Marta Weigle, ed., *Two Guadalupes: Hispanic Legends and Magic Tales from Northern New Mexico* (Santa Fe: Ancient City Press, 1987), 42–43.

123. Edith L. Crawford, "Pioneer Story," NMFWP, May 5, 1939, WPA#210, NMSRC. On Lorencita Herrera de Miranda and others, see Darlis A. Miller, "The Women of Lincoln County, 1860–1900," in *New Mexico Women: Intercultural Perspectives,* ed. Joan M. Jensen and Miller (Albuquerque: University of New Mexico Press, 1986), 169–200. This and many other NMFWP manuscripts are collected in Robert F. Kadlec, ed., *They "Knew" Billy the Kid: Interviews with Old-Time New Mexicans* (Santa Fe: Ancient City Press, 1987).

124. Janet Smith, "Interview with José García y Trujillo," NMFWP, August 26, 1936, reprinted in Weigle, *New Mexicans,* 28–29.

125. Lynda A. Sánchez, "Recuerdos de Billy the Kid," *NM,* July 1981, 71, 70–71.

126. Stephen Tatum, *Inventing Billy the Kid: Visions of the Outlaw in America, 1881–1981* (Albuquerque: University of New Mexico Press, 1982), 9. Tatum cites Amy Hogeboom, *The Boy's Book of the West* (New York: Lothrup, Lee and Shepard, 1946), 235.

Tatum is severely criticized by Jon Tuska in *Billy the Kid: A Bio-Bibliography* (Westport, Conn.: Greenwood Press, 1983), who calls Tatum's book "the only complete failure" among the works that attempt to assess the nature and significance of the Kid legend. Essentially, Tuska denies the validity of Tatum's methodology, specifically Tatum's working notions that historical narrative is only a version of reality; that myth and legend are shaped into different forms of reality; that each generation has produced popular materials about the Kid to satisfy its own psychological and sociocultural needs. Tuska, on the other hand, argues that "there is such a thing as past historical reality, and we, as human beings, are capable of constructing a comprehensive model of it" (pp. 193–97). Tuska is more lenient with Kent Ladd Steckmesser's analysis of the Kid's legend as fact and fiction in his *The Western Hero in History and Legend* (Norman: University of

Oklahoma Press, 1965). Tuska's chapter on "The Legend of Billy the Kid" (pp. 189–207) takes issue with most such analysis, and he is obviously more comfortable with historical "facts," appending a useful "Billy the Kid Chronology" (pp. 213–21). See also Robert M. Utley, *Four Fighters of Lincoln County* (Albuquerque: University of New Mexico Press, 1986).

127. Tatum, *Inventing the Kid,* 9, 10.

128. Tatum's (ibid.) note 20 (p. 207): Frank G. Applegate, "New Mexican Legends," *Southwest Review* 17 (1932): 199–208.

129. Tatum's (ibid.) note 21 (p. 207): W. Eugene Hollon, *Frontier Violence* (London: Oxford University Press, 1974), 188.

130. Tatum's (ibid.) note 23 (p. 207): "'Walk-along' Smith told J. Frank Dobie that Pat Garrett, the Kid, and Lew Wallace staged the Kid's death and buried two bags of sand in the coffin. See Dobie's *Apache Gold and Yaqui Silver* (1939; rpt. Albuquerque: University of New Mexico Press, 1976), pp. 188–89. 'Brushy Bill' Roberts claimed to be the Kid in 1950, and petitioned then New Mexico Governor Mabry for a pardon (it was denied). See C. L. Sonnichsen and William V. Morrison, *Alias Billy the Kid* (Albuquerque: University of New Mexico Press, 1955)."

131. Tatum's (ibid.) note 24 (p. 207): F. Stanley, *Desperadoes of New Mexico* (Denver: World Press, 1953), 97–98.

132. Tatum's (ibid.) note 25 (p. 207): Las Vegas (N.M.) *Optic,* 25 July 1881.

133. Tatum's (ibid.) note 26 (p. 207): Phil Lenoir, *Rhymes of the Wild and Wooly* ([Santa Fe, New Mexico: privately printed, 1920]), n.p.

134. Tatum's (ibid.) note 27 (p. 207): J. W. Hendron, "The Haunted House of Lincoln Town," *NM* 25 (1947): 22–23, 41; Edwin Corle, "The Ghost of Billy the Kid," in *Mojave* (New York: Liveright, 1934), 163–69; N. Howard Thorp, *Pardner of the Wind,* 168.

135. Tatum, *Inventing the Kid,* 11, 12–13.

136. Emerson Hough, *The Story of the Outlaw* (New York: Outland Publishing, 1907), 311–12.

137. Metz, Metz, *Pat Garrett: The Story of a Western Lawman* (Norman: University of Oklahoma Press, 1974), 306.

138.   Andrew Jenkins and Irene Spain were commissioned by Polk C. Brockman to write "Billy the Kid." By January 1, 1927, Jenkins and Spain had composed the text and the tune for the ballad, using Walter Noble Burns, *The Saga of Billy the Kid* (Garden City, New York: Doubleday, 1926). D. K. Wilgus traces the history of the folk and commercial recordings of this song and notes that on March 18, 1954, "Billy the Kid was copyrighted in the name of Andrew Jenkins, who, as of 1970, had never been compensated by producers or publishers of this song" ("The Individual Song: 'Billy the Kid,'" *WF* 30 [1971]: 226–34). The version given here is that of Ray Reed, Roswell, as recorded by John D. Robb (Robb#197) on May 8, 1949. Reed claims to have heard the song first from his father in San Jon. Reed sings "Billy the Kid" without stanza four on Folkways Record FD5329.

139. Metz, *Pat Garrett,* 307.

140. Thorp, *Pardner of the Wind,* 189–90.

141. Metz, *Pat Garrett,* 304.

142. Simmons, *Ranchers, Ramblers, Renegades,* 37–39.

143. Tobias Duran, "Francisco Chávez, Thomas B. Catron, and Organized Political Violence in Santa Fe in the 1890s," *NMHR* 59 (1984): 291–92, 296–97.

144. Howard Roberts Lamar, *The Far Southwest, 1846–1912: A Territorial History* (1966; reprint, New York: W. W. Norton, 1970), 194–95. Duran cites Richard Maxwell Brown's claim that New Mexico may have been "the only place in America where assassination became an integral part of the political system" (*Strain of Violence* [New York: Oxford University Press, 1975], 14).

145. The 1884 murder of Lincoln County leader Juan Patrón also remains unsolved, but it does not have as much currency in folklore as Fountain's and Cháves's mystery killings (Duran, "Political Violence," 291, 307 [note 2]).

146. *Santa Fe New Mexican* accounts, reprinted in Oliver La Farge, *Santa Fe: The Autobiography of A Southwestern Town* (Norman: University of Oklahoma Press, 1959), 159, 161. Residents of Capitan told R. D. Jameson's student "J. M." of Highlands University that on the White Sands near La Luna, "the ghosts of Colonel Fountain and his son come up from the sands on windy nights and cry for revenge" (in Robe, *Hispanic Legends from New Mexico,* 102).

147. Erna Fergusson, *New Mexico: A Pageant of Three Peoples,* 2d ed. (1964; reprint, Albuquerque: University of New Mexico Press, 1973), 287. See also A. M. Gibson, *The Life and Death of Colonel Albert Jennings Fountain* (Norman: University of Oklahoma Press, 1965).

148. Marc Simmons, "The Murder of José Francisco Chaves—An Unsolved Mystery," in his *Taos to Tomé: True Tales of Hispanic New Mexico* (Albuquerque: Adobe Press, 1978), 81, 84. See also Maurilio E. Vigil, *Los Patrones: Profiles of Hispanic Political Leaders in New Mexico History* (Washington, D.C.: University Press of America, 1980), 56–62.

149. Kenneth Fordyce, "Pioneer: 'Early Crimes and Tragedies in Northern New Mexico,'" NMFWP, December 4, 1937, WPA#188, NMSRC; WPA5-4-6#5, H-MNM.

150. Simmons, *Ranchers, Ramblers, Renegades,* 50. See also three Bonito City legends reported by residents of Capitan to R. D. Jameson's student "J.M." at Highlands University (in Robe, *Hispanic Legends from New Mexico,* 103–4).

151. Clay W. Vaden, "Early Days in Magdalena," NMFWP, May 29, 1936, WPA#231, NMSRC.

152. As quoted in Ron Hamm, "A. B. Baca's Uncle Elfego," *NM,* December 1981, 27, 30. See also Betty Woods, "He Man's Town," *NM,* April 1941, 12–13, 37–38; George Fitzpatrick, "The Real Elfego Baca," *NM,* April 1960, 2–6, 40; Marc Simmons, "Sheriff's Savior," *Santa Fe Reporter,* n. d.

153. Jack Schaefer, *Heroes Without Glory: Some Goodmen of the Old West* (Boston: Houghton Mifflin, 1965), as reprinted in *Furia y Muerte: Los Bandidos Chicanos,* ed. Pedro Castillo and Albert Camarillo, Monograph no. 4, Chicano Studies Center, University of California, Los Angeles (Los Angeles: Aztlán Publications, 1973), 67. See also Kyle Crichton, *Law and Order, Ltd.* (Santa Fe: Santa Fe Publishing, 1928).

154. Marc Simmons, *Albuquerque: A Narrative History* (Albuquerque: University of New Mexico Press, 1982), 356.

155. Barbara A. Babcock, ed., *The Reversible World: Symbolic Inversion in Art and Society* (Ithaca, N.Y.: Cornell University Press, 1978), 14, 27–28.

Chapter 7. A Sense of Time: Texts of Community and Celebration

1. Charles F. Lummis, *The Land of Poco Tiempo* (1893; reprint, Albuquerque: University of New Mexico Press, 1966), 3, 258–59. For a dated discussion of *"mañana,"* see Arthur L. Campa, "Mañana Is Today," *New Mexico Quarterly* 9 (1939): 3–11; reprinted in Campa, *Hispanic Culture in the Southwest* (Norman: University of Oklahoma Press, 1979), 211–16.

2. Edmund R. Leach, "Two Essays Concerning the Symbolic Representation of Time," 1961, in *Reader in Comparative Religion: An Anthropological Approach,* ed. William A. Lessa and Evon Z. Vogt, 3d ed. (New York: Harper & Row, 1972), 113, 115; Beverly J. Stoeltje, "Festival in America," in *Handbook of American Folklore,* ed. Richard M. Dorson (Bloomington: Indiana University Press, 1983), 240.

3. Victor Turner, "Introduction," in *Celebration: Studies in Festivity and Ritual,* ed. idem (Washington, D.C.: Smithsonian Institution Press, 1982), 16, 14.

4. Mrs. Benton (May Price) Mosley, "Ranching in the Later 1880's," NMFWP, n.d.; "Customs and Conditions of Early Ranch Life (Lea County)," NMFWP, December 7, 1936; "Customs and Conditions of Early Ranch Life (cont'd) (Lea County)," NMFWP, December 21, 1936; reprinted in her *"Little Texas" Beginnings in Southeastern New Mexico,* ed. Martha Downer Ellis (Roswell, New Mexico: Hall-Poorbaugh Press, 1973), 14, 32, 33.

5. Sally Yerkovich, "Conversational Genres," in Dorson, *Handbook of American Folklore,* 280–81.

6. Gary Witherspoon, *Language and Art in the Navajo Universe* (Ann Arbor: University of Michigan Press, 1977), 62.

7. S[ergeij] A. Tokarev, "Toward a Methodology for the Ethnographic Study of Material Culture," trans. Peter Voorhis, in *American Material Culture and Folklife: A Prologue and Dialogue,* ed. Simon J. Bronner (Ann Arbor, Mich.: UMI Research Press), 81, 82, 84.

8. Henry Glassie, *Passing the Time in Ballymenone: Culture and History of an Ulster Community,* Publications of the American Folklore Society, n.s., vol. 4 (Philadelphia: University of Pennsylvania Press, 1982), 36, xiii, 461–62.

9. James F. Downs, *The Navajo,* Case Studies in Cultural Anthropology (New York: Holt, Rinehart and Winston, 1972), 119–20.

10. Lucius Dills, in James D. Shinkle, *Reminiscences of Roswell Pioneers* (Roswell, New Mexico: Hall-Poorbaugh Press, 1966), 119–20.

11. Mosley, "Customs and Conditions," December 7, in *"Little Texas" Beginnings,* 29–30.

12. Ruleen Lazzell, "Life on a Homestead: Memories of Minnie A. Crisp," *NMHR* 54 (1979): 61, 63.

13. Carolyn Niethammer, *American Indian Food and Lore* (New York: Collier Books, 1974), 135.

14. B. A. Reuter, "Natz-szing in Keresan by Us Called Paper Bread," NMFWP, January 6, 1939, WPA5-4-15#7, H-MNM.

15. Niethammer, *American Indian Food,* 143. According to Frank Hamilton Cushing: "For no art or industry within the range of the domestic duties of Zuñi, is so much care and instruction bestowed by the old women on the young, as for every process in the making of the *he'-we,* or wafer breads. Year in and year out, too, while these lessons are being plied, it is told how the famed and beloved Goddess of the White

Shells taught not a few of her graces—and some secrets—in connection with the daily occupation which forms their theme. Of these secrets a chosen few old women of the tribe are the keepers. With many a mysterious rite and severe penance, they quarry and manufacture the enormous baking-stones on which the flaky, toothsome *he'-we* is made. Garrulous enough, mercy knows, are these old crones on most other subjects; but they guard with sphinx-like jealousy such of their methods and observances as add prestige to experience in their occasional calling" (*Zuñi Breadstuff,* Indian Notes and Monographs, vol. 8 [1920; reprint, New York: Museum of the American Indian Heye Foundation, 1974], 317–18).

16. Reyes N. Martínez, "The Old-Time Miller," NMFWP, reprint, *EP* 81, 1 (Spring 1975): 10. See also the description of a mill built by Juan Sandoval in Lou Sage Batchen, "Juan of Tecolote," WP, September 25, 1940, WPA 5-5-49#40, H-MNM; Moises Racl, "Molinos Flourished in Northern Region," *The Taos News,* July 5, 1979, B-1.

17. Stanley L. Robe, ed., *Hispanic Legends from New Mexico: Narratives from the R. D. Jameson Collection,* Folklore and Mythology Studies, 31 (Berkeley: University of California Press, 1980), 172–73.

18. Nan Elsasser, Kyle MacKenzie, and Yvonne Tixier y Vigil, *Las Mujeres: Conversations from a Hispanic Community* (Old Westbury, New York: Feminist Press; New York: McGraw-Hill, 1980), 67.

19. Campa, *Hispanic Culture,* 278. Cleofas M. Jaramillo notes that in Arroyo Hondo: "These crisp *chicharones* [*sic*] . . . were kept to be used instead of bacon, and were also given to the poor when children were sent to beg for a soup bone to boil with their beans. The soup bone was sometimes passed from house to house to their neighbors, as lard was a luxury possessed only by the rich" (*Shadows of the Past* [1941; reprint, Santa Fe: Ancient City Press, 1980], 39).

20. Lorin W. Brown, "Agua Fria," from Nicolás López, NMFWP, August 11, 1937, reprinted in *New Mexicans in Cameo and Camera: New Deal Documentation of Twentieth-Century Lives,* ed. Marta Weigle (Albuquerque: University of New Mexico Press, 1985), 13.

21. Jaramillo, *Shadows of the Past,* 41.

22. N. Howard Thorp, "A Chuck-Wagon Supper," NMFWP, November 4, 1937, WPA#118, NMSRC.

23. May Mosley, "Son-of-a-Gun or Rascal," *NMFR* 3 (1948–49): 26–27. See also N. Howard (Jack) Thorp with Neil M. Clark, *Pardner of the Wind* (1941; reprint, Lincoln: University of Nebraska Press, 1977), 271; Marc Simmons, "A Stew Fit for the Gods," *The Santa Fe Reporter,* January 25, 1984, 15.

24. Marie Carter, "Old Timers Stories—Charles C. Geck (Wife: Ramona Geck)," NMFWP, May 24, 1937, reprinted in Weigle, *New Mexicans,* 62.

25. Franc Johnson Newcomb, *Navaho Neighbors* (Norman: University of Oklahoma Press, 1966), 111, 113–14.

26. Jaramillo, *Shadows of the Past,* 54.

27. Lou Sage Batchen, *"El Hombre Alegre* (The Jolly Man) (As told by Rumaldita Gurule)," NMFWP, n.d., WPA#224, NMSRC.

28. John P. Harrington, "The Tewa Indian Game of 'Cañute,'" *AA* 14 (1912): 253.

29. Lorin W. Brown, "Games of Chance," NMFWP, n.d., WPA#177, NMSRC.

30. Virginia Wayland, *Apache Playing Cards,* Southwest Museum Leaflets, no. 28 (Los Angeles, 1961), 18.

31. Agnes Morley Cleaveland, *No Life for a Lady* (Boston: Houghton Mifflin, 1941), 160. Cleaveland maintains: "Now, poker has always seemed to me to be the only game of cards worth wasting time over—if one is determined to waste time. Poker is the ultimate of individualism. One goes it alone" (p. 195).

32. Thorp, *Pardner of the Wind,* 114, 115.

33. Lorin W. Brown, "Trompos are Trumps," in Brown, with Charles L. Briggs and Marta Weigle, *Hispano Folklife of New Mexico* (Albuquerque: University of New Mexico Press, 1978), 68–71. See also Frances Leon Swadesh, "Toys and Games," *EP* 81, 1 (Spring 1975): 32–33.

34. Aileen O'Bryan, *The Díné: Origin Myths of the Navajo Indians,* BAE Bulletin 163 (Washington, D.C.: Government Printing Office, 1956), 49, 50.

35. Arnold van Gennep, *The Rites of Passage,* trans. Monika B. Vizedom and Gabrielle L. Caffee (Chicago: University of Chicago Press, 1960), 2–3.

36. Jean M. Burroughs, "Courtships, Weddings and Chivarees," *NM,* September 1980, 25, 49.

37. Reyes N. Martínez, "Rural Weddings," NMFWP, WPA 5-5-2#2, H-MNM; WPA 457, NMSRC; reprinted in *EP* 81, 1 (Spring 1975): 12–13, 15. See also N. Howard Thorp, "A Wedding Feast," NMFWP, WPA 5-5-23#2, H-MNM; Carol Jensen, "Cleofas M. Jaramillo on Marriage in Territorial Northern New Mexico," *NMHR* 58 (1983): 153–71; Paul Kutsche and John R. Van Ness, "Casorio," in their *Cañones: Values, Crisis, and Survival in a Northern New Mexico Village* (Albuquerque: University of New Mexico Press, 1981), 122–26.

38. Juan B. Rael, "New Mexican Wedding Songs," *Southern Folklore Quarterly* 4 (1940): 55. Rael notes that "New Mexicans invariably use the archaic form *entriega* instead of the modern literary one," and that "the name *pueta* is usually given to one who improvises *coplas* as he sings."

39. Louise Lamphere, *To Run After Them: Cultural and Social Bases of Cooperation in a Navajo Community* (Tucson: University of Arizona Press, 1977), 71.

40. Ruth Benedict, *Tales of the Cochiti Indians,* BAE Bulletin 98 (1931; reprint, Albuquerque: University of New Mexico Press, 1981), 86–87. See also "Marriage," in Charles H. Lange, *Cochiti: A New Mexico Pueblo, Past and Present* (Carbondale: Southern Illinois University Press, 1959), 411–15.

41. Morris E. Opler, "The Apachean Culture Pattern and Its Origins," in *Handbook 10,* 376–77.

42. Elsie Clews Parsons, *Isleta, New Mexico,* BAE 47th Annual Report (1932; reprint, Albuquerque: Calvin Horn Publisher, 1974), 248–49. The aunt referred to is the father's sister.

43. "Villanueva," New Mexico Rural Council (Las Vegas, February 1938), 36–37. A similar study was also done in nearby San Geronimo (Marta Weigle, ed., *Hispanic Villages of Northern New Mexico* [Santa Fe: The Lightning Tree, 1975], 251).

44. Lorin W. Brown, "The Wake," NMFWP, April 9, 1937, reprinted in Lorenzo de Córdova, *Echoes of the Flute* (Santa Fe: Ancient City Press, 1972), 48–50. See also Kutsche and Van Ness, "Death," in *Cañones,* 130–33.

45. Mosley, "Customs and Conditions," December 21, 1936, in *"Little Texas" Beginnings,* 24.

46. Cleaveland, *No Life for a Lady,* 156–57.

47. Ortiz, *The Tewa World: Space, Time, Being, and Becoming in a Pueblo Society* (Chicago: University of Chicago Press, 1969), 103.

48. Gertrude Prokosch Kurath with Antonio Garcia, *Music and Dance of the Tewa Pueblos,* MNM Research Records, no. 8 (Santa Fe: Museum of New Mexico Press, 1970), 23.

49. Don L. Roberts, "A Calendar of Eastern Pueblo Indian Ritual Dramas," in *Southwestern Indian Ritual Drama,* ed. Charlotte J. Frisbie (Albuquerque: University of New Mexico Press, SAR Book, 1980), 109.

50. Thomas J. Steele, S.J., "Naming of Places in Spanish New Mexico," in *Hispanic Arts and Ethnohistory in the Southwest,* ed. Marta Weigle with Claudia Larcombe and Samuel Larcombe (Santa Fe: Ancient City Press; Albuquerque: University of New Mexico Press, 1983), 300.

51. Ruth L. Bunzel, *Zuñi Katcinas: An Analytical Study,* BAE 47th Annual Report (1932; reprint, Glorieta, New Mexico: Rio Grande Press, 1973), 874. Bunzel notes: "This medicine is also a love charm. Mothers use it in the same way on their girls before they go out to watch a dance, 'to make them beautiful, so that everyone will like to look at them.'"

52. James Seavey Griffith, "Kachinas and Masking," in *Handbook 10,* 766.

53. Jill D. Sweet, *Dances of the Tewa Pueblo Indians: Expressions of New Life* (Santa Fe, New Mexico: School of American Research Press, 1985), 89–90. See also Flavia Waters Champe, *The Matachines Dance of the Upper Rio Grande: History, Music, and Choreography* (Lincoln: University of Nebraska Press, 1983); John Forrest, *Morris and Matachin: A Study in Comparative Choreography* (London: The English Folk Dance and Song Society; Sheffield: The Centre for English Cultural Tradition and Language, University of Sheffield, 1984).

54. Jaramillo, *Shadows of the Past,* 49–50. See also Brown, *Hispano Folklife,* 175–76.

55. J. D. Robb, "The Matachines Dance—a Ritual Folk Dance," *WF* 20 (1961): 91–92.

56. John Donald Robb, *Hispanic Folk Music of New Mexico and the Southwest: A Self-Portrait of a People* (Norman: University of Oklahoma Press, 1980), 198–99.

57. Blanche C. Grant, *Taos Today* (Taos, New Mexico: Author, 1925), 30–31.

58. Thomas J. Steele, S.J., "The Spanish Passion Play in New Mexico and Colorado," *NMHR* 53 (1978): 245, 246. See also Thomas J. Steele, S.J., *Holy Week in Tomé—A New Mexico Passion Play* (Santa Fe: Sunstone Press, 1976).

59. Evon Z. Vogt, "A Study of the Southwestern Fiesta System as Exemplified by the Laguna Fiesta," *AA* 57 (1955): 820, 822.

60. "Spanish Fiestas in New Mexico," NMFWP, *EP* 51 (1944): 101–3.

61. Charles L. Briggs, "A Conversation with Saint Isidore: The Teachings of the Elders," in Weigle et al., *Hispanic Arts,* 110–11. See also the NMFWP account of "San Ysidro's Day in Córdova," in "Fiestas in New Mexico," *EP* 48 (1941): 239–42.

62. Jaramillo, *Shadows of the Past,* 85.

63. "Spanish Fiestas in New Mexico," 103, 104. According to the anonymous NMFWP writers: "In an earlier day, women used to engage in the *corrida* on St. Ann's day and at the little village of Agua Zarca, San Miguel County, *galleras* (women riders) may still be seen engaging in this picturesque folk custom, heritage of the Moorish tradition" (p. 104).

64. Marc Simmons, "Pity the Poor Rooster," *The Santa Fe Reporter,* May 18, 1983, 17. See also references to rooster racing in Josiah Gregg, *Commerce of the Prairies,* ed. Max L. Moorhead (Norman: University of Oklahoma Press, 1954), 169–70; John G. Bourke, "Notes on the Language and Folk-Usage of the Rio Grande Valley," *JAF* 9 (1896): 101–2; Ruth Laughlin, *Caballeros* (New York: D. Appleton and Co., 1931), 198–99; S. Omar Barker, "La corrida del gallo," *NM,* March 1932, 22–23; Juan B. Rael, "New Mexican Spanish Feasts," *California Folklore Quarterly [WF]* 1 (1942): 88.

65. Reyes N. Martínez, "San Geronimo Celebrations during the Nineties," NMFWP, January 1, 1937, WPA5-5-47#34, H-MNM; WPA#50, NMSRC.

66. Campa, *Hispanic Culture,* 50–51.

67. Reyes N. Martínez, "Entertainments of the Past: *Los Titeres," Over the Turquoise Trail,* NMFWP, 1, 2 (1937): 4–5.

68. Marc Simmons, *Taos to Tomé: True Tales of Hispanic New Mexico* (Albuquerque: Adobe Press, 1978), 25.

69. "Spanish Fiestas in New Mexico," 104–5.

70. Laughlin, *Caballeros,* 240. See also Aurora Lucero-White Lea, *Literary Folklore of the Hispanic Southwest* (San Antonio, Texas: Naylor, 1953), 10–12, 52–65. According to John S. Englekirk: "The oldest extant New Mexican copy of *Adán y Eva* is that made from the Monclova manuscript by José Longino Galindre, signed and dated at Las Vegas, January 11–February 20, 1886. It was from this Galindre manuscript of 1886 that the Baca troupe obtained the copy later transcribed by don Próspero at Bernalillo between August 12 and November 17, 1924. And it was from this Baca copy of 1924—or that of 1896—that the UNM edition of the play was taken. We know of only a few scattered performances of *Adán y Eva* by the Baca troupe in and about Las Vegas at the turn of the century, and in Mora and Taos upon the occasion of their triumphal tour during the winter of 1903–1904. I have not yet uncovered the identical Mexican text, manuscript or printed, from which the Monclova copy was made" ("The Source and Dating of New Mexican Spanish Folk Plays," *WF* 16 [1957]: 253–54). See also *Comedy of Adam and Eve,* trans. Julián Josué Vigil (n.p., 1980).

71. Campa, *Hispanic Culture,* 229. See also Reyes N. Martínez, "Las Posadas," NMFWP, WPA5-5-44#1, H-MNM; Pedro Ribera Ortega, *Christmas in Old Santa Fe,* 2d ed. (Santa Fe: Sunstone, 1973), 9–13.

72. Englekirk, "Source and Dating," 245–46. Englekirk identifies three basic New Mexican shepherds' plays, associated with Las Vegas, San Rafael, and Abeyta.

73. Lea, *Literary Folklore,* 7–8.

74. Arthur L. Campa, *Spanish Religious Folktheatre in the Southwest, Second Cycle,* University of New Mexico Bulletin Language Series, vol. 5, no. 2 (June 15, 1934), 9–10.

75. Lea, *Literary Folklore,* 12–13. According to Englekirk: "The original New Mexican manuscript of this play is likewise the property of the Tenorio family of Taos, and from it have come all other copies in the state—including those of the San Luis Valley in Colorado. The Tenorio copy . . . was said to have been taken sometime in the 1880's from a forgotten Mexican source. . . . The Tenorio play has been localized largely in the Taos–San Luis Valley region. However, Epifanio Espinosa of Cleveland made a copy of the Tenorio manuscript sometime prior to 1903. And it was from this Espinosa copy that Próspero Baca took his original sometime in 1903 or 1904. The extant Baca copy, transcribed from his original and dated at Las Vegas June 26, 1917, is

the one from which the Campa edition and the Santa Fe Reyes Martínez copy were made. According to my informants, the play has had few performances over the years. Próspero S. Baca, for example, one of the most active impresarios in the state . . . has never presented it" ("Source and Dating," 244–45).

76. Mary R. Van Stone and E. R. Sims, ed., "Canto del Niño Perdido," in *Spur-of-the-Cock,* ed. J. Frank Dobie, Texas Folklore Society Publication no. 11 (Austin, 1933), 48–49. According to Englekirk: *"El Niño Perdido,* confined to the sparsely populated region from Taos north to the San Luis Valley of Colorado, has also been cited as another drama of the second cycle of New Testament plays. . . . All who have reported on *El Niño Perdido* concur in that, with the exception of an occasional early fall presentation, it is customarily played around Easter time. The original New Mexican copy from which all other manuscript, typed, and printed copies have come was taken from a Mexican copy of the play by the Tenorio family of Taos sometime in the 1880's. I have not yet succeeded in tracing this lead to the Mexican source, nor have I located an approximate Mexican equivalent. That the New Mexico play is of nineteenth-century Mexican authorship is patently undeniable" ("Source and Dating," 243–44).

77. Lea, *Literary Folklore,* 16–17; Englekirk notes: "Several nineteenth-century Mexican Guadalupe plays have been fairly popular in New Mexico since the first manuscript copy of one of those plays was brought to Las Vegas in the 1880's to become a part of the [Próspero S.] Baca repertoire" ("Source and Dating," 241).

78. Gaspar Pérez de Villagrá, *History of New Mexico,* trans. Gilberto Espinosa (Los Angeles: Quivira Society, 1933), 148–49.

79. Lea, *Literary Folklore,* 22. See also T. M. Pearce, "Los Moros y Los Cristianos: Early American Play," *NMFR* 2 (1947–48): 58–65; Josie Espinosa y Lujan, "Los Moros y Cristianos," *NM,* July 1977, 34–35.

80. Mary Austin, "A Drama Played on Horseback," *The Mentor,* September 1928, 39.

81. Aurelio M. Espinosa and J. Manuel Espinosa, "The Texans: A New Mexican Spanish Folk Play of the Middle Nineteenth Century," *New Mexico Quarterly Review* 13 (1943): 299–300. The Espinosas knew "of only one manuscript of the New Mexican historical play *Los Tejanos,* the one obtained by [them], in the summer of 1931, from Doña Bonifacia Ortega of Chimayo, New Mexico, who kept it with other manuscripts and family letters in an old trunk" (p. 299).

82. Lorin W. Brown, "Los Comanches," NMFWP, January 3, 1939, in *Hispano Folklife,* 40–41. Campa notes that the religious *Los Comanches* "is often confused with the eighteenth-century historical drama of the same name. . . . [It] first appeared in north-central New Mexico about the turn of the century. It was composed, as a manuscript states, 'recalling the Indian chief Victorio who attacked in 1880 and Nana in '81.' In the late 1920's and early 1930's it was presented in Arenales, a small settlement adjoining Albuquerque. It was also very popular in San Rafael. . . . The story is sung and danced in its entirety. All the members of the cast except those representing the Holy Family are in full Indian costume. There is hardly any dialogue; the participants . . . weave in snake-like patterns and tell the story with unmistakable mimicry. At times it is difficult to tell whether it is an Indian dance or a religious play. . . . The Indians kidnap the Child. The settlers pursue and overtake them, and, after bartering . . . , they buy back the Child for a blanket. The Indians become interested in the Spanish ceremony . . . and end by joining the settlers in adoration at the manger" (*Hispanic Culture,* 230–31).

83. Campa, *Hispanic Culture,* 232. See also Jaramillo, *Shadows of the Past,* 46. Paul G. Martínez provided Lester B. Raines with a text of the Ranchos de Taos *Comanches,* annually performed on January 25, San Pablo Fiesta ("Los Comanches," NMFWP, August 31, 1936, WPA#122, NMSRC). See also Scottie King, "Los Comanches de la Serna," *NM,* January 1979, 26–27, 42.

84. Eric Hobsbawm, "Introduction: Inventing Traditions," in *The Invention of Tradition,* ed. Hobsbawm and Terence Ranger (Cambridge: Cambridge University Press, 1983), 1, 4.

85. Betty Reich, [untitled], NMFWP, July 9, 1937, WPA#213, NMSRC.

86. Georgia B. Redfield, "Old Timers' Day, Eastern New Mexico State Fair, Friday, Oct. 9, 1936," NMFWP, October 19, 1936, WPA#185, NMSRC. See also James D. Shinkle, *Fifty Years of Roswell History* (Roswell, New Mexico: Hall-Poorbaugh Press, 1964), 249–50.

87. Georgia B. Redfield, "Old Timers' Reunion and Barbecue," NMFWP, November 22, 1937, WPA5-5-50#34, H-MNM.

88. Mrs. Belle Kilgore, "Clovis Pioneer Days Celebration, Curry County, New Mexico, June 5, 1935," NMFWP, April 26, 1937, WPA#191, NMSRC.

89. "The Santa Fe Fiesta," *EP* 7 (1919): 99–101.

90. "Fiesta Proclamation," *EP* 19 (1925): 26.

91. "The 1925 Santa Fe Fiesta," *EP* 18 (1925): 88–91.

92. Thomas E. Chávez, "Santa Fe's Own: A History of Fiesta," *EP* 91, 1 (Spring 1985): 13.

93. Ronald L. Grimes, *Symbol and Conquest: Public Ritual and Drama in Santa Fe, New Mexico* (Ithaca, New York.: Cornell University Press, 1976), 207–8, 210–11. See also his "The Lifeblood of Public Ritual: Fiestas and Public Exploration Projects," in *Celebration,* ed. Turner, 272–83.

94. J. Wesley Huff, "A Quarter Century of Ceremonials," *NM,* July 1946, 56–58.

95. Unidentified newspaper clipping, August 22, 1936, WPA#59, NMSRC.

96. Huff, "Quarter Century Ceremonials," 59.

97. Ibid., 13–14.

98. *Coronado Cuarto Centennial: What It Will Mean to New Mexico* (Albuquerque: University of New Mexico, 1938), 3–4.

99. Erna Fergusson, "The Coronado Cuarto Centennial," *New Mexico Quarterly* 10 (1940): 67, 68–70.

100. "Coronado Monument Dedication," *EP* 47 (1940): 144–45. For contemporary Hispanic commentary, see Arthur L. Campa's articles translated by Clarabel Márquez in *Arthur L. Campa and the Coronado Cuarto Centennial,* ed. Anselmo F. Arellano and Julián Josué Vigil (Las Vegas, New Mexico: Editorial Telaraña, 1980).

101. Unidentified newspaper clipping, October 7, 1936, in WPA#101, NMSRC.

102. Edmund Sherman, "New Mexico Celebrates," *NM,* June 1940, 11–13, 15.

103. Hobsbawm, "Inventing Traditions," 5.

104. Terry Lee Carroll, "Gallup and Her Ceremonials," Ph.D. diss., University of New Mexico, December 1971, 127–28.

105. Chávez, "Santa Fe's Own," 10–11.

106. Beatrice Chauvenet, *Hewett and Friends: A Biography of Santa Fe's Vibrant Era* (Santa Fe: Museum of New Mexico Press, 1983), 149–51, 152–53.

107. Special Coronado Cuarto Centennial edition, *Albuquerque Journal,* April 30, 1940, A-2.

108. *Coronado Magazine: Official Program of the Coronado Cuarto Centennial in New Mexico* (Albuquerque: Valliant Printing, 1940).

109. Hobsbawm, "Inventing Traditions," 4.

110. In Shinkle, *Reminiscences Roswell Pioneers,* 165–66.

111. "What the Coronado Cuarto Centennial Means to New Mexico," 1938 booklet.

112. John DeWitt McKee, "The Unrelenting Land," *New Mexico Quarterly* 3 (1957), reprinted in *The Spell of New Mexico,* ed. Tony Hillerman (Albuquerque: University of New Mexico Press, 1976), 74–75.

113. Erna Fergusson, *Our Southwest* (New York: Alfred A. Knopf, 1940), 345–46.

PLACE INDEX

County names are in parentheses.

PERSON INDEX

SUBJECT INDEX

acequia. *See* irrigation

"Adán y Eva" (drama), 353, 382, 436

adobe, 381

alabado (hymn), 14, 136, 244, 310, 331, 344; first
line: "God save thee, beautiful moon!", 136;
"Let's sing the dawn/ Cantémos él álba", 136;
"The rocks break in two/ Las piedras se
parten", 17; "Saint Isidore, Husbandman/ San
Ysidro Labrador", 132; title: "Hail, Lady of
Sorrows/ Salve de Dolores", 17. *See also*
singing; song

Alvarado Hotel, 78, 79, 399

Anglos, 7, 18, 60, 133, 229, 230, 288, 398

Apache Indians, 7, 11, 32, 42, 148, 169, 190–92,
195–97, 221, 246, 262, 288, 319, 328–29, 348,
373, 377. *See also* Chiricahua Apache Indians;
Jicarilla Apache Indians; Lipan Apache Indians;
Mescalero Apache Indians

apparition, 216, 357

architecture, 78, 82, 83, 151, 412, 421–22

art colonists, 84, 212, 368

Atchison, Topeka & Santa Fe Railway, 73, 76, 77,
79, 81, 82, 88, 89, 92, 105, 115, 162, 166, 168,
373, 383, 400, 411, 414

Atocha, Holy Child of, 67–68

atomic bomb, 7, 21–23, 24

automobile, 71, 84–85, 105, 109, 117, 211, 212, 348,
372, 386

Aztec Indians, 46, 92, 96, 99, 214, 225–26, 234,
402–403

baile. See dance; Hispano

ballad, 270, 343, 379; first line: "I'll sing you a true
song", 290–91; "I'll tell you a story", 43;
"Plantonio", 43–45; title: "Little Joe the
Wrangler", 19–20; "We'd driven to red river

and the weather had been fine", 19–20. *See also*
corrido; singing; song

baptism, 193, 235, 284, 324, 345, 347

barbed wire, 163–64

bell, 40, 46, 85, 246, 266, 270, 330, 359, 371

Blessingway Chant, 250

buffalo (hunting), 18, 20, 40, 54, 76, 140, 163,
183–86, 204, 229, 268, 358, 414

Bureau of American Ethnology, 131

burro, 58, 146–47, 212, 242, 270, 418

captivity, 194–97, 233, 420

Castañeda Hotel, 78, 80, 84, 89

Cathedral of St. Francis, 237, 239–40

cattle (herding), 18–20, 141, 163, 169–81, 185, 191,
199, 276, 280, 284, 295, 316. *See also* cowboy;
ranching

cemetery. *See* grave(yard)

Changing Woman (Navajo deity), 13, 154, 192,
228

chapel, 41, 62, 63, 66, 159, 160, 237, 335, 343, 402

Chautauqua, 384

children, 21, 27–28, 32–33, 53, 58, 69, 193, 198–99,
208, 249, 260, 320, 337, 433

chile, 61, 62, 63, 311, 313

Chiricahua Apache Indians, 192, 196, 205

chivaree, 324

Christ (*Cristo*), 14–17, 23, 32, 63, 64, 115, 138, 233,
267, 341, 342, 345, 356–57, 437

Christmas, 256, 335, 337, 353, 355

chuckwagon, 176, 314–15, 317, 363

clown(ing), 34, 338, 351, 391

Comanche Indians, 48, 169, 190, 193, 204–205,
359

"Los Comanches" (drama), 358–59, 437

Conquistador, 31, 36–41, 54, 92, 106, 226, 237, 367, 378

La Conquistadora. See Our Lady (Virgin)

contest, 35–36, 50, 234, 374, 379. *See also* gambling; game; racing; rodeo

copla (verse), 50, 327. *See also* singing; song

copper, 45, 46, 197, 218, 221. *See also* mining

corn, 154–55, 233, 248, 249, 307, 309–311, 334

Coronado Cuarto Centennial, 113, 129, 360, 364, 378–82, 383, 384–85

Coronado Monument, 379

Corpus Christi, 334, 365

corrido (ballad), 173, 344; first line: "Oh my sorrel colored horse/ Caballo alazan tostado", 18. *See also* ballad; singing; song

cowboy, 18–20, 43, 50, 86, 90, 116, 120, 146, 185, 198, 262, 275, 296, 314–15, 332, 364, 383

Coyote, 228, 232, 247; coyotes, 199, 333

cross, 38, 156–62, 181, 235, 237, 239, 269, 330, 341, 358, 371, 421. *See also* Way of the Cross

crucifix(ion), 63, 64, 66, 237, 265, 281, 338, 342

culture hero(ine), 10, 12–14, 18, 20, 23, 28, 31, 42, 135, 191, 193, 231–45, 288, 298. *See also* myth

dance, 302, 379; Anglo, 316, 317; Hispano, 313, 314, 326, 335, 343, 344, 350, 368, 382; Indian, 33, 112, 114, 115, 233, 249, 334, 335, 336, 338, 342, 350, 368, 373, 377, 379, 405, 435. *See also* Devil Dance; Harvest Dance; Matachines; Shalako; Turtle Dance

death, 49, 161, 162, 163, 215, 245–47, 371. *See also* funeral; outlawry

deer (hunting), 12, 35–36, 181, 328

Denver & Rio Grande Railroad, 62, 74

devil, 259, 310–11, 354, 355

Devil Dance (Apache), 373, 377. *See also* dance

dowsing, 141, 142–43, 407

drama, 302, 335, 352–60, 368, 378, 436–37. *See also* "*Adán y Eva*"; "*El Niño Perdido*"; "*Las Posadas*"; "*Los Comanches*"; "*Los Pastores*"; "*Los Tejanos*"; "*Los Tres Reyes*"; "Moors and Christians"; passion play

dress, 27, 58, 80, 84, 86, 103, 174, 235, 237, 328, 336, 338, 343, 348, 350, 352, 357, 358, 359, 363, 382, 399, 413, 421

drum, 309, 338, 350

Eagle Dance (Santa Clara), 112. *See also* dance

"*El Niño Perdido*" (drama), 356–57, 382, 437

emergence mythology, 6, 7, 9–13, 23, 27, 32–34, 114, 117, 125, 135, 152, 232, 247, 335. *See also* myth

Esquípulas, Our Lord of, 63–64

fair, 25, 28, 48, 57, 159, 379, 382, 386

fandango. See dance, Hispano

Farmington Gang (outlaws), 279

feast day. *See* fiesta

festival, 123, 302, 360. *See also* fiesta

fiddle(r). *See* violin(ist)

fiesta, 106, 113, 115, 237, 302, 335, 342–50, 352, 379, 382, 386. *See also* festival; Santa Fe Fiesta

flute, 318, 352, 357

food, 35, 47, 57, 78, 80, 81, 103, 114, 155, 204, 248, 302, 304, 307–317, 326, 328, 332, 343, 361, 363, 382, 399, 433

Franciscans, 14, 16, 27, 64, 129, 234–38, 241, 244, 337, 366, 368, 371

Fred Harvey Company, 72, 76–88, 89, 92, 105, 373, 399

funeral, 324, 328–32. *See also* death

Gallup Inter-Tribal Ceremonial, 343, 360, 372–76, 383, 385

gambling, 35–36, 205, 228, 250, 276, 317, 319, 322–24, 324. *See also* contest; game

game, 205, 317, 319–22, 343, 351, 357, 374, 434. *See also* contest; gambling; top

geophagy (earth eating), 63

ghost, 288, 329

Girls' Puberty Ceremony (Mescalero), 154

gold, 36, 40, 197, 204, 207, 216, 218, 223, 224, 281, 419. *See also* mining

Good Friday, 60, 341–42

Las Gorras Blancas, 200

grave(yard), 160–61, 244, 269, 289, 290, 295, 330

Guadalupe. *See* Our Lady (Virgin)

guitar(ist), 317, 326, 338, 358, 371, 382, 395

gypsies, 209–10

Harvest Dance (Pueblo), 343, 373. *See also* dance

healing, 10, 24, 54, 60, 63, 67–70, 73–75, 89, 114, 206, 208, 213, 248, 250, 260–62, 263, 267, 298–99, 335, 345, 424, 426. *See also* sickness; witch(craft)

Hispanos, 7, 10, 18, 24, 60, 113, 133, 157, 172, 183, 229, 230, 287, 331–32, 335

hoedown. *See* dance, Anglo

hogan, 107, 317, 373

Holy Week, 14, 16, 17, 23, 115, 268, 335, 341

homesteading, 18, 24, 163, 164, 166, 198

horse, 18, 41–45, 48, 50, 52, 170, 177, 181, 191–92, 200, 203, 210, 220, 234, 253, 255, 277, 279, 280, 321, 328, 346, 347, 359

humor, 174, 325, 331, 346, 359

hunting, 18, 20, 35–36, 40, 103, 114, 140, 181–90, 274, 328, 334. *See also* buffalo (hunting); deer (hunting)

Grateful acknowledgment is made for permission to quote from the following copyrighted material:

Ruth Laughlin Barker, "New Mexico Witch Tales," in *Tone the Bell Easy,* ed. J. Frank Dobie, by permission of the Texas Folklore Society.

E. Boyd, *Popular Arts of Spanish New Mexico* (Santa Fe: Museum of New Mexico Press, 1974). Copyright © 1974 by E. Boyd. Used by permission of David H. Snow, Santa Fe.

Hispanic Culture in the Southwest, by Arthur L. Campa. Copyright © 1979 by the University of Oklahoma Press.

Treasure of the Sangre de Cristos: Tales and Traditions of the Spanish Southwest, by Arthur L. Campa. Copyright © 1963 by the University of Oklahoma Press.

Ruben Cobos, "The New Mexican Game of Valse Chiquiao," *Western Folklore* 15 (1956). Used by permission of the California Folklore Society.

No Life for a Lady by Agnes Morley Cleaveland. Copyright 1941 by Agnes Morley Cleaveland. Copyright © renewed 1969 by Loraine Lavender. Reprinted by permission of Houghton Mifflin Company.

"The War God's Horse Song," from The Navajo Indians by Dane Coolidge and Mary Roberts Coolidge. Copyright 1930 by Dane Coolidge and Mary Roberts Coolidge.

Richard I. Ford, "Inter-Indian Exchange in the Southwest." By permission of the Smithsonian Institution Press from *Handbook of North American Indians,* vol. 10. © Smithsonian Institution, 1983. Washington, D.C.

James Seavey Griffith, "Kachinas and Masking." By permission of the Smithsonian Institution Press from *Handbook of North American Indians,* vol. 10. © Smithsonian Institution, 1983. Washington, D.C.

Ronald L. Grimes, *Symbol and Conquest: Public Ritual and Drama in Santa Fe, New Mexico.* Copyright © 1976 by Cornell University. Used by permission of the publisher, Cornell University Press.

Navaho Witchcraft by Clyde Kluckhohn. Copyright © 1972 by the President and Fellows of Harvard College. Reprinted by permission of Beacon Press.

Louise Lamphere, "Southwestern Ceremonialism." By permission of the Smithsonian Institution Press from *Handbook of North American Indians,* vol. 10. © Smithsonian Institution, 1983. Washington, D.C.

John A. Lomax, *Adventures of a Ballad Hunter* (New York: Macmillan Co., 1947) and *Cowboy Songs and Other Frontier Ballads* (New York : Macmillan Co., 1938). Used by permission of Alan Lomax.

Haniel Long, *Piñon Country.* Copyright © 1941 by Haniel Long; renewal copyright © 1969 by Anton V. Long. Used by permission of Anne Caiger, Special Collections, University Research Library, University of California at Los Angeles.

James A. McKenna, *Black Range Tales,* first published in 1936; reissued by the Rio Grande Press, Inc., Glorieta, New Mexico, in 1965, 1971, 1976, 1979, 1985, and currently in print.

María: The Potter of San Ildefonso, by Alice Marriott. Copyright © 1948 by the University of Oklahoma Press.

Pat Garrett: The Story of a Western Lawman, by Leon C. Metz. Copyright © 1974 by the University of Oklahoma Press.

Joseph Miller, *New Mexico: A Guide to the Colorful State* (New York: Hastings House, 1940).

Morris E. Opler, "The Apachean Culture Pattern and Its Origins" and "Mescalero Apache." By permission of the Smithsonian Institution Press from *Handbook of North American Indians,* vol. 10. © Smithsonian Institution, 1983. Washington, D.C.

———. "The Jicarilla Apache Ceremonial Relay Race," *American Anthropologist* 46 (1944).

T. M. Pearce, "The Bad Son *(El Mal Hijo)* in Southwestern Spanish Folklore," *Western Folklore* 9 (1950). Used by permission of the California Folklore Society.

Juan B. Rael, "New Mexican Wedding Songs," *Southern Folklore Quarterly* 4 (1940).

By permission from Gladys A. Reichard, *Navaho Religion: A Study of Symbolism* (Tucson: University of Arizona Press, 1983).

Hispanic Folk Music of New Mexico and the Southwest: A Self-Portrait of a People, by John Donald Robb. Copyright © 1980 by the University of Oklahoma Press.

J. D. Robb, "The Matachines Dance—A Ritual Folk Dance," *Western Folklore* 20 (1961). Used by permission of the California Folklore Society.

Stanley L. Robe, ed., *Hispanic Legends from New Mexico: Narratives from the R. D. Jameson Collection,* Folklore and Mythology Studies 31 (Berkeley: University of California Press, 1980). © The Regents of the University of California.

Helen H. Roberts, "The Reason for the Departure of the Pecos Indians for Jemez Pueblo," *American Anthropologist* 34 (1932).

Marc Simmons, *The Little Lion of the Southwest: A Life of Manuel Antonio Chaves* (Swallow Press, 1973). Reprinted by permission of Ohio University Press.

Thomas J. Steele, S.J., "The Spanish Passion Play in New Mexico and Colorado," *New Mexico Historical Review* 53 (1978).

Dennis Ernest Tedlock, "The Ethnography of Tale-Telling at Zuni" (Ph. D. dissertation, Tulane University, 1968). Used by permission of Dennis Tedlock.

———. *Finding the Center: Narrative Poetry of the Zuni Indians* (New York: Dial Press, 1972). Reprinted by permission of the Balkin Agency, New York.

———. "The Spoken Word and the Work of Interpretation in American Indian Religion." Reprinted from Karl Kroeber, ed., *Traditional American Indian Literatures: Texts and Interpretations* by permission of the University of Nebraska Press. Copyright © 1981 by the University of Nebraska Press.

Jim Bob Tinsley, *He Was Singin' This Song* (Orlando: University Presses of Florida, 1981).

Mary R. Van Stone and E. R. Sims, "Canto del Niño Perdido," in *Spur-of-the-Cock,* ed. J. Frank Dobie, by permission of the Texas Folklore Society.

Evon Z. Vogt, "A Study of the Southwestern Fiesta System as Exemplified by the Laguna Fiesta," *American Anthropologist* 57 (1955).

Frank Waters, *To Possess the Land: A Biography of Arthur Rochford Manby* (Swallow Press, 1973). Reprinted by permission of Ohio University Press.

Gary Witherspoon, *Language and Art in the Navajo Universe* (Ann Arbor: University of Michigan Press, 1977). Reprinted by permission of the University of Michigan Press.